11 7/12
$40.20

The Natural Philosophy of Chu Hsi
(1130–1200)

The Natural Philosophy of Chu Hsi (1130–1200)

Yung Sik Kim

Memoirs
of the
American Philosophical Society
Held at Philadelphia
For Promoting Useful Knowledge
Volume 235

ISBN: 0-87169-235-x
US ISSN: 0065-9738

Library of Congress Cataloging-in-Publication Data

Kim, Yung Sik.
   The natural philosophy of Chu Hsi (1130–1200) / Yung Sik Kim.
   p.   cm. − (Memoirs of the American Philosophical Society held at Philadelphia for promoting useful knowledge, ISSN 0065-9738; 235)
   Includes bibliographical references and index.
   ISBN 0-87169-235-x
   1. Chu, Hsi, 1130–1200.   2. Neo-Confucianism.   3. Philosophy and science.
I. Title.   II. Series: Memoirs of the American Philosophical Society; 235.
B128.C54K55   2000
181'.112−dc21   99-37252

To the memory of my father
Woo Bong Kim (1918–1984)

Contents

Illustrations

Figures

Tables

Acknowledgments

I have been indebted to many people during the long period in which this book has been in the making. Foremost among them is Charles C. Gillispie, my unfailing mentor. It is from him that I learned what it means to be a scholar in the humanities, having come from years of training in the natural sciences. He also taught me by example what it means to be a teacher. He always found time, from the book's beginning as a doctoral dissertation in the mid-1970s, to read all the successive versions, to listen to what I had to say, and to provide numerous comments and suggestions on every aspect of writing and publishing a study on a subject very different from that of his own research. Without his continuing care, support, and encouragement—and those of Emily Gillispie—the project would not have survived all the difficulties that I have encountered in the course of completing it.

While writing the dissertation, I benefited greatly from the generous guidance of two other scholars, Willard J. Peterson and James T. C. Liu. Willard has since read a few postdissertation versions and provided very useful criticisms. I would also like to thank Michael S. Mahoney, Thomas S. Kuhn, and Gerald L. Geison, who conscientiously trained me while I was a graduate student in the Program in History of Science at Princeton University. They showed continuous interest in the project and welcomed me warmly whenever I returned for a visit.

The following persons have read part or all of one or more versions of the draft, sometimes in the form of separate papers: Derk Bodde, Peter Bol, Wing-tsit Chan, Karine Chemla, Julia Ching, Jacques Gernet, Edward Grant, Peng-yoke Ho, Chun-chieh Huang, Ira E. Kasoff, D. C. Lau, G. E. R. Lloyd, Thomas A. Metzger, Joseph Needham, Conrad Schirokauer, Benjamin I. Schwartz, Nathan Sivin, and Hoyt C. Tillman. Their comments, criticisms, and suggestions have helped me in various ways to improve the content of the book, although many of them will find that I have not always agreed with them.

Fellowship support from the Harvard-Yenching Institute (March 1982–February 1983 in Princeton), the Alexander von Humboldt Foundation (July–December 1987 in Munich), and the Japan Foundation (March–June 1994 in Kyoto) made it possible for me to leave my university and spend uninterrupted time working on the book. I would like to thank Edward Baker, Paul U. Unschuld, and Yoshinobu Sakade, who helped me to obtain the fellowships; Professors Unschuld and Sakade were very generous as hosts during my stays in Munich and Kyoto. Back home in Korea, research grants from the Korea Science and Engineering Foundation, the Korea Research Foundation, and Seoul National University supported the research that portions of the book are based upon.

I would like to thank the journals that have given me permission to use in revised forms the following previously published materials: "Some Aspects of the Concept of *Ch'i* in Chu Hsi," *Philosophy East and West 34* (1984), 25–36 (for sections 3.1 and 3.2); "*Kuei-shen* in Terms of *Ch'i*: Chu Hsi's Discussion of *Kuei-shen*," *Tsing Hua Journal of Chinese Studies*, new ser., *17* (1985), 149–163 (for chapter 6); "Chu Hsi (1130–1200) on Calender Specialists and Their Knowledge: A Scholar's Attitude toward Technical Scientific Knowledge in Traditional China," *T'oung Pao 78* (1992), 94–115 (for sections 12.1 and 12.2).

Special thanks also go to Lee Jungrye of Seoul National University, who typed the earliest versions of the book, the writing of which began before the age of word processing, and to Carole LeFaivre-Rochester of the American Philosophical Society, who has patiently edited the long manuscript written by a nonnative speaker.

And finally, I would like to thank my family for their understanding and support, in particular my wife, Sun-Kyung Chu, who made numerous sacrifices, including her own career, to accommodate my irresponsible and unending negligence of household responsibilities.

Y. S. K.

CHAPTER 1

Introduction

The importance of Chu Hsi (1130–1200), the subject of this book, does not need to be emphasized. Generally considered as the one who "completed" the Neo-Confucian "synthesis," he further developed the new trends of thought and learning that had emerged in the Northern Sung and worked out a new Confucian philosophical system.[1] In doing so, he laid out what was to become an established "program of learning," with a fixed set of classical texts and commentaries, anthologies of important Northern Sung thinkers, and advice concerning the proper method of reading them.[2] He also played a major part in the rise of private academies as centers of teaching, study, and discussion and in the emergence of the role of the scholar as a teacher.[3] In all these, he saw ways to solve the problems of his day—the barbarian occupation of the north, the misgovernment, the moral decline, the threat of Buddhism, and above all, the splintering of the true Confucian Way.[4] And in his efforts to restore and redefine the Confucian Way (*Tao*), he helped to establish the school of Ch'eng I (1033–1107), which had been but one of many alternatives in the eleventh century, as the mainstream of Confucianism.[5] He emerged as the undisputed leader of the school, which was eventually to become the orthodoxy accepted by scholars and adopted by the state.[6]

The question remains, however, why one should study his natural knowledge. It may be said, of course, that any aspect of such an important figure holds an inherent interest and, moreover, that previous studies of Chu Hsi, focused on moral and social problems, have generally neglected his knowledge of the natural world.[7] Yet, some explanation for doing what others have chosen to ignore is still needed. For that purpose, in the first section I turn to the role and significance of natural knowledge in the whole body of Chu Hsi's thought and learning. The next section enlarges on the question and looks at Chu Hsi's natural knowledge in the context of Sung society and culture and of the Neo-Confucian tradition as a whole—its development after Chu Hsi in particular. I treat these questions only tentatively, however, and rather than attempting to find full answers to them, try only to put the content of the following chapters in perspective. I end the chapter commenting on the limits of the book.

1.1. Natural Knowledge in the Thought of Chu Hsi

The role that natural knowledge played in Chu Hsi's thought and learning can be best discussed in terms of his doctrine of "investigation of things" (ke-wu), the basis of his entire endeavor to become a sage.[8] Since Chu Hsi took the term ke-wu to mean investigating "the li of things" (wu chih li),[9] and since every "thing" (wu) has its li—which is but a manifestation of the single universal li—every thing was worth investigating.[10] To be sure, he glossed the word "wu" as "events" (shih),[11] and his discussions of ke-wu were weighted heavily toward moral and social concerns. But "the things"—objects and phenomena—of the natural world were not excluded from his conception of the "wu," and thus, knowledge and understanding of natural phenomena did have a place in his ke-wu endeavor.

Closely related to this aspect of ke-wu was the notion that a moral order underlay the natural world and provided a kind of "cosmic basis" for morality. This ancient idea, which gained a renewed importance, in part in response to the Buddhist challenge of the time, has been recognized by many modern scholars as the foundation of Neo-Confucian moral philosophy.[12] Some have even considered this shift in emphasis as the key achievement of the Ch'eng I school. With Ch'eng I and Chu Hsi, the Way and the li began to be "conceived of as something that exists independent of the cultural tradition," which had been the source of "literati value" till then; their existence was now "confirmed by the processes of nature rather than the records of culture."[13]

The main outcome of this shift, to be sure, was an increased importance of moral self-cultivation in comparison with literary and cultural accomplishments. But there also was a growth of interest in the natural world of heaven and earth. Confucian discussions, formerly centered around human and social problems, now began to touch on certain cosmological issues. So although Chu Hsi's interest became focused more on morality and self-cultivation, the character of his endeavor grew increasingly more intellectual. And though he was more inclined to speculative philosophy than his contemporaries, the scope of his speculation broadened to cover much of the natural world. Indeed, as the following chapters show, he had much to say and write about natural phenomena and attained a considerable degree of understanding in certain scientific and technical subjects.

Yet, if the natural world thus provided a basis of morality, the actual objects and phenomena in that world do not seem to have mattered very much to Chu Hsi. To be sure, he did advocate the study of the natural world as part of the ke-wu endeavor. There were even times when he appeared to consider natural phenomena more important than human affairs. He mentioned, for example, "the profundity of 'the Way of heaven' (t'ien-tao)" as an example of what is "grand" (ta) and "the complications of 'human affairs' (jen-shih)" as what is "minute" (hsi).[14] He also said: "As for what is grand, heaven and earth and the myriad things; as for what is small, getting up, residing, eating and resting. All [these] are the li of the supreme ultimate (t'ai-chi) and yin-yang."[15] But the expressions "the Way of heaven" and "heaven and earth and the myriad things" (t'ien-ti wan-wu) referred to the entire world and its working as a whole, and not to particular concrete objects or phenomena. The activities mentioned in these examples, however, were really trivialities of daily life rather than matters that would constitute significant moral and social problems for Chu Hsi. What was important as the "cosmic basis," then, were global notions, not concrete "natural" objects and phenomena.

The point, however, is not that such objects and phenomena were unimportant but that they were unproblematic. They were not excluded but were taken for granted and hence simply accepted without discussion.[16] This is evident in the manner in which Chu Hsi discussed natural phenomena. Frequently, as we shall see, he spoke of them not for their own interest but for some external purposes. He alluded to them mainly in the course of discussing moral and social problems, by adducing analogies between those familiar and obvious natural phenomena and the latter problems, which are usually more complicated and difficult. Only rarely did he mention such common natural phenomena for themselves.

We shall see numerous examples of such analogies. Among the most typical and frequent is that of a cart. Chu Hsi noted that once a cart has started to move, no great exertion of force is needed to keep it moving; he argued that in study also a great exertion of effort is needed only at the beginning, after which it becomes easy.[17] Similarly, to explain that when impurities enter the mind it loses "sincerity" (*ch'eng*) and falls into "self-deception," he used the analogy that when gold is mixed with a small amount of silver, the whole quantity of the gold loses its worth as gold.[18] On "the method of reading books" (*tu-shu-fa*), especially on the need for "careful reading" (*shu-tu*), two different analogies argued for the same point:

> Generally, in reading books, it is necessary to read carefully. When read carefully, the essences [of the books] will spontaneously become familiar; after the essences have become familiar, the *li* will spontaneously be seen. It is like eating a piece of fruit. When one first bites it, one does not know the taste; one simply eats it. One has to chew it into tiny and soft pieces; then the taste spontaneously comes out, and one begins to know whether it is sweet or bitter. . . . [It is also like] a gardener watering gardens. One who is good at watering waters each tree, following its vegetables and fruits. After a while the watering becomes sufficient; then water and soil are mixed and the things [i.e., vegetables, fruits, and trees] get nourishment and grow naturally. One who is not good at watering administers it hurriedly.[19]

It is not impossible to learn from these examples something about Chu Hsi's views on natural phenomena—the tendency of moving objects, the properties of a mixture of metals, the perception of tastes, and the nourishment of plants. But his real concern lay elsewhere—to argue for the strong exertion of effort at the beginning stage of study, for the importance of sincerity and purity of the mind, and for the necessity of careful reading, by showing that these were analogous to the natural phenomena. In none of the examples were the phenomena themselves what Chu Hsi was really interested in.

Much of what is contained in the following chapters, especially the concrete natural phenomena and objects, came up in this context in Chu Hsi's writings and conversations.[20] Thus, we shall note that his frequent references to the effects of medicines and to the clarity of water were usually intended for similar discussions, by way of analogy, of human nature and the state of mind.[21] We shall also see him resorting to the fixed sequence of the seasons to make the point that the constant human virtues cannot be changed.[22] Even the retrograde motion of planets came up in a similar context, that is, to illustrate that man's mind, normally compassionate, can sometimes become cruel.[23] He went as far as to invent natural phenomena to support his points concerning analogous human problems. He said, for example, that a tree will die if it stops growing for a single day, in order to illustrate his point that one should keep studying every day.[24]

Of course, common and familiar phenomena used in this type of analogy were not limited to the natural world; Chu Hsi drew on obvious facts of social and human affairs in a similar manner. For example, in arguing for the importance of purity of mind, for which he used the analogy of mixing silver with gold, he said: "It is like a man uttering ten sentences, [of which] nine are true and one is false. The truth of those nine sentences is all destroyed by the falsity of this one sentence."[25] For the importance of careful reading, he said: "It is like men meeting one another and scattering right away without exchanging a word. [If it is] like this, what good [is the meeting]?"[26] There were other examples also; the most frequent kind involved official positions and duties, to the various aspects of which he compared such terms as "decree" (*ming*), "human nature" (*hsing*), "mind" (*hsin*), "feelings" (*ch'ing*), and *ch'i*. Typically, Chu Hsi said:

> A decree is a kind of directive. Human nature is the official task that ought to be carried out. . . . Mind is the official. "*Ch'i* and tangible quality" (*ch'i-chih*) are the customs of the official, some generous and some severe. Feelings are the affairs that ought to be dealt with at the office.[27]

Military tactics, to which Chu Hsi compared the method of reading books, was another kind.[28] Other examples included eating rice, drinking wine, cutting meat for cooking, washing rice, writing, weaving, lighting candles, building houses, purchasing lands, and minting coins.[29]

At times, the common phenomena Chu Hsi mentioned in such contexts were in themselves trivial. The obvious fact that without a bridge one cannot cross a river was mentioned to illustrate that in the program of self-cultivation in the *Great Learning* (Ta-hsueh), the step of "making the mind correct" (*cheng-hsin*) is necessary between the stages of "extending the knowledge" (*chih-chih*) and "making the intention sincere" (*ch'eng-i*).[30] The alternation of the two feet while walking was used to show that both "broad culture" (*po-wen*) and "restraining propriety" (*yueh-li*) are essential.[31] That most natural phenomena were adduced by Chu Hsi in a similar manner suggests, then, that they also must have been considered comparably "common," "obvious," and often "trivial."

Certain features of the basic ideas and assumptions discussed in part 1 will help one understand how natural phenomena could have appeared so obvious. For example, for Chu Hsi the qualities and activities of *ch'i* were innate; thus, once certain phenomena had been attributed to certain qualities and activities of *ch'i*, they were deemed sufficiently accounted for—without any need to look for external causes or hidden mechanisms. Furthermore, the concept of *li* did not facilitate detailed analysis of objects and phenomena of which it is the *li*; the *li* of a thing or an event was accepted in its entirety. When he noted regularity in nature, for example, he was concerned only with the existence, but not with the concrete detail, of that regularity.

The dichotomy of what is "above physical form" (*hsing-erh-shang*) and what is "below physical form" (*hsing-erh-hsia*) also facilitated the ready acceptance of natural phenomena. According to that dichotomy, the Way, *li*, humaneness (*jen*), mind, and human nature—abstract and sublime concepts without manifest "physical forms" (*hsing*)—belong to what is "above physical form," whereas concrete things with tangible physical forms belong to what is "below physical form."[32] It was commonly assumed that what has physical form and is visible is easy to understand, whereas what is without physical form is difficult. Chu Hsi said, for example: "What is above physical form refers to *li*; what is below physical form refers to things and events. . . . The things and events can be seen, but their *li* are difficult to know."[33] It was natural that what was difficult to understand was thought to be important and thus worthy of further consideration; what was easy to understand was considered obvious and even trivial. It was with this idea in mind that Chu Hsi commented:

> Things are easy to see; mind has no physical form or measure. The weight and length of things are easy to measure; the weight and length of the mind are difficult to measure. When a thing is in error, only [that] one thing is in error. When the mind is in error, myriad things are in error.[34]

Since most common natural phenomena are accompanied by tangible qualities and physical effects and thus belong to what is "below physical form," it is understandable that they were thought to be obvious and were simply accepted in the way they were perceived; no further investigation was attempted beyond the surface of the phenomenal realities of empirical data.[35] Such ready acceptance of commonly observed natural phenomena was facilitated further by the characteristic Confucian emphasis on the reality of the external world.[36]

Chu Hsi's discussion of natural phenomena was not always in the context we have seen so far; natural knowledge had different roles when it came up in different contexts. For instance, when he commented upon certain natural phenomena referred to in classics supposedly written by—or which at least contained the intentions of—the sages (*sheng-jen*), his interest in them seemed to be more genuine. We shall see many such examples, in which natural objects and phenomena were discussed in some detail, and Chu Hsi's interest in them appeared quite strong, though his actual concern was with elucidating the sages' intentions.

Then there were the traditions of various branches of specialized knowledge involving natural phenomena, such as calendrical astronomy, harmonics, geography, and medicine. These subjects claimed the attention of Confucian scholars and officials such as Chu Hsi for various reasons. The *ke-wu* doctrine, for example, kept them mindful of the need to study concrete things and events in all areas of human concern. Some of the specialized subjects, knowledge of which was available in the texts widely studied by scholars—the standard commentaries of the classics and the official dynastic histories, for example—were considered even a part of the Confucian tradition. Besides that, knowledge of some topics was actually needed for performing official duties. Chu Hsi had a strong interest in these specialized subjects, and in some of them his understanding reached a fairly high level of sophistication (see chapter 12), although, of course, such topics could not be his primary concern.

1.2. Chu Hsi's Natural Knowledge in Sung Society and Neo-Confucian Tradition

Having considered the role and significance of natural knowledge in Chu Hsi's thought and learning in general as an indirect means of explaining why we study his *natural knowledge*, we may now broaden the question and ask about its role and significance in a larger context—that of Sung society and culture and the Neo-Confucian tradition as a whole. This may provide an indirect justification for studying Chu Hsi's natural knowledge. I do not deal with this complex question fully here, but offer only some tentative observations that may have relevance to various aspects of the question.

First, we may note the breadth of Chu Hsi's learning. Not only was he a great philosopher, but he was also a scholar well versed in a wide range of subjects. His scholarship was not confined to such conventional areas as classical studies and history; it covered nearly all branches of knowledge then available. What is especially notable for us is that he attained a considerable degree of understanding in many scientific and technical subjects and had an exceptional knowledge about the natural world.[37] To be sure, there were many other well-informed Sung scholars. Shao Yung (1011–1077), Shen Kua (1031–1095), Su Sung (1020–1101), and even Chang Tsai (1020–1077) (all of the Northern Sung), and Ts'ai Yüan-ting (1135–1198), a contemporary and a friend of Chu Hsi, all showed familiarity with certain scientific and technical subjects. But Chu Hsi studied them all and incorporated their knowledge in his own. If in his understanding in any one branch he did not reach the level of any of those men, he covered the broadest ground. And although his knowledge in these various areas did not form a coherent system, his sayings and writings reveal a most comprehensive understanding of them, or at least a very serious effort to achieve it.

This broad scope of Chu Hsi's learning appears even more marked when it is compared with what happened after him. For such breadth did not continue. To be sure, the traditions of specialized knowledge did persist within specialist circles. But when later generations of scholars adopted Chu Hsi's philosophy, they did not maintain his exceptional scope of interest and knowledge. Their interest narrowed, and Chu Hsi's kind of breadth became rare. In particular, most of them more or less ignored his knowledge about the natural world. Although they were engaged in heated debates over many ideas and problems that they inherited from him, they were hardly ever concerned with natural phenomena or scientific subjects.[38] It appears, even, that the scholars' interest in natural knowledge dropped off right after it had reached a peak with Chu Hsi. One is tempted to ask why this happened.

This "why" question is difficult to treat in a manner that is not overly speculative.[39] It would be better to postpone the question till we learn more about "what"—that is, what Chu Hsi knew, or what the post-Chu Hsi scholars knew. Clearly, to ask what was in the Chu Hsi corpus—and was then ignored by later generations—would be more fruitful than to ask why it was ignored. The former, therefore, is what I take as my main task in this book.

Yet, we do not have to suppress the "why" question completely. We can even reach some tentative answers to it while dealing with the "what" question. For example, we can see what happened to Chu Hsi's natural knowledge as part of the more general pattern of "change and stabilization" in Sung China. For in eleventh- and twelfth-century China, we see many changes and new trends in various areas of man's life, society, and culture that did not continue.

There is now general agreement concerning the major developments in this period, although their details, and the extent to which they occurred, are debated.[40] To begin with, there were technical advances in such areas as mining and metal-working as well as printing and porcelain manufacture. Agricultural production increased rapidly, owing to the introduction of new crops, techniques, and lands. These advances resulted in large-scale production and regional specialization and propelled the growth and diversification of commercial activities, both domestic and foreign. Such changes, in turn, contributed to the development of a monetary economy, including the widespread use of paper currency. A great increase in wealth and population followed. In particular, large cities emerged as centers of flourishing economic and cultural activities. Along with them came new developments in culture and lifestyle. Painting, calligraphy, and pottery-making reached new heights. New literary styles and genres were introduced in both poetry and prose writing. New forms of entertainment were added to these and enriched the lives of both the elite and the masses, both urban and rural. These developments, especially printing, contributed to increased opportunities and facilities for education and the growth of literacy. The civil service examination was institutionalized as the main gate to official positions in the centralized bureaucracy and gave rise to a new kind of elite rooted in literary education. Finally, there was a fundamental reorientation of the Confucian philosophy, with changes in the views of major Confucian thinkers of the period as to what constituted important problems and texts.[41]

Characteristically, however, these changes and new trends did not develop further. If some of the developments noted above did continue, they remained within certain limits and did not lead to further, related changes in other areas.[42] Indeed, in certain areas it is possible to see decline rather than development in the post-Sung periods.

Sung thought and learning showed this same pattern. There were many changes and flourishing new developments in the eleventh century.[43] New philosophical questions were raised, and there were lively discussions and debates about them. An important problem was that of the source, or the basis, of morality, which led many eleventh-century thinkers to search for the moral basis in man's nature, classics, history, or the world of heaven and earth and to struggle with the problem of the relationship between man and the world. Another important new concern was with the method of apprehending, or attaining, this basis—the *li* or the Way—through study, reading books, meditation, or other means. In the course of discussing these new problems, certain ancient texts, notably the *Four Books* (Ssu-shu) and the *Book of Changes* (I-ching), gained new importance and emerged eventually as key Confucian texts. Particularly notable was the breadth of learning: many eleventh-century scholars showed a very broad range of interest and knowledge in various fields, including specialized scientific and technical subjects. Yet again, though these developments continued into the twelfth century, the vitality, creativity, and breadth accompanying them did not. Twelfth-century thought and learning began to "turn inward" to "introspection and retrospection," in the words of James T. C. Liu; thinkers of the time were confined in "narrow perimeters," while emphasis was placed on "refining, improving, elaborating, or specializing."[44]

This pattern, of course, does not explain what happened. It can by no means constitute an answer to the "why" question. Rather, it introduces a new "why" question, on an even greater scale: why—or how—did this general pattern of change and stabilization develop? Yet, the fact that later scholars did not continue the broad interest and knowledge of men like Chu Hsi becomes more understandable when one sees how what happened to his natural knowledge fits into this pattern of development in the larger society and culture.

Paradoxically, the very breadth of Chu Hsi's learning may have been a factor in the subsequent narrowing of scholars' interests.[45] His followers could have felt that everything they might wish to know about the natural world had already been included in the corpus of their master. It was almost as if, once Chu Hsi had produced a corpus of knowledge that covered everything, those who came after him did not feel the need to worry about problems other than their principal concern, morality and self-cultivation; everything else, including knowledge of the natural world, was, after all, already there in Chu Hsi. Or it may have been that once Chu Hsi had established "the cosmic basis of morality," it was not necessary to concern themselves with the natural world that had provided that basis.

Yet, in view of the discussion in section 1.1, what happened turns out to be not so paradoxical after all. We have noted, for example, that most natural phenomena were obvious and unproblematic for Chu Hsi and were simply accepted by him. We have also noted some characteristics of his basic ideas and assumptions that could have facilitated this attitude. In a sense, in ignoring natural phenomena Chu Hsi's followers followed Chu Hsi himself, who was not concerned very much with detailed knowledge about the objects and phenomena of the natural world, which he took for granted.

In the remaining pages of this book, I discuss the sort of natural knowledge that the post–Chu Hsi scholars would have found in his sayings and writings. We cannot say whether they actually studied or tried to master the great volume of natural knowledge they found in Chu Hsi, but their silence about it cannot hide the fact that it was readily available to them in their master's corpus. Moreover, it must have appeared sufficient for them, since they were not interested in going further. This is the sense in which we can still take Chu Hsi, however exceptional the scope of his interest and knowledge was, as representative of the place of natural knowledge among the Neo-Confucian literati in general.

1.3. Limits of the Book

This study is limited to only a part, a rather small part, of Chu Hsi's thought and learning. But there are further limits imposed on the book. To begin with, there is the difficulty—or even impossibility—of distinguishing those objects and phenomena that are "natural" from those that are not. The difficulty is that of dividing the thought of a traditional thinker into compartments based on distinctions that are not his own. Chu Hsi himself did not have clear-cut distinctions between "natural" and "nonnatural."[46] He did not even have a single word that would denote "natural" or "the natural world."[47] Although he did use the expression "*tzu-jan*," the standard word for "natural" in modern Chinese, for him the word never meant much more than its literal meaning—"so by itself." He also frequently employed the expression "*t'ien-ti*" (heaven and earth), which referred to "the natural world."[48] But it was always used in a quite global sense, referring to the natural world as a whole without leaving much room for its details—"the myriad things" (*wan-wu*) and man.

Thus, although I have drawn an imaginary boundary to separate objects and phenomena that belong to the natural world from those that do not, it is essentially an artificial, and even an arbitrary, line. Indeed, in Chu Hsi's conversations and writings, there were objects, phenomena, and concepts lying in the border areas that to us would appear clearly nonnatural or "supernatural" but which nevertheless cannot be separated unequivocally from those inside the demarcation line. For example, the alchemical and divinatory theories and practices discussed by Chu Hsi are of the sort that would be difficult to reconcile with modern conceptions of the "natural" world, but many of the objects and phenomena they dealt with clearly belong to it. There also were such concepts as *kuei-shen*, heaven (*t'ien*), and the sages, whose principal meanings lie outside but which nevertheless touch upon objects and phenomena inside the "natural" realm.

In dealing with such border-area phenomena and concepts, I have made my selection of topics quite inclusive. For understanding Chu Hsi's ideas about them will not only show us what he thought about the subjects themselves but will also reveal his ideas about what lies inside the border and throw light on his understanding of the things and the events therein. Thus, from his sayings and writings, I have taken into consideration any passage about objects and phenomena in the external world that occur independently of man's subjective will and emotions and of which objective accounts can be given. This includes human beings, because man's physical and material qualities and functions can be observed and objectively discussed. Not even human thought and feelings have been left out altogether: as we shall see, they can be accounted for by qualities and activities of *ch'i*, the common basic stuff of everything in the world. What I have excluded are social affairs, historical events, and moral concerns, subjects that necessarily involve human emotions and subjective judgments. When cases have come up that are problematic as to whether they are "natural" or not, I have not tried to make a decision but have chosen to include them.

Not only does my choice of materials use a criterion that was not Chu Hsi's own, but my presentation arranges them in a way quite different from the way they appeared in his works. His discussions of natural phenomena are scattered all over his conversations and writings; in the two basic Chu Hsi sources, the *Classified Conversations of Master Chu* (Chu-tzu yü-lei) and the *Collected Writings of Chu Wen-kung* (Chu-wen-kung wen-chi), they are completely mixed in with discussions of other problems. Although I separate his knowledge about natural phenomena from the rest and organize the isolated pieces of information in a more or less systematic way, it has to be borne in mind that such a system was never in Chu Hsi's own mind.

Comparisons that I have occasionally made between Chu Hsi's ideas and those of Western scientific traditions have at times placed me in the perspective of the latter. This has led me, as readers of various drafts of this book have sometimes observed, to speak about what Chu Hsi did *not* (or even failed to) do or what his ideas were *not* rather than what he did or what his ideas were. Yet I have decided to include such comparisons, understanding their dangers fully. They are not entirely avoidable for anyone who tries to discuss traditional ideas in the modern world using modern words. I believe also that comparisons of this sort will enhance our understanding of how Chu Hsi's thought differed from ours, which, if it can be achieved with minimum distortion, will keep us from imposing our own standards upon him and will help us to understand his thought better in its own context. I have even included a chapter (13) in which I consider what Chu Hsi thought about certain ideas that turned out to be important in Western scientific traditions and in modern science, and I allow myself frequently to make comparisons, sometimes quite speculative ones, between Chu Hsi's ideas and those of his Western counterparts.

My own limits of understanding have imposed another restriction on the selection of materials for inclusion in the book. I have chosen to discuss only what I have understood clearly and can express clearly. Some of Chu Hsi's topics that fall inside the imaginary boundary that I mentioned—numerology, divination, and alchemy, for example—have not been adequately dealt with because I have not fully digested the difficult and often highly ambiguous passages containing his ideas about them. This book, then, has been written with the belief that what is contained in those more or less straightforward passages that I have understood clearly will shed sufficient light on Chu Hsi's understanding of the natural world.

I have not been able to trace fully the development of Chu Hsi's natural knowledge throughout his life.[49] To be sure, this is not an altogether impossible task, because we can date most of his recorded conversations and writings, owing largely to the works of scholars who have studied the relationship between Chu Hsi and the disciples with whom he conversed and corresponded.[50] It is obvious that his interest in and attitude toward knowledge of the natural world cannot have remained unchanged during his rather long and intellectually active life. We know, for example, that his interest in natural phenomena and specialized scientific topics deepened late in his life. Much of his discussion on calendrical astronomy and other scientific subjects took place in the late 1190s, when he and his school suffered a vicious political persecution.[51] Yet such "developmental" studies have not always been possible or manageable. The results of such attempts, which I have made when faced with different accounts given by Chu Hsi on the same subject, have often failed to be conclusive.[52] Sometimes the passages could not be dated at all; sometimes only a very wide range of dates could be given; sometimes passages recording different, conflicting views turned out to belong to the same period. Even when different dates were obtained for passages expressing different views about a given natural phenomenon, it could not be determined clearly whether Chu Hsi had changed his view consciously in the course of that period or whether the difference merely reflects a lack of positive interest on his part in the particular phenomenon. After all, it was entirely possible, because he did not intend to construct a coherent system of natural knowledge, for him to have and express different views at different times without worrying about the possibility of conflicts between them.[53] On the whole, it does not appear practicable at this stage to attempt a full-scale "developmental" study of the changes and developments that Chu Hsi's ideas about the natural world underwent. I have contented myself with noting, when and where I can, the changes of his views over time.

I have also not tried to identify all the sources of Chu Hsi's thought about the natural world. Not all of the ideas attributed to him here are his own original contributions. He shared most of them with other thinkers: he derived the bulk of them from his Northern Sung forerunners; a significant portion can be traced back to ancient sources. This was inevitable because these ideas came up as he discussed—in conversations or correspondence with his contemporaries—classical passages or ideas of earlier thinkers. Yet, I have decided that to trace and identify the sources of all of his ideas, which is certainly possible since Chu Hsi was usually explicit about his sources, is neither practical nor necessary. To do so, even in the notes, would hopelessly increase the length of the book without contributing much to its purpose. And after all, these ideas gained importance as Chu Hsi chose to include them in his corpus. Thus, I have commented upon Chu Hsi's sources only when to do so is clearly called for.

Translating Chinese words and sentences into English has imposed still another kind of limit on the book. For instance, I have adopted the policy of sticking to one English translation for a particular Chinese word whenever possible. In this way, readers will know what Chinese characters the English words they are reading stand for. Of course, exceptions cannot be avoided altogether: I have had to resort to different translations for such characters as *hsin*, which means both "heart" and "mind"; *t'ien*, both "heaven" and "sky"; and *chih-chüeh*, both "perception" and "consciousness."[54] I have also tried to avoid using multiword translations—which are more like explanations than translations—for single Chinese characters. Thus, for such terms as *li*, *ch'i*, *kuei-shen*, and so forth, I have opted for transliterations rather than inventing multiword explanations. As a result of following these policies more or less consistently, my translations have frequently become stilted and too literal. For instance, I have chosen to render *tao-li* consistently as "way and *li*," rather than as "moral principle," which would be more idiomatic. On the whole, I do not succeed in providing fully polished, idiomatic English translations. But though sacrificing this goal, my translation policies help to preserve some of the flavors of the original Chinese expressions of Chu Hsi. I believe that they also help to present Chu Hsi's views more faithfully, avoiding distortions that my own interpretations might cause, while retaining all the ambiguities and inconsistencies that were present in the original.

Finally, I have followed the age-old, and now largely out of date, convention of using the words *man* and *he*, when what I actually mean are *human being* (*person*) and *he or she*. I have chosen to do so mainly to avoid burdening my already stilted English. But I believe that the outcome turns out to be a more accurate representation of the male-centered world in which Chu Hsi—and practically all the other persons whose names appear in the book—lived.[55]

Notes

For complete authors' names and for titles and publication data of works cited, as well as the relevant Chinese characters and abbreviated forms of citations, see the bibliography.

1. E.g., Chan, "Chu Hsi's Completion of Neo-Confucianism"; Gardner, *Learning to Be a Sage*. Some useful references on Chu Hsi's thought and learning in general are Ch'ien, *Chu-tzu hsin hsueh-an*; Morohashi and Yasuoka, *Shushigaku taikei*; Chang, *Chu Hsi ssu-hsiang yen-chiu*; Chan, *Chu Hsi and Neo-Confucianism*; Ch'en, *Chu Hsi che-hsueh yen-chiu*.

2. See, e.g., de Bary, "Chu Hsi's Aims as an Educator"; Gardner, *Learning to Be a Sage*, pp. 35–56.

3. On Chu Hsi and academies, see, e.g., Chan, "Chu Hsi and the Academies"; Chaffee, "Chu Hsi and the Revival of the White Deer Grotto Academy." For Sung education in general, see, in addition to the articles in de Bary and Chaffee, *Neo-Confucian Education*, the following two recent monographs: Chaffee, *The Thorny Gates of Learning in Sung China*; Lee, *Government Education and Examinations in Sung China*. See also Terada, *Sōdai kyōikushi gaisetsu*. For an interesting thesis on the changing situation of Sung scholars who found it increasingly difficult to gain official positions, see Bol, "The Sung Examination System and the

Shih." See also Hymes, *Statesmen and Gentlemen*.

4. On the problems confronting the Confucians of Chu Hsi's time, see, e.g., Gardner, *Learning to Be a Sage*, pp. 10–22.

5. For a careful discussion of this complicated process, see Tillman, *Confucian Discourse and Chu Hsi's Ascendancy*. See also Bol, "Chu Hsi's Redefinition of Literati Learning."

6. On the "ascendancy" of Chu Hsi as the leader of the "*Tao-hsueh*" (Learning of the Way) school, see Tillman, *Confucian Discourse and Chu Hsi's Ascendancy*, esp. pt. 3. On the emergence of the Chu Hsi school as the state orthodoxy, see, e.g., Liu, "How Did a Neo-Confucian School Become the State Orthodoxy?"; Schirokauer, "Neo-Confucianism under Attack"; de Bary, *Neo-Confucian Orthodoxy and the Learning of the Mind-and-Heart*, pt. 1.

7. Perhaps the single exception is Yamada's pioneering work: *Shushi no shizen-gaku*. But its coverage is more or less restricted to the astronomical and meteorological knowledge, and in it Yamada adopts a modern scientific perspective, which occasionally makes his interpretation of Chu Hsi's understanding overenthusiastic.

8. In the famous *Ta-hsueh* program of self-cultivation, which Chu Hsi made a core of his teaching, the steps of "making the

mind correct" (*cheng-hsin*) and "making the intention sincere" (*ch'eng-i*), which were prerequisites for the subsequent steps of "cultivating the self" (*hsiu-shen*), "regulating the family" (*ch'i-chia*), "ordering the country" (*chih-kuo*), and "bringing peace to all under heaven" (*p'ing-t'ien-hsia*), were made to be based on "the investigation of things" and the consequent "extension of knowledge" (*chih-chih*). SSCC (*Ta-hsueh*), p. 1b–2a.

9. E.g., *YL*15.2a3.

10. For detailed discussion on the concepts of *li* and *ke-wu*, see chap. 2.

11. E.g., SSCC (*Ta-hsueh*), p. 2a.

12. E.g., Metzger, *Escape from Predicament*, secs. 3i and 3p; Kasoff, *Thought of Chang Tsai*, pp. 71–72, passim; Gardner, *Learning to Be a Sage*, p. 72, passim; Bol, "Chu Hsi's Redefinition of Literati Learning"; Smith et al., *Sung Uses of I Ching*, p. 209.

13. Bol, "Chu Hsi's Redefinition of Literati Learning," pp. 184–185. This point has become a key theme in Bol's book, *"This Culture of Ours."*

14. *YL*34.26b2.

15. *YL*6.5a4.

16. Thus, the lack of interest in detailed natural knowledge did not contradict the idea of a "cosmic basis of morality." Furthermore, since natural objects and phenomena were "obvious" things that needed no further consideration, the knowledge of them could never challenge or threaten the search for morality but would rather accord with, or even reinforce, it. Such a "challenge" was felt, for example, by the medieval church toward the "rationalistic" natural philosophy of Aristotle.

17. E.g., *YL*31.8a0, 1; 8b0, 1, 2; 9a1; 9b2; 78.35b1; *CS*1.19a4; 2.11a1. For more details on this, see chap. 13, sec. 13.2.

18. E.g., *YL*16.19b0; 59.36a2. For more details on this, see chap. 13, sec. 13.3.

19. *YL*10.6a1. All translations in this book are my own. See also *YL*80.19b1.

20. For a rich illustration of how certain things—a stream, a mirror, a plant, and so forth—were used as "images" in Chu Hsi's analogical discussions of human nature, see Munro, *Images of Human Nature*. See also Levey, "The Clan and the Tree."

21. See chap. 10, sec. 10.2; chap. 11, sec. 11.7.

22. See chap. 13, p. 306.

23. *YL*57.12a1.

24. E.g., *YL*72.24a2, 3. For more on this and other examples, see chap. 10, sec. 10.5. John E. Murdoch has mentioned instances in medieval Europe in which certain theological points appear to have been used as excuses to discuss such natural phenomena as light, motion, and celestial spheres, cases that appear to be exactly opposite to what Chu Hsi did. "From Social into Intellectual Factors," esp. pp. 278–279.

25. *YL*16.19b0.

26. *YL*80.19b1.

27. *YL*4.8a1. See also *YL*4.7a1, 19a0; *WC*59.28a; 74.20a; *CS*43.32a2–32b0.

28. E.g., *YL*10.2b3, 3a3; *CS*3.30b0; 6.29b2–30a0.

29. E.g., *YL*4.20b1; 14.1b2, 2a2, 3, 4; 27b3, 4; 20.9a1; 24.6a2; 25.27a1; 44.20a1; 101.33a6. In *YL*4.20b1 Chu Hsi even made a comment that is close to Gresham's law of coins—that "pure ones are always rare and impure ones are always plenty"—in illustrating that great men (*chün-tzu*) are always rare and small men (*hsiao-jen*) are always plentiful.

30. *YL*15.16a2–16b0.

31. *YL*118.19a1. The two expressions come from the *Analects:* "A great man broadly studies culture and restrains it with propriety" (6.25).

32. One source of this dichotomy was the remark from the "Hsi-tz'u chuan" commentary of the *I-Ching:* "What is above physical form is called the Way; what is below physical form is called 'the concrete things' (*ch'i*)" (A12). Chu Hsi's comments on this are gathered in *YL*75.19b4–20b2. See also *YL*95.6a0.

33. *YL*75.20a3. See also *YL*6.11b1; 59.26a3; 78.29b1.

34. *YL*51.5a1. Earlier in the same pas-

sage, he expressed the same idea differently: "The error in things has no harm; the error in the mind has harm." In the passage Chu Hsi is commenting on the *Mencius* passage: "After weighing, one knows the weight; after measuring, one knows the length. Things are all thus; mind is especially so" (1A7).

35. Typical was Chu Hsi's comment on the famous dialogue between Ch'eng I and Shao Yung about where thunder comes from: Ch'eng I said, "Thunder comes from where it comes from," in response to Shao Yung's question, "Where do you think [thunder] comes from?" Chu Hsi commented, "Why must one know where it comes from?" See *YL*100.11a0. The dialogue is recorded in *Ho-nan Ch'eng-shih i-shu*, ch. 21a (*ECC*, p. 270).

36. For more discussion of this, see chap. 13, sec. 13.5.

37. The broad scope of Chu Hsi's learning can be seen in Ch'ien, *Chu-tzu hsin hsueh-an*. For his natural knowledge, in particular in astronomy and meteorology, see Yamada, *Shushi no shizen-gaku*.

38. Note that here I am referring only to a subset of scholars in post–Chu Hsi China, namely those who followed the main emphasis of Chu Hsi. I thus exclude authors of the "encyclopedias," whom Hoyt C. Tillman has discussed in "Encyclopedias, Polymaths, and *Tao-hsueh* Confucians." Tillman's account of them, especially on pp. 106–107, also shows, however, that the kind of narrowing that I refer to in this paragraph did indeed occur. For a brief account of the post–Chu Hsi intellectual atmosphere in general, see Tillman, *Confucian Discourse and Chu Hsi's Ascendancy*, chap. 10.

39. The question is essentially of the same nature as Needham's famous grand question about "the failure of China to give rise to distinctively modern science while having been in many ways ahead of Europe for some fourteen previous centuries," of which it can constitute a part, or the even more grand, and more speculative, "why not" question –"Why did the 'scientific rev-

olution' not take place in China?" or "Why did modern science not develop independently in China?" These grand questions underlie all volumes of Joseph Needham's monumental series, *Science and Civilisation*, but see esp. p. xxiii of the author's note to vol. 5, pt. 2. See also Bodde, *Chinese Thought, Society, and Science*. For discussion of various problems concerning the "why not" question, see my "Natural Knowledge in a Traditional Culture." See also Graham, "China, Europe, and the Origins of Modern Science"; Sivin, "Why the Scientific Revolution Did Not Take Place in China."

40. The changes and new trends in Sung have been amply discussed in books of general history and in monographs on particular aspects of the period: e.g., the works excerpted in Liu and Golas, *Change in Sung China*. For accounts covering longer periods, see, e.g., Elvin, *Pattern of Chinese Past*; Hartwell, "Demographic, Political, and Social Transformations of China." They have also been succinctly summarized in the introductory sections of some recent works on the Sung intellectual history: e.g., Kasoff, *Thought of Chang Tsai*; Smith et al., *Sung Uses of I Ching*; de Bary and Chaffee, *Neo-Confucian Education*; Hymes and Schirokauer, *Ordering the World*.

41. This is an impressive list. And given all these developments, it was almost inevitable that one would think of the parallel developments in early modern Europe, characterized by the growth of commerce, the rise of cities, the centralized states, the "new philosophy," the Renaissance, the Reformation, and so on; indeed, the characterization of the period as "early modern China" did appear. See, e.g., Reischauer and Fairbank, *East Asia*, pp. 220–225. One can find numerous other early modern European parallels to the changes and new trends of Sung China. Thus, two of the trends that Daniel K. Gardner has noted in his recent article on the Sung *yü-lu*– the use of colloquial language in philosophical discourse, and the increased relative

importance placed on the views of the contemporaries compared with the ancient sages—have close parallels in early modern Europe: the vernacular movement and the "ancients versus moderns" debate that ended with the victory of the latter. "Modes of Thinking and Modes of Discourse in the Sung." The point I stress, however, is that although the changes and new trends in early modern Europe continued and even accelerated, ultimately to usher in modern Europe, those of "early modern" China did not bring about "modern" China.

42. James T. C. Liu, in a recent book dealing with this very subject, which he has characterized as "China turning inward," has even said: "Whatever may be described as early modern features were frozen inside a rigid cultural pattern; they continued to grow, not by reaching out to new ideas and technologies but by modifying those within. . . . Something must have happened to turn many broad sweeps of outward-reaching advance into an intricate weaving of inward refinement and reinforcement." *China Turning Inward*, p. 9. He concluded: "In short, the elite culture developed; but stayed *within* accepted categories. Its creativity was contained" (p. 11, original italics). Elvin, in an earlier, more controversial, book, even spoke of China's ultimately reaching "the high-level equilibrium trap." *Pattern of Chinese Past*, p. 298.

43. Good brief surveys of Sung intellectual background are available in the following recent studies: Tillman, *Utilitarian Confucianism*, chap. 1, esp. pp. 30–59; Kasoff, *Thought of Chang Tsai*, chap. 1; Gardner, *Learning to Be a Sage*, pp. 57–81; Smith et al., *Sung Uses of I Ching*, chap. 2; Bol, *"This Culture of Ours,"* chaps. 1, 5–6.

44. Liu, *China Turning Inward*, pp. 35, 72, 128, passim.

45. Cf. de Bary, "Chu Hsi's Aims as an Educator," pp. 209–210, where he sees a different sort of paradox, not altogether unrelated to the present one.

46. Nor did he have a clear-cut distinction between matter and mind; thus, we cannot use that distinction as our criterion, either.

47. The meaning of the word "natural" is by no means straightforward in English, either. For example, it is used in such idiomatic expressions as "it is *natural* that . . ." Translation of the character *hsing*, one of the most important philosophical terms for Chu Hsi, into "human nature," or simply "nature," imposes even more ambiguity upon the English word.

48. Willard J. Peterson has proposed the use of this expression as a single word, "heaven-and-earth," referring to "the physical cosmos as a whole." "Making Connections," p. 84. For more on the expression *t'ien-ti*, see chap. 7, sec. 7.2.

49. Chu Hsi himself at times admitted that he had changed his views on some topics, e.g., YL92.10a3–10b0.

50. E.g., Tanaka, "Shumon teishi shiji-nen kō"; Ch'en, *Chu-tzu men-jen*.

51. See, e.g., Yamada, *Shushi no shizen-gaku*, p. 1. Of the many biographies of Chu Hsi, the most recent and complete is Shu, *Chu-tzu ta-chuan*. But I have found Miura's account in his *Shushi*, pp. 35–263, most interesting. Wang Mao-hung's (1668–1741) *Chu-tzu nien-p'u* is the standard source. Among the excellent brief biographies are those contained in Gardner, *Learning to Be a Sage*; and in Chan, *Chu Hsi and Neo-Confucianism*. The political aspect of his life is discussed in Schirokauer, "Chu Hsi's Political Career." Ch'en, *Chu-tzu hsin t'an-so*, contains various pieces of information on many particular aspects of Chu Hsi's life. See also the English version of Ch'en's work, Chan, *Chu Hsi: New Studies*.

52. For more on this point, see chap. 14, sec. 14.3.

53. Nor has it been possible for me to see what were Chu Hsi's real intentions in studying and discussing specialized scientific subjects in his late life, as can be seen in *Ts'an t'ung-ch'i k'ao-i* and *Ch'u-tz'u chi-chu*. When his intellectual development is understood more fully, the political situation surrounding him may turn out to have

been significant. For example, his interest in the abstruse and speculative topics in the above two books might very well have been more genuine in this difficult period of his life than is generally depicted in the present book.

54. For each of these words, however, it is not always possible to distinguish which of the two senses Chu Hsi was referring to. Indeed, in many cases he did not seem to be conscious of such distinctions. I have translated the character *hsin* as "the mind," except when it clearly refers to the physical organ, in which case it is translated as "the heart." The character *t'ien* has been rendered always as "heaven" unless it refers only and unambiguously to the physical sky. For the word *chih-chüeh*, I have alternated rather freely between the two translations as the context dictates.

55. Information on Chu Hsi's own attitudes toward women can be found in Birge, "Chu Hsi and Women's Education"; Ch'en, *Chu-tzu hsin t'an-so*, pp. 781–792; Chan, *Chu Hsi: New Studies*, pp. 537–547.

Basic Concepts of Chu Hsi's Natural Philosophy

I discuss in part 1 some key concepts—*li*, *ch'i*, yin-yang, the five phases (*wu-hsing*), images and numbers, and so on—that form the basic vocabulary of Chu Hsi's natural knowledge. They were the fundamental concepts in terms of which he presented his ideas about the natural world; I also use them in my own discussion.

Most of these concepts have been discussed to a degree—some more intensively than others—in the current literature. My reasons for covering this rather familiar ground include the obvious one, that I have found new and important points to discuss that other scholars have overlooked. But there are other reasons also. First, whereas the existing accounts have usually taken only one or a few of these terms at a time, I consider them together, albeit in several separate chapters. Second, much of the earlier work has been fairly general, often covering many thinkers over long periods of time, in certain cases over the whole period of traditional Chinese history; I focus my discussion on Chu Hsi's understanding and use of the terms. Finally, I concentrate on those aspects that bear on our understanding of the content and context of Chu Hsi's knowledge about the natural world, and in so doing I am able to suggest that his ideas about these basic concepts both reflected and enforced certain characteristic attitudes of Chu Hsi toward natural phenomena and the knowledge of them.

The list of terms forming this vocabulary should have also included such concepts as the Way (*tao*), human nature (*hsing*), mind (*hsin*), humaneness (*jen*), righteousness (*i*), propriety (*li*), and so forth. For these were key concepts of Chu Hsi's moral philosophy, in which there was no definite boundary between the natural and the human worlds. Yet, his ideas about all these terms have been extensively discussed, and I do not attempt to add my own account. Rather, I use them in my discussions of other concepts, assuming that readers are more or less familiar with them. Even with regard to the term *li*, which is one of the topics of part 1, I discuss only some particular aspects relevant to the understanding of Chu Hsi's *ke-wu* endeavor, which in turn provides a general context for the rest of my discussion in the book. The term "mind" (*hsin*), excluded from part 1, is taken up in chapter 11, which deals with Chu Hsi's ideas about man as an object in the natural world.

Chapters 6 and 7 discuss Chu Hsi's ideas of *kuei-shen*, heaven, and the sages. I include them here because, although the principal meanings of these terms lie outside the natural world, they nevertheless touch upon natural objects and phenomena; also, perhaps more importantly, what he thought about these border-area concepts helps us to understand better his thought about what lies inside the border.

2

Li and *Ke-wu* (Investigation of Things)

Among the most fundamental and frequently used concepts in Chu Hsi's discussion of natural phenomena are *li* and *ch'i*. In fact, in the standard Neo-Confucian schemes of classification, these concepts, grouped into one word, *li-ch'i*, designated a category covering basic topics in what can be called cosmology and natural philosophy. The first two *chüan* (volumes) of Chu Hsi's *Classified Conversations* are titled *Li-Ch'i* and cover the topics of the supreme ultimate (*t'ai-chi*) and heaven and earth. The *Complete Works of Master Chu* (Chu-tzu ch'üan-shu) also has two *chüan* (49–50) titled *Li-Ch'i* that are devoted to such topics as the supreme ultimate, heaven and earth, yin-yang, the five phases (*wu-hsing*), astronomy, calendars, geography, tides, and meteorology. My discussion begins with these two concepts—*li* in this chapter, and *ch'i* and its relation to *li* in the next.

The concept of *li* has a wide variety of characteristics with meanings of various shades and dimensions, by no means confined to the domain of natural philosophy. Yet, since such various aspects of the term have been abundantly treated in many modern studies,[1] I shall restrict my discussion in this chapter to aspects of *li* that bear upon our understanding of the contents and contexts of Chu Hsi's natural knowledge, the relation of his ideas of *li* with the *ke-wu* endeavor in particular.

2.1. *Li:* The One Universal *Li* and the Many Individual *Li*

The term *li* is difficult to define. It is difficult even to translate, because there is no single word in Western languages that covers all facets of what *li* meant to the traditional Chinese mind. The existence of many translations for the term, which often leaves transliteration as the only viable option, bespeaks the difficulty.[2]

Chu Hsi himself did not provide any explicit definition of *li*. He came the closest to defining it when he said:

> When it comes to things under heaven, for each [of the things] there must be a "reason (*ku*)[3] by which [a thing is] as it is" (*so-i-jan chih ku*) and "a rule (*tse*) according to which [a thing] ought to be" (*so-tang-jan chih tse*). [These are] what are called "*li*."[4]

But he did not elaborate on these two different aspects of the concept that he characterized by the expressions "that by which a thing is as it is" (*so-i-jan*) and "that which a thing ought to be" (*so-tang-jan*). He spoke of them only in terms of particular examples. For instance,

> In treating one's parents, one ought to be filial, and in treating one's elder brother, one ought to be brotherly. Such are "the rules according to which [one] ought to be." But in treating one's parents, why should one be filial, and in treating one's elder brother, why should one be brotherly? These are "the reasons by which [a man is] as he is."[5]

An aspect of *li* that Chu Hsi emphasized greatly was the idea that there are many individual *li* for individual objects and phenomena and the one *li* for the whole of those objects and phenomena. Every object and phenomenon of the world—"a blade of grass, a tree, or even an insect,"[6] to use Chu Hsi's own expression—has its individual *li*; all individual *li* are manifestations of the one *li*. He praised Ch'eng I's famous expression "*Li* is one and its manifestations are many" (*li i fen shu*) and said, "Speaking of heaven and earth and the myriad things together, [they] simply are the one *li*; when it comes to [the *li*] in man, then again each man has [his own] one *li*."[7] Chu Hsi himself expressed the idea in various other ways: "All things have [their] *li*; as a whole [they are] simply the one *li*";[8] "Heaven and earth, yin and yang, life and death, day and night, and *kuei* and *shen*—[all these] are simply the one *li*";[9] and "Myriad things all have this *li*; all the *li* come from the one source. Yet, if the positions in which they reside are different, the functions of their *li* are not one."[10]

The one *li* is a kind of "universal" *li* that somehow covers all the individual *li* of things and events. And as such, it is a concept difficult to discuss in a straightforward manner. Chu Hsi sometimes equated it with the concept of the supreme ultimate.[11] The latter, for him, was "the original *li* of heaven and earth and of the myriad things,"[12] or simply the name given to "the sum of [all] the *li* of heaven and earth and of the myriad things."[13] It is called the "supreme ultimate" (*t'ai-chi*) because it is the "ultimate" (*chi*), the "extreme" (*chih* or *chih-chi*), or the "acme" (*chi-chih*) of the *li*.[14] Chu Hsi said, for example, that "the supreme ultimate is simply the ultimately fine and extremely good way and *li*."[15]

Chu Hsi identified the one *li* with "the heavenly *li*" (*t'ien-li*) also:

> The heavenly *li* flows and moves. Wherever one touches, it is the heavenly *li*. Hot weather goes and cold weather comes; rivers flow and mountains stand erect. Fathers and sons have love; rulers and subjects have righteousness, and things like that. There is nothing that is not this *li*. "To learn and at times to practice it," for example, is to investigate this *li* exhaustively. That "filial piety and brotherly respect are the root of the humaneness" also is in substance this *li*.[16]

The heavenly *li* is what the original human nature manifests in the form of such ethical virtues as humaneness and righteousness; it is because the heavenly *li* is obstructed and blocked by "human desires" (*jen-yü*) that man loses the virtues and shows evil traits. This dichotomy of "heavenly *li*" versus "human desires," which can be traced back to the ancient times,[17] became the basis of Chu Hsi's moral philosophy; thus, a state of mind free from human desires was for him the ultimate goal of man's self-cultivation.[18] When that goal is attained, man's mind fully manifests the heavenly *li*.[19]

2.2. *Ke-wu:* Mind and the *Li* of Things and Events

It is not only the original human nature that manifests the heavenly *li;* every thing and event in the world has its *li*, which is but a manifestation of the one universal, "heavenly" *li*. Therefore, man can aim at the heavenly *li* through the method of "*ke-wu*" also, because for many Neo-Confucians, including Chu Hsi, that term, translated usually as "the investigation of things," meant reaching the *li* in "things."[20] Chu Hsi said, "'*Ke-wu*' is exhaustively investigating the ultimate *li* of every thing,"[21] or "One who 'investigates things' simply wants to exhaust the *li* of things."[22]

Ke-wu, however, did not involve primarily intellectual procedures. To be sure, the characters "*ke*" and "*wu*," and Chu Hsi's occasional illustrations of the term with actual examples, make one think of processes of examination and analysis of things and events with the goal of understanding of their *li*. Chu Hsi even said, "Scholars must know, in general, how heaven can be high, how the earth can be thick, how *kuei-shen* becomes hidden and manifest, and how mountains can be fused. This simply is *ke-wu*."[23] Yet, the emphasis of Chu Hsi's *ke-wu* endeavor was overwhelmingly on moral and social problems. Even in the above examples, he spoke of natural objects and phenomena to illustrate *ke-wu*, more or less rhetorically; rarely was he thinking of actual investigations or analyses of the objects and phenomena.[24]

In fact, the mind's reaching the *li* of things was, for Chu Hsi, a kind of "resonance" between the mind's *li* and the things' *li*.[25] This was so because the heavenly *li* resides both in man's mind and in things and events. And since the many individual *li* of things and events are but manifestations of the one *li*, Chu Hsi could say that man's mind in its original state contains all "the myriad *li*."[26] He even went on to equate the *li* in the mind and the *li* in things and events:

> The *li* in things and in my mind are originally one thing. The two do not have even a small gap [between them]. But it is necessary that I should respond to them [i.e., the *li* in things], and that is all. Things and the mind share this *li*.[27]

Thus, when a man reached the *li* of a thing or an event as a result of *ke-wu*, it was described by Chu Hsi usually as "seeing" (*chien* or *k'an*) the *li* rather than as "knowing" it.[28] In other words, what he gained was not so much a knowledge of the *li* as an insight into it.

For that sort of resonance to take place, the mind needs to be in certain states— "empty" (*hsü*), "bright" (*ming* or *kuang*), "tranquil" (*ching* or *ning*), "settled" (*ting*), or "peaceful" (*p'ing*). These are the original states of man's mind, manifesting the heavenly *li* fully, free from blockings by human desires. In such states the mind spontaneously sees the *li* in things and events, which are nothing but manifestations of the heavenly *li* contained in the mind itself. Thus, Chu Hsi said: "When the mind is bright, it can spontaneously see that this event has this *li* and this thing has this *li*";[29] "When this mind is empty, bright, and tranquil, the way and *li* circulate spontaneously."[30] Also, "when the mind is peaceful and the *ch'i* is settled, one can see the way and *li*."[31] When "the mind is not settled, . . . one cannot see the *li*."[32] Chu Hsi emphasized the "empty" state of mind in particular: "If one has emptied the mind, one can see the way and *li* clearly";[33] "Empty the mind and see the *li*."[34] Therefore, in reading books, an "empty" mind is required, as he repeatedly stated.[35] He even said, "To 'investigate the *li* exhaustively' (*ch'iung-li*), one takes the empty mind and tranquil thought as the basis."[36]

Moreover, this "resonance" is a two-way process. Not only does one's mind in those states see the *li* in things and events; but also the state of one's mind changes as the result of seeing the *li*. For example: "Once it is settled on the *li*, the mind can be tranquil. If it is not settled on the *li*, then this mind will simply go east and run west."[37] And "After the mind is ripe (*shu*), there will spontaneously be cases in which it will see the *li*. When ripe, the mind is refined and subtle. When it does not see the *li*, this mind will be coarse just because of that."[38]

2.3. The Heavenly *Li*: The Ultimately Moral Purpose of *Ke-wu*

Understanding the many *li* of individual things and events, however, was not the real aim of Chu Hsi's *ke-wu* endeavor. The ultimate purpose of *ke-wu*, for him, was to reach the one universal *li*—the heavenly *li*—via the individual *li*. That was how, for example, he characterized the "extension of knowledge" (*chih-chih*), the intended consequence of the *ke-wu*: "[One] must reach all the *li* of heaven and earth and the myriad things, and 'penetrate through it by one' (*i i kuan chih*)."[39] The key step in the *ke-wu*, then, was not to see the *li* of things and events by studying them, although that was important and difficult enough; it was to move from those individual *li* to reach the one heavenly *li*, which ensures the moral virtues of the original state of man's mind.

Yet, the connection between the many individual *li* and the one universal *li* was not quite traceable. It was never clear exactly how a grasp of the many individual *li* could lead to the apprehension of the one heavenly *li*. Chu Hsi's idea about this process was basically that of Ch'eng I, who described it as a "sudden" (*t'o-jan*), "thorough penetration" (*kuan-t'ung*). Chu Hsi praised, and frequently quoted, the following remark of Ch'eng I:

> One must investigate one item today and another item tomorrow. After one has accumulated, and familiarized oneself with, many [of them], suddenly and spontaneously there will be a "thorough penetration."[40]

But Chu Hsi did not have much to say about the actual process that "suddenly" takes man from the many *li* to the one *li*; he merely repeated that after much accumulation and familiarization it would come "spontaneously."[41] For example,

> Although myriad *li* are simply one *li*, scholars still need to proceed to the myriad *li* and understand all the thousand ends and the myriad beginnings. [When one has] managed to collect them together on four sides, [one can] see spontaneously that [they] are the one *li*.[42]

In this situation, it is no wonder that there could be no agreement among Chu Hsi's followers on details of this key step in the *ke-wu* endeavor, and such disagreement was at the center of the perennial controversy over the correct method of *ke-wu* throughout the history of Neo-Confucianism.[43]

A point on which all seemed to agree, however, was that the step described by such expressions as "sudden," "spontaneous," and "thorough penetration" must involve something more than a purely intellectual process. In Chu Hsi's words, one needs "laborious efforts" (*kung-fu*) and "nourishing" (*yang*) in addition to "knowing" (*chih*) and "understanding" (*li-hui*). "In investigating things, one must not merely understand the meaning of the text. One should really exert laborious efforts and go on investigating."[44] "One who is to extend knowledge has to nourish knowledge first."[45]

This is why the mental state of "reverence" (*ching*) was required for the *ke-wu* endeavor. Chu Hsi praised Ch'eng I's saying "There is no one who has extended knowledge but does not reside in reverence."[46] He said himself that "maintaining reverence is the root of the exhaustive investigation of the *li*."[47] This was so because, for Chu Hsi, when a man is reverent, his mind is "bright," "alert" (*hsing-hsing*), "alive" (*ts'un*), "uniform" (*i*), and "transparent" (*chan-jan*),[48] the heavenly *li* is "brilliant" (*ts'an-jan*),[49] and all *li* are in the mind.[50] He even said: "When one is reverent, the heavenly *li* will be always bright, and spontaneously, human desires will be curbed and will vanish."[51] It must have been to attain this state of reverence that Chu Hsi recommended, and himself resorted to, the practice of "quiet sitting" (*ching-tso*).[52]

Thus, the moral and intellectual endeavors of Chu Hsi converged in his search of *li*—the many individual *li* and the one heavenly *li*—through *ke-wu*.[53] And in this convergence, the moral side was clearly the more important.[54] Of course the intellectual aspect could not be ignored. When a disciple said, "When one is reverent, the mind becomes empty and bright, and afterward one can investigate things and judge right and wrong," Chu Hsi responded: "Although it is so, one must nevertheless investigate things also and not allow it [i.e., the mind] to be blocked by [even] the slightest amount of selfish desire. [Only] afterward, the mind can become empty and bright."[55] Yet, on the whole, the intellectual elements of the *ke-wu* endeavor were fused into its ultimately moral aims. For Chu Hsi, it was to uphold morality and to avoid errors that one investigates things: "When one has accumulated laborious efforts [by investigating many things], . . . one will spontaneously see this way and *li* clearly, and one will not make errors in dealing with affairs."[56] One who has exhaustively investigated the *li* also "knows that by which [things and events] are as they are, and therefore [his] will is not confused. [He] knows that according to which they ought to be so, and therefore [his] actions are not in error."[57] The same thing was true in terms of learning in general:

> When one is not versed in learning, the mind will be confused by human desires. If one is already versed in learning, the heavenly *li* will be spontaneously manifest, and human desires will disappear gradually.[58]

Attainment of moral virtues that are manifestations of the heavenly *li* was the ultimate goal of learning for Chu Hsi and for the Neo-Confucians who followed him.

It is natural, then, that much of Chu Hsi's illustration of *li* was in terms of normative moral rules. What came up most frequently were the rules governing the basic human relations—between rulers and subjects, fathers and sons, husbands and wives, elder and younger persons, and between friends.[59] The constant virtues of "humaneness," "righteousness," "propriety," and "knowledge" were other frequently mentioned examples of *li*: "Propriety is that spontaneous *li* of heaven and earth";[60] "Humaneness is the correct *li* of my mind."[61] Chu Hsi's discussion of where *li* can be found reflects the same orientation:

> If one reads books in order to teach and clarify the way and righteousness, then the *li* exists in the books. If one discusses men of the past and present and distinguishes the right and wrong, the wicked and correct, then the *li* exists in the men of past and present. If one deals with events and things and examines and judges whether they are proper or not, then the *li* exists in dealing with events and things.[62]

Furthermore, in discussing the two aspects of *li*, namely "that by which a thing is as it is" and "that which a thing ought to be," his illustrations were frequently in terms of the latter alone. He said, for example:

> In general, seeing has the rule of [what one] ought to see, and hearing has the rule of [what one] ought to hear. To see when it is so [i.e., when one ought to see], and to hear when it is so, it is right; to see when it is not so [i.e., when one ought not see] and to hear when it is not so, it is not right. . . . Inferring from this to the mouth on tastes and the nose on smells, [each] cannot but have the rule [according to which it] ought to be. What is called "exhaustively investigating the *li*" is nothing other than exhaustively investigating this.[63]

Indeed, the context in which the term originally appeared in *Great Learning* (Ta-hsueh) showed the moral purpose of *ke-wu* clearly, which Chu Hsi noted in his comment on the classic:

> For this, it is said that when one investigates things and reaches things, the *li* of the things are exhaustively investigated. When all the *li* of things are exhaustively investigated, my

knowledge will be broad and will thoroughly penetrate [the *li*]. There will be no blocking or obstruction; the intention will have nothing that is not sincere and the mind will
have nothing that is not correct. This is the meaning of the main classic of the *Great
Learning*.[64]

2.4. The Content and Substance of *Li*

One aspect of the concept *li* fits in well with the nature of the *ke-wu* endeavor discussed in the previous section — the convergence of moral and intellectual endeavors and the supremacy of the moral side. This aspect of *li* has not been covered adequately in the current literature. As I deal with it in this section, I speak more about
what *li* is not than about what it is.

The *li* of an object or a phenomenon is not a simple idea or principle that can
provide an explanation or an understanding of the object or the phenomenon at a
level more fundamental than the object or the phenomenon itself. It is merely that
because of which the object exists or the phenomenon takes place as it actually
does: when and only when there is *li* for it, does it exist or take place. In Chu Hsi's
own words, "If there is 'this' *li*, only then does 'this' thing or event exist. It is like
[the fact that] if the plants have seeds, only then they can produce [new] plants."[65]
The analogy between the *li* of a thing or event and the seeds of plants makes it even
clearer that for a thing or event to exist or to occur there has to be the *li* for it first.
In one passage Chu Hsi expressed this same idea in the following four different
ways:[66] (1) "If there is 'this' *li*, then there is 'this' thing"; (2) "There cannot be [such
a case in which there is] 'this' thing while there is no *li* for 'this'"; (3) "If there is no
li for 'this,' then although there may be 'this' thing, it is as though there were no
such thing"; (4) "If there is no *li* for 'this,' then there [can]not be 'this' thing." Thus,
every thing has to have its *li* in order to exist. There have to be *li* for heaven and
earth, for example, so that there can be heaven and earth.[67] Only when there is *li*
for the *ch'i*, is there that *ch'i*.[68] Chu Hsi said: "When there is *li* for 'this,' then 'this'
ch'i flows, moves, grows, and nourishes the myriad things."[69] He also said: "Their
li are various, so the things are also various."[70] Even such strange phenomena as
ghost whistles and ghost fires occur when there are *li* for them.[71]

This aspect was so overwhelming in Chu Hsi's thought about *li* that for him the
expression "there is *li* for 'this'" (*yu tz'u li*) usually meant that "this" can exist, that
"this" can take place, or even simply that "this" is true.[72] Frequently, after mentioning certain phenomena or facts, Chu Hsi added the remark, "Perhaps there is *li*
for this," which meant that perhaps "this" was possible.[73] Or he asked the question,
"Is there *li* for this?" which was really asking whether "this" was possible.[74] When
he said, "There is no *li* for this," or questioned, "How could there be *li* for this?" it
meant that "this" could not exist or take place or that "this" was not possible.[75]

Therefore, the *li* of a complex object or phenomenon is not conceptually simpler
or more fundamental than the object or phenomenon itself. Indeed, *li* refers to a
given object or phenomenon as a whole in its totality. The *li* of a complicated object or phenomenon is not what can be employed in the explanation or analysis of

that object or phenomenon in simpler terms. When *li* is mentioned, it is merely invoked to assure the existence or occurrence of the object or the phenomenon. Nor is the content of *li* analyzed or studied; it is grasped as a whole. As we have noted, when a man is faced with a thing or an event, his mind "sees"—rather than "understands" or "knows"—its *li.*

Thus, when Chu Hsi mentioned "the *li* of movement and rest," it was not something that could facilitate an analytical explanation of the nature and details of movement and rest; it was only that because of which there is the movement and the rest. He said: "There is this *li* of movement, then [the supreme ultimate] can move and produce the yang. There is this *li* of being at rest, then [it] can be at rest and produce the yin."[76] Similarly, when he said, "The reason that [flying birds] fly and [jumping fish] jump is the *li,*" this *li* referred to the particular acts of the birds' flying and the fish's jumping and did not embrace any simpler or more fundamental understanding of the acts.[77] His conception of *li* seemed to assume a more general form when he said, "That the complex interconnection of the yin and yang and the five phases does not lose its order is simply [because of] the *li*";[78] but this *li* did not tell anything about that order except that it existed.

Sometimes Chu Hsi appeared to have something more in mind when he spoke of *li,* even something like the notion of "law" or "rule." For instance, he spoke of the following examples of *li:* "A boat can move only on water; a cart can move only on land."[79] Superficially, those sound like laws governing the movements of boats and carts. But these *li* really refer to the whole fact that boats move on water or that carts move on land, and not to any general and simple principles according to which boats and carts move or which can be used in analyses of the movements of boats and carts.[80] What his sentence really says, therefore, is simply that a boat can move only on water because the *li* of a boat is that it should move on water and that a cart can move only on land because the *li* of a cart is that it should move on land. Yet, that a boat should move on water and a cart on land is really a condition for being a boat or a cart. Thus, in the end, the sentence amounts to nothing more than the mere statement that a boat or a cart exists and functions as such because there is the *li* of a boat or a cart, exactly the aspect of *li* stressed here. The same point can be made with Chu Hsi's assertion "Winter is cold and summer is hot. This is because 'the constant *li*' (*ch'ang-li*) must be like this."[81] He even said that, because there are the *li* of them, "rhubarb cannot become wolfsbane and wolfsbane cannot become rhubarb."[82] In other words, because there is the *li* of rhubarb, rhubarb is rhubarb and cannot be wolfsbane.

Thus, *li* has little additional content beyond the phenomenon or object of which it is the *li.* In a sense, *li* is very much like a definition. What Chu Hsi frequently referred to as the *li* of a chair, "that it has four legs and that one can sit on it," is a good example.[83] Similarly, the *li* of a fan, for him, was "that the fan is made like this and ought to be used like this," again a kind of definition of a fan.[84] Like a definition, the *li* of a thing includes its functions: that one can sit on it is a function of a chair; as for "the *li* of a man," Chu Hsi referred to "speech and activities."[85]

This aspect of *li* was not so marked from the beginning of the evolution of the concept. It began to be noticeable only in the thought of the Ch'eng brothers and became prominent only in Chu Hsi.[86] Nor did the concept of *li* enjoy a great importance during the early phase of Sung Neo-Confucianism; it gained such importance only gradually, again first with the Ch'eng brothers.[87] But once this aspect of *li* became prominent after Chu Hsi, and as the concept itself gained importance, a tendency developed that took *li* to have an existence apart from the phenomenon or the object of which it is the *li*. Chu Hsi, of course, did not approve such notions; he expressed his disapproval frequently. For example, he said: "Cold and hot weather, day and night, opening and closing, going and coming—'the real *li*' (*shih-li*) flows and moves in them. Without them, the real *li* does not have [a place] where it can be put."[88] He meant the same thing when he said that "*li* is everywhere between heaven and earth and the myriad things."[89] Thus, Chu Hsi said repeatedly that *li* does not constitute an additional thing, for *li* is in *ch'i* (which constitutes every thing of the world) or in the mind (which perceives every thing of the world).[90] His saying that if there is no *ch'i* or mind, there is no place to which *li* can be attached or adhered expressed the same point.[91]

Yet, these sayings of Chu Hsi could not prevent the persistence of the idea of the separate existence of *li*. That he had to assert repeatedly that *li* is only in *ch'i* testifies to this, for it came up really as his response to those who, assuming a separate existence of *li*, asked where it could be found. He even had to respond to such questions as where *li* existed before there was any man or any thing.[92] His assertion that *li* is only in the mind, though it was meant as rejection of the existence of *li* as a separate substance, could still be interpreted as referring to a separate existence of *li* apart from actual things and events. Chu Hsi himself was not free from such a tendency. He said, for example, that the heart, the physical site for the mind, has empty spaces in it so that it can contain and store ways and *li* abundantly.[93] His firm opposition to the Buddhist doctrines of the void (*k'ung*) and nothingness (*wu*) also reinforced the tendency, for it made him defend the reality and actuality of *li*, which could easily lead to the implication of separate existence of *li*.[94]

Chu Hsi's contemporaries and followers were more prone to side with such implications. From their interest in questions as to whether there is a *li* for a certain thing or event (for only then can there be that thing or event), they were readily led to ask questions like "Where does the *li* exist?" "Where can one find the *li*?" and even "How can one attain the *li*?" clearly implying a separate existence of *li*. These, then, were the kinds of questions that continued to be asked by Chu Hsi's followers, who regarded the search for—and the attainment of—*li* as the key to their moral-intellectual endeavor of *ke-wu*. And it is not surprising that those interested in asking this sort of questions should concentrate themselves on the moral side of the endeavor.

Notes

1. For recent discussions of various aspects of the concept of *li*, in Chu Hsi as well as other Neo-Confucian thinkers, see, e.g., Wittenborn, "*Li* Revisited and Other Explorations"; Cheng, "Chu Hsi's Methodology and Theory of Understanding"; Peterson,

"Another Look at *Li*." For some earlier useful discussions, see Chan, "Evolution of the Concept *Li* as Principle"; Graham, *Two Chinese Philosophers*, pp. 8–22.

2. *Li* is most often translated as "principle," but it is also rendered as "reason" and "law." For the list of translations of *li*, see Chan, *Reflections on Things at Hand*, p. 367. Willard J. Peterson has suggested "coherence" as an alternative. "Another Look at *Li*."

3. The character *ku*, translated here as "reason," has other meanings as well: see chap. 13, p. 305. But Chu Hsi said that *ku* also "has the meaning of that by which a thing is as it is." E.g., *YL*57.13a1, 13b1.

4. *Ta-hsueh huo-wen*, 1.11b–12a. He expressed the same idea in a slightly different way: "One who exhaustively investigates the *li* wishes to know that by which events and things are as they are and that according to which they ought to be so." *WC*64.33a.

5. *YL*18.21b1.

6. *YL*15.12a2. See also *YL*15.12a3.

7. *YL*1.1b6. Ch'eng I's saying appears, e.g., in *Ts'ui-yen*, ch. 1 (*ECC*, pp. 1202–1203); *I-ch'üan wen-chi*, ch. 5 (*ECC*, p. 609), where Chang Tsai's discussion of the idea is praised.

8. *YL*94.8b0.

9. *YL*25.13b1.

10. *YL*18.8a1.

11. For Chu Hsi's ideas about this ancient concept, which occupied an important place in the early phase of Neo-Confucianism, see, e.g., Yamanoi, "The Great Ultimate and Heaven in Chu Hsi's Philosophy."

12. *WC*36.14a.

13. *WC*78.19a. See also *YL*94.9b1.

14. E.g., *YL*94.6a2; *WC*36.8b; 37.31b.

15. *YL*94.6a1. At times "the supreme ultimate" was equated with *li* in general, not just with the single universal *li*: "The supreme ultimate is simply *li*." E.g., *YL*94.1b3, 2a3, 5a0. Chu Hsi even said, "Each man has one supreme ultimate; each thing has one supreme ultimate." *YL*94.6a1.

16. *YL*40.8a1. The phrase "To learn and

at times to practice it" comes from the first sentence of the *Analects*, 1.1. See also *YL*41.7a0.

17. E.g., *Li-chi*, 37.10a–10b: "A man who is transformed to a thing is one who destroys the heavenly *li* and exploits human desires."

18. Chu Hsi's discussions of this dichotomy can be found, e.g., in *YL*13.2a6–3b2; 31.14b2; 40.7a0; 41.5b1, 7a0, 20b2; 68.10a2; 90.7a5–7b0; *WC*39.20a; 73.42b; *CS*3.3a3.

19. Chu Hsi even said that "the entire body of the Sage [i.e., Confucius] is the heavenly *li*." *YL*58.1a1. See also *YL*44.18b1.

20. E.g., *SSCC* (*Ta-hsueh*), 2a. For some brief discussions of what *ke-wu* meant in the Sung times, see, e.g., Graham, *Two Chinese Philosophers*, pp. 74–82; Lau, "A Note on *Ke Wu*"; Tillman, "The Idea and the Reality of the 'Thing' during the Sung." For Chu Hsi's own account of some earlier thinkers' ideas about *ke-wu*, see *YL*18.23b1–24b2.

21. *YL*15.8a5.

22. *YL*63.7a0. Daniel K. Gardner has made this aspect explicit by translating the term as "apprehension of the principle in things": *Learning to Be a Sage*, pp. x–xi, 52–53, 88 n, 117–118, and passim.

23. *YL*18.8b2. See also *YL*15.4b2.

24. Chu Hsi's sayings and writings about *ke-wu* are scattered all over *YL* and *WC*, but especially in *YL*16 and 18. They are gathered and discussed by Ch'ien, *Chu-tzu hsin hsueh-an*, 2:504–550.

25. In Daniel K. Gardner's apt words that sum up his discussion in *Learning to Be a Sage*, pp. 46–53, "[T]he mind of man, after all, embraced the myriad manifestations of principle [i.e., *li*]; thus as it confronted things, the mind—if fully attentive, fully concentrated—could through a sort of resonance sense the principle in those things. A natural response occurred between principle in one's mind and in the things before that mind" (p. 53). Gardner even said that "apprehending principle either in things out there or in oneself was nothing but *self-realization*" (p. 53, my italics).

26. E.g., *YL*9.6a3; *CS*44.5a3–5b0; *SSCC* (*Meng-tzu*), 7.1a.

27. *YL*12.17b3.

28. E.g., *YL*11.2a2, 3b5; 12.8b3–9a0.

29. *YL*12.8b3–9a0.

30. *YL*67.12b1. Such is the state of mind that Thomas A. Metzger characterized with the expression "*hsü-ling ming-chüeh*" and described as "intelligent awareness in its pure, naturally given, cosmically indivisible form, empty of any consciously specific concepts or sensations." *Escape from Predicament*, p. 58, passim.

31. *YL*11.3a1.

32. *YL*11.2a2.

33. *YL*11.3a5–3b0.

34. *YL*9.6a5.

35. E.g., *YL*11.3a4–4b1.

36. *YL*9.6a4.

37. *YL*14.12b1.

38. *YL*9.7b3.

39. *WC*42.16b. The phrase "penetrate through it by one" is from the *Analects*, 4.15.

40. *Ho-nan Ch'eng-shih i-shu*, ch. 18 (*ECC*, p. 188). The remark is quoted in various different forms, and discussed, by Chu Hsi in, e.g., *YL*18.2a1, 2; 2b1, 2; 2b3–3a0; 3a2–3b0; 3b1–4a0; 4a1; 6b1–7a0; 25b0. See also *YL*44.20a4; 115.14a4. Cf. *YL*18.4b3; 5a1; 5b1; 6a0, 1; 6b0, where Chu Hsi quoted and discussed similar sayings by Ch'eng Hao.

41. Although Chu Hsi frequently mentioned the so-called method of "analogical extension" (*lei-t'ui*) while speaking of the process, it was not clear how this method of inferring what one does not know from what one already knows enables one to proceed from many individual *li* to reach the one *li*: e.g., *YL*18.3a1; *WC*42.16b. For more detailed discussion of the *lei-t'ui* method, see my forthcoming article, "'Analogical Extension' in Chu Hsi's Methodology."

42. *YL*117.12b0. Chu Hsi even compared the process to man's walking:

When the left foot has advanced one step, the right foot also advances one step; when the

right foot has advanced one step, the left foot also advances. Continuing without a stop [like this], [there] spontaneously [comes] a thorough penetration. (*YL*18.3a1)

43. The long-standing division of the Neo-Confucian tradition into the Ch'eng-Chu and the Lu-Wang schools, though too simplified, illustrates such disagreement: see, e.g., Fung, *History of Chinese Philosophy*, 2:585–592. For more recent, and nuanced, discussions of this division, see, e.g., Ch'ien, *Chu-tzu hsin hsueh-an*, 3:359–489; T'ang, *Chung-kuo che-hsueh yüan-lun, Yüan-hsing-p'ien*, pp. 531–643; Mou, *Hsin-t'i yü hsing-t'i*, 1:43–60; Shimada, *Shushigaku to Yōmeigaku*; Yü, "Ts'ung Sung Ming ju-hsueh ti fa-chan lun Ch'ing-tai ssu-hsiang-shih. Shang-p'ien."

44. *YL*18.7a0.

45. *YL*18.13b4.

46. E.g., *YL*18.11a2–11b1.

47. *YL*9.3a2.

48. E.g., *YL*12.10a7, 9, 11; 18.11a2, 4.

49. E.g., *YL*12.10a11.

50. E.g., *YL*12.10a4; 18.11a4.

51. *YL*12.11a10.

52. For Chu Hsi's ideas and practices of quiet sitting, see Ch'en, *Chu-tzu hsin t'an-so*, pp. 299–313; Chan, *Chu Hsi: New Studies*, pp. 255–270. For more on quiet sitting as a "religious dimension" of Confucian self-cultivation, see Taylor, *Religious Dimensions of Confucianism*, chaps. 6–7.

53. Thomas A. Metzger has described such convergence in this manner: "The goal of Neo-Confucians . . . was to obtain a living, immediate, emotionally soothing, and elitist sense of cosmic oneness and power by achieving moral purification together with a comprehensive cognitive grasp of the cosmos as a coherently linked whole. With this state of mind, one would realize social oneness and put the whole world in order." *Escape from Predicament*, p. 81.

54. Nearly all the recent studies of Chu Hsi and Neo-Confucianism agree on this point. See, e.g., de Bary, "Chu Hsi's Aims as an Educator"; Bol, "Chu Hsi's Redefinition

of Literati Learning"; Tillman, *Confucian Discourse and Chu Hsi's Ascendancy.*

55. *YL*18.11a5.

56. *YL*18.20a0.

57. *WC*64.33a.

58. *YL*13.3b1.

59. In addition to the examples we have already come across, see, e.g., *YL*18.8a1; 95.6b1.

60. *YL*41.7a0.

61. *YL*45.4b3.

62. *YL*18.2a1.

63. *YL*59.6b1–7a0.

64. *WC*44.37a–37b.

65. *YL*13.12a1.

66. *YL*64.17a2.

67. E.g., *YL*1.1b0.

68. E.g., *YL*1.1b7; 87.23b2; *WC*58.10b.

69. *YL*1.1b0.

70. *YL*94.19a0.

71. E.g., *YL*3.4b0. The references cited in note 1, which discuss many different aspects of the concept of *li*, do not explicitly note the aspect I stress in this section. The following characterizations of the concept in studies not cited there seem to come closer to it: "Principles [i.e., *li*] were not properties but functions, or the reason why, of a thing or relationship, that is to say, the task it must perform in the natural order." Tillman, *Utilitarian Confucianism*, p. 41. "It [i.e., *li*] seems to be the plan by which things become what they are. . . . *Li* is the reason why of the world and it is also the plan by which this reason finds entrance into the world." Berthrong, "The Thoughtlessness of Unexamined Things," p. 134.

72. The expression "There is *li* for . . ." has become an idiomatic phrase in modern Korean with exactly the same meaning.

73. E.g., *YL*86.10b0; 92.6a3.

74. E.g., *YL*97.3b1.

75. E.g., *YL*3.4b0; 16.18b0; 18.2a2; 86.10b0; 89.14a0.

76. *YL*94.8a1. Here, Chu Hsi is commenting on Chou Tun-i's *T'ai-chi-t'u shuo.* See also *WC*45.11b.

77. *YL*63.12b2.

78. *YL*1.2b2.

79. *YL*4.5b3.

80. Of course Chu Hsi's discussions contain some very general ideas about lawlike regularities in the natural world: for example, *ch'i* seeks the same *ch'i*, i.e., *ch'i* with the same attributes; the yin and yang characteristics alternate ceaselessly. These ideas are at the basis of his understanding of many natural phenomena. But Chu Hsi did not call them "*li*." For Chu Hsi's ideas about the regularities in the natural world, see chap. 13, pp. 305ff.

81. *YL*79.6b2.

82. *YL*4.5a2. Both rhubarb and wolfsbane are dried medicinal plants.

83. E.g., *YL*62.15a1; 77.5a1; *CS*3.2b1.

84. *YL*62.15a1–15b0.

85. *YL*77.5a1. That the *li* of something covers its potential and normative, as well as actual and descriptive, aspects, as we have seen repeatedly in this chapter, shows still another way in which *li* is similar to "definition." See also Peterson, "Another Look at *Li*," pp. 23, 27.

86. Before Chu Hsi, *li* could still be viewed as some kind of law or principle that governs objects and phenomena or according to which they behave or take place. Even some early Sung thinkers like Chang Tsai had such a conception of *li*. Chang said, "Although the *ch'i* of heaven and earth aggregates and disperses, attracts and repulses in a hundred ways, nevertheless its *li* is smooth and unerring." *Chang-tzu ch'üan-shu*, 2.2a.

87. For a brief account of the historical development of the concept, see Chan, "Evolution of the Concept *Li* as Principle."

88. *YL*95.6b1.

89. *YL*18.23a2.

90. E.g., *YL*1.2b1; 5.3b6; 9.6b1.

91. E.g., *YL*1.2b1, 2; 5.3a6; *WC*58.10b; *CS*49.4b2.

92. E.g., *YL*1.2a0; 94.7a2.

93. *YL*98.7b1.

94. E.g., *YL*94.2b1.

CHAPTER

3

Ch'i

Ch'i also is a term of extremely broad scope and is thus nearly impossible to define. It is also very difficult to come up with a translation for *ch'i*, perhaps even more so than for *li*.[1] Unlike *li*, however, *ch'i* does not seem to have been a difficult or problematic concept for Chu Hsi himself. Except when used in such technical subjects as medicine, geomancy, and divination, *ch'i* was not even a technical concept. Chu Hsi and his interlocutors used the term in a quite matter-of-fact manner; I have not detected, from their use of it, that they expected questions or disagreements to arise concerning its meaning. They must have thought they completely understood the concept and agreed with one another on it; questions about the exact and accurate meaning of *ch'i* simply did not occur to them. Thus, the term did not appear prominently in Chu Hsi's many debates with contemporary scholars.[2] Indeed, Chu Hsi and other Neo-Confucians used *ch'i* rather freely in discussing other concepts that did appear problematic to them—*li*, mind, and human nature, for example.[3] My discussion of *ch'i* in this chapter therefore derives from a reconstruction based on Chu Hsi's various uses of the term in his discussion of such more problematic concepts.

Again, I do not attempt to provide a complete general account of the complex concept;[4] I comment mainly upon those aspects relevant to the formation and understanding of Chu Hsi's natural knowledge. Nor is my discussion of *ch'i* complete in the present chapter; I use the term throughout the remaining chapters of the book, which should further enhance the reader's understanding of the concept.

3.1. *Ch'i:* Its Qualities and Activities

In Chu Hsi's use of the word *ch'i*, we can distinguish two different senses. When used in the narrower sense, *ch'i* does not have "physical form." The *ch'i* that constitutes "heaven" (*t'ien* in the sense of "the sky") is a good example, for, according to Chu Hsi, heaven does not have physical form: Heaven is "merely *ch'i*"[5] or "rotating wind" (*hsüan-feng*).[6] This formless *ch'i* acquires physical form through "aggregation" (*chü*), and it is the aggregated *chi*, or "*ch'i* with physical form" (*hsing-ch'i*), that constitutes men and things.[7] Chu Hsi used the word "tangible quality" (*chih*) in referring to aggregated *ch'i* and contrasted it with formless *ch'i*, which he called simply "*ch'i*."[8] Perhaps the best example of tangible quality for him was that of the earth; he frequently mentioned the contrast between heaven and earth in this respect: "Heaven is *ch'i* and earth is tangible quality";[9] "If one eliminates a foot from the earth, one will have a foot of *ch'i* [i.e., heaven] in its place."[10]

Chu Hsi did not always stick to this dichotomy of *ch'i* versus tangible quality, however. He frequently used the same word *ch'i* to cover both formless and aggregated *ch'i*. When the two characters were combined into one word, *ch'i-chih*, it referred to the tangible quality of aggregated *ch'i*. It is in this broader sense of *ch'i* that he said, "Some *ch'i* has physical form,"[11] implying that other *ch'i* does not possess physical form. He also said, "The clear (*ch'ing*) portion of *ch'i* is *ch'i*, whereas its turbid (*cho*) portion is tangible quality";[12] "What is clear is *ch'i*, and what is turbid is physical form."[13] On heaven and earth, he said, "The light and clear portion [of *ch'i*] became heaven, while the heavy and turbid portion became the earth."[14] Mountains and rivers, for example, are "sediments" (*cha-tzu*) of *ch'i*.[15]

From Chu Hsi's use of the character *hsing* (physical form), which distinguishes aggregated *ch'i* from formless *ch'i*, it can be gathered that the concept of physical form referred to corporeal aspects of aggregated *ch'i*. For example, it referred to visibility. Chu Hsi said, "It simply is that if *ch'i* aggregates, the eyes can see [it]; if [*ch'i*] does not aggregate, [the eyes] cannot see."[16] It is because heaven does not have physical form that man cannot see it.[17] Color seems to have been included in Chu Hsi's idea of physical form, for he said that "the physical forms of birds and beasts naturally have the colors of the birds and beasts."[18] He even spoke of "the physical form of heaven," which he usually considered to be lacking physical form, as blue.[19] The notion of physical form also included the tangibility of corporeal objects. For example, in classifying different kinds of sound, which is produced as "*ch'i* and physical form grind each other," Chu Hsi spoke of the following examples of (formless) *ch'i* and physical forms:

> [Examples of the mutual grinding of] two *ch'i* are things like wind and thunder. Two physical forms [grinding each other] are things like drumsticks and drums. *Ch'i* grinding physical form are things like bamboo pipes. Physical form grinding *ch'i* are things like [the sounds of] feather fans and arrows.[20]

It is obvious here that the term "physical form" referred to tangible and visible corporeal objects like drums, pipes, fans, and arrows.

This passage shows that for Chu Hsi air was formless *ch'i*. Obviously, air, which makes wind and constitutes a part of heaven, appeared to him to be invisible and intangible and thus lacking physical form. Sometimes he even denied that bright objects like stars and candle lights had physical form or tangible quality; they were "merely 'congelations' (*ning-chü che*) of 'the exquisite' (*ching-ying*) [portions of formless] *ch'i*."[21] To Chu Hsi these bright things were not solid objects made of aggregated *ch'i* but mere gaseous existence made of formless *ch'i* and endowed with brightness. Thus, "the clear portion of *ch'i* becomes heaven, the sun, the moon and the stars";[22] and "the extremely clear portion of the Fire [*ch'i*] produces things like wind, thunder, lightning, the sun, and the stars."[23]

Chu Hsi was not interested, however, in the details of the process of aggregation, which accords physical form and tangible quality to formless *ch'i* and by which men and things come into being. Of course, his remarks about the formation of the earth and the emergence of life hint that these processes may represent modes of such aggregation: the former, for Chu Hsi, was the turning of *ch'i* resulting in the compression of sediments at the center, and the latter was spontaneous congelation of the essences of yin and yang *ch'i*. But, as we see later in the chapter, his remarks about them do not really touch on details of the processes.

Nor was Chu Hsi rigorous or explicit about actual qualities and activities of *ch'i*.[24] We can only collect information about them that is implicit in his scattered discussions involving the concept.

In some passages of Chu Hsi, *ch'i* has to be interpreted to be extremely minute, or (what is the same) extremely "permeating" (*t'ou*): some *ch'i* can "permeate even gold and stone."[25] Thus, wind, made of *ch'i*, can enter any object, a wooden coffin for example.[26] The commonest image of *ch'i* for Chu Hsi was what the character means in its most frequent modern usage, namely air or gaseous substances in general. Air that man inhales in respiration, for example, is *ch'i*.[27] Since *ch'i* was thus viewed as gaseous, it is natural that *ch'i* should manifest pressure when condensed: in an extremely pent-up state, *ch'i* can explode, in the form of thunder, for example.[28] When its movement is extremely rapid, *ch'i* becomes stiff like a solid, as the stiff wind at a high altitude exemplifies.[29] Of course, *ch'i* can actually be solid, for *ch'i* forms, through aggregation, all things of the world, including solid objects. Some *ch'i* can be moist, and through congelation it forms rain.[30] In fact, we shall see that not only rain, but snow, frost, dew, and fog are all manifestations of moist *ch'i*.[31] *Ch'i*, according to Chu Hsi, is also responsible for other physical qualities, such as light and color. Some *ch'i* has brightness and forms luminaries in the sky.[32] Sound is also produced by *ch'i*, as we have seen.

The preceding paragraph constitutes essentially all that can be gathered from Chu Hsi on the "material" or "physical" aspects of *ch'i*. But *ch'i* constitutes and underlies all—not just physical or material—objects and phenomena in the world. It is also responsible for the physiological phenomena connected with life, for example.

To begin with, *ch'i* is the source of life. Chu Hsi accepted the common view of his time that life results from aggregation of *ch'i* and death from the dispersion (*san*).[33] Through what is called "the transformation of *ch'i*" (*ch'i-hua*), *ch'i* is transformed into a primeval form of life. It is through this process that the first man and other species came into being:

> When things first came into being, the essences of yin and yang [*ch'i*] congealed spontaneously to form "two [of a thing]." They were thus produced through the transformation of *ch'i*. Like lice, [they] spontaneously popped out. Once there were these two—one male and one female. Afterward [they] continue to be produced one by one from the seeds.[34]

In fact, an important quality of *ch'i* is that it moves and turns constantly and forms man and "the myriad things."[35] Since these "things" include animate as well as inanimate things, *ch'i* is both the material basis of all things in the world and the ultimate source of the nonphysical or nonmaterial qualities, including life. Thus, for men and things to come into being, there first has to be *ch'i*.[36]

Ch'i not only forms life but also nourishes living beings. For example, the earth receives the *ch'i* of heaven and nourishes the myriad things with it.[37] The *ch'i* of dew, which, according to Chu Hsi, nourishes living beings, may be an example of such *ch'i*.[38] *Ch'i* also nourishes men. The interior of man's body is filled with *ch'i*.[39] Indeed, man's body is filled with various "*ch'i* varieties"—usually with names coined by attaching some labels to the character *ch'i*—that possess various qualities and perform various functions (see chapter 11). This *ch'i* that fills man is essential to his life: although *ch'i* can come in and out all the time, man dies if the *ch'i* completely leaves his body.[40] Man's physical motion is also the activity of his *ch'i*,[41] and *ch'i* is the source of his physical strength as well.[42] Thus it is natural that, when a man damages his *ch'i*, he becomes ill.[43] Man's life span depends on the endowment of his *ch'i*.[44] "It is possible to know a man's life and death," for example, by looking "simply at the flourishing and decaying of [his] *ch'i*."[45]

Ch'i also constitutes man's mind. Mind, for Chu Hsi, was really nothing but *ch'i*—its "essential and refreshing" (*ching-shuang*) or "numinous" (*ling*) portion, to be more specific.[46] Thus, *ch'i* is endowed with qualities of mind. "Perception" (*chih-chüeh*), for example, "is the activity of physical form and *ch'i*."[47] "To perceive is the *li* of mind, and that which can perceive is the numinous part of *ch'i*."[48] Chu Hsi took *ch'i* to be responsible for other activities of the mind as well, such as thought, knowledge, and understanding (considered in more detail in chapter 11). He used the expression "the power of *ch'i*" (*ch'i-li*) in referring to man's mental abilities. He complained, for example, that as he grew old he did not have the power of *ch'i* to see and speak clearly, as well as to move around.[49] He also said that he wasted the power of *ch'i* in explaining difficult problems to others.[50] He even mentioned the "weakness" (*jo*) of *ch'i* in speaking of literary styles.[51]

Chu Hsi attributed morality also to qualities of man's *ch'i*. When the *ch'i* is clear, man has "the good mind" (*liang-hsin*), because then the ways and *li* in the mind are manifest; when the *ch'i* is dark (*hun* or *cho*), the ways and *li* are blocked.[52] Selfish human desires arise when the physical form is "fettered" (*ku*) and the *ch'i* is "impure" (*tsa*).[53] Other personal characteristics also depend on the "endowments" (*ping*) of man's *ch'i*. When a man is endowed with clear *ch'i*, he is wise; when he has turbid *ch'i*, he is stupid.[54] When a man's *ch'i* is "flourishing" (*sheng*), he is "strong and vigorous" (*ch'iang-chuang*); when it is weak, he is "dispirited and subservient" (*wei-mi hsün-no*).[55] "Vigorous" or "grand" *ch'i* makes man courageous.[56] But when the *ch'i* is excessively "hard" (*kang*), man is incapable of self-command (*tzu-k'e*).[57] Haughtiness and laziness are also due to the "habit" (*hsi*) of the *ch'i*.[58] He even attributed the ability to recognize musical notes to the completeness (*ch'üan*) of the endowed *ch'i*.[59]

Indeed, Chu Hsi attributed differences among men in general to the differences of their endowed *ch'i*—being dark or bright, clear or turbid, deep or shallow, thick or thin, and so on.[60] "Small men," for example, are preoccupied with profits (*li*), because "in the endowment of their *ch'i*, there originally are many coarse, decayed, evil, and turbid things."[61] The sages are endowed with clear, "balanced" (*chung*) and exquisite *ch'i*."[62] Thus it is that when a wise ruler reigns, "the *ch'i* blazes greatly, cauterizes and steams, and cultivates men."[63] Differences between the qualities of the *ch'i* of men and of animals, or between those of different animals, also account for the differences between them: man's *ch'i* is clear, bright, and balanced, whereas the *ch'i* of animals and other things is turbid, dark, and one-sided (*p'ien*).[64]

At times *ch'i* was directly invested with moral qualities and other personal characteristics. Chu Hsi mentioned "good (*hao*) *ch'i*," "bad (*pu-hao* or *o*) *ch'i*," "wicked (*hsieh*) *ch'i*," "evil (*li*) *ch'i*," "degenerated (*t'ui-to*) *ch'i*," and "the lazy, haughty, and perverse (*t'o-man hsieh-p'i*) *ch'i*."[65] He said, for example: "Bad *ch'i* is always plentiful; good *ch'i* is always rare";[66] "[When] a *ch'i* is deficient, it simply forms 'dissatisfied' (*k'an-jan*) *ch'i*; when it is not harmonious, it simply forms 'angry and evil' (*fen-li*) *ch'i*."[67] He attributed such unusual meteorological phenomena as hail and yellow fog to the "wicked and bad" (*hsieh-o*) *ch'i*.[68]

The connection of *ch'i* with moral qualities can be traced back to Mencius, especially to his idea of the "magnanimous *ch'i*" (*hao-jan chih ch'i*).[69] Chu Hsi accepted Mencius's theory in attributing moral qualities to *ch'i*: man receives magnanimous *ch'i* from "the correct *ch'i* of heaven and earth" (*t'ien-ti chih cheng-ch'i*) and fills himself with it. Thus, for Chu Hsi, magnanimous *ch'i* was the same as the *ch'i* that fills man's body except that it has righteousness.[70] Man can cultivate magnanimous *ch'i* through nourishing the Way, accumulating righteousness, abstaining from desires, and guarding himself from falling into disgrace.[71] Chu Hsi said, for example: "Where one has collected righteousness to the extent that it is full and flourishing, one can be strong and vigorous. This *ch'i* spontaneously becomes 'magnanimous.'"[72] One who has cultivated magnanimous *ch'i* possesses mental and moral, as well as physical, strength. Magnanimous *ch'i* makes man daring and fearless, for example.[73]

3.2. The "Non-Inertness" of *Ch'i* and Its Consequences

From the discussion in the previous section, it can be said that for Chu Hsi there existed no discontinuity between matter and life or between matter and mind. If he saw differences between what we would call "physical," "physiological," and "psychical" phenomena, they were different only in degree, not in kind. The qualities and activities of *ch'i* that produced these different phenomena were of course different. But they did not result from different kinds of *ch'i* or from discontinuous differences in qualities and activities of *ch'i*. The same *ch'i*, with its various qualities and activities, produces all phenomena. Thus, the series of Western categories and distinctions that I employ in this section, such as matter/life/mind, material/nonmaterial, inanimate/animate, and physical/physiological/psychical, were alien to the minds of traditional Chinese thinkers like Chu Hsi. To them these aspects were not separate but formed a single whole, and *ch'i* always meant all of them at once. Indeed, the purview of *ch'i* was not limited to the aspects covered by these Western categories. For example, Chu Hsi accepted the interaction of man's *ch'i* and the outside *ch'i* that enables man to understand and to influence what happens in the external world. Even those apparently mysterious and inexplicable phenomena referred to as "*shen*" or "*kuei-shen*" were nothing but manifestations and activities of *ch'i* (see chapter 6). It is clear, then, that Chu Hsi's idea of *ch'i* is quite different from the Western concept of matter. A key difference between the two concepts is that *ch'i* is not inert.

First, *ch'i* is not inert in that it is endowed with qualities and activities not only of "inert matter" but of life and mind also. More importantly, these qualities and activities are innate to *ch'i*: *ch'i* is noninert because it is endowed with them as its innate tendencies and capacities. Thus, most material qualities and activities were simply accepted by Chu Hsi in a matter-of-fact manner, as "natural" qualities and tendencies of *ch'i*. There was no need for him to be concerned with them any further—either to understand them at a deeper level or to explain them in terms, for example, of external causes or hidden mechanisms. He simply accepted that *ch'i* had such qualities and tendencies.

Of these innate qualities and tendencies of *ch'i*, many involve movement—contracting or expanding, aggregating or dispersing, ascending or descending, and so on. Thus, *ch'i* is endowed with the inherent capacity for movement, and it is this aspect of *ch'i* that has often been referred to as "energetic" by many modern scholars.[74] This had an interesting consequence, namely that Chu Hsi did not need to study or analyze various movements of *ch'i* to find their external causes. For example, he referred to the rapid rotation of *ch'i* as being responsible for the formation of the earth:

> In the beginning of heaven and earth, there was only the *ch'i* of yin and yang. This one *ch'i* moved and turned around continuously. When the turning became rapid, a large quantity of the sediments of *ch'i* were compressed. Inside, there was no outlet [for the sediments], and thus they congealed to form the earth in the center.[75]

But he never paid attention to the cause of such rotation. It was almost as if rotation was the natural activity for *ch'i*. Similarly, as we have seen from an earlier quotation, Chu Hsi simply accepted the production of life through congelation of the essences of yin and yang *ch'i*—"transformation of *ch'i*"—without worrying about the causes of the congelation. The consequence did not stop there. The notion of the inherent capacity of *ch'i* for movement also precluded, by eliminating the need to look for causes, an interest in details of those movements, which would have naturally raised the question of why certain movements of *ch'i* should produce a particular phenomenon. Chu Hsi simply accepted that those movements of *ch'i* produce that phenomenon without asking why it should be so.

Chu Hsi's acceptance of the qualities of life as innate to *ch'i* had a similar consequence. It was not necessary for him to look for an external agent that created life. A living being could come into being from *ch'i* without such an agent because, for him, *ch'i* was endowed with qualities of life. The "transformation of *ch'i*" is such an example. And in his discussion of that process, he did not need to ask how the congelation of the essences of *ch'i* produced life.

The interaction of *ch'i* and mind is another consequence of this wide purview of *ch'i*. This is nothing remarkable for Chu Hsi, for whom *ch'i* is endowed with qualities of mind. But what is worth noting is that such mutual influence is not restricted to man's *ch'i* and his own mind but is extended to the *ch'i* of the outside world and to the minds of others. This is so because man receives his *ch'i* and his mind from heaven and earth: man partakes of "the *ch'i* of heaven and earth" (*t'ien-ti chih ch'i*) and "the mind of heaven and earth" (*t'ien-ti chih hsin*)."[76] This made it possible for Chu Hsi to discuss, all in terms of the interaction of *ch'i* and mind, various kinds of mutual influence and interaction between man's mind and the things and events of the outside world (see chapter 11 for more detail).[77]

3.3. *Ch'i* versus *Li*

Some of the points discussed in the previous section could be pertinent to the relation between *ch'i* and *li*, for *li* may appear as a kind of simple, basic "principle" in terms of which the qualities and activities of *ch'i* can be analyzed and explained. But this is exactly what we have rejected in chapter 2. In particular, *li* is not a "law" that qualities and activities of *ch'i* should follow. Chu Hsi even said that "although *ch'i* is 'the product' (*so-sheng*) of *li*, once *ch'i* has come into being, *li* cannot control it."[78] It is thus not surprising that when Chu Hsi explained some natural phenomena in terms of the qualities and activities of *ch'i*, he never used *li* in an analysis for a deeper understanding or explanation of them; *li* was merely invoked. Frequently, Chu Hsi even did not need to invoke *li*; once the phenomena were attributed to those innate qualities and activities of *ch'i*, they were deemed to have been sufficiently understood. The discussion of Chu Hsi's ideas about the *li-ch'i* relation in this section will make that clearer.

There are two opposite sides of the relationship between *li* and *ch'i*. One is that in order for *ch'i* to exist, there has to be the *li* for *ch'i*. That is the aspect stressed in section 2.4, and Chu Hsi's repeated statement, "Only after there is 'this' *li*, there is 'this' *ch'i*,"[79] clearly meant this. The other, exactly opposite, side of the relation was also touched upon in section 2.4: there has to be *ch'i* in order for *li* to exist. For *li* does not exist separately, apart from the things of which it is the *li*. *Li* has to exist in things themselves, or in the *ch'i* that constitutes the things. *Li* needs *ch'i* for its existence.

The former side of the *li-ch'i* relationship has been emphasized in chapter 2, but Chu Hsi did not neglect the latter side. For example, he said, "*Li* dwells within *ch'i*";[80] "Once there is *ch'i*, *li* also exists inside the *ch'i*."[81] Sometimes Chu Hsi was more explicit about the way *li* exists in *ch'i*: "Once there is 'this' *ch'i*, 'this' *li* has a place to 'be settled in' (*an-tun*)";[82] "When 'this' *ch'i* is not there, 'this' *li* has no place to 'be attached to' (*kua-ta*)";[83] "*Li* acts while 'being attached to the *ch'i* (*ta yü ch'i*)";[84] "When *ch'i* does not congeal or aggregate, *li* also has nowhere 'to be adhered to' (*fu-cho*)";[85] "When there is *li* but no *ch'i*, *li* has nowhere 'to stand' (*li*). Only after there is *ch'i*, *li* has somewhere to stand."[86] For Chu Hsi, then, *ch'i* provides a place for *li* to be "settled in," "attached," "adhered to," or to "stand on."

It can be said that the former of the above two sides shows the logical aspect of the *li-ch'i* relationship, whereas the latter shows its ontological aspect; but they are two sides of a single relationship. Chu Hsi frequently combined both aspects in a single sentence. Some of the sentences quoted above to illustrate the two different aspects were really parts of longer sentences involving both sides of the *li-ch'i* relation. For example, Chu Hsi said in one sentence, "Only after there is 'this' *li*, there is 'this' *ch'i*; once there is 'this' *ch'i*, 'this' *li* has a place to be settled in."[87] He also said, "Once there is *li*, then there is *ch'i*; once there is *ch'i*, *li* also exists inside the *ch'i*."[88] Sometimes he even put the two sides of the relationship in parallel phrases: "Under heaven there is no *ch'i* without *li*; and there is no *li* without *ch'i*."[89]

Chu Hsi's discussions, however, do not make it clear how the two sides of the *li-ch'i* relationship are related to each other. Sometimes combining them in one sentence creates confusion. For example, it is difficult to understand what Chu Hsi really meant by such assertions as "After there is 'this' *li*, there is 'this' *ch'i*; if there is 'this' *ch'i*, there necessarily is 'this' *li*";[90] and "Before there is 'this' *ch'i*, there is 'this' *li*; once there is 'this' *li*, there necessarily is 'this' *ch'i*."[91]

It is natural, then, that questions continued to be raised concerning the *li-ch'i* relationship. The question most frequently asked by Chu Hsi's interlocutors was about the meaning of the saying that in order for *ch'i* to exist there first has to be *li* for it. Chu Hsi's characteristic response was that this does not refer to a temporal order. He said, for example: "In short, one still [has to say that] first there is *li*; but one cannot say that today there is 'this' *li* and tomorrow there is 'this' *ch'i*."[92] He also said: "Basically [*li* and *ch'i*] cannot be spoken of as 'first' and 'later.' But if one insists on tracing where they have come from, one has to say that there first is this *li*."[93]

The two sides of the *li-ch'i* relationship already discussed do not exhaust all the ways *li* and *ch'i* are related to each other. Chu Hsi also spoke of other aspects of the *li-ch'i* relationship and provided illustrations for them. For example, he emphasized that *li* has no visible form or traces, whereas *ch'i* has them. Also, *ch'i* can change, move, and operate in various ways, whereas *li* cannot:

> Whereas *ch'i* can congeal and operate, *li* does not have feeling, does not plan and does not operate. . . . As for *li*, it simply is a clean and spacious world. It has no physical form or traces. It cannot operate. As for *ch'i*, it can brew, congeal, and aggregate to produce things.[94]

Ch'i, then, is responsible for all phenomena and tangible effects. Of course there has to be the *li* for these phenomena and activities, but *ch'i* is their actual agent. Chu Hsi illustrated this, using perception as an example:

> QUESTION: Is perception like this because of mind being numinous, or is it the activity of *ch'i*?
> ANSWER: It is not entirely *ch'i*. There first is the *li* for perception. [But] *li* does not perceive. *Ch'i* aggregates and produces physical form. *Li* and *ch'i* combine, and then [one] is able to perceive. It can be compared to this candle light. It is because it gets this fat that it can have much light and flame.[95]

Yet, there are different roles for *li* and *ch'i*. The various aspects of the *li-ch'i* relationship discussed so far really show different ways of representing such different roles. Sometimes *li* appears to play the more important role. *Li* is logically prior to *ch'i* and lies at the "basis": "When there is this *li*, then there is this *ch'i*. But *li* is the basis (*pen*), and therefore now one speaks of *ch'i* from the perspective of *li*."[96] Sometimes the role of *ch'i* appears more important. Not only is *ch'i* responsible for the visible and tangible aspects of things, but the *ch'i* in a thing even determines how the *li* in the thing should be: "The *ch'i* that [things] receive are different, therefore their *li* are also different."[97]

Given such assertions by Chu Hsi, it is natural that subsequent discussions of the *li-ch'i* relationship tended to emphasize one or the other of the pair. There even arose controversies over the question of which of the *li-ch'i* pair is more important.[98] This, however, was not what Chu Hsi himself had in mind. For him, both *li* and *ch'i* were important. They referred to two different layers of reality, as can be seen from the following passage, in which Chu Hsi spoke of the different roles of *li* and *ch'i* in a more neutral, balanced manner:

> Between heaven and earth, there is *li* and there is *ch'i*. That which is *li* is "the Way of what is above physical form" and is the basis of the coming into being of things. That which is *ch'i* is "the concrete things (*ch'i*) of what is below physical form" and is the implement (*chü*) of the coming into being of things. For this reason, in coming into being, men and things are necessarily endowed with this *li*, and only then have their nature (*hsing*). They are necessarily endowed with this *ch'i*, and only then have their physical form.[99]

Notes

1. For various translations of *ch'i*, see Onozawa, Fukunaga, and Yamanoi, *Ki no shisō*, pp. 557–567. In addition to the more familiar translations, such as "ether," "material force," "vital force," "matter," and "matter-energy," there have been even such translations or overtranslations as "configurational energy" and "ether of materialization": see Porkert, *Theoretical Foundations of Chinese Medicine*; Metzger, *Escape from Predicament*. It has to be noted, however, that Porkert and Metzger emphasize aspects of the term that I have not done justice to in this chapter.

2. For a good account of the major debates between Chu Hsi and his contemporary scholars, see Tillman, *Confucian Discourse and Chu Hsi's Ascendancy*.

3. It is perhaps for this same reason that most modern studies of *ch'i* in East Asian languages, which do not need to translate the term, have dwelled mainly on the philosophical role of *ch'i* and on its relation to other concepts, rather than on the meaning of the term itself.

4. So far the most comprehensive historical discussion of *ch'i* is Onozawa, Fukunaga, and Yamanoi, *Ki no shisō*. See also Kuroda, *Ki no kenkyū*. For shorter discussions of this concept in some individual thinkers, see Graham, *Two Chinese Philosophers*, pp. 31–43; Kasoff, *Thought of Chang Tsai*, pp. 36–43; Yasuda, "Shushi no 'ki' ni tsuite." My own article, "Some Aspects of the Concept of *Ch'i* in Chu Hsi," is an earlier version of a part of the present chapter.

5. E.g., *YL*2.13bo; *CS*49.21a4.

6. E.g., *YL*45.7bo.

7. E.g., *WC*52.15b; *CS*49.5a3.

8. E.g., *YL*94.12a0.

9. *CS*49.28a1.

10. *YL*98.1a2. For Chu Hsi, "heaven" includes the atmospheric space above the earth's surface as well as the blue firmament. See chap. 9.

11. *YL*2.10b3.

12. *YL*3.4a0.

13. *YL*83.21a2.

14. *YL*1.5a1.

15. *YL*98.1a2.

16. *YL*99.2b3.

17. E.g., *YL*98.1a2.

18. *YL*60.24a2.

19. *YL*68.16b4.

20. *YL*99.4a1.

21. *YL*2.13b0.

22. *YL*1.4b3.

23. *YL*1.5b2.

24. Although some modern scholars have characterized *ch'i* in more specific ways, referring, for example, to its "continuous"—rather than "corpuscular"—character, and to its "energetic" aspect, these characterizations result from the imposition of distinctions that were alien to traditional ideas about *ch'i*. Yasuda, for example, argued that *ch'i* is continuous rather than corpuscular. "Shushi no ki ni tsuite," pp. 33 ff. Yamada endorsed Yasuda in this respect. *Shushi no shizen-gaku*, p. 38. The "energetic" aspect of *ch'i* is emphasized in Porkert, *Theoretical Foundations of Chinese Medicine*, pp. 166–196.

25. It has to be noted, however, that to "permeate gold and stone" is not a quality of *ch'i* in general but that of some particular *ch'i*—*yang-ch'i* (*YL*8.8a3, 4; 74.24b2) and "the *ch'i* of heaven and earth" (*t'ien-ti chih ch'i*) (*YL*8.8a5; 52.19b2), for example.

26. E.g., *YL*89.13b1.

27. E.g., *YL*1.6b2; 74.10b1.

28. E.g., *YL*2.10b1; 72.18a1.

29. E.g., *YL*2.6a0, 10a0, 13b0.

30. E.g., *YL*2.10a2; 70.11b2.

31. See chap. 9, sec. 9.8.

32. E.g, *WC*70.3a; *CS*49.27b2.

33. E.g., *YL*3.3b3; 126.5b2; *WC*52.15b.

34. *CS*49.26a1. See also *YL*1.6a2; 94.13a0, 13b1; 97.4a2; *WC*52.15a.

35. E.g., *YL*1.3b1; 74.18a2; *CS*49.24b2.

36. E.g., *YL*16.2b4.

37. E.g., *YL*74.24b2.

38. *CS*50.49b0. The *ch'i* of frost can kill things. See chap. 9, p. 158.

39. E.g., *YL*5.12a4; *CS*49.5a2.

40. *YL*74.10b1. See also *YL*1.6b2.

41. E.g., *WC*50.30a.

42. E.g., *YL*52.19b2.

43. E.g., *WC*48.25b.

44. E.g., *YL*1.6b3; 4.18b3, 20a2; *WC*56.35a–35b; *CS*23.5a1.

45. *YL*100.4b1.

46. E.g., *YL*5.3b2, 4b2; 60.8a0.

47. *WC*50.30a–30b.

48. *YL*5.3b1. See also *CS*49.5a3.

49. *YL*104.10b3.

50. E.g., *YL*109.10b0; *CS*27.5b0.

51. E.g., *YL*101.11a2, 3. For discussion of the concept of *ch'i* in Chinese literary theory, see, e.g., Pollard, "*Ch'i* in Chinese Literary Theory."

52. E.g., *YL*4.19a0; 59.15b2.

53. *WC*73.41b.

54. E.g., *YL*4.15a2.

55. *YL*52.11b1–12a0.

56. E.g., *YL*34.24a1; 52.19b2.

57. E.g., *WC*64.27b.

58. *YL*16.30b2.

59. *YL*92.11b2.

60. E.g., *YL*4.9a1, 11b5–12a0; 17.5b2–6a0; 23.12b5; 52.11b1; 59.13a1.

61. *YL*27.29a2.

62. E.g., *YL*4.15a2, 16b1, 18b4.

63. *YL*108.6a4.

64. E.g., *YL*5.4b2; 6.2b1; 32.8a1; 57.8b0; 74.20b0; 109.3a1; 117.14a0; *CS*43.19a0.

65. E.g., *YL*17.5b2–6a0; 52.14a0; 60.10b3; 63.22a1; 73.11b1; 103.1a1; *CS*2.8b1.

66. *YL*59.11a0.

67. *YL*52.13b0.

68. *YL*99.3a4.

69. *Mencius*, 2A2. Chu Hsi glossed the adjective "*hao-jan*," which I translate as "magnanimous," as "an air of being 'mag-

nificent and flowing' (*sheng-ta liu-hsing*)"
(*YL*52.9b1) and as "vast (*hao-hao*) like
rivers and oceans" (*YL*52.14a1).

70. E.g., *YL*52.11b1, 13b0.

71. E.g., *YL*18.29a2; 46.2b3–3a0;
52.13a1, 13b0, 14a0, 19b2.

72. *YL*52.14a0. See also *YL*52.13b0.

73. E.g., *YL*52.19b2.

74. E.g., Porkert, *Theoretical Foundations of Chinese Medicine*, esp. pp. 166–196.
But I do not feel the need to go beyond recognizing this aspect to calling *ch'i* "energetic" or even to translating it as some kind
of "energy." To do so, especially outside the
technical context, such as that of Porkert,
would be to introduce an alien and too
technical idea into the common nonproblematic traditional concept.

75. *YL*1.4b3.

76. See chap. 7, pp. 112, 116; chap. 11,
pp. 206–207.

77. In emphasizing this aspect of *ch'i* in
a letter to me of 11 August 1988, Thomas A.
Metzger used such expressions as "an indivisible cosmic consciousness" and "tremendous efficacy."

78. *YL*4.13b0. To be sure, there is a
passage that contains an idea of *li* that
sounds rather close to the concept of law:
"[I] suspect that this *ch'i* moves 'relying on'
(*i-pang*) this *li*." *YL*1.2b3. But this sentence
is followed immediately by the remark
that "when this *ch'i* aggregates, then *li* also
exists." The discussion then goes on to emphasize that *ch'i* can move, change, and
operate in various ways, whereas *li* cannot
(see note 94). These subsequent sentences
make it quite clear that the similarity of
li to "law" is only apparent and cannot
be real.

79. E.g., *YL*1.1b7; 4.15a2; 95.13a2;
*WC*58.10b.

80. *YL*4.13b0.

81. *YL*94.8a1.

82. *WC*58.10b. See also *YL*74.17b5.

83. *YL*1.2b1.

84. *YL*94.10a3.

85. *YL*1.2b2.

86. *YL*94.14a2.

87. *WC*58.10b (the same passage as in
note 82).

88. *YL*94.8a1 (the same passage as in
note 81).

89. *YL*1.1b4.

90. *YL*4.15a2. It is possible to interpret
the second half of the sentence to mean that
if there is this *ch'i*, there must have been the
li for this *ch'i*, namely the first of the two
"sides" of the *li-ch'i* relationship. But the
subsequent sentences make it clear that
that is not the intended meaning.

91. *YL*93.11b1. See also *YL*95.18b4,
19a1, where he said that "before there is
'this' event, there is 'this' *li* first."

92. *YL*1.3a1.

93. *YL*1.2b1.

94. *YL*1.3a0. In *WC*56.33b Chu Hsi has
an assertion that could be interpreted as referring to movement of *li*. But it turns out,
on a closer look, that what the expression
"*Li* has movement and rest" (*Li yu tungching*) really means is that "[among] *li* there
is [the *li* for] movement and [the *li* for]
rest." The passage continues as follows:
"Therefore *ch'i* has movement and rest. If
[among] *li* there is no [*li* for] movement or
rest, how can the *ch'i* itself have movement
and rest?"

95. *YL*5.3a4. It cannot be known exactly
what Chu Hsi meant by his assertion that *li*
and *ch'i* "combine" (*ho*). The candlelight
analogy in which he compared *ch'i* to fat
and *li* to light and flame does not help us in
this regard.

96. *YL*1.1b7.

97. *YL*4.2a1.

98. Such controversies were especially
frequent among Chu Hsi's Korean followers:
see, e.g., Hwang, *Han' guk-ŭi yuhaksasang*,
chaps. 6–8; Kim, "Yi Hwang-ŭi igigwankwa sinyuhak chŏnt'ongsang'-esŏŭi kŭ
wich'i." For an account in English, see
Ching, "Yi Yulgok on the 'Four Beginnings
and the Seven Emotions.'"

99. *WC*58.4b.

CHAPTER 4

Yin-Yang and the Five Phases

The distinction between formless *ch'i* and aggregated *ch'i* or between clear *ch'i* and turbid *ch'i* was highlighted in chapter 3. Chu Hsi's discussions of natural phenomena frequently employed other pairs of qualities and characteristics of *ch'i*—moving and being at rest, advancing and retreating, growing and vanishing, bright and dark, light and heavy, hard and soft, and so on. At the basis of all these dualities lay the most important and fundamental of them all—yin and yang. Originally meaning the shadowy and the sunny sides of mountains and rivers in ancient times, yin and yang subsequently came to be connected with various dual and polar aspects of the world. By Chu Hsi's time, the two terms had become associated with all kinds of dualistic qualities and characteristics, by no means limited to the natural world.[1]

Chu Hsi frequently referred to another set of categories, *wu-hsing*, usually translated as "the five phases." Again, from very ancient times many characteristics of the phenomenal world were grouped in five categories and were associated with one of the five phases, Water, Fire, Wood, Metal, and Earth. This scheme was also fairly well established by Chu Hsi's time, and almost any set of objects, phenomena, or concepts of the world that could conceivably be classified in fives came to be connected with the five phases.[2]

In this chapter I discuss Chu Hsi's ideas about the yin-yang and the five phases together, because, as we shall see, the two sets of categories, with apparently separate origins, came to be closely connected to each other. But again, I do not attempt a complete and general account of these concepts; I focus on the aspects that are relevant to understanding the contents and contexts of Chu Hsi's natural knowledge.[3]

4.1. The Yin-Yang and Five-Phase Associations

As can be seen from table 4.1, which lists all the yin-yang associations mentioned by Chu Hsi, what he connected with yin and yang included almost all things, events, aspects, and concepts that come in pairs. In his own words,

> [B]etween heaven and earth, what else is there? [Everything] is merely the two characters "yin" and "yang." Whatever thing or event one may look at, one cannot separate [yin

and yang] from it. If one looks at one's own body, as soon as one opens the eyes, it is either yin or yang.[4]

This was so for Chu Hsi because in his view everything in the world had its opposite (*tui*), or something that made a pair with it:[5] yin had yang as its opposite; what
was large had something small; clear, turbid; high, low; good, bad; speech was opposed to silence, movement to rest, and so on. His belief in this idea was so strong
that he even included such pairs as humaneness versus righteousness, "the one"
versus "the two," and "above physical form" versus "below physical form" as examples of pairs of opposites.

Yet, associating every thing and aspect of the world with yin and yang could not
be simple or straightforward. First, yin and yang could be divided further. Chu Hsi
said: "In yin there also are both yin and yang; and in yang there also are both yin
and yang."[6] For example, whereas day is yang and night is yin, both day and night
have their yin and yang parts: the daytime hours from noon on are the yin part of
the day, and the night hours from midnight on form the yang part of the night.[7]
Though plants receive yin *ch'i* and animals receive yang *ch'i*, both are divided further: of plants, grasses receive yin *ch'i* and trees receive yang *ch'i*; of animals, the
earthbound animals receive yin *ch'i* and birds receive yang *ch'i*."[8] And although in
general man belongs to yang and woman to yin, man's body also has its yin part and
woman's body its yang part, because *ch'i* in the human body—both man's and
woman's—is yang and "blood" (*hsueh*) is yin.[9] Chu Hsi even said, "Although *ch'i*
belongs to yang, it has both yin and yang, and though 'blood' belongs to yin, it has
both yin and yang."[10] Similarly, although the human body is yang when alive and
yin when dead, the living body has its yin part, *p'o*, and the dead body its yang
part, *ch'i*.[11]

Sometimes, the use of different criteria led to different ways of associating a given
set of categories with yin and yang. For example, Chu Hsi spoke of two different yin-
yang assignments of the twelve terrestrial branches (*shih-erh-chih*)[12]:

> In discussing the twelve hexagrams,[13] yang begins with *tzu* (the 1st branch) and ends with
> *ssu* (the 6th); yin begins with *wu* (the 7th) and ends with *hai* (the 12th). However, in dis-
> cussing the *ch'i* of the four seasons, yang begins with *yin* (the 3rd) and ends with *wei* (the
> 8th), whereas yin begins with *shen* (the 9th) and ends with *ch'ou* (the 2nd).[14]

He also noted two different ways of associating the twelve musical pitches with yin
and yang: in the "great yin-yang" (*ta yin-yang*) scheme, the pitches from *huang-
chung* (the first) to *chung-lü* (the sixth) belong to yang, and those from *jui-pin*
(the seventh) to *ying-chung* (the twelfth) belong to yin; in the "small yin-yang"
(*hsiao yin-yang*) scheme, the odd-numbered pitches are yang and the even-
numbered, yin.[15]

Chu Hsi noted other kinds of exceptions. For example, although in general yang
is lucky and yin is unlucky, yang can at times be unlucky and yin, lucky. Chu Hsi
even provided an explanation for this: "There are what one should do and what one
should not do. If one does not do what one should do or if one does what one should

TABLE 4.1
Yin Yang Associations Mentioned by Chu Hsi

Yang	Yin	References[a]
movement (*tung*)	rest, stillness (*ching*)	YL94.5a0
dispersion (*san*)	aggregation (*chü*)	CS49.32a1
divergence (*fa-san*)	convergence (*shou-lien*)	YL74.10b1
emitting (*fa-ch'ang*)	collecting (*lien-chü*)	YL94.13b4
dissipating (*hui-san*)	achieving (*ch'eng-chiu*)	YL94.13b4
expanding (*shen*)	contracting (*ch'ü*)	YL3.1b2[b]
opening (*p'i*)	closing (*hsi*)	YL94.13b4
advancing (*chin*)	retreating (*t'ui*)	YL74.4b0
growing (*chang*)	vanishing (*hsiao*)	YL74.4b0
growing (*hsi*)	vanishing (*hsiao*)	WC38.12a
man	woman	YL94.9a0
husband	wife	YL70.10a4
bright (*ming*)	dark (*an*)	YL94.9b2
strong (*ch'iang*)	weak (*jo*)	WC38.12a
light (*ch'ing*)	heavy (*chung*)	YL76.18a3
great (*ta*)	small (*hsiao*)	YL69.17b1
clear (*ch'ing*)	turbid (*cho*)	YL76.18a3
hard (*kang*)	soft (*jou*)	YL94.9b2
gentle (*wen-hou*)	severe (*yen-ning*)	WC38.10b
smooth (*p'ing-t'an*)	hazardous (*hsien-tsu*)	YL74.13b1
ch'i	blood (*hsueh*)	YL94.9a0
ch'i	physical form (*hsing*)	YL94.13a0
ch'i	tangible quality (*chih*)	YL94.13a0
ch'i	essence (*ching*)	YL74.14a4
shen	essence (*ching*)	YL95.6b0
shen	*kuei*	YL63.25a0
man (*alive*)	*kuei*	YL87.30a0
hun	*p'o*	YL87.26b1
shen and knowledge (*shen-chih*)	physical form and body (*hsing-t'i*)	YL94.13b4
perception and physical activities (*chih-chüeh yün-tung*)	physical form and body (*hsing-t'i*)	YL3.4a0
spring and summer	autumn and winter	YL94.9b2
from winter solstice to summer solstice	from summer solstice to winter solstice	YL65.1b3
before the full moon (*wang-ch'ien*)	after the full moon (*wang-hou*)	YL74.18a2
day	night	YL65.3a1
sun	moon	YL74.13b1
the earth and water	fire and wind	YL3.8b1
the light of gold and silver	the ore of gold and silver	YL94.13a0
animals	plants	YL4.5b5
trees	grasses	YL4.5b5
birds	land animals	YL4.6a0

TABLE 4.1 (*continued*)

Yang	Yin	References[a]
dragon	tiger	YL63.20b0
exhalation	inhalation	YL74.10b1
odd number	even number	YL67.1b1
one	two	YL34.24b2
left	right	YL94.9b2
above (*shang*)	below (hsia)	YL94.9b2
east	west	CS49.34a1
south	north	CS49.34a1
Wood and Fire (phases)	Metal and Water (phases)	WC46.11b
Water and Wood (phases)	Fire and Metal (phases)	WC49.27b–28a
ch'ien (1st hexagram)	*k'un* (2nd hexagram)	YL76.9b2
chia (1st celestial stem), *ping* (3), *wu* (5), *keng* (7), and *jen* (9)	*i* (2), *ting* (4), *chi* (6), *hsin* (8), and *kuei* (10)	YL30.13a2
from *tzu* (1st terrestrial branch) to *ssu* (6)	from *wu* (7) to *hai* (12)	WC38.10a
from *yin* (3) to *wei* (8)	from *shen* (9) to *ch'ou* (2)	WC38.10b
from *huang-chung* (1st pitch) to *chung-lü* (6)	from *jui-pin* (7) to *ying-chung* (12)	YL92.2a1
1st, 3rd, 5th, 7th, 9th, and 11th pitches	2nd, 4th, 6th, 8th, 10th, and 12th pitches	YL92.2a1
yüan, heng (of the four cosmic qualities)	*li, chen*	YL94.11b1
door, passage (of the five domestic spirits)	gate, kitchen	YL3.16b1
lucky (*chi*)	unlucky (*hsing*)	YL34.25b1
good (*hao*)	bad (*pu-hao*)	YL69.21b5
good (*shan*)	evil (*o*)	WC62.8a
virtue (*shu*)	evil (*t'e*)	YL69.21b5
noble (*tsun*)	humble (*pei*)	YL68.1a3
original (*fu*)	accidental (*kou*)	YL65.6a3
public, unselfish (*kung*)	private, selfish (*ssu*)	WC76.1a
righteousness (*i*)	profit (*li*)	WC76.1a
humaneness (*jen*)	righteousness (*i*)	YL17.4a2
propriety (*li*)	knowledge (*chih*)	YL17.4a2
music (*yüeh*)	propriety (*li*)	YL17.4a2
will (*chih*)	intention (*i*)	YL5.12b1
function (*yung*)	substance (*t'i*)	YL1.1a1
vigorous (*chien*)	obedient (*shun*)	YL17.4a2
joy and happiness (*hsi-le*)	anger and sadness (*nu-ai*)	YL94.4b1
love and desire (*ai-yü*)	fear and hatred (*chü-wu*)	YL87.13b4
reward (*shang*)	punishment (*hsing*)	WC67.4a
above physical form (*hsing-erh-shang*)	below physical form (*hsin-erh-hsia*)	YL94.21b0

(*continued*)

TABLE 4.1 *(continued)*

Yang	Yin	References[a]
great man (*chün-tzu*)	small man (*hsiao-jen*)	YL65.2b4
men (*jen*)	things (*wu*)	YL100.9a3
father	son	YL65.8b6
ruler (*chün*)	subject (*ch'en*)	YL65.8b6
guest (*k'e*)	host (*chu*)	YL65.2b2
astronomy (*t'ien-wen*)	geography (*ti-li*)	YL74.13b1
honorable (*kuei*)	wealthy (*fu*)	YL66.16a3
regretful (*hui*)	stingy (*lin*)	YL66.16a4
waving a fan	holding a fan	YL65.2b5
to have the back of the hand up	to have the palm of the hand up	YL94.9b2
facing the bright place	turning one's back to the bright place	YL94.9b2
going forward (*hsiang-ch'ien*)	withdrawing (*shou-t'ui*)	YL65.4b2
moving and utilizing (*yün-yung*)	storing and receiving (*ts'ang-shou*)	YL87.26b1
taking action (*shih*)	receiving action (*shou*)	YL74.6a1
answering	stopping	YL12.16b0[c]
giving birth and nourishing (*sheng-yü chang-yang*)	disease and killing (*i-shang ts'an-sha*)	WC76.1a
extension of knowledge (*chih-chih*)	strenuous exertion of efforts (*li-hsing*)	YL76.18b0
opening up things (*k'ai-wu*)	completion of tasks (*ch'eng-wu*)	YL76.18b0
to control the self and return to the propriety (*k'e-chi fu-li*)	to maintain seriousness and to practice considerateness (*chu-ching hing-shu*)	YL42.6b1[d]
to have action (*yu-wei*)	to keep on guard (*chih-shou*)	YL42.6b1[d]
aroused and coming forward (*fen-fa*)	tranquil and grave (*ching-chung*)	YL42.6b1[d]

Notes

[a] Only one representative reference is given for each pair of yin-yang associations.

[b] Indirectly, through associations with *shen* (yang) and *kuei* (yin).

[c] Indirectly, through associations with movement (yang) and rest (yin).

[d] Indirectly, through associations with *ch'ien* (yang) and *k'un* (yin).

not do, then even though it may be yang it is still unlucky."[16] Also, whereas in general earthbound animals are yin and live in grasses (associated with yin) and birds are yang and live in trees (yang), gibbons and monkeys, though earthbound, live in trees and are thus yang, and pheasants live in grasses and are yin.[17]

It has to be kept in mind also that yin and yang were always defined relative to each other. A given thing can be yang relative to one thing but yin relative to another. We have seen above that the *wei* hour (1–3 P.M.) is yang relative to the night hours, say the *hai* hour (9–11 P.M.) but yin relative to the forenoon hours, the *ssu* hour (9–11 A.M.) for example. Earthbound animals are yin relative to birds but yang relative to water animals.[18] Similar examples involve righteousness and propriety: humaneness and propriety are yang relative to righteousness and knowledge, which are yin; but righteousness becomes yang when opposed to profit, and propriety becomes yin when opposed to music.[19]

Thus, most yin-yang associations are attributes — qualities or aspects — of objects and phenomena, not objects and phenomena themselves. Even when the associations were with such pairs as great man and small man, animals and plants, and the sun and the moon, it was not man, things, and luminaries themselves but qualities and aspects of them that were called yin and yang. In particular, when "yin *ch'i*" and "yang *ch'i*" were mentioned, it did not mean that there exist two different kinds of *ch'i*; rather, those terms referred to yin and yang characteristics of the same *ch'i*. Chu Hsi said, "Division of the two *ch'i* is really movement of the one *ch'i*."[20] He elaborated on this elsewhere:

> Though yin-yang is [made of] two characters, they are merely vanishing and growing of the one *ch'i* — one advancing and one retreating, one vanishing and one growing. Where [the *ch'i* is] advancing, it is yang; where retreating, it is yin; where growing, it is yang; where vanishing, it is yin. They merely are what is produced by the vanishing and growing of this one *ch'i*.[21]

The list of Chu Hsi's five-phase associations in table 4.2 is rather incomplete. It includes only some of the most common five-phase associations; for some sets, Chu Hsi did not mention all five.[22] But what are included are sufficient to show that they cover all kinds of things, events, and concepts; they include not only the ones that can be placed in the "natural" or "material" realm, such as the seasons, weather, tastes, and the compass directions, but also such nonmaterial ones as human virtues, sentiments, and behavioral characteristics. Chu Hsi asked rhetorically, "Between heaven and earth, what things are not five phases?"[23]

Like the yin-yang associations, it was mostly qualities, processes, and aspects, not objects and phenomena, that were associated with the five phases. Most scholars now agree that the five phases are not five sorts of basic materials or five "elements."[24] They also generally agree on the adoption of the word *phase* as a translation of the Chinese character *hsing*, which literally means "to go" or "to act."[25] It is not possible, however, to provide a rigorous description of what the "phases" actually refer to.[26] We will have to be content with a rather general and vague characterization that the five "phases" are attributes of things, events, and ideas; that they

TABLE 4.2

The Five-Phase Associations Mentioned by Chu Hsi

Wood	Fire	Metal	Water	Earth	References[a]
bending and straightening (ch'ü-chih)	blazing and uprising (yen-shang)	obeying and changing (ts'ung-ke)	soaking and descending (jun-hsia)	planting and harvesting (chia-se)	YL79.16a3
soft (juan)		solid (ying)	moist (shih)		YL1.7b4 / WC38.12b
spring	summer	autumn	winter		
east	south	west	north	center	CS16.33b1
blue	red	white	black	yellow	CS16.33b1
sour (suan)		bitter (hsin)			YL79.16f2
beginning of yang (yang chih ch'u)	flourishing of yang (yang chih sheng)	beginning of yin (yin chih ch'u)	extreme of yin (yin chih chi)		WC38.12b
hun		p'o			YL3.9a1
The Five Notes					
chiao	chih	shang	yü	kung	YL92.4a2
The Five Storing Viscera (wu-tsang)					
liver (kan)	heart (hsin)	lung (fei)	kidneys (shen)	spleen (p'i)[b]	YL68.5b3
The Ten Celestial Stems (shih-kan)					
chia (1st), i (2nd)	ping (3rd), ting (4th)	keng (7th), hsin (8th)	jen (9th), kuei (10th)	wu (5th), chi (6th)	YL65.7b1
The Eight Trigrams (pa kua)					
sun (☴)		ch'ien (☰)			YL72.19b3
tui (☱)		chen (☳)			YL72.19b3
The Five Constant Virtues (wu-ch'ang)					
humaneness (jen)	propriety (li)	righteousness (i)	knowledge (chih)	faith (hsin)	YL6.5a4

TABLE 4.2 (continued)

	Wood	Fire	Metal	Water	Earth	References[a]
The Four Beginnings (ssu-tuan)						
	mind of commiseration (ts'e-yin chih hsin)		mind of shame and dislike (hsiu-o chih hsin)			YL4.16b1
The Four Cosmic Qualities						
	yüan	heng	li	chen		YL94.15b3
The Seven Sentiments (ch'i ch'ing)						
	love (ai), sadness (ai), and fear (chü)	joy (hsi)	hatred (wu) and anger (nu)	desire (yü)		YL87.14a0
	humaneness (jen)	centrality (chung)	righteousness (i)	correctness (cheng)		YL94.15b3
	bright (ming)	penetrating (t'ung)	fair (kung)	extensive (p'u)		YL94.34a2
	penetrating	fair	extensive	bright		YL94.33b0
	seeing (shih)	speech (yen)	hearing (t'ing)	appearance (mao)	thought (ssu)	YL79.16b3
					intention (i)	See below[b]
	regret (hui)	good luck (chi)	planning (mou)	respectfulness (k'ung)		YL120.27b0
	gentle (wen-hou)		parsimony (lin)	bad luck (hsiung)		YL74.9b0[c]
	kind (tz'u-hsiang)		tough (kang)			YL59.12a2
			strong (ch'iang)			YL64.11a2
	warm (nuan)	clear (ch'ang)	cold (han)	rainy (yü)	windy (feng)	YL79.17a1
	nature of generation (fa-sheng chih hsing)			substance of purity and tranquility (cheng-ching chih t'i)	monther of surrounding and nourishing (pao-yü chih mu)	WC72.2b

Notes

[a] Only one representative reference is given here for each set of five-phase associations.

[b] Ts'an-t'ung-ch'i k'ao-i, p. 11b.

[c] Indirectly, through associations with the four seasons.

can represent five sorts of basic processes, qualities, and aspects of the world; and that they are never separate substances themselves.[27]

Thus, it is possible that a single object or phenomenon has characteristics of more than one of the five phases, or even all of them. Chu Hsi indeed believed that everything of the world has characteristics of all five. He said, for example, that "each of the single things also has the *li* of the five phases"[28] and that "the five phases and yin-yang, these seven rotate and unite and are the 'raw materials' (*ts'ai-liao*) of producing things."[29] Of course, the five phases are not present equally in everything; there are differences in the degree—or proportion—that they are present in each object or phenomenon. According to Chu Hsi:

> The *ch'i* of the five phases.... What fills [the world] between heaven and earth is all this. Pick up one thing. There is nothing that does not have these five. Only, there are more or less different portions among them.[30]

Since the objects, phenomena, and concepts associated with the five phases are associated with yin and yang also, it is natural that the yin-yang and the five-phase schemes should be connected with each other. Indeed, they were combined into something like a single scheme.[31] Chu Hsi said, "It is not that there additionally are the five phases outside yin and yang."[32] He even said that "discarding the five phases, there is no other place for discussing yin and yang."[33]

Chu Hsi saw two different ways in which the two sets are related with each other: "The five phases are yin and yang to one another, and each of them is [both] yin and yang."[34] In the following quotation he was more explicit:

> [As for] yin and yang becoming the five phases, there are those who talk about it by dividing them: for example, Wood and Fire are yang and Metal and Water are yin. There [also] are those who talk about it by combining them: for example, *chia* (i.e., the 1st of the ten stems) of Wood, *ping* (the 3rd) of Fire, *wu* (the 5th) of Earth, *keng* (the 7th) of Metal, *jen* (the 9th) of Water are all yang; and *i* (the 2nd), *ting* (the 4th), *chi* (the 6th), *hsin* (the 8th), *kuei* (the 10th) are all yin.[35]

The first of these two methods associates the five phases with subdivisions of yin and yang. To be more specific, of Wood and Fire, which belong to yang, Wood is the beginning of yang and Fire is the "flourishing" of yang; of Metal and Water, which belong to yin, Metal is the beginning of yin and Water is the "extreme" of yin.[36] The second method divides each of the five phases further into yin and yang and connects the resulting ten with the ten stems: of *chia* and *i*, which belong to Wood, *chia* is yang and *i* is yin; and of *ping* and *ting*, which belong to Fire, *ping* is yang and *ting* is yin; and so forth.[37] *Chia*, then, is the yang of Wood, and *i* is the yin of Wood; *ping* is the yang of Fire, *ting* the yin of Fire.[38]

Chu Hsi did not say much, however, about the exact relationship between the yin-yang and the five-phase schemes that are connected in this manner. He frequently spoke of one difference between the two schemes, that yin and yang are *ch'i* whereas the five phases are tangible qualities (*chih*). Yet, it is not clear what Chu Hsi meant by this distinction.[39] All that can be gathered from his statements is that the five phases are more tangible than yin and yang. For he made use of the dichotomy of formless *ch'i* versus tangible quality and identified yin-yang with the former and the five phases with the latter. He said, for example:

> To say it in terms of man's body, the *ch'i* of respiration is yin-yang; body, blood, and flesh are the five phases. The *ch'i* is *ch'i* and the tangible quality is tangible quality. It is not permissible to discuss them mixed together.[40]

But Chu Hsi did not stick to this distinction.[41] For him the five phases were special among tangible qualities in that they were the first that came into being when heaven and earth produced things.[42] In fact, we have already seen that Chu Hsi regarded the five phases, along with yin and yang, as the "raw material" that formed things, which might mean that the five phases were more elementary and less tangible than actual things. They could even have the characteristics of formless *ch'i*: "Although the five phases are tangible qualities, they also have the '*ch'i* of the five phases,' and only then the production of this thing can be achieved."[43]

4.2. Cyclical Alternation and Opposition: Relations between Yin and Yang

Some of the quotations in the previous section illustrated a key feature of the yin-yang scheme, namely that yin and yang alternate and follow each other continuously. Chu Hsi referred to this alternation as "the circulation" (*hsün-huan*) of yin and yang:[44] At the extreme of yin emerges yang; as yang grows and reaches its extreme, yin reemerges; and this process continues.

Since yin and yang keep following each other, there cannot be a distinction of what is earlier or later between the two. Chu Hsi noted this and frequently quoted Ch'eng I's saying that "movement and rest have no ends; yin and yang have no beginnings."[45] He even said that yin and yang, "like a ring, have no endpoint."[46] The idea of continuous alternation of yin and yang is also closely connected with Chou Tun-i's saying in the *Explanation of the Diagram of the Supreme Ultimate* (T'ai-chi-t'u shuo) that "yin and yang . . . act as roots of each other," which Chu Hsi frequently quoted and commented upon.[47] He said, for example: "Before the supreme ultimate moved, there was only yin. Inside the stillness of yin, there spontaneously were roots of yang. Inside the movement of yang, there also were roots of yin."[48]

Thus, there cannot be yin or yang completely devoid of each other: yin has to contain at least a trace of yang mixed with it, and vice versa.[49] Chu Hsi frequently illustrated this idea with the progression of "the twelve hexagrams." When the yang line at the top of the *po* hexagram (☶☷, corresponding to the ninth month) disappears to become *k'un* (☷☷, the tenth month), it is not completely devoid of yang because at the same moment a yang line begins to grow at the bottom to become the *fu* hexagram (☷☳, the eleventh month).[50] He even called it "the *li* of the impossibility of completely exhausting the yang"[51] and provided another illustration of it:

when leaves fall down in autumn, new buds have already sprouted.[52] Chu Hsi also mentioned "the *li* that yang cannot come into being suddenly [from a complete absence]."[53]

Indeed, Chu Hsi seemed to view alternation of opposites as the most important characteristic of phenomena in the natural world. He frequently spoke of cyclical alternations of movement and rest, going and coming, opening and closing, contracting and expanding, growing and vanishing, day and night, the sun and the moon, life and death, hot and cold weather, rainy and fine weather, exhalation and inhalation, and even the bending and stretching movements of the measuring worm, all of which he embraced with the general idea of alternating repetition of "stimulus and response" (*kan-ying*).[54] Thus, he illustrated "the substance of the Way" (*tao-t'i*) in the following manner.

> After it is cold, it is hot; after it is hot, it is cold. The sun goes and the moon comes. Spring and summer are yang, autumn and winter are yin. One yin and one yang keep changing into each other.[55]

He even explained the presence of seashells on high mountains by the idea of alternation of opposite characteristics — in this case the low (i.e., the sea bottom) and the high (the high mountain), and the soft (the mud) and the hard (the stone in which the seashells are found).[56]

This, then, was one way of looking at the yin-yang relation: yin and yang as two "sides" or "phases" of one entity, one *ch'i*, for example. But there was a different way of looking at the yin-yang, namely taking it as two entities. The yin-yang pairs that are difficult to view as alternating in the manner discussed above — heaven and earth, east and west, and man and woman, for example — call for such a view. Chu Hsi, of course, was aware of this possibility and expressed it in the following words:

> In yin-yang, there is "what flows and moves" (*liu-hsing-ti*) and there is "what is fixed in position" (*ting-wei-ti*). Movement and rest becoming roots of each other is "what flows and moves"; the coming and going of hot and cold weather is [also] this. Dividing yin and yang so that the two forms are established is "what is fixed in position." Heaven and earth, above and below, and the four directions are this.[57]

> In yin-yang, there is "what refers to the opposite." For example, east as yang and west as yin, south as yang and north as yin are [examples of] this. And there is "what refers to the intermixed." For example, day and night, cold and hot weather, and one being sideways and one being straight are [examples of] this.[58]

It is in referring to this difference that Chu Hsi said, "The yin-yang can be considered as one; it can also be considered as two."[59] Viewing it as "one" corresponds to "what flows and moves" or to "what refers to the intermixed," namely, what undergoes continuous alternation; viewing it as "two" corresponds to "what is fixed in position" or to "what refers to the opposite," namely, what does not alternate.

The yin and yang that stand in such opposition can interact. Congelation of the essences of yin and yang, which, as we have seen, leads to the "transformation of *ch'i,*" is an example of such interaction. It must be in referring to this "interacting" aspect of yin-yang that, in a similar, and parallel, division of the concept of "*i*" (change) into two kinds, one is called "the intersecting *i*" (*chiao-i*): "*I* has two meanings. One is the 'changing *i*' (*pien-i*), which is 'what flows and moves.' One is the 'intersecting *i*,' which is 'what opposes each other.'"[60]

In both of these points of view, yin and yang are symmetric. Yin and yang are in balance; they are of equal status and on the same level. Not only are they in balance; they are also supposed to be kept in balance. When the balance is disturbed, it has to be restored. Thus, for Chu Hsi, it is following "the way and *li* of yin-yang" that men should "cut yang trees in midsummer [when yang is excessive] and cut yin trees in midwinter."[61]

Yin and yang cannot always be so symmetrical, however. Chu Hsi said, for example:

> Between heaven and earth, there is no *li* of "two standing together" (*liang-li*). Either yin is superior to yang, or yang is superior to yin. There is nothing not like this. There is no time when [it is] not like this.[62]

It should be noted that this remark still kept a kind of balance between yin and yang, for in it Chu Hsi spoke of possibilities both for yang's being superior to yin and for yin's being superior to yang. But there were times when the imbalance between yin and yang was more clearly noticeable. For example, as can be seen from table 4.1, some yin-yang associations suggest an obvious supremacy of yang over yin. What was good, great, virtuous, lucky, and noble, for example, was associated with yang, whereas what was bad, small, evil, unlucky, and humble was classified as yin. In yin-yang pairs such as father as yang and son as yin or ruler as yang and subject as yin, the yang supremacy would have been even more apparent.

Indeed, Chu Hsi himself recognized such imbalance between yin and yang and concluded that "therefore, one supports yang and restrains yin," after a discussion that had begun as follows:

> Yin and yang are the basis of "the creative transformation" (*tsao-hua*) and thus cannot be absent. But there is the distinction of "virtuous" versus "evil." In general, yang is virtuous and yin is evil; yang is good and yin is bad. It is similar to the fact that if there is day, there must be night; if there is hot weather, there must be cold weather.[63]

He spoke of applying this conclusion to an actual situation: "Advance the good and extinguish the evil; use great men and expel small men."[64] The supremacy of yang is evident also in his sayings that "yang is always in possession of yin, but yin cannot be so, yang is great and yin is small. Yin must depend on yang"[65] and that "there is less yin than yang; *ch'i, li,* and *shu* (number) are all like that."[66] He even made a remark that appears to contradict the assertion that yin and yang have no beginning or end: "Yin and yang basically have no beginning. But if one discusses the opposites in terms of yang and movement versus yin and rest, yang is first and yin is later, yang is the beginning and yin is the end."[67]

4.3. Gradations and Sequences: Relations among the Five Phases

The relationships among the five phases are more complex than that between yin and yang. To begin with, the five phases also show a cyclical character, but unlike the simple yin-yang pair, there are a large number of sequences that the five phases can form.[68] Two of those sequences are frequently mentioned by Chu Hsi. One is the so-called "mutual production sequence" (*hsiang-sheng-hsü*): Wood, Fire, Earth, Metal, Water, the sequence in which a phase is viewed as producing the phase that follows and as the product of the preceding phase. In Chu Hsi's own words, "Water produces Wood, Wood produces Fire, Fire produces Earth, Earth produces Metal, Metal also produces Water, Water again produces Wood. [They] circulate and mutually produce one another."[69] It is also the sequence of the seasons associated with the five phases: spring for Wood, summer for Fire, autumn for Metal, winter for Water, and Earth being inserted in the middle between summer and autumn. The other sequence is the so-called "mutual conquest sequence" (*hsiang-sheng-hsü* or *hsiang-k'e-hsü*): Wood, Metal, Fire, Water, Earth, in which a phase is viewed as "conquering" or "destroying" the preceding phase while being conquered or destroyed by the following phase.[70]

In these two sequences, the five phases are clearly cyclical: the phase or phase characteristic at the end of a sequence is followed by the one at its beginning, giving rise to an endless repetition of the five-phase cycle. When any set of five successive phases is taken from such infinite cyclical repetition, those phases form a finite sequence, to be sure. But this sequence does not have a fixed beginning or end phase; any phase can be the beginning or the end. Thus, although it is customary to start the mutual conquest sequence with Wood, the same sequence can be expressed as "Fire, Earth, Metal, Water, Wood" or in three other ways beginning with Earth, Metal, or Water.

It can be seen that in these sequences each of the five phases has a status equal to the others; the five phases stand on equal footings. Yet this is not the case for all five-phase sequences. For instance, in the first of the two methods of associating the five phases with yin and yang, discussed in the previous section, the phase Earth is left out and given a special status. For Earth does not belong to either yin or yang or to their subdivisions. This, of course, is a consequence of trying to divide five phases into two groups: because five is not divisible by two, one phase is left out.[71] A similar problem comes up when the five phases are associated with what obviously come in fours, such as the seasons and the compass directions. In dealing with this problem, Chu Hsi followed the generally accepted solution and regarded the phase Earth either as neutral or as the basis of the other four.[72] He said, for example: "Each of the four out of the five phases already has a place to belong to. But Earth resides in the 'middle palace' and becomes the ground of the four phases and the master of the four seasons."[73] In associating the five phases with the compass directions, Chu Hsi put Earth at the center: "Earth . . . resides at the center and responds to the four directions."[74] For the seasons, he accepted the common practice of assigning Earth to the eighteen days at the end of each of the four seasons.[75] In this manner, then, Earth is given a status different from that of the other four phases. Chu Hsi even spoke of a division of the five phases in which Earth alone stands on one side and all the other four phases stand on the other.[76]

The remaining four phases are further divided into two groups: Water and Fire form the primary group, and Metal and Wood the secondary one. This leads to a three-layer grouping because Earth by itself forms still another group. This grouping is in accord with the notion that Water and Fire are the extreme phases of yin and yang and Wood and Metal are intermediate between the two, whereas Earth is their neutral balance. But the idea also reflects different relations of the four phases with Earth. Chu Hsi said, for example: "Water and Fire at first came into being by themselves. As for Wood and Metal, they 'are supplied by' (*tsu yü*) Earth."[77] For him, "The body and the tangible quality (*t'i-chih*) of Metal and Wood belong to Earth, but [those of] Water and Fire do not belong to Earth."[78] "Those that belong to Wood and Metal all turn around and come into being from Earth,"[79] whereas "Water and Fire do not come from Earth."[80] Thus, "Earth contains plenty of Metal, Wood, and what is like them."[81] This difference also shows the difference in their material qualities:

> Water and Fire are *ch'i*. They are flowing, moving, flashing, and burning. Their body is rather empty. Their complete physical form is still not fixed. . . . Wood and Metal, [on the other hand,] clearly have fixed physical forms.[82]

To Chu Hsi, the phases of Water and Fire obviously lacked some qualities that the phases of Wood and Metal possessed, namely that which is "supplied by" Earth.

This gradation of the phases—and the difference in their qualities—fits in well with, and was probably derived from, the supposed order of the coming into being of the five phases in the beginning of the world:

> Generally speaking, heaven and earth, in producing things, began with what is light and clear and then reached what is heavy and turbid. Heaven first produced Water; earth second produced Fire. [These] two things are the lightest and the clearest of the five phases. Metal and Wood are much heavier than Water and Fire; Earth is still heavier than Metal and Wood.[83]

The five phases in this order form another "sequence," which is generally referred to as "the production sequence" (*sheng-hsü*): Water, Fire, Wood, Metal, Earth. It is the sequence Chu Hsi spoke of most frequently.[84] But it has to be pointed out that, unlike the other sequences, this one is not cyclical; it has fixed beginning and end phases.

4.4. Explaining the Associations and Relations

It is difficult to provide a simple, clear-cut delineation of the yin-yang and five-phase characteristics. Of course, some common yin and yang characteristics can be listed: we can tell from table 4.1 that yang stands for what is male, bright, strong, warm, expanding, and acting upon something, for example, whereas yin represents what is female, dark, weak, cold, contracting, and responding to something.[85] But such a list cannot be exhaustive or predictive. Table 4.1 contains many examples that illustrate this point. For instance, although assigning the sun to yang and the moon to yin, spring to yang and autumn to yin, or east to yang and west to yin will be easily predictable from such a list, and though assigning divergence to yang and convergence to yin, exhalation to yang and inhalation to yin, astronomy to yang and geography to yin, or even righteousness to yang and profit to yin may still be understandable, it is impossible to predict assignments like humaneness to yang and righteousness to yin, or will (*chih*) to yang and intention (*i*) to yin, which indeed appear quite arbitrary.

Yet, this arbitrariness is a problem only for us, not for Chu Hsi himself. There were times when Chu Hsi felt that he had to explain some yin-yang associations, as we shall see, but they never remained real problems for him. He held the view that when one is versed in the yin-yang assignments, they become natural and obvious: "The *li* of yin-yang and the five phases, if we constantly look at them before our eyes, will naturally become obvious [to us]."[86]

For the five-phase associations, it is even more difficult to construct a list of general defining characteristics. For there are five categories to assign, and as A. C. Graham has noted, "Larger sets are also harder to fit to the facts and to develop consistently."[87] Indeed, examination of table 4.2 does not yield the kind of rough characterizations that are possible for yin-yang. The table even shows an outright contradiction between Chu Hsi's remarks made at different times about associating a single set of characteristics—"bright," "penetrating," "fair," and "extensive" for example—with the five phases.[88] For some sets, he did not mention all five associations.

Of course, connections can be seen between some five-phase associations and the corresponding five basic materials. Many of the associations that have come up so far are the ones that can be derived in a more or less straightforward manner from qualities of the five materials. The "Hung-fan" (Great plan) chapter of the *Book of Documents* (Shu-ching), one of the earliest sources of the five-phase ideas, associated some typical qualities of the five materials with the five phases, and Chu Hsi quoted them frequently:

> [As for] Water, [it] is said to be soaking and descending (*jun-hsia*); Fire is said to be blazing and uprising (*yen-shang*); Wood is said to be bending and straightening (*ch'ü-chih*); Metal is said to be obeying and changing (*ts'ung-ke*); and Earth is said to be planting and harvesting (*chia-se*).[89]

He also used qualities of the five materials in explaining the reason for there being different phases.

> [As for heaven] producing Water, originally it was simply meant to be provided with what is moist. Wood was simply to produce a thing that is soft. Metal was simply to produce a thing that is solid.[90]

The three qualities mentioned in this manner — moistness, softness, and solidness — must have been the most basic material qualities for Chu Hsi. For the other two phases, Fire and Earth, he spoke of other aspects: "Fire is just a thing in the void";[91] "Earth is the physical form and the tangible quality of the earth (*ti*)."[92]

There are many associations whose connections with the five-phase materials are not so straightforward but can still be reasoned. The five-phase association of the seasons is a typical example. Once that is accepted, extension to the compass directions is quite straightforward. The color association, blue[93] with Wood, red with Fire, white with Metal, black with Water, and yellow with Earth, is not difficult to accept, either. These three associations — with the seasons, the compass directions, and the colors — were the commonest and most basic five-phase associations, and some associations that are difficult to connect directly with qualities of the corresponding materials can be explained indirectly through connection with these basic associations. For example, the association of humaneness with Wood can be readily accepted when the association of spring with the phase is taken into consideration: humaneness is the virtue characterized frequently by the qualities of life and production (*sheng*),[94] and spring is the season for the same characteristics. Some of the five-phase sequences and relations can also be understood in terms of qualities and activities of the five-phase materials. All the three sequences mentioned in the previous section are examples of this kind.

More often, however, five-phase associations and relations are not unequivocally predictable from qualities and activities of the corresponding materials. Even among the commoner ones just mentioned, there are some whose connections with the five-phase materials can be questioned. For example, of the associations with the seasons, the latter two, autumn with Metal and winter with Water, are not as obvious as the former two. Nor can the assignment of blue with Wood be as easily accepted as the other color assignments. And although most of the mutual production and conquest relations are easily acceptable, some, Metal producing Water, for example, are not as obvious as the others. There are some associations, white with Metal and black with Water, for example, that can be interchanged and still be accepted. Similarly, the mutual conquest relation, Earth conquering Water, may appear just as reasonable when it is turned around. Chu Hsi even said: "When Fire is flourishing, it conquers Water; when Water is flourishing, it conquers Fire."[95]

Of course, it is not impossible to come up with explanations for those associations and relations that appear questionable. There has been no lack of such explanations in discussions of the five phases, including those by modern scholars.[96] Chu Hsi himself provided some of them. For example, Metal is associated with bitter taste because "its *ch'i* is cutting and piquant," and the association of sour taste with Wood can be checked by the fact that "after two pieces of wood have been rubbed against each other, the teeth can taste sourness."[97] In explaining how Metal produces Water, he said, "Metal is a thing that is durable and congealing, and after its inside is solidified, it can wring out water."[98] After associating Earth with the eighteen days at the end of every season, he said, "during the eighteen days of the summer season, the *ch'i* of Earth is most flourishing and thus can produce the Metal of autumn."[99]

Yet, these explanations appear to us essentially ad hoc justifications; at times they look arbitrary and forced. The following exchange of questions and answers between Chu Hsi and a disciple shows how far such explanations could go.

QUESTION: How does the appearance (*mao*) [of man] belong to Water?
ANSWER: Appearance must be lustrous and therefore belongs to Water.[100] Speech comes out from *ch'i* and therefore belongs to Fire. Eyes take charge of the liver, and therefore [seeing] belongs to Wood. The sound of metal is clear and bright, and therefore hearing belongs to Metal.
QUESTION: In general, the above four affairs all originate from thought, which is also like [the fact that] Water, Fire, Wood, Metal all come from Earth.
ANSWER: Yes, that is so.
QUESTION: How does propriety belong to Fire?
ANSWER: By means of its brightness.
QUESTION: Does righteousness belong to Metal by means of its solemnness?
ANSWER: Yes.[101]

It is difficult to believe that these associations actually originated or came to be accepted for the reasons given here. But Chu Hsi himself—and his interlocutors engaged with him in discussions on these topics—did not seem to have problems in accepting such explanations. To them, the five-phase associations and relations must have appeared well supported—either directly by qualities and activities of the corresponding materials or through indirect connections with them. Moreover, the five-phase scheme, at least by Chu Hsi's time, carried with it a long and time-honored tradition, so that it would be unthinkable to question the appropriateness of those associations and relations.

4.5. Interconnections and Extensions: The Use of the Yin-Yang and Five-Phase Schemes

Characteristics associated with yin and yang are connected among themselves: A yin characteristic is connected with other yin characteristics, and the same is true for yang. When an object or a phenomenon is known to have a yang characteristic, it is generally assumed that its other characteristics are also yang.[102] Thus, a yang characteristic is supposed to accompany, respond to, and interact with other yang characteristics; it is also supposed that a yang characteristic can be counteracted and held in check by yin characteristics. For example, Chu Hsi said: "The night belongs to yin. For instance, evil birds are all yin kinds, and all cry at night."[103] For another example, having accepted the associations of "will" with public (*kung*), a yang characteristic, and "intention" with private (*ssu*), a yin characteristic, Chu Hsi connected "will" with other yang characteristics such as clearness, hardness, and the *ch'ien* hexagram and "intention" with other yin characteristics such as turbidness, softness, and the *k'un* hexagram.[104]

Such interconnections were frequently used by Chu Hsi. For example, in his explanation of why men and women seek each other, the yin-yang associations of the odd-even and the movement-rest dualities were connected in the following manner:

> [According to] the *li* under heaven, what is single must move and what is two must be at rest. For instance, man [when alone] necessarily seeks woman and woman [when alone] necessarily seeks man; there spontaneously is movement. If one man and one woman reside in the room, there must be rest afterward.[105]

The same kind of interconnections were used by Chu Hsi in explaining yin-yang associations that do not appear obvious. In explaining the association of softness and hardness with yin and yang, for example, he used other yin and yang characteristics in the following way:

> Yang is mainly advancing and yin mainly retreating. Yang is mainly growing and yin dying out. The *ch'i* of what is advancing and growing is strong. The *ch'i* of what is retreating and dying out is weak. This is the reason why yin and yang are softness and hardness.[106]

Similarly, in explaining the association of humaneness with yang and righteousness with yin, he noted that the main features of the former are initiating (*fa-tung*) and growing, that is, yang characteristics, whereas those of the latter are converging (*shou-lien*) and vanishing, yin characteristics.[107]

The five-phase scheme also makes frequent use of interconnections among its various associations. Different characteristics associated with the same phase are connected among themselves. For example, spring, the season associated with Wood, is connected with other Wood characteristics such as the direction east, the color blue, and the musical note *chiao*. These Wood associations are further connected with various other Wood associations, such as humaneness, gentleness, kindness, penetration (*t'ung*), the "mind of commiseration," the cosmic quality *yüan*, and so on. Of course, there are similar interconnections among the associations of the other phases.

Such interconnection exists not only among the associations but also among the yin-yang and five-phase relations. For example, the continuous cyclical alternation of yin and yang is extended to that of the dualistic qualities and aspects associated with them. We have seen that Chu Hsi spoke of cyclical alternations of numerous pairs of yin-yang characteristics. That yin and yang cannot be completely devoid of each other was also frequently transferred in a similar manner. For example, from the fact that yang has to contain some yin, Chu Hsi inferred that humaneness has to contain some righteousness.[108] He even noted that hot weather must exist inside cold weather and that night must exist inside the day.[109] This relation, of course, holds for movement and rest, the commonest yin-yang pair: "One movement and one rest are roots of each other. . . . Amid the extreme rest there always is the beginning of movement."[110] The supremacy of yang over yin was also employed in

Chu Hsi's explanation of other problems. He argued that, though both parents should be respected in a household, the mother cannot equal the father, as the noble yang and the base yin cannot be equal to each other.[111] And as we have seen, he based his suggestion to use great men (associated with yang) and to expel small men (associated with yin) on the supremacy of yang.[112]

Relations and sequences within a set of five-phase characteristics are also transferred to other sets. The mutual conquest relations of the five phases are thus transferred to the relations among the colors: black, the color for Water, conquers red, the color for Fire, which in turn conquers white, the color for Metal.[113] Similarly, the sequence of the seasons is transformed into the sequence of the "four beginnings": "As there is summer only after there has been spring, so is there [the mind of] 'shame and dislike' only after there has been [the mind of] 'commiseration.'"[114]

The resulting discussions could give rise to a very complex, elaborate network consisting of all kinds of mutually connected two-fold or five-fold—at times four-fold or seven-fold—categories. For example,

> To talk about these four characters [i.e., "balance," "correctness," "humaneness," and "righteousness"] by associating them with Metal, Wood, Water, and Fire, "balance" has the principle of "propriety," "correctness" has the principle of "knowledge." It is like *yüan, heng, li, chen* [i.e., the four cosmic qualities] of the *ch'ien* [hexagram of *I-ching*]. *Yüan* is humaneness, *heng* is balance, *li* is righteousness, *chen* is correctness. All are these *li*.[115]

Speaking of one of the two ways of associating the four sagely qualities, Chu Hsi said:

> "Brightness" is to be bright with oneself; it is Water, and has the meaning of *cheng* [this should be *chen*, one of the four cosmic qualities]. When "penetrating" [one's] activity does not have obstacles; it is Wood and has the meaning of *yüan*. "Fairness" (*kung*) is to be fair with oneself; it is Fire and has the meaning of *heng*. When "extensive" (*p'u*), it means that each thing gets its satisfaction; it is Metal and has the meaning of *li* [of the four cosmic qualities].[116]

Problems could arise with this kind of interconnections because different sets of yin-yang or five-phase associations may not always agree with one another. At times some discussion was called for to explain the problems—or to explain away the contradictions. For example, the interconnection of the humaneness-righteousness and the hardness-softness pairs, which led to the association of hardness with humaneness and softness with righteousness, caused such a problem, because it contradicted the common feeling that humaneness is soft and righteousness is hard.[117] The association of humaneness with yang and knowledge with yin posed a similar problem because of the common view that knowledge has a certain feature of movement, a yang characteristic, and humaneness has that of stillness, a yin characteristic.[118]

Yet, these were problems that Chu Hsi could easily deal with. He frequently discussed the former of those two problems, and his typical explanation was as follows.

> Humaneness is originally a soft thing but comes up [here] as hard. Yet, if we see that the myriad things come out this swiftly at the time of their coming into being, [we can understand that] it has the sense of hardness. Righteousness is originally a hard thing but comes up [here] as soft. Yet, if we see that the myriad things contract this haggardly at the time of their solemn declining, it has the sense of softness.[119]

In his typical answer to the latter problem, he said:

> If one must associate them [humaneness and knowledge] with yin and yang, humaneness is associated with spring, is mainly coming forth (*fa-sheng*), and is thus associated with yang and movement. Knowledge is associated with winter, is mainly hiding and storing (*fu-ts'ang*), and is thus associated with yin and rest.[120]

Thus, the above sort of problems were never considered to be serious enough to threaten the whole yin-yang or five-phase scheme. Nor was it intended by Chu Hsi that the yin-yang and five-phase schemes should provide a rigorous and coherent system. As the flexible and ambiguous nature of the concept *ch'i* enabled it to take account of all kinds of things and events, the flexibility and the lack of rigor of the yin-yang and five-phase schemes enabled them to accommodate all kinds of concepts, objects, and phenomena.

In this situation, interconnections and extensions like those discussed here were precisely what made these schemes useful as conceptual tools for understanding and explaining many complex phenomena and difficult problems. For such interconnections made it possible for one to see relationships between the various characteristics thus connected and to transfer a relation that held within a particular yin-yang or five-phase set to other sets. Indeed, the principal use of the yin-yang and five-phase schemes, for Chu Hsi, was in this mode of transfer and extension.[121]

Finally, it has to be noted that these extensions were not confined to what can be referred to as "natural." More frequently found in Chu Hsi's discussions involving the yin-yang and five-phase schemes were extensions from the natural to the nonnatural—the social, moral, and other—realms. In numerous cases, associations and relations derived from common, familiar, natural phenomena were transferred to those concerning more difficult, nonnatural problems.[122] We have already seen many such examples, but more can be added. From the association of the heart with Fire, he inferred: "Thus, [the heart] is a bright, 'initiating' thing. Therefore, [it] is provided with many ways and *li*."[123] His comment on the "Hung-fan" chapter is more elaborate:

> [Of] the five events of the "Hung-fan," hearing is said to be clear (*ts'ung*). To hear clearly produces a plan (*mou*). To make a plan belongs to Metal. Metal has the sense of being quiet and hidden (*ching-mi*). Man, in making a plan, also desires to be quiet and hidden.

> Manner is respectful (*kung*). To be respectful produces solemnness (*su*). Being respectful belongs to Water. Water has the sense of being delicate and enriching (*hsi-jun*). Man, in his behavior, also desires to be delicate and enriching.[124]

In fact, the main use of the yin-yang and five-phase schemes in Chu Hsi's discussion seems to have been of this type rather than explanations of natural phenomena.

The examination of what was associated with the yin-yang and the five phases provides some explanation for the direction of the extensions. As we see in table 4.1, the majority of the yin-yang associations are with characteristics that do not belong to what can be called the "natural" world. But it was these "nonnatural" associations that were considered more important and were used more frequently. For they were more problematic and thus called for explanations and discussions. The "natural" associations were rather obvious for Chu Hsi and were thus readily accepted; they provided the basis for the nonnatural ones, to which they were extended.

It is not surprising, then, that many of the examples concerning the yin-yang scheme in this chapter involved phenomena and problems that fall outside the "natural" world. It can even be suggested that the yin-yang associations in the "natural" realm played the role of rationalizing the use of the yin-yang scheme. The natural phenomena, from which these associations were derived, or which were explained in terms of them, really served as illustrations of the yin-yang scheme rather than themselves being the object of Chu Hsi's interest.[125]

The situation was similar, perhaps more pronounced, for the five-phase scheme. Table 4.2 shows that the majority of the five-phase associations do not belong to what can be called "natural." But again, these "nonnatural" associations were the more important, and more frequently discussed, ones. For Chu Hsi used the five-phase associations not so much in understanding or explaining natural phenomena as in explaining or justifying problems outside the natural realm, usually social, moral, and philosophical ones.[126] And the associations used in these discussions were not the ones directly connected with the corresponding five-phase materials; those more directly connected functioned as the basis for these applications.

At times, Chu Hsi went as far as introducing new five-phase relations to accommodate established moral or philosophical theories into the five-phase scheme. For example, to maintain agreement with the accepted theory that humaneness is the basis of the other human virtues, such as righteousness, propriety, and knowledge, and thus contains them, he argued that Wood, the phase associated with humaneness, contains Fire, Metal, and Water, the phases associated with the three other virtues.[127] This relation led him to accept further relations that spring, associated with Wood, contains all the four seasons[128] and that *kung*, the musical note associated with Wood, controls all the five notes.[129] But that this five-phase relation is in conflict with the one discussed earlier, that is, that Earth contains Wood and Metal, does not seem to have been a problem for Chu Hsi. Nor did this relation prevent him from agreeing with a disciple's idea that all the four other phases come from Earth, the relation that itself had come up in discussing the supremacy of thought (associated with Earth) over other human features such as seeing, hearing, speaking, and appearance (associated with the other four phases).[130] While discussing still other five-phase associations, he could even come up with explanations of how the phase Water can be viewed as containing all the five phases.[131] Obviously, for Chu Hsi, the problem of which particular phase contains the other four phases was not as important as the social, moral, and philosophical problems that he discussed using these relations of a particular phase containing the other four.

Notes

1. For the origin and historical development of the ideas of yin and yang, see, e.g., Needham, *Science and Civilisation*, 2:273–278; Rubin, "Concepts of Wu-Hsing and Yin-Yang," esp. pp. 139–141; Graham, *Yin-Yang and Correlative Thinking*, pp. 9–15, 70–74; Kobayashi, *Chūgoku jōdai in'yō gogyō shisō*, pp. 247–300; Hsü, *Chung-kuo jen-hsing-lun shih: Hsien-Ch'in-p'ien*, pp. 509–587.

2. For the origins and the historical development of the concept of the five phases, see, e.g., Needham, *Science and Civilisation*, 2:232–253; Graham, *Yin-Yang and Correlative Thinking*, pp. 74–92; Kobayashi, *Chūgoku jōdai in'yō gogyō shisō*, pp. 19–246; Hsü, *Chung-kuo jen-hsing-lun shih: Hsien-Ch'in-p'ien*, pp. 509–587. Throughout this book I capitalize the names of the five phases in order to distinguish them from the ordinary materials (including fire, which was considered as material substance by the traditional Chinese) of their namesakes. This is only for the convenience of our discussion and does not mean that Chu Hsi actually distinguished the two all the time. Often, especially when he was not directly concerned with the five-phase scheme itself, it is difficult to tell which of the two senses he actually had in mind, or even whether he had such a distinction in mind at all.

3. For brief general discussions of yin-yang and the five phases, see the references cited in note 1. Sivin, *Traditional Medicine in Contemporary China*, pp. 59–83, is also a good brief account with emphasis on medical contexts. For a more extensive and rigorous analysis of the yin-yang associa-

tions, see Porkert, *Theoretical Foundations of Chinese Medicine*, chap. 1.

4. *YL*65.4b2.

5. E.g., *YL*6.19b2; 53.8b1; 62.2b3; 95.16b4–17a0, 17a1; *CS*46.16a0.

6. *YL*119.4b0. For subdivisions of yin-yang, see, e.g., Sivin, *Traditional Medicine in Contemporary China*, pp. 66–70. Chu Hsi, however, did not speak of the six-fold subdivision of yin-yang frequently used in medical contexts: cf. Sivin, *Traditional Medicine in Contemporary China*, pp. 80–83; Porkert, *Theoretical Foundations of Chinese Medicine*, pp. 34–43.

7. E.g., *YL*65.3a1.

8. E.g., *YL*4.5b5–6a0.

9. E.g., *YL*65.3a1; 94.9a0. The character "hsueh," which ordinarily meant "blood," is used here in a technical sense to refer to yin parts of the bodily content; see chap. 11, table 11.1.

10. *YL*94.9a0.

11. *YL*74.14a4–14b0. On *p'o* and the *p'o-ch'i* dichotomy, see chap. 11, sec. 11.6. Some of these subdivisions became necessary as different yin-yang dualities were combined. For example, the last two subdivisions were the result of combining the male-female and the *ch'i*-blood pairs and the alive-dead and the *ch'i-p'o* divisions.

12. On the twelve branches, see chap. 5, sec. 5.4.

13. Here, Chu Hsi is referring to the twelve terrestrial branches associated with "the twelve hexagrams" discussed in chap. 5, p. 82. On the hexagrams in general, see chap. 5, sec. 5.3.

14. *WC*38.10a–10b.

15. *YL*92.2a1. In *WC*72.1b, Chu Hsi

referred to all the twelve pitches as yang; the yin sounds were the "clear sounds," whose pitch pipe lengths do not reach half that of the principal *huang-chung* pitch. For more on this, and on the twelve pitches in general, see chap. 12, sec. 12.3.

16. *YL*65.5a0. See also *YL*34.25b1.

17. E.g., *YL*4.6a0.

18. E.g., *YL*4.5b4, 5b5–6a0.

19. E.g., *YL*17.4a2; *WC*76.1a.

20. *YL*63.23b1.

21. *YL*65.1a1. See also *YL*74.4b0; 95.4a1; *WC*50.1b.

22. For an extensive list of five-phase associations, see Eberhard, "Beitrage zur kosmologischen Spekulation Chinas in der Han Zeit," esp. pp. 48–50.

23. *YL*94.3a0.

24. Although Needham has clung to the use of the expression "five elements," he was one of the earliest who made this point clear: "[T]he conception of . . . [*wu-hsing*] was not so much one of a series of five sorts of fundamental matter, as of five sorts of fundamental processes." *Science and Civilisation*, 2:243.

25. On the choice of "five phases" as the translation of *wu-hsing*, see, e.g., Sivin, *Traditional Medicine in Contemporary China*, pp. 72–76. For other translations, see, e.g., Rubin, "Concepts of *Wu-Hsing* and Yin-Yang," pp. 132–133.

26. To be sure, there is the following, quite detailed definition by Manfred Porkert:

> The five evolutive phases . . . constitute stretches of time, temporal segments of exactly defined qualities that succeed each other in cyclical order at reference positions defined in space. Or . . . [they] define conveniently and unequivocally energetic qualities changing in the course of time. They typify the qualities of energy by the use of five concepts (wood, fire, earth, metal, water) which, because of the richness of their associations, are ideally suited to serve as the crystallizing core for an inductive system of relations and

correspondence. (*Theoretical Foundations of Chinese Medicine*, pp. 45–46)

Although this definition is no doubt very rigorous and perhaps correct in the context of technical medical knowledge for which it was intended, it is questionable whether the concepts of the five phases were used in this rigorous manner outside such technical contexts—by Chu Hsi for example. Nathan Sivin's characterization is in a similar vein but is less rigorous and perhaps more generally applicable: "[The] *wu hsing* theory provides a language for analysis of configurations into five functionally distinct parts or aspects. The names of the phases refer both to these spatial and cyclic relations and to the energies, the *ch'i*, that make them possible, maintain them, and guide their change." *Traditional Medicine in Contemporary China*, p. 76.

27. This aspect of the five phases accords well with the idea of the inherent capacity of *ch'i* for movement, discussed in chap. 3. As *ch'i*, the basic stuff of the world, constantly moves on its own without external causes, what gives rise to the different phenomena is the differences in the ways *ch'i* moves rather than differences in the kinds of *ch'i* that take part in the phenomena. Thus, naturally, the characteristics of the processes involving the movements of *ch'i* were more important than the different kinds of materials.

28. *YL*1.7b3.

29. *YL*94.3a0.

30. *WC*47.11a.

31. For speculations about how the yin-yang and the five-phase systems came to be connected with each other historically, see, e.g., Rubin, "Concepts of *Wu-Hsing* and Yin-Yang," pp. 144, 151; Loewe, *Ways to Paradise*, p. 6.

32. *YL*1.7a3.

33. *YL*30.13a2.

34. *YL*1.7b1. He meant the same thing when he said, "Yin and yang spread and become the five phases, and in each of the

five phases there are yin and yang."
*YL*1.6b3.

35. *WC*46.11b. On the ten stems, see chap. 5, sec. 5.4.

36. E.g., *WC*38.12b.

37. E.g., *YL*30.13a2.

38. E.g, *YL*94.13a0. There was yet another method of assigning the five phases to yin and yang: when the five phases are numbered in the "mutual production" sequence (Wood, Fire, Earth, Metal, Water), the odd-numbered ones (Wood and Water) are yang, and the even-numbered ones (Fire and Metal) are yin. See, e.g., *WC*49.27b–28a. For discussions of various five-phase sequences, see sec. 4.3. See also *YL*1.8b2, where it is said: "The black inside fire is yin inside yang. Water is black and clear outside, but is bright inside. [That] is yang inside yin. Therefore, it is also all right if Water is called yang and Fire is called yin."

Of course, yin-yang and the five phases are associated also with other categorical sets—the eight trigrams (*pa-kua*) and the ten celestial stems, for example. We have already seen the yin-yang and the five-phase associations of the latter set; Chu Hsi mentioned two different ways of associating the former set with the five phases (e.g., *YL*72.19b3).

39. E.g., *YL*1.7a3; 94.3a0, 11a4. Nor have discussions of this distinction by modern scholars clarified it much. See, e.g., Yasuda, "Shushi no 'ki' ni tsuite," pp. 16–25; Yamanoi, "Shushi no shisō ni okeru ki," p. 439; Yamada, *Shushi no shizen-gaku*, pp. 109ff.

40. *YL*94.11b2–12a0.   See   also *YL*94.11a4.

41. The distinction is in conflict also with the common association of *ch'i* with yang and tangible quality with yin: e.g., *YL*94.13a0.

42. E.g., *YL*94.3a0.

43. *YL*1.7a3.

44. E.g., *YL*74.17b4; 98.2b2. Needham refers to this as "a wave-like succession." *Science and Civilisation*, 2:274. Vitaly A.

Rubin prefers the words "pulsation" and "rhythmical succession." "Concepts of Wu-Hsing and Yin-Yang," p. 141. For Nathan Sivin, it is "the shifting predominance of opposed characteristics." *Traditional Medicine in Contemporary China*, p. 70.

45. E.g., *YL*1.1a1; 94.3a0; 4a0; 7a4–7b0; 7b2, 3; 17a1; *WC*49.7a.

46. E.g., *YL*76.1b3; 94.17a1.

47. E.g., *YL*32.17a0; 94.17a1.

48. *CS*49.10a1.

49. *YL*98.5b1.

50. E.g., *YL*62.31a4; 65.2a0; 71.6b1. It is obvious here that in the strict sense the *k'un* hexagram corresponds not to the entire tenth month but to a moment at the middle of the month. For the association of the twelve hexagrams with the twelve months, see chap. 5, table 5.4.

51. *YL*71.6b1.

52. *YL*71.7b0.

53. *YL*71.8a1. This aspect of yin and yang reflects the notion of the continuity of nature, or that all changes in the natural world take place in a continuous manner, not in discontinuous sudden steps. Chu Hsi's discussion of the above-mentioned *li* in the same passage shows this idea clearly:

> Not a single *ch'i* advances suddenly; not a single form wanes suddenly. We perceive neither their formation nor their waning. In general, in the gradual disappearance and gradual flourishing of yin and yang, and in man's body from youth to old age, there is nothing that is not like this.

54. For detailed discussions on Chu Hsi's idea of "stimulus and response," see chap. 8.

55. *YL*95.7a2. See also *YL*95.7a0.

56. *YL*94.3a0. Nor was it only in the natural world that Chu Hsi saw such alternating repetitions. We shall see that his examples of the stimulus-response alternation included such things as sleeping and waking up, speaking and silence, good and bad personal characters, and flourishing

and decaying historical periods. See chap. 8, sec. 8.1.

57. *YL*65.1a6–1b0.

58. *YL*65.1b1.

59. *YL*65.1a2.

60. *YL*65.1b0. See also *YL*65.3b1. The examples he provided to illustrate these two kinds of *i* are similar to the ones we have seen for the two kinds of yin-yang:

> The intersecting *i* is yang intersecting at yin and yin intersecting at yang. . . . "Heaven and earth fixed in position," and "Mountains and marshes passing the *ch'i*" are [examples of] it. The changing *i* is yang changing into yin and yin changing into yang. . . . Day and night, cold and hot weather, contraction and expansion, and going and coming are [examples of] it. (*YL*65.3b2–4a0)

61. *YL*15.12b1. See also *YL*15.12a3.

62. *YL*65.2b1.

63. *YL*69.21b5–22a0. For discussion of the term *tsao-hua*, see chap. 6, p. 101.

64. *YL*71.7a0.

65. *YL*69.17b1. Cf. *YL*100.7a2, where it is said, "Before 'the ultimate of nothing-ness' (*wu-chi*), yin contained yang; after there being 'images' (*hsiang*), yang was separated from yin." This, however, cannot be interpreted as a yin supremacy over yang.

66. *YL*65.9a1. For various meanings of *shu*, see chap. 5, sec. 5.1.

67. *YL*94.10b5.

68. Wolfram Eberhard arranges the five phases in all of the thirty-six theoretically possible sequences in his "Beitrage zur kosmologischen Spekulation Chinas in der Han Zeit," p. 45.

69. *YL*94.5a0. See also *YL*94.3a0.

70. *WC*32.12a.

71. Cf. *YL*94.13a0, where Chu Hsi appears to be saying that of the five phases, "three belong to yang and two belong to yin." He did not mention particular phases.

72. To see how the Chinese dealt with this problem in the earlier times, see, e.g., Henderson, *Development and Decline of Chinese Cosmology*, pp. 10–11.

73. *WC*38.12b–13a.

74. *WC*72.3a.

75. E.g., *YL*1.8a3, 4; 94.3a0. This practice dates at least as far back as the first century A.D., the time of Pan Ku; see, e.g., Henderson, *Development and Decline of Chinese Cosmology*, p. 11. Chu Hsi did not mention other ways—assigning the second half of summer to Earth, for example, following the mutual production sequence.

76. *CS*46.15b0.

77. *YL*94.11a1.

78. *YL*1.7b5–8a0. The source of this idea for Chu Hsi is Chang Tsai's *Cheng-meng* (*Chang-tzu ch'üan-shu*, 2.11a–11b). In another passage, however, Chu Hsi said that "Earth is what Water and Fire are consigned to (*chi*), and that by which Metal and Wood are supplied." *WC*72.3a.

79. *YL*94.11a1.

80. *YL*1.7b4.

81. *YL*94.3a0. See *WC*72.2b–3a, however, in which Chu Hsi mentioned the ways that Wood and Water can also be considered to contain all the five phases.

82. *YL*94.11a1.

83. *YL*94.14b4–15a0. See also *YL*1.8a1. One of the sources of this idea is the theory of the beginning of the world in the *Huai-nan-tzu*, according to which there were only water and fire at the beginning, and the earth was produced from the sediments of water; see chap. 9, sec. 9.1.

84. E.g., *YL*94.5a0, 9a0; *WC*49.27b. Chu Hsi did not explicitly use the name "production sequence," however. Needham, in his list of the four most important sequences of the five phases, calls this "the cosmogonic sequence." *Science and Civilisation*, 2:253–261.

85. Manfred Porkert has performed an elaborate analysis of yin and yang aspects and qualities and has come up with a rigorous and analytical list of yin and yang characteristics, which could be summed up by his characterization of the "active" aspect of yang and the "structive" aspect of yin. *Theoretical Foundations of Chinese Medi-*

cine, chap. 1, esp. pp. 14–31. Such a listing could of course enhance our understanding of the yin-yang. But it could also be misleading if it creates an impression that yin-yang associations and relations can be subjected to such a rigorous and exact analysis. Cf. Nathan Sivin, who has the following to say concerning the aspect Porkert referred to as "structive": "'Latent,' 'reactive' and 'responsive' are better English counterparts of yin than 'passive,' since yin not only accepts yang stimuli but responds to them." *Traditional Medicine in Contemporary China*, p. 61.

86. *YL*1.7a2. In this respect, yin-yang assignments are similar to gender assignments of nouns in European languages. For in the latter case, too, there are certain predictable characteristics, and it would be possible to construct a list of characteristics of masculine and feminine nouns. But no such list would be capable of predicting the genders of all nouns. Many gender assignments appear arbitrary to persons other than native speakers of the language. Yin-yang assignments are similar to gender assignments also in that they become non-problematic for those who are versed in them. Although for us many yin and yang assignments appear quite arbitrary and unpredictable, for those who constantly used the yin-yang framework these assignments seem to have been natural. The similarity between yin-yang and gender assignments should not be pushed too far, however, for the two are essentially different: the former are basically conceptual associations whereas the latter are linguistic. There are thus many differences between them, which should not be overlooked. The most notable is that yin-yang assignments are relational and thus occur always in pairs; gender assignments are not necessarily so. For example, the French word for "head," *tête*, is feminine; what can be its opposite masculine noun?

87. Graham, *Yin-Yang and Correlative Thinking*, p. 42.

88. The contradiction occurs between the set of associations mentioned in *YL*94.33b0, 34a1, on the one hand, and that in *YL*94.34a2, on the other. In the latter passage, however, Chu Hsi rejects the alternative set of associations given in the former passages as a "mistake in recording." For more on this, see p. 60.

89. E.g., *YL*79.16a3, 4; 16b1; 97.5a0.

90. *YL*1.7b4.

91. *YL*1.8a0.

92. *YL*94.11a3.

93. It has to be kept in mind that the character *ch'ing*, which I translate as "blue," does not exactly correspond to our notion of blueness; it covers a rather wide range in our color spectrum from blue to green.

94. E.g., *YL*5.3b4; 17.11b3–12a0; 20.16a1; 100.8b1; 116.8b0. For a discussion of the historical development of this and other aspects of the concept *jen*, see Chan, "Evolution of the Concept *Jen*."

95. *YL*73.3b1.

96. Needham, for example, gives such explanations for the five-phase associations of tastes and colors (*Science and Civilisation*, 2:244, 261), and for the mutual production and conquest relations (255–256). Graham, *Yin-Yang and Correlative Thinking*, chap. 4, also contains a sufficient number of such explanations.

97. *YL*79.16b2.

98. *YL*100.5b2.

99. *YL*94.3a0.

100. Cf. *YL*79.16b3, where Chu Hsi quotes Wu Jen-chieh's explanation that "appearance is what is moistening, and thus is Water."

101. *YL*79.17a1. Cf. *YL*17.12a0 for a long discussion explaining the associations of humaneness with Wood and righteousness with Metal.

102. It has to be pointed out again, however, that yin and yang are defined relative to each other. The yin-yang is not an inherent polarity of qualities, like that of the positive and negative electric charges in the classical electromagnetic theory. A phe-

nomenon or an object with a yang quality does not necessarily have all the other yang characteristics; it can even have some yin qualities if it is yin relative to another phenomenon or object.

103. *YL*3.2a3.
104. E.g., *YL*5.12b1; *CS*45.17b2, 3.
105. *YL*65.6a4.
106. *WC*38.11b–12a.
107. E.g., *YL*6.18b7, 19a3.
108. E.g., *YL*64.1a2.
109. E.g., *YL*98.6a0.
110. *CS*2.47b0.
111. E.g., *YL*68.1a3.
112. *YL*71.7a0.
113. *WC*32.12a.
114. *YL*97.15b0.
115. *YL*94.15b3. On the four cosmic qualities, see chap. 5, sec. 5.4.
116. *YL*94.34a1. See also *YL*94.33b0. The four sagely qualities appear in Chou Tun-i's *T'ung-shu*, ch. 20.
117. E.g., *YL*6.6b1; 77.5a4, 5b1; *WC*38.12a.
118. E.g., *YL*17.4a2, 4b1; 32.16a4, 16b1.
119. *YL*77.5a4–5b0.
120. *YL*32.17a0. See also *YL*6.7a1, where Chu Hsi notes that the converging quality of knowledge is even more pronounced than that of righteousness.
121. For example, the extension from what is known to what is unknown could be found right from the supposed origin of the five-phase scheme in Tsou Yen (ca. 305–240 B.C.), who, according to the biography in *Shih-chi,*

> always examined small objects first and then extended (*t'ui*) [the knowledge obtained from] them to large ones until he reached what is without limit. He began with the present and from this went back to the time of the Yellow Emperor (Huang-ti), all of which had been recorded by scholars. Then he followed great events in the rise and fall of the ages, and by examining the omens and systems, extended it [i.e., his knowledge of the recorded times] far backward to the time when heaven and earth had not yet come into being and

it was mysterious and impossible to investigate. He first listed China's famous mountains, great rivers, connecting valleys, birds and beasts, the products of her waters and soils, her rare products, and based on these extended it to what is beyond the seas and cannot be seen by men. (*Shih-chi*, ch. 74, p. 2344)

Tsou Yen thus "extended" knowledge obtained from small objects to the infinitely large ones, from recorded times to the beginning of the world, for which there was no record, from common objects to rare ones that cannot be seen: in short, from what is experienced and directly understood by men to what cannot be experienced or directly understood. Such extension was also the essence of the method of "analogical extension" (*lei-t'ui*), a key method in Chu Hsi's discourses. On the "*lei-t'ui*" method, see my forthcoming article, "'Analogical Extension' in Chu Hsi's Methodology."

122. Chu Hsi could see this direction of extension right from the "Hung-fan" chapter: "'Hung-fan' first spoke about the five phases and next talked about the five events. Generally speaking, in [the realm of] heaven they are the five phases; in [the realm of] men they are the five events." *YL*23.22b1–23a0. Indeed, the wide dissemination of the five-phase scheme in the Han times was largely due to the possibility of applying the scheme to political considerations, a typical example of which used the five-phase associations of successive dynasties or historical periods in combination with the mutual production or conquest sequences in explaining and predicting the fortunes of the dynasties and the periods. Chu Hsi discussed debates concerning the actual determination of phases for different periods and the problem of selection between the mutual production and conquest sequences. See, e.g., *YL*24.25b0; 87.12a0–12b0. For numerous examples of various early political and social applications of the five-phase scheme, see, e.g., Henderson, *Development and Decline of Chinese Cos-*

mology, chap. 1; Graham, *Yin-Yang and Correlative Thinking*, chap. 4. Graham concludes his chapter with the observation that the five-phase scheme was more suitable for "social than . . . scientific application." "Wearing the wrong colour or standing at the wrong cardinal point will not act causally on the seasons and disrupt the natural order, but within Chinese society they will indeed act causally on the ruler's capacity to perform his seasonal duties" (p. 66). Elsewhere, he even offers the following speculation concerning the origin of the scheme: "[S]uch correlations are more likely to emerge from the problems of organising ritual than from protoscientific speculation. May we not be insulting the intelligence of Tsou Yen and the rest of them if we suppose them to be explaining natural phenomena by correspondences fancied in their own heads rather than rooted in traditional practice?" (p. 82).

123. *YL*5.5a0.

124. *YL*120.27b0.

125. Porkert's elaborate analysis of yin and yang characteristics, his distinction of the "primary" and "secondary" correspondences in particular, throws light on this point: "We call those correspondences primary that result from a sensuous experience of values and consequently concern natural phenomena; and we qualify as secondary those that are evidently derived from the primary experiences by a speculative process." *Theoretical Foundations of Chinese Medicine*, pp. 23–24. Yin and yang

associations that concern natural phenomena are usually the ones resulting rather directly from experiences. The "secondary" correspondences are derived from the "primary" correspondences by speculative processes. They are based less directly on experience and cannot be accepted so readily. Thus, between the two, it is the latter that calls for explanations and discussions.

126. The use of various five-phase associations and relations in such specialized subjects as medicine, divination, and alchemy, some of which Chu Hsi himself discussed, does not quite constitute genuine exceptions, for the associations and relations employed in dealing with technical problems in these branches were not common ones connected directly to qualities and activities of the five-phase materials. Furthermore, the ways in which they were used were very complex and abstract, quite similar to the ways they were used in complicated social and philosophical problems. For such discussions in medicine, see, e.g., Porkert, *Theoretical Foundations of Chinese Medicine*. For some of the other branches, see chap. 12 of this volume.

127. E.g., *YL*6.8a1. For Chu Hsi's discussion of the theory that humaneness contains all the other virtues, see, e.g., *YL*25.4a1.

128. E.g., *YL*6.9a1; 20.18b1.

129. E.g., *WC*72.3a.

130. *YL*79.17a1.

131. *WC*72.2b–3a.

CHAPTER 5

Shu, Images (*Hsiang*), and Other Categories

We have seen in the previous chapters how *ch'i*, which constitutes all things and events of the world, is endowed with various physical forms and tangible qualities and can be described in terms of the categories of yin-yang and the five phases. There were two other fundamental concepts, *shu* and images (*hsiang*), that Chu Hsi frequently resorted to in speaking of things and events of the world. Of course, *shu* and images are manifested in qualities and activities of *ch'i* and thus in yin-yang and the five phases. But they are also manifested in numbers and various other sets of concepts, symbols, and categories (see table 5.1).

Particularly important among these were the diagrams of the *I-ching* (Book of changes). Indeed, all the other concepts and categories discussed in this chapter were either derived from or connected to the *I-ching*; in this sense, the *I-ching* was a source of all of them. This chapter thus reveals some of Chu Hsi's ideas about the book *I-ching* itself, which underlay much of his discussion of natural phenomena.[1]

5.1. *Shu* and Images (*Hsiang*)

To the traditional Chinese mind, the character *shu* meant much more than "number," its ordinary modern meaning. For men like Shao Yung, *shu* was the key concept that underlay all things and events of the world and represented the order and harmony behind the complexity of the phenomenal world.[2] Chu Hsi basically accepted this view.

Thus, for Chu Hsi, *shu* ranked with such fundamental concepts as *li* and *ch'i*. He said, for example, that one can see "the *li* of yin and yang flourishing and decaying, vanishing and growing" by means of the "great *shu*."[3] Shao Yung, according to Chu Hsi, "could simply exhaust the *li* of heaven and earth full and empty, vanishing and growing, and thereby make these *shu* clear."[4] Chu Hsi even said, "In general, *li* is in *shu*, and *shu* also is in *li*."[5] On the relation between *shu* and *li*, he simply mentioned the difference: "Looking at [things] through *li*, the effect is large, [whereas] *shu* is naturally detailed."[6] On *ch'i* and *shu*, he said, "If there are *ch'i* and physical form, then there is *shu*."[7] To be more specific, "what is called *shu* is simply the way in which *ch'i* is divided, limited, joined, and measured."[8] At times he even said that

TABLE 5.1
The Systems of Categories Treated in Chapter 5

Eight Trigrams (pa-kua 八卦)

1. *ch'ien* (乾 ☰)	5. *ken* (艮 ☶)
2. *k'un* (坤 ☷)	6. *sun* (巽 ☴)
3. *chen* (震 ☳)	7. *li* (離 ☲)
4. *k'an* (坎 ☵)	8. *tui* (兌 ☱)

Sixty-four Hexagrams (liu-shih-ssu-kua 六十四卦) (combination of the two trigrams) [a]

1. *ch'ien* (乾 ䷀)	4. *meng* (蒙 ䷃)
2. *k'un* (坤 ䷁)	5. *hsü* (需 ䷄)
3. *chun* (屯 ䷂)	. . .

Numbers

1. *i* 一	4. *ssu* 四
2. *erh* 二	5. *wu* 五
3. *san* 三	. . .

Four Cosmic Qualities

1. *yüan* 元	3. *li* 利
2. *heng* 亨	4. *chen* 貞

Ten Celestial Stems (shih-kan 十干)

1. *chia* 甲	6. *chi* 己
2. *i* 乙	7. *keng* 庚
3. *ping* 丙	8. *hsin* 辛
4. *ting* 丁	9. *jen* 任
5. *wu* 戊	10. *kuei* 癸

Twelve Terrestrial Branches (shih-erh-chih 十二支)

1. *tzu* 子	7. *wu* 午
2. *ch'ou* 丑	8. *wei* 未
3. *yin* 寅	9. *shen* 申
4. *mao* 卯	10. *yu* 酉
5. *ch'en* 辰	11. *hsü* 戌
6. *ssu* 巳	12. *hai* 亥

[a] For a list of all the sixty-four hexagrams, see Needham, *Science and Civilisation*, 2:315–321.

"*ch'i* is *shu*."[9] He summed up all this when asked about the relation between *li* and *shu:* "If there is this *li*, then there is this *ch'i*; if there is this *ch'i*, then there is this *shu*."[10]

As *shu* is thus related to *ch'i*, and as man's *ch'i* determines his physical and mental qualities, it is to be expected that man's *shu* also determines various aspects of him. When asked about "the *shu* of spontaneity" (*tzu-jan chih shu*), Chu Hsi said:

> [As for] a man whose endowed *ch'i* is thick, [his] happiness (*fu*) is thick; if the *ch'i* is thin, the happiness is thin. If the endowed *ch'i* is luxurious, he is rich and flourishing; if [the *ch'i*] is declining, he is lowly. If the *ch'i* is long, he lives long; if the *ch'i* is short, he dies early. This is a "*li* that is necessarily so" (*pi-jan chih li*).[11]

He frequently spoke of "the *shu* of *ch'i*" (*ch'i-shu*) responsible for man's lot. For example:

> [T]here can be a man whose *ch'i* is clear and bright but who has no happiness or wealth. There can also be a man whose *ch'i* is turbid but who has happiness and wealth. [The reason for this is that] the *shu* of his *ch'i* makes it so.[12]

In particular, it is "the *shu* of the *ch'i* with which he is endowed at the time of birth [that] fixed it like this."[13]

Of course, *shu* determines aspects not only of men but also of nonhuman things. Chu Hsi said: "When things are produced, they also meet 'the situation of *ch'i* (*ch'i-hou*). Therefore they all have *shu*."[14] Thus, one can know, by inferring through *shu*, the "declining (*shuai*) and prospering (*wang*)" of things, the life span of a tree for example.[15] He even believed that the *shu* of the *ch'i* of a historical period determined its many aspects,[16] and he spoke of "the *shu* of a state's *ch'i* flourishing and declining."[17]

In this sense, the term *shu* can be equated with fortune (*yün*) and fate (*ming*).[18] And such fortunes and fates can be known by man. Chu Hsi said, "[If there is *shu*], the declining and flourishing of things can be known by inferring its beginning and end," and added that "the inferring also is simply to start 'numbers' (*shu*) with the year, month, day, and hour of just now."[19] He even said flatly that "once it is called '*shu*,' I suppose there must be the *li* of the possibility of understanding it exhaustively."[20] For him, Shao Yung was a person who understood *shu* in such a way.[21] Thus, *shu* could be used in divination and fortune-telling. Indeed, as *shu* was also "numbers," it was possible to calculate fortunes and fates and even to use numerical manipulations in doing so. Chu Hsi spoke of "calculating the fate" (*suan-ming*), based on "the inference from the interactions of the *ch'i* of the five stars and yin-yang,"[22] or on "the calculation by means of the five phases and the [ten] stems and [twelve] branches."[23]

The term *hsiang*, which I translate as "image," also represented various aspects of the structure and workings of the world. Chu Hsi believed that images expressed something that words cannot convey. While commenting on the phrases of "Hsi-tz'u chuan" (Commentary on the appended words), "words not exhausting the meaning (*yen pu chin i*)," and "establishing images to exhaust the meaning (*li hsiang i chin i*)," he said: "Scholars who can get it [i.e., the meaning] in words are shallow; those who can get it in images are profound."[24] Chu Hsi also used the expression "the image of *ch'i*" (*ch'i-hsiang*) in referring to such human attributes as sageness or goodness[25] and even to the situation of historical times.[26]

Thus, *shu* and image were closely connected. Chu Hsi said, for example: "When there is this *li*, there is this image; when there is this image, its *shu* is naturally there."[27] The two terms were combined to form a single expression, *hsiang-shu* (images and numbers), which came to be ranked among the most fundamental concepts referring to the workings—or the order, or the secrets, or even the mysteries—of the world. Indeed, there appeared a specialist tradition of those who attempted to master the secrets of the world by means of study and manipulations of "images and numbers."[28]

What was aimed at in these attempts was, of course, the *li*. It could be arrived at by various other means also; but to those who preferred "the study of images and numbers" (*hsiang-shu-hsueh*), their method seems to have appeared to be more concrete than others because it used numbers and diagrams rather than mere ideas and concepts. In any case, no post-Han scholar ignored it entirely, and most Sung Neo-Confucians showed considerable interest in it. Chu Hsi also studied it and advised others to do so.[29]

Chu Hsi's ideas about "images and numbers" were usually expressed in terms of numbers and the *I-ching* diagrams, the subjects of the next two sections. Yet, I have not fully mastered the content of his discussions, which frequently became quite elaborate, often involving very difficult and complicated discussions of divination and alchemy. They appear to have been difficult even to Chu Hsi himself. He said, for example, that he did not understand *shu*[30] and that the images of the *I-ching* were difficult to understand,[31] something he did not say about yin-yang and the five phases. He even said that the theories of the "*shu* specialists" (*shu-chia*) could be "delusive" (*huo*).[32] Thus, I shall restrict my discussion in the next sections to the more straightforward portions of Chu Hsi's sayings and writings about numbers and diagrams. There will be an occasion in chapter 12 to deal with his ideas about and attitudes toward the specialist traditions of the study of images and numbers, along with discussions of divination and alchemy, which applied them.

5.2. Numbers

Since the character *shu*, designating "number," possessed such a broad range of meaning, it was natural that numbers were associated with various nonquantitative characteristics. The most fundamental set of such qualities was the dichotomy of the odd versus the even numbers. Chu Hsi quoted Ts'ai Yüan-ting's remark "The myriad numbers under heaven come from the odd and even"[33] and said himself that "between heaven and earth there simply are the odd and even."[34] In fact, the odd-

TABLE 5.2
Qualitative Characterizations of Numbers by Chu Hsi

Number	Qualities	References
1	beginning of the numbers	See below[a]
	Water	YL125.8b1
	p'o	YL125.8b1
2	the opposite of one	See below[a]
	the earth	YL75.5a1
	Fire	YL125.8b1
	hun	YL125.8b1
3	circumference of a circle	YL77.1b0
	heaven	YL75.5a1
	hun	YL3.9a1
4	circumference of a square	YL77.1b0
5	"the extreme of the number of production" (sheng-shu chih chi)	YL75.5a1
6	"spontaneous number of heaven and earth" (t'ien-ti tzu-jan chih shu)	YL2.10a1
	number of water	YL65.6b2
7	p'o	YL3.9a1
8	number of yin-yang	YL75.4b1
9	"the extreme of the yang number" (yang-shu chih chi)	See below[b]
10	end of the numbers	See below[a]
	number of the five phases	YL75.4b1
	"the extreme of the number of completion" (ch'eng-shu chih chi)	YL75.5a1
55	"number of heaven and earth"	WC38.1a
360	"the correct number of heaven and earth" (t'ien-ti chih cheng-shu)	YL65.7a3

Notes:
[a] SSCC (Lun-yü), 3.3a.
[b] Ch'u-tz'u chi-chu, 3.96.

even dichotomy was one of the key yin-yang pairs and was associated with many yin-yang dualities. Chu Hsi duly quoted the *I-ching* passage that associates the odd numbers 1, 3, 5, 7, 9 with heaven and the even numbers 2, 4, 6, 8, 10 with the earth[35] and accepted the particular choice that originated from the *I-ching* phrase "three for heaven and two for the earth" (*san-t'ien liang-ti*).[36] The first pair of odd and even numbers, one and two, were frequently associated with other dualistic pairs, *p'o* and *hun* and Water and Fire, for example.[37]

Chu Hsi spoke of qualitative characterizations of many integers, as can be seen in table 5.2. He frequently discussed the significance of the numbers associated with various categorical schemes. For example, to illustrate the significance of four, he mentioned all kinds of things that come in fours:

> Inside yin there naturally are yin and yang; inside yang also, there naturally are yin and yang. All things are inseparable from these four. Now see, for example, that heaven and earth have the four directions. To talk about it in terms of one year, there are the four seasons. To talk about it in terms of one day, there are the day, the night, the dusk, and the dawn. To talk about it in terms of the twelve double-hours, they are four threes. As for man, they are just these four [virtues] of humaneness, righteousness, propriety, and knowledge. [It is] like the way this fire stove has four legs.[38]

He called eight "the number of yin-yang" and ten "the number of the five phases" and explained:

> One yin and one yang are two. If one puts two upon two, then it is four. To put four upon four, it is eight. The five phases originally are just five. But there are times when they are ten. [It is because] in general one phase contains two: for example, Wood contains *chia* (the 1st of the ten stems) and *i* (the 2nd); Fire contains *ping* (the 3rd) and *ting* (the 4th); . . . Therefore they are ten.[39]

Chu Hsi noted that sixty is the number of ways in which the ten celestial stems and the twelve terrestrial branches are paired and that sixty is the product of multiplication of the five musical notes (*wu-sheng*) and the twelve pitches (*shih-erh-lü*).[40] On the significance of thirty-six, he used the numbers of two particular types of hexagrams: the fifty-six hexagrams (twenty-eight pairs) that produce different hexagrams upon inversion (e.g., ䷀ → ䷁, ䷂ → ䷃, etc.) and the eight that invert into identical ones (e.g., ䷀ → ䷁, ䷂ → ䷃, etc.). Thirty-six was, Chu Hsi pointed out, the sum of these two numbers, twenty-eight and eight.[41]

Chu Hsi maintained, however, that manifestations of numbers in the world were "spontaneously so"; he rejected the possibility that they might have been "arranged" (*an-p'ai*) beforehand by some nonnatural agents: "Grasses and woods came into being spontaneously like this; they had not waited to be arranged."[42] Thus, he insisted that the hexagonal shape of snowflakes and the numbers of streaks on the back of the tortoise—five at the center, eight on the two sides, and twenty-four in the rear—were "spontaneously so" and not "arranged."[43] Nor can man change those things in the world that are based on numbers: "All [the seven musical notes] are mutual productions of numbers. They are spontaneously like this and are not what man's power can increase or decrease."[44]

Endowed with such qualitative characteristics, numbers were used in what may be called "numerological" discussions. A foremost example was the various series of numbers that symbolized the process of things coming into being in the beginning of the world. Chu Hsi mentioned the series of Shao Yung, 1, 2, 4, 8, 16, 32, 64, . . . , and that of Yang Hsiung (53 B.C.–18 A.D.), 1, 3, 9, 27, 81, . . . , in alluding to the way things and changes came into being at the beginning.[45] Chu Hsi also quoted the *Lao-tzu* passage "The Way produces one; one produces two; two produces three; and three produces the myriad things," in the same vein.[46] Numbers appeared explicitly in his discussion of the production sequence of the five phases as well: "Heaven, one, produced Water; the earth, two, produced Fire; heaven, three, produced Wood; the earth, four, produced Metal."[47] Chu Hsi must have been referring to all these when he asserted, "Heaven and earth produced numbers."[48]

The numbers five and ten were prominent in Chu Hsi's numerological discussions. He referred to five, the sum of three (the number of heaven) and two (the number of the earth), as "the extreme of the number of production" (*sheng-shu chih chi*) and to ten as "the extreme of the number of completion" (*ch'eng-shu chih chi*).[49] His description of the production of numbers by heaven and earth also accorded special status to five and ten:

> In creating numbers, heaven and earth stopped after reaching five. Those one, two, three, and four met with five, and formed six, seven, eight, and nine. Five paired with itself, however, and [thus] five formed ten.[50]

Of the two numbers, ten seems to have been more important to Chu Hsi. He even said, "Although the trigrams are eight, the numbers must be ten."[51] For him, "One is the beginning of the numbers, and ten is the end of the numbers."[52] He also spoke of pairs of numbers that add up to ten in the following ways: "One hides (*ts'ang*) nine, two hides eight . . ."; "One begets (*te*) nine, two begets eight . . ."[53]

Some of these examples refer to simple relations among integers. Chu Hsi used some arithmetic operations involving them also: for example, that the sum of the numbers from one to ten is fifty-five, "the number of heaven and earth."[54] In the course of such discussions, he even mentioned something like the "exchange rule of multiplication": "Five multiplied by ten is fifty, and ten multiplied by five is also fifty."[55] He approved a disciple's use of the ancient value of three for the ratio (π) of the circumference of a circle to its diameter in explaining the above-mentioned association of "three for heaven and two for the earth":

> If the diameter of the heaven's circle is one, then from the fact that the circumference is three, consider it [i.e., heaven] as three. If the side of the earth's square is one, then from the fact that the circumference is four, consider it [i.e., the earth] as two.[56]

Most of Chu Hsi's numerological remarks appear in his discussions on the *I-ching*, especially the two commentaries "Hsi-tz'u chuan" and "Shuo-kua chuan" (commentary on the explanation of the diagrams). They were often combined with his discussions of the *Ho-t'u* (Yellow River chart) and the *Lo-shu* (Lo River diagram), charts of mysterious and obscure origin that arrange the numbers (in dots) from one to ten.[57] I do not deal with details of these numerological discussions. For my discussion of Chu Hsi's attitudes toward them, see section 12.5, where it is clear that he did not fully accept them. In later chapters I show quantitative and "mathematical" uses of numbers by Chu Hsi, in calendrical astronomy and harmonics, for example.[58]

5.3. The *I-ching* Diagrams (*Kua*)

Although it is difficult to say exactly what Chu Hsi's idea of "image" (*hsiang*) was, one thing at least is clear, namely that the *I-ching* diagrams and their various associations represented "images" at various levels.[59]

The origins of the sixty-four hexagrams (composed of six horizontal lines that are either solid [—] or broken [— —]) and the eight trigrams (composed of three such lines) are not clear. The age-old tradition, which Chu Hsi did not reject, holds that the legendary sage Fu Hsi drew the sixty-four hexagrams.[60] According to it, the scheme of constructing trigrams and hexagrams by combining the single lines (*yao*) one by one (from the two kinds of single lines, to the four kinds of double lines, to the eight trigrams, and so on all the way to the sixty-four hexagrams), often referred to as the "*hsien-t'ien*" (prior to heaven) sequence, actually represents how the diagrams were first drawn up by the sages.[61] Chu Hsi said, after outlining this scheme, "The basic wonder of heaven and earth was originally like this," which was then drawn up "borrowing the hands of the sages."[62]

Chu Hsi believed that once the trigrams and hexagrams were drawn up in this manner, they were viewed as representing various things and events of the world. He emphasized, however, that only "after the sixty-four hexagrams had been complete, [the sages] could see that they could exhaust the changes of the world"; he denied the possibility that the sages, after seeing that the eight trigrams alone could not cover all things and events of the world, paired the trigrams to form the sixty-four hexagrams.[63] He was also of the view that relations among the diagrams were noted only after all the diagrams had been drawn up. For example, the fact that all the eight trigrams can be derived from the two trigrams of *ch'ien* and *k'un*, that is, by successive substitution of the three lines by their opposite lines, was noted only after all of them had been drawn up.[64]

It is not possible to determine the truth of these beliefs held by Chu Hsi concerning the traditions about the beginnings of the diagrams and their interpretations.[65] In any case, however, by Chu Hsi's time, all kinds of phenomenal characteristics of the world, and relations among them, had been associated with the trigrams and hexagrams; there thus emerged a system of diagrams, associations, and relations, which Joseph Needham has called "a universal concept-repository."[66] And with such associations, the idea, already present in "Hsi-tz'u chuan," that the term *i* itself represents changes involving various things, events, and relations in the world was reinforced.[67] Chu Hsi said, "'*I*' is the 'spontaneous creative transformation' (*tzu-jan tsao-hua*). The original intention of the sages is simply to speak about the flowing and moving of 'spontaneous creative transformations.'"[68]

Of all the trigrams and hexagrams, *ch'ien* and *k'un* were the most basic and important. The same names refer to the hexagrams (☰ and ☷), to the trigrams (☰ and ☷) and even to the single yang and yin lines (— and — —). Composed solely of either the yang or the yin lines, they were considered virtually the same as yang and yin themselves. Chu Hsi even said: "The meaning of the character '*i*' is simply yin and yang";[69] "'*I*' simply is one yin and one yang bringing forth many kinds and manners."[70]

Thus, *ch'ien* and *k'un* were routinely associated with various yin and yang characteristics and were thought to account for every thing and event of the world. For example, *ch'ien* is hard and vigorous, whereas *k'un* is soft and obedient.[71] *Ch'ien* and *k'un* were also associated with father and mother, and Chu Hsi frequently quoted the beginning sentence of Chang Tsai's *Western Inscription* (Hsi-ming): "*Ch'ien* designates father and *k'un* designates mother."[72] The most frequent *ch'ien-k'un* association, however, was with heaven and earth. The three pairs, *ch'ien-k'un*, yang-yin, and heaven-earth, were often regarded as almost synonymous. Chu Hsi tried to explain the relationship among them in the following manner:

> *Ch'ien* is a yang thing and *k'un* is a yin thing. The yin and yang are what is "below physical form"; *ch'ien* and *k'un* are what is "above physical form."[73]

> *Ch'ien* and *k'un* are what is above physical form; heaven and earth are what is below physical form. Heaven and earth are the "external shape" (*hsing-k'o*) of *ch'ien* and *k'un*; *ch'ien* and *k'un* are the "disposition" (*hsing-ch'ing*) of heaven and earth.[74]

Ch'ien and *k'un* represented for Chu Hsi the least tangible—the farthest of what is "above physical form"—of the three pairs.

Of course, other diagrams were involved in various kinds of associations. For example, Chu Hsi frequently spoke of the common trigram associations—with the compass directions, great natural objects, the moon's phases, the ten celestial stems, and the five phases—as table 5.3 shows.[75] Hexagram associations were mentioned more fragmentarily, except for those with the twelve lunar months listed in table 5.4.[76] Yet, like yin-yang and five-phase associations, these associations did not form a coherent system. There were different, conflicting ways of associating trigrams with the same sets of categories—the compass directions and the five phases, for example, as Chu Hsi himself recognized.[77]

It is not possible to determine how these associations came about. Obviously, the shapes of the diagrams played some role, and this must have been the reason why the diagram associations were referred to as "*hsiang*," which also means "shape." Indeed, resemblances between hexagrams and certain objects had been noted right from the beginning of the *I-ching* tradition, notably in "Hsi tz'u chuan."[78] Chu Hsi mentioned the associations based on such resemblances: for example, *ting* (☲)

TABLE 5.3
The Common Trigram Associations Mentioned by Chu Hsi

Ch'ien (☰)	K'un (☷)	Chen (☳)	K'an (☵)	Ken (☶)	Sun (☴)	Li (☲)	Tui (☱)	References
				Compass Directions				
				Scheme 1[a]				
South	North	North-east	West	North-west	South-west	East	South-east	YL65.12b1 YL65.13a1
				Scheme 2[b]				
North-west	South-west	East	North	North-east	South-east	South	West	YL72.19b3 YL77.7b2
				Great Natural Objects and Phenomena				
Heaven	Earth	Thunder	Moon Water Fountain River Cloud Rain	Mountain	Wind	Sun Brightness Lightning Fire	Marsh	YL65.12b1 CS27.45b1
				Moon's Phases				
full moon on the 15th day	30th day	3rd day		half moon on the 23rd day	after the full moon		half moon on the 8th day	YL65.12b0
				Ten Celestial Stems				
chia (1st)	i (2nd)	keng (7th)	kuei (10th)	ping (3rd)	hsin (8th)	jen (9th)	ting (4th)	YL65.12a2 YL67.23b1
				Five Phases				
				Scheme 1[c]				
Metal					Wood			YL72.19b3
				Scheme 2[d]				
		Metal					Wood	YL72.19b3

Notes
[a] The Fu Hsi system.
[b] The King Wen system.
[c] "The five phases of the eight trigrams": associations based on the shapes.
[d] "The five phases of the five phases": associations based on the compass directions.

TABLE 5.4
The Twelve Branch–Twelve Hexagram Associations

Twelve Branches	Twelve Hexagrams	Twelve Lunar Months
tzu	*fu* (☲)	11th month
ch'ou	*lin* (☲)	12th
yin	*t'ai* (☲)	1st
mao	*ta-chuang* (☲)	2nd
ch'en	*kuai* (☲)	3rd
ssu	*ch'ien* (☲)	4th
wu	*kou* (☲)	5th
wei	*t'un* (☲)	6th
shen	*p'i* (☲)	7th
yu	*kuan* (☲)	8th
hsü	*po* (☲)	9th
hai	*k'un* (☲)	10th

with the tripod cauldron, *ko* (☲) with the cooking stove, *hsiao-kuo* (☲) with the bird, *chung-fu* (☲) with the egg.[79] He even provided detailed descriptions of such resemblances for some of these associations. He compared the shape of the *ching* hexagram (☲) with that of the toad in the following manner:

> The top [line of the hexagram] is the two front legs [of the toad]. The fifth [line counting from the bottom, i.e., the second line from the top] is the head. The fourth is the eyes. The third and the second are the body. The first is the two hind legs.[80]

The *chung-fu* hexagram resembled an egg because, for Chu Hsi, "the four yang lines are outside and the two yin lines are inside; being solid outside and empty inside, it has the appearance of an egg."[81] He also gave similar line-by-line comparisons of the *ko* hexagram with the cooking stove[82] and of *hsien* (☲) and *ken* (☲) with the human body.[83]

Chu Hsi could explain some trigram associations also through shape resemblance.[84] For example, the *tui* trigram was likened to a marsh because "the gap on top has the appearance of the mouth of the marsh, whereas the two lower lines have the appearance of the bottom of the marsh"; the *ken* trigram resembled a mountain because "the one yang line on top has the image of the earth and the empty [spaces] in the two lower yin lines are the image of water infiltrating [the earth]."[85] He could explain the *I-ching* phrase "The river becomes marsh when blocked up" in the same vein:

K'an is the river, *tui* is the marsh. The marsh is that whose water does not flow. When the bottom one line of *k'an* is closed up, it forms the *tui* trigram. This is the shape of "the river becoming marsh when blocked up."[86]

Some of the resemblances Chu Hsi spoke of are on a more conceptual level, usually using the yin-yang associations of the constituent single lines. For example, he explained the associations of the *li* trigram with Fire and *k'an* with Water by calling the middle yin line of the former "false darkness amid fire" and the middle yang line of the latter "false brightness amid water."[87] The trigram associations with the moon's phases (and thus with the days of a lunar month) are obviously also based upon the associations of brightness and darkness (i.e., the bright and dark portions of the moon's surface) with the yang and yin single lines. The hexagram associations with the twelve lunar months could be explained by taking the yang and yin single lines to be yang (warm) *ch'i* and yin (cold) *ch'i*. The space of the entire heaven and earth is thought to have six layers in this scheme, each single line corresponding to the *ch'i* of each layer.[88] A year is represented by the consecutive changes of a yin line to a yang line from *k'un* (associated with the tenth month) to *ch'ien* (fourth) and the successive changes of a yang line to a yin line from *ch'ien* back to *k'un*.[89] Chu Hsi considered that, of the six layers, the bottom two are under the surface of the earth. Thus, though yang lines are present in *fu* (☷, eleventh) and *lin* (☷, twelfth), it is not until *t'ai* (☷, first) that yang *ch'i* appears above the ground.[90] As it takes one month for a full yang line to grow from a yin line, its daily growth amounts to one-thirtieth.[91] Chu Hsi also compared the formation of yang lines to the process of heaven and earth producing things. Thus, he could see "the mind of heaven and earth [producing things]" in the *fu* hexagram, in which the first yang line appears out of the six yin lines.[92]

5.4. The Four Cosmic Qualities, the Ten Stems, and the Twelve Branches

A set of four characters, which originated from the *I-ching*, formed another categorical scheme frequently resorted to by Chu Hsi: *yüan, heng, li,* and *chen.* We have already encountered them in discussing their associations with yin-yang and the five phases; we referred to them as "the four cosmic qualities."

In the *I-ching* the four terms appeared in the "hexagram text" (or "word on judgment" [*kua-tz'u*]) of many hexagrams and were the first four characters of that text for the first hexagram, *ch'ien.*[93] Chu Hsi was of the view that originally these four characters were a pair of two-character divinatory judgments, "*yüan-heng*" and "*li-chen*"—meaning "great success" (*ta-heng*) and "advantage from correctness" (*li yü cheng*)—and that only later they were made (by Confucius) "the four qualities" (*ssu-te*).[94] In any case, by Chu Hsi's time, the four characters had developed into a set of four categories associated with all kinds of things and events.[95] He said:

To speak about them in terms of "the Way of heaven" (*t'ien-tao*), [they] are *yüan, heng, li,* and *chen.* To speak about them in terms of the four seasons, [they] are spring, summer, autumn, and winter. To speak about them in terms of "the Way of men" (*jen-tao*), [they] are humaneness, righteousness, propriety, and knowledge. To speak about them in terms of weather, [they] are warmth, coolness, dryness, and wetness. To speak about them in terms of the compass directions, [they] are east, west, south, and north.[96]

Table 5.5 lists all the characteristics associated by Chu Hsi with the four cosmic qualities.

The four cosmic qualities were connected closely with the four seasons and thus were routinely associated with characteristic attributes of the seasons. The life cycle of plants was the most frequent example. Chu Hsi said:

> *Yüan* is the time when the buds are first sprouting; *heng* is the time when they have grown [to become] branches and leaves; *li* is the time when [the growth is] complete and accomplished; *chen* is the time when they bear fruits and settle themselves down.[97]

The four characteristics abstracted in this manner, that is, birth (*sheng*) for *yüan*, growth (*chang*) for *heng*, completion (*ch'eng*) for *li*, and latency (*ts'ang*) for *chen*, became the standard attributes of the four qualities.[98] Chu Hsi praised a similar characterization of them by Ch'eng I: *yüan* is "the beginning of the myriad things," *heng* their "growth," *li* their "continuation" (*sui*), and *chen* their "settling down" (*ch'eng*).[99]

As the four cosmic qualities were associated with many of the standard five-phase characteristics, such as the four seasons, the five constant virtues, and even the five storing viscera (*wu-tsang*),[100] much of what has been noted for the five-phase scheme holds for the four qualities as well. For example, the four qualities form a cycle that repeats continuously: after *chen*, *yüan* appears again, and before *yüan* there is another *chen*.[101] Chu Hsi compared this to the birth of a new plant (*yüan*) from the seed of fruits or grains (*chen*), adding that "the circulation is endless."[102] A relation among the four qualities could also be translated into that among the associated characteristics: for example, "If there is no *chen*, *yüan* has no place to rise from. How [then] can there be humaneness [associated with *yüan*] if there is no knowledge [associated with *chen*]?"[103]

The origin of "the ten celestial stems" (*shih-t'ien-kan* or *shih-kan*) and "the twelve terrestrial branches" (*shih-erh-ti-chih* or *shih-erh-chih*) is not clear. But they were in wide use by Chu Hsi's time, frequently in combination with yin-yang, the five phases, and the *I-ching* diagrams.[104]

The ten stems were associated with yin-yang and the five phases, the two-fold and five-fold schemes that naturally combine into a ten-category system. The odd-numbered stems were associated with yang and the even-numbered ones with yin; *chia* (the first) and *i* (the second) are associated with Wood, *ping* (the third) and *ting* (the fourth) with Fire, and so forth.[105] Chu Hsi also spoke of the associations of the ten stems with the eight trigrams, through them with the phases of the moon, and then with the days of the lunar month.[106]

The twelve branches also were associated with yin and yang, of which we have seen two different schemes, but not with the five phases. Their most characteristic association was with "the twelve hexagrams" (*shih-erh-kua*); through them,

TABLE 5.5

The Four-Cosmic-Quality Associations Mentioned by Chu Hsi

yüan	*heng*	*li*	*chen*	*References* [a]
"chief of the good" (*shan chih chang*)	"gathering of the beautiful" (*chia chih hui*)	"harmony of righteousness" (*i chih ho*)	"main part of events" (*shih chih kan*)	YL68.17b2 [b]
beginning (*shih*) of the myriad things	growth (*chang*) of the myriad things	continuation (*sui*) of the myriad things	completion (*ch'eng*) of the myriad things	YL68.6b0 [c]
Wood	Fire	Metal	Water	YL68.5b3
spring	summer	autumn	winter	YL68.8a1
warm	hot	cool	cold	YL68.6b2
humaneness (*jen*)	propriety (*li*)	righteousness (*i*)	knowledge (*chih*)	YL68.8a1
humaneness (*jen*)	balance (*chung*)	righteousness (*i*)	correctness (*cheng*)	YL94.15b3
liver	heart	lungs	kidneys	YL68.5b3
head	limbs	chest and abdomen	"the place where the *yüan-chi* returns"	YL68.5b3
birth (*sheng*)	growth (*chang*)	completion (*ch'eng*)	latency (*ts'ang*)	YL53.11b1 [d]
birth (*sheng*)	growth (*chang*)	"complete but not perfect" (*ch'eng erh wei-ch'üan*)	complete and ripened (*ch'eng-shu*)	YL68.5b1

(continued)

TABLE 5.5 (continued)

yüan	heng	li	chen	References[a]
first sprouting of the buds	growing of the branches and leaves	completion of the growing	bearing the fruits and settling down	CS44.7b0
beginning of the buds	growing of the branches and leaves	forming fruits but not yet ripe	bearing the fruits and firm	YL68.16a2
buds [of a tree]	flowers and leaves	branches and leaves being firm and strong	ripening of the fruits	WC50.1a
forming the buds [of a grain]	seedling	ear [of the grain]	complete grain	YL68.5b4
first formation [of a plume]	blooming of the flowers	formation of seeds	completion of fruits	YL68.5b1
obtaining the *ch'i* and forming the physical form	manifestation (*chang-chu*) [of the *ch'i* and physical form]	forming and aggregating (*chieh-chü*)	converging (*shou-lien*)	YL68.13b1

Notes

[a]Only one representative reference is given for each set of associations.

[b]Source: "Wen-yen chuan" of *I-ching*.

[c]Source: *Chou-i Ch'eng-shih chuan*, ch. 1.

[d]Associated indirectly, through their associations with the four seasons.

the twelve branches were further associated with the twelve lunar months (see table 5.4).[107] Chu Hsi connected this association with the yin-yang scheme in the following manner:

> If one speaks about them in terms of the waning and waxing of *ch'i*, then *tzu* (the first branch, associated with the *fu* hexagram) is the extreme of yin and the beginning of yang, *wu* (the seventh, *kou*) is the extreme of yang and the beginning of yin. *Mao* (the fourth, *ta-chuang*) is the middle of yang, *yu* (the tenth, *kuan*) is the middle of yin.[108]

This then led to the twelve-branch associations with the four seasons and the four compass directions:

> *Yin, mao*, and *ch'en* belong to east and are spring; *ssu, wu*, and *wei* belong to south and are summer; *shen, yu*, and *hsü* belong to west and are autumn; *hai, tzu*, and *ch'ou* belong to north and are winter.[109]

Chu Hsi went on to speak of seasonal characteristics of animals and plants and of their "life-*ch'i*" (*sheng-ch'i*) in connection with the twelve branches.[110] The twelve branches were used also in designating the twelve double hours of the day, which Chu Hsi connected with the plant life cycle.[111] He also spoke of Shao Yung's theory of the twelve epochs (*hui*), according to which a cosmic cycle of 129,600 years from the beginning of the world to its end is constituted of twelve epochs (of 10,800 years each), designated by the twelve branches.[112]

The ten stems and the twelve branches were often used in combination, forming a sexagenary cycle of the "stem-branch" pairs: the cycle begins with the *chia* (first stem)–*tzu* (first branch) pair, goes on to *kuei* (tenth stem)–*yu* (tenth branch), then to *chia*–*hsü* (eleventh branch), *i* (second stem)–*hai* (twelfth branch), and *ping* (third stem)–*tzu*; it proceeds to *kuei*–*wei* (eighth branch), *chia*–*shen* (ninth branch), and so forth, until finally it reaches *kuei-hai*, after which the *chia-tzu* pair begins again. These pairs were used mainly in designating and counting days, months, and years and thus also in various methods of fate calculations.[113] Chu Hsi mentioned one such method, called "*huo-chu-lin*," in which each of the single lines of a hexagram is assigned a different stem-branch pair.[114]

Notes

1. For general discussions of the *I-ching* and its diagrams, see Needham, *Science and Civilisation*, 2:304–345. Shchutskii, *Researches on the I Ching*; Smith et al., *Sung Uses of I Ching*, esp. chap. 1; Kao, *Chou-i ku-ching t'ung-shuo*. The two books by Hellmut Wilhelm—*Eight Lectures on the I Ching*; and *Heaven, Earth, and Man in the Book of Changes*—often contain some free-wheeling speculations. On Chu Hsi's own ideas about the *I-ching*, see Chang, "Analysis of Chu Hsi's System of *I*"; Smith et al., *Sung Uses of I Ching*, chap. 6.

2. For Shao Yung's thought about *shu*, see, e.g., Smith et al., *Sung Uses of I-ching*, chap. 4, esp. pp. 110–127; Birdwhistell,

Transition to Neo-Confucianism, chap. 4. For opinions on Shao Yung held by contemporary and later thinkers, including Chu Hsi, see, e.g., Birdwhistell, *Transition to Neo-Confucianism*, chap. 9. For Chu Hsi's views in particular, see, e.g., Wyatt, "Chu Hsi's Critique of Shao Yung." See also chap. 12, sec. 12.5, of this volume.

3. *YL*4.19b1. See also *YL*100.4a2.

4. *YL*100.11a0.

5. *YL*100.4a2.

6. *YL*93.6a4. According to Chu Hsi, Chou Tun-i looked at things through *li*, whereas Shao Yung did so through *shu*.

7. *YL*65.7b4.

8. *YL*67.1b1. Cf. *YL*65.6b1, where he said, "In general, *shu* is where it is divided, demarcated, and limited."

9. *YL*65.6b2.

10. *YL*65.6b1. See also *YL*65.6b2.

11. *YL*4.21a1. See also *YL*4.18b4–19a0, where Chu Hsi spoke of similar things, referring to them as "the fate decreed by heaven" (*t'ien so ming*).

12. *YL*1.7a0. This came up as Chu Hsi's explanation of how a sage like Confucius remained poor and failed to occupy a high position; see chap. 11, p. 208. See also *YL*72.17b3–18a0, 127.4a1.

13. *YL*4.22a2.

14. *YL*138.7a4.

15. *YL*65.7b4–8a0. See also *YL*67.4b1.

16. E.g., *YL*4.21a0; *WC*56.35b.

17. *YL*94.34b0.

18. E.g., *YL*65.12a2, where Chu Hsi said:

A day has the day's fortune, a month has the month's fortune, and a year has the year's fortune. [To talk about] great [matters], the beginning and end of heaven and earth; as for small [matters], life and death of men and things; as for distant [matters], changes of the ancient and present times. None of these lie outside this [i.e., fortune]. It simply is a single *li* of fullness, emptiness, waning, and waxing.

19. *YL*65.7b4–8a0.

20. *WC*37.27a.

21. E.g., *YL*4.19b1; 100.4a2. See chap. 12, pp. 267ff.

22. *YL*4.17a0.

23. *YL*4.17b1. See also *WC*75.4a, 12a. For brief discussions of various methods of Chinese fate calculation, see Chao, "Chinese Science of Fate-Calculation"; Smith, *Fortune-Tellers and Philosophers*, esp. chap. 5. Huang, "Court Divination and Christianity in the K'ang-hsi Era," also contains some relevant information. For the ten stems and the twelve branches, see sec. 5.4 of this volume.

24. *YL*66.18a2. The two phrases, both of which are attributed to Confucius, appear in "Hsi-tz'u chuan," ch. A12.

25. E.g., *YL*103.1a2; *CS*10.32a4, 33b0. Cf. Graham, *Two Chinese Philosophers*: "[T]he style, manner, air, by which the temperament of any human type is revealed are the outward signs of the ether (*ch'i-hsiang*)" (p. 38).

26. *YL*135.1a4.

27. *YL*67.1b1.

28. The most conspicuous examples of such attempts in Chinese history before Chu Hsi's time were those made by Yang Hsiung and Shao Yung: see, e.g., Nylan and Sivin, "First Neo-Confucianism"; Smith et al., *Sung Uses of I-ching*, chap. 4; Birdwhistell, *Transition to Neo-Confucianism*.

29. On the attitudes of Sung Neo-Confucians toward "*hsiang-shu*," see, e.g., Smith et al., *Sung Uses of I-ching*; Also see chap. 12 of this volume, sec. 12.5.

30. E.g., *YL*100.4b1.

31. E.g., *YL*66.19a1, 2, 4.

32. *YL*67.5b2.

33. *YL*65.7a4. For a more complete quotation, see note 71.

34. *CS*58.31b0.

35. E.g., *YL*65.6b1. The *I-ching* passage comes from "Hsi-tz'u chuan," ch. A9.

36. *YL*77.1b0. The *I-ching* phrase comes from the "Shuo-kua chuan" commentary, ch. 1.

37. E.g., *YL*87.27a0; 125.8b1. It has to be noted, however, that these associations

are in conflict with the yin-yang associations of the two pairs, according to which *p'o* and Water are yin, with which the even numbers are associated, and *hun* and Fire are yang, associated with the odd numbers. On the *hun-p'o* dualities, see chap. 11, sec. 11.6.

38. *YL*119.4b0–5a0.　　See also *YL*20.14b0.

39. *YL*75.4b1.

40. *YL*65.7a2. For the ways the ten stems and the twelve branches are combined into pairs, see p. 85.

41. *YL*100.9b1, in which Chu Hsi gives the names of all the eight hexagrams of the latter type.

42. *YL*65.6a5.

43. E.g., *YL*65.6b1, 2.

44. *YL*92.2b0.

45. E.g., *YL*67.3b4–4a0; 100.1b3–2a0, 3b3, 4a1, 5b1; *WC*37.28a, 38.3a–3b. For Yang Hsiung and his theory, see, e.g., Nylan and Sivin, "First Neo-Confucianism."

46. E.g., *YL*65.7b2; 100.3b3; 125.10b1, 2; *WC*37.35a. The *Lao-tzu* passage comes from ch. 42. One can think of another series that incorporates the yin-yang, five-phase, and various other categories in a single scheme. According to it, the one *ch'i* is divided and becomes yin and yang. Each of the yin and yang is further divided and yields the four phases. When Earth is added as the neutral phase, it completes the five phases. The dividing goes further to the eight trigrams, the ten celestial stems, the sixty-four hexagrams, and so forth, eventually covering all the myriad things.

47. *YL*94.5a0.

48. *YL*65.8b1.

49. *YL*75.5a1.

50. *YL*65.8b1.

51. *YL*75.4b1.

52. *SSCC* (*Lun-yü*), 3.3a.

53. *YL*65.8b3. Cf. *YL*65.9a2, in which he mentioned pairs of numbers that add up to fifteen: "If one talks about it with fifteen, nine pairs with six, and seven pairs with eight."

54. *WC*38.1a. Here Chu Hsi was elaborating upon "Hsi-tz'u chuan," ch. A9.

55. *YL*75.5a1.

56. *YL*77.1b0. Here Chu Hsi is using another ancient idea, "the circular heaven and the square earth" (*t'ien-yüan ti-fang*). See also *Chou-i pen-i*, 10.1a.

57. The two diagrams are presented, along with other diagrams, in the appendix of Chu Hsi's *I-hsueh ch'i-meng* and are discussed in detail in ch. 1 of that work. They are discussed also in *YL*65.8a1–9a5; *WC*37.36a; 38.1a–3a, 4b–5a; 44.7b–8a; 45.38a–38b; 84.3b–4a. See also *YL*65.9a2, where Chu Hsi asserted that "the *Ho-t'u* and the *Lo-shu* were just what heaven and earth drew up." For modern discussions of these diagrams, including their origins and developments, see Needham, *Science and Civilisation*, 3:56–69; Camman, "Magic Square of Three in Old Chinese Philosophy and Religion"; Saso, "What Is the *Ho-t'u?*"; Henderson, *Development and Decline of Chinese Cosmology*, pp. 82–86; Chang, "Analysis of Chu Hsi's System of *I*," pp. 301–305. Most of these references include the diagrams themselves. In *YL*87.10b4–11b0 and *WC*68.11a–12a, Chu Hsi discussed the related diagram called "*ming-t'ang*." For the *ming-t'ang* diagram, see Henderson, *Development and Decline of Chinese Cosmology*, pp. 75–82.

58. See chaps. 9 and 10. See also sec. 12.8 for Chu Hsi's attitude toward the specialist tradition of mathematics.

59. E.g., *YL*66.18b2, 3; 18b4–19a0; 19b1; *WC*67.1a–1b.

60. E.g., *YL*65.15a1; *CS*26.8b2. The source of this tradition can be traced to "Hsi-tz'u chuan," ch. B2.

61. For a brief discussion on the *hsien-t'ien* sequence, see Smith et al., *Sung Uses of I Ching*, pp. 112–119. Chu Hsi's own discussion appears, e.g., in *I-hsueh ch'i-meng*, ch. 2. This sequence is logically and mathematically very neat. Many commentators on the *I-ching*, from Shao Yung down to modern scholars, have found it possible to

discuss the construction of the diagrams and the relations among them in purely mathematical or numerical manners; see, e.g., McKenna and Mair, "Reordering of the Hexagrams of the *I Ching*." Some even compared the scheme to the binary number system of Leibniz: see, e.g., Aiton and Shimao, "Gorai Kinzo's Study of Leibniz and the *I ching* Hexagrams"; Needham, *Science and Civilisation*, 2:340–345. The most recent comparative analysis of the two systems is Ryan, "Leibniz' Binary System and Shao Yong's *Yijing*."

62. *YL*65.3b1.

63. *WC*38.7b.

64. *YL*65.3b1. Nor was the relation between the trigrams on the two sides of the so-called *Hsien-t'ien-t'u*, that is, that those on one side produce those on the other side if the yin and yang lines are changed into each other, in the sages' mind until all the trigrams had been completed. The *Hsien-t'ien-t'u* is also given in the appendix of Chu Hsi's *I-hsueh ch'i-meng*, along with various other charts made of the *I-ching* diagrams, and is discussed in the passages gathered in *YL*65.9b1–15a2. For more on these charts, see Phelan, "Neo-Confucian Cosmology."

65. For the actual development of the *I-ching* diagrams, see, e.g., Shchutskii, *Researches on the I Ching*, pt. 2, chap. 1, esp. pp. 144 ff. Wilhelm, *Eight Lectures on the I Ching*, chap. 4, contains more speculations concerning the problem.

66. Needham, *Science and Civilisation*, 2:322.

67. For a good discussion of the intentions of "Hsi-tz'u chuan," see Peterson, "Making Connections."

68. *YL*96.3a3.

69. *YL*65.3a2.

70. *YL*65.4b1.

71. E.g., *YL*69.5a3, 5b2, 13a1, 17b2. In *YL*65.7a4, Chu Hsi approvingly quoted Ts'ai Yüan-ting's saying:

The myriad sounds under heaven come from the opening and closing; the myriad *li* under heaven come from the movement and rest;

the myriad numbers under heaven come from the odd and even; the myriad images under heaven come from the square and circle. These all arise from the two diagrams, *ch'ien* and *k'un*.

72. E.g., *YL*47.2b1, 98.12a4. *Ts'an-t'ung-ch'i* also begins with the saying "*Ch'ien* and *k'un* are the gates of the *I-ching*, and are the father and mother of many diagrams." See also *YL*65.12b0 and *WC*37.29b for Chu Hsi's own remarks about the association. It was because of this association with father and mother that the *ch'ien* and *k'un* were employed in metaphors of human reproduction.

73. *YL*76.9b2.

74. *CS*49.26a2.

75. Many of the trigram associations originated from the "Shuo-kua chuan" commentary of the *I-ching*. Henderson, *Development and Decline of Chinese Cosmology*, pp. 14–18, discusses the development of these trigram associations briefly. Needham, *Science and Civilisation*, 2:312–321, gives a more complete listing of the trigram and hexagram associations.

76. E.g., *YL*62.31a4; 67.23b1; 68.1a4; 71.6a0; 74.25a0.

77. E.g., *YL*72.19b3; *WC*37.36a–36b. Nor is it possible to see general defining characteristics for these associations. They appear even more arbitrary than the yin-yang and five-phase associations. This must have been in part the reason that Needham has regarded the *I-ching* diagrams as a "hindrance" to the development of scientific ideas, while believing that the yin-yang and the five phases "helped" it. E.g., *Science and Civilisation*, 2:304.

78. E.g., "Hsi-tz'u chuan," ch. B2.

79. E.g., *YL*66.20b1, 2, 3; 73.4b1, 21a3. Chu Hsi even used these associations in explaining a sequence of two hexagrams: "The bird comes from the egg. This is the reason why *hsiao-kuo* comes after *chung-fu* [in the *I-ching* text]." *YL*73.21a3.

80. *YL*66.21a1.

81. *YL*66.20b3.

82. E.g., *YL*66.20b2; 73.4b1.

83. E.g., *YL*72.1a2.

84. There were explanations that even linked the shapes of the single yin and yang lines with the odd-even and the circle-square dichotomies of heaven and earth or that related the broken yin line to the empty spaces inside the earth. E.g., *YL*65.4a0. Chu Hsi was not fully willing to accept such explanations, however; he said, for example, that "heaven is originally one and the earth is originally two" (*YL*65.4a0) and that "*ch'ien* simply is a single thing, solid and full everywhere: *k'un* has an opening." *YL*67.17a5.

85. *YL*72.1b1.

86. *YL*66.20a1.

87. *YL*71.24a1.

88. E.g., *YL*65.1b3.

89. This sequence of associations can be traced to the "*kua-ch'i*" technique of Ching Fang (79–37 B.C.), discussed in Ch'ü, *Hsien-Ch'in Han Wei i-li shu-p'ing*, pp. 82–98; Lo, *Chung-kuo che-hsueh ssu-hsiang-shih, Liang-Han Nan-pei-ch'ao p'ien*, pp. 469–481.

90. *WC*38.10b. For more on this, see chap. 9, p. 156.

91. E.g., *YL*71.6b1, 2.

92. E.g., *YL*71.9a1, 9b1. For more on "the mind of heaven and earth producing things," see chap. 7, sec. 7.4.

93. For the origins, meanings, and development of these four terms, see, e.g., Shchutskii, *Researches on the I Ching*, pp. xv–xx, 136–156.

94. E.g., *YL*66.3a0; 105.1a1–1b0; *WC*50.1a. The four characters appeared frequently in pairs in the *I-ching* text itself, and Chou Tun-i was still speaking of the two pairs, saying that "*yüan-heng* is 'the penetration (*t'ung*) of sincerity' and *li-chen* is 'the return (*fu*) of sincerity.'" *T'ung-shu*, ch. 1. For Chu Hsi's comments on this remark, see, e.g., *YL*69.17a0; 94.22b1–23a2. See also *YL*69.16a4–17a0, where he discussed the two pairs. But already in the "Wen-yen" (Words of the text) commentary of the *I-ching* (for the *ch'ien* hexagram) the

four terms were given separate significances: "*yüan* is 'the chief of the good' (*shan chih chang*); *heng* is 'the gathering of the beautiful' (*chia chih hui*); *li* is 'the harmony of righteousness' (*i chih ho*); *chen* is 'the main part of events' (*shih chih kan*)." The meanings of the four characters given here are quite obscure, however, and Chu Hsi's own discussions of the passage, e.g., in *YL*68.17b2–23a1, are not much clearer.

95. Chu Hsi even titled a brief essay "Explanation of *Yüan, Heng, Li*, and *Chen*" (Yüan-heng-li-chen shuo). *WC*67.1a.

96. *YL*68.6b1.

97. *CS*44.7b0. See also *WC*50.1a.

98. E.g., *YL*53.11b1. In Derk Bodde's translation, these four standard attributes are nicely combined with the usual meanings of the characters: "original growth" for *yüan*, "prosperous development" for *heng*, "advantageous gain" for *li*, and "correct firmness" for *chen*; see Fung, *History of Chinese Philosophy*, 2:636.

99. E.g. *YL*68.6a1, 6b0; 69.17a0. Ch'eng I's original remark comes from his *Chou-i Ch'eng-shih chuan*, ch. 1 (ECC, p. 695).

100. E.g., *YL*6.7a3; 53.11b1; 60.2a1; 68.5b3, 6b1, 2; 8a1. On the five storing viscera, see chap. 11, sec. 11.2.

101. E.g., *YL*68.6a2, 3; *CS*44.7b0.

102. E.g., *YL*68.5b4; *WC*50.1a.

103. *YL*60.2a1.

104. For brief discussions of the ten stems and the twelve branches, see, e.g., Needham, *Science and Civilisation*, 2:358–359, 3:396–398; Chao, "Chinese Science of Fate-Calculation"; Shinzō, "Kanshi Gō-gyōsetsu to Senkyokureki."

105. See chap. 4, table 4.1.

106. See table 5.3. This scheme of associations is called "*na-chia*" and is discussed in Lo, *Chung-kuo che-hsueh ssu-hsiang-shih, Liang-Han Nan-pei-ch'ao p'ien*, pp. 481–484. Chu Hsi spoke of the *na-chia* scheme in, e.g., *WC*38.19a; *Ts'an-t'ung-ch'i k'ao-i*, pp. 4a–5a.

107. E.g., *WC*38.10a–10b.

108. *WC*58.38b. Chu Hsi also said, "*Mao* and *yu* are [the hexagrams in which]

the yin and yang are not yet settled; *tzu* and *wu* are [those whose] yin and yang are already settled." *YL*74.10a4.

109. *YL*53.3b1. Of the twelve branches, however, Chu Hsi called the four, *tzu* (north), *wu* (south), *mao* (east), and *yu* (west), "the correct positions of the four directions" (*ssu-fang chih cheng-wei*). *WC*58.38b.

110. *YL*53.3b1–4a0. For more on life-*ch'i*, see chap. 10, p. 173.

111. *YL*68.13b1. For a brief discussion of the traditional Chinese double-hour system, see Needham, Wang, and Price, *Heavenly Clockwork*, appendix (pp. 199–205)

112. See chap. 9, sec. 9.1.

113. For brief discussions of the sexagenary cycle of the stem-branch pairs and their uses, see, e.g., Needham, *Science and Civilisation*, 3:396–398; Chao, "Chinese Science of Fate-Calculation."

114. *YL*65.12b0.

Kuei-Shen

In selecting topics thus far, I have assumed an implicit distinction between what is "natural" and what is "nonnatural" (or "supernatural") and have discussed those that can be placed inside the imaginary boundary that includes only the "natural." But we have noted repeatedly that the key concepts in Chu Hsi's natural philosophy could not be confined to the "natural" realm. For example, *ch'i* was what constituted all objects and underlay all phenomena in the world, not only those that could be called "natural." Yin-yang, the five phases, and other concepts were also associated with all kinds of things, again not limited to the "natural." We now turn to those concepts that must be placed in the border area—*kuei-shen*, heaven (*t'ien*) and the sages (*sheng-jen*). The principal meanings of these concepts lie outside the "natural" realm; but they nevertheless touch on natural phenomena and objects, and what Chu Hsi thought about these border-area concepts will help us to understand better his thought about what lies inside the boundary.

   I take up *kuei-shen* first in this chapter and discuss Chu Hsi's ideas about the concept and about the beliefs and practices associated with it. Since there is no satisfactory general account of *kuei-shen* that I can refer to, my discussion here is more general than those in the previous chapters.[1]

6.1. Different Meanings of *Kuei-Shen* and *Shen*

In his frequent characterizations of *kuei-shen*, Chu Hsi stressed that it is difficult to see or to understand. For example, he said that *kuei-shen* "has no physical form or shadow (*ying*) and is difficult to understand"[2] and that it is "what cannot be inferred in terms of *li*."[3] Thus, in comparison with things like rituals and music, which are bright (*ming*), *kuei-shen* is dark (*yu*): the former are "what can be seen," whereas the latter is "what cannot be seen."[4] The character *shen* by itself also has similar meanings. Chu Hsi frequently quoted and commented on characterizations of *shen* by earlier thinkers, from the famous "Hsi-tz'u chuan" phrase that "what is unfathomable in [terms of] yin and yang is called *shen*"[5] and Mencius's assertion that *shen* is what is "sagely and not possible to know"[6] to Chou Tun-i's that "[its] manifestation is subtle and it cannot be seen; [it] fills everywhere and cannot be known completely"[7] and Chang Tsai's repeated sayings that *shen* is "subtle and mysterious" and "unfathomable."[8] Chu Hsi's own characterizations emphasized suddenness and the lack of fixity and constancy. Typically, he said: "*Shen* is suddenly like this [and suddenly not like this]. It is all unfathomable. It comes suddenly and goes suddenly. It is suddenly here and suddenly there."[9] For Chu Hsi, then, *kuei-shen* and *shen* refer to things and events that are so subtle, sudden, strange, and mysterious that they are difficult to see, understand, or accept.[10]

Yet, *kuei-shen* has a meaning much broader than this. Chu Hsi illustrated the breadth of the concept in the following words:

> Rain, wind, dew, and thunder, the sun, the moon, day, and night. These are "traces" (*chi*) of *kuei-shen*. These are "the fair, even, correct, and straight" (*kung-p'ing-cheng-chih*) *kuei-shen* of the bright day. For example, what are called "ghosts shouting on the beams [of houses] and touching the chests [of people]"—these refer to those [*kuei-shen*] that are "incorrect, wicked, and dark" (*pu-cheng-hsieh-an*), "sometimes existing and sometimes not," "sometimes going and sometimes coming," and "sometimes aggregating and sometimes dispersing." There also are sayings that [when one] offers a prayer to them, it is responded to, and [when one] makes a wish to them it is obtained. These are also what are called *kuei-shen*. And they are [all] the same *li*. The myriad things and events in the world are all this *li*; there only are differences of being exquisite or coarse, and small or large.[11]

Chu Hsi distinguished, in this manner, three different kinds of *kuei-shen:* first, "the fair, even, correct, and straight" *kuei-shen;* second, "the incorrect, wicked, and dark" *kuei-shen;* and third, the *kuei-shen* that respond to prayers.[12]

In the first and broadest sense, *kuei-shen* refers to all objects and phenomena of the world. For each of them can be considered subtle and mysterious in that none can be known completely: everything that exists or takes place in the natural world—including what appears to be normal and regular—manifests subtle and mysterious workings of the world and thus is *kuei-shen* or *shen*. This is how Chu Hsi interpreted the *I-ching* phrase "Looking at 'the heaven's way of *shen*' (*t'ien chih shen-tao*), the four seasons do not err": "Looking at the heaven's way of *shen*, it is nothing but the way and *li* of spontaneous operation. The four seasons spontaneously do not err."[13] He also said, "The earth's *shen* is merely coming into being of the myriad things."[14] Thus, for Chu Hsi, "between heaven and earth are all *shen*."[15] He even asked, "What thing is not *kuei-shen?*"[16] To give more specific examples, the sun, the moon, and the stars, which are manifestations of clear and bright portions of *ch'i*, are all *shen*.[17] Such weather phenomena as the wind, rain, dew, thunder, lightning, and darkness are all *kuei-shen*, too.[18] "Things like flowers and trees appear suddenly. [They] all blossom when [they should] blossom; [they] all produce fruits when [they should] produce fruits. . . . This is *shen*."[19] Even in the human realm, the ability to speak, laugh, and to possess intelligence and knowledge is all *kuei-shen*.[20] Man's perception—feeling pain, for example—is also *shen*.[21] Chu Hsi even said that "in happiness and goodness, misfortune and licentiousness, one can also see the way and *li* of *kuei-shen*."[22]

More often, however, Chu Hsi used the words *kuei-shen* and *shen* in a more restricted sense, in which their subtle and mysterious nature is more marked and thus more difficult to understand. He illustrated the difference of this second sense from the first in the following manner:

> To discuss the correct *li*, it is similar to the sudden blooming of flowers and leaves on trees. It is "a trace of creative transformation" (*tsao-hua chih chi*). Also, there suddenly are thunder, wind, or rain in the sky, for example—they are all [*kuei-shen*]. But people see them often and thus do not feel strange about them. [As for] things like the sudden hearing of ghost whistles and ghost fires, [people] regard them as strange but do not know that they are also traces of creative transformations. Only, they are not correct *li*.[23]

He also said:

> The *kuei-shen* phenomena are considered to be strange. In the world, there naturally are ways and *li* like these. It cannot be said that there are none [of them]. It is only that they are not correct "creative transformations," and these are what received the incorrect *ch'i* of yin-yang.[24]

This sense of *kuei-shen* was what Chu Hsi had in mind when he said, "Metal, Wood, Water, Fire, and Earth are not *shen*."[25] The five phases and what can be cast into them were not *shen* in this sense, because for him they fell under the purview of the "proper" *li*.

Yet, *kuei-shen* phenomena in this second sense are also workings of yin and yang *ch'i*, albeit "incorrect" ones. They could not transcend the domain of *ch'i*, which constitutes all objects and underlies all phenomena of the world. Chu Hsi thus provided, for many *kuei-shen* and *shen* phenomena, explanations in terms of qualities and activities of *ch'i*. He even went as far as saying flatly that "*kuei-shen* is merely *ch'i*"[26] or "the exquisite [part of] *ch'i*."[27] But more typically, *kuei-shen*, for him, was "nothing but the vanishing and growing of yin and yang,"[28] "the contraction and expansion, going and coming of the two *ch'i* [i.e., yin and yang *ch'i*],"[29] or, adopting Chang Tsai's characterization, "the innate ability (*liang-neng*) of the two *ch'i*."[30] He even said that "[*kuei-shen*] is like spirits (*shen-ling*) inside this *ch'i*."[31] Chu Hsi characterized *shen* in similar ways: *shen* also is "the essence of *ch'i*,"[32] "the place where *ch'i* is 'essential and subtle' (*ching-miao*),"[33] "the 'essential and bright' (*ching-ming*) [portion] of *ch'i*,"[34] and "the clear and bright [portion] of *ch'i*."[35]

Examples of the third sense of *kuei-shen* mentioned most frequently by Chu Hsi were the spirits of dead ancestors responding to sacrificial services (*chi*). Since the offering of sacrificial services was among the most important duties of a Confucian gentleman like Chu Hsi, he had a great deal to say and write about this sense of *kuei-shen*, a lot more than about the other two.

6.2. Sacrificial Services and Spirits

Underlying Chu Hsi's discussion of sacrificial services to dead ancestors was the common belief, which he also accepted, that man's *ch'i* is "dispersed" (*san*) or "exhausted" (*chin*) upon death.[36] But this occurs only at a normal death, for those who have died peacefully, the sages like Yao and Shun, for example.[37] The *ch'i* of those who die abnormally is not dispersed or exhausted. Chu Hsi mentioned many such cases: those who die suddenly, especially from sudden diseases; those who die in battlefields; those who are executed, murdered, or drowned; and those who commit suicide.[38] He even spoke of a person whose *ch'i* was not exhausted upon death because his endowed *ch'i* was very flourishing.[39]

Of course, such undispersed *ch'i* does not remain indefinitely; it becomes dispersed "eventually," "after a long time."[40] But while it stays undispersed, it can produce various strange effects: "Monstrous and evil [ghosts] are often [those who] could not get their *ch'i* dispersed upon death. Therefore [the *ch'i*] is pent-up and congealed to form the monstrous and evil [effects]."[41] For example, the undispersed *ch'i* of dead persons and horses at old battlefields can form "ghost fires" (*kuei-huo*) or even ghosts in the shape of humans.[42] Some men die violently without exhausting their *ch'i*, which can form evil spirits (*li*) possessing evil power that can be destroyed only through such means as firecrackers.[43] An example is the case of Po Yu, whom Chu Hsi discussed on several occasions.[44] Chu Hsi also mentioned a certain Ch'ang Hung who turned into emerald after death because his extreme loyalty kept his *ch'i* from being dispersed.[45]

Sometimes the dispersion of *ch'i* upon death can produce strange effects. For example, Chu Hsi told of a man whose *ch'i*, after his death, became warm, smoky, and steamy and filled a room for several days: "His *ch'i* was flourishing. Therefore it was like this."[46] He spoke of another man's death, upon which there were blasts of wind and thunder and it became very dark with cloud and fog, because the man had nourished his *ch'i* and made it so strong that it produced such violent effects while being dispersed.[47] In fact, Chu Hsi interpreted the famous phrase of the *Record of Rites* (Li-chi) "bright, fuming up, and pathetic" (*chao-ming hsün-hao ch'i-ch'uang*) as referring to such effects of the *ch'i*—or the *hun-ch'i*—of a dead person: "This refers to the way in which *ch'i* of *kuei-shen* stimulates and touches man."[48]

Chu Hsi's explanation of sacrificial services was based on the belief that ancestors and their descendants have the same *ch'i*, which is passed from father to son, to grandson, and so on.[49] Since the same *ch'i* respond to each other, the ancestors' *ch'i* can respond to the descendants' and come back to aggregation.[50] Yet, the notion that *ch'i* is dispersed upon death poses a problem for such explanations. For if the ancestors' *ch'i* has already been dispersed, there can be no way for the descendants to reach them through sacrificial services. This became the key problem in Chu Hsi's discussion of the topic—How does the sacrificial service reach the dead ancestors whose *ch'i* has already been dispersed?

Chu Hsi's answer can be seen in the following typical discussion of the sacrificial service:

> When a man dies, although [his *ch'i*] eventually returns to [the state of] dispersion, there also is [some part that is] not dispersed or exhausted. Therefore, the sacrificial service has the *li* of reaching and moving [the ancestor]. Whether the *ch'i* of an ancestor of a generation far removed [still] exists or not, it is not possible to know. But since the person

who offers the sacrificial service is his descendant, [their *ch'i*] must be the same *ch'i*, and therefore there is the *li* of stimulating and penetrating [the ancestor].[51]

The point was that the *ch'i* dispersed upon death does not vanish completely but lingers for some time. Chu Hsi did not reject an analogy, offered by a disciple, that it is like the *ch'i* of lantern smoke going up and gradually disappearing but still remaining inside the room, in a dispersed form.[52]

Yet, for sacrificial services to reach dead ancestors, something more than the mere presence of ancestors' and descendants' *ch'i* is needed. The mind of the descendants offering the services must be "sincere" (*ch'eng*) and "reverent" (*ching*) in order for them to reach their ancestors' dispersed *ch'i* and to call them back to respond.[53] Chu Hsi said: "Although his [i.e., the ancestor's] *chi* is dispersed, its roots exist here. If [the descendant] accomplishes his sincerity and reverence to the utmost, he can still call back that *ch'i* to aggregate here."[54] He asked, "If sincere mind reaches and moves, how can his [i.e., the ancestor's] *ch'i*, which is not completely exhausted or dispersed, not come to receive?"[55] He even said that during the services "one should not seek [the response] with the physical form but seek it with this sincere intention."[56]

This does not mean, however, that Chu Hsi went beyond the realm of *ch'i* to account for what takes place during sacrificial services. Since, as we have seen in chapter 3, man's mind and *ch'i* can interact, it is possible that descendants' minds are capable of moving their ancestors' *ch'i*. Chu Hsi said, "The presence or absence of the *shen* [of the ancestors] always depends on whether this mind is sincere or not."[57] He also said: "When the mind is set, even a *kuei-shen* obeys";[58] "Where this mind [of a descendant] is manifest, that [ancestor] responds with the *ch'i*."[59] He even explained the effect of a gathering of many people at a sacrificial service: "Where many minds converge, these become hot."[60]

Since mental qualities like sincerity and reverence play such an important role, it is not surprising that Chu Hsi would take the "mental spirit" (*ching-shen*) as the agent that operates during sacrificial services. For him, ancestors "come and reach [us]" during the services, as "[we] move their mental spirits with our mental spirits."[61] The descendant "must have his mental spirit aggregate" so that "afterward he can arrive at the shrine and receive the ancestors' [mental spirits that aggregate there]."[62] Chu Hsi did not reject the explanation that one observes "purification and abstinence" (*chai-chieh*) in order to "have one's mental spirit aggregate."[63]

While discussing sacrificial services in this manner, Chu Hsi said frequently that the topic was difficult to discuss.[64] But at the same time, it was very important for him; indeed, there could hardly be anything more important than the sacrificial service for him. That he took it to be so important can be seen from the persistence—rarely found in his discussions of other subjects—that he and his disciples showed in pursuing some problems related to the subject. For example, Chu Hsi dealt with the problem of the number of generations that people should go back in offering sacrifices, the answer to which was based on the belief that the *ch'i* of the recent ancestors could be reached, but the *ch'i* of those far removed could not.[65] Similarly, when a disciple asked how one could reach one's maternal ancestors and the ancestors of one's wife, who did not have the same *ch'i* as one's own, Chu Hsi re-sponded by pointing out that all mental spirits and *ch'i* in the world originated from a single source.[66] Another question led to a discussion of whether the dispersed *ch'i* of ancestors could be called back to aggregation during sacrificial services only: "The ancestor's *ch'i* exists only when the descendant's *ch'i* exists. On the other hand, when it is not the time of sacrificial service, how can it be aggregated?"[67] Chu Hsi even discussed the effects of money, foods, and drinks offered in the services: "Are they just to express the sincerity of my mind, or does *ch'i* really come [from these objects] to reach [the ancestors]?"[68] Chu Hsi accepted neither of these choices. But as for the use of living things or blood and meat as sacrificial objects, he said that it was to borrow their "life-*ch'i*."[69] He even attributed the ancient custom of using im-ages of dead persons to the belief that "the image and the dead person were origi-nally [made of] the same *ch'i*," which then enabled the mental spirits of living per-sons to contact and move the mental spirits of the dead.[70] Obviously, these are questions that could come up in discussing the sacrificial service; but they would not have been taken up and pursued in this manner if it had not been a topic of great importance for Chu Hsi and his disciples.

Chu Hsi mentioned other spirits that also are objects of sacrificial service and worship. Great natural objects and phenomena—heaven and earth, the four seasons, the sun, the moon, stars, lands, valleys, mountains and rivers, cold and hot weather, flood and drought, crops, and so on—were believed to have spirits associated with them so that they must be offered sacrifices.[71] The world (*t'ien-hsia*, literally "[all] under heaven"), countries, and households also have spirits for each of them.[72] Chu Hsi even spoke of the "five domestic spirits" (*wu-ssu*), that is, the spirits of five dif-ferent parts of a house: the eaves (*liu*), the gate (*hu*), the doors (*men*), the passage (*hsing*), and the kitchen (*tsao*).[73]

Chu Hsi did not reject the common belief that these spirits can respond to deeds of the people who are supposed to be under their purview. "The spirits of the world," for example, can cause abnormal effects to stars in the sky and to moun-tains and rivers on earth if the emperor indulges in pleasure without restraint.[74] Sometimes these spirits sounded like personified deities with occult powers. Chu Hsi did not reject expressions that invested spirits with feelings such as joy, fear, and anger. When they are joyous, they respond favorably to sacrifices and prayers. This is how Chu Hsi interpreted the phrase from *Mencius* "The hundred spirits receive it with joy": "[It refers to the cases] like praying for clear weather producing clear weather, and praying for rain producing rain."[75] He also spoke of *kuei-shen* with-drawing the anger when the sky is clear and bright,[76] and even of *kuei-shen*'s fear of music in the *shang*-tune.[77] Indeed, while serving as local governor, Chu Hsi duly followed the customs of offering sacrificial services to the spirits of the land and of praying for rain; his *Collected Writings* contain invocations that he wrote on such occasions.[78]

Of course, Chu Hsi did not go along completely with the popular beliefs in spir-its and deities.[79] On a visit to a village near his ancestral tomb, he was quite skep-tical about the deities worshiped in a local temple, which he refused to visit.[80] He even said: "I usually do not like to enter temples of deities and do not even view them. All this is what the stupid and ignorant do."[81] But Chu Hsi could not rule out the existence of spirits completely, because they could always be accounted for in terms of *ch'i*. Indeed, for him, spirits were also manifestations of qualities and activities of *ch'i*, just as *kuei-shen* in the first two senses were. He could see the same *kuei-shen* both in "the wind, thunder, mountains, and waters" and in "the sacrificial services in temples."[82] This is what Chu Hsi meant when he said, "The way of *kuei-shen* is just the way of a great man. It is not that there are two [different ways]."[83] Thus, he took the view that the practice of sacrificial services was established (by the sages) in accordance with "the *li* of heaven and earth."[84] He also said (as quoted at the beginning of this section), "[those that respond to prayers] are also what are called *kuei-shen*. And they are the same *li*." For him, "prayers are correct rituals, and naturally have responses."[85]

Chu Hsi explained the effect of sacrificial services to nonancestral spirits also in terms of interactions between the *ch'i* of the spirits and those who offer sacrifices. In praying for rain, for example,

> one acts upon the *ch'i* of them [i.e., the spirits in charge of rain] with one's sincerity. [As for] prayers to spirits and Buddha, for example, it is also that the *ch'i* of mountains and rivers where they reside can be acted upon. [The places] where today's spirits and Buddha reside are all excellent and numinous [parts] of mountains and rivers.[86]

Shrines "where the *ch'i* of mountains and rivers converge and aggregate" are particularly numinous and thus are responsive to sacrifices and prayers, but when these places "are damaged by digging and boring by people . . . [they] are no longer numinous."[87] Chu Hsi even explained "visitations of spirits" (*chiang-shen*) invoked by shamans (*wu*) as "mutual stimulation of their similar *ch'i*."[88]

There are, however, certain rules as to who can offer sacrifices to which spirits in order for the sacrifices to reach the spirits and to elicit their responses:

> The emperor offers sacrifices to heaven and earth; princes offer sacrifices to mountains and rivers; high officials offer sacrifices to the five domestic spirits. All these are [the cases in which] one's own mental spirit is appropriately content with them [i.e., the spirits to whom one offers sacrifices] and is able to stimulate and call them to come. If princes offer sacrifices to heaven and earth, or if high officials offer sacrifices to mountains and rivers, then it is meaningless.[89]

When appropriate spirits are chosen, said Chu Hsi, "they [i.e., the spirits] belong to me, and therefore I can reach them by offering sacrifices. If [they] do not belong to me, then [since my] *ch'i* [and theirs] do not mutually stimulate, how can I reach them by offering sacrifices?"[90] He discussed this topic frequently in commenting upon the *Analects* passage "When one offers sacrifices to spirits that are not one's own, that is obsequious" (2.24).[91] In this context he even discussed the problem of who should offer sacrifices to those without descendants.[92] He said that it is not proper to offer sacrifices to "idle *shen* and wild *kuei*" (*hsien-shen yeh-kuei*).[93]

Not only prayers and sacrificial services but also divination and fortune-telling involve *kuei-shen* in the third sense. Chu Hsi used the term *kuei-shen* in his discussions of those topics also. For example, "In human affairs, in things like happiness, goodness, misfortune, and licentiousness, one can also see the way and *li* of *kuei-shen*."[94] Thus, divinatory practices are "in accord with the *li* of *kuei-shen*."[95] He even said that shamans "interact with *kuei-shen*."[96] In this sense, divination and fortune-telling are activities parallel to prayers and sacrificial services. The difference is only that in the latter, man attempts to be heard and responded to by *kuei-shen*, whereas in the former he attempts to "question" and "listen to" them.[97] It follows that the reverence of mind required for sacrificial services is required for divination as well.[98] Indeed, Chu Hsi explained divination in much the same way as he did sacrificial service:

> Once man's mind moves, it must reach the *ch'i* [of heaven and earth]. And with this [*ch'i*] contracting and expanding, coming and going, it mutually stimulates and moves. Things like divination are all thus.[99]

6.3. Retaining Strange Phenomena While Rejecting "Superstitious" Beliefs about Them

A theme can be discerned that pervades all of Chu Hsi's discussion of *kuei-shen*: his opposition to "superstitious" beliefs and practices. Dedicated to constructing a philosophical basis of reality that would stand up against what he saw as empty and speculative tenets of Buddhists and Taoists, Chu Hsi was firm in his rejection of what appeared superstitious to him. In particular, he was staunchly opposed to admitting "occult" beings and powers beyond the qualities and activities of *ch'i*, which he believed underlay every object and phenomenon of the world.

This led Chu Hsi to offer explanations, in terms of *ch'i*, for many strange phenomena that could have been attributed to some occult causes. The strange phenomena taking place upon man's death discussed in the previous section are examples of this kind. But more can be found. For instance, the "thunder ax" (*lei-fu*), an ax-shaped object commonly believed to accompany thunder and lightning and fall down from the sky, striking men and things on earth, is formed by the condensation of *ch'i*.[100] Chu Hsi's explanation of the popular belief that dragons carry rain is another example: it can rain when a dragon appears because the dragon is an animal associated with Water and can thus produce wet *ch'i* when it encounters yang *ch'i*.[101] Dragons can also ride clouds and rise up in the sky by combining themselves with yang *ch'i*, for they are the most flourishing of what are yang.[102] Not only dragons but also men could fly. Such men, according to Chu Hsi, had refined their *ch'i* so much that their bones and flesh melted to become formless *ch'i*, which then became extremely light and clear; when the *ch'i* was exhausted, they could no longer fly.[103] Chu Hsi also spoke of a man who received the *ch'i* of the pig; he had pig's hair on his chest and made the noise of a pig while sleeping.[104]

In all these cases, however, Chu Hsi accepted the things and events in question: whether they were possible or not was seldom a problem for him. In other words, his antisuperstitious stand led him to reject "superstitious" beliefs about strange things and events but rarely to reject the things and events themselves. On the contrary, by attributing them to qualities and activities of *ch'i* rather than to occult causes, Chu Hsi accepted and "rationalized" their existence and occurrence. In fact, given the wide purview and adaptability of the concept *ch'i*, it was possible for him to come up with explanations for any phenomena, however strange they may appear.[105]

Thus, Chu Hsi was never dogmatic concerning the question of the existence of "ghosts" (designated by the same word, *kuei-shen*). To a disciple who asked whether ghosts exist, he responded: "How can this be discussed so simply?"[106] The problem for Chu Hsi was summarized in his own words in the following manner:

> Among people, those who believe in ghosts all say they really exist between heaven and earth. Those who do not believe in them think positively that there are no ghosts. Yet, there also are those who have seen real ghosts.[107]

Chu Hsi's view was basically that one cannot say they do not exist. He noted that "whether there are ghosts or not, the Sage [i.e, Confucius] did not say definitely."[108] Even the Ch'eng brothers "at first did not say that there were no ghosts"; what the Ch'engs rejected were those things that common people of the day called "ghosts."[109] Since many people have seen ghosts, Chu Hsi concluded, "How can one say there are no ghosts? It is merely that they are not correct *li*."[110] He even narrated, without either accepting or rejecting it, a story of a one-legged ghost that entered a house, causing death to a son within several days.[111]

Chu Hsi had the same attitude toward other strange things and events. To be sure, he was skeptical about most of them. In his view, out of ten of such strange stories current among the common people, about eight were nonsense and only two had the *li* for their occurrence.[112] After pointing out that Buddhists had many strange stories, he said that "these do not necessarily exist."[113] He was skeptical about such Buddhist theories as "cyclical transmigration" (*lun-hui*) and rebirth.[114] On other strange stories—for example, about a person who obtained a written answer from a deity by placing a question in a sealed envelope in the temple where he worshiped the deity,[115] or about some adverse effects of a damaged casket on the descendants' fortunes[116]—he had the same response: "I do not know how this could be so."

Sometimes Chu Hsi explained the strange effects by attributing them to the mental state of the person experiencing them. About the story of someone who was known to have seen ghosts, Chu Hsi explained: "It is simply [because his] mental spirit is not complete [that he] is like this";[117] what the person saw must have been "things like rainbows and colored clouds."[118] On the ghosts' ability to speak, he said, "[The speech] comes out relying on man's mental spirit [i.e., owing to the incomplete state of the mental spirit of the man who hears the ghosts speak]."[119] Incantations (*chou*) have effects because, according to Chu Hsi, those who "shout them angrily . . . have strong and resolute look, and therefore can move *kuei-shen* to obey."[120]

On the whole, however, Chu Hsi rarely rejected reported facts outright. In a long conversation on stories of various strange events, Chu Hsi did not commit himself definitely on the question of whether such things and events as footmarks of giant monsters; monstrous ghosts living in "thick mountain forests and deep waters"; a creature with a half-man, half-horse body; lizards making hail; prior and subsequent lives; or persons coming back to life after death could actually exist or occur.[121] His characteristic attitude toward them was that they needed to be "thoroughly understood." Nor did he reject the stories by Ch'eng I, recorded in *Ho-nan Ch'eng-shih i-shu* (Surviving works of the Ch'engs of Honan), about a man appearing in an island without parents, about a primeval man with an ox head and a snake body, and about a dragon egg. For him "they are not so strange"; he could "accept that perhaps there may be those."[122] On the mountain monsters, called "*wang-liang*" and mentioned in miscellaneous ancient texts, he said that "if they indeed exist, then they must be" the same things as the one-legged monster "*k'uei*."[123] He suggested that it is those who do not understand the *li* of such things that stubbornly refuse to believe them and insist on their nonexistence; if one understands their *li*, their strangeness will be resolved.[124] He even seemed to accept the existence of "immortals" (*shen-hsien*): "Who say they do not exist? Truly, there is *li* for them. Only, those efforts of theirs are very difficult to make."[125]

Concerning all these, the important question for Chu Hsi was whether they were actually seen. He was basically of the view that if a thing or an event is seen, its existence cannot be rejected. He confronted a disciple who was skeptical about the existence of such strange things with the remark "It is merely that you have never seen them."[126] Indeed, these things could always be explained in terms of *ch'i*, which was endowed with such flexible qualities and activities. We have already seen—and shall see—numerous examples in which Chu Hsi explained strange phenomena with attributes of *ch'i*. The island man born without parents, for example, came into being through "the transformation of *ch'i*."[127] The strange light, called "Buddha candle" (*fo-teng*), was seen because "the *ch'i* is flourishing and has brightness."[128]

This attitude of Chu Hsi was derived ultimately from these two remarks of Confucius in the *Analects:* "Respect ghosts and spirits and keep them at a distance" and "Till one has learned to serve men, how can one serve ghosts?"[129] These were the sources for the basically skeptical and even agnostic attitude toward spirits and ghosts held by many Confucians up to Chu Hsi's time: that one should not devote too much effort to trying to understand and master them, for what is more important and urgent are human affairs, which are difficult enough. Chu Hsi himself quoted the Confucian remarks frequently and endorsed such an attitude.[130] But he could not always remain so aloof from discussions of spirits and ghosts as could Confucius and other earlier Confucian thinkers; with the rival systems of Buddhists and Taoists to compete against, Neo-Confucian thinkers could no longer avoid dealing with these ideas. They had to either reject spirits and ghosts or show that they could find a place for them in their philosophical system. In his all-encompassing synthesis, Chu Hsi chose to include them. To do so, however, Chu Hsi needed to explain them by means of *ch'i* without positing extra beings and powers beyond *ch'i*. The concept of *kuei-shen* thus had to be broadened to embrace the first two meanings discussed earlier in this chapter. The notion of spirits and ghosts was still included in the concept, but the two broader senses could now provide it with a basis in terms of *ch'i*. The different senses of *kuei-shen* that we have seen came to be connected with one another in this manner.[131]

Chang Tsai's and Ch'eng I's characterizations of *kuei-shen*, the former as "the innate ability of the two *ch'i*" and the latter as "traces of creative transformation," played important roles in this development and formed the basis of Chu Hsi's broad interpretation of *kuei-shen*. Chu Hsi glossed Chang Tsai's "innate ability" as the ability of *ch'i* for "contraction and expansion, and going and coming," making it clear that *kuei-shen* phenomena were attributable to qualities and activities of *ch'i*.[132] He characterized "creative transformation" also as "nothing but the ending and beginning, flourishing and declining of yin and yang *ch'i*."[133] Thus, his examples for "traces of creative transformation" were nothing other than the sun, the moon, the stars, the four seasons, wind, rain, thunder, lightning, the blooming of flowers, the forming of fruits, and so on, the same examples we have seen for the first and broadest sense of *kuei-shen*.[134]

6.4. *Kuei* versus *Shen*

As the ideas of *kuei-shen* evolved in this manner, discussions about it became increasingly more elaborate, and there were a few different lines of development. Chu Hsi's discussions on *kuei-shen* reflect some of these developments.

For one, the characters *kuei* and *shen* were separated from each other, were given separate meanings, and were associated with other pairs of things, events, and concepts. In particular, *kuei* and *shen* were associated with yin and yang and with various pairs of yin-yang characteristics. Chu Hsi even said, "*Kuei* is what is numinous of the yin and *shen* is what is numinous of the yang."[135] The yin-yang pairs most frequently associated with *kuei* and *shen* were the ones that Chu Hsi used in explaining the expression "the innate ability of the two *ch'i*": contraction and going for *kuei* and expansion and coming for *shen*. Combined with another set of characterizations by Chang Tsai, "To arrive at it is called *shen*, on account of its expanding [nature]; to turn back from it is called *kuei*, on account of its returning [nature],"[136] these became the basis of Chu Hsi's dualistic *kuei-shen* associations. He said, "That which arrives at and expands is *shen*; that which turns back and returns is *kuei*."[137] "In general, *ch'i* coming and having just expanded is *shen*; *ch'i* going and having already contracted is *kuei*."[138] He used them in explaining other *kuei-shen* associations: "Rituals are restraining and contracting, and so they are *kuei*; music is enhancing and harmonious, and so it is *shen*."[139]

Table 6.1 lists various other *kuei-shen* associations mentioned by Chu Hsi. But this list looks like a shorter version of table 4.1, because nearly all the *kuei-shen* pairs are those found in the yin-yang associations. Indeed, some of the features noted concerning the yin-yang scheme can be repeated here for *kuei-shen*. For instance, *kuei* and *shen* characteristics undergo continuous cyclical alternations. Chu Hsi said, for example, that "the *ch'i* that has already contracted can expand again"

TABLE 6.1
Kuei-Shen Associations Mentioned by Chu Hsi

Kuei	Shen	References[a]
yin	yang	YL63.24b1
contraction (*chü*)	expansion (*shen*)	YL3.1b2
going (*wang*)	coming (*lai*)	YL63.22b1
going (*chü*)	coming (*lai*)	YL3.7a1
returning (*kuei*)	expanding (*shen*)	YL63.23a3
the *ch'i* that has gone and already contracted	the *ch'i* that has come and just expanded	YL63.23b1
turning back from it (*fan chih*)	arriving at it (*chih chih*)	YL98.4b4[b]
what turns back and returns	what arrives and expands	See below[c]
dark (*yu*)	bright (*ming*)	YL74.10b1
hidden (*yu*)	manifest (*hsien*)	WC62.39a
dead	alive	YL3.2a2
vanishing (*hsiao*)	growing (*hsi*)	YL68.3a2
rest (*ching*)	movement (*tung*)	YL68.3a2
inhalation	exhalation	YL68.3a2
dispersing (*san*) and becoming changes (*pien*)	aggregating (*chü*) and becoming things	YL74.14a4
night	day	YL3.2a2
after noon	before noon	YL63.24b1
after the 16th of a lunar month	from the 3rd of a lunar month[d]	YL63.24b1
autumn and winter	spring and summer	YL68.3a2
withering and declining (*tiao-ts'an shuai-lo*)	generation (*fa-sheng*) of grasses and trees	YL63.24b1
old and declining years of life	from youth to the prime years of life	YL63.24b1
end of wind, rain, thunder, and lightning	beginning of wind, rain, thunder, and lightning	Y3.1b2
subsiding of wind and thunder	stirring up of wind and thunder	YL63.25a0
juice of sugarcane	fragrance of sugarcane	YL93.11b1
rituals (*li*)	music (*yüeh*)	YL93.11b1
p'o	*hun*	WC44.30b
p'o	*ch'i*	YL63.25a0
essence (*ching*)	*ch'i*	YL3.7a1
silence	speech	YL68.3a2

Notes

[a]Only one representative reference is given for each pair of associations.

[b]Quotation of Chang Tsai; see note 136.

[c]*SSCC* (*Chung-yung*), p. 9a

[d]This association refers both to the days of a lunar month and to the phases of the moon on the given days.

in explaining how the *ch'i* of a dead man can come back to respond to sacrificial services.[140] He also noted that the simple *kuei-shen* dichotomy can be divided further into the fourfold system of *kuei* of *kuei*, *shen* of *kuei*, *shen* of *shen*, and *kuei* of *shen*.[141]

Kuei and *shen* were associated with another important pair of concepts, *p'o* and *hun*. According to Chu Hsi, the latter pair refers to phenomena inside the human body, whereas *kuei* and *shen* refer to all things and processes of the world.[142] In a sense *p'o* and *hun* are *kuei-shen* inside man's body, and thus Chu Hsi used *p'o* and *hun* mostly in discussing human physiological and mental phenomena, which are discussed in chapter 11. There, we also see that *kuei* and *shen* were associated with various other pairs of terms designating human bodily contents — the essence-*ch'i* dichotomy, for example.[143]

In another, related line of development, the character *shen* by itself came to be identified with the subtle and unfathomable aspect of *kuei-shen*; there emerged a kind of contrast between this aspect of *shen* and the compound term *kuei-shen*, though both terms continued to be used interchangeably. Ch'eng I, for example, distinguished them: "In terms of tangible effect (*kung-yung*), it is called *kuei-shen*; in terms of subtle effect (*miao-yung*), it is called *shen*."[144] In his comments on this, Chu Hsi characterized *shen* as something "unfathomable," "changing and unknowable," "sudden," and "having no trace," in contrast to *kuei-shen*, which was "visible," "constant," and "gradual and having physical forms and traces."[145] In sum, "when we say '*kuei-shen*,' we talk about it from that which has traces. When we say '*shen*,' we simply talk about its being subtle and being impossible to fathom or understand."[146]

The aspect of change and suddenness of *shen* was contrasted with another term, *hua*, which denotes a gradual change. This distinction of *shen* versus *hua* was related, in turn, to another distinction of sudden versus gradual change, *pien* and *hua*. See chapter 8 for a discussion of Chu Hsi's ideas about both of these distinctions.

Notes

1. My own article, "*Kuei-shen* in Terms of *Ch'i*," is an earlier version of this chapter.

2. *YL*3.1a1.

3. *YL*3.2b0.

4. *YL*78.21b6. See also *YL*93.11b1.

5. E.g., *YL*74.22b0; 94.26a2. The "Hsi-tz'u chuan" phrase comes from ch. A5. This phrase and others involving the concept of *shen* in the "Hsi-tz'u chuan" are discussed in Peterson, "Making Connections," pp. 102–110.

6. E.g., *YL*61.9b1. The *Mencius* phrase comes from 7B25.

7. E.g., *YL*94.26a2, 4; 26b1. Chou Tun-i's phrase comes from *T'ung-shu*, ch. 3.

8. E.g., *YL*87.14b3; 98.8b4, 9a0. Chang Tsai's characterizations of *shen* appear in the "Shen-hua" (4th) chapter of *Cheng-meng*. For a brief discussion of Chang Tsai's ideas about *shen*, see Kasoff, *Thought of Chang Tsai*, pp. 60–65.

9. *YL*68.2b3. See also *YL*68.2b1, 2, 4; 74.17a1, 2; 94.26b2; 95.8a1. In *YL*5.2b0 Chu Hsi quoted Chou Tun-i's saying that "moving without movement and being still without stillness, that is *shen*." *T'ung-shu*, ch. 16.

10. Thus, Chu Hsi called the imaginary man who could place himself up in the sky between the sun and the moon a *"shen man"* (*shen-jen*). *Ch'u-tz'u chi-chu*, 3.101.

11. *YL*3.2a4.

12. In his brief discussion of *kuei-shen*, Wing-tsit Chan refers to the classification of Ch'en Ch'un (1159–1223), who divides it into four kinds: "that in the Confucian classics, that in ancient religious sacrifices, that in latter-day religious sacrifices, and that referring to demons and gods." *Source Book in Chinese Philosophy*, pp. 789–790. See also Chan, *Neo-Confucian Terms Explained*, pp. 142–168.

13. *YL*70.29b1. The *I-ching* phrase is a comment on the *kuan* hexagram.

14. *YL*3.16a4.

15. *YL*90.3a0.

16. *YL*3.1b3.

17. E.g., *YL*3.12b2.

18. E.g., *YL*3.1b3, 6b1; 73.15a1.

19. *YL*95.8a1.

20. *YL*3.6b1.

21. *YL*94.26b2.

22. *YL*34.30a2.

23. *YL*3.4b0. Here, Chu Hsi is using Ch'eng I's characterization of *kuei-shen* as "traces of creative transformations," discussed later.

24. *YL*3.5b0. See also *YL*83.21b0.

25. *YL*1.7b2.

26. E.g., *YL*3.1b4; 62.19b0.

27. *YL*63.19b2.

28. *YL*3.1b3.

29. E.g., *YL*34.30a2; 39.4b2.

30. E.g., *YL*63.22b3; 68.3b21. Chang Tsai's phrase comes from the "T'ai-ho" (1st) chapter of *Cheng-meng* (*Chang-tzu ch'üan-shu*, 2.4a).

31. *YL*3.2a1. I have translated the expression *"shen-ling,"* literally meaning *"shen* and numinous" or "numinous *shen,"* as "spirits," its common everyday meaning.

32. *YL*1.7b2.

33. *YL*95.6b0.

34. *YL*140.15b3.

35. *YL*3.12b2.

36. E.g., *YL*3.3b3, 9a6; 63.25b0; 126.5b2. This idea can be traced to *Chuang-tzu*: "Man's coming into being is the aggregation of *ch'i*. When [the *ch'i*] aggregates, [he is] born; when [it is] dispersed, [he] dies" (7.23a).

37. E.g., *YL*3.6a0, 9b2.

38. E.g., *YL*3.5a0, 9b2, 10a2; 63.25b0; 87.16a1.

39. *YL*63.25b0.

40. E.g., *YL*3.10a1, 2; 10b1; 63.25b0.

41. *YL*3.10b1.

42. E.g., *YL*3.5a0; 63.21a0.

43. *YL*3.5b0.

44. E.g., *YL*3.4b0, 9b3–10b0. The story of Po Yu (formal name, Liang Hsiao) is recorded, for example, in *Ch'un-ch'iu*, Yang-kung, 11th, 26th, 27th, and 30th years (31.14b; 37.1a; 38.1a; 40.1b, respectively).

45. E.g., *YL*3.11a1; 63.20b0. Ch'ang Hung's story is recorded, for example, in *Tso-chuan*, Ai-kung, 3rd year (57.18a).

46. *YL*3.6a0. See also *YL*87.28b3.

47. *YL*3.6a0.

48. *YL*87.29a1. For more discussion on this phrase, see chap. 11, p. 224.

49. E.g., *YL*17.11b3; 63.21a1; 90.18b0; *WC*52.16a.

50. E.g., *YL*3.12b1, 13a1; 63.21a1.

51. *YL*3.4a0.

52. *YL*3.9b1.

53. E.g., *YL*3.11b3; 63.26a0.

54. *YL*3.13a1.

55. *YL*3.5a0.

56. *CS*51.47a1.

57. *YL*25.15a0.

58. *YL*87.29b0.

59. *YL*87.29a0.

60. *YL*87.28b4, 29b0.

61. *YL*3.12b2.

62. *YL*72.23b4. See also *YL*3.15a1.

63. *YL*101.9a0. See also *YL*3.17a1.

64. E.g., *YL*3.11b3, 13a1, 13b0.

65. E.g., *YL*25.12a2–12b0; *WC*57.8a.

66. *YL*3.17a1.

67. *YL*3.15a5–15b0.

68. *YL*3.16a1.

69. E.g., *YL*3.15b4–16a0, 18b1; 87.29b0.

70. *YL*90.18b1. See also *YL*3.16a0.

71. E.g., *YL*24.28a2–28b0; 25.15a1; 78.17a6–17b0, 35a2; 90.1a2–2b0; 98.4b5; *CS*58.4a2. In *YL*78.17b0 Chu Hsi mentioned "the six worships" (*liu-tzung*), that is, offering sacrificial services to the four seasons, cold and hot weather, the sun, the moon and the stars, and flood and drought.

72. E.g., *YL*38.6b0; 90.2a1.

73. E.g., *YL*3.16b0; 24.28b1; 25.16b2; 90.2b2. In *YL*24.28b1 Chu Hsi provided some discussion on these spirits, the spirit for the eaves in particular. He also said, "The *wu-ssu* are all 'house spirits' (*shih-shen*)."

74. *YL*38.6b0. In some of his memorials to the throne, he used reports of natural disasters in admonishing the emperor to act properly. *WC*13.6a–7a, 14.23a–24b.

75. *YL*58.3a4. See also *YL*58.3a3, in which Chu Hsi said: "The time when yin and yang are harmonious and [bring] wind and rain is [the time when] 'the hundred spirits receive it with joy.'" The *Mencius* passage (5A5) runs as follows: "When he [i.e., Yao] was made to take charge of the sacrificial service, the hundred spirits received it with joy. This is [because] heaven received him."

76. *WC*13.7a.

77. *YL*86.18b1.

78. E.g., *WC*85.21a; 86.9a, 16a–16b. Thus, from Chu Hsi we do not find the "ill-concealed skepticism and a trace of annoyance" toward these duties of a local governor that James T. C. Liu could discern in Ou-yang Hsiu (1007–1072) for example. *Ou-yang Hsiu*, p. 156.

79. For the popular beliefs about deities in the Sung, see, e.g., Hansen, *Changing Gods in Medieval China*.

80. *YL*3.18a2. This passage is discussed in Hansen, *Changing Gods in Medieval China*, pp. 141–142.

81. *YL*106.7a1.

82. *YL*63.20a1.

83. *YL*63.26b0.

84. *YL*3.1b1.

85. *CS*15.38a1.

86. *YL*90.4a1.

87. *YL*3.16b0.

88. *YL*90.18b0.

89. *YL*3.12b2. See also *YL*3.13a0, 16a5; 24.28a1; 25.8b3; 78.35a2.

90. *YL*25.8b3. See also *YL*3.13a0, 90.3a0.

91. E.g., *YL*24.28a1, 2; 28b1; 39.3b3.

92. *YL*25.8b3.

93. *YL*101.9a1.

94. *YL*39.4b2. See also *YL*34.30a2; 70.21a6.

95. *YL*64.28a2.

96. *SSCC* (*Lun-yü*), 7.6a–6b.

97. *WC*45.7a; Chu Hsi's comment on the "Hung-fan" chapter of *Shu-ching* is recorded in *Ch'in-ting Shu-ching chuan-shuo*, 11.36a.

98. E.g., *WC*45.7a. For more discussion of Chu Hsi on divination, see chap. 12, sec. 12.5.

99. *YL*3.2a0.

100. E.g., *YL*2.10a3.

101. E.g., *YL*2.10a2; 3.3a0.

102. *YL*63.20b0.

103. *YL*63.20b0–21a0. See also *YL*125.13a2–13b0.

104. *YL*3.11b1.

105. On this aspect of *ch'i*, see chap. 3. Yamada Keiji has noted a similar point about Chu Hsi's "rationalistic" attitude, referring to it as "unbound rationalism" or "the trap of rationalism." *Shusi no shizen-gaku*, pp. 390, 398.

106. *YL*3.1a3.

107. *YL*3.3b1.

108. *YL*63.24a3. Here Chu Hsi was commenting on *Chung-yung*, ch. 16.

109. *YL*3.1b1.

110. *YL*3.5a0.

111. *YL*3.11a2.

112. *YL*63.25b0.

113. *YL*126.22a2.

114. E.g., *YL*126.22a5, 22b1. In *YL*126.22a3, while speaking about a form of rebirth called "robbing the fetus" (*to-t'ui*), Chu Hsi even said that "in *li* there is none [for] this."

115. *YL*3.19a1.

116. *YL*89.14a0.

117. *YL*138.9b1. This story of a son of Hsueh Ch'ang-chou seems to have been circulated widely among Chu Hsi's circle at the time. A disciple even wondered how a learned man like Hsueh could believe such a story of his son.

118. *YL*3.3b1.

119. *YL*3.11a2.

120. *YL*126.8b0. Chu Hsi even said that "incantations are entirely methods of thought." Ch'ien Mu said that Chu Hsi "interpreted incantations psychologically." See his *Chu-tzu hsin hsueh-an*, 5:405.

121. *YL*3.2b2–3b0.

122. *YL*97.4a2. Cf. *Ho-nan Ch'eng-shih i-shu*, ch. 15 (*ECC*, p. 161); ch. 18 (*ECC*, pp. 198–199). On the story of a man turning into a tiger, recorded in the same passage, however, Chu Hsi said that "it cannot be believed" and rejected a disciple's suggestion of an explanation in terms of the man's *ch'i* that was as wicked as that of a tiger.

123. *YL*3.3b2.

124. *YL*138.10a3. Chu Hsi even praised the saying of Hsieh Liang-tso (1050–1103), "When I want them to exist, they exist; when I want them not to exist, they do not exist."

125. *YL*4.21a1. For more on immortals, see chap. 12, pp. 274–275.

126. *YL*3.2b2.

127. On the "transformation of *ch'i*," see chap. 3, p. 33; chap. 10, pp. 187ff.

128. *YL*126.23b2.

129. *Analects*, 6.20, 11.11.

130. E.g., *YL*3.1a1, 2; 14b0; 32.12a1; 39.3b2, 4a1; 83.21b0.

131. Wing-tsit Chan maintains, however, that the "naturalistic and philosophical meaning should always be kept entirely distinct from the other meaning, namely *kuei-*

shen as spiritual beings." *Source Book in Chinese Philosophy*, p. 790.

132. E.g., *YL*63.22b3, 24b1; 95.4b3.

133. *WC*76.1a. The Ch'eng I phrase comes from the Ch'eng brothers' *Chou-i Ch'eng-shih chuan*, ch. 1. For Chu Hsi's quotation of the phrase, see, e.g., *YL*63.22a1; 22b1, 2, 4; 23a1, 2; 25b0; 83.21b0. Sometimes, especially in pre-T'ang texts, the word *tsao-hua* had a meaning quite close to that of "Creator." But that meaning occurred much less frequently in Neo-Confucian writings, including those of Chu Hsi. I have chosen a rather literal translation, "creative transformation."

134. E.g., *YL*63.22a1, 22b1; 83.21b0; 95.4b3. In *YL*63.22b2 Chu Hsi said, however, that "the wonder of creative transformation cannot be seen," because its subtleness is visible only through "the going and coming, contraction and expansion of its *ch'i*." He even added that *kuei-shen* is "no trace of creative transformations" (*tsao-hua wu chi*). Of the two characterizations, Chu Hsi thought Chang Tsai's to be clearer than Ch'eng I's; see, e.g., *YL*63.22b4; 93.11b1.

135. E.g., *YL*63.23a3, 23b1. It is in this sense that Wing-tsit Chan translates *kuei* and *shen* as "negative and positive spiritual forces." *Source Book in Chinese Philosophy*, p. 790.

136. "Tung-wu" (5th) chapter of *Cheng-meng* (*Chang-tzu ch'üan-shu*, 2.16a).

137. *SSCC* (*Chung-yung*), p. 9a. It is to be noted that the character for "expanding" has the same pronunciation as *shen* and that for "returning" has the same one as *kuei*.

138. *YL*63.23b1. See also *YL*18.5a0.

139. *YL*78.21b6.

140. *YL*3.5b1. See also *YL*63.21a1.

141. E.g., *YL*63.23b1. Of course the *kuei-shen* and the yin-yang schemes of associations are not always consistent with each other. For example, dispersion, a yang characteristic, is associated with *kuei*, whereas aggregation, a yin characteristic, is associated with *shen*: e.g., *YL*74.14a4.

142. E.g., *WC*44.30b.

143. See chap. 11, sec. 11.6.

144. *Chou-i Ch'eng-shih chuan*, ch. 1 (*ECC*, p. 695).

145. E.g., *YL*68.2b1, 2, 3, 4; 3a1, 2; 3b1. In *YL*68.2b4, Chu Hsi contrasted *shen* not with *kuei-shen* but with *kuei*. But the context of the discussion makes it clear that what Chu Hsi intended was comparison of *shen* with *kuei-shen*.

146. *YL*63.23a2.

7

Heaven and the Sages

The term "*t'ien*" (heaven) also had a very broad range of meanings, spanning both sides of our imaginary boundary that encloses the "natural" world. Chu Hsi's ideas about "heaven" in the sense of the physical sky are discussed in chapter 9; in this chapter I consider those aspects of his ideas about the term that fall outside the border but bear upon what he thought about the things and events inside it. These include man's relation to "heaven," and in dealing with it I discuss another concept, "the sages" (*sheng-jen*), which supplemented and overlapped some aspects of "heaven."

7.1. Different Meanings of *T'ien*

From its origin as a term designating the ancestor-deity of the early Chou royal family, the concept of *t'ien* had gone through a long and complicated historical development by Chu Hsi's time.[1] One line of this development was centered in the aspect of deity. It can be characterized by the gradual weakening of the anthropomorphic character of the concept, which over time came to represent more general, abstract, and even conceptual deity. But *t'ien* continued to mean something that controls, rules, and presides over everything in the world. As the development along this line proceeded further, *t'ien* was also thought to be what produced the men and the things of the world. *T'ien* even referred to "decree" (*ming*) and "nature" (*hsing*), which were endowed to men and things when they were produced. And in all of this, the term retained the moral aspect present in its original meaning.

Another line of development resulted from the association of the word with the supposed site of the original ancestor-deity, the physical sky. It went with the separation of the moral character from the concept. But this meaning was also expanded gradually, first to the whole natural world, including the sky, then to the events and processes of that world, and eventually to the *li* underlying the workings of the natural world.

When the two lines of development had proceeded this far, their outcomes converged, and the two aspects were connected again. This connection of the physical, naturalistic aspect of the concept of heaven with its moralistic aspect came to provide a basis for the belief in the moral character of the natural world. Because of this connection, the concept of heaven could supplement the morally neutral character of the world composed of *ch'i*; processes of the natural world, covered by the term "heaven," could be taken for a standard upon which human ethical behavior should be based.[2]

In the course of these developments, the term *t'ien* came to have various different meanings. They can be classified in four categories: (1) the physical sky; (2) the natural world, including the things and events in it; (3) the *li* of both natural and human realms; and (4) a concept or a being that rules or presides over the world.[3] All of these meanings appeared in Chu Hsi's sayings and writings. He was explicit that the concept has three of the four meanings—(1), (3), and (4):

> Heaven certainly is *li*. But the blue sky (literally, "what is blue" [*ts'ang-ts'ang-che*]) is also heaven. [That which is] up there and has what "presides" (*chu-tsai*) is also heaven. Each discusses [heaven] following a different aspect.[4]

And though he did not explicitly say so, there were numerous occasions when he used the term in the second sense.

Of the above meanings, the most problematic—both for us and for Chu Hsi and his interlocutors—is the fourth, namely heaven as what "rules" or "presides over" the world, "*chu-tsai*" in Chinese characters. The *Classified Conversations* records numerous discussions he was engaged in with others on what "*chu-tsai*" meant. He recognized that it was not easy to explain. He said, for example: "[On topics] like this [i.e., *chu-tsai*], it is necessary for one to understand them for oneself. It is not what words can explain fully";[5] "After all, as to what this *li* [of *chu-tsai*] is like, scholars can never answer."[6] Thus, Chu Hsi seldom said explicitly what *chu-tsai* meant; nor did he provide concrete examples that show the *chu-tsai* aspect of heaven.

We can find some hints that show why Chu Hsi used the expression "*chu-tsai*." He said, after mentioning such regularities of the natural world as the succession of the four seasons, the alternation of day and night, and the way plants flourish on the sunny side and wither on the shadowy side, "This is clearly as if a person were in [heaven] and 'presided over' [these regularities]."[7] But he was explicit that actually there is no such person up there: "If one now says that a person is in heaven and blames crimes, it certainly is not acceptable";[8] "It is as though a person were up there like that. . . . But [the truth] is simply that the *li* is like this."[9] Thus, Chu Hsi rejected the idea of heaven as an anthropomorphic deity with concrete human faculties. He denied that heaven spoke, saw, heard, thought, or knew as a human being does; heaven did not have organs like the ears, eyes, heart, or intestines that are needed for such human faculties.[10]

What Chu Hsi emphasized instead was that the *chu-tsai* aspect of heaven is somehow responsible for the "naturalness" and spontaneity of the phenomena and processes of the natural world. When a disciple asked, "What is *chu-tsai*?" he responded:

> There naturally is *chu-tsai*. In general, heaven is a thing of extreme hardness and yangness. Spontaneously, it rotates like this without stopping. To be like this, there must be what "presides over" it.[11]

The term *t'ien* itself could also refer to "natural" and spontaneous behaviors and tendencies of man. Chu Hsi said that "to know heaven is to know the spontaneity of the *li* . . . [of the relationships] . . . between rulers and subjects, fathers and sons, elder and younger brothers, husbands and wives, and between friends."[12] He even thought that such inborn human tendencies as eating when hungry and drinking when thirsty, wearing furs in winter and linens in summer were taught by heaven.[13]

This aspect of *chu-tsai* is not very far from the idea of heaven as *li*. Indeed, as we have seen, Chu Hsi's explanation of phenomena that make people suspect the existence of a person in heaven in charge of them was that "the *li* is like this."[14] He even identified *chu-tsai* with *li:* "What is called '*chu-tsai*' is simply *li*."[15] This meant, then, that the most basic and important meaning of *t'ien* for Chu Hsi was that of *li*. For him, "To act in accordance with the *li*, that is heaven."[16] He even asserted that "heaven is simply *li*" and elaborated on it: "The reason that heaven is heaven is the *li* and nothing else. If heaven did not have this way and *li*, it could not be heaven. Therefore, the blue sky is simply the heaven of this way and *li*."[17]

Yet, equating *chu-tsai* with *li* shows only one side of Chu Hsi's ideas about heaven; he had many things to say about its other aspects. Most frequently, Chu Hsi repeated the common idea that heaven "produced" (*sheng*) men and things.[18] He mentioned an example of heaven producing a particular person, King T'ang, the founder of the Shang dynasty.[19] He even said that the *Ho-t'u* and *Lo-shu* diagrams were drawn by heaven and earth.[20] Yet, he denied that heaven has conscious intentions in producing particular men and things. Differences in "the endowment of *ch'i*," responsible for men's different qualities, were for him "accidental" (*ou-jan*) and not a result of conscious assignment by heaven.[21] While admitting that heaven might appear to have an "intention" to produce a sage, Chu Hsi asked, "Where did heaven and earth say that it would specifically produce a sage to come into being?"[22] Sometimes he even sounded as though he were rejecting the very idea of heaven's producing things: "Heaven simply is the flow and movement of the one *ch'i*. The myriad things spontaneously come into being, grow, and take physical forms and colors."[23] In this way Chu Hsi emphasized, as he did with the idea of *chu-tsai*, the natural and spontaneous character of the activities of heaven, which does not possess conscious intentions.[24]

The production of men and things by heaven cannot be random, however. There are "rules" (*tse*) that heaven follows in producing them. Chu Hsi said, for example: "In heaven's production of things, there is none that does not have the shell. For example, men have bodies, and fruits have skins."[25] Of course, the rules are not the same for different things. He gave the reason for this, again in terms of the endowment of *ch'i*: "In heaven's production of things, their *li* certainly do not have differences or distinctions. But the *ch'i* endowed by men and things are different."[26] Thus, "when heaven and earth produce things, there are [times when] extremely fine and delicate things are obtained, and also there naturally are rough, steep, coarse, and clumsy things."[27] For Chu Hsi, then, each thing has a rule for it.

One source of this idea is the passage from the *Book of Poetry* (Shih-ching), "When heaven produces masses of people, if there is a thing, there is a rule," which Chu Hsi quoted frequently.[28] In commenting on this passage, he said:

In heaven's production of this thing, there must be a "rule according to which it ought to be so." Therefore, people hold it and take it as a constant way. . . . In general, kings have the rule of kings; subjects have the rule of subjects. Being a king of people, stay in humaneness. That is the rule of kings. Being a subject of someone, stay in reverence. That is the rule of subjects. Ears have the rule of ears, eyes have the rule of eyes. . . . Of the four limbs, the hundred bones, the myriad things, and the myriad events, there is none that does not have the rule according to which they ought to be so.[29]

These rules are what constitute the natures (*hsing*) of things: "Heaven produces things. Then they have constant 'natures.'"[30] When men and things come into being, they receive such natures that "heaven endows to men and things."[31] Chu Hsi also mentioned "the decree" and "the many ways and *li*" with which heaven endowed men.[32] It must be in referring to all these that he said, "In the beginning of man, he comes into being thanks to heaven."[33]

The discussion so far in this section appears to preclude the idea of heaven as an anthropomorphic deity. And that seems to be in line with Chu Hsi's overall views. To be sure, it is possible to find, in the voluminous records of his conversations and writings, assertions by him that smack of anthropomorphism. For example, "Goodness and crimes, heaven knows all of them";[34] "If heaven wanted to use Confucius. . .";[35] "[At] the wrath of heaven, thunders also occur";[36] "[They] are what heaven taught me";[37] "[It] is what heaven originally ordered."[38] But all these he was led to say while commenting, usually in response to disciples' questions, on some problematic expressions in the classics: the first two assertions came up in his comments on *Analects* passages; the third appeared in his response to a question whether the sages can show anger in their faces; the last two were parts of his explanations of the phrases "heaven's duty" (*t'ien-chih*), from *Mencius*, and "heaven's bright decree" (*t'ien chih ming-ming*), from the *Great Learning* (Ta-hsueh).[39] It does not appear likely that Chu Hsi meant what he said literally, for none of the passages containing these assertions show a sense of conviction about such an anthropomorphic notion of *t'ien*.[40] There were, however, plenty of places where he was explicit about his rejection of the idea of the personified heaven. For example, as we have seen, he explicitly stated that heaven cannot know because it does not have a heart or intestines.[41] Also, though he protested against interpreting heaven only as *li* while commenting upon the expression of the *Book of Documents* "Heaven sees with our people's eyes; heaven hears with our people's ears,"[42] he was nevertheless firm against attributing concrete human faculties to heaven: "How can heaven have ears and eyes to see and hear?"[43] Thus, Chu Hsi took the *Analects* phrase "to commit a crime against heaven" simply to mean "to offend the *li*."[44]

7.2. Man versus Heaven

When used in the second of the four senses mentioned above, the character *t'ien* was often combined with the character *ti* (earth), and the resulting expression, "heaven and earth" (*t'ien-ti*),[45] as well as the single term "heaven," designated the whole natural world. And as words referring to the natural world, "heaven and earth" and "heaven" were often contrasted with the human world.

The relation between man and the natural world—"heaven" or "heaven and earth"—had many sides. For one, there was the idea of the parallelism of macrocosm-microcosm, the notion that man as the small universe is an epitome of the great universe, heaven and earth.[46] Chu Hsi frequently made assertions that contain this idea. He said, for example, that "heaven simply is a great man, and man simply is a small heaven" and went on to compare the four human virtues with the four cosmic qualities.[47] He also said: "Man simply is a small child, and 'heaven and earth' is a large child";[48] "'Heaven and earth' is a great 'myriad thing,' and a 'myriad thing' is a small 'heaven and earth.'"[49] This idea was expressed using *ch'ien* and *k'un* also: "*Ch'ien* and *k'un* are the parents of the world, and [one's own] parents are the parents of oneself."[50] His discussion involving *ch'ien* and *k'un* in the metaphors of human reproduction reflects the same idea.[51] Chu Hsi also made more direct comparisons between man and the world. For example, he compared man's navel to the supposed center of the earth, the Sung Mountain (*sung-shan*), and the umbilical cord to the axis of rotation of the heavens.[52] He even offered a direct comparison between the shapes of man and the universe: "Man's head is circular and is like heaven; man's feet are square and are like the earth."[53]

The parallelism between man and heaven and earth even turned into an identity and into a mystical notion that man is one with the whole universe and everything of the universe is within himself. Chu Hsi said that "they [i.e., man and heaven and earth] are one body from the beginning till now."[54] The same idea can be found in his following remark:

> Heaven is simply man; man is simply heaven. In the beginning of man, he comes into being thanks to heaven. Once [heaven] has produced this man, then heaven is also in man. In general, speech, action, seeing, and hearing are all heaven. Now [while I am] speaking, heaven is just here.[55]

This notion is also in line with his ideas about "the *ch'i* of heaven and earth" and "the mind of heaven and earth," which man receives and makes his own *ch'i* and mind.[56] At times, the identity was not limited to man but was extended to all the myriad things: "In general, heaven and earth and the myriad things are originally my one body."[57]

The most pronounced aspect of the relationship between man and heaven and earth, however, was the idea of the triad of "heaven-earth-man," that is, the notion of the world in which man lives harmoniously between heaven and earth. A source of this view is the passage from the *Doctrine of the Mean* (Chung-yung): "If [a man] can assist the transforming and nourishing of heaven and earth, he can form a triad with heaven and earth" (ch. 22). Chu Hsi interpreted the latter half of the passage to mean "standing side by side with heaven and earth and becoming three [with them]."[58] Commenting upon the passage, he wrote elsewhere:

> Man came into being between them (i.e., heaven and earth), where [things] are mixed and indistinguishable. If [he] fully accomplishes the achievement of harmonizing the *li*, then

there will be seasonable winds and rains and no abnormal *ch'i*, drought, or damages by locusts. There will be five grains, mulberry trees, and hemp, and no weeds, darnels, or poisonous vines. This is the reason why man becomes three with heaven and earth and assists their transforming and nourishing. Because of this, heaven and earth waits for man and becomes "the three talents" (*san-tsai*).[59]

The relationship displayed by the idea of the triad is basically that man and heaven and earth complement each other. To be sure, heaven, or heaven and earth, produces man and things and presides over them.[60] But heaven (and earth) does not do everything alone; there are some things that heaven cannot do, which man does for heaven. The former half of the above passage from the *Doctrine of the Mean* expressed this idea, and Chu Hsi commented on it as follows:

> Man is in the middle of heaven and earth. Although [they] are just one *li*, heaven and man each has its own role. [There is something which] man can do but heaven cannot do. For example, heaven can produce things but must use man for sowing seeds. Water can moisten things, but [heaven] must use man for irrigation. Fire can burn things, but [heaven] must use man for [gathering] firewood and for cooking.[61]

Chu Hsi spoke of the relationship using more general attributes of heaven and earth. For example, "Heaven is simply movement and earth is simply rest. . . . Man combines movement and rest."[62] He also said: "Heaven can 'cover' (*fu*) but cannot 'sustain' (*tsai*); earth can sustain but cannot cover"; only man can do both.[63]

In man's role of complementing heaven and earth, "the sages" are supreme examples. Chu Hsi frequently said that the sages did what heaven and earth could not do and thus complemented heaven and earth.[64] He rephrased the above expression of the *Doctrine of the Mean:* "The sages [i.e., rather than man] assist in the transforming and nourishing of heaven and earth."[65] Discussion of Chu Hsi's ideas about the sages is thus in order.

7.3. The Sages

The concept of "the sages" also underwent a long historical development, during the course of which it acquired various different meanings, including the common designations of legendary kings and moral exemplars who possessed wisdom, moral virtues, talents, and abilities.[66] Chu Hsi's use of the term reflected these various meanings.[67]

To begin with, the sages are men also; man can become a sage, although it requires a very difficult process of study and cultivation, so difficult that few men in history attained the goal.[68] Since they are men, Chu Hsi was of the view that the sages are also produced by heaven (and earth).[69] Furthermore, heaven makes the sages do things that it cannot do itself—"cultivating the Way and establishing the teaching in order to edify people," for example.[70] Thus, Chu Hsi said: "The sages assist in the transforming and nourishing of heaven and earth; the function of heaven and earth is in waiting for the sages [to do these things]."[71] "The trans-

formation of heaven and earth flows endlessly. Like the metallic fluid in one furnace, it [i.e., heaven and earth] melts and transforms without stopping. As for the
sages, they cast and form tools for it [i.e., heaven and earth]."[72] Of the things that
the sages do, "there is not a single item that the sage does on his own; all are [what]
heaven has laid out [beforehand]."[73] He even said: "Heaven and earth simply cannot speak, and [therefore] have the sages appear and speak for them";[74] "The sages
are to heaven and earth as a son is to his father and mother."[75]

The sages, in turn, depend on heaven in carrying out their activities. They imitate
heaven's activities. Chu Hsi said, "The sages 'model themselves on heaven' (*fa t'ien*)
and carry out these various procedures."[76] He also said: "[As for] heaven's decree
and heaven's punishment (*t'ao*), the sages never added even a trace of selfish intention to them. They simply perform them respectfully according to heaven's 'model'
(*fa*)."[77] He characterized this aspect of the sage as "inheriting (*chi*) the will of
heaven and earth and following (*shu*) the events of heaven and earth"; he elaborated:

> To know in what way to live and in what way to die; to know in what way to vanish and
> in what way to grow—these are all "inheriting the will of heaven and earth." . . . To talk
> about small matters, [they consist in] eating when hungry, drinking when thirsty, taking
> action when going out, and taking rest when coming in. To talk about great matters, [they
> consist in] rulers and subjects having righteousness, fathers and sons having humaneness.
> These are all "following the events of heaven and earth."[78]

What the sages "inherit" and "follow," which Chu Hsi called by various names—
heaven's "decree," "will," and "model"—can be subsumed in a word, namely "the *li*
of heaven." Chu Hsi said, "The sages merely act depending on that *li* of heaven."[79]
He even said, "The sage simply is the *li* of heaven that stands 'in the form of human body' (literally, 'one piece of red bone')."[80] Confucius, for example, whom Chu
Hsi frequently called "the Sage" because he was, for Chu Hsi, the person most characteristic of a sage, "was entirely the *li* of heaven."[81] In this sense, the sages are the
supreme examples showing the identity of man with heaven.

Therefore, what the sages did manifested the *li* of heaven. For example, they
wrote books, the classics in particular, to teach posterity.[82] Chu Hsi said, "[The
sages] simply spoke about the *li* that ought to be so; they also wrote them in books
lest people should not understand."[83] Yet, "the words of the sages" that can be read
from the classics are "all [about] the *li* of heaven [which is] spontaneously so."[84]
The sages first observed heaven and earth before writing the *I-ching*, for example.[85]
Thus, "by reading books, one sees the intention of the sages. Based on the intention of the sages, one sees the *li* of spontaneity."[86] He even said that "what the sages
said is pure and cannot be doubted."[87] The classics, the *Rites of Chou* (Chou-li) for
example, "cannot be erroneous."[88]

The sages not only wrote books but also produced many other things. Chu Hsi
did not reject the "Hsi-tz'u-chuan" tradition that the sages produced cultural arti-
facts, inventions, and institutions.[89] For example, "the sages produced various compositions, institutions, rites and music."[90] But in producing these also, the sages
manifest the *li* of heaven. Chu Hsi said that "the sages instituted the sacrificial ser-

vice . . . [because] the *li* of heaven should be so."[91] He also added to his remark about "the compositions, institutions, rites and music" that "they all are just what this 'one way and li' (*i-ke tao-li*) produced."[92] Of course, it is clear that "the *li* of spontaneity," "the *li* that ought to be so," and "the one way and *li*" are all equivalent to the *li* of heaven.

As the sages thus follow the *li* of heaven, their activities are in accord with heaven. They share heaven's characteristic attributes of naturalness and spontaneity and are thus superior to other men. Chu Hsi said: "[What] the sages do all flows, moves, and comes out spontaneously; as for scholars, . . . [they] keep using exertion. The sages move by means of heaven; wise men move by means of men."[93] Even in irrigating, "the sages make [water] flow out spontaneously and irrigate 'the hundred things,' whereas other men must push out [water] to irrigate."[94] He summed up this aspect of the sages in the following manner:

> A sage simply comes out from the one great origin and source. The vision [of the sage] is spontaneously bright; the hearing is spontaneously clear; the look is spontaneously warm; the appearance is spontaneously respectful. When it is between fathers and sons, it is humaneness; between rulers and subjects, it is righteousness. Flowing out from within the great origin, [the sages] form many ways and *li*. [But] it is simply that this one [i.e., the one *li* of heaven] keeps penetrating through [them].[95]

7.4. The Mind of Heaven and Earth

As noted in the first section, Chu Hsi said that heaven does not have heart (*hsin*) and thus cannot know Confucius.[96] On the question of whether heaven has mind (designated by the same character, *hsin*),[97] his answer was generally affirmative. To be sure, there were times when he thought otherwise. For example, commenting on the Ch'eng brothers' saying "Heaven and earth do not have mind but complete the transformation," he said:

> This is discussing the aspects in which heaven and earth do not have mind. For example, when the four seasons proceed [regularly] and the hundred things come into being [regularly], for what would heaven and earth allow mind?[98]

Also, for him, "when the myriad things come into being and grow, that is the time when heaven and earth have no mind."[99] Yet in the same passage, he also spoke of "the time when heaven and earth have mind," namely, "the time when dried and withered things desire life." Moreover, Chu Hsi frequently discussed the concept of "the mind of heaven and earth."[100] He said, for example: "The mind of heaven and earth cannot be said to be not numinous. But it does not think like men."[101] Thus, it is clear that he saw some aspects of heaven and earth as some sort of "mind," which, however, is different from man's ordinary mind. What, then, does it mean that heaven and earth have mind, that is, the mind of heaven and earth?[102]

First, it refers to the "*chu-tsai*" aspect of heaven and earth and thus ultimately to "the *li*." Chu Hsi said, for example: "The mind [of heaven and earth] certainly has the meaning of a ruler (*chu-tsai*). But what is called a ruler is simply the *li*,"[103] Also, "the teacher of heaven and earth is the mind of heaven and earth. The *li* exists within it."[104] He spoke of "the mind of heaven" also in the same terms: "That which rules (*chu-tsai*) and controls (*kuan-she*) this *li* is just the mind [of heaven]."[105] The role of the mind of heaven and earth, then, is to ensure that things and events of the world conform to the *li*. For example, "if heaven and earth have no mind, then probably oxen will give birth to horses and plum flowers will blossom on peach trees."[106]

More often, however, the mind of heaven and earth refers to some kind of cosmic mind, a source of the minds of all things in the world. Men and things receive this cosmic mind and have it as their minds. Thus, for Chu Hsi, "my mind simply is the mind of heaven and earth."[107] He even said that "man is the mind of heaven and earth," adding, "If this man were not there, heaven and earth would have no one that would control [it]."[108] He also said: "The minds of the myriad things are simply like the mind of heaven and earth. . . . Inside one thing, there simply is one mind of heaven and earth."[109] He summed up all of these in the following manner:

> Heaven and earth provide the myriad things with this mind [of heaven and earth]. When man acquires it, then it becomes man's mind. When a thing acquires it, it becomes the mind of the thing. When grasses, trees, birds, and beasts receive it, then it becomes the mind of grasses, trees, birds, and beasts. [All these] are just one mind of heaven and earth.[110]

It can be inferred from this, then, that when a sage acquires this mind, it becomes "the mind of the sage." Chu Hsi spoke of the mind of the sage and the mind of heaven and earth in a parallel manner: "[When] heaven and earth produce things, inside one thing there is one mind of heaven and earth. [When] the sages deal with all under heaven, inside one man there is one mind of sage."[111]

The mind of heaven and earth refers also to the aspect of heaven and earth that produces men and things and gives life to them. In this sense it is called "the mind of heaven and earth producing things" (*t'ien-ti sheng-wu chih hsin*).[112] Men and things first acquire this mind so that they come into being and have life.[113] Chu Hsi said: "Having this mind [of heaven and earth], it is equipped with this physical form and comes into being";[114] "If there is no mind of heaven and earth producing things, then this body is not there."[115] It is in referring to this aspect of the mind of heaven and earth that Chu Hsi said, in a passage quoted earlier: "When dried and withered things desire life, that is the time when heaven and earth have mind."[116]

For Chu Hsi, to produce things was the most important and characteristic activity of heaven and earth. This is why he frequently said that "heaven and earth regard producing things as the mind."[117] He meant the same thing by the remark "Heaven and earth regard continuous producing as their power."[118] He even said: "Heaven surrounds the earth and has nothing else to do. It simply produces things and that is all. At all times in the past and present, it continues to produce [things] without end."[119] The mind of heaven and earth producing things, therefore, never ceases. In Chu Hsi's view, even in winter when the weather is severe and plants are withered, this mind exists. It is simply that men do not see this mind till spring, when it is manifest, just as men can see the yang line only from the *fu* hexagram.[120]

The mind of heaven and earth producing things is associated with the virtue of humaneness, since the aspect of life and producing things is commonly associated with that virtue.[121] For Chu Hsi, it is because man partakes of this mind that he has such characteristics of humaneness as "the mind unable to bear [other] men['s suf- ferings]" (*pu-jen-jen chih hsin*), and "the mind of affection and commiseration."[122] He even asserted that "humaneness is the mind of heaven and earth producing things."[123] In this manner, the concept of the mind of heaven and earth reinforced the connection between the physical and the moral aspects of heaven; that connec- tion is fundamental to the notion of "the cosmic basis of morality."

Notes

1. Among the various hypotheses con- cerning the origin of the term, the one I find most plausible is H. G. Creel's in *Ori- gins of Statecraft in China*, appendix 3. For other theories, see Eno, *Confucian Creation of Heaven*, esp. appendix A; Miura, "Keisho yori mita ten no shisō." For a brief dis- cussion of the historical development of the concept, see, e.g., Lamont, "Early Ninth Century Debate on Heaven," esp. pt. 1.

2. For such a role of the concept of *t'ien*'s providing a link between natural processes and human morality, see, e.g., Ch'ien, *Chu-tzu hsin hsueh-an*, 1:366–376; Kasoff, *Thought of Chang Tsai*, pp. 57–60; Tillman, "Consciousness of *T'ien* in Chu Hsi's Thought."

3. Fung Yu-lan has provided a some- what different classification into five cate- gories: (1) a material or physical *t'ien*, (2) a ruling or presiding *t'ien*, (3) a fatalistic *t'ien*, (4) a naturalistic *t'ien*, (5) an ethical *t'ien*. *History of Chinese Philosophy*, 1:31. See also Shih, "Metaphysical Tendencies in Mencius," esp. pp. 320–328, for different meanings of *t'ien* in *Mencius*; and Machle, *Nature and Heaven in the "Xunzi,"* for those in *Hsün-tzu*.

4. *YL*79.13b5–14a0. See also *CS*49.25a3. In *YL*5.1a1 Chu Hsi criticized the contemporary habit of excluding the physical sky from the meanings of heaven.

5. *YL*68.2a1.

6. *YL*79.10a3.

7. *YL*4.4b5.

8. *YL*1.4b2.

9. *YL*4.6b4.

10. E.g., *YL*16.1b0; 44.18b1; 65.9a2; *CS*49.22b3.

11. *YL*68.2a1.

12. *YL*60.4b1.

13. E.g., *YL*96.11a3.

14. E.g., *YL*1.4a2; 4.6b4.

15. *YL*1.3a4.

16. *YL*25.15b3.

17. *YL*25.16a1. The assertion "Heaven is simply *li*" appears in his comments upon the *Analects* phrase "to commit a crime against heaven" (3.13). *SSCC* (*Lun-yü*), 2.4b. The supremacy of *li* for Chu Hsi can also be seen in his assertion that "under heaven nothing is higher than the *li*, and therefore it is called 'the ruler' (*ti*)." *YL*4.6b4–7a0.

18. E.g., *YL*14.9b2; 59.6b1; 68.16a2; *WC*44.37a; 58.13a; 63.24b; *CS* 10.28b0. This idea was so commonly held by the Chinese in ancient times that it is both impossible and unnecessary to trace its sources.

19. E.g., *CS*35.63b1.

20. *YL*65.9a2. In *YL*65.8b1 Chu Hsi said that "heaven and earth produced numbers."

21. E.g., *YL*55.1b3.

22. *YL*4.21a0.

23. *YL*45.2a1.

24. Chu Hsi actually mentioned the similarity of such aspects of the two terms *t'ien* and *chu-tsai:* after the above-mentioned rejection that endowments of *ch'i* are the result of conscious assignment, he said, "It is just the same as *chu-tsai* discussed earlier." *YL*55.1b3.

25. *YL*68.16a2.

26. *WC*58.13a.

27. *YL*67.9a1.

28. E.g., *YL*18.17b1; 59.6b1; *WC*44.37a. The passage is originally from *Shih-ching*, no. 260, which is quoted in *Mencius*, 6A6.

29. *YL*18.17b1–18a0. It might be noted, however, that this idea of "rule" is not the same as the Western concept of "the law of nature." For whereas the latter is a law provided by the creator-god for his creatures to follow, the former has the character of a rule to be followed by heaven in producing things. See chap. 13, p. 306.

30. *WC*63.24b.

31. E.g., *YL*94.6b1. In *YL*60.6a3 he even said that "when one knows nature, . . . the nature has that heaven."

32. E.g., *YL*4.18a4; 14.9b2; 16.2b4; *CS*17.3b1. Again, however, he rejects that there is a person in heaven who endows the decrees to men; see *YL*4.6b4.

33. *YL*17.14b3.

34. *YL*50.1a2.

35. *YL*34.6b2–7a0.

36. *YL*95.25b3.

37. *YL*96.11a3.

38. *YL*16.2b4.

39. In *YL*50.1a2 and *YL*34.6b2–7a0, Chu Hsi was asked to comment on the *Analects* passages "The decision is in the mind of the ruler" (20.1) and "My decay has gone far. It has been long since I dreamt of Chou-kung"(7.5). The assertion in *YL*95.25b3 comes amid his comment that there are times when even the sages can show anger. In *YL*96.11a3 he was asked how "eating when hungry, drinking when

thirsty, wearing furs in winter and linens in summer" can be called "heaven's duty," the expression that first appeared in *Mencius*, 5B3. The expression "heaven's bright decree," discussed in *YL*16.2b4, appears in *Ta-hsueh*, ch. 1.

40. It is more likely that those expressions were merely idiomatic for Chu Hsi, who simply spoke as though heaven had consciousness or personality though not actually accepting that possibility, as modern men do when they use such expressions as "Heaven knows," "Heaven forbid," and so on. Lamont has provided examples of T'ang dynasty officials who made similar assertions though not believing them literally. "Early Ninth Century Debate on Heaven," p. 194.

41. *YL*44.18b1. See note 10.

42. E.g., *YL*79.13b4 ("If heaven is taken completely to be *li*, how could one also say 'as our people see and hear'?"); *YL*79.14a0 ("How could *li* also see and hear?"). The *Shu-ching* phrase comes from the spurious "T'ai-shih" (Great oath) chapter and is quoted in *Mencius*, 5A5.

43. *YL*16.1b0.

44. E.g., *YL*25.15b3, 16a1. The *Analects* phrase comes from 3.13. See note 17.

45. See chap. 1, note 48, on Willard J. Peterson's proposal for using this expression as a single word, "heaven-and-earth," referring to "the physical cosmos as a whole."

46. For a brief discussion of Chinese thought on this idea and a comparison with Western thought, see Needham, *Science and Civilisation*, 2:294–303. Bodde, "Harmony and Conflict in Chinese Philosophy," p. 55, has listed examples of such parallelism from Tung Chung-shu. Other early examples can be found in Sivin, *Traditional Medicine in Contemporary China*, pp. 54–59; Tjan, *Po Hu T'ung*.

47. *YL*60.4b3.

48. *YL*53.4a1.

49. *YL*68.16a3. Here the word *wan-wu* refers not to all the myriad things but just to one of them.

50. *WC*37.29b.

51. See chap. 11, p. 222.

52. *YL*2.6b2.

53. E.g., *YL*4.9a1; 53.4a1.

54. *YL*33.20a1. This remark came up in his discussion of an *Analects* passage (4.28), but sources of the idea can be located in *Mencius* (7A4: "All the myriad things are there in me") and in Chang Tsai's *Hsi-ming* (*Chang-tzu ch'üan-shu*, 1.2a: "What fills heaven and earth, I regard as my body").

55. *YL*17.14b3. See also *YL*90.3a0.

56. For further discussion on Chu Hsi's ideas about "the mind of heaven and earth," see sec. 7.4.

57. *SSCC* (*Chung-yung*), p. 2a. Chu Hsi added, "If my mind is correct, the mind of heaven and earth is also correct; if my *ch'i* is smooth, the *ch'i* of heaven and earth is also smooth." This is the aspect that Thomas A. Metzger has emphasized in his *Escape from Predicament*, pp. 72, 81, passim, using such expressions as "linkage" of all things and "cosmic oneness."

58. *SSCC* (*Chung-yung*), p. 17a. While commenting upon it, Chu Hsi even discussed the question "How can [a man with] a body of blood and *ch'i* [with the height] of seven feet stand side by side [with heaven and earth] and become three [with them]?" *YL*118.3a0. See also *YL*118.8b1.

59. *WC*73.40a.

60. For Chu Hsi's remarks that heaven and earth produce men and things, see, e.g., *YL*17.11b3; *WC*73.44b.

61. *YL*64.10a3.

62. *YL*100.6b3–7a0. See note 108.

63. *YL*110.4b2. Here Chu Hsi is referring to the *Chung-yung* phrase "[w]here heaven 'covers' and where the earth 'sustains'" (ch. 31).

64. E.g., *YL*14.9b2; 64.10a4–10b0; 67.3b2; 110.4b2.

65. E.g., *YL*64.10a4–10b0; 67.3b2.

66. For a brief discussion of the origins, various meanings, and early historical development of the concept, see Ch'in, "'Sheng' tsai Chung-kuo ssu-hsiang-shih

nei te to-chung i-i." See also Taylor, *Religious Dimensions of Confucianism*, chap. 3, for various Confucian perceptions of the concept; and Kasoff, *Thought of Chang Tsai*, pp. 23–26, for a brief survey of Northern Sung attitudes to the concept. Chapter 4 of Kasoff's book discusses various aspects of Chang Tsai's ideas about it in more detail.

67. According to Ch'ien Mu, "Master Chu considered the four things, i.e., virtuous conduct, intelligence, talents, and achievements, to be important and called those [with these qualities] 'the sages.'" *Chu-tzu hsin hsueh-an*, 1:72. See also 1:377–394.

68. Most eleventh-century Neo-Confucian thinkers had this kind of attitude; see, e.g., Kasoff, *Thought of Chang Tsai*, pp. 24–26, 104–106. Chu Hsi seems to have been more conservative than these earlier thinkers concerning the attainability of sagehood, however. Although he never denied the possibility, he emphasized its difficulty. See, e.g., *YL*104.1a4, where he recalled that when, in his teens, he read the phrase from *Mencius* "The sage and I are of the same kind" (6A7), he was hopeful that it would be easy to become a sage; but he soon realized that it was in fact very difficult. In *YL*90.11a0, 12a0, he noted that becoming a sage had become more difficult in the later ages.

69. E.g., *YL*4.21a0.

70. *YL*14.9b2.

71. *YL*67.3b2.

72. *YL*74.16a4.

73. *YL*78.35b1.

74. *YL*65.9a2.

75. *CS*5.23a1. In contrast, what is referred to as *shen* or *kuei-shen* is what heaven does itself. For example, "Where the sages are producing, [they] are rituals and music; where the creative transformation [takes place, they] are *kuei-shen*." *YL*87.23a2. Thus, in *Ch'u-tz'u chi-chu*, 3.101, Chu Hsi referred to the imaginary person that could rise up in the sky and place himself between the sun and the

moon as a "*shen*" man, and not a "*sheng*"
man (a sage), see chap. 9, p. 142.

76. *YL*73.19a2.
77. *YL*78.35b1.
78. *YL*116.7b0–8a0.
79. *YL*78.35b1
80. *YL*31.16a1.
81. *YL*44.18b1. It is not necessary to cite
examples of Chu Hsi's calling Confucius
"the Sage," for they are too numerous and
scattered all over his conversations and
writings. In *YL*36.9a3–9b0 Chu Hsi even
mentioned "the aspects in which 'the Sage'
[i.e., Confucius] was wiser than Yao and
Shun," as if only Confucius, and not Yao
and Shun, was a sage.
82. E.g., *YL*10.1a2; *WC*78.16a–16b,
82.24a. On the relation of the sages and the
classics, see, e.g., Taylor, *Religious Dimensions of Confucianism*, chap. 2.
83. *CS*6.28b2.
84. *CS*6.5a2.
85. This is one of the basic positions
held in the "Hsi-tz'u chuan," which Chu
Hsi adopted, e.g., in *YL*67.1b1.
86. *YL*10.1b3.
87. *YL*18.3b0.
88. *YL*58.12a0.
89. Some eleventh-century thinkers
showed a more skeptical attitude toward
such a belief; see, e.g., Kasoff, *Thought of
Chang Tsai*, pp. 23–24.
90. *YL*64.28b0. See also *YL*87.23a2.
91. *YL*3.1b1.
92. *YL*64.28b0. In *YL*35.23b1 Chu Hsi
illustrated the case of music: "Man's voice
naturally has [what is] high and [what is]
low. The sages established the five notes to
embrace them. . . . The sages also established the twelve pitches to regulate the five
notes."
93. *YL*27.15b0.
94. *YL*27.21a1.
95. *YL*45.2a1–2b0.
96. *YL*44.18b1.
97. It is not always possible to tell in
which of the two senses the character was
used. But the contexts of most of the uses of

the character discussed in this section make
it clear that it was in the sense of "mind."
For Chu Hsi's ideas about the character *hsin*
in these two senses, see chap. 11, sec. 11.3.
98. *YL*1.3b1–4a0.
99. *YL*1.4a1.
100. A source of this can be traced back
to the *I-ching* remark "In the *fu* hexagram
one sees 'the mind of heaven and earth.'"
Chu Hsi's comments on the remark are
found, e.g., in *YL*71.9a1–12a1, 13b1–14a4;
*WC*42.17b–18a; *CS*29.30a1.
101. *CS*49.22b3.
102. For a discussion of the mind of
heaven and the mind of heaven and earth
from a different perspective, see Tillman,
"Consciousness of *T'ien* in Chu Hsi's
Thought," esp. pp. 38–42.
103. *YL*1.3a4–3b0,
104. *WC*58.5a.
105. *CS*45.6a1.
106. *YL*1.3b0.
107. E.g., *YL*36.24a1; 97.4b2.
108. *YL*45.14b0. See also *YL*100.6b3–
7a0, in which Chu Hsi said:

> In general, heaven is simply movement
> and earth is simply rest. When it comes to man,
> he combines both movement and rest. This is
> where [man] is more subtle (*miao*) than
> heaven and earth. Therefore, it is said that
> man is the mind of heaven and earth.

109. *YL*27.18a3.
110. *YL*1.4a0.
111. *YL*27.18a3. This is a continuation of
the passage cited in note 109. See also
*YL*71.13b1, 14a4.
112. E.g., *YL*53.3a1; 71.10b1, 11a1.
113. E.g., *YL*95.21b2, 3.
114. *YL*53.18b4.
115. *YL*53.3a1.
116. *YL*1.4a1.
117. E.g., *YL*53.3a3, 4a1; 71.1b0;
*WC*42.18a, 67.20a; *CS*29.30a1.
118. *YL*71.10b3.
119. *YL*53.3a3.
120. *YL*71.10b1. See also *YL*27.27a1,
71.9b1.

121. E.g., *YL*5.3b4; 17.11b3–12a0; 100.8b1; 116.8b0.

122. E.g., *YL*53.3a1, 3b1. Chu Hsi also interpreted the Ch'eng brothers' remark "The mind of commiseration is the way of producing life of man" (*Chin-ssu-lu*, ch. 1) in the same way. *Chin-ssu-lu chi-chu*, p. 1.16a. See also *YL*95.21b2, 3.

123. E.g., *YL*5.3b5; 53.18b4 (quoted by a disciple); 95.8b1. However, in *WC*40.29b, in a letter difficult to date, Chu Hsi wrote that this assertion was a conjecture that he had once held. See also *YL*95.21b2, where he said, "The mind of heaven and earth producing things is humaneness."

CHAPTER

8

Stimulus-Response (*Kan-Ying*) and *Pien-Hua*

Two pairs of concepts, "stimulus" (*kan*)–"response" (*ying*) and *pien-hua*, were used by Chu Hsi to refer to various interactions and changes in the world. In discussing his ideas about those concepts, we can observe some of the characteristic modes in which Chu Hsi perceived and interpreted things and events of the natural world. Examination of his thought about the former pair, for example, enhances our understanding of the two general features—namely the categorical-associative and the cyclical—that we have noted concerning various key concepts of his natural philosophy. In particular, it throws light on the nature of the categorical associations and the cyclical sequences formed by them. Chu Hsi's sayings and writings about the latter pair show how he distinguished and classified changes in the world, rather than describing and explaining them.

8.1. Two Kinds of Stimuli and Responses

Although the two general features were prominent in Chu Hsi's discussion of natural phenomena, he was not clear about the exact nature of the two corresponding relations, namely, the relation among the things, events, and concepts that belong to a category and the relation among those that form sequences, following one another continuously. He adopted the concept of "stimulus and response" to describe both kinds of relationship. And from his various remarks involving the terms, we can see two kinds of stimuli and responses roughly corresponding to the two features.

First, there was the stimulus-response interaction among things, events, and concepts that belong to a single category and are associated with one another. It is, to borrow John Henderson's characterization, a kind of "cosmic resonance," according to which "things of the same category but in different cosmic realms were supposed to affect one another by virtue of a mutual sympathy, to resonate like properly attuned pitchpipes."[1] This idea was widespread in the Han times and was especially pronounced in the writings of Tung Chung-shu (ca. 179–104 B.C.), whose *Ch'un-ch'iu fan-lu* (Luxuriant dew of the *Spring and Autumn Annals*) contains a chapter titled "[Things of] the Same Category Move Each Other" (T'ung-lei hsiang tung).[2] Chu Hsi referred to it when he said, though not explicitly using the words "stimulus and response," that "the same sounds respond to each other; the same *ch'i* seek each other."[3] He illustrated his statement with the following kinds of remarks: "Cloud follows dragons and wind follows tigers";[4] "Auspicious men do good things and naturally have [other] auspicious men to be in company with. Those of evil quality also have evil men to be together with."[5] Speaking of the sacrificial service, he was more explicit: "[It] stimulates with [things of the same] category and responds with the category."[6] Commenting on alchemical procedures, he used different words to refer to the same idea: "[Things of] the same category change each other; . . . [things of] different categories cannot form (*ch'eng*) each other."[7]

These examples show that the stimulus-response interactions were not restricted to things and events that could be called "natural." Chu Hsi more frequently mentioned cases of mutual interactions and influences between men or between men and natural things and events. He spoke of "the mind of commiseration" coming out of man's body, stimulated by an external thing or event;[8] he also mentioned a certain Wang Hsiang whose extraordinary filial devotion to his ailing stepmother stimulated a fish to respond by coming out of frozen water;[9] the purpose of praying for rain, for him, was to stimulate the *ch'i* with the sincerity of those who pray.[10] Numerous examples in chapter 6 illustrated how the sincerity of descendants' minds can stimulate their ancestors' *ch'i* or mental spirit to respond by aggregating and returning.

The most frequently mentioned example, however, is the idea that man's conduct can affect the course of natural events. We have seen, also in chapter 6, Chu Hsi's remarks that licentious conduct on the part of the ruler can influence the spirits of heaven to cause natural calamities. Sometimes Chu Hsi did not have recourse to spirits but simply said that men have "brought about" (*chih*) or "beckoned" (*chao*) the calamities.[11] For example, he resolutely approved a disciple's remark that "if the ruler of people accumulates sins and mistakes, these stimulate and beckon inauspicious events and bring about the calamities of eclipses of the sun and moon, the collapse of mountains and drying of rivers, and drought and famine."[12] Thus it is that "if the ruler cultivates virtue and [good] government, . . . this can make yang flourish so that [it] overcomes yin and [makes] yin decay [so that it] cannot invade yang. . . . Therefore, [the moon] does not eclipse [even when] it is supposed to eclipse."[13]

These, then, are instances of the "mutual stimulation of heaven and man" (*t'ien-jen hsiang-kan*), the basic idea of which was spelled out in *Ch'un-ch'iu fan-lu*:

> Heaven has yin and yang. Man also has yin and yang. When the yin *ch'i* of heaven and earth rises, man's yin *ch'i* responds to it and rises. When man's yin *ch'i* rises, the yin *ch'i* of heaven and earth also must respond to it and rise.[14]

Chu Hsi did not cite this passage, because he did not believe that the book was written by Tung Chung-shu;[15] nor did he actually use the expression "mutual stimulation of heaven and man" in referring to the above-mentioned examples. But his saying that "the mutual stimulation of heaven and man can be understood from the 'Hung-fan' (Great plan) [chapter of the *Book of Documents*]," a key source of the five-phase categorical scheme, clearly reflects his belief that stimulus and response occur between men and natural events of the same category.[16] Commenting on the remark in *Analects* (7.5) about Confucius's "decline" (*shuai*), Chu Hsi attributed it to the decline of the world at the time, adding that "Confucius and heaven and earth responded to each other."[17]

Of course, Chu Hsi did not believe that all natural calamities are caused by men. He said, for example, that "there are times when human conduct brings them about, and also when they occur accidentally [i.e., by accident of natural events]."[18] He had the following explanation for people's being struck dead by lightning:

> There are [those who are struck] accidentally. There are [those who,] by evil acts, stimulate and beckon it [i.e., the striking of lightning]: for example, a man who encountered it while [secretly] desiring to kill another man with a knife.[19]

Nor did he believe that all natural events can be affected by human conduct:

> Great events cannot be affected disastrously (for example, things like the sun and moon). Only small events can be affected. (For example, things like winter's cold and summer's heat. Great heat in winter and snowfall in the sixth month are these.)[20]

Thus, he was skeptical about a report of an omen involving a variation in the position of the fixed star "*kuei-hsing.*"[21]

The second kind of stimulus-response relation occurs among things, events, and concepts that repeat continuously in fixed sequences, especially the dualistic ones that undergo continuous alternation. Chu Hsi spoke of this kind of stimulus-response relation far more frequently than the first kind. Typical examples may be found in the following remark:

> For example, when the sun goes [down], it stimulates and gets the moon to come [up]. When the moon goes, it stimulates and gets the sun to come. When the cold [weather] goes, it stimulates and gets the hot [weather] to come. When the hot goes, it stimulates and gets the cold. One stimulus and one response, one going and one coming—the *li* of this is endless. The *li* of stimulus and response is like this.[22]

In this manner Chu Hsi viewed the successive appearance and disappearance of the sun and the moon and the alternation of cold and hot weather as resulting from their mutual actions as stimuli and responses. He mentioned numerous other alternating pairs acting as stimulus and response to each other: for example, expanding and contracting, movement and rest, vanishing and growing, going and coming, exhaling and inhaling, day and night, life and death, rainy and fine weather.[23] With regard to the cycle of the seasons, he mentioned two different ways of viewing them as stimulus and response: (1) spring and summer as stimuli, of which the responses are autumn and winter; and (2) spring as a stimulus and summer as the response, summer as a stimulus and autumn as the response, and so on.[24]

A source of this idea is the text for the *hsien* hexagram of the *I-ching*: "The two *ch'i* stimulate and respond, thus helping each other." Much of Chu Hsi's discussion on stimulus and response came from his comments on this phrase, or on the Ch'eng brothers' discussions of the phrase and the subsequent texts on the same hexagram.[25] Chu Hsi even said that "the discussion of the *li* of stimulus and response in the [Ch'eng brothers'] *Commentary on the I-ching* is complete in [their comments on] the fourth, yang line of the *hsien* hexagram."[26] Another source is the remark supposedly made by Confucius and recorded in the "Hsi-tz'u chuan":

> When the sun goes, the moon comes; when the moon goes, the sun comes. The sun and the moon alternate, and the brightness comes into being. When the cold [weather] goes, the hot [weather] comes; when the hot goes, the cold comes. The cold and hot weather alternate, and the year comes into being. That which goes is contracting; that which comes is expanding. Contracting and expanding stimulate each other and the *li* [i.e., the third of the four cosmic qualities] comes into being. The contracting of the measuring worm is to seek for expanding; the hibernating of dragons and snakes is to preserve their bodies. (ch. B5)

Commenting on this passage, one of the Ch'eng brothers, possibly Ch'eng I, said:

> This [passage] sheds light on the *li* of stimulus and response, using coming and going and contracting and expanding. When [something] contracts, there is expanding; when it expands, there is contracting. This is what is called "stimulus and response."[27]

Chu Hsi subscribed to this interpretation and relied heavily on it in his own discussion of the alternating aspect of the stimulus-response relation.

Since stimulus and response follow each other continuously in this manner, there is no end to their cyclical alternation. The response to a stimulus acts, in turn, as a new stimulus, which brings another response; and this cycle goes on without end. In Ch'eng I's words,

> Stimulus is that which moves [other things]. When there is a stimulus, there must be a response. In general, moving [other things] always acts as a stimulus. When stimulated, there must be a response. That which responds acts again as a stimulus. The stimulus has a response again. Therefore, [the cycle] does not end.[28]

Again, Chu Hsi's discussion of the idea is found in his comments on this passage:

> When [something] contracts, it stimulates expansion. When it expands, it stimulates contraction. [This] is the spontaneous *li*. Now, look at this, taking [the example of] respiration through the nose. When [the *ch'i*] comes out, it must enter. [This is so because] coming out stimulates entering. When it enters, it must come out. Entering stimulates coming out. Therefore, [Ch'eng I] said: "When stimulated, there is a response. Response acts again as a stimulus. That which stimulates has a response again."[29]

This second type of stimulus-response relationship was not restricted to what happens in the natural world. Chu Hsi said, for example: "Both the creative transformations [in the natural world] and human affairs are thus."[30] The examples he mentioned after this assertion included the alternation of sleeping at night and waking up in the morning, and the alternation of activity during the daytime and rest at night.[31] When a disciple referred to examples from the natural world as the stimulus-response of "those that do not have 'feelings' (*ch'ing*)" and distinguished them from that of "those that have feelings," Chu Hsi mentioned, as an example of the latter, the mutual reinforcement of the father's love and the son's filial piety.[32] He also spoke of the alternations of speaking and silence of man, goodness and badness of man's nature, and even flourishing and decaying periods and peaceful and troubled periods in history.[33]

Indeed, everything in the world could be viewed as stimulus and response. Chu Hsi quoted Ch'eng Hao's saying "Between heaven and earth there is only stimulus and response"[34] and made such comments as "Every event and every thing has stimulus and response";[35] "Between heaven and earth, there is nothing that is not the *li* of stimulus and response";[36] "There is no place where this *li* [of stimulus and response] does not exist."[37]

8.2. How Does a Stimulus Stimulate a Response to Respond?

It is possible to figure out the nature of the first kind of stimulus-response relation from Chu Hsi's discussions, in particular from its most typical example of the same musical notes responding to each other—or "resonating," to use a modern expression.[38] But it is difficult to see how pairs of continuously alternating things, events, and concepts act as stimulus and response to each other. Chu Hsi used such expressions as "the way and *li* of spontaneity" or "the *li* of necessity" in referring to such cyclical alternations.[39] For him, alternating appearances of the sun and the moon and of cold and hot weather occur because they "spontaneously stimulate and respond like this."[40] He was not clear about the nature of such interactions, however. His writings and sayings merely reveal a belief that what comes first in a stimulus-response sequence somehow "causes" that which follows to occur. For example, "A movement and a stillness circulate without end. Therefore, it is said that when the movement is extreme, it is still again; when the stillness is extreme, it moves again."[41]

There were times when Chu Hsi's expressions were stronger. For example, commenting on the above-quoted "Hsi-tz'u chuan" example of the measuring worm, he said, "If the measuring worm does not bend [i.e., "contract"], then it cannot stretch [i.e., "expand"]."[42] He also said, "If the sun does not go, the moon does not come; if the moon does not go, the sun does not come. Cold and hot weather is also like this."[43] We have seen from an earlier quotation that the going down of the sun can stimulate the moon to come up and vice versa. In that passage and elsewhere Chu Hsi also spoke of the ability of day and night, cold and hot weather, rainy and fine weather, contraction and expansion, exhalation and inhalation, and even a father's love and a son's filial piety to stimulate each other to appear or exist.[44] He even said, "When the cold [weather] becomes extreme, it 'produces' (*sheng*) the warm [weather]."[45]

Sometimes Chu Hsi discussed more general aspects of stimulus-response relations. For example:

Owing to this one event, there also comes about another event. They simply are stimulus and response. Owing to this second event, a third event also comes about. The second event is also a stimulus, and the third event is also a response.[46]

He pointed out further that a great or small stimulus brings about a great or small response, respectively.[47] Expressed in this manner, the relationship between stimulus and response sounds very much like that between cause and effect in our modern ideas. In fact, of the pairs that Chu Hsi called "stimulus and response," some do appear to us as cause and effect. "For example, coming [i.e., blowing] of the wind is a stimulus; moving of the tree is the response. Shaking the tree is also a stimulus; moving of the things below is also the response."[48] He viewed the sowing of seeds and the appearing of sprouts similarly as stimulus and response.[49] One of his examples identified acquiring a concubine as a stimulus; the response was purchasing silver utensils.[50] But he did not seem to be aware of differences between these examples and the pairs that are simply sequences. For instance, after mentioning the stimulus-response relation of the wind and the tree, he added the stimulus and response of day and night, as if the relation were the same kind: "When the day reaches the extreme, it must stimulate and get the night to come; when the night is at its extreme, it also stimulates and gets the day to come."[51]

At times Chu Hsi did make distinctions between different kinds of stimuli, but the criteria were of a different sort. For example, he spoke of a difference between "the internal stimulus" (*nei-kan*) and "the external stimulus" (*wai-kan*):

Among things there certainly are those that stimulate from inside. But they are not always internal stimuli. There certainly are those that stimulate from outside. The "internal stimuli" are, for example, one movement and one stillness, one going and one coming. This is simply that the earlier and the later [characteristics] of one thing naturally stimulate each other. For example, when a man speaks to an extreme degree, he must become silent; when he becomes silent to an extreme degree, he must speak. This is simply an internal stimulus. [But] if a man comes from outside to summon me out and succeeds [in doing so], one can simply regard the summoning as an external stimulus.[52]

His examples in this passage make the distinction appear very similar to that between the two kinds discussed in the previous section. But he seemed to be more interested in distinguishing between the stimulus coming from the self and that coming from outside, as he said elsewhere: "Some [stimuli] come out from this [i.e., my body] and act on the outside; some come from the outside and act on me."[53] He also spoke of the distinction between the normal use of the word "stimulus" for stimuli alone and the habitual but inexact use of the same term "stimulus" both for stimuli and responses.[54]

The second kind of stimulus-response relation leads one to consider Chu Hsi's ideas about regularities in the natural world. For most of the examples he provided—the rising of the sun and the moon, cold and hot weather, and so on—were phenomena that occur regularly in nature. It could hardly be otherwise since cyclical repetitions occur always in the same fixed orders. He said: "For example, the movement of the four seasons. Warm, cold, mild, and hot weather, each [moves] according to its order."[55] There may be slight aberrations of unseasonable weather, to be sure, but the order of the four seasons can never be altered.[56] As we have seen, Chu Hsi referred to such cyclical repetitions as "the way and *li* of spontaneity,"[57] and he saw regularities of cyclical alternation in social and historical realms— peaceful and troubled periods following each other in history, for example—as "a necessity of events and powers" or "spontaneously . . . [as] circulation of the way of heaven."[58] See chapter 13 for a more detailed discussion of this idea; there it is also compared with similar ideas in the West.

8.3. *Pien* and *Hua*

Both *pien* and *hua* refer to change. For Chu Hsi, however, the two words repre-sented two different kinds of change. A source for this distinction was the "Hsi-tz'u chuan": "To 'transform' (*hua*) and to conclude on it is called 'change' (*pien*)" (*Hua erh ts'ai chih wei chih pien*) (ch. A12); Chu Hsi's thought about it appears in his com-ments on the statement.[59] For example:

> [The progression] from the first day to the thirtieth day [of a lunar month] is *hua* (trans-formation). Having reached this thirtieth day, concluded and made one month, the next day belongs to the next month. This is *pien* (change).[60]

Thus, for Chu Hsi, *hua* is a slow, gradual process like the progression of the days in a lunar month, from the first to the second, to the third, and so on to the thirtieth, whereas *pien* is a rapid, sudden change like the transition from the thirtieth day of one month to the first day of the next.[61] Similarly, a gradual cooling of the weather is *hua*, whereas the sudden change from summer to autumn is *pien*.[62] He also com-pared the gradual progression of the hours in a day to *hua* and the change of one day to the next to *pien*.[63]

Chu Hsi provided characteristic images of *pien* and *hua* in terms of mutual changes of yin and yang lines in the *I-ching* diagrams. He said:

> *Pien* is from a yin [line] to a yang [line]. [It] changes suddenly. Therefore, it is called "change" (*pien*). *Hua* is from a yang to a yin. [It] gradually vanishes and wears out. Therefore, it is called "transformation" (*hua*). [The change] from yin to yang naturally grows to become sudden. Thus it is called change. From yang to yin, it gradually goes on vanishing and wearing out.[64]

It must have appeared to Chu Hsi that the transformation of a solid yang line to a broken yin line is a gradual process of "wearing out," whereas the change between the opposites can only be sudden. Thus it is that for him "*pien* belongs to growth and *hua* belongs to vanishing."[65] He expressed the same idea utilizing the yin-yang association of soft and hard: "The hard [line] 'transforms' and becomes the soft [line]; the soft 'changes' and becomes the hard."[66] Still of the same idea was his characterization of *pien* as a change "from nothing to something" (*tzu wu erh yu*) and of *hua* as that "from something to nothing" (*tzu yu erh wu*).[67]

Chu Hsi had other characterizations for the *pien-hua* distinction. For example, a sudden change, *pien*, is short, whereas a slow transformation, *hua*, is long.[68] Also, a sudden change is accompanied by manifestations, whereas slow transformation leaves no traces.[69] Commenting on a difficult passage from the *Doctrine of the Mean*, "When moved, it is changed; when changed, it is transformed" (ch. 23), he said: "When changed, its old conventions have already been altered, but there still are traces. When transformed, they have completely vanished and transformed, and there are no longer any traces."[70] The same passage led him to speak of still another way of distinguishing *pien* and *hua:* "As for *pien*, things follow [the movement] and change. As for *hua*, there are cases in which one does not know the [reason] by which things are as they are."[71] He also contrasted the "spontaneous" (*tzu-jan*) process of "transforming" (*hua*) with the "artificial" (*jen-wei*) one of "concluding" (*ts'ai*), which in turn leads to change (*pien*).[72]

Characterized as gradual transformation, the concept of *hua* was contrasted with *shen*, which, as we have seen in chapter 6, had aspects of change and suddenness. For Chu Hsi, "*Shen* naturally is a rapid affair. . . . *Hua* is [what is] gradually transformed."[73] He also quoted Chang Tsai as saying, "As the two *ch'i* of yin and yang act upon each other, what is gradual is called *hua;* what is unfathomable in opening and closing is called *shen*."[74] Another, more ambiguous, phrase of Chang Tsai, "One, therefore *shen* (*i ku shen*); two, therefore *hua* (*liang ku hua*)," provided a more important occasion for Chu Hsi's discussion of the *shen-hua* distinction.[75] But Chu Hsi's frequent comments on it do not help us to gather a clear meaning for it, except that he had "the transformation of *ch'i*" in mind as an example of *hua:*

> In general, as for things and events under heaven, "one" cannot transform. Only after [there are] "two," can they transform. For example, [only when] there is one yin [thing] and one yang [thing], can they begin to transform and produce the myriad things.[76]

Chu Hsi discussed the *shen-hua* distinction also while commenting upon a remark of Mencius: "That which passes (*kuo*) is *hua;* that which remains (*ts'un*) is *shen*" (7A13).[77] This appears to be in line with the above-mentioned comment on the passage of the *Doctrine of the Mean* (that *hua* has no traces). But again, his various comments on this remark do not help make the distinction clearer.

See chapter 13 for my discussion of Chu Hsi's ideas of change in general.

Notes

1. Henderson, *Development and Decline of Chinese Cosmology*, p. 20.
2. Ch. 57 of *Ch'un-ch'iu fan-lu*, which begins with the following words:

> Now pour water on a level ground. It will avoid dry [areas] and follow wet [areas]. Apply fire to identical [pieces of] firewood. It will avoid the damp [piece] and follow the dry one. The hundred things avoid what is different from them and follow what is similar to them. Therefore, if the *ch'i* are the same, they come together; if the sounds are in [proper] ratio, they respond [to each other]. The proof is extremely clear. Try tuning the lute and the harp and polishing them. Strike its *kung* [note], then other *kung* [i.e., the *kung* notes from other instruments] respond

to it. Strike its *shang*, then other *shang* respond to it. The five notes are in [proper] ratio and resonate by themselves. It is not that there are spirits (*shen*) but that their numbers are so. Good things call up [other things of] the good category; evil things call up the evil category. This arises [because things of] the same category respond to each other. For example: If a horse whinnies, [another] horse responds; if a cow lows, [another] cow responds. (p. 13.3a)

Cf. Needham, *Science and Civilisation*, vol. 5, pt. 4, p. 307). For further discussion of the early Chinese ideas about this kind of "resonance," see, e.g., Needham, *Science and Civilisation*, vol. 5, pt. 4, pp. 305–323; Henderson, *Development and Decline of Chinese Cosmology*, pp. 22–28.

3. E.g., *YL*27.32a4; 69.15a4. In both of these passages, Chu Hsi was commenting on the *Analects* phrase "Virtue is not alone; it must have neighbors" (4.25), which also appears in the "Wen-yen" commentary for the *ch'ien* hexagram of the *I-ching*.

4. *YL*69.15a4.

5. *YL*27.32a4.

6. *WC*45.19b.

7. *Ts'an-t'ung-ch'i k'ao-i*, pp. 12a–12b. For more on Chu Hsi's ideas about alchemy, see chap. 12, sec. 12.5.

8. E.g., *YL*53.6a1, 7a1. It was while discussing this kind of response that Chu Hsi distinguished proper and improper responses: "Responding when one should respond, that is stable. If one responds when one should not, that is out of order. If one does not respond when one should, that also is deadly." *YL*95.23b2. He was also of the view that when a stimulus contains selfish intention, it cannot lead to proper stimulus-response interaction; e.g., *YL*72.2a2, 3b1, 5a1–5b0. Most of Chu Hsi's discussions along this line occurred in his comments on the cryptic *I-ching* phrase "If you go and come while your mind is not settled, then friends will follow your thought" (the *hsien* hexagram, on the fourth line).

9. *YL*136.8b2. See also *YL*97.16a1. The story of Wang Hsiang appears in the *Chin-shu*, ch. 33, p. 987.

10. E.g., *YL*90.4a1.

11. E.g., *YL*79.6b2; 87.11b1.

12. *YL*62.19b0.

13. *Shih chi-chuan*, p. 132.

14. *Ch'un-ch'iu fan-lu*, p. 13.3b. For discussion of the early instances and subsequent development of this idea, see, e.g., Henderson, *Development and Decline of Chinese Cosmology*, pp. 24ff; Lamont, "Early Ninth Century Debate on Heaven."

15. E.g., *YL*83.27a0.

16. *YL*79.22b4. Indeed, Chu Hsi added: "Many evidences can prove [that they] respond with [things of the same] category."

17. *YL*34.6b2.

18. *YL*79.6b2.

19. *YL*138.7b1.

20. *YL*79.6b2–7a0. The examples in the parentheses are in small print, indicating that they were added by the recorder, or even by the compiler, and do not represent verbatim records of Chu Hsi's sayings. For the presence of this same belief in the T'ang times, in Po Chü-i (772–846) for example, see Lamont, "Early Ninth Century Debate on Heaven," pp. 57ff.

21. *YL*138.8a1.

22. *YL*72.2b3. *Kuei-hsing* is a star designating one of the twenty-eight lunar mansions (*hsiu*), discussed in chap. 9, p. 150.

23. E.g., *YL*1.1a1, 6b2; 12.17b1; 72.2b2, 3; 2b4–3a0, 3b1, 3b2–4a0, 4b1, 5a1; 74.4b0; 76.6b2; 94.7a3; 95.20a2; 115.10a2–11a0; 116.7b0.

24. E.g., *YL*1.8b6; 72.4b1–5a0.

25. E.g., *YL*72.1b2–9a1. For the Ch'eng brothers' discussions, see *Chou-i Ch'eng-shih chuan*, ch. 3 (*ECC*, pp. 855–860). In these comments the Ch'eng brothers sometimes used the character *t'ung* (penetration) instead of *ying*, and Chu Hsi at times followed this usage; e.g., *YL*72.3b1, 2; 4a1; 76.6b0.

26. *YL*72.2b1.

27. *ECC*, p. 858.

28. Ibid.

29. *YL*72.2b2. See also *YL*72.3b2, 4a2, 4b1–5a0.

30. *YL*72.2b4.

31. See also *YL*95.20a2.

32. *YL*72.2b3.

33. E.g., *YL*1.4a2; 24.25b2; 70.16a2, 24b1; 72.3a0; 95.20a2.

34. E.g., *YL*65.5b0; 95.20a1, 2. Ch'eng Hao's saying appears in *Chin-ssu-lu*, ch. 1 (*Chin-ssu-lu chi-chu*, 1.14a).

35. *YL*95.20a2.

36. *YL*72.2b4 (just before the remark cited in note 30).

37. *YL*72.3a0.

38. Modern scholars have generally characterized this mode of interaction as "resonance." E.g., Needham, *Science and Civilisation*, vol. 5, pt. 4, p. 308; Henderson, *Development and Decline of Chinese Cosmology*, p. 20. Porkert used the word "inductive" to refer to this mode of mutual interaction. *Theoretical Foundations of Chinese Medicine*, p. 1. Graham uses the word "rhythm":

> In the sense that a regular recurrence exciting an impulse to corresponding movement is called a "rhythm," the cycle of the seasons is not merely a recurrence usable for prediction but a rhythm with which man like other creatures stays in step. When the ruler issues largesse in spring and punishes in autumn, it is not at all that he has inferred how to act from a set of artificial analogies and a dubious jump from "is" to "ought"; he is spontaneously moved to generosity by the kindly breath of spring and to just wrath by the breath of autumn which kills the leaves when their time has come. (*Yin-Yang and Correlative Thinking*, pp. 63–64)

39. E.g., *YL*72.2a3, 5a0; 76.5b6.

40. *YL*72.4b1.

41. *YL*12.17b1.

42. *YL*72.5a0.

43. *YL*72.4b1. See also *YL*76.5b6.

44. E.g., *YL*72.2b3, 4; 3b1; 76.6b2.

45. *YL*24.24a1.

46. *YL*72.4a2.

47. *YL*53.6a1.

48. *YL*72.3b1.

49. *YL*72.5b0.

50. *YL*72.4a2–4b0.

51. *YL*72.3b1.

52. *YL*95.20a4.

53. *YL*136.9a0.

54. *YL*95.20a3. The example provided by Chu Hsi was "stimulating [i.e., responding to] the favors" (*kan en* or *kan te*).

55. *WC*73.2a

56. E.g., *YL*24.a1, 64.30b0.

57. *YL*76.5b5–6a0.

58. E.g., *YL*70.16a2, 24b1.

59. Chu Hsi's discussion of this phrase and another similar phrase from the same chapter, "To transform and to conclude on it lies in change" (*Hua erh ts'ai chih ts'un hu pien*), appears in *YL*75.20b2–22a2. Another possible source is the *Kuan-tzu* phrase "[The sages] change in accordance with the times but are not transformed" (49.270). For these and many other ancient sources for the words, see Sivin, "Change and Continuity in Early Cosmology."

60. *YL*75.21b1. See also *YL*71.5b1; 75.20b3.

61. This interpretation of Chu Hsi is different from, and appears even opposite to, the one offered by K'ung Ying-ta in his commentary on the *ch'ien* hexagram: "Gradually moving and altering is called *pien*; . . . suddenly altering is called *hua*." *Chou-i cheng-i*, 1.7a. Other ancient sources, which Sivin has analyzed in his "Change and Continuity in Early Cosmology," appear to be along the same line. Obviously, as Sivin has noted, "From the Sung on, new intellectual trends . . . so greatly altered the understanding of change that the usage of *pien* and *hua* often has little in common with that of earlier periods" (p. 18).

62. E.g., *YL*74.11a1; 75.21b0.

63. E.g., *YL*75.21a2, 21b2.

64. *YL*74.10b2–11a0. See also *YL*75.21a1.

65. *YL*74.10b1. See also *YL*74.3a1.

66. *YL*74.11a1.

67. E.g., *YL*74.10b1, 11a1.

68. *YL*71.5b1.

69. *YL*75.21a1.

70. *YL*64.13a0.

71. *SSCC* (*Chung-yung*), p. 17a.

72. *YL*75.21a1. Not all of Chu Hsi's characterizations of *pien* and *hua* conform to what has been outlined so far. For example, in his *Chou-i pen-i*, completed in 1177, he made a statement that says exactly the opposite: "Change (*pien*) is that which is gradual of transformation (*hua*); transformation is the completion of change." Chu Hsi himself recognized later that it contradicted his other characterizations. Such contradictions even made him admit that *pien* and *hua* can be used in common: "When changed, [it is] also transformed. [It simply] is that transformation is long and change is short." *YL*71.5b1; see also *YL*74.11a1. Chang Li-wen concluded from such contradictions that "in [the idea of] gradual transformation, the [idea of] sudden change is 'infiltrated' (*shen-tou*); in the sudden change, the gradual transformation is infiltrated." *Chu Hsi ssu-hsiang yen-chiu*, p. 366.

73. *YL*99.3b3.

74. E.g., *YL*98.9a0. Chang Tsai's original remark, which is slightly different from Chu Hsi's quotation, appears in the "Shen-hua" (4th) chapter of *Cheng-meng* (*Chang-tzu ch'üan-shu*, 2.13b).

75. E.g., *YL*98.5a3–6b1. The Chang Tsai phrase comes from the "San-liang" (2nd) chapter of *Cheng-meng* (*Chang-tzu ch'üan-shu*, 2.5b).

76. *YL*98.5b2.

77. E.g., *YL*60.15a3–17a1.

PART TWO

Chu Hsi on the Natural World

9. Heaven and Earth
10. The Myriad Things
11. Man

In part 2 I consider Chu Hsi's actual knowledge about the natural world. My division of the discussion into three chapters, namely, heaven and earth, the myriad things, and man, is a scheme that Chu Hsi himself would have accepted.

We have already looked at his views on how these three are related. In chapter 7, while dealing with his ideas about heaven, we have seen how he thought about the relationship between heaven and the other two—man and things—which heaven "produced." In chapter 10 we look at the relationship between man and things and at their place between heaven and earth.

Because chapter 7 deals with the nonphysical aspects of the term *t'ien*, my discussion in chapter 9 is restricted to the physical aspects of the world of "heaven and earth." However, reflecting the lack, in Chu Hsi's thought, of clear distinctions between matter and life and between matter and mind, I include both living and non-living things in chapter 10 and deal with the mental, as well as the physical and physiological, aspects of man in chapter 11.

CHAPTER

Heaven and Earth

In the chapter 7 discussion of Chu Hsi's ideas about the concept of "heaven" in several different senses, I left out the sense of the physical sky. Heaven in this sense and the earth constituted the whole world for Chu Hsi, however; the word for "heaven and earth" designated the entire universe. In this chapter I look at Chu Hsi's ideas about this universe of "heaven and earth."

9.1. The Beginning of Heaven and Earth

A most important ancient source of the Chinese views about the beginning of heaven and earth is the following account in the chapter titled "T'ien-wen hsün" (Teaching on the pattern of heavens) in *Huai-nan-tzu*, which was generally accepted in Chu Hsi's time:

> When heaven and earth did not yet have physical form, [there was only] undifferentiated formlessness. Therefore it is called the great beginning. The Way began from the empty extensiveness, and this empty extensiveness produced the universe (*yü-chou*). The universe produced *ch'i*. The *ch'i* had limits. That which was clear and light drifted upward and became heaven; that which was heavy and turbid congealed and became the earth. The union of the clear and refined is especially easy, whereas the congelation of the heavy and turbid is extremely difficult. Therefore, heaven was formed first and then the earth was fixed later.[1]

Chu Hsi's own account was essentially an elaboration of this. He also held that there was a state of undifferentiated chaos before the beginning of heaven and earth. In this state, "there was not a thing; there simply was the *ch'i* that was blocked."[2] It was quiet and dark. Only with the differentiation of the *ch'i* into yin and yang *ch'i*, the bright light shone forth:

> When [it was in a state of] chaos and not yet differentiated, yin and yang *ch'i* were mixed together and it was quiet and dark. After [they were] differentiated, it could become spacious and bright in the middle, and "the two modes" (*lang-i*) [i.e., yin and yang] began to be established.[3]

Once yin and yang *ch'i* came into being, heaven, the earth, and the luminaries were produced in the following manner:

> In the beginning of heaven and earth, there was only the *ch'i* of yin and yang. This one *ch'i* moved and turned around continuously. When the turning became rapid, a large quantity of the "sediments" of *ch'i* were compressed. Inside, there was no outlet [for the sediments], and thus they congealed to form the earth in the center. The clear portions of the *ch'i* became heaven, the sun and the moon, and the stars. They simply exist outside and constantly turn around and move. The earth simply exists in the center and does not move. It is not that [the earth exists] down below.[4]

The dichotomy of clear versus turbid *ch'i* plays an important role in this account. Chu Hsi repeatedly said that the clear, light, and hard *ch'i* made heaven and the luminaries, whereas the turbid and heavy *ch'i* made the earth.[5] He put this idea in terms of water and fire, the two primary five-phase materials, in the following manner:

> In the beginning of heaven and earth, when it was in a state of chaos and not yet differentiated, I suppose that there were just the two, namely water and fire. The sediments of water formed the earth. . . . The extremely turbid [portions] of water formed the earth; the extremely clear [portions] of fire formed wind, thunder, lightning, the sun, the stars, and the like.[6]

The earth formed from water in this manner was very soft in the beginning but gradually became hard.[7]

On the timing of this beginning, Chu Hsi frequently quoted Shao Yung's theory of cosmic cycles, according to which the greatest cosmic cycle, called *yüan*, was of the duration of 129,600 years. One "cosmic cycle" (*yüan*) consisted of twelve "epochs" (*hui*) of 10,800 years each; one epoch, in turn, was made of thirty *yün* (revolutions), each lasting 360 years; one *yün* consisted of twelve *shih* (generations), each of which was 30 years long.[8] Shao Yung named the twelve epochs of a cosmic cycle by the twelve terrestrial branches and assigned various cosmic events to specific epochs.[9] As summarized in table 9.1, heaven came into being, or "began" (*k'ai*), in the first (*tzu*) epoch. The earth then "opened up" (*p'i*) in the second (*ch'ou*) epoch, and men and things appeared in the third (*yin*). Shao Yung placed his own time in the eighth (*wei*) epoch, thus situating the events of the beginning of heaven and earth six to seven epochs earlier, or 64,800 to 75,600 years in the past. The sage kings Yao and Shun were assigned to the seventh (*wu*) epoch.[10] The cycle was completed by assigning the disappearance of men and things and the end of heaven and earth to the eleventh (*hsü*) and twelfth (*hai*) epochs, respectively. The entire cycle can be divided into two parts, of which "one half is bright and one half dark; about fifty or sixty thousand years good, and about fifty or sixty thousand years bad, like day and night."[11]

This theory of Shao Yung's provided Chu Hsi an occasion to speak more about the beginning of the world, especially about the order in which heaven, the earth,

TABLE 9.1
The Twelve Epochs of a Cosmic Cycle

Epoch	Duration	Event	Corresponding Lunar Month
1st (*tzu*)	1–10,800 years	Beginning of heaven	11th
2nd (*ch'ou*)	10,801–21,600	Beginning of the earth	12th
3rd (*yin*)	21,601–32,400	Beginning of men and things	1st
4th (*mao*)	32,401–43,200		2nd
5th (*ch'en*)	43,201–54,000		3rd
6th (*ssu*)	54,001–64,800		4th
7th (*wu*)	64,801–75,600	Yao and Shun	5th
8th (*wei*)	75,601–86,400	Sung Dynasty	6th
9th (*shen*)	86,401–97,200		7th
10th (*yu*)	97,201–108,000		8th
11th (*hsü*)	108,001–118,800	Disappearance of men and things	9th
12th (*hai*)	118,801–129,600	End of heaven and earth	10th

Note: This table contains only the items mentioned by Chu Hsi. For a more complete list, following Shao Yung himself, see Fung, *History of Chinese Philosophy*, 2:471.

and men and things began. He said that there was an order and a sequence to what happened during the gradual brightening of darkness at the time of the "great beginning" (*k'ai-p'i*).[12] For example,

> if one infers the meaning of the saying that man came into being in the *yin* (third terrestrial branch) hour [of the *yin* day] of the *yin* month of the *yin* year, it must be that first there was heaven, and then there was the earth. When heaven and earth exchanged stimulation, then [they] began producing men and things.[13]

On the order of the coming into being of other natural objects, he had the following tentative remarks, in his comments on a passage of the *Record of Rites:*

> [It is said in the *Record of Rites:*] "Heaven holds yang and hangs out the sun and stars. The earth holds yin and gives vent to it in mountains and rivers. They [i.e., heaven and earth] spread the five phases over the four seasons. When they were harmonious, the moon came into being." The changes and transformations of yin and yang were unleashed at the same time. It is not that this was produced today and that was produced tomorrow. It is only that [if one is] to discuss the order of their being earlier and later, it ought to be like this.[14]

Shao Yung's theory led Chu Hsi to speak also of the end of the world. For Chu Hsi, at the time of the disappearance of things, or "the closing of things" (*pi-wu*) that is to occur in the eleventh epoch, "there is nothing at all between heaven and earth."[15] He mentioned the theory proposed by Hu Hung (1105–1155) of "the immense turbulence" (*hung-huang*) after the disappearance of men and things:

> The one *ch'i* stops immensely, shaking without boundary. Great oceans change and move. Mountains [collapse] suddenly and rivers are blocked. Men and things disappear completely. The old traces are greatly destroyed.[16]

The cosmic cycle repeats itself: after one cosmic cycle, a new one occurs. Therefore, after the end and destruction of this heaven and earth, a new heaven and earth comes into being, leading to a new "great beginning."[17] Before this cosmic cycle, there was another cosmic cycle: "Before the supreme ultimate [i.e., the great beginning], there must have been a world, just like yesterday's night followed by today's daytime."[18] On the problem of how long the cosmic cycles had been in operation, Chu Hsi said: "From what he [i.e., Shao Yung] said, it must be that heaven and earth have been turning around for several hundred thousand years."[19]

While quoting and commenting upon Shao Yung's theory in this manner, however, Chu Hsi never endorsed it explicitly. When asked about Shao Yung's assignments of epochs to cosmic events, Chu Hsi replied, "The appearance is perhaps like this;"[20] or "This is discussed in the *Huang-chi ching-shih* (Supreme rules governing the world), but now it is not possible to know. He [i.e., Shao Yung] simply used numbers and could infer that [it] was like this."[21] Chu Hsi's discussions of the theory occurred mostly in his conversations recorded around and after the mid-1190s. In an earlier conversation (recorded by Pao Yang some time between 1183 and 1185), he did not reject the assertion that it had been less than ten thousand years since the great beginning of heaven and earth, and he maintained that heaven and earth "cannot be destroyed [literally, become bad]" and that only men and things disappear and reappear.[22]

Chu Hsi and his interlocutors seem to have been satisfied with the level of discussion outlined here. They did not speak of further details of the processes of the formation and the destruction of heaven and earth, or of other cosmic events. For example, Chu Hsi did not seem to have a concrete thought about how one cosmic cycle followed another.[23] Obviously, the above discussions, sketchy as they may appear to us, were sufficient for Chu Hsi, because they were in line with commonly held beliefs and also fit in well with everyday experiences. Moreover, many of the features of them were constructed by analogy to commonly observed phenomena, the compression of sediments toward the center in a whirling fluid, for example.

The account so far of Chu Hsi's thought about the beginning of heaven and earth contains basic elements of his ideas about the structure and movement of the world: notably, that the earth was at the center of heaven, which rotated around it. The following sections look at the details.

9.2. The Structure of Heaven and Earth

In Chu Hsi's use of the term "heaven" denoting the physical sky, we can discern two different senses. In the broader sense, heaven included the atmosphere of the earth as well as the blue firmament, whereas in the narrower sense it referred only to the latter. Thus, "heaven" in the broader sense extended from the earth's surface all the way up to the vault and was made of *ch'i*; it was merely rotating *ch'i*, just as the wind was merely movement of *ch'i*.[24] Chu Hsi denied that heaven had physical form or tangible quality; it did not have tangible body and thus could not be seen by man.[25] This is what he had in mind when he said: "If one eliminates a foot from the earth one will have a foot of *ch'i* (i.e., heaven) in its place. But men do not see [this *ch'i*]. This is what does not have physical form."[26]

This atmospheric heaven surrounds the earth, which is at its center.[27] Thus, heaven is not only above earth but below earth also.[28] The *ch'i* of heaven turns around the earth constantly. In fact, it is the rapid rotation of the *ch'i* of heaven that sustains the weight of the earth: if the rotation stopped for a moment, the earth would fall.[29]

Chu Hsi believed that the rotation of the *ch'i* of the atmospheric heaven was slow near the earth and fast further out; there is a gradual variation in the speed of this rotation according to the altitude. When it is fast, the *ch'i* possesses a great force and becomes hard and tense. Thus, the variation of the rotating speed leads to a variation in the hardness of the *ch'i*, and along with it, variations in the clarity and brightness also. In this manner, the dichotomy of the clear *ch'i* of heaven versus the turbid *ch'i* of earth is extended to cover the internal structure of the atmospheric heaven. Toward the top, or in the outer portions, the *ch'i* is clear, hard, and bright; at the bottom, or in the inner portions, it is turbid, soft, and dark.[30] According to Chu Hsi, one can see this by climbing up a high mountain; there the *ch'i* is extremely tense and men cannot stand still.[31] Closer to the earth's surface, on the other hand, the *ch'i* is softer so that men and things can be in it: "If the *ch'i* here were [also] tense, then men and things would all have been rubbed away."[32]

Chu Hsi used this idea also in explaining such notions as "the hard wind" (*kang-feng*) and "the nine heavens" (*chiu-t'ien*). He noted that the former, sometimes called "the hard wind of ten thousand *li*," was found in Taoist sources and was nothing but the extremely hard *ch'i* rotating very high in the sky.[33] The latter was found in the chapter of the *Ch'u-tz'u* (Songs of Ch'u) titled "T'ien-wen" (Questions on the heavens) and merely refers to nine layers of *ch'i* differing in hardness, clarity, and brightness:

> According to what I see, they [i.e., the nine heavens] are just nine layers. The movement of heaven has many layers. The inside layers are relatively soft; reaching toward the outside, they become gradually hard. I imagine that when the ninth layer is reached, it simply forms [something] like a hard shell. There the rotation becomes still greater [i.e., faster] and tenser.[34]

It is obvious that the ninth layer refers to the vault by which the atmospheric heaven is bounded on top. This is what Chu Hsi meant also when he said, "At an extremely high place on top, [the *ch'i*] is extremely clear and also bright, and is mutually in contact with heaven," now using the word "heaven" in the narrower sense.[35] The vault is also very thick so that the *ch'i* inside may be secure.[36] Concerning the shape of heaven's vault, Chu Hsi was never explicit. There is no reason to doubt, however, that he held the commonly accepted view that it was spherical. Although there were occasions when he compared it to nonspherical objects, such as an eggshell or a drumhead,[37] what he really had in mind was not the shapes of those objects but the fact that they had external shells. On the size of the vault, different remarks of Chu Hsi gave different numbers, which seems to suggest that it was not the actual numbers that interested him. In his comments on Ch'eng I's theory that "the sun ascends and descends for [the distance of] 30,000 *li*," Chu Hsi made assertions that took the number both as the distance between the sun's positions at summer and winter solstices (in which case the radius of the vault comes out as approximately 36,350 *li*) and as the distance between the ecliptic and the equator (with a radius of 72,700 *li*).[38] He also spoke of someone's saying that heaven's height was about 84,000 *li*, adding that "it cannot be known."[39] On another occasion, he praised the theory of Hu Yüan (993–1059) that included the remark that heaven moves more than 900,000 *li* during a day (corresponding to a radius of more than 140,000 *li*).[40]

With the notion of a shell-like vault that bounds the atmospheric heaven from outside, it was only natural that the question of what lies outside heaven should arise. Chu Hsi recalled that this question bothered him even when he was only five or six *sui* old.[41] His views concerning the problem seem to have changed over time.[42] At first he had no answer. In a conversation recorded in 1179, for example, he said, "I do not know what things are there beyond that wall [i.e., the vault]."[43] The final answer he came up with was that there was nothing outside it. He rejected, for example, the theory of the *History of the Chin Dynasty* (Chin-shu) that there was water outside heaven.[44] Instead, Chu Hsi spoke of Ts'ai Yüan-ting's idea of "the supreme empty void" (*t'ai-hsü-k'ung*):

> To discuss the sun and the moon, they exist inside heaven; to discuss heaven, it exists inside the "supreme empty void." If one were to go out to the "supreme empty void" and look at heaven, [one would see that] the sun and the moon rotate and do not stay where they were at an earlier time.[45]

But Chu Hsi did not say anything about the nature of this "supreme empty void," for example whether it was devoid even of formless *ch'i*.[46] He simply said that "the outside of heaven is inexhaustible";[47] outside the extremely hard ninth layer, that is, the vault, "there is no other boundary."[48]

Concerning the shape of the earth, Chu Hsi believed that it was flat. To be sure, he discussed a remark that could be interpreted as implying a spherical earth: "The shape of heaven and earth is like a bird's egg. The earth resides at the center. Heaven surrounds the earth from the outside, like the yellow [yolk] inside the shell. It is round like a pellet."[49] But although the remark compares the earth to the egg yolk, its emphasis is on the spherical and shell-like shape of heaven's vault and on the complete enclosure of the earth by heaven, and not on the shape of the earth.[50] Indeed, Chu Hsi's comments following this quotation were focused upon heaven's surrounding the earth and could be better understood in terms of a flat earth:

This theory holds that one half of heaven covers the earth from above, the [other] half is below the earth. [The portion of] heaven that is visible above the earth is a little more than 182½ degrees; [the portion] below the earth is also the same.

Chu Hsi's explanations of some phenomena that we know result from the spherical shape of the earth also show that such an idea was alien to him. For example, he knew that there were regions in the far north where the nights were short and not quite dark. But the idea of a spherical earth, which would have explained the phenomenon easily, did not occur to him. Instead, his explanation was that near the north pole, where the earth's surface is convex and pointed upward, the sun's light could not be blocked very well.[51] He had a different explanation also, namely that that was "the place where the earth is broken off and the sunlight is emitted through [the gap]."[52] Similarly, although he spoke of the record of a man who navigated to the far south and observed many bright stars not seen in China, this did not make him imagine the possibility of a spherical earth.[53] His explanation was again quite ad hoc: "It is that in the south there is a certain 'Old man star' (*lao-jen-hsing*). When the south pole is high, it can float and rise up."[54] He also knew that the distance of the north pole star from the horizon varied: in Fu-chou it was twenty-four degrees; in his own place it was twenty-eight degrees; and in Yüeh-t'ai, the supposed center of the earth, it was thirty-six degrees. But about this he merely said, "I do not know the reason why."[55] The very fact that Chu Hsi never had to worry about the problems that the idea of a spherical earth would have posed is ample evidence that he did not deviate from the common-sense notion of a flat earth, consonant with ordinary experiences.

Furthermore, Chu Hsi frequently mentioned, as we shall see, that China was at the center of the earth, which makes sense only if the earth has a flat surface. We shall also see that his explanation of the seasonal changes was based upon the idea of a flat earth. It can be said that the flat-earth idea conditioned his whole picture of the world. Yet, Chu Hsi did not say what was the actual shape of this flat earth. For example, he did not offer an explicit opinion about the ancient notion that heaven is round and the earth is square ("*t'ien-yüan ti-fang*").[56] Although he frequently used the words "four sides" (*ssu-pien* or *ssu-p'ang*) of the earth, they referred merely to the existence of the boundaries on four sides of the earth, and not to an actual square shape.[57]

Of course, Chu Hsi did not think that the earth's surface was perfectly flat. There were convex places, for example near the north pole, as we have seen, where the earth's surface was pointed and very close to heaven.[58] He even thought that there the earth was so close to the vault that no one could reach the extreme point in the northern sea.[59] The regions of high mountains are also convex: "The shape of the earth is like a dumpling, its knotted and pointed place being K'un-lun."[60]

Chu Hsi was not very exact about the size of the earth, either. He said that it was not very large compared with heaven. For example, it is smaller than the sun, so that even when the sun is below the earth, the sunlight can reach and brighten the moon's surface.[61] Thus, the small earth is not extended in the horizon all the way to the vault; there are empty spaces surrounding the earth.[62] But as to what exists in those empty spaces, Chu Hsi's views vacillated. He said frequently that the earth was floating on water: both below the earth and surrounding its four sides is water, namely the underground water and the far-away sea waters whose boundaries touch heaven's vault.[63] But there were also times when he said that *ch'i* surrounded the earth.[64]

What has been said about heaven and earth in this section constitutes the basics of Chu Hsi's picture of the world.[65] And although he did not explicitly say so, it is based essentially on the *Hun-t'ien* theory, which had been widely accepted ever since the *History of the Chin Dynasty* adopted it in the early seventh century.

9.3. The Luminaries

The earth is not the only body in the heavens; the heavens contain such other bodies as the sun, the moon, and the stars. It is these luminaries that brighten the sky; without them the sky would be completely dark. Chu Hsi said, "The sky has no brightness; the black darkness of midnight is the correct color of the sky."[66]

For Chu Hsi, the sun was the most important of all the luminaries. It was the source of all the lights of the world: "All lights of heaven and earth are the sun's light."[67] "When the sun comes above the earth, then it is bright; when it enters below the earth, then it is dark."[68] The light of the sun was also the strongest. He spoke of the brief moment of complete darkness at daybreak, when the sun has not yet risen but has already "melted away" the lights of the moon and stars.[69]

The moon does not have its own light. Chu Hsi said repeatedly that the moon reflected the light that it received from the sun.[70] He also stressed that although the moon appears to wax and wane, it looks that way because man sees only the bright part of its surface receiving the sunlight; the actual body of the moon remains perfectly round.[71] He even suggested that if a man could rise up in the sky and place himself between the sun and the moon, the man would see a full moon on the half-moon and moonless days.[72]

Yet, even on full-moon days, there are relatively dark spots on the moon's surface. Chu Hsi rejected the popular beliefs that attributed the spots to the existence on the moon of such things as rabbits and cinnamon trees;[73] he explained them in terms of "the earth's shadow" (*ti-ying*) as is depicted in figure 9.1:

> The physical form of the earth is small. When the sun is below the earth and the moon is in the sky, the sun is very large and its light rises from [below around] the four sides of the earth. The shadowy [spots on the moon] are "the earth's shadow." The earth is blocking the light of the sun.[74]

He refused to interpret the expression "*ti-ying*" as "image" of the earth. To illustrate the point, he spoke of a situation in which light shines upon a round mirror before which a paper doll is placed. The reflected light on the wall, a bright circle, has a dark spot in the shape of the doll that blocks the light. It is a "shadow" of the doll and not an "image" of it.[75]

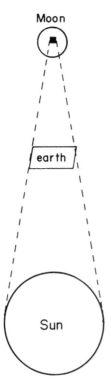

FIGURE 9.1
The Dark Spots on the Moon

Chu Hsi distinguished two different kinds of stars: the fixed stars and the planets. He called the former "regular stars" (*ching-hsing*) and the latter "irregular
stars" (*wei-hsing*). A basic criterion for this distinction was the source of the light.
The five planets do not have their own light but receive and reflect the light of the
sun, whereas the fixed stars have light of their own.[76] Although fixed stars also receive the sunlight, what they receive from the sun is only a small fraction of their
light. Having their own light, they are glistening and twinkling, whereas the light of
the planets is fixed.[77] Chu Hsi summed up all this in the following manner:

> The irregular stars are yang inside yin; regular stars are yin inside yang. In general, the
> five [irregular] stars are all formed through rising up and congealing of the *ch'i* of Wood,
> Fire, Earth, Metal, and Water on earth. Yet, they receive the sun's light. Regular stars, on
> the other hand, are what are [formed through] congelation of extra yang *ch'i* [of heaven].
> I suspect that they can also receive the sunlight. Regular stars, however, twinkle and
> shine on and off, and their light is not fixed. The irregular stars are not so: although [they]
> have twinkling glows, the light of their own bodies nevertheless does not vary sponta-
> neously. If one observes them in detail, one will see that.[78]

The beginning remarks of the passage show Chu Hsi's views about the composition of stars: fixed stars are formed of the yang *ch'i* of heaven, whereas the planets

are formed of the yin *ch'i* of earth. He used the dichotomy of the bright and heavenly aspect of yang versus the dark and earthly aspect of yin in distinguishing bodies that have their own light from those that do not. Thus, he approved Shao Yung's designation of the sun as "the supreme yang" (*t'ai-yang*), the moon as "the small yin," and (regular) stars simply as "yang."[79] Also, the moon, a yin object, did not appear on his list of what is formed by the extremely clear portions of the *ch'i*—namely, wind, thunder, lightning, the sun, and (regular) stars.[80] The earthly yin *ch'i* making the five planets can be divided into the *ch'i* of the five phases. Hence the association of the five stars with the five phases. They are called by the phase names: Mercury is "the Water star" (*shui-hsing*) and Venus is "the Metal star" (*chin-hsing*), for example.[81] Chu Hsi even said that one could tell the five stars from one another by their colors, which were associated with the five phases.[82]

Chu Hsi referred to both the planets and the fixed stars as "*hsing*" (star) and mentioned actual names of many individual stars and constellations.[83] In *Ch'u-tz'u chi-chu* (Collected commentaries on the *Songs of Ch'u*), for example, he identified many star names appearing in the *Songs of Ch'u*.[84] The ones he mentioned most frequently were the north pole star (*pei-chi-hsing*) and other stars and constellations near the north pole: for example, the *T'ai-i* star (often identified as the pole star), the *Pei-tou* star (the Big Dipper), the *Wu-ti* constellation, and the *Tzu-wei-han* constellation.[85] These star names came up often in his comments on the *Analects* passage in which the ruler is compared to the north pole or the north pole star: "[The ruler] is like the north *ch'en*, which resides in its place while a multitude of stars pay homage to it" (2.1).[86] He said, for example, "The *T'ai-i* star is like the ruler of men; the pole is like the imperial capital."[87] He even discussed star maps (*hsing-t'u*); he preferred circular ones over square ones.[88] He also knew about special kinds of "stars." For example, he mentioned "stars . . . [which] fall down to earth, whose light brightens the sky and is dispersed, and some of which change into stones," in an obvious reference to meteors and meteorites.[89] A disciple spoke of a "guest star (*k'e-hsing*) . . . invading the *Ti* constellation," apparently a nova.[90]

9.4. The Surface of the Earth

We have seen that Chu Hsi considered the earth to be a small body in the heavens. That was the perspective he adopted when he thought about the earth in an abstract manner, placing himself outside heaven and earth. But he also had a different conception of the earth, an actual physical body on which he lived. In this conception, the earth lay under heaven, facing it and dividing it into two halves; indeed, the earth constituted one-half of the whole world of heaven and earth. Thus, men knew much more about it, a great deal more than about other bodies, and Chu Hsi spoke of various features of the earth and its more or less flat surface.

The Chinese traditionally believed that China lay at the center of the earth's surface. They even spoke of the exact location of "the earth's center (*ti-chung*) and had a method to determine it. The method of "*t'u-kuei*" is mentioned in the chapter "Ti-kuan" (Official of the earth) of the *Rites of Chou* (Chou-li): "Using the method of *t'u-kuei*, [an official] measures the depth of the earth [from the sun], and corrects [the length of] the sun's shadow in order to obtain the earth's center."[91] Chu Hsi discussed this method in his comments on the passage.[92] For example,

> [According to] the method of *t'u-kuei*, one erects a gnomon of eight feet and extends a template of one foot five inches horizontally down on earth. When the sun is at the center [of heaven] and its shadow [exactly] covers the template, then this is the earth's center.[93]

It is clear that the method of *t'u-kuei* can fix only the latitude, and not the exact location, of the earth's center. But the method was actually used in identifying a specific location as the earth's center. The location adopted in this way in the Sung times was Chün-i, near K'ai-feng in the present Honan province. Chu Hsi mentioned, as the earth's center, Chün-i and some other locations near it that have the latitude of approximately thirty-six degrees—the Sung Mountain (Sung-shan) and Ying-ch'uan, for example.[94] He was not firm about this, however. Once, having said that the *t'u-kuei* method gave Chün-i, he added a doubt as to whether "Chün-i is really the earth's center or not."[95]

Chu Hsi spoke of other regions of the earth. For example, he said that in the northwestern region the earth was extremely high, though it did not correspond to the center of heaven.[96] We have also seen his views about the extremely northern parts of the earth, where the earth's surface is convex and nights are short and not very dark, and about the southern sea, where different stars can be observed. In his view, beyond these far regions are the oceans, which surround the earth and are extended outward to touch heaven's vault.[97] The earth itself is extended for some distance under the sea water, but it stops at a point:

> Where there are islands and many barbarian countries out in the ocean, the earth is still continuous. In those places, the sea still has the bottom. [But] when [one] reaches where the sea has no bottom, the physical form of the earth ceases.[98]

Chu Hsi thought, as we have seen, that the earth was made of sediments of turbid *ch'i*.[99] It is thus to be expected that the earth is not a perfectly solid body like the vault of heaven, which is made of clear *ch'i*, for example. Chu Hsi noted that the earth was not full inside but had empty spaces and thus could receive and contain the *ch'i* of heaven.[100] He approved of comparing the earth to the lungs, which also have empty spaces inside for respiration of *ch'i*.[101] The earth can be characterized as "vast" (*kuang*) because it has enough such spaces to accommodate all the *ch'i* of heaven. Chu Hsi agreed when an interlocutor made the following remark:

> To discuss it in terms of physical form, heaven surrounds the earth [from] outside; the earth is in the center of heaven. Therefore, it is said that the tangible quality of heaven is "great." To discuss it in terms of *li* and *ch'i*, the earth is contained by heaven; the *ch'i* of heaven is completely inside the earth; the earth completely receives that *ch'i* of heaven. Therefore it is said that the volume (*liang*) of the earth is "vast."[102]

This was an elaboration of Chu Hsi's own remark in *Chou-i pen-i* (Original meaning of the *Book of Changes*):

> The *ch'ien* [i.e., the yang line of the *I-ching*] is one and full. Therefore, talking about it in terms of tangible quality, it is said [to be] "great." The *k'un* [i.e., the yin line] is two and empty. Therefore, talking about it in terms of volume, it is said [to be] "vast."[103]

Here Chu Hsi compared the empty spaces of the earth with the broken shape of the yin line. It was in this context also that he associated "two" with the earth in contrast with "one" for heaven.[104] He mentioned the earth's production of things as an evidence for the "twoness" of the earth: "To open is to open up into two. To close is to combine the two. For example, when things are produced and come up [from below] the earth's surface, the earth's surface must open up."[105]

The movement of *ch'i* causes wind inside the earth, which can be very strong, so strong that it can move and damage coffins. This is so because, according to Chu Hsi, *ch'i* is accumulated under the earth's surface. When the wind comes out above the earth's surface, it is dispersed.[106] The *ch'i* inside the earth is also very hot. Chu Hsi seemed to take it for granted when a disciple spoke of "the steamy heat of the earth's *ch'i*."[107] There is more than just *ch'i* inside the earth; there is water as well. Chu Hsi mentioned well drillers who look for such underground water[108] and damage caused to coffins by the water.[109]

Chu Hsi's discussion of the features of earth's surface centered around mountains and rivers. As he believed that the earth was formed of sediments of the turbid portions of water, he thought that mountains were formed of water also.[110] He had evidence for this: "Climbing up high and looking [around, one will see that] mountains are all in the shape of waves. It is simply [because] water floated [the sediments] like this." And when it was suggested that the process was similar to "tides heaping up sand," he agreed.[111] Mountains were formed also by the elevation of sea bottoms, which was proved by the presence of seashells on top of mountains.[112]

Chu Hsi frequently spoke of mountains and rivers together. For example, "When two mountains run parallel to each other, there must be a river between them. When two rivers run parallel, there must be a mountain between them."[113] Quoting Ts'ai Yüan (1148–1236), Ts'ai Yüan-ting's son, he said: "A mountain is the same at the origin and different at the ends, whereas a river is different at the origins and the same at the end," obviously referring to the fact that a mountain range is separated into ridges, whereas the branches of a river are combined into a single river.[114] He also mentioned the erosion of mountains by water, which results in the gradual thinning of the mountains and the rising of the riverbeds.[115]

On rivers, most of Chu Hsi's remarks were about the flow of water from the source downward. For example, "Water does not flow back to its source";[116] "Seeing that the flow of water is clear, one knows that its source must be clear."[117] He also noted that the amount of water, small in the upper reaches of a river, grew gradually larger until it became a great flow.[118] In the end, all rivers flow into the ocean. When this prompted someone to wonder why the ocean does not overflow, Chu Hsi replied:

"In general, it is [so because the ocean] dries. [But] there is [also] someone who saw a whirlpool formed in the ocean to absorb the water down."[119]

Mountains and rivers influence the winds and the climates of a region. Chu Hsi said, for example, that in the eastern regions on the seaside,

> wind is extremely abundant. Always, it blows according to the times. For example, in spring there must be the eastern wind; in summer there must be the southern wind. . . . [There,] the land is broad. There is no obstruction of high mountains. Therefore, each wind arrives according to each direction.[120]

Indeed, mountains and rivers were the key elements of the unique Chinese tradition of "wind and water" (*feng-shui*), the practice of selecting auspicious sites for residences and graves.[121]

9.5. Motions of the Heavens and the Earth

A basic ingredient of Chu Hsi's picture of the world, as we have seen, is the rotation of the heavens—both the vault and the *ch'i* inside it. But there are other bodies in the heavens that also rotate. He even believed that the earth had some kind of motion.

Heaven rotates once a day around the imaginary axis connecting the north and south poles of the earth. Fixed stars ("regular stars") rotate in the same way, and they thus encircle the north pole.[122] According to Chu Hsi, the rotation of heaven itself can be observed through the rotation of such stars, the Big Dipper, for example.[123] But these stars are "not attached to [the vault of] heaven"; it is merely that "men below see the stars move following [the rotation of] heaven."[124]

The pole star (*chi-hsing*), or "the north pole star" to be exact, does not move, though it is a "regular" star. It does not move because the pole is the center of rotation around which heaven and the stars turn, and thus it does not move itself.[125] Chu Hsi used the expressions "the pivot" (*shu-niu*) and "the pivotal axis" (*shu-chou*) of heaven, in referring to the pole;[126] he compared it to the center of a rotating wheel or a millstone.[127] There is, however, no star located exactly at the north pole; the pole star had to be chosen near, but not exactly at, the pole:

> At the north *ch'en* there is no star. Because people wanted to choose this as the pole, and because there must be something [by which] to recognize [it], [they] simply chose a small star nearby and called it "the pole star."[128]

Therefore, the pole star actually moves around the pole. Its movement is not discerned by people because the movement is very slight on account of its extreme proximity to the pole.[129] Chu Hsi mentioned Shen Kua's observation of the movement of the pole star by the sighting tube: only when the tube was large enough, the entire movement of the pole star could be covered by it.[130] Chu Hsi illustrated the situation by referring to rotating umbrellas and round candy trays. The pole, like the centers of those objects, does not move; the pole star is near the center and moves only slightly.[131]

The sun, the moon, and the five planets also rotate following the rotation of heaven. For Chu Hsi, these luminaries all rotate in the same direction as heaven, but the rates of their rotations are slower: the sun lags behind heaven one degree a day, and the moon by 13⁷/₁₉ degrees a day.[132] Thus he rejected the view of "the calendar specialists" (*li-chia*) that they move rightward whereas heaven turns leftward; instead, he accepted the theory of Chang Tsai that the sun, the moon, and the five stars all rotate leftward. According to Chu Hsi, the calendar specialists merely took the difference between the faster leftward rotation of heaven and the slower leftward rotation of the sun or the moon and regarded the latter as rotating rightward with respect to heaven by as much as the difference between the two rotations.[133] Chapter 12 discusses more details about these theories and about Chu Hsi's views of them and calendar specialists. But it can be noted here that his insistence on the leftward rotation of the luminaries enabled him, for example, to solve the problem of why the movement of the sun, associated with yang (and thus with movement), appears to be smaller (1 degree a day) than that of the moon (13⁷/₁₉ degrees a day), associated with yin (and thus with stillness): these numbers do not represent the actual rotations but merely were the numbers of degrees by which the sun and the moon fall behind heaven in one day in their leftward rotations.[134]

Since one day is defined as the length of time it takes the sun to return to the same position in heaven, it is the sun that makes exactly one rotation, or moves 365¼ degrees, per day; heaven is faster than the sun by 1 degree, and thus its rotation amounts to 366¼ degrees per day.[135] Chu Hsi noted that this choice, and not the alternative one proposed by Ts'ai Yüan, which assigned 365¼ degrees for heaven and 364¼ degrees for the sun, was the correct choice, because it provided an explanation of the variation in the positions of the stars at the same time of the day over the year, a phenomenon that in turn served as the basis for determining the day of the year:

> If it were supposed that heaven makes [exactly] one rotation a day, how would one explain the fact that the position of the stars [at the same time of the day] differs over the four seasons? Furthermore, if it were so, [the position of the stars] would be the same every day, and how would one count the year; which seasonal point should one take as the definite boundary [of the year]? If it were supposed that heaven does not exceed [one full rotation a day] and that the sun does not reach [one full rotation, but lags] one degree [per day], then [the clock] would become faster and faster so that in the future it would strike midnight at noon.[136]

On the rotations of the planets, Chu Hsi did not provide detailed numbers. He only noted that "the Year star (*Sui-hsing*, i.e., Jupiter) rotates thirty degrees [a year]," adopting the rightward movement theory.[137] About the Metal star (Venus) and the Water star (Mercury), he noted that they "always move attached to the sun, sometimes [moving] in front and sometimes behind."[138]

For an actual, more detailed description of the motions of heaven and the luminaries, more concrete data were necessary. For that purpose Chu Hsi took the numbers obtained at the latitude of the Sung Mountain, one of the supposed centers of the earth's surface. Thus, for him, the north pole on the vault is located at thirty-six degrees above the northern horizon; the south pole is at the opposite point, thirty-six degrees below the southern horizon.[139] The rotation of heaven around the axis joining these two poles, which is neither parallel nor perpendicular to the supposedly flat surface of the earth, Chu Hsi characterized as "slant rotation" (*ts'e-chuan*).[140] Consequently, the visible portion of the vault, that is, the portion that lay above the horizon, changes constantly. But the portion within thirty-six degrees of the north pole remains always above the horizon and thus always visible, whereas that within thirty-six degrees of the south pole remains below the horizon and can never be seen.[141] Chu Hsi referred to these two portions as "the lid" and "the bottom" of heaven.[142] He also noted that the sun could never be seen in the northern direction, for there it was always below the horizon.[143]

Chu Hsi compared the equator, called "the Red Path" (*ch'ih-tao*), to the suture of a spherical box.[144] The daily paths of the sun and the moon vary every day as they undergo "rightward rotations," lagging behind heaven. At the spring and fall equinoxes the sun's daily path coincides with the Red Path; at the summer solstice it is at twenty-four degrees to the north; at the winter solstice it is at twenty-four degrees to the south. The path of the sun's rightward rotation projected onto the vault, called "the Yellow Path" (*huang-tao*), or the ecliptic, thus makes twenty-four degrees with the Red Path.[145] The moon's path is different from the sun's. Chu Hsi approved of a disciple's quotation of Shen Kua's theory:

> In spring, [the moon is] to the east [of the Yellow Path] and follows the blue path; in summer [it is] to the south and follows the red path; in autumn [it is] to the west and follows the white path; in winter [it is] to the north and follows the black path. The movements of the sun and the moon are not [along] the same path.[146]

In addition to these paths, there were various sets of reference positions on the vault that were used in describing the movements of bodies in heaven. Of these Chu Hsi spoke of the three that were the most important, namely the twelve branch points (*chih*), the twelve Jupiter stations (*tz'u*), and the twenty-eight lunar mansions (*hsiu*).[147]

The twelve branch points divide the earth's horizon into twelve, assigning the twelve terrestrial branches to each of them: for example, *tzu* for the north, *wu* for the south, *mao* for the east, and *yu* for the west. These positions were then used in naming the twelve double hours of the day: "When the sun reaches the *wu* point, it is called the *wu* hour [i.e., 11 A.M.–1 P.M.]; when it reaches the *wei*, it is called the *wei* hour [1 P.M.–3 P.M.]. The twelve hours are all like this."[148]

The twelve Jupiter stations were originally based on the yearly positions of Jupiter, which has the period of rotation of about twelve years. Chu Hsi mentioned the names of a few of them—*hsing-chi*, *yüan-hsiao*, and *shun-huo*, for example—and noted that whereas the twelve branch points of the horizon are fixed to the earth, heaven's positions change: "Only when the *shun-huo* [position] of heaven is placed on the *wu* position of the earth, [heaven] combines [harmoniously] with the earth and gets the correctness of the movement of the heavens."[149]

The twenty-eight lunar mansions are made of twenty-eight divisions of the Yellow Path and are defined by the constellations lying on these positions. Sometimes Chu Hsi used the word for "twenty-eight lunar mansions" in referring to stars themselves and said that "the twenty-eight lunar mansions are the body of heaven," which "does not have [tangible] body."[150] He actually mentioned many of their names in his various discussions, though he did not show all twenty-eight of them in the fixed order.[151]

Chu Hsi also spoke of the twelve *ch'en*, which originally referred to the twelve positions where the sun and the moon meet during a year, and related them to the twelve Jupiter stations. For example, "the *ch'en* of the eleventh month is on *hsing-chi* [position] and the *ch'en* of the twelfth month is on *yüan-hsiao*."[152] Yet, when used alone, the character *ch'en* referred to a small area in heaven: "Domains of stars are also called *ch'en*. For example, the twelve *ch'en* are twelve domains."[153] It was mostly in this sense that Chu Hsi interpreted the expression "the north *ch'en*" (*pei-ch'en*) in the *Analects* passage quoted earlier, traditionally translated as the north pole star:[154] "The north *ch'en* is that place in the middle where there is no star";[155] "In the middle of the north *ch'en* there is a star which is very small."[156]

Chu Hsi also used "degree" (*tu*) to describe positions in heaven. One degree was defined as the difference between the rotation of heaven and that of the sun during a day, or as the magnitude of the sun's daily "rightward rotation." As the sun returned to the same position every 365¼ days, there are 365¼ degrees in a full circle, "the circumference of heaven" (*chou-t'ien*).[157]

The picture of heaven outlined so far was summed up in Chu Hsi's quotation of the *Hun-t'ien* theory of Wang Fan (fl. third century A.D.), part of which has been quoted already:

One-half of heaven covers the earth from above; the [other] half is below the earth. [The portion of] heaven that is visible above the earth is a little more than 182½ degrees; [the portion] below the earth is also the same. The north pole rises 36 degrees above the earth; the south pole enters also 36 degrees below the earth. And the Sung-kao [Mountain] corresponds exactly to the center of heaven: [the point] 55 degrees to the south of the [north] pole corresponds to [the point] above the Sung-kao. 12 degrees more to the south is the sun's path on the summer solstice; 24 degrees more to the south is the sun's path on the spring and autumn equinoxes; 24 degrees more to the south is the sun's path on the winter solstice. [From there] it is only 31 degrees from the earth['s horizon] down south. [Thus,] it is that on the summer solstice the sun is in the north, 67 degrees from the [north] pole; on the spring and fall equinoxes it is 91 degrees from the pole; on the winter solstice it is 115 degrees from the pole. These are the general points. The south and north poles constitute the two end-points [of the axis]; and heaven, the sun, the moon, and the stars rotate [around it] slantwise.[158]

Figure 9.2 illustrates this. It shows that the idea that China was at the center of the flat earth conditioned Chu Hsi's whole picture of heaven and earth, as it depicts the

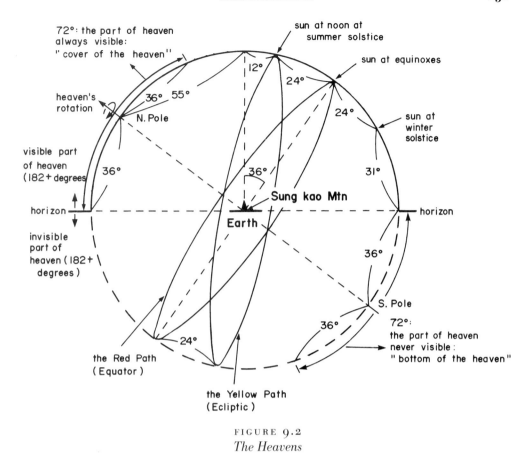

72°: the part of heaven always visible: "cover of the heaven"

sun at noon at summer solstice

sun at equinoxes

heaven's rotation

N. Pole

visible part of heaven (182+ degrees)

sun at winter solstice

Sung kao Mtn

Earth

horizon

horizon

invisible part of heaven (182+ degrees)

S. Pole

72°: the part of heaven never visible: "bottom of the heaven"

the Red Path (Equator)

the Yellow Path (Ecliptic)

FIGURE 9.2
The Heavens

north and south poles, the equator (the Red Path), and the ecliptic (the Yellow Path), all based upon the latitude of the Sung-kao Mountain without allowing for change according to the variation of latitude.

The motions of heaven, the sun, the moon, and the stars, observed on earth and measured against the above-mentioned reference positions, were not uniform, however. We now know that various causes combine to give rise to this lack of uniformity, the main cause being that the actual movements of these bodies are nonuniform rotations along heliocentric elliptical orbits. Chu Hsi, who had no way of knowing this, simply said that the motions of the heavens had deviations.[159] He thought that whereas the sun's motion was "absolutely fixed," the motions of the moon and the stars were sometimes slow and sometimes fast.[160] For example, he mentioned deviations caused by the phenomenon that we now call the "precession of the equinoxes," the long-term variations in the positions of stars in the heavens and the position of the earth's center.[161] He also mentioned the change in the speed of heaven's rotation as a possible cause of the seasonal change of weather:

I suppose that during spring and summer heaven rotates a little more slowly. Thus the weather is mild and slumberous, and in the south it is particularly so. When autumn and winter come, heaven rotates more rapidly. Thus the weather is clear and bright, the world is clear and wide. The reason that it is said that "the sky is high and *ch'i* is clear" is that the rotation [of heaven] is rapid and *ch'i* is tense.[162]

Chu Hsi at times mentioned movement of the earth, but it is difficult to know exactly what kind of motion he had in mind. For example, in a conversation recorded by Shen Hsien in the late 1190s, attributing the above-mentioned long-term change in the position of the earth's center to the deviations in heaven's motion, Chu Hsi said that "the earth rotates following heaven, and [its movement also] has deviations."[163] He added: "It is simply that now we sit like this and simply think that the earth does not move. How can we know for sure that [while] heaven moves outside, the earth does not follow it and rotate?" In this remark, he appeared to have in mind a rotation of the earth around its own axis, which was also the axis of heaven's rotation.[164] But in another conversation, recorded by Shen Hsien also, Chu Hsi spoke of the earth's motion in connection with the age-old theory of the "four wanderings" (*ssu-yu*), which, according to him,

> refers to the four wanderings and ascending and descending of the earth. . . . In spring, [the earth] wanders to the east for thirty thousand *li*; in summer it wanders to the south for thirty thousand *li*; in autumn it wanders to the west for thirty thousand *li*; in winter it wanders to the north for thirty thousand *li*.[165]

Later in the same conversation, when Shen Hsien illustrated these motions with the motion of an empty vessel floating around on water, Chu Hsi approved it.[166] In a passage recorded earlier, probably in 1179, he said: "The motion of the earth now is a motion at just one place, and the motion also does not reach far."[167] Exactly what he had in mind cannot be known, but it is clear that he was thinking about still another kind of movement, smaller than the two already mentioned.

Discussed so far in this section have been the basics of Chu Hsi's knowledge about the structure and motions of the heavens. Of course Chu Hsi knew more than this as he read and studied the works of calendar specialists. For a discussion of them, see chapter 12.

9.6. The Moon's Phases and Eclipses of the Sun and the Moon

The most important consequence of the motions of the bodies in heaven is the alternation of day and night. But that was too obvious to require explanation. Chu Hsi took it so much for granted that he could say, as we have seen: "If it were day for a long time and there were no night, how could [one get] rest? And if there were no day, how could there be this brightness?"[168] The consequences of the motions of the luminaries that he spoke of frequently and in detail were the phases of the moon and the eclipses of the sun and the moon.

According to the modern theory, both phenomena are explained in terms of the position of the moon relative to the sun and the earth. Figure 9.3 shows four such relative positions at equal time intervals during a lunar month. At position 1 the moon appears completely dark to an observer on earth; at positions 2 and 4 it is half

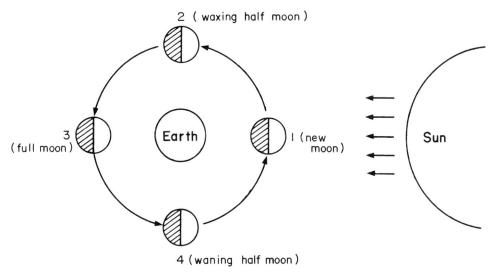

FIGURE 9.3
Phases of the Moon (Modern Explanation)

dark and half bright; at position 3 it is fully bright. A solar eclipse can be observed at position 1, because the sun may be blocked by the moon; a lunar eclipse can be observed at position 3, because the moon may be blocked by the earth. The common explanation of the lunar phases that Chu Hsi adopted was essentially the same. He said, for example:

> On the first day of a lunar month, the moon and the sun pile up on each other. Reaching the third [day] they begin to separate from each other gradually. When men below look at [the moon] slantwise, its light has deficiency. Reaching the full-moon day, the moon and the sun are exactly opposite to each other. When men in the middle look at [the moon] straightly, its light is a full circle.[169]

Chu Hsi understood the solar eclipse also in terms of the relative positions of the sun and the moon; such understanding of the solar eclipse had been available since ancient times.[170] According to that understanding, on a new-moon day the moon was below the sun and above the earth, so that the sun could be blocked from man's sight by the moon.[171] With such an explanation he rejected the alternative explanation that the sunlight was dispersed during eclipses;[172] he endorsed an earlier imperial edict pronouncing that solar and lunar eclipses were not "abnormal disasters" (*tsai-i*).[173] Solar eclipse did not occur on every new-moon day; in fact it occurred quite rarely. Chu Hsi knew the reason: because the moon's path did not coincide exactly with the sun's, so that even on the new-moon days, the moon's position on the vault was usually to the north or to the south, not precisely where it could block the sun.[174]

For the lunar eclipse, at different times Chu Hsi had different explanations,[175] which can be grouped into two kinds. One adopts the yin-yang scheme: a lunar eclipse occurs because on a full-moon day the moon, a yin thing, dares to compete with the sun, a yang thing, in the quality of brightness, a yang aspect; this invites the reaction of the sun, which takes away the moon's light.[176] Commenting on Ch'eng Hao's explanation that "[during the lunar eclipse] the moon does not receive the sun's light" because "yin flourishes and exceeds yang," Chu Hsi said, "It is because yin does not yield a little to yang."[177] This clearly carried a connotation of personifying the moon. Chu Hsi at times went as far as saying that "if the moon gave in a little, then there simply would be no eclipse,"[178] or that "if yin had an intention of retreating, then it would not reach [the situation in which yin and yang] oppose each other and produce an eclipse."[179]

In the other kind of explanation, Chu Hsi attributed the lunar eclipse to the presence of a dark place on the sun. The moon is eclipsed when it comes to the exact position to reflect the light from this part of the sun's surface:

> In the extreme brightness [of the sun], there is a dark place whose darkness is extremely weak. At the time of a full moon, [when] the moon is exactly opposite this place without a slight difference, [then] the moon is lighted by this dark part [of the sun], and therefore it is eclipsed.[180]

It is this explanation that was held by Chu Hsi in his late years and thus seems to have been the explanation he finally adopted.[181] In another version of the same text, he used the expression "dark gap" (*an-hsü*) in referring to the dark part of the sun's surface.[182] Originally, that term had referred to a supposedly dark part of the vault opposite the sun (where the sunlight was blocked by the earth) and had been used in explaining the lunar eclipse in the following manner, which is basically the same as the modern view:

> [As for the place which,] corresponding to the opposite point (*ch'ung*) of the sun, the light never reaches, [it is because the place] is blocked by the earth. This is called the "dark gap." When a star exists in it, it becomes feeble. If the moon passes it, it is eclipsed.[183]

It is interesting to note that Chu Hsi, by changing the original meaning of the term, moved the "dark gap" from the vault to the sun's surface and thereby precluded the possibility of an alternative, and eventually correct, explanation of the lunar eclipse in terms of the earth blocking the sunlight.[184]

9.7. The Seasons and the Tides

The four seasons and the sea tides, like the moon's phases and the eclipses, are consequences of the motions of the sun and the moon. But whereas the lunar phases and the eclipses are the phenomena in the sky, the seasons and the tides are observed on earth.

The regularity in the coming and going of the four seasons is among the most obvious ones in the natural world. To use Chu Hsi's own words,

As for the movement of the four seasons, after spring it necessarily is summer; after summer it necessarily is autumn. Although cold and hot weather during the seasons cannot be free of deviations, the movement of the four seasons can never be altered.[185]

In fact, his conceptions about the whole natural world were conditioned by the idea of the four-season year, and as we have seen in earlier chapters, many of the basic categorical schemes—such as yin and yang, the five phases, the four cosmic qualities—were associated with the four seasons.

We know that the deviation of the sun's path from the equator is the cause of the periodic variation in such seasonal characteristics as temperature, the length of the day, and the length of the sun's shadow. Chu Hsi also knew that the sun's path varied over a year. It is difficult to imagine that he did not see the connection of the seasonal variation of the sun's height with the variations in the length of the sun's shadow and in the length of the day. Indeed, Chu Hsi approved of a disciple's remark that "when yang is in charge, the sun advances to the north, and the day advances to become longer. When yin is in charge, the sun retreats to the south, and the day retreats to become shorter."[186] And when Chu Hsi mentioned, in a passage discussed earlier, "the four wanderings" of the earth (thirty thousand *li* to the south in summer and thirty thousand *li* to the north in winter), a disciple concluded that this movement of the earth was the cause of the variation in the lengths of the day and the night, thus assuming a connection between the consequent apparent change of the sun's height and the change in the length of the day.[187] Yet, Chu Hsi never said explicitly that the former was the cause of the latter. In the case of seasonal temperature changes, a connection with the change in the sun's height was not even implicitly mentioned by him.

Far more frequently, Chu Hsi saw various seasonal changes in terms of the yin-yang cyclical alternation. We have already seen that hot and cold weather was among the most frequent examples of alternating yin-yang characteristics. And in the above-quoted remark of Shen Kua, approved by Chu Hsi, other seasonal variations were also seen as examples of the yin-yang alternation. For Chu Hsi, then, all these seasonal variations—the sun's path, the sun's height, the length of the sun's shadow, the length of the day, and the temperature—were equally manifestations of the yin-yang cyclical alternation; no one of them was selected as a cause for the rest.[188]

The sequence of the twelve hexagrams, which, associated with the twelve lunar months, was used in explaining the temperature change during a year, can also be seen as an elaboration of the cyclical alternation of the yin and yang parts of the year. Chu Hsi said, commenting upon the twelve-hexagram sequence: "When yang becomes extreme, it vanishes and yin comes into being; when yin becomes extreme, it vanishes and yang comes into being."[189] He elaborated:

Between heaven and earth, there simply is one *ch'i*. From this year's winter solstice until next year's winter solstice, it is that the earth's *ch'i* turns one round. When one takes this, folds it, and makes two sections, then what is on the front side is yang and what is on the back side is yin. When one folds them again and makes four sections also in the same way, then they are the four seasons. Between heaven and earth there are just six layers. . . .

When yang grows and reaches that sixth position [i.e., the top layer], it becomes extreme and has no place to go. So on top it gradually vanishes. When a few vanish on top, then a few come into being at the bottom. They are yin.[190]

Similarly, after yin has become extreme,

on the winter solstice in the eleventh month (corresponding to [䷗]), the first layer begins to rise from the bottom. When it reaches the sixth layer on top, the extreme reach of the heavens, it is the fourth month [☰].[191]

Of the six layers of the *ch'i* of heaven and earth, Chu Hsi considered the bottom two to be under the earth's surface. He used this to explain why the warm *ch'i* cannot be felt until the first lunar month corresponding to the *t'ai* hexagram (䷊):

Although the first yang line [from the bottom] in the *tzu* position (the 11th month, ䷗) has come into being, it has not yet come out of the earth['s surface]. When it reaches the *t'ai* hexagram of the *yin* position (the 1st month), the third yang line comes into being and comes out above the earth. The gentle *ch'i* (*wen-hou chih ch'i*) begins from this. Although the sixth yang line of the *ch'ien* hexagram in the *ssu* position (the 4th month) has become extreme, the gentle *ch'i* does not end. Thus, although the first yin line in the *wu* position (the 5th month, ䷀) has come into being, it does not damage yang. It has to reach the *t'un* hexagram (䷠) in the *wei* position (the 6th month). [Only] after that, the gentle *ch'i* begins to be exhausted. In the *wu* position the yin line has already come into being, but the severe *ch'i* (*yen-ning chih ch'i*) only begins when it reaches the *shen* (the 7th month, ䷋). Although the sixth yin line in the *hai* position (the 10th month, ䷁) has become extreme, the severe *ch'i* only becomes exhausted when it reaches *ch'ou* (the 12th month, ䷗). . . . The *ch'i* inside the earth is difficult to see. The *ch'i* above the earth is easy to recognize.[192]

It is obvious from these remarks that Chu Hsi envisioned a yearly cycle of movement of yin and yang *ch'i* stretching over the entire space of heaven and earth—the rise of yang *ch'i* from the bottom of the earth to the top of heaven, followed by a similar rise of yin *ch'i*. His statements show again that, for him, the four seasons were not simply a consequence of particular facts concerning the sun's motion but were themselves direct manifestations of the basic yin-yang alternation of heaven and earth. He took this as actual movement of the cosmic yin and yang *ch'i* and referred to it even as "the great turning" (*ta-chuan*), apparently contrasting it with the daily, small rotation.[193]

Of course, the four seasons occur only in the temperate zone of the earth. Chu Hsi knew about geographical variations of weather. For example, he said: "In the south, the sun is near and yang flourishes; therefore, there is much warmth. In the north, the sun is far and yin flourishes; therefore, there is much cold."[194] For him, it is "not strange that there are places," south of Yüeh and north of Yen for example, "where winter is warm or summer is cold." Yet, he did not distinguish these general features from local aberrations. He spoke of them in a way not much different from the way he spoke of the western region of Hsi-ch'üan, where snow did not melt in the fifth lunar month, an aberration caused by the narrowness of the space between heaven and that part of the earth's surface.[195] And although he knew, as we have seen, that nights were short and not very dark in the extremely northern regions, he attributed this also to certain local features of the earth's surface and did not seem to realize that it was so only during the summer half of the year.

Chu Hsi's understanding of the phenomena of the sea tides was also in terms of the yin-yang cyclical alternation. He based his understanding on the writings of such scholars as Shen Kua and Yü Ching (fl. 1025).[196] He was aware of the periodicity of the tidal phenomena, that is, the twice daily rising of the tides and the twice monthly maxima in the height of tides.[197] He also noted the dependence of these phenomena on the moon's position:

> *Tzu* (the 1st terrestrial branch), *wu* (the 7th), *mao* (the 4th) and *yu* (the 10th) are the correct positions of the four compass directions; and the advancing and retreating of tides take [the times when] the moon reaches these positions as [their] nodes.[198]

To be more specific, "when the moon is placed on the *tzu* and *wu* [positions], the tide is long."[199] As to why it is so, Chu Hsi turned to the yin-yang alternation:

> To discuss it in terms of "vanishing and growing of *ch'i*," *tzu* is the extreme of yin and the beginning of yang, *wu* is the extreme of yang and the beginning of yin; *mao* is the middle of yang, and *yu* is the middle of yin.[200]

9.8. "Meteorological" Phenomena

In addition to motions of the luminaries, there are other sorts of phenomena observed in the atmospheric heaven: namely, those that we would call "meteorological," such as wind, thunder, lightning, clouds, rain, snow, and so on. Chu Hsi even considered some of them, wind, thunder, and lightning, for example, which arose from the clear portions of the *ch'i* of heaven, as belonging to the same category as the sun and the stars.[201]

Most of Chu Hsi's discussion of these phenomena derives from the writings of earlier scholars.[202] For example, he considered Chang Tsai's discussion in *Cheng-meng* (Correct teaching for youth) to be the clearest.[203] In particular, he accepted, and elaborated upon, Chang Tsai's meteorological theory based on the dichotomy of the light, dispersing yang *ch'i* versus the heavy, aggregating yin *ch'i*.[204] According to this theory, when rising yang *ch'i* encounters yin *ch'i* on top and is pressed by the yin *ch'i*, it falls down as rain; when rising yin *ch'i* encounters yang *ch'i* on top, it is sustained by the yang *ch'i* to float as clouds. When yang *ch'i* is surrounded by yin *ch'i* and is prevented from coming out, it bursts out like an explosion as thunder; when yin *ch'i* is congealed inside and yang *ch'i*, unable to get inside, turns around it, it is wind. The wind, in turn, blows and disperses the congealed yin *ch'i*. When the dispersion is harmonious, the resulting phenomena are rain, snow, dew, and frost, that is, those that are considered normal. When it is inharmonious, the resulting *ch'i* is "deviant and incorrect" (*hsieh-o pu-cheng*) and produces abnormal phenomena such as hail, dark mist, and "yellow fog" (*huang-wu*).

When Chu Hsi encountered Ch'eng I's remark on the difference between frost and dew, Chu Hsi made comparisons between various related pairs of meteorological phenomena.[205] For example, according to Chu Hsi, the *ch'i* of dew is different from that of frost in that dew can "nurture" (*tzu*) animals and plants, whereas frost can kill them. Snow and frost are also different because snow cannot kill things. Apparently, for him, the *ch'i* of dew and frost had organic qualities—of nurturing and killing animals and plants—that the *ch'i* of snow and rain did not have. Dew is different from rain in still another respect: the *ch'i* of dew is clear in contrast to the unclear, muddled *ch'i* of rain. Chu Hsi had an explanation for the difference between rain and fog also: when the steamy *ch'i* is blocked, it turns into water and falls down as rain; when it is not blocked, it remains dispersed as fog. He compared the two cases to the boiling of water in a pot: when the lid is closed, the result is like rain; in an open pot, it is like fog. Finally, the difference between dew and fog was that the *ch'i* of dew was clean and that of fog was muddled.

These ideas suggest certain classification schemes. First, Chu Hsi's acceptance of Chang Tsai's theory suggests a division into those that are workings of the yang *ch'i* of heaven and those of the yin *ch'i* of earth: wind and thunder are examples of the former, and clouds, rain, snow, dew, and frost are examples of the latter.[206] Chu Hsi's response to Ch'eng I's remark implies a further division of the yin-*ch'i* phenomena: clouds, rain, snow, and fog are formed in heaven as products of the moist *ch'i* that has risen from the earth; dew and frost are different in that, rather than falling down from above, they rise directly from below the earth's surface. Thus, Chu Hsi said, "The *ch'i* of marshes rises above mountains and becomes cloud and rain."[207] He rejected "the ancient saying that dew is the *ch'i* of stars and moon," insisting that "dew is simply that which steams up from below."[208] His attribution of such organic qualities of nurturing and killing to dew and frost can also be understood from his belief that they come directly from below the earth.[209]

Chu Hsi also had more detailed, and at times different, things to say about particular meteorological phenomena. Wind, to begin with, was a movement of yang *ch'i* in general, not just a turning of yang *ch'i* around a congealed yin *ch'i*, as characterized in Chang Tsai's scheme. Chu Hsi said: "In general, wind arises following yang *ch'i*."[210] The *ch'i* of heaven was an example of yang *ch'i*, and we have seen that he referred to the turning of the *ch'i* of heaven as "wind."[211] There was always wind in heaven because the *ch'i* of heaven turned ceaselessly: "If there is no wind here now, it may be turning over there, or may be up there."[212] There is a strong wind on a high mountain where *ch'i* is clear and hard, as we have seen.[213] Wind varies over time. Chu Hsi explained the change of wind during a day in terms of change in the strength of yang *ch'i*: in the morning, when yang *ch'i* comes into being, the wind also comes into being; at noon, when yang *ch'i* flourishes, the wind is strong; in the afternoon yang *ch'i* is weak, and so is the wind.[214] He mentioned a seasonal change in the direction of the wind: eastern wind (i.e., wind from the east) in spring, southern wind in summer, and northern wind in winter.[215] He also noted a geographical variation in the wind. On the eastern coast, for example, there was much wind and its seasonal variation was regular.[216]

On thunder also Chu Hsi had something to add to Chang Tsai's theory. When a disciple quoted the Ch'eng brothers that thunder and lightning "are merely mutual 'rubbing and grinding' (*mo-ya*) of *ch'i*," Chu Hsi approved.[217] For him, thunder is like the explosion of a firecracker; it is an explosive dispersion of the closed and condensed *ch'i* in an extremely pent-up state.[218] On lightning, he followed the Ch'engs more closely: "Lightning is a mutual grinding of yin and yang [*ch'i*]. It is like stones rubbing each other and producing fire."[219]

On rain, Chu Hsi stayed with Chang Tsai's theory. While commenting upon the *I-ching* phrase "Dense clouds do not make rain but move still further," he made a few additional remarks as to when rain is formed from the steamy *ch'i* and when it is not. For example, "[That] is when yin [*ch'i*] cannot contain it [i.e., yang *ch'i*]. Yang *ch'i* is dispersed further and cannot form rain. Therefore, it 'moves still further.'"[220] We have seen that such *ch'i* left in a dispersed state is fog. Chu Hsi mentioned the ancient distinction of two kinds of fog: "When the *ch'i* of heaven descends but the *ch'i* of earth does not receive it, then it becomes *wu*; when the *ch'i* of earth rises but the *ch'i* of heaven does not receive it, then it becomes *meng*."[221]

Rain freezes and changes into snow when it becomes cold. Chu Hsi said, "If it snows, it simply is that rain has met cold and congealed. Therefore, in high and cold places, snow is formed first."[222] He explained the hexagonal shape of snowflakes in the following manner:

> As for the reason why the snowflake must come out in six [i.e., in the shape of a hexagon], in general, it is simply that [the congealed rain] is broken off by a strong wind and falls down. Therefore, it produces "six." [It is] like a man throwing a lump of mud on the ground. The mud must break and form angular pieces. Also, "six" is a yin number. . . . It is the natural number of heaven and earth.[223]

Dew is formed from the steamy *ch'i* coming directly from below the earth's surface. Thus, dew can be formed on clear days as well as cloudy ones. In fact, Chu Hsi seemed to think that one could expect to see dew on any clear day, for he said, "on top of high mountains, there is no dew *even on clear* days."[224] He accepted the common belief that frost was merely frozen dew.[225] Thus, on high mountains there is no frost, either. He said that "on high mountains there is no dew or frost, but only snow" and explained: "On top, *ch'i* becomes gradually clearer and wind becomes gradually tenser. Even if there is a little moist *ch'i*, it is all blown and dispersed away. Therefore, [frost and dew] are not formed."[226] Unlike rain and snow, which fall down from above, dew and frost, coming directly from below the earth's surface, can be blown away and dispersed by strong wind on high places.[227]

Chu Hsi took hail as an example of abnormal phenomena, produced when the congealed yin *ch'i* is dispersed in a disharmonious way. He even added that the water of melted hail was "dirty, turbid, and sometimes of blue and black colors."[228]

He seems to have considered rainbows also to be abnormal, for he said that they are produced when "yin and yang *ch'i* should not meet but still meet." He even went on to call a rainbow "the licentious (*yin*) *ch'i* of heaven and earth," or "the debauching (*yin-te*) *ch'i* [which] damages the harmony of yin and yang."[229]

Concerning these abnormal phenomena, there were popular beliefs among the common people of Chu Hsi's time. For example, Chu Hsi spoke of beliefs that hail is made by lizards and that rainbows can stop rain.[230] But his attitude toward those beliefs was similar to that we have seen concerning *kuei-shen* phenomena and superstitious beliefs about them: he did not completely reject the beliefs but tried instead to provide explanations for them in terms of qualities and activities of *ch'i*.

For example, in a long passage, he reported many stories of people who saw lizards making hail, including the following:

> On top of the mountain all lizards held water [in their mouths]. When they spat water, the water became hail. After a while there were great winds and rain, and all the hail that was spat [by the lizards] disappeared. The next day, upon coming down the mountain, I [the person who told this story] saw people saying that the night before there had been a lot of hail.[231]

He had begun the passage with the remark that this was not impossible:

> I-ch'üan [i.e., Ch'eng I] said that people say hail is made by lizards. At first I had suspected that there was no *li* for that. [But afterward] it appeared that there also is such [*li*]. [If] it is said that all [hail] is made by lizards, it is wrong. There is naturally [hail] that is congealed and formed up [in the sky]; and there is also [hail] that is made by lizards.[232]

Chu Hsi seems to have found an explanation for this in the association of a lizard with yin, as he said later in the passage:

> The shape of a lizard is also like that of a dragon[, which is a yin thing]. It is of the yin category. [The fact] is that these *ch'i* [i.e., the yin *ch'i* of the water held by the lizard and the yang *ch'i* of heaven(?)] mutually stimulate and respond and let [the lizard] make them like this. It is exactly the time when yin and yang meet and contend with each other. Therefore, when hail falls, it is necessarily cold.[233]

He then continued with an explanation of the angular shapes of hailstones:

> Now, the two sides of hailstones are both sharp and have angular forms. Supposedly, at first they were circular. [But] when yin and yang meet and contended with each other up [in the sky], they struck each other and were broken like this.[234]

In the case of the rainbow, Chu Hsi's attitude changed over time. In *Shih chi-chuan* (Collection of commentaries on the *[Book of] Poetry*), compiled in 1177, he seemed both to know how the rainbow is formed and to accept the popular belief. There he explained:

The sun meets rain and forms the tangible quality [i.e., the rainbow] in a flashing manner. . . . The rainbow follows the projection of the sun. Therefore, in the morning [it appears] in the west, and in the evening, in the east.[235]

But he also said: "Now common people say that rainbows can stop rain. It appears believable." In a conversation recorded later (but not earlier than 1193), he was aware that rainbows "ordinarily are merely reflections produced by thin raindrops when the sun shines upon them."[236] He added: "Yet, [rainbows] also have physical form and can absorb water and wine. When people have them, some consider them evil and some, auspicious." Apparently, it was through its ability to absorb water that the rainbow could stop rain.[237] The following remark by Chu Hsi, recorded still later, explicitly rejects the popular belief and tries to explain why people believed it:

> The rainbow is not what can stop rain. But when the *ch'i* of rain has reached the extreme [i.e., the end], it is already very thin. [Then] also, the colors of the sun shine on, and are dispersed by, the *ch'i* of rain.[238]

Chu Hsi showed a similar attitude toward popular beliefs concerning other meteorological phenomena. For example, he explained the belief that dragons cause rain in terms of the association of dragons with Water: "The dragon is a Water thing. When it appears, it meets yang *ch'i* and forms steam. Therefore it can produce rain."[239] But he added that "the common rains . . . are not necessarily the doings of dragons." He also rejected the idea that rain comes out directly from a dragon's mouth: "It simply is that when a dragon moves, there is rain following it."[240] On a question concerning the belief that thunderclaps strike and kill wrongdoers, he responded that there was *li* for such events: "It must not be thought that there is no [such *li*]."[241] He spoke of the "thunder axes" (*lei-fu*), ax-head shaped objects believed to be formed during the striking of thunder that kill men and animals.[242] For him, they were merely aggregated *ch'i*, which contained sediments and thus could not be dispersed through explosions of thunder.[243] He also mentioned Ts'ai Yüan-ting's view that thunder axes were formed after the striking of *ch'i*: "It is not that [heaven] employs these to strike things."[244] Finally, Chu Hsi had an explanation for the belief that heavy snow is an omen for a good harvest: "Generally, [snow] can congeal yang *ch'i* inside the earth. [This yang *ch'i*] develops the next year and produces and grows the myriad things."[245]

Notes

1. *Huai-nan-tzu*, 3.1a. For the most recent and most extensive discussion of this chapter of *Huai-nan-tzu*, see Major, *Heaven and Earth in Early Han Thought*, chap. 3.

2. YL45.7a2.

3. YL94.2b2. This remark came up in his comments on Chou Tun-i's *T'ai-chi-t'u shuo*.

4. YL1.4b3.

5. E.g., Y1.4b4, 5a1.

6. YL1.5b2.

7. E.g., YL1.5b2; 45.7b0.

8. E.g., YL24.25a1; 45.7a1; 94.2b2–3a0; 100.5a2. Shao Yung's theory is contained in his *Huang-chi ching-shih*, an extremely

difficult work involving complex numerological associations with the *I-ching* hexagrams. For brief discussions of its content, see, e.g., Fung, *History of Chinese Philosophy*, 2:469–474; Chan, *Source Book in Chinese Philosophy*, pp. 481–494; Birdwhistell, *Transition to Neo-Confucianism*, pp. 138–144. I have adopted these authors' translation of the terms *yüan* (cycle), *hui* (epoch), *yün* (revolution), and *shih* (generation).

9. E.g., *YL*24.24b4; 45.6b2, 7a1, 2; 7b1.

10. In *YL*45.7a1, however, Chu Hsi assigned Yao to the time between the sixth (*ssu*) and the seventh (*wu*) epochs, which is not consistent with the assignment of his own time to the eighth.

11. *YL*24.25a1.

12. *YL*94.4a0.

13. *YL*45.6b2. The associations of heaven, the earth, and men with *tzu*, *ch'ou*, and *yin* were extended to the lunar months associated with these branches, which the Chou, Shang, and Hsia dynasties chose as the first month of a year. These months were thus called *t'ien-cheng* (the first month of heaven), *ti-cheng* (of the earth), and *jen-cheng* (of man), corresponding to the eleventh, the twelfth, and the first month of the current lunar calendar that adopted the *jen-cheng* of the Hsia dynasty; see, e.g., *YL*24.24b4; *WC*31.1a; 42.12a, 13a–13b; 43.22b; *SSCC* (*Lun-yü*), 1.11b.

14. *YL*87.14b3. The *Li-chi* passage is from the "Li-yün" chapter, 22.5b.

15. *YL*24.24b4.

16. *YL*94.3a0.

17. E.g., *YL*1.6a2; 24.25a1; 45.7a1; *CS*49.27b2.

18. *YL*94.4a0.

19. *YL*24.24b4. But the conversation stopped with this remark; neither Chu Hsi nor the interlocutor seems to have pursued the question any further.

20. *YL*45.7a2.

21. *YL*45.7a1.

22. *YL*1.6a2.

23. Cf. *YL*94.13a1–13b0; 126.16b0, in which Chu Hsi speaks of a Buddhist account, which appears in *Leng-yen-ching*, about the reappearance of human beings after the end of the world.

24. E.g., *YL*2.9b2, 13b0; 45.7b0.

25. E.g., *YL*2.3b1, 13b0; 45.7b0. Yamada Keiji, in *Shushi no shizen-gaku*, p. 33, has traced this idea to the following passage from *Ch'un-ch'iu fan-lu*: "Between heaven and earth, there is the *ch'i* of yin and yang. It constantly soaks men, as water constantly soaks fish. That by which it is different from water is [the difference between] what can be seen and what cannot be seen" (17.6b).

26. *YL*98.12a2.

27. E.g., *YL*1.5a2, 4; 2.5b0, 6a0; 65.4a0; 74.24b2, 25b1; 98.1a2; *CS*50.8b0.

28. E.g., *YL*2.1a1; 18.5a0.

29. E.g., *YL*1.5a1, 2; 2.13b0; 68.4a1–4b0; 100.6b2; *Ch'u-tz'u chi-chu*, 3.97.

30. E.g., *YL*2.10a0, 13b0; 45.7b0.

31. E.g., *YL*2.6a0, 10a0.

32. *YL*2.6a0. In *YL*2.5b0, Chu Hsi spoke of empty spaces between the top and the bottom parts of the atmospheric heaven that allowed movements of the sun and the moon.

33. *YL*2.10a0. See also *YL*45.7b0. One source, *Pao-p'u-tzu*, mentioned "hard wind" four thousand *li* high in heaven. One *li* is approximately four hundred meters.

34. *YL*2.10a0. See also *YL*45.7b0; *Ch'u-tz'u chi-chu*, 3.97.

35. *YL*45.7b0.

36. *YL*100.6a2.

37. E.g., *YL*74.24b2; *CS*50.8b0.

38. E.g., *YL*2.5a2, 5b1, 6b1.

39. *YL*2.5b1.

40. *YL*68.16b4.

41. E.g., *YL*45.7b0; 94.10b6–11a0. In the Chinese system of counting age, *sui* refers to the number of calendar years in which one has lived. Thus, a newborn baby's age is one *sui* at birth and becomes two *sui* on the next New Year's Day.

42. For a hypothesis concerning the change in Chu Hsi's ideas on this and other problems about the heavens, see Yamada, *Shushi no shizen-gaku*, pp. 143–150, 181.

43. *YL*94.11a0. Cf. Yamada, *Shushi no*

shizen-gaku, p. 210, note 154, however; he dates the passage 1193, following Tanaka Kenji, "Shumon teishi shijinen kō." I follow the dating of Ch'en Jung-chieh (Wing-tsit Chan) in his *Chu-tzu men-jen*.

44. *YL*45.7bo.

45. *YL*2.3b1. See also *YL*2.12b2.

46. There are at least two passages that appear to imply that heaven, or the formless *ch'i* of heaven, was boundless and was extended outward indefinitely:

> There is no "outside" to heaven and earth. [Thus] it is said that though there is a boundary to the physical form [of heaven] [i.e., the apparent vault of heaven(?)], there is no boundary to the [formless] *ch'i* [of heaven]. (*YL*100.6a2)

> Heaven is great, and has no "outside." There is nothing that is not contained in it. (*YL*98.11a4)

But what Chu Hsi meant by these difficult short passages cannot be known clearly. He made the statements in the first passage only in commenting upon Shao Yung's even more ambiguous passage, "Heaven depends on physical form and earth is attached to *ch'i*" (*t'ien i hsing ti fu ch'i*). *Yü-ch'iao wen-tui*, 13.4b. It is thus possible that Chu Hsi may have overstated what he really intended to say, that is, that there is nothing outside heaven and earth. In fact, just before the quoted remark, Chu Hsi said, "[Shao Yung said this] only [because he] was afraid that people may go to other places outside heaven and earth to investigate." The second passage above came up in Chu Hsi's comments on Chang Tsai, in which Chu Hsi emphasized that to find the *li*, one had to look at actual things.

47. *WC*62.39a.

48. *Ch'u-tz'u chi-chu*, 3.97.

49. *CS*50.8bo. The passage comes from the subcommentary (*shu*) on the "Shun-tien" (2nd) chapter of *Shu-ching*. The author of the passage is Wang Fan of the third century A.D.

50. Christopher Cullen has argued this point in connection with a similar *Huai-nan-tzu* passage. "Chinese Erastosthenes of the Flat Earth," esp. pp. 107–109. Although Needham, in his discussion of an imperial commission for the exact determination of the changes in the length of gnomon's shadow over varying latitudes, bases his interpretation on the idea of a spherical earth, nowhere in his long discussion can we find any actual evidence for the spherical earth; the whole discussion can be repeated in terms of a flat earth. *Science and Civilisation*, vol. 4, pt. 1, pp. 43–55.

51. E.g., *YL*1.5b4, 6; 86.10b1.

52. *YL*1.5b5. It is difficult to know exactly what Chu Hsi meant by this remark. But perhaps it is more important to note the ad hoc nature of his different explanations for a single phenomenon. In *Ch'u-tz'u chi-chu*, 3.108–109, Chu Hsi rejected outright a suggestion in an earlier commentary on *Ch'u-tz'u* that in the northwest "there is a country which is dark and has no sun," saying: "The sunlight fills heaven. Its motion encircles the earth. Certainly, there is no place where it does not reach."

53. *YL*2.7a2. The record appears in *Chiu T'ang-shu*, ch. 35, pp. 1303–1304.

54. *YL*23.2bo. "Lao-jen-hsing" is the common name for the south pole star (*nan-chi-hsing*).

55. *WCH*2.6a.

56. For a brief account of this idea in ancient China, see Major, *Heaven and Earth in Early Han Thought*, pp. 32–35. Chu Hsi himself mentioned it, e.g., in *CS*24.27bo–28ao.

57. E.g., *YL*2.5bo, 13a1, 13bo; *Ch'u-tz'u Chi-chu*, 3.101.

58. E.g., *YL*1.5b4, 6.

59. *YL*2.13bo.

60. *YL*86.8bo. K'un-lun is a legendary mountain thought to be in western China; it is frequently mentioned in *Ch'u-tz'u chi-chu*, e.g., 2.83; 3.96, 108.

61. E.g., *YL*2.5bo, 6ao; 79.27ao.

62. E.g., *YL*2.5bo, 13a1.

63. E.g., *YL*2.13bo, 14a1; 45.7bo; *Ch'u-tz'u Chi-chu*, 3.101. See also *YL*86.10bo, in

which he compared the "four wanderings"
(*ssu-yu*) of the earth to the movement of an
empty vessel floating on water. On the theory of "four wanderings," see p. 152.

64. E.g., *YL*1.5a2; 94.11a0.

65. For brief accounts of various early
Chinese cosmological theories, including
the *Kai-t'ien* and the *Hun-t'ien*, see, e.g.,
Needham, *Science and Civilisation*, 3:210–
227; Nakayama, *History of Japanese Astronomy*, pp. 24–43; Yamada, *Shushi no
shizen-gaku*, pp. 13–36; Ch'eng and Hsi,
Chung-kuo li-shih shang te yü-chou li-lun,
chap. 3.

66. *YL*1.5a7.

67. *YL*79.27a0.

68. *YL*74.13b2.

69. *YL*2.9a5.

70. E.g., *YL*2.5b0, 7a3, 7b2; 70.29b5;
79.26b2–27a0. I have found two passages
from Chu Hsi that may be interpreted as
implying that the moon had its own light.
But in both of them Chu Hsi was merely
referring to the moon together with the
sun as bright objects; whether the moon
had its own light was not the point. See
*YL*101.24a2: "The humaneness exists in the
mind as before. It is similar to the fact that
the sun and the moon are originally bright."
See also *Ch'u-tz'u chi-chu*, 3.101, where Chu
Hsi approved someone's view that the sun
and the moon are in the sky, "shining upon
each other like two mirrors."

71. E.g., *YL*2.5b0, 7a3, 4; 79.27a0. In
*YL*79.27a0 Chu Hsi rejected a suggestion
that the moon's shape is like a rice cake.

72. *Ch'u-tz'u chi-chu*, 3.101.

73. E.g., *YL*2.3a2–3b0; *Ch'u-tz'u chi-
chu*, 3.101. Of course, we know that the dark
spots appear because the moon's surface is
not completely smooth and does not reflect
the sunlight evenly.

74. *YL*79.27a0. See also *YL*2.3a2–3b0,
5b0, 6a0.

75. *YL*2.8a2.

76. Chu Hsi's remarks on the source of
the light of stars are found, e.g., in *YL*2.5a0,
6a0, 8a0; 79.27a0.

77. E.g., *YL*3.6a0, 9a2.

78. *YL*2.9a3.

79. *YL*2.8a3.

80. *YL*1.5b2.

81. E.g., *YL*2.9a4; 81.21b2.

82. *YL*2.6a0.

83. The character *hsing* was frequently
combined with the character *ch'en*, and the
word *hsing-ch'en* also meant stars; see, e.g.,
*YL*1.4b3. For more on Chu Hsi's ideas about
ch'en, see p. 150.

84. E.g., *Ch'u-tz'u chi-chu*, 1.12; 2.82;
5.206, 208.

85. E.g., *YL*1.9a0; 23.1b2–2a0, 3a0, 1;
101.32a1; *WC*44.6a–6b, 72.1a–1b.

86. Chu Hsi's comments on this passage
are contained, e.g., in *YL*23.1b1–3b1.

87. *YL*23.3a0.

88. E.g., *YL*2.9b1. For the traditional
Chinese star maps, see, e.g., Needham,
Science and Civilisation, 3:276–282;
Ch'en Tsun-kuei, *Chung-kuo t'ien-wen-
hsueh-shih*, 2:205–257.

89. *YL*2.9a6. For brief discussions of
traditional Chinese views about meteors
and meteorites, see, e.g., Needham, *Science
and Civilisation*, 3:433–434; Ch'en Tsun-
kuei, *Chung-kuo t'ien-wen-hsueh-shih*, 3:
358–366.

90. *YL*38.6b0. For brief discussions of
traditional Chinese views about novae, see,
e.g., Needham, *Science and Civilisation*, 3:
423–429; Ch'en Tsun-kuei, *Chung-kuo
t'ien-wen-hsueh-shih*, 3:344–357.

91. *Chou-li*, 10.10a. For a brief discussion of this method, see Needham, *Science
and Civilisation*, 3:286ff.

92. E.g., *YL*78.12b6; 86.7b2–11a1. See
also *WC*43.20a, where Chu Hsi spoke of his
plan to try the method himself.

93. *YL*86.10b1.

94. E.g., *YL*2.6b2; 86.10b1; *CS*50.8b0.
Chu Hsi also noted the variation of the
earth's center over a long period of time,
from Yang-ch'eng in the Han times to
Yüeh-t'ai [in Chün-i] in the Sung, for example, and attributed it to the deviations in
the movement of the heavens and the consequent deviations in the accompanying
movement of the earth. *YL*86.9a1. For Chu

Hsi's ideas on the movements of the earth, see p. 152.

95. *YL*86.10b1. Chu Hsi also had the notion of "the center of heaven and earth" (*t'ien-ti chih chung*) and mentioned different places as that center: the K'un-lun mountain, the capital of Chi-chou in the present Hopei province, and possibly even his own Fu-chien and Che-chiang area. E.g., *YL*2.13b0, 14a8; *WCH*2.6a.

96. *YL*1.5b3.

97. E.g., *YL*2.13b0, 14a1. Chu Hsi did not concern himself, however, with the problem of how the earth, the oceans, and the heaven's vault were connected to one another.

98. *YL*2.13a3.

99. E.g., *Ch'u-tz'u chi-chu*, 3.97. In *YL*98.1a2, in commenting on Chang Tsai's expression "the melting and coagulation, dregs and ashes of mountains and rivers" (*Chang-tzu ch'üan-shu*, 2.2b), he said that they were "just sediments of *ch'i*."

100. E.g., *YL*1.5a4; 65.4a0; 74.24a1, 24b2, 25b1.

101. *YL*74.24b2.

102. *YL*74.24b2. Cf. *YL*18.5a0, where Chu Hsi characterized the earth variously as "great," "deep," and "thick."

103. *Chou-i pen-i*, 7.5b. This, in turn, was Chu Hsi's comment on the "Hsi-tz'u chuan" theory that the *ch'ien* produced what was great and the *k'un* produced what was vast (ch. A6).

104. In *YL*65.4a0, however, Chu Hsi said: "It is not particularly so. Heaven is naturally one; the earth is naturally two."

105. *YL*74.24a1.

106. E.g., *YL*73.16a3; 89.13b1–14a0.

107. *YL*89.13b0.

108. *YL*2.14a7.

109. E.g., *YL*89.13a2–13b0.

110. E.g., *YL*1.5b2; 45.7a2–7b0.

111. *YL*1.5b2. These remarks are the omitted portions in the passage quoted on p. 136 (note 6). See also *YL*45.7a2–7b0.

112. E.g., *YL*94.3a0, 4a0. Chu Hsi's source for this was Shen Kua's *Meng-hsi pi-t'an*, 21.18. Many modern scholars have interpreted this as implying a geological theory about mountain formation and fossils. E.g., Needham, *Science and Civilisation*, 3:598ff.; Ch'ien, *Chu-tzu hsin hsueh-an*, 5:385; Yamada, *Shushi no shizen-gaku*, pp. 161–163. But Chu Hsi himself was not interested in the question of how and when such elevations occurred; he took this simply as an example of the cyclical alternation of opposite characteristics: "What was low changed and became high; what was soft changed and became hard." *YL*94.3a0. See also *YL*94.4a0.

113. *YL*79.3a1–3b0.

114. *YL*2.14a6. Cf. *YL*27.7a0, however, where he said, "Water from a single source flows down into myriad branches." He may not have been referring to the actual flow of a river with this remark, which he made to illustrate the theory that "the *li* is one but its manifestations are many."

115. *YL*70.21a3. Here Chu Hsi was commenting on the *ch'ien* hexagram (the 15th) of *I-ching*. He quoted the remark "Mountains are diminished [to become] thinner, rivers grow higher" and attributed it to Yang Hsiung, but I have been unable to locate it in Yang Hsiung's sources.

116. *YL*117.18a0.

117. *YL*5.7a1.

118. *YL*34.34a3.

119. *YL*2.14a1.

120. *YL*86.7b2–8a0. See also *YL*2.15a5.

121. For brief discussions of the *feng-shui* tradition, see, e.g., March, "Appreciation of Chinese Geomancy"; Bennett, "Patterns of the Sky and Earth"; Smith, *Fortune-Tellers and Philosophers*, chap. 4. For Chu Hsi's mention and discussion of the *feng-shui*, see chap. 12 of this volume, p. 266.

122. This was how Chu Hsi interpreted the above-mentioned *Analects* phrase "A multitude of stars pay homage to it [i.e., the north ch'en]" (2.1). E.g., *YL*23.1b0, 1b2–2a0, 2a1, 3a0.

123. *YL*1.9a0.

124. *YL*2.4b1.

125. E.g., *YL*23.1b2, 2b0, 3a0; 101.31b4.

126. E.g., *YL*23.1b2, 2a2, 3a0. In these passages Chu Hsi used the word "the north *ch'en*" for the north pole.

127. E.g., *YL*2.6b2; 23.3a1; 101.32a3; *WC*72.1a. In *YL*2.6b2 Chu Hsi called the north and south poles "the pivot of the heavens" and went on to compare them to the umbilical cord in man's body.

128. *YL*23.2a2.

129. E.g., *YL*23.2a1, 2; 3a1; 5b0. On the traditional Chinese ideas about the pole star, see Huang, "Chi-hsing yü ku-tu k'ao."

130. *YL*23.3a1. Shen Kua's observation is reported in his *Meng-hsi pi-t'an*, 7.18.

131. E.g., *YL*23.2a1, 2a2–2b0; 86.11a1.

132. E.g., *YL*2.3a2, 4a0; *Ch'u-tz'u chi-chu*, 3.99. Chu Hsi also used the traditional Chinese convention of counting degrees, according to which the full circumference of a circle is 365¼ degrees. See p. 150.

133. E.g., *YL*2.3a2; 4b1, 2; 9a2.

134. *YL*2.5a1.

135. E.g., *YL*2.1b1, 3a2, 4a0, 5a1; *Ch'u-tz'u chi-chu*, 3.98–99.

136. *YL*2.3b1. See also *WCH*3.10b.

137. *YL*2.3a2.

138. *Shih chi-chuan*, p. 148. See also *YL*2.9a4, in which Chu Hsi added: "Therefore it [i.e., the Metal star] is seen on half-moon days"; this remark is impossible to accept, because Mercury can actually be seen either shortly before the sunrise or shortly after the sunset on any clear night. In *YL*81.21b2 he also made an unlikely comment on the movement of these "minor planets":

> The Metal [star] is located to the west of the sun. Therefore, when the sun is about to rise, it is seen on the east. The Water [star] is located to the east of the sun. Therefore, when the sun is about to set, it is seen on the west.

For a brief discussion of the consequences of the proximity of the minor planets to the sun, see Kuhn, *Copernican Revolution*, pp. 48–49.

139. E.g., *YL*68.16b4; *CS*50.8b0.

140. *YL*23.2b0. See also *CS*50.9a0.

141. E.g., *YL*2.6b3–7a0, 7a2; 23.2b0, 3a0; *WC*72.1a.

142. *YL*2.1a3.

143. *YL*78.13b0.

144. E.g., *YL*2.1a4, 5.

145. E.g., *CS*50.9a0, 23b3–24a0.

146. *WC*45.37b. Shen Kua's own remark appears, in a different form, in his *Meng-hsi pi-t'an*, 8.5–6. Whereas Shen Kua mentioned two each of the four different paths, thus making nine paths in heaven, including the Yellow Path, Chu Hsi spoke of "the five paths," counting each of the four just once. *YL*2.1a4. See *CS*50.23b3–24a0, where a passage is reproduced from *Ching-chi wen-heng* (A9.10a), compiled by T'eng Kung, a disciple of Chu Hsi, which says that the moon's path deviates from the Yellow Path by as much as six degrees.

147. For a discussion of various reference positions in heaven, see, e.g., Needham, *Science and Civilisation*, 3:229–262, esp. fig. 91 on p. 243, which shows the three sets. See also Ch'en, *Chung-kuo t'ien-wen-hsueh-shih*, vol. 2, esp. pp. 51–136, 167–176.

148. *YL*1.8b7. See also *YL*97.3b1; *WC*58.38b; *Ch'u-tz'u chi-chu*, 3.98.

149. *Ch'u-tz'u chi-chu*, 3.98.

150. *YL*2.3b1–4a0. See also *YL*36.23b0; *Ch'u-tz'u chi-chu*, 3.99.

151. E.g., *YL*2.1b0, 2a0, 4a0; 138.8a1, 10b3; *Ch'u-tz'u chi-chu*, 5.200, 206.

152. See *Ch'u-tz'u chi-chu*, 3.98, where Chu Hsi traced this idea to *Tso-chuan* and its commentary. See also *YL*2.1a2; 23.2b0.

153. *YL*23.2a1. See also *YL*23.2b0.

154. E.g., Waley, *Analects of Confucius*, p. 88. See p. 144 of this book. There are passages in which Chu Hsi equated the north *ch'en* with the north pole (e.g., *YL*23.1b2, 3a0; *WC*72.11a), but he never referred to the pole star itself as the north *ch'en*. Cf. *YL*23.2a1: "*Ch'en* is a great star."

155. *YL*23.2a2. See also *YL*23.2b0.

156. *YL*2.5b0.

157. E.g., *YL*2.1a2, 1b1, 12b2. Chu Hsi used the convention of referring to the right angle as "near by one and far by three" (*chin-i yüan-san*). E.g., *YL*2.6b0; 7b1, 2;

79.27a0; *WC*45.38a. It was so called because the right angle divides the circumference of a circle into two segments whose lengths are in the ratio of one to three. Moreover, in the 365¼-degree system, the number of degrees in the right angle does not amount to a neat 90 but would come out as 91.31 . . .

158. *CS*50.8b0–9a0. See note 49.

159. E.g., *YL*1.9a0; 36.23b0; 73.3b2; 86.9a1.

160. *YL*1.9a0.

161. *YL*86.9a1. But Chu Hsi did not explicitly attribute these phenomena to the precession of equinoxes.

162. *YL*2.13b1.

163. *YL*86.9a1.

164. Yamada Keiji thinks it natural that Chu Hsi should take the earth to be rotating along with the *ch'i* of heaven, which also rotated. *Shushi no shizen-gaku*, pp. 175, 179. It is possible to trace this idea back to a remark in an apocryphal treatise, *Ch'un-chiu yüan-ming-pao*, that the earth turns rightward while heaven rotates leftward. Quoted in, e.g., *I-wen lei-chü*, 6.100. Yamada rejects this possibility, however, and sees a great originality in the similar idea of Chang Tsai, which is likely to have been Chu Hsi's source. *Shushi no shizen-gaku*, pp. 29, 40–45.

165. *YL*86.10a1. Yamada considers this movement of the earth to be "revolution" (*kung-chuan*) as opposed to rotation around its own axis (*tzu-chuan*); he emphasizes that Chu Hsi had both ideas: *Shushi no shizen-gaku*, p. 179.

The idea of "the four wanderings" appeared in various ancient sources, including the *Chou-pei suan-ching*, and was variously interpreted as movements of the earth, heaven, or the luminaries. For brief discussions of "the four wanderings" and the movement of the earth in general, see, e.g., Yamada, *Shushi no shizen-gaku*, pp. 29–31, 171–184; Chung-kuo t'ien-wen-hsueh shih cheng-li yen-chiu hsiao-tsu, *Chung-kuo t'ien-wen-hsueh shih*, pp. 171–173.

166. *YL*86.10b0.

167. *YL*100.6a2.

168. *YL*72.4b1.

169. *YL*2.7a4. See also *YL*2.5b0, 6a0, 7a3, 7b2; 79.27a0; 137.12a2–12b0; *WC*45.38a; *Ch'u-tz'u chi-chu*, 3.100. We have already seen Chu Hsi's reason that the moon could receive the light of the sun that was below the earth on a full-moon day: the earth covered only a very small portion of the plane of the horizon so that the sunlight could reach the moon, passing through the empty spaces around the earth. See, e.g., *YL*2.5b0, 6a0, 13a1; 79.27a0. Also see p. 142. In *YL*2.7b2 an interlocutor attributes this explanation to Ts'ai Yüan-ting and Chu Hsi accepts it.

170. For brief discussions of the early Chinese understanding of eclipses and their records of them, see, e.g., Needham, *Science and Civilisation*, 3:409–423; Chung-kuo t'ien-wen-hsueh shih cheng-li yen-chiu hsiao-tsu, *Chung-kuo t'ien-wen-hsueh shih*, pp. 120–127.

171. E.g., *YL*2.1b0; 5b0; 8b2, 3; 79.27a0; *Shih chi-chuan*, p. 132.

172. *WC*47.10b.

173. *YL*2.9a1. It is to be noted, however, that here Chu Hsi characterized the eclipses as "decay of yin and yang *ch'i*."

174. E.g., *YL*2.5b0; 79.27a0. There was a time when Chu Hsi added another reason, namely that even when the sun's and the moon's apparent positions on the vault exactly coincided with each other, the sun might sometimes be inside the moon's path and thus could not be blocked by the moon. *WC*45.38a. He illustrated this by comparing it to a situation in which one person holding a candle (representing the sun) and one holding a fan (the moon) pass each other while still another person is looking at them from inside (the observer on earth):

When the two persons are at a distance from one another, the fan cannot block the candle even if the fan is inside and the candle is outside. On the other hand, if the person holding the candle is inside and the one holding the fan is outside, then the fan cannot block the candle even when [they] are close [to each other].

Chu Hsi attributed this idea to the sub-commentary of K'ung Ying-ta (574–648) to *Shih-ching*:

> Every month [the sun and the moon] always meet each other. But the moon is sometimes on the outside of the sun's path and sometimes on the inside of the sun's path, and therefore [the moon] is not eclipsed. (12B.3a)

> While the sun and the moon move in heaven, each has its own path. Even when they meet on the new-moon days, their paths have inside and outside. If the moon is inside, [there are] many cases in which it lies inside the boundary and is eclipsed. If the moon is outside, even when it lies inside the boundary, [there are] a small number of cases in which it is eclipsed. (12B.4a)

Yamada Keiji interprets the words "inside" and "outside" in these quotations as referring to "the north" and "the south" of the sun's path and not to "farther" and "nearer" from the earth. *Shushi no shizen-gaku,* pp. 259–260.

The above idea of Chu Hsi's appears to have been a passing thought, which did not recur in his discussions. In fact, in a conversation that records his established view in late years, Chu Hsi said, "The moon is always below, and the sun is always above." *YL2.1bo.* Nor did he pursue its consequence on the problem of the relative distances of the sun and the moon from the earth. Always concerned with the apparent positions of the sun and the moon projected onto the vault, and not with their actual positions, he treated the actual distances of these bodies very casually. He does not seem to have realized that the possibility of the larger distance for the moon than for the sun was in conflict with his own explanation, for example, of the phase of the new moon, which was based on the fact that the sun is farther from the earth than the moon is. Apparently, once he was satisfied with his explanation in each case, whether the two were

compatible with each other in terms of the relative distances of the sun and the moon did not concern him very much. For a more general discussion of this tendency in Chu Hsi's thought, see chap. 14, sec. 14.3.

175. For the development of and changes in Chu Hsi's views on the lunar eclipse, see, e.g., Yamada, *Shushi no shizen-gaku,* pp. 256–266.

176. E.g., *YL2.1bo;* 8b2, 3; *Shih chi-chuan,* p. 132. One source of this idea is the *Huai-nan-tzu* passage "When the moon is full, the sun takes away its light. [It is because] yin cannot mount on [top of] yang" (16.3a).

177. *YL2.8a3–8bo.* There Chu Hsi wrongly attributes the explanation to Ch'eng I. Ch'eng Hao's saying appears in *Ho-nan Ch'eng-shih i-shu,* ch. 11 (*ECC,* p. 130).

178. *YL2.8b3.*

179. *YL79.27bo.* Thus, it was in discussing this explanation that Chu Hsi spoke of the virtuous conduct of the ruler preventing lunar eclipses by making "yang flourish so that [it] overcomes yin and yin decay [so that it] cannot invade yang." *Shih chi-chuan,* p. 132. See chap. 8, p. 123.

180. *YL79. 27ao–27bo.*

181. E.g., Yamada, *Shushi no shizen-gaku,* p. 264.

182. *YL79.27ao* (in small print – see chap. 8, note 20). See also *YL2.1bo,* in which Chu Hsi explained the expression "dark gap," in the following manner: "Fire and the sun have reflections outside and real darkness inside them."

183. E.g., Chang Heng, *Ling Hsien.*

184. It might have been that for Chu Hsi, the earth, a dark and heavy body, was different from the bright luminaries and thus could not interfere with them in the manner that they interfere with one another: the moon, a luminary, could cause an eclipse of another luminary, the sun, by blocking it, but the earth could not block the moon in a similar way. In fact, when, in a remark recorded earlier (*YL2.6bo,* perhaps in 1179), Chu Hsi did attribute the

lunar eclipse to a blocking, it was the sun, and not the earth, that blocked the moon from inside, a situation rather difficult to understand:

> Only when the moon moves outside the sun and blocks the sun from inside, there is a solar eclipse. When the sun moves outside the moon and blocks the moon from inside, there is a lunar eclipse.

185. *YL*24.26a1.

186. *WC*45.37b.

187. *YL*86.10b0.

188. In *YL*2.13b1, which has been quoted on pp. 151–152 (note 162), however, Chu Hsi mentioned another such variation —that is, of the speed of the heaven's rotation—as a possible cause of the seasonal change of weather.

189. *YL*74.25a0.

190. *YL*65.1b3–2a0. See also *YL*65.1b2. Although Chu Hsi is speaking of consecutive divisions of a year defined as a period from one winter solstice to the next one, the twelve lunar months do not result from these divisions; they are based on the motion of the moon, whereas the winter solstice is defined by that of the sun. An actual result of such consecutive divisions is the system of the twenty-four seasonal periods, defined by the twenty-four seasonal points (*chieh-ch'i*) with names alluding to seasonal characteristics, such as "beginning of spring" (*li-ch'un*), "small cold" (*hsiao-han*), and "great heat" (*ta-shu*). For the names and approximate dates of all the twenty-four seasonal points, see, e.g., Needham, *Science and Civilisation*, 3:405. For Chu Hsi's mention of the seasonal points, see, e.g., *YL*2.12a4, 7; 71.12b1; 78.12b6–13a0, 13a1.

191. *YL*74.25a0.

192. *WC*38.10b. From this Chu Hsi went on to explain why people of the Hsia dynasty chose the *yin* position (corresponding to ☶) as the first month of a year. In *WC*38.8b Chu Hsi referred to this association of the twelve hexagrams with the twelve terrestrial branches as the theory of "the calendar specialists" and contrasted it

with the theory of "the ritual specialists" (*li-chia*) that "the gentle *ch'i* flourishes in the southeast, while the severe *ch'i* flourishes in the northwest" and with the theory of the "Shuo-kua chuan" commentary of the *I-ching* that associates the southeast with the *sun* trigram and the northwest with the *ch'ien* trigram.

193. *YL*74.25b0.

194. *Ch'u-tz'u chi-chu*, 3.109.

195. *YL*138.5a1. In fact, as we have seen, the seasonal weather was among "the small events" that, unlike "the great events," can be altered. *YL*79.6b2. See chap. 8, p. 124.

196. E.g., *YL*2.14a4, 5; *WC*58.38b; *CS*50.46a1–47a0. A long quotation from Yü Ching's *Hai-chao t'u-lun* is appended to *CS*50.46a1. For a brief historical discussion of the tidal theories in China, see Needham, *Science and Civilisation*, 3:483–494; Yamada, *Shushi no shizen-gaku*, pp. 387–390.

197. E.g., *YL*2.14a5; *Ch'u-tz'u chi-chu*, 4.195.

198. *WC*58.38b.

199. *YL*2.14a4.

200. *WC*58.38b, immediately following the passage cited in note 198.

201. E.g., *YL*1.5b2.

202. For a brief discussion of meteorological knowledge in traditional China, see Needham, *Science and Civilisation*, 3:462–483. See also Yamada, *Shushi no shizen-gaku*, pp. 373–375.

203. E.g., *YL*2.10a2.

204. *YL*99.3a4. Chang Tsai's theory appears in *Chang-tzu ch'üan-shu*, 2.10b–11a.

205. *YL*100.6b1. Ch'eng I's remark (*Ho-nan Ch'eng-shih i-shu*, ch. 18: *ECC*, p. 238) is not explicit about the actual difference between dew and frost:

> Frost and dew are different. Frost is Metal *ch'i*; it is the *ch'i* of stars and moon. Dew is also the *ch'i* of stars and moon. Looking at them, one can perceive which *ch'i* makes dew and which *ch'i* makes frost. To say that dew is congealed to become frost is wrong.

206. We have also seen Chu Hsi's acceptance of Chang Tsai's division of meteorological phenomena into harmonious ones (rain, snow, dew, and frost) and inharmonious ones (fog and hail). Cf. *Huai-nan-tzu*, 3.1b, which speaks of related, but still different, divisions:

> The raging [portion] of the one-sided *ch'i* of heaven becomes wind; the harmonious [portion] of the *ch'i* contained by the earth becomes rain. Yin and yang clashing against each other, stimulated they become thunder, roused they become lightning, and confused they become fog. When yang *ch'i* prevails, it is dispersed to become rain and dew; when yin *ch'i* prevails, it is congealed to become frost and snow.

207. YL77.6a3. This is a comment on the "Shuo-kua chuan" passage "Mountains and marshes exchange the *ch'i*." (ch. 3).

208. YL2.9b3. This is in direct opposition to Ch'eng I's view that both frost and dew were the *ch'i* of stars and moon: cf. note 205. Chu Hsi agreed with Ch'eng I, though, that dew was Metal *ch'i*; he explained, "Dew naturally has the appearance of *ch'i* that is clear and clean." YL100.6b1.

209. Shao Yung's associations of rain with land animals, wind with birds, dew with grasses, and thunder with trees, about which a disciple asked a question to Chu Hsi, could be understood in terms of such divisions. As we have seen in chapter 4, land animals were animals (yang things) receiving yin *ch'i*, whereas birds received yang *ch'i*; trees were plants (yin things) receiving yang *ch'i*, and grasses received yin *ch'i*. Chu Hsi's reply was that it was "choosing and matching what are large and small." See YL100.6b1. Shao Yung referred to these meteorological phenomena as "transformed things" (*hua-wu*).

210. YL86.8a0.

211. E.g., YL2.13b0; 45.7b0.

212. YL2.9b2.

213. E.g., YL2.6a0, 9b4–10a0. See p. 139.

214. YL86.8a0.

215. E.g., YL2.9b2; 86.7b2.

216. YL86.7b2.

217. YL2.10a3. The Ch'engs' actual saying appears in *Ho-nan Ch'eng-shih i-shu*, ch. 2B (*ECC*, p. 57):

> Lightning is a mutual grinding of yin and yang; thunder is a mutual striking (*ch'i*) of yin and yang. Grinding is like stones rubbing each other so that fire and light come out. [The reason that when there is] lightning, there is a striking of thunder is [because of] this.

218. E.g., YL2.10b1; 72.18a1.

219. YL97.3b1.

220. YL70.11b3. See also YL2.10a2; 70.11b2. The *I-ching* phrase comes from the comments on the *hsiao-ch'u* hexagram.

221. YL99.4a1. In the ancient sources, however, the distinction was made in the opposite way: e.g., in *Erh-ya*, 6.9a, where it is said that "when the *ch'i* of heaven descends but the earth does not respond, then it is called *meng*; when the *ch'i* of earth goes forth but the heaven does not respond, then it is called *wu*."

222. YL2.9b4–10a0.

223. YL2.10a1. In the omitted portion of the passage, Chu Hsi mentioned a certain stone, *t'ai-yin hsüan-ching-shih*, whose crystal is also of a hexagonal shape. The hexagonal shape of a snowflake was known as early as the second century B.C., as it is mentioned in Han, *Han-shih wai-chuan*: "In general, flowers of plants come often in five; only snowflakes come in six (quoted in *T'ai-p'ing yü-lan*, ch. 2).

224. YL2.9b3.

225. YL2.9b3. Thus, Chu Hsi could not agree with Ch'eng I, who rejected this belief: "In the ancient sayings, it is said that dew is congealed to become frost. To look at it now, it appears to be true. I-ch'üan said it is not so. I do not know the reason why." YL100.6b1. For Ch'eng I's remark, see note 205.

226. YL2.9b4. The word that I translate here as "the moist *ch'i*" is "*wu ch'i*," literally "the fog *ch'i*."

227. In *YL*2.9b3 Chu Hsi spoke of the high mountains in the extreme western region, where, it is said, there is no snow or rain.

228. *YL*99.3a4.

229. *Shih chi-chuan*, p. 32.

230. E.g., *YL*2.10b5–11a0; 3.2b2–3a0; *Shih chi-chuan*, p. 32.

231. *YL*2.11a0.

232. *YL*2.10b5. Ch'eng I's remark and Chang Tsai's skeptical response appear in *Ho-nan Ch'eng-shih i-shu*, ch. 10 (ECC, p. 112).

233. In *YL*3.3a0, which is likely to have been recorded later, Chu Hsi is more skeptical: "If the creative transformation used this thing [i.e., a lizard] to make hail, then this creative transformation is small indeed."

234. After this he ends the passage with the following remark: "The character *pao* (hail) is [made] from [the characters] *yü* (rain) and *pao* (to surround). [The reason] is that this *ch'i* surrounds and stops and thus makes the hail."

235. *Shih chi-chuan*, p. 32.

236. *YL*2.10b3.

237. See also *YL*3.3b1, in which Chu Hsi says: "If it can drink water, it must have intestines and stomach. When dispersed, there is none." Shen Kua also mentioned the popular belief that "the rainbow can enter a mountain stream and drink water." *Meng-hsi pi-t'an*, 21.1.

238. *YL*2.10b4. See also *Ch'u-tz'u chi-chu*, 1.37. This idea can be traced back to a remark by Sun Ssu-kung (1015–1076), which Shen Kua quoted in his *Meng-hsi pi-t'an*, 21.2: "The rainbow is the sun's reflection in raindrops. When the sun shines on the rain, then there is it [i.e., the rainbow]."

239. *YL*2.10a2.

240. *YL*3.3a0.

241. *YL*97.3b1. Here Chu Hsi was discussing Ch'eng I's remarks about such a belief. Ch'eng I said, for example: "When a man does an evil [act], he has evil *ch'i*. [This *ch'i*] and the evil *ch'i* of heaven and earth strike each other, and then shake [the man] to death." *Ho-nan Ch'eng-shih i-shu*, ch. 18 (ECC, p. 237).

242. E.g., *YL*2.10b0; 3.3b1; 87.14b3; 125.5a2.

243. *YL*2.10b0.

244. *YL*125.5a2.

245. *YL*2.10b2.

CHAPTER 10

The Myriad Things

Chu Hsi's idea of "the myriad things" (*wan-wu*) covers both living beings—animals and plants—and inanimate things, although by that word he almost always referred to living beings, especially animals. This is to be expected because for him, as we have noted, there was no clear distinction between life and matter. A key to his lack of distinction is the concept of *ch'i*, which was endowed with qualities of life. For Chu Hsi, the same *ch'i* was responsible both for the physical and the material aspects of nonliving things and for the physiological and the psychic aspects of the living world.

10.1. Differences among the "Myriad Things"

An idea that Chu Hsi used in distinguishing living beings was "life intent" (*sheng-i*). According to him, only living things had life intent; lifeless or dead things did not have it.[1] I translate the term as "life intent" because with it Chu Hsi seemed to refer to some kind of latent potential, power, or even intention that living beings possess to be alive.[2] For example, it was because plants had life intent that they could sprout buds and leaves and produce flowers.[3] And once there was life intent, it could not be stopped:

> When the sun shines upon [the flowering trees] in the morning, they flourish joyfully [i.e., blossom]. Once there is this life intent, the skin cannot contain and hold it [inside]. It spontaneously squeezes out.[4]

> When [a planted seed that] is about to sprout has not [done so] for the lack of a little rain, and [if it] suddenly gets that little rain, then how can the life intent be held in check?[5]

Yet, it appears that what Chu Hsi had in mind was not the distinction between life and matter in general but that between the living and dead states of living beings. The examples that he mentioned as things without life intent were not inanimate objects but typically were such things as grain seeds that had been steamed, plant sprouts that had been stepped upon and broken, and dried and rotten things that had once been alive.[6]

Chu Hsi seemed to believe that life intent actually existed inside living things. For example, it existed in the plant body throughout a year from spring to winter:

> To speak of grain, in spring it comes out, in summer it forms sprouts, in autumn it produces crops, in winter it is stored up. Life intent is contained inside as always.[7]

> Come winter, one [may] suspect that the tree does not have life intent. But [this is so because one] does not know that life intent is spontaneously converged at the bottom.[8]

Moreover, life intent existed in all parts of the plant body:

> To speak of a tree, every branch and every leaf, there is none that does not have life intent. If there is just a small place where [the life intent] is interrupted, the branches and leaves will have a place where they are not flourishing.[9]

He also said, "After sprouts have come out from [the seeds], their skins contain [life intent] inside."[10]

As something that actually exists, life intent must have its basis in *ch'i*. Chu Hsi suggested that living things made "the *ch'i* converge and congeal . . . life intent."[11] He sometimes used the expression "life-*ch'i*" (*sheng-ch'i*), to refer to such *ch'i*:

> When one has planted a seed in the soil, life-*ch'i* spontaneously gathers around it. If it is already placed upside down [i.e., separated from the soil], life-*ch'i* has no place to attach itself to. From where can it come to contact [with life-*ch'i*]? It is like a man who has a disease. If he has life-*ch'i* himself, the *ch'i* of the power of medicine will rely on it [i.e., the life-*ch'i*], and life intent will grow. If [his condition] has already become dangerous, life-*ch'i* will scatter away and not gather again.[12]

To be more specific, the branches and leaves of a tree flourish when life-*ch'i* flows into them from the roots;[13] life-*ch'i* is manifest also when flowers bloom and fruits are formed.[14] Thus, life-*ch'i* was among Chu Hsi's criteria that distinguished "the dried and withered" things (which do not have life-*ch'i*) from plants and animals (which have it).[15] And, as we have seen, it is to borrow their life-*ch'i* that living things or blood and meat are used as sacrificial objects.[16]

Chu Hsi also used the word "*sheng-li*" (which could be rendered literally as "life-*li*") in a way more or less similar to the way he used "life intent." He said, for example: "Each fruit possesses *sheng-li*. Then one sees 'the intent of ceaselessly coming into being' (*sheng-sheng pu-ch'iung chih i*)."[17] But he did not restrict its use to living things alone. Without any clear distinction between living and inanimate things, *sheng-li*, for him, was the *li* by which things—both living and lifeless—came into being as they were. Thus, even a piece of dried wood must have "the *li* of coming into being as it is" (*sheng-li*), though it does not have life intent or life-*ch'i*.[18] He said: "When one burns a certain wood, it becomes a certain *ch'i*, and for each [wood, the *ch'i*] is not the same. This is because [for each *ch'i*] the *li* [of coming into being] is originally like this."[19]

Although Chu Hsi did not make a clear distinction between living and nonliving things, he did speak of various other differences among the myriad things. First, there was the idea of differences in the levels or statuses of things—indeed, of all beings including man. We can even detect from Chu Hsi a notion of the "scale of beings," in which man was at the top; below man are animals and plants, and inanimate objects are at the bottom.[20] He said, for example:

> In heaven's production of things, there are those that have blood-*ch'i* (*hsueh-ch'i*) and perception (*chih-chüeh*): men and animals are those. There are those that do not have blood-*ch'i* and perception but have life-*ch'i*: grasses and trees are those. There are those whose life-*ch'i* is already extinct but which have physical form, tangible qualities, smells, and tastes: the dried and withered [things] are those. . . . Therefore, men are the most numinous and are complete with the nature of the five constant virtues. Birds and beasts are dark and cannot be complete. As for grasses, trees, and dried and withered things, they are also equal to those with perception, but [their perception] is lost.[21]

This, of course, is a consequence of difference, and gradation, in the endowments of *ch'i* in different things:

> Speaking in terms of their *ch'i*, those that receive what is correct and penetrating become men. Those that receive what is one-sided and obstructed become things. This is why some are noble and some humble, and cannot become equal.[22]

These quotations show Chu Hsi's various distinction schemes for men and the myriad things: men–things; men and animals–plants–inanimate things; men–animals–plants and inanimate things. Of these he was most interested, of course, in the distinction between men and nonhuman things. For him, man was unique among all living beings. Man was not even considered as part of "the myriad things"; he never referred to man with the character *wu*. Chu Hsi repeatedly said that man was endowed with *ch'i* that was correct, clear, complete, penetrating, balanced, numinous, and excellent (*hsiu*), whereas things were endowed with *ch'i* that was turbid, one-sided, dark, obstructed, and screened (*pi*).[23] Because of these differences, man is bright, numinous, and complete, whereas things are dark, muddled, ignorant, and one-sided.[24]

For Chu Hsi the key difference that distinguished man from nonhuman things lay in the human ethical virtues.

> For example, to eat when hungry and to drink when thirsty, and to seek profits and to avoid damages—man can do these, and so can birds and beasts. If [a man] did not discern righteousness and *li*, he would be the same as them.[25]

Chu Hsi also mentioned the five human relationships (*wu-lun*) as what distinguished man from animals:

> The difference of man from birds and beasts is the fact that fathers and sons have affection, rulers and subjects have righteousness, husbands and wives have distinction, elders and youths have order, and friends have trust.[26]

Chu Hsi admitted that animals could have some human virtues; but they could not have all of them:

> [As for] perception and motion, man is capable of them, and so are things. However, [to speak of] humaneness, righteousness, propriety, and knowledge, although things certainly have them, how can they be complete with [all of] them?[27]

The difference most frequently mentioned by Chu Hsi was that man manifests all the ethical virtues, whereas nonhuman things can at best be one-sided in their virtues. He said:

> Man's mind is empty and numinous and can contain and circulate many ways and *li* in it; there is no obstruction. Even if there is some *ch'i* inside whose endowments are dark, [man's mind] can still overcome and make it bright. The mind of myriad things does not contain and circulate many ways and *li*. Although there is [a part] inside it [that] can be endowed with *ch'i* that is a little correct, it still stops at being bright in one or two aspects [literally, "routes"]. For example, among birds and beasts there are those kinds that have mutual love between fathers and sons and a distinction between male and female [partners]. [But] they have only one or two aspects [in which their *ch'i* are] bright. The other ways and *li* are all obstructed.[28]

Chu Hsi frequently mentioned examples of particular ethical virtues manifested by animals, and even by some plants. For example, tigers show humaneness and know the proper relationship between fathers and sons; otters offer sacrifices to ancestors; cats nurse other cats' kittens; some birds show filial piety; *chü-chiu* birds[29] manifest the proper distinction between male and female partners; ants and bees manifest righteousness and the ruler-subject relationship.[30] Chu Hsi even saw the father-son relationship between tall and short trees.[31] He also mentioned the lichee and the peony as plants that "manifest various exquisiteness."[32] Yet, his point in all these was that these "things" manifest only these particular virtues and no others.

Chu Hsi pointed out the one-sidedness also in the knowledge and the abilities of animals: "Dogs can [only] watch guards; cows can only till lands. As for man, there is nothing that he does not know or cannot do."[33] A consequence of this was that whereas nonhuman things can "penetrate" (*t'ung*) the single aspects that they concentrate on, "man can understand all events to some degree but superficially, so that [the understanding] becomes easily muddled."[34] In contrast, even though man is at times endowed with *ch'i* that is turbid or obstructed, it can be opened up and penetrated, through edification by sages, for example; the obstructed *ch'i* of animals cannot be opened up or penetrated.[35]

Of course, there are other features distinguishing man from animals. Chu Hsi took the ability to speak as such a characteristic. Speech is what distinguishes man from the macacus monkey, for example, "the shape [of which] is similar to man, and [which] is more numinous than other things. It is simply that it cannot speak."[36] Man's upright stance is another example mentioned by Chu Hsi. He had a scheme of distinguishing man, animals, and plants based on the stance:

> What is based on heaven is inclined upward; what is based on earth is inclined down-ward. For example, man's head faces upward, and thus [man] is the most numinous. The heads of grasses and trees face downward, and thus they are the most ignorant. The heads of birds and beasts are sideways, and they are ignorant. Gibbons and monkeys are numi-nous to some degree, for sometimes their heads are like man's and thus can face upward to some degree.[37]

He even attributed the difference in the qualities of the *ch'i* of man and things to the difference in their stance: man stands upright and receives the correct and clear *ch'i* of heaven and earth, whereas "things" do not stand upright and thus receive the one-sided and turbid *ch'i*.[38]

Chu Hsi noted the similarity of monkeys to man in these quotations. He also spoke of the wild fox, which can stand upright like man and walk a few steps in that stance.[39] But he also thought that some men were close to animals: "If [a man] loses his numinous [nature] and muddles it, then how can he be distinguished from birds and beasts?"[40] He even said: "When it comes to barbarian tribes, they lie in be-tween men and animals."[41] Thus, the remark that man manifests all virtues was not a descriptive but rather a normative statement. Not all men can manifest all virtues; such an ideal man appears very rarely. In fact, there are differences in the quality of men owing to differences in the endowments of their *ch'i*: "To talk about [the *ch'i* with which] men are endowed, there also are the differences of dark versus bright and clear versus turbid."[42] Chu Hsi had a classification of men according to their ethical qualities:

> A great man (*chün-tzu*) is one who accomplishes every affair. Thus it is said, "a great man is not a [mere] instrument." As for a good man (*shan-jen*), he does not reach [the level of] a great man. [He] merely is one who knows that some things are good and some bad and is willing to do good and unwilling to do bad. A common man (*ch'ang-che*) does not even reach [the level of] a good man. He is merely one who more or less complies with his own role.[43]

Differences in the endowments of *ch'i* cause differences among nonhuman beings also. For example, Chu Hsi attributed the difference in the natures of the dog and the cow, or of the gibbon and the pig, to the difference in their endowed *ch'i*.[44] But he also spoke of divisions and subdivisions of nonhuman things more generally. We have already seen some distinguishing characteristics between plants and animals:

stance, blood-*ch'i*, and perception (*chih-chüeh*), for example. What he seems to have considered the most important, however, was that animals have knowledge whereas plants do not.[45] Even such small animals as lice have knowledge, "biting men when hungry, for example,"[46] but plants do not have it. Chu Hsi admitted that plants have a quality similar to knowledge, referring to the fact that when they are injured they become dry, never to flourish again; but for him this merely represented the effect of the loss of life intent, not the capacity for knowledge.[47] He also held that plants do not have perception, as we have seen. Thus, the fact that plants facing the sunny side flourish, whereas those facing the shadowy side wither, made him willing to admit that plants have mind but not perception.[48] That belief also caused him to consider it strange that plant bodies are durable and do not decay easily, whereas the bodies of animals, which have perception, decay quickly after death.[49]

Exactly what Chu Hsi thought about the word *chih-chüeh* is not clear, however. Sometimes it had the rather broad meaning of "consciousness."[50] His ideas about it seem to have varied over time, also. For in a conversation recorded very late in his life (later than 1198), he was willing to say that not only plants but even decayed things have perception, thus greatly broadening the meaning of the word:

> QUESTION: Do grasses and trees also have perception?
> ANSWER: They also do. For example, if a flower in a pot gets a little water sprayed on it, it blossoms. If [it is] injured and pressed upon, it dries up. Is it possible to say that it does not have perception? . . . It is simply that the perception of birds and beasts is different from that of man, and the perception of grasses and trees is still different from that of birds and beasts. For another example, the rhubarb, when eaten, can cause diarrhea; wolfsbane, when eaten, can cause fever. It is simply that their perceptions are effective in these aspects [literally, "go only along these single routes"].
> QUESTION: Do rotten and decayed things also have perception?
> ANSWER: They also do. If they are burnt by fire to form ashes, made into soup and eaten, [they taste] hot and bitter.[51]

Chu Hsi used the yin-yang scheme in making divisions and subdivisions of animals and plants, as we have seen:

> Grasses and trees all receive yin *ch'i*. Land animals and birds all receive yang *ch'i*. To divide each [further], grasses receive yin *ch'i* and trees receive yang *ch'i*. Therefore, grasses are soft and trees are hard. Land animals receive yin *ch'i*; birds receive yang *ch'i*. Therefore, land animals lie on grasses and birds live in trees. Yet, among land animals there also are those that receive yang *ch'i*. Animals like gibbons and monkeys are those. Among birds there also are those that receive yin *ch'i*. Birds like pheasants are those. Although grasses and trees all receive yin *ch'i*, there nevertheless are yin inside yang and yang inside yin.[52]

He also spoke of the difference between the straight, hard plants that are endowed with the "vigorous" yang *ch'i* and the soft and weak plants endowed with the "obedient" yin *ch'i*.[53]

10.2. Inanimate Things

We cannot enumerate all the inanimate things that Chu Hsi mentioned. Some things came up more frequently in his conversations, however, either because they were familiar or because they were useful in discussing problems that he deemed important. For example, he often spoke of water and fire and their various qualities in discussing the human mind and human nature. The mirror, with its light and the dust that covers it, is another example frequently employed by Chu Hsi in similar discussions. There were also houses and bridges, such everyday items as rice, salt, silk, and liquor, and such moving things as carts, boats, waterwheels, and millstones.[54] Of course there were many more. These, along with animals and plants, were what constituted "the myriad things" for Chu Hsi.

Of these examples, water and fire are different from the rest in that they are not concrete objects but material substances. They came up in Chu Hsi's discussion much more frequently than the others because they were endowed with many general qualities that could be used in discussing other problems. Chu Hsi also spoke of many other material substances and their qualities. To give just a few examples, he mentioned the use of different kinds of substances from the earth—such as sand, mud, lime, coal, and pitch—for making graves: coal repels moisture and plant roots, whereas mud attracts the roots; pitch cannot stand the underground heat; when lime is mixed with sand, it becomes as hard as stone.[55] Metals like gold, silver, and iron were frequently mentioned in his discussions of mental states: the loss of the quality of gold when a small amount of silver is mixed illustrated the loss of "sincerity"; iron covered with silver outside illustrated the state of "self-deceit."[56] He also mentioned mercury in illustrating the ceaseless "flow" of the *li* of heaven, because mercury constantly rolls and escapes and cannot be seized by hand.[57] He spoke of vinegar that had lost its acidity and compared this "unworthy" vinegar to a man unworthy of his high position.[58]

The substances most frequently mentioned by Chu Hsi, however, were water and fire. He referred to many qualities and tendencies of them—not only that fire is hot and water is cold,[59] but also that water is deep and wet, it moistens things, and it tends to move downward, whereas fire tends to move upward, boils, and dries and burns things.[60] He considered these qualities and tendencies innate to water and fire; for him they were "natures" or "virtues" (*te*) of water and fire. He said:

> One only knows that ministers ought to be loyal, that sons ought to be filial, that the nature of fire is originally hot, and that the nature of water is originally cold. One does not know the reasons why ministers are loyal, sons are filial, fire is hot, and water is cold.[61]

He also said: "As for the warmth of spring, heaven produces it naturally so. It is like fire. When it burns, it is hot in itself; it is not that [burning] makes it hot."[62]

A few characteristics of water were particularly suited for use in analogies having to do with moral and philosophical problems. One is the dichotomy of clear versus turbid water. Chu Hsi frequently compared water to the mind in such a manner that its clarity is translated into clarity of mind. For example, water is originally clear; it is mud, sand, and other sediments that make the originally clear water turbid.[63] Turbid water becomes clear as those things making it turbid are gradually removed, which suggested for Chu Hsi a method of changing a turbid state of mind into a clear one.[64] He also noted that when clear water is placed inside turbid water, its clarity cannot be seen, illustrating the difficulty of discerning the moral mind that is mixed with selfish desires.[65] Another tendency often employed in such analogical use is that water flows and does not stay the same, which is the "nature" of water.[66] Chu Hsi used the character *liu* (to flow) frequently in referring to the *li* of heaven, to human nature, or to the human mind, in which cases the character had such various meanings as "to move," "to operate," and "to be in effect." Selfish desires and an evil mind appear, for example, when the flow of the *li* of heaven or of the human mind is faulty.[67]

Chu Hsi seemed to take fire to be a gaseous substance, merely a kind of *ch'i*, and thus to be less corporeal than other material substances formed through the aggregation of *ch'i*. He approved an assertion that fire is "the warm and hot *ch'i*" and said himself that "fire is a thing in the empty void (*hsü-k'ung*)."[68] He used qualities and tendencies of fire also in analogies relating to other problems. He spoke of the use of fire in cooking, in boiling medicine, in forging metals, and in alchemical processes while discussing man's exertions in study and in reading books.[69] For a typical example:

> Reading books is like alchemy (*lien-tan*). In the beginning one smelts fiercely with a strong fire. Afterward one nourishes gradually with a slow fire. [It is] also like boiling things. In the beginning one boils with a strong fire, but [afterward] nourishes with a slow fire.[70]

These uses of fire are based on the ability of fire, and its heat, to change—burn, boil, and so forth—material substances. Chu Hsi had other examples of changes caused by fire and heat: in a furnace, gold melts and turns into a liquid form that is malleable;[71] underground heat melts pitch;[72] in a rice kettle, water boils and becomes steam, which is dispersed when the lid is open;[73] above a stove, *ch'i* becomes light and rises upward.[74] He was not interested, however, in the details of how these changes proceed. He did not have much to say about the phenomenon of burning or combustion, for example. Of course he knew that fire is produced by rubbing two stones against each other,[75] but he did not concern himself with the exact relation of fire and burning materials on the one hand and the process of combustion on the other. Obviously, for him the fact that fire burns and that it burns other things was its natural quality, requiring no further explanation. Thus, he simply said: "As for this candlelight, because it gets this fat it has much light and flame."[76] In his illustration of the process of study, he made the following casual remark:

> Study . . . is like burning of fire. One must blow and start fire first and add firewood afterward. Then the fire becomes bright. If one first adds firewood and blows the fire afterward, then the fire disappears.[77]

10.3. Sensible Material Qualities

Chu Hsi thought that light was an innate quality of certain *ch'i*. He praised a passage from *Lieh-tzu*: "Heaven is accumulated *ch'i*. . . . The sun, the moon and the stars are also portions of the accumulated *ch'i* that have 'brightness and shining' (*kuang-yao*)."[78] He said himself: "If heaven has this *ch'i*, then it must have 'the brightness and shining' of the sun, the moon, and the stars."[79] He also approved the explanation that the sun's *ch'i* reaching the moon's surface is responsible for the light of the moon.[80] At times he even used expressions like "light *ch'i*" (*kuang-ch'i*) and "fire *ch'i*" (*huo-ch'i*) in referring to the brightness of the luminaries.[81]

Certain objects contain light or light *ch'i* in them and are therefore bright. The example that Chu Hsi mentioned most frequently is the mirror.[82] He said repeatedly that a mirror originally had light and brightness. When it is covered with dust, the light and brightness inside it is screened and not visible; but when the dust is wiped off, the mirror is again bright and its light shines on other things.[83] Thus, "the brightness of a mirror is not to be obtained from outside";[84] "When one polishes [a mirror] a little today and a little tomorrow, it becomes bright of itself without one's noticing it."[85] He even spoke of "the ability [of a mirror] to be bright" (*neng kuang*).[86] A mirror not only contains light inside it but keeps light from being dispersed:

> To talk about light for example, there must [first] be a mirror, then there is light afterward. There must be water, then there is light afterward. Light is nature; mirror and water are *ch'i* and tangible quality. If there is no mirror or water, then light would also be dispersed.[87]

This passage suggests that light exists in water also. Indeed, that is how Chu Hsi interpreted the *Huai-nan-tzu* phrases "Fire and the sun cast the shadow outside" (*huo je wai ying*) and "Water and the moon cast the shadow inside" (*shui yüeh nei ying*). He said, "Water is bright inside and dark outside, whereas fire is dark inside and bright outside."[88] He even altered the original *Huai-nan-tzu* phrases to fit them to his own views:

> *Huai-nan-tzu* said: "Metal and water are bright inside; the sun and fire are bright outside." The *ch'i* is inclined toward inside. Therefore it is bright inside. If the *ch'i* is inclined toward outside, it is bright outside.[89]

That *ch'i*, or light *ch'i*, is responsible for the light or brightness of certain objects is again obvious from this. Chu Hsi spoke of the existence of light in other objects as well, such as the luminaries in the sky and man's eyes.[90] An object such as a wooden board, however, does not have light in it and thus does not shine upon other things.[91]

Chu Hsi did not think that the light present in actual objects was stationary. For example, light is continuously regenerated: "The light *ch'i* [of the sun and the moon] constantly renews itself. [The renewal occurs] not just once a day; [light *ch'i*] does not stay still for even a single moment."[92] It is obviously for this reason that stars twinkle.[93] Chu Hsi sometimes referred to the movement of light as a "flow."[94] About the actual course of such motion, or flow, however, he was not explicit. To be sure, his references to the blocking of light by objects—the sunlight blocked inside a house or during eclipses or the shadow of the earth on the moon or of an object on a mirror, for example[95]—imply a generally rectilinear character of the flow of light. And for us, his remark that "when one sees the shadow [of an object] one knows [its] shape"[96] is not explainable unless the flow of light is rectilinear. But whether it is rectilinear, or whether light flows in well-defined rectilinear rays, was not a problem for Chu Hsi. Sometimes he made remarks that could even suggest deviations from the rectilinearity: the sunlight rising from below the earth around its four sides[97] or the light of jewels reaching out in four directions from inside a pagoda.[98]

Objects block light because light cannot pass through them. Chu Hsi said, for example: "The earth is a piece of a real thing. Therefore, the light [of the sun] shone upon [the earth] does not pass through [it], and there is this dark shadow [on the moon]."[99] Some objects can reflect the light shone upon them. Chu Hsi said, "When the sun shines upon it, the light on the surface of water is reflected onto a wall"; he compared this to the reflection of the sunlight by the moon.[100] He also spoke of a mirror reflecting candlelight onto a wall.[101] Objects could also "disperse" light. For example, as we have seen, rainbows are formed when the sunlight is dispersed by thin water drops.[102]

Chu Hsi's remarks about colors were usually quite casual. For example, he referred to darkness as "color," calling "the black darkness of midnight" "the correct color of the sky."[103] He also said that "when the five colors happen to be in a place where there is much black, then all become black; when they enter a place where there is much red, then all become red."[104] His conversation even touched upon a divination method involving color, by which colors can be discerned in a dark room.[105] But Chu Hsi was not interested in the exact nature of colors or in the question of how colors are produced. He simply accepted them as qualities of things that needed no explanation.

To be sure, Chu Hsi had a rather long discussion in which he spoke of the production of "the five intermediary colors" (*wu-chien-se*) by mixing various pairs of "the five regular colors" (*wu-cheng-se*):

Blue, red, yellow, white, and black are the regular colors of the five [compass] directions. Green, vermillion red (*hung*), emerald-blue (*pi*), violet (*tzu*), and horse brown (*liu*) are the intermediary colors of the five directions. Now, with the blue of Wood [one can] conquer the yellow of Earth. [Thus,] combining blue and yellow produces green, . . . the intermediary color of east. With the white of Metal [one can] conquer the blue of Wood; combining blue and white produces emerald blue, . . . the intermediary color of west. With the red of Fire [one can] conquer the white of Metal; combining red and white produces vermillion red, . . . the intermediary color of south. With the black of Water [one

can] conquer the red of Fire; combining red and black produces violet, . . . the intermediary color of north. With the yellow of Earth [one can] conquer the black of Water;
combining yellow and black produces horse brown, . . . the intermediary color of the
center.[106]

But Chu Hsi was not interested in the actual processes by which the colors are
mixed to produce new ones. What prompted him to discuss this was the problem of
the proper colors to be used for the clothes of great men. It is natural, then, that he
should be interested in classifying the colors – according to whether they are regular or intermediary and according to their five-phase associations.[107]

Whereas Chu Hsi considered light to be a quality of a certain kind of *ch'i*, he did
not conceive of a separate kind of *ch'i* for sound; for him, sound was produced by
motions of *ch'i* in general, not of a special kind of *ch'i*. He even said that "sound and
musical pitches are simply *ch'i*."[108] Although a disciple used the expression "sound
ch'i" (*sheng-ch'i*) in a question about sound, the word was not present in Chu Hsi's
response.[109] On the exact nature of *ch'i*'s motions that produce sound, Chu Hsi was
not clear. He adopted Chang Tsai's theory that sound is produced by "mutual grinding of *ch'i* and physical form."[110] He also quoted Ts'ai Yüan-ting's saying that "the
myriad sounds come from the opening and closing."[111] When speaking of thunder,
he said that the sound occurs as *ch'i* in an extremely pent-up state "is exploded and
dispersed."[112] But he was not interested in discussing details of such grinding,
opening, closing, explosion, or dispersion.

Instead, Chu Hsi was interested in the qualitative characteristics of sound. In his
elaboration of the above-mentioned theory of Chang Tsai, which has been quoted
once already, Chu Hsi distinguished different kinds of materials producing sound:

> [Examples of the mutual grinding of] two *ch'i* are things like wind and thunder. [Ex-
> amples of] two physical forms are things like drumsticks and drums. [Examples of] *ch'i*
> grinding physical form are things like bamboo pipes. [Examples of] physical form grind-
> ing *ch'i* are things like feather fans and arrows.[113]

He also spoke of different qualities of sound produced by different materials. A
phrase from *Mencius*, "Metal propagates sound and jade collects sound" (*Chin
sheng yü chen*, 5B1), provided an occasion for him.[114] Commenting on this phrase,
Chu Hsi mentioned eight kinds of materials used in producing musical sounds:
metal, stone, silk string, bamboo, gourds, earth, leather, and wood.[115] He added that
of these materials, metal and stone, which make metal bells (*chung*) and jade tubes
(*ch'ing*), are the most important for music.[116] He spoke frequently of the qualities of
sound produced by these two materials. The sound of metal is gradually decreasing,
whereas that of jade remains constant until it ends abruptly.[117] The sound of bamboo, heard in the pan pipe for example, is "large," and the sound of silk string, as
in the lute, is "thin."[118]

The quality of sound depends not only on the kinds of materials but also on the
dimensions of the objects producing the sound. It was well known that the pitches
of musical notes are determined by the lengths of the pipes producing them.[119] The

character *lü*, designating a series of pitch pipes producing a set of musical notes, was even considered as part of the standard system of measures, which Chu Hsi frequently referred to as "*lü-tu-liang-heng*" (meaning literally "pitch pipe, length, volume, and weight").[120]

Chu Hsi used the "clear" versus "turbid" dichotomy in characterizing the high and low pitches: "When [the pipe] is long, the sound is turbid; when it is short, the sound is clear."[121] But he also used other qualities: high pitches are not only clear, but also light, large, and pointed; low pitches are not only turbid, but also heavy, deep, thin, and broad.[122] He even said, "If a sound is too high, it is 'anxious and fierce' (*chiao-sha*); if it is too low, it is 'plentiful and slow' (*ang-huan*)."[123]

There were two sets of names for pitches used in traditional Chinese music. One is composed of "the five notes" (*wu-sheng*)—*kung, shang, chiao, chih,* and *yü*—at characteristic intervals of pitch; the other is the set of "the twelve pitches" (*shih-erh-lü*) at approximately equal intervals. The lengths of the pitch pipes producing these notes and pitches are related to one another by simple numerical ratios, which had been well known ever since the "pitch numbers" (*lü-shu*) were first given in the *Record of the Historian* (Shih-chi) by Ssu-ma Ch'ien.[124] Chu Hsi quoted that work and gave "the five-note numbers" (*wu-sheng-shu*) that explain the production of the five notes:

> Nine times nine, eighty-one, is taken as [the length for] *kung*. Dividing this into three parts and subtracting one [part from the three], one gets fifty-four and takes it as *chih*. Dividing this into three parts and adding one [part to the three], one gets seventy-two, which can be taken as *shang*. Dividing this into three and subtracting one [part], one gets forty-eight, which can be taken as *yü*. Dividing this into three and adding one [part], one gets sixty-four, which can be taken as *chiao*.[125]

Table 10.1 illustrates this. From the length of *kung*, the lengths of the other four notes are obtained through multiplication, alternately by $\frac{2}{3}$ and $\frac{4}{3}$. The five notes thus produced can be arranged as in table 10.2 in order of decreasing lengths and thus of ascending pitches. In it we have added another *kung* note with half the length of the original *kung*, for, as Chu Hsi recognized, taking half of the length of a note produces the same note.[126] Continuing the above procedure, two more notes can be added to the five mentioned above: multiplying the length for *chiao* ($^{64}/_{81}$) by $\frac{2}{3}$ produces *pien-kung* ("changed *kung*," $^{128}/_{243}$); multiplying that by $\frac{4}{3}$ produces *pien-chih* ("changed *chih*," $^{512}/_{729}$). Those two notes conveniently fall in the intervals between *yü* and *kung* and between *chiao* and *chih*, which, as can be seen from the last column of table 10.2, are larger than the other intervals. Chu Hsi also recognized this[127] and said that the two additional notes were there for "the harmony (*ho*) of music."[128] When the same procedure is continued, twelve more or less evenly spaced pitches result. Table 10.3 shows the entire procedure and all the names of "the twelve pitches."[129]

To Chu Hsi, however, the five notes had qualitative characteristics as well. For example, the five notes were associated with the five phases and thus with such five-phase characteristics as the seasons and the five constant virtues.[130] The most

TABLE 10.1
Production of the Five Notes

Five Notes	kung 宮	shang 商	chiao 角	chih 徵	yü 羽
Length	81	72	64	54	48
First step (81 × 2/3 = 54)	•————————————→ •				
Second step (54 × 4/3 = 72)		• ←————————— •			
Third step (72 × 2/3 = 48)			•—————————————→ •		
Fourth step (48 × 4/3 = 64)				• ←—————————— •	

TABLE 10.2
The Five Notes Arranged
according to Their Pitches

Name (Length)	Ratio[a]
kung (1 = 81/81)	
	8/9
shang (8/9)	
	8/9
chiao (64/81)	
	27/32
chih (2/3)	
	8/9
yü (16/27)	
	27/32
kung (1/2)	

Note
[a]Ratio of the lengths of the two adjacent notes.

frequently mentioned by Chu Hsi were the associations of the *kung* note with rulers (*chün*), *shang* with ministers (*ch'en*), *chiao* with people (*min*), *chih* with events (*shih*), and *yü* with things (*wü*).[131] This set of associations best reveals a characteristic feature of the five notes, which do not merely form a linear scale of notes related to one another by numerical ratios but also represent a harmonious ensemble of sounds with characteristic qualities.[132] With such associations in mind, Chu Hsi felt it necessary to explain why the *chiao* note, rather than *kung*, is in the middle of the five-note sequence.[133] He also considered it to be natural that "[the length for] *kung*, belonging to rulers, should be the greatest, whereas [the length for] *yü*, belonging to things, should be the smallest."[134] While explaining why one should avoid having the length of the *shang* pitch pipe exceed that of *kung*, he even said that "the most deplorable thing in music is ministers' abusing [their] rulers."[135]

TABLE 10.3
The Twelve Pitches

Order of Lengths (Names)	Length	Order of Production
1 (*huang-chung* 黃鐘)	1	1 (*kung*) [a]
2 (*ta-lü* 大呂)	$512/729 \times 4/3 = 2{,}048/2{,}187$	8
3 (*t'ai-ts'ou* 太簇)	$2/3 \times 4/3 = 8/9$	3 (*shang*)
4 (*chia-chung* 夾鐘)	$4{,}096/6{,}561 \times 4/3 = 16{,}384/19{,}683$	10
5 (*ku-hsien* 姑洗)	$16/27 \times 4/3 = 64/81$	5 (*chiao*)
6 (*chung-lü* 仲呂)	$32{,}768/59{,}049 \times 4/3 = 131{,}072/177{,}147$	12
7 (*jui-pin* 蕤賓)	$128/243 \times 4/3 = 512/729$	7 (*pien-chih*)
8 (*lin-chung* 林鐘)	$1 \times 2/3 = 2/3$	2 (*chih*)
9 (*i-tse* 夷則)	$2{,}048/2{,}187 \times 2/3 = 4{,}096/6{,}561$	9
10 (*nan-lü* 南呂)	$8/9 \times 2/3 = 16/27$	4 (*yü*)
11 (*wu-i* 無射)	$16{,}384/19{,}683 \times 2/3 = 32{,}768/59{,}049$	11
12 (*ying-chung* 應鐘)	$64/81 \times 2/3 = 128/243$	6 (*pien-kung*)
13 (*huang-chung* 黃鐘)	$131{,}072/177{,}147 \times 2/3 = 262{,}144/531{,}441 \approx 1/2$	3 (*kung*)

[a] In the parentheses are the corresponding notes, when the *kung* note is fixed at *huang-chung*.

Sound produces echoes (*hsiang*) when it meets other objects and is reflected by them. Chu Hsi interpreted this process as "the echo responding to the sound."[136] He seems to have believed that empty spaces were needed to produce such responses of echoes, for he said: "To speak of the emptiness of valleys, when sounds reach there, echoes respond to them."[137] The more typical of the mutual responses of sound for him, however, were those that take place between the same sounds: "Same sounds respond to each other; same *ch'i* seek each other."[138] For example, he spoke of the method of tuning string instruments by matching the sounds of the strings with those of the standard pitch pipes.[139] He also interpreted the ancient practice of "watching for *ch'i*" (*hou-ch'i*) as an instance of such mutual response: twelve pitch pipes are buried in soil in different lengths corresponding to the twelve pitches; at a certain point of time in each lunar month the *ch'i* of that month rises from under the ground, and the *ch'i* inside the pitch pipe of the corresponding length responds to this rising *ch'i* (by causing the ashes inside to come out of the pipe, which is what man "watches for"); as the months go by, the *ch'i* of the twelve pitch pipes respond in order.[140] Underlying this practice is the belief in the association of the twelve pitches with the twelve lunar months.[141] Chu Hsi noted that, in tuning the strings, ancient people chose different pitches in different months in accordance with this association: the *huang-chung* pitch in the eleventh lunar month and *ta-lü* in the twelfth, for example.[142] He even spoke of an ancient ritual that suggests that each moment of time had its characteristic pitch of sound: "In the ancient times, when a crown prince was born, a grand master blew a pitch pipe to measure the sound. He examined which [of the twelve] pitches and lengths it matches."[143]

Whereas two sounds respond to each other when they are of the same pitch, different sounds can be in harmony with one another. And when different sounds are played together in harmony, they produce music.[144] We look at more of Chu Hsi's ideas about music and "the music specialists" in chapter 12.

Chu Hsi attributed taste directly to the material substance of food. Man perceives taste directly when he eats food: "When one eats a sour [food], one knows that it is sour; when one eats a salty [food], one knows it is salty."[145] Chu Hsi also said: "The taste of a food exists completely inside [the food]. If one only licks and bites the outside, one will not get its taste."[146] He emphasized that food has to be chewed well, cut into small pieces, and made soft, before its taste can be perceived.[147] When one swallows a large piece of food, one cannot know its taste;[148] the more one chews, the more one perceives the taste.[149]

Many of those remarks were made by Chu Hsi to illustrate, by way of analogy, the reading of books (food) and understanding of the *li* (taste) in them. Most of his other remarks touching on tastes were also made to illustrate similar matters. For example, to illustrate the uselessness of aimless study, he said that if one ate something without knowing its taste, it would not matter whether one ate it or not.[150] He could even say that after eating a sweet thing, there always remained an acid aftertaste, whereas a bitter thing left a sweet aftertaste; but his real point was something else: "The rituals are originally the most solemn [things] under heaven; [but] when they are carried out so that each one gets his share, then they are the most gentle."[151]

Chu Hsi had much less to say about smell, and what he said showed similar features. He noted, for example, that a bad smell of water from a certain spring could be eliminated by passing the water many times through a bamboo pipe filled with sand.[152] He did not reject an interlocutor's comment on this that smell is like mud.[153]

10.4. The Coming into Being of the Myriad Things

As Chu Hsi did not have a clear distinction between living and nonliving things, he did not in principle distinguish the processes of the coming into being of the two kinds. Yet, the coming into being of living beings seems to have been more problematic for him, because he discussed it often.

In chapter 7 we came across Chu Hsi's repeated saying that heaven (or heaven and earth) "produced" men and things. His descriptions of the actual process of such "production," however, were in terms of the inherent movement of the *ch'i* of heaven and earth rather than of any supernatural creative power of heaven and earth. He described the process in the following various ways:

> Between heaven and earth, the two *ch'i* [i.e., yin and yang *ch'i*] simply keep moving and turning. Without realizing, they produce one man. Without realizing, they also produce one thing.[154]

> Yin-yang and the five phases circulate, intermix, rise and fall, and go and come. Thus, they produce the myriad differences of men and things and establish the great meaning of heaven and earth.[155]

"The *ch'i* of one origin" (*i yüan chih ch'i*) moves, turns, flows, and passes, and there is not even a slight moment of rest. [In this manner] it simply produces many of the myriad things.[156]

He also compared it to various common processes of everyday life:

[It can be] compared to a cauldron for cooking rice. *Ch'i* moves from below to the top and moves down again. [But it] keeps moving inside [the cauldron] and can boil [rice] to be cooked. Heaven and earth simply contains much *ch'i* inside, for which there is no way out. [The *ch'i*] turns once, then it produces one thing.[157]

[It is] exactly like a millstone for noodles. Its four sides keep scattering out layer after layer [of noodles]. It is exactly like the *ch'i* of heaven and earth, [which] moves and turns without rest and keeps producing layer after layer of men and things.[158]

He even compared the production of men and things to a fan's producing wind.[159] In all of these descriptions, however, he only implied some kind of movement of *ch'i*; he was never explicit about the details of such movement.

Chu Hsi's descriptions of the "transformation of *ch'i*" were also in very general terms. He referred mainly to the transformation of *ch'i* into primeval forms of life. In a passage also quoted in chapter 3, he said: "When things first came into being, the essences of yin and yang congealed spontaneously to form two [of a thing]. They were thus produced through the 'transformation of *ch'i*.'"[160] He believed that the first human being emerged through this process: "The transformation of *ch'i* is [the process in which] in the beginning a man came out spontaneously without a parent [literally, 'a seed' (*chung*)]."[161] The first man came into being "as the essences of the two [i.e., yin and yang] and the five [phases], by means of the transformation of *ch'i*, combined and took physical form."[162] He emphasized that the first human being could not have been born from parents:

About the beginning of heaven and earth, how can one discuss a seed [and thus parents] of man? After *ch'i* congealed to form a pair of men, it produced many of the myriad things. . . . If there had not been this pair of man in the beginning, how can there be many men now?[163]

As the appearance of the first human being was thus considered a result of the movement of *ch'i*, Chu Hsi was led to admit the possibility of its recurrence: for example, the appearance of a man without parents on an uninhabited island.[164] He also compared the process to what he considered to be the spontaneous appearance of lice: "The pair of men [produced through transformation of *ch'i*] are like the lice now on man's body [which] come out by spontaneous change and transformation."[165] Nor was the process restricted to that which produces life; Chu Hsi used the term in referring also to the production of such other things as "cold and hot weather, day and night, rain, dew, frost and snow, mountains and rivers, woods and stones, metal, water, fire, and earth."¹⁶⁶ This was to be expected because of the breadth of Chu Hsi's concept of *ch'i*.

A common component in Chu Hsi's descriptions of the transformation of *ch'i* was that the process transformed *ch'i* into physical form. He referred to this process variously as "combination" (*ho*), "aggregation," and "congelation" (*ning* or *ning-chieh*) of *ch'i*.¹⁶⁷ But once living beings have been produced through it, giving them physical form, the production of life can go on through the normal reproductive processes, which Chu Hsi referred to as "transformation of physical form" (*hsing-hua*):

> Once there existed these two, one female and one male; afterward [things] gradually kept coming into being from the seeds. This is [production] through "transformation of physical form." The myriad things are all thus.¹⁶⁸

He contrasted this with the "transformation of *ch'i*" in the following way:

> Harmony and prosperity of heaven and earth refer to the transformation of *ch'i*; sexual union [literally 'building an essence' (*kou-ching*)] of man and woman refers to the transformation of physical form.¹⁶⁹

This process posed even less of a problem to Chu Hsi, who had no concrete description of it:

> When *ch'i* aggregates and produces physical form, the physical form interacts with and stimulates the *ch'i*. Thereupon, men and things keep coming into being through the transformation of physical form.¹⁷⁰

Chu Hsi followed Chang Tsai and associated the transformation of *ch'i* with the supreme void (*t'ai-hsü*), the original state of the world when there was only formless *ch'i*.¹⁷¹ In his comments on Chang Tsai's saying "From the supreme void, one has the name of heaven; from the transformation of *ch'i*, one has the name of the Way," Chu Hsi made such remarks as "[The transformation of *ch'i*] simply is that supreme void," or "The transformation of *ch'i* actually cannot be separated from the supreme void."¹⁷² He approved a subsequent suggestion by a disciple that "[while] the supreme void corresponds to the circle on top of 'the Diagram of the Supreme Ultimate' (*T'ai-chi-t'u*), the transformation of *ch'i* corresponds to the stillness of yin and the movement of yang inside the circle." Thus, the transformation of *ch'i* was a process of transforming the formless *ch'i* in the supreme void.

Chu Hsi used another term taken from Chang Tsai, "the wandering *ch'i*" (*yu-ch'i*), in designating the *ch'i* that produced men and things.¹⁷³ Chang Tsai had said: "The wandering *ch'i*, which is varied and disorderly, combines and forms tangible qualities. Thus, it produces the myriad differences of men and things."¹⁷⁴ Chu Hsi glossed Chang Tsai's phrase "varied and disorderly" (*fen-jao*) variously as "irregular," "disunited," "diverged," "coarse," and "turbid."¹⁷⁵ The character *yu* ("wandering") implied some kind of movement: Chu Hsi noted that "*yu* has the meaning, 'to flow and to move' (*liu-hsing*), also"¹⁷⁶ and compared the movement of wandering *ch'i* to such moving objects as fans, waterwheels, and millstones.[177] Yet, the wandering *ch'i* is not a separate kind of *ch'i* distinct from the usual yin and yang *ch'i*:

> How can there also be wandering *ch'i* apart from yin and yang [*ch'i*]? What is called "the wandering *ch'i*" refers to that which is endowed to the myriad things. Each thing gets one life, and has one "physical form and tangible quality." These are all that this *ch'i* combines and produces.[178]

We came across Chu Hsi's use of the expression "the *ch'i* of one origin" in discussing heaven's production of men and things. He also spoke of "the great source" (*ta-yüan*) and "the one source" (*i-yüan* or *i-ke yüan-t'ou*), from which all things, including men, come forth.[179] Chang Tsai had gone further and held that men and things returned to this source upon death:

> The supreme void cannot but have *ch'i*. *Ch'i* cannot but aggregate and become the myriad things. The myriad things cannot but disperse and become the supreme void.[180]

> Physical form aggregates and becomes a thing; physical form scatters and returns to the source. "Returning to the source"—does this not refer to "the wandering *hun* making a change" (*yu-hun wei pien*)?[181]

But this idea of Chang Tsai's created a problem for Chu Hsi and other Neo-Confucians, for it implied continuous regeneration of life from the source, which smacked of the Buddhist belief in "cyclical transmigration" (*lun-hui*).[182] Ch'eng I had criticized Chang Tsai's theory of dispersion and regeneration of *ch'i* on this account, maintaining instead that *ch'i* was constantly produced anew.[183] Chu Hsi generally sided with Ch'eng I in this respect. His comment upon this Chang Tsai passage ended by endorsing Ch'eng I.

> Heng-ch'ü's [i.e., Chang Tsai's] theory that "physical form scatters and returns to the source" holds [the following]: When a man is born he gets "this thing"; and when he is dead this thing goes back to the great source again; still another is pulled out from inside [the source] and produces a man. [It is] like a lump of mud. After one has made a pellet from it, one puts it back in the mud as before, and one [can] still make another pellet. What I-ch'üan said was: "[It is] not necessary to take it to mean that the already contracted *ch'i* becomes the expanding *ch'i*." When we look at it from the Sage's [i.e., Confucius's] saying, "The essence and *ch'i* become things; wandering *hun* makes a change," I-ch'üan's theory is correct. In general, when man dies, the *ch'i* is dispersed. When he is born, again, it comes out forth from inside the great source.[184]

Chu Hsi even characterized Chang Tsai's view with the expression "the great cyclical transmigration" (*ta-lun-hui*):

> Heng-ch'ü criticized the Buddhist theory of cyclical transmigration. But when he [himself] spoke of aggregation and dispersion, contraction and expansion, its harm was still [great enough to be called] "great cyclical transmigration." The Buddhist [theory] is that

each individual [undergoes] cyclical transmigration. Heng-ch'ü's [view] mixes everything in a round. All the same, it is a great cyclical transmigration.[185]

Although I discuss plants and animals separately in the next two sections, there are certain points that are common to both. For example, Chu Hsi held that all living beings had life intent. We have also seen that he broadened the meanings of words like "mind" and "perception" to such a degree that he was able to say that all "things"—including even inanimate things—had mind and perception. He maintained also that all living beings—men, animals, and plants—had to have "seed" in order to be born.[186] Another such belief was that all living beings had shells surrounding their bodies, by means of which they could protect what was inside: man's outside body and the skin of fruits and grains, for example.[187]

10.5. Plants

Chu Hsi's knowledge about living beings was centered around man. Many phenomena involving plants were brought up by Chu Hsi to illustrate analogous human problems. Even when they were not used in such analogical discussions, what he really had in mind was very often human-related, such as the edibility, medicinal effects, and other uses of plants. Thus, he spoke frequently of grains, fruits, flowers, medicinal herbs, and fiber plants. For example, grains are edible, whereas darnels are not; the roots of ginseng and the *chu* plant cure diseases, whereas those of the *kou-wen* plant kill men.[188] He even seemed to consider usefulness for men as part of the "nature" of certain plants, for he said, "Beans and grains necessarily make [man's stomach] full; cloths and silks necessarily make [man] warm,"[189] in exactly the same manner as he said that water is necessarily cold and fire is necessarily hot.

Ancient texts, especially the *Book of Poetry* and the *Songs of Ch'u*, which contain many names of plants, also provided occasions for Chu Hsi to speak of various plant species. Confucius had already said that by studying the *Book of Poetry* one could acquire "a broad knowledge about the names of birds and beasts, grasses and trees."[190] From the third century A.D., there even emerged as a legitimate branch of classical scholarship a tradition of identifying and describing the plants and animals whose names appear in the *Book of Poetry*.[191] Although Chu Hsi did not speak directly about Confucius's assertion, his comments on the *Book of Poetry* and the *Songs of Ch'u* contain many references to plant names.[192] In those and other contexts, Chu Hsi mentioned many more plant species than we can include here.

The feature of plants that Chu Hsi referred to most often is the yearly life cycle. For example, "a tree flourishes in spring and spreads in summer; in autumn it forms fruit, and in winter it settles down."[193] "As for a grain, in spring it starts life, in summer it forms a seedling, in autumn it forms grains, and in winter it is gathered and stored."[194] The fruits and grains harvested and stored in winter contain seeds that repeat the cycle again the next spring. The plant life cycle, of course, constitutes a typical example of the cyclical alternation of dualistic characteristics, which we have seen repeatedly. Chu Hsi said, for example:

Now, when it is autumn and winter, each of the myriad things spontaneously gathers and stores [itself]; it dries and withers like that. When spring comes, all of a sudden each of them spontaneously starts life and flourishes in good order. This simply is the single *chi*, one vanishing and one growing.[195]

We have also seen that seasonal features of plants formed a key set of associations with the four cosmic qualities of *yüan*, *heng*, *li*, and *chen*. Chu Hsi compared the plant life cycle to the cycle of the twelve double hours also:

At the *tzu* (1st) double-hour at midnight, though this thing exists, there is still no movement there. At the *yin* (3rd) and *mao* (4th) hours, it comes to life. At the *ssu* (6th) and *wu* (7th) hours, it is manifest. At the *shen* (9th) and *yu* (10th) hours, it congeals. At the *hai* (12th), *tzu*, and *ch'ou* (2nd) hours, it forms fruits. When it reaches the *yin* hour, it comes to life again.[196]

The idea of the yearly life cycle was so predominant in Chu Hsi's thought about plants that at times he even seemed to think that there must be four seasons in order to accommodate the plant life cycle:

If there were no winter, it could turn out that [a plant] does not grow or flourish in spring and summer. . . . If things come to life but there is no winter, then the things will just go on living, and the original *ch'i* (*yüan-chi*) can also be exhausted.[197]

If there were spring and summer but no autumn or winter, how could a thing settle down? [If there were] only autumn and winter but no spring or summer, then how could it come into being?[198]

In other words, plants needed not only spring and summer but also autumn and winter to restore the original *ch'i*, to settle down, and to form seeds. But Chu Hsi also noted seasonal features of certain plants that deviate from the usual cycle. For example, there are trees that remain green in winter, whose leaves fall down only after the buds have sprouted.[199] When an interlocutor spoke of the loquat, which "forms flower-buds in autumn, blooms in winter, forms fruits in spring, and ripens in summer, after which it again forms flower buds," Chu Hsi accepted it as an illustration of the "circulation of the life-*li*."[200]

The entire process of plant growth outlined in the idea of the plant life cycle was considered by Chu Hsi to be natural or spontaneous. He kept saying that plants sprout, grow, and ripen naturally or spontaneously.[201] For him these processes were simply manifestations of life intent, which exists in every part of the plant body all year round and cannot be stopped. He even said that a tree had to grow every day and would die if it stopped growing for a single day; he used this to back up his point that one should study consistently without stopping for a single day.[202] Thus, he did not feel it necessary to explain these spontaneous processes. Or at best, he referred to them as "*shen*," implying that they showed the mysterious workings of nature that could not be explained: "A flowering tree suddenly comes out. When it is time for blooming, all bloom; when it is time for forming fruits, all form fruits. The life-*ch'i* comes out. This simply is *shen*." 203

Plants need water and nourishment to manifest life intent and to sprout, grow, or ripen.204 They also need the sunlight to grow and flourish.205 Chu Hsi said: "In a blade of grass and a tree, the place facing the sunny [yang] side is alive, and the place facing the shadowy [yin] side is emaciated." 206 When plants are broken, stepped on or otherwise damaged, or when their roots are separated from the soil, they lose life intent and wither or die.207 As we have seen, such responses of plants made Chu Hsi suspect that plants had knowledge; he even concluded, late in life, that plants had "perception."

Concerning the various parts of a plant, what Chu Hsi said consisted mostly of casual observations about outward appearances or behavioral patterns. This is not surprising, for he spoke of the plant parts mainly to illustrate analogous human problems, not from any interest in their structures and functions. In a typical example, he noted that when a branch of a large tree is tugged, all its branches and leaves move, to illustrate that if one understands a basic point, one will be able to see all the other related things and events.208 We have also seen that he compared the parts of a plant directly to man's body—the root to the head, and the branches to the limbs—and spoke of the "upside-down" stance of plants in a perspective that is clearly man-centered. But the most characteristic examples of this kind appeared in his illustrations of the relationship between various human virtues, in which different parts of a plant were compared to different virtues.209

Phrases from the classics frequently provided the occasion for such comparisons. For example, to explain the phrase from the *Analects* "As for my Way, it is penetrated through by one" (4.15), Chu Hsi referred to the fact that "a tree of one root produces many branches and leaves." 210 He also said: "The thousand branches and myriad leaves are all fine. All this is [because] the life-*ch'i* in this root flows into and penetrates through them." 211 To explain the term "considerateness" (*shu*), which appears in the same *Analects* passage, he compared it to the *ch'i* flowing through and penetrating the branches and leaves and contrasted it with faith (*hsin*), which he compared to the leaves and branches receiving the life-*ch'i* or to the flowers necessarily forming fruits.212 To illustrate the expression from the *Doctrine of the Mean* "to accomplish by oneself" (*tzu-ch'eng*), he spoke of "a grass plant or a tree having many roots, branches, leaves, and stems." 213 On the phrases from "Hsi-tz'u chuan" "to manifest it in humaneness" (*hsien chu jen*) and "to store it in function" (*tsang chu yung*) (ch. A5), he had the following comment:

> To compare it to a tree, one root produces many branches, leaves, flowers, and fruits. This is where "it is manifested in humaneness." When it forms fruits, one kernel forms one seed. This is where "it is stored in function." 214

Chu Hsi was of the view that the different parts of the plant differed in relative importance. The most important part of a plant, to him, was the roots. He considered the roots to be the basis of the entire plant: because a plant has roots, it can have the other parts, stem, branches, leaves, flowers, and fruits; without roots these other parts will all die:

> A tree must have roots. And then, it will spontaneously have branches, leaves, flowers, and fruits. If it does not have roots, then even though it has branches, leaves, flowers, and fruits, they will wither and fall immediately.[215]

He even said that the root "produces" the other parts of a tree.[216]

These remarks show that Chu Hsi considered it "natural" or "spontaneous" for all parts of a plant to grow from the roots.[217] He seemed to know, though he never said so explicitly, that plants absorb something from the soil through the roots. He said, for example, that after a tree takes root in the soil, it grows gradually.[218] He also mentioned plant nutrients formed from water and mud: "When [vegetables and fruit trees are] watered sufficiently, then the mud and water harmonize with each other; things [i.e., the plants] obtain nutrients from them and are born and grow spontaneously."[219] He even spoke of roots coming into contact with, and receiving, the "correct *ch'i*" of nearby dead trees.[220]

What the roots absorb—*ch'i*, water, nutrients—is transmitted to the other parts. We have seen, for example, Chu Hsi's remark that the branches and leaves flourish when the life-*ch'i* in the roots flows and penetrates them. When the *ch'i* has already passed out, old branches and leaves become emaciated.[221] His interpretation of the *I-ching* phrase "There is water above a tree" also alluded to the upward movement of water and nutrients from the roots to the branches and leaves: "In the life of a grass plant or a tree, juices and nutrients all move upward, all the way to the ends of the tree. [This] is the meaning of [the phrase] 'There is water above a tree.'"[222] He attributed the water droplets found in the morning on leaves, of calamus for example, to such a rise of water.[223]

On other parts of the plant, which, Chu Hsi believed, grew naturally from the roots, he had less to say. On stems, branches, and leaves, for example, he said nothing special except what we have already come across. On flowers, he had some remarks about withering—for example, about the difference in the withering of different kinds of flowers:

> In winter, flowers do not wither easily. For example, narcissuses are extremely weak but still endure long. Plum blossoms and winter plums are all like this. When it comes to spring flowers, they wither easily. If they are summer flowers, it is especially so. For example, sunflowers, pomegranates, and lotus plants bloom just for one day. It must be that in winter their *ch'i* is "pure and firm" (*cheng-ku*) and therefore difficult to wither. During spring and summer, as soon as [their *ch'i*] comes out, it comes out completely and therefore cannot last long.[224]

He added that flowers with large petals, such as pear blossoms, wither easily.

When certain flowers wither, fruits are formed. According to Chu Hsi, "when this flower forms a fruit, one flower naturally forms one fruit."[225] He believed that the fruit received *ch'i* from the tree, and he compared the transmission of *ch'i* from human ancestors to their descendants to "the *ch'i* of a tree [being] transmitted to fruits."[226] He seemed to think that the tree itself died if too much *ch'i* was transmitted in this manner, for he said that trees with large fruits like pears "could get weakened extremely easily": "When [a pear tree] is about to die, it must form one year's [crop of] fruits rapidly and die. This is also [because] the *ch'i* is about to depart."[227] In other words, the *ch'i* departs from a tree to form fruits. Chu Hsi thus said that when a fruit ripened, it had its own life separate from the tree, unlike flowers, which shared a single life with the tree.[228]

This new life, fruit, begins a new life cycle because it contains seeds. According to Chu Hsi, a fruit contains a kernel inside, which forms seeds and spontaneously falls off from the fruit when it is ripe.[229] Grains also begin new life cycles, as the grains themselves act as seeds:

> For example, one grain comes to life and becomes a seedling; the seedling produces flowers; flowers form crops and produce grains again and return to the original form. One stalk has a hundred grains, each of them complete. If these hundred grains are planted again, each of them in turn produces a hundred grains.[230]

Grains must ripen first, however, in order to function as seeds. Chu Hsi said, for example: "In case a grain is nine-tenths ripe and one-tenth not ripe, it will still die if it is cut off. If it is cut when it becomes completely ripe, this life intent is still stored inside."[231] In a different version of the same remark, he added: "If a grain has two parts [out of ten that are] not ripe, it will only produce a grain seven- or eight-tenths [complete]."[232] As for fruits, he said that they must pass winter to form seeds:

> Even though it is said that it [i.e., a tree] has formed fruits, if it has not passed winter, seeds will not form. It has to keep receiving *ch'i* sufficiently. Then it will be the time when they [i.e., the tree and the fruits] are about to be separated from each other. If one plants a thousand fruits, they will form a thousand trees.[233]

10.6. Animals

What Chu Hsi said about animals was also very much centered around human concerns, even more so than his comments about plants. In fact, his remarks about animals provide an excellent set of examples showing the predominantly human bearing of his concerns even while dealing with natural phenomena. Again, I cannot discuss here all the animal species mentioned by him; I focus on the general features of his ideas about animals.

A key theme is the distinction between the nature of man and the nature of animals. In particular, he contrasted the one-sidedness of the virtues and abilities of animals with the completeness of those of men. It was to illustrate this contrast that, as we have seen, he frequently spoke of animals possessing some particular human virtue. To repeat typical examples, tigers manifest the father-son relationship, ants show the ruler-subject relationship, otters offer sacrifices to ancestors, and *chü-chiu* birds show the proper distinction between husband and wife.[234] Chu Hsi referred to these animals as "humane animals" (*jen shou*) and "righteous animals" (*i-shou*).[235] He also compared behavioral characteristics of certain animals to those of men:

> Lambs "kneel to suck" (*kuei-ju*), [which means that they] have [the relationship between] father and son. Crickets and ants govern their kinds, [which means that they] have rulers and subjects. Some reside in front and some reside in the rear, [which means that they] have elder and younger brothers. Dogs, horses, cows, and sheep form groups and unite into teams, [which means that they have] friends.[236]

He even said that insects had all the four basic human virtues of humaneness, righteousness, propriety, and knowledge; it is simply that their virtues are "only one-sided and not complete."[237] For example, even lice must have knowledge, for they bite when hungry.[238] In all these examples, however, Chu Hsi's point was that these animals manifest only these specific virtues and abilities, whereas men manifest all of them.

Of course, there are differences among animals, which are due to different endowments of their *ch'i*. Thus it was that Chu Hsi's specification of the differences between birds and earthbound animals and between land and water animals were in terms of yin and yang *ch'i*. He also spoke of differences in the natures of different animals endowed with different *ch'i*. The nature of the dog is different, for example, from that of the cow, which, in turn, is different from that of the horse.[239] To give an example with more specific description, "Even when a tiger is hit by a poisoned arrow and dies, it keeps going and does not return. A tiger is a hard and strong thing. Even in dying it can be fair and correct."[240] Differences in the endowed *ch'i* lead also to differences within a single animal species. Chu Hsi said, for example: "Dogs that can bite men are those that are endowed with that strong nature. Those that do not bite are those endowed with that obedient nature."[241] In the case of the human species, we have already seen that Chu Hsi attributed all kinds of different qualities to differences in the endowed *ch'i*.

Chu Hsi's comments on the *I-ching* contain frequent remarks about animals. In particular, the "Hsi-tz'u chuan" passage "The bending of the measuring worm is to seek stretching; the hibernation of the dragon and the snake is to secure the body" (ch. B5) provided him with key examples illustrating the continuous alternation of yin and yang aspects. He said, for example: "If the measuring worm does not bend, it cannot stretch; if the dragon and the snake do not hibernate, they cannot save the body."[242] He stressed the necessity of such alternation by adding: "Nowadays in forests when winter is warm, some snakes come out. Frequently, many [of them] die."[243] He spoke of the movement of a snail in and out of the shell in the same context.[244] His comments on the *I-ching* also contained some numerologically significant facts about certain animals: for example, the number of scales on a carp is thirty-six, a yin number, and that of a dragon is eighty-one, a yang number.[245] He also spoke of various numbers (e.g., 4, 5, 8, 24, etc.) of the lines making the pattern on the back of a tortoise.[246] He compared, as we have seen, the shapes of a bird and an egg and the birth of a bird from an egg to certain hexagrams and to their sequence.[247]

What really interested Chu Hsi in all these were not the actual shapes and behaviors of animals but such systems as the yin-yang, the numbers, and the *I-ching* diagrams. When he spoke of the hibernation of snakes and the birth of birds from eggs, for example, his actual interest did not lie in the problems of animal hibernation or reproduction, but in illustrating the yin-yang and the *I-ching* schemes. Some facts mentioned by him appear even to have been devised to illustrate such schemes. It is difficult, for example, to believe that the numbers of scales and lines on the carp, the dragon, and the tortoise were obtained by actually counting. His remark that snails die when they leave their shells completely must also have been an invention to illustrate the point that the expansion and contraction of *ch'i* should alternate ceaselessly.[248] It is thus not surprising that Chu Hsi spoke of the number of scales of an imaginary animal like a dragon, which, he said, he "had never seen."[249] We have also noted how he resorted to the association of the dragon with Water in explaining the theory that dragons accompany rain.

To be sure, there were times when Chu Hsi gave rather detailed descriptions of animal shapes and behaviors. As was the case with plants, the appearance of various animal names in the *Book of Poetry* provided occasions for him to say various things about them. For example, in his comments on the first poem of the *Book of Poetry*, in which the name of the *chü-chiu* bird appears, he included the following description of it:

> I have seen people on the Huai River say that there are those [*chü-chiu* birds] on the Huai River. Their shapes are like pigeons here, the difference [being that they] are smaller and longer. There always are a female and a male, and the two do not lose each other. Although the two do not lose each other, never is there a place, however, where they stand close to each other. [They] necessarily come down to the ground with the distance of one *chang* (10 feet) apart [from each other].[250]

In the same passage, a disciple added a comment on "*i-yao*" and "*hsiao-hsing*," the words appearing in another poem from the *Book of Poetry:* "'*Hsiao-hsing*' is simply a worm with lights at night. It moves on the ground at night. '*I-yao*' refers simply to its light."[251] His comments on the *Songs of Ch'u* also contain many remarks about various animal species—a kind of monkey that can speak, living in the southern mountains,[252] and the numinous bird phoenix (*feng*),[253] for example.

Other miscellaneous records of various facts concerning animals also prompted Chu Hsi to comment on them. For example, it was in speaking of such records, by Su Shih (1036–1101) and others, that Chu Hsi mentioned the strange and suspicious character of the wild fox, the brain of a fish that is full before the full moon and empty afterward, the reaction of a tiger encountering a man who does not show fear, and the pheasant that "[fore]knows thunder."[254] In his preface to the collected works of Wang Shih-p'eng (1112–1171), Chu Hsi mentioned such insects as earthworms, leeches, and lice.[255] When asked about the word "*i-feng,*" appearing in one of his own essays, Chu Hsi responded with the following detailed description of anthills:

> It is "anthill" (*i-tieh*). In the northern regions, it is called "ant tower" (*i-lou*). It is like a small mountain. It is [formed as] ants dig under the ground. The mound of earth rises like a hill. The inside is bending and winding like small alleys. . . . When the sky is dark and rain falls, ants come out. So a stork sings at the anthill, waits for ants to come out, and eats them. Wang Ching-kung [i.e., Wang An-shih] first explained the hill as a natural hill and did not believe the theory of the anthill. [But] seeing one himself afterward in the northern region, he changed his explanation.[256]

Yet, far more frequent among Chu Hsi's remarks about animals were those made quite casually concerning some very common empirical facts—sometimes incorrectly understood—used mainly for illustrating human problems. A typical example had to do with the relationship of fish with water. He said man lived in *ch'i* as fish live in water. Man inhales and exhales *ch'i*, which is what fish do with water.[257] Thus, Chu Hsi said:

> This body [of mine] is simply a shell. Both inside and outside, there is nothing that is not the yin and yang *ch'i* of heaven and earth. It is like fish in water. The water outside is simply the water inside the belly [of the fish].[258]

In this way, water nourishes fish, which Chu Hsi compared to the *ch'i* cultivating man's mind:

> This *ch'i* goes to cultivate that mind of humaneness and righteousness. It is like water nourishing fish. When water is plenty, the fish is tasty; when water is drying up, the fish falls sick. When this *ch'i* gets cultivated, the mind of humaneness and righteousness is also good; when the *ch'i* is scarce, the mind of humaneness and righteousness is also weak.[259]

In another example, he spoke of the hearts of pigs and chickens, which have empty spaces inside, in arguing that "man's heart is also thus, so that these empty spaces can contain and store many ways and *li*."[260] He also compared the scholar's effort in study to the hen sitting on eggs to hatch them.[261]

Notes

1. E.g., *YL*4.5b1; 20.16a1; 53.10a.

2. Although Needham's less awkward translation of the term as "vital impulse" (*Science and Civilisation,* 2:568) aptly conveys this aspect, it also carries many extra connotations. "Life principle" may be a smoother translation, but the word "principle" implies an unnecessary association with *li*, often translated as "principle." Cf. note 17. In *YL*89.13b0, Chu Hsi used the expression "*ch'ing*" (feelings) in distinguishing living beings from inanimate

things: "Coal is a dead thing and does not have 'feelings.' Therefore, plant roots do not enter [i.e., penetrate the coal]." But elsewhere, what the word distinguished was human affairs from natural events. *YL*72.2b3. See also chap. 8, p. 126.

3. E.g., *YL*4.6a2; 16.2b4.

4. *YL*4.6a2.

5. *YL*34.14b2.

6. E.g., *YL*4.5b1; 20.16a1; 53.10a0.

7. *YL*20.16a1. See also *YL*6.5b0.

8. *YL*69.17a0.

9. *YL*43.8b1. See also *WC*44.38b.

10. *YL*16.2b4.

11. *YL*76.12a1.

12. *YL*63.26b2.

13. *YL*27.11a1.

14. *YL*95.8a1.

15. E.g., *WC*59.35a–35b.

16. See chap. 6, p. 96.

17. *YL*69.17a0. See also *YL*100.8b1. "The mind of heaven and earth producing things," which, as we discussed in chapter 7, referred to the ability of heaven and earth to produce men and things and give life to them, is another concept similar to "life intent." In *YL*16.2b4–3a0 Chu Hsi even said that life intent was "the decree" of heaven, or was "originally consigned by heaven." But the mind of heaven and earth was responsible for the coming into being of everything, whether it had life or not. Also, whereas life intent had actual existence in the living body, the mind of heaven and earth was a more or less abstract idea.

18. E.g. *YL*4.5b1; *WC*59.35a–35b.

19. *YL*4.5b1.

20. For a classical discussion of the same idea in Western intellectual history, see Lovejoy, *Great Chain of Being*.

21. *WC*59.35a–35b.

22. *YL*4.3b0. We have seen the same kind of gradation in the variation of clarity, hardness, and speed of rotation of the layers of *ch'i* between heaven and earth. See chap. 9, p. 139.

23. E.g., *YL*4.1a4, 5; 3a4; 3b0; 9a1; 15a1; 17.4b3–5a0; 30.13a2; 57.7b2; 59.2a2;

63.20b0; 94.17b3; 98.12b2; *WC*39.24b; 50.30a; 62.8a; 73.44b; *CS*43.19a0.

24. E.g., *YL*4.15a1; 63.20b0; 98.12b2; *WC*58.13a, 13b; 59.35a–35b.

25. *YL*59.12b1.

26. *YL*57.8b0.

27. *YL*4.3b0. See also *YL*4.1a5, where Chu Hsi said that even insects have those virtues: "Only, [they] are one-sided and not complete."

28. *YL*57.7b2. See also *YL*4.2b1; 14.13a1; 17.5a0; *WC*58.13b.

29. The word "*chü-chiu*" appeared in the first poem of *Shih-ching* and is generally interpreted as the name of a waterfowl (osprey?) believed to observe fidelity in marital life.

30. E.g., *YL*4.2a0; 2b0, 1; 4a2; 9a1; 15a2–15b0; 17a0; 59.2b0; 62.10a3; 97.4b0; *CS*42.35a0.

31. *YL*59.2b0.

32. *YL*97.4b0. Chu Hsi did not elaborate, however, on what was the "exquisiteness" that these plants manifest.

33. *YL*4.9a1.

34. *YL*4.4a2.

35. E.g., *YL*4.2b1; 64.9b2.

36. *YL*4.2b1. See also *YL*97.4b0.

37. *YL*98.8b1. Here it is obvious that Chu Hsi took the roots of plants as their "heads." See also *YL*4.6a2, 9a1.

38. E.g., *YL*4.6a2, 9a1.

39. E.g., *YL*97.4b0; 138.9b3.

40. *YL*60.15a1. See also *YL*4.2b0; 8.3b2–4a0.

41. *YL*4.2b1.

42. *YL*4.9a1.

43. *YL*34.33b1. The quotation in this passage comes from the *Analects*, 2.12, although in the passage Chu Hsi was commenting on the *Analects*, 7.25. It is to be noted that Chu Hsi did not mention those men who do not reach the level of common men, that is, those who do not even comply with their roles. Obviously, he did not think those men worth the name "man."

44. E.g., *YL*59.2b2; 98.8b1.

45. E.g., *YL*4.4b3, 6a2.

46. *YL*17.5ao.
47. *YL*4.6a2.
48. *YL*4.4b5.
49. *YL*4.5a1.
50. For further discussion on perception, see chap. 11, pp. 213, 219ff.
51. *YL*60.8ao.
52. *YL*4.5b5–6ao.
53. *YL*17.4b2. Clearly, as Chu Hsi himself realized, the simple yin-yang scheme cannot fully accommodate all the varieties of living beings. Although Chu Hsi apparently based his yin-yang associations on the fact that yang *ch'i* comes from heaven, whereas yin *ch'i* comes from below (Yamada Keiji has added the movement of animals and the stillness of plants as their yang and yin characteristics. *Shu-shi no shizen-gaku*, p. 435), this is in conflict with his other belief that the earth can contain much yang *ch'i*, which it has received from heaven and with which it nourishes the myriad things; e.g., *YL*2.10b2; 74.24b2. Chu Hsi also mentioned Ts'ai Yüan-ting's yin-yang division of land and water animals, which is in conflict with the above yin-yang characterizations of land animals and birds: "Those on land have much yang and a little yin; those on water have much yin and a little yang." *YL*4.5b4.
54. It would be pointless to cite all the sources where Chu Hsi spoke of these things, but the following passages will illustrate the different ways they were utilized in his discussions of various problems: *YL*4.5b3; 14.2a2, 3; 27b3, 4; 15.16bo; 23.1b1, 2a2; 24.6a2; 25.27a1; 31.8a1, 8b1, 9b2; 41.16a1; 78.35b1; 101.32a3; 116.7bo, 8ao; 121.12a1; *WC*24.6b–9a; *CS*1.19a4; 2.11a1; 50.12a1.
55. *YL*89.13bo. See also *WC*45.31b–32a.
56. E.g., *YL*16.10b3, 11a1, 19bo; 59.36a2; *CS*63.12bo–13ao.
57. E.g., *YL*113.5a1; 117.18ao.
58. *YL*25.29bo.
59. E.g., *YL*14.14b3; 68.4a1; 73.2b1; 120.12b2; *WC*56.10a.
60. E.g., *YL*14.23ao; 23.1a2, 10a1; 57.11b2; *WC*60.18a; *CS*42.11bo.

61. *YL*120.12b2. See also *YL*14.14b3.
62. *YL*95.27b1.
63. E.g., *YL*16.17ao; 26.3a2; 95.11bo, 34a4; 113.7bo; 117.6ao.
64. *YL*9.9b4.
65. *YL*78.28bo.
66. E.g., *YL*32.15b3; 101.24a2; 117.24bo; 126.11a2.
67. E.g., *YL*4.15a1; 29.22ao, 23b3; 30.11a1; 31.14b2; 59.32ao; *WC*40.39b; *CS*6.46b1; 47.14b1.
68. *YL*1.8ao.
69. E.g., *YL*8.7b3; 114.12a2; 121.4ao; 138.5a1; *CS*2.3b4–4ao; 42.11ao–11bo.
70. *YL*114.12a2. See also *YL*71.7bo.
71. E.g., *YL*74.16a4.
72. E.g., *YL*89.13bo.
73. E.g., *YL*70.11b2; 100.6b1.
74. E.g., *YL*72.15a2.
75. E.g., *YL*97.3b1.
76. *YL*5.3a4.
77. *CS*2.3b4–4ao.
78. *CS*49.27b2. The *Lieh-tzu* passage appears in 1.15.
79. *WC*70.3a.
80. *YL*2.7b2.
81. E.g., *YL*81.20a4; *CS*50.4ao.
82. Donald J. Munro mentions "the family and the stream," "the mirror and the body," "the plant and the gardener" as examples that Chu Hsi used for "images of human nature"; see his *Images of Human Nature*.
83. E.g., *YL*11.2a2; 14.12a1–12bo, 15b1; 15.1b3; 17.7a1; 31.2b1, 7b4; 95.33b2; 101.24a2.
84. *YL*95.33b2.
85. *YL*5.9bo.
86. *YL*95.8ao.
87. *YL*4.8a1.
88. *YL*1.8b3. See also Chu Hsi's comments in *Chang-tzu ch'üan-shu*, 2.11b. The *Huai-nan-tzu* phrases appear in 3.1b. In *YL*1.8b2 Chu Hsi explained: "The darkness inside fire is yin in yang. Outside water it is dark and transparent, but inside, it is bright: [that is] yang in yin." In *YL*1.8b4 he referred to the brightness inside metal and

water as "clear brightness" and to the outside brightness of the sun and fire as "turbid brightness."

89. *YL*4.16b3.

90. E.g., *YL*2.8ao; 41.10ao; 101.24a2.

91. *YL*95.8ao.

92. *WC*47.10b–11a.

93. E. g., *YL*2.9a3.

94. E.g., *YL*41.10ao.

95. E.g., *YL*2.7b2, 8a2; 4.2b1; 79.27ao; *WC*47.10b.

96. *YL*5.7a1.

97. E.g., *YL*2.7b2, 8a2.

98. *YL*53.10bo.

99. *YL*2.8a2.

100. *YL*2.7b2–8ao.

101. *YL*2.8a2.

102. See chap. 9, p. 161.

103. *YL*1.5a7.

104. *YL*4.8bo.

105. *YL*19.13a2. The method is called "*hsiang ch'i-se.*"

106. *WC*32.12a. Although the reason that the intermediary color, green, is associated with east is not spelled out by Chu Hsi in the passage, it is not difficult to guess. From the two phases Wood and Earth, associated with the two regular colors, blue and yellow, the intermediary color green will select the phase that conquers rather than the one that is conquered. Green is thus associated with Wood and then with east.

107. The difficulty in imagining that some of the intermediary colors can be produced in the manner described by Chu Hsi —violet from red and black, horse brown from yellow and black, for example—also bespeaks his lack of interest in the actual process of mixing colors.

108. *YL*92.10b1.

109. *YL*92.3ao.

110. See chap. 3, p. 32.

111. *YL*65.7a4.

112. *YL*2.10b1.

113. *YL*99.4a1. Chang Tsai's original discussion appears in the "Tung-wu" (5th) chapter of *Cheng-meng* (*Chang-tzu ch'üan-shu*, 2.17a).

114. E.g., *YL*58.10a2, 3; 10b1; 92.5ao; *WC*40.17a–17b. For the translation of the *Mencius* phrase, I have used Chu Hsi's glossaries in *SSCC* (*Meng-tzu*), 5.14a.

115. *SSCC* (*Meng-tzu*), 5.14a. See also *YL*35.22bo.

116. *SSCC* (*Meng-tzu*), 5.14a. He even said that metal and stone were 'the principles" (*kan-chi*) of the multitude of sounds.

117. E.g., *YL*58.10a2, 3. In *YL*58.10a2 he went on to say that metal bells are used at the beginning of music and jade tubes at the end. See also *YL*58.10b1; 92.5ao; *SSCC* (*Meng-tzu*), 5.14a.

118. *YL*92.4b2.

119. E.g., *YL*92.8bo.

120. E.g., *YL*78.17b4; 18ao, 1; 18b1; 21b5. The expression first appeared in the "Shun-tien" chapter of *Shu-ching*, p. 3.9a. The compilers of the *YL* even chose a passage about the old measuring rulers as the first one in the volume on music: *YL*92.1a1. See also *YL*92.1a2, 3; 1b1.

121. *YL*92.3ao. See also *YL*92.4b4.

122. E.g., *YL*92.1b4, 6; 4b2, 3; *WC*72.1b. Although high pitches are generally characterized as "large" and low ones as "thin," Chu Hsi had them the opposite way in *WC*72.1b, where what is characterized is not the pitches themselves but the sizes of the pitch pipes. See also *YL*78.36bo, where the *kung* note, the lowest one, is said to be the largest and the highest *yü* note the smallest.

123. *YL*92.1a3.

124. *Shih-chi*, ch. 25, p. 1249.

125. *WC*66.27b.

126. E.g., *YL*92.1b5; 2bo, 1; 10bo; *WC*45.36b. They are called "the half sound" (*pan-sheng*), "the son sound" (*tzu-sheng*) or "the clear sound" (*ch'ing-sheng*). For more on this, see chap. 12, p. 260.

127. *YL*92.3a2.

128. *YL*92.2bo.

129. The procedure is described, e.g., in *WC*66.27b–28a.

130. *YL*87.11b2; 92.4a1, 2; *WC*72.1b–3a.

131. E.g., *YL*78.36bo; 92.10b3.

132. Needham has aptly characterized this feature of the five notes in the following manner:

[T]he earliest Chinese conception of a scale was not, as in the West, that of a ladder ascending from low to high or descending from high to low pitch, but of a court in which the notes are ranged on either side of the chief or *kung* note. (*Science and Civilisation*, vol. 4, pt. 1, p. 159)

We shall see a similar qualitative character in Chu Hsi's conception of space, in which different qualitative characteristics were associated with the four compass directions; see chap. 13, p. 304.

133. *WC*72.1b.

134. *YL*78.36bo.

135. *YL*92.3ao. See also *YL*25.20ao; 39.1a1–1bo; 92.2b1, 3a1, 10bo.

136. *YL*75.7b1.

137. *YL*125.8a1. Here, Chu Hsi was commenting on the *Lao-tzu* phrase "The valley spirits (*ku-shen*) do not die" (ch. 6). He added, "This is a spontaneous [process] of the *shen* and transformation." See also *YL*125.7b1, where he said: "Valleys are empty. There are spirits (*shen*) in the valleys. They receive sounds; thus they can produce echoes. They receive things; thus they can produce things."

138. E.g., *YL*27.32a4; 69.15a4. These phenomena, which we would now refer to as "acoustic resonance," were, for Chu Hsi, simply an example of mutual responses taking place universally between two things of the same category. See chap. 8.

139. E.g., *YL*92.8b2–9ao; *WC*44.10bo. Similarly, when cutting a jade tube, the workmen adjust its dimensions so that its sounds match the standard twelve pitches. See *YL*92.4b3, where Chu Hsi is commenting on a *Chou-li* passage (41.9a).

140. E.g., *YL*74.25ao; *WC*45.37a, 66.30b–31a. For brief discussions of this practice, see Bodde, "Chinese Cosmic Magic Known as 'Watching for the Ethers'";

Huang and Chang, "Chung-kuo chuant'ung hou-ch'i-shuo te yen-chin yü shuai-t'ui"; Huang and Chang, "Evolution and Decline of the Ancient Chinese Practice of Watching for the Ethers."

141. E.g., *YL*87.11b2.

142. *YL*92.9ao.

143. *YL*92.5b1.

144. E.g., *YL*25.24bo. In *YL*22.9a1 Chu Hsi even said that "harmony is the basis of music."

145. *YL*115.13ao.

146. *YL*120.13a3.

147. E.g., *YL*8.13a3; 10.6a1, 8ao; 14.5a1.

148. *YL*10.8ao.

149. *YL*14.5a1. These remarks, however, should not be considered as suggesting a microscopic, or even a corpuscular, mechanism for the perception of taste.

150. *YL*8.3b1.

151. *YL*138.14a2.

152. *YL*95.11bo.

153. But again, these remarks did not necessarily imply a microscopic mechanism for the perception of smell. Nor is it quite clear what Chu Hsi meant when he said: "Sound and smell have *ch'i* but do not have physical form. Among the things [they] are the most subtle, and one may as well say they do not exist." *SSCC* (*Chung-yung*), p. 24b. It may be that he was simply referring to the fact that smell, like sound and unlike light or color, is not visible.

154. *YL*98.3a1.

155. *YL*98.3b5.

156. *YL*1.3b1.

157. *YL*53.4a1.

158. *YL*98.1b1. See also *YL*53.4a1.

159. *YL*98.3b2.

160. *CS*49.26a1. See chap. 3, p. 33.

161. *YL*94.13b1.

162. *YL*1.6a2.

163. *YL*94.13a1.

164. *YL*97.4a2.

165. *YL*94.13a1. See also *YL*1.6a2; *CS*49.26a1. In *CS*49.26a1 Chu Hsi even said that "lice popped out spontaneously."

166. *YL*60.7b1.

167. E.g., *YL*1.6a2; 62.21b0; 94.13a1; 98.2b1; *WC*52.15b; *CS*49.26a1.

168. *CS*49.26a1. This is the continuation of the passage cited in note 160. See also *YL*94.13b1.

169. *YL*76.9a2.

170. *WC*52.15b. There was still another related expression, *hua-sheng*, which could be rendered as "production of life through transformation." The expression had appeared in the following sentence of Chou Tun-i's: "The two *ch'i* interact and stimulate each other and produce the myriad things through transformation." *T'ai-chi-t'u shuo.* Chu Hsi had the same sentence in *YL*53.8b1. In his commentary on the *T'ai-chi-t'u shuo*, Chu Hsi equated the expression with "transformation of physical form." But in *YL*1.6a2 he attributed the expression to Buddhists and used it in referring to the "transformation of *ch'i*" and to the spontaneous appearance of lice, to which, elsewhere, he compared the process of the transformation of *ch'i.*

171. For a brief discussion of Chang Tsai's ideas on the supreme void, see Kasoff, *Thought of Chang Tsai*, pp. 37–43.

172. *YL*60.7b1. Chang Tsai's saying appears in the "T'ai-ho" (1st) chapter of *Cheng-meng* (*Chang-tzu ch'üan-shu*, 2.3b).

173. E.g., *YL*98.3a2; 3b2, 3.

174. *Chang-tzu ch'üan-shu*, 2.4b. Most of Chu Hsi's comments on this passage, cited below, are also gathered and appended to *Chang-tzu ch'üan-shu*, 2.4b–5a.

175. E.g., *YL*98.2a1–2b0; 3a1, 2.

176. *YL*98.3a2.

177. E.g., *YL*98.2b2; 3a1; 3b2, 3.

178. *YL*98.2b1.

179. E.g., *YL*36.24a1; 62.10a3; 126.22b0; *CS*39.18a1. In *YL*138.7a3 Chu Hsi spoke of the *ch'i* of "the true origin" (*chen-yüan*), but this referred to the origin of the *ch'i* produced continuously inside man's body. See chap. 11, pp. 221–222.

180. *Chang-tzu ch'üan-shu*, 2.2a.

181. Ibid., 3.23b. The phrase "the wandering *hun* making a change," comes from "Hsi-tz'u chuan," ch. A4, where it pairs with a parallel phrase, "the essence *ch'i* becoming things" (*ching-ch'i wei wu*). For Chu Hsi's discussion on these phrases, see, e.g., *YL*83.21a2.

182. For Chu Hsi's remarks on *lun-hui*, see, e.g., *YL*126.22a4; 22b1, 2.

183. For the different views of Chang Tsai and Ch'eng I on this, see, e.g., Graham, *Two Chinese Philosophers*, pp. 41–42; Kasoff, *Thought of Chang Tsai*, pp. 139–140.

184. *YL*126.22b0.

185. *YL*99.5b1. See also *WC*54.34b.

186. E.g., *YL*1.3a0; 13.12a1; 23.10a1.

187. E.g., *YL*68.16a2; 116.8b0.

188. *WC*43.10b. The *chu* and the *kou-wen* plants have been identified as *Atractylodes chinensis* and *Gelsemium elegans*, respectively. Needham, *Science and Civilisation*, vol. 6, pt. 1, pp. 481, 487–488.

189. *YL*16.2a1.

190. *Analects*, 17.9.

191. For such a context of scholars' interest in plant species, see, e.g., Needham, *Science and Civilisation*, vol. 6, pt. 1, pp. 440–471, where Needham also points out another context, namely the availability of new plants as the result of the southward expansion of China.

192. Chu Hsi's comments on the *Shih-ching* are gathered in *YL*80–81. For his comments on the *Ch'u-tz'u*, see *Ch'u-tz'u chi-chu.*

193. *YL*69.16b3.

194. *YL*20.16a1.

195. *YL*116.8a0.

196. *YL*68.13b1.

197. *YL*94.16a2.

198. *YL*72.4b1.

199. *YL*71.7b0.

200. *YL*4.6b1.

201. E.g., *YL*10.6a1; 52.31a0; *WC*38.36b.

202. E.g., *YL*72.24a2, 3.

203. *YL*95.8a1.

204. E.g., *YL*10.6a1; 34.14b2; 60.8a0; 120.1b0. In *YL*80.19b1; *WCP*9.4a, Chu Hsi spoke of the use of human manure to supply plant nutrients.

205. E.g., *YL*4.6a2; 52.31a0.

206. *YL*4.4b5. See also *YL*76.4b0.

207. E.g., *YL*4.6a2; 23.19a1; 53.10a0; 60.8a0; 95.2b0.

208. *YL*36.24a1.

209. Chu Hsi usually compared what he considered to be the basic virtue to the root and the derivative virtues to other parts. For example: "Humaneness is the root. Commiseration is the sprout coming forth from the root. To be filial to parents, to be benevolent to people, to love things—these are the branches and leaves." *YL*119.4a0. Of the latter three virtuous conducts, "being filial to parents is the root, being benevolent to people is the stem, and loving things is the branches and leaves." *YL*20.23a0. See also *YL*20.13b2. He also compared humaneness to the grain (seed) that produces a seedling, which, in turn, was compared to filial piety and brotherly love, both of which are manifestations of humaneness. *YL*20.23a0. Other virtues that were considered basic and compared to the root in this manner were loyalty (*chung*) and faith. E.g., *YL*27.11a1; 69.3b2.

At times Chu Hsi's interest lay so much in the analogous human problems that the direction of the analogy became inverted and he tended to make up, or even distort, facts about plant parts to make them appear analogous to the human problems in question. For example, in a passage discussing the four constant virtues and their manifestations in the four feelings, Chu Hsi drew a comparison to quite an unlikely fact: "Suppose a tree has four branches, then even though it [appears as though it] had just one large root, there must [actually] be four roots. For one branch must have one root." *YL*120.24b0. To illustrate the theory that the *ch'i* of ancestors reaches the descendants during sacrificial services, he said, "When a tree has already dried and decayed, a new root comes up nearby, contacting and continuing this correct *ch'i* [of the dead tree]." *YL*25.14a3. Another similar example is his remark that one kernel of fruit forms one seed. *YL*74.19b2.

210. *YL*27.7a0.

211. *YL*27.11a1.

212. Ibid.

213. *YL*64.14a5–14b0. The *Chung-yung* sentence "That which is sincere accomplishes by itself" appears in ch. 25.

214. *YL*74.19b2. See also *YL*74.20a1.

215. *YL*25.5b1. See also *YL*20.13b2; 25.6b1; 69.3b2; *WC*43.10b.

216. *YL*74.19b2. See also *YL*27.7a0.

217. See also *YL*20.13b2; 25.6b1.

218. *YL*23.19a1.

219. *YL*10.6a1. See also *YL*89.13b0, where Chu Hsi says that roots are attracted by "yellow mud."

220. *YL*25.14a3. See note 209.

221. *YL*4.6a2.

222. *YL*73.2b2. The *I-ching* phrase is on the *ting* hexagram, constituted of the *k'an* trigram (associated with water) placed on top of the *sun* trigram (associated with wood).

223. E.g., *YL*73.2b1, 2. In the latter passage, he rejected that the water droplets are dew, for they were formed even when the plants were in a closed room. Later in the same passage, when someone told the following story, Chu Hsi did not reject it:

> Every morning, the taro leaves also contained water jewels. Only when the sun rose, shone on, and dried them, was there no damage. If the sun did not shine on them, and if they were torn apart and fell down by other things, then the taro fruits withered and had no taste. Sometimes they produced worms.

224. *YL*4.6b2. It is to be noted that the withering of flowers was treated here more as a kind of behavioral pattern of flowers than as a physiological process.

225. *YL*74.20a1.

226. *WC*52.16a.

227. *YL*4.6b2.

228. *YL*74.20a1.

229. E.g., *YL*12.18a0; 16.19a0; 74.19b2; 116.8b0. As we have seen, however, Chu Hsi said that "one kernel forms one seed." *YL*74.19b2.

230. *YL*94.8a1–8b0. See also Y20.16a1; 116.8b0.

231. *YL*95.2a2.

232. *YL*95.2b0.

233. *YL*69.16b3. On details of the processes of seed formation and the sprouting of seeds, however, Chu Hsi did not have any more to say. They were, for him, among the most natural processes in the world and required no explanation. In other words, there was no problem of plant reproduction for him. To be sure, he said at least that plants also have sexuality, speaking of the existence of male and female plants in such species as bamboo, hemp, ginko, paulownia, and mulberry. But his real point in speaking of them was that everything in the world has its yin and yang aspects. See, e.g., *YL*65.2b4; 74.3b3; 76.4b0; 94.13a0, 13b2. There is no reliable reference on traditional Chinese knowledge about the sexuality and reproduction of plants. Needham, *Science and Civilisation*, sec. 38h (to be written by Georges Métailié), which will deal with these topics, has not been published yet.

234. See p. 175.

235. *YL*4.15a2–15b0.

236. *YL*24.26a0. The expression "*kuei-ju*" (to kneel to suck) even became an idiom with the meaning of "to show filial piety."

237. *YL*4.1a5.

238. *YL*17.5a0.

239. E.g., *YL*59.2b2; 62.11a0, 1, 3.

240. *YL*4.4b1.

241. *YL*17.4b2.

242. *YL*72.5a0. See also *WC*42.2a–2b. For Chu Hsi's other comments on the *I-ching* remark, see, e.g., *YL*76.6b1–3.

243. *YL*72.5a0.

244. *YL*74.10b1.

245. *YL*76.4a4.

246. *YL*76.4b0.

247. See chap. 5, pp. 80, 88 (note 79).

248. *YL*74.10b1.

249. *YL*76.4a4. *YL*138.10b4–11a0 contains reports by Chu Hsi and his disciples on various recorded appearances of dragons. In one of them, Chu Hsi quoted the following record: "[When] the dragon first came out of the water, there first was a thing like the shape of a lotus blossom, and afterward the water gushed up. A strange thing appeared, [with] lights on both eyes like copper discs."

250. *YL*81.3a3.

251. *YL*81.3b0. The *Shih-ching* phrase appears in the poem titled "Tung-shan."

252. *Ch'u-tz'u chi-chu*, 3.109.

253. Ibid., 1.37.

254. E.g., *YL*138.7b2, 3; 8a2; 9b2, 3. *YL*138 is titled "Miscellaneous category" (*tsa-lei*).

255. *WC*75.28a.

256. *YL*105.8a2. The essay, "Ching-chai chen," is contained in *WC*85.5b–6a.

257. It was also to illustrate the alternation of inhalation and exhalation that Chu Hsi mentioned the continuous movement of a snail exiting and entering its shell.

258. *CS*49.5a2.

259. *YL*59.17b2.

260. *YL*98.7b1. Chu Hsi saw these animal hearts because they were, as he said, common foods.

261. *YL*8.3b1. Again, as was the case with plants, the human-centeredness of Chu Hsi's knowledge about animals was so predominant that the direction of analogical inference was sometimes inverted—from man to animals. For example, Chu Hsi spoke of "a baby [fish] inside a fish" in an obvious parallelism with the human case. *YL*74.20a1. But his point was that "a baby [fish], when it is inside the mother fish, is one life with the mother," whereas it formed a separate life itself when it came out of the mother fish, and with it he illustrated the above-mentioned "Hsi-tz'u chuan" phrases, "to manifest it in humaneness" and "to store it in function." It is unlikely that he had in mind the actual mode of reproduction of fish, for then it would have been impossible for him not to think of fish eggs, which were available as a common food, perhaps more common than chicken or pig hearts. Nor can the above remark be in-

terpreted as suggesting that Chu Hsi knew of the existence of viviparous fish, which Joseph Needham proposed in a private communication to me (dated 17 December 1981). Cf. *YL*126.17a2, where Chu Hsi quoted a passage from the Buddhist canon, *Chin-kang-ching*, that mentions different modes of reproduction: viviparous birth (*t'ai-sheng*), oviparous birth (*luan-sheng*) "the wet birth" (*shih-sheng*), and "the birth through transformation" (*hua-sheng*). On the last of these terms, see note 170.

CHAPTER 11

Man

Chu Hsi made abundant remarks about man. Indeed, almost all of his sayings and writings were in some sense about man, because as a good Confucian he was constantly concerned with human problems. But he was not interested in all aspects of man equally. His goal was to answer the question of how man should live in the world as a true human being.[1] Thus, his concern was usually with social, moral, or metaphysical problems. The parts, functions, and activities of the human body—what we would call physiological or anatomical—were rarely his primary concern;[2] his remarks about them are scattered in various places where he discussed other problems. This chapter is based on my attempt to construct a systematic account from those scattered remarks.

I have discussed in earlier chapters some of Chu Hsi's general ideas about man: the trichotomy of heaven-earth-man; the parallelism of the world as macrocosm and man as microcosm; the distinction between man and nonhuman things, with sets of distinguishing characteristics. Another general point to be added here, before we look at concrete ideas about the human body, is that Chu Hsi did not make a clear distinction between physical and physiological phenomena on the one hand and mental and moral phenomena on the other, or between body and mind.[3] This will be most clearly seen in his ideas about the interaction between mind and *ch'i*, discussed in section 11.4.

11.1. Man's Body and Its Constituents

The basis of Chu Hsi's ideas about the human body is that it is made of *ch'i*. He said, for example, that "man also is simply *ch'i*."[4] This point is unexceptionable, because everything in the world is made of *ch'i*. But the statement could mean different things. It could mean simply that man's body is formed by the aggregation of formless *ch'i*, as is everything else in the world; but it also meant that man's body was filled with *ch'i*.[5]

To Chu Hsi, this *ch'i* that forms and fills man's body—man is "endowed with" this *ch'i*—is nothing but the *ch'i* of heaven and earth: "There is no place where the *ch'i* of heaven and earth does not reach [or] . . . penetrate. . . . Man simply is endowed with this *ch'i*."[6] He also said: "The *ch'i* of heaven and earth . . . is that which I receive and fill the body with";[7] "Man is born, receiving the *ch'i* of heaven and earth."[8] Thus it is that both "inside and outside [man's body], there is nothing that is not the yin and yang *ch'i* of heaven and earth."[9] "The *ch'i* of man and the *ch'i* of heaven and earth are constantly in contact with each other, [between which] there is no gap."[10] Chu Hsi even said that "man's *ch'i* is simply the *ch'i* of heaven and earth."[11] It is natural, then, that man's *ch'i* can have qualities of the *ch'i* of heaven and earth—for example, its extreme hardness that enables it to penetrate anything, even gold and stone.[12]

The *ch'i* constituting different men is different in its quality. "Differences of being shallow, deep, thick, and thin"[13] or "of being dark, bright, clear, and turbid"[14] in the endowed *ch'i* give rise to the differences in men. For example, as we saw in chapter 3, different endowments of *ch'i* are responsible for such behavioral characteristics as vigor, courage, and subservience, such moral qualities as goodness and evilness, and such intellectual qualities as wisdom, intelligence, and stupidity. We have also seen that Chu Hsi attributed all the other kinds of differences—from the difference in life span to that between sages and "small men"—to differences in the quality of man's endowed *ch'i*.

These differences arise because man's *ch'i* is frequently one-sided. Chu Hsi said, "Although men's natures are the same, the endowed *ch'i* cannot but have one-sidedness," and added:

> As for those who got Wood *ch'i* heavily, [their] mind of "commiseration" (associated with Wood) is always abundant, but the minds of "shame and dislike" (Metal), of "respect and reverence" (Fire), and of "right and wrong" (Water) are blocked and do not come forth. As for those who got Metal *ch'i* heavily, [their] mind of "shame and dislike" is always abundant, but [the other] minds . . . are blocked and do not come forth. [With] Water and Fire [*ch'i*], it is also the same.[15]

This is so because, as Chu Hsi said elsewhere, "when a man gets [the yin and yang *ch'i* and the five-phase *ch'i*], they simply are hardness and softness and the five constant virtues."[16] Sages are those in whom all of these are in balance: "Only after yin and yang have combined their power and the five natures have been completely provided, the balance is correct and one becomes a sage."[17] For Chu Hsi, the reason that all men cannot become sages is that their originally good nature "has been damaged by the endowments of their *ch'i*": "For example, when the endowment of *ch'i* is inclined to hardness, then one is only tough and fierce; when it is inclined to softness, then one is only soft and weak, and so on."[18] It is also because of such one-sidedness that "some men can know exhaustively about profits and losses of the world but do not know righteousness and *li*, and [that] some are skilled in hundreds of skills and techniques but do not understand books."[19] When a disciple attributed women's proneness to fear to the one-sidedness of their endowed *ch'i*, Chu Hsi commented: "The humaneness of women flows only through love."[20]

Man gets the *ch'i* of heaven and earth, determining his various qualities, at the time of his birth: "When a man is born, he meets the [yin-yang and the five-phase]

ch'i [of heaven and earth]. There are some who get the clear *ch'i*, and some who get
the turbid *ch'i*."[21] To be more specific,

> When the sun and the moon are clear and bright, and the weather is harmonious and cor-
> rect, and if a man is born and is endowed with this *ch'i*, then it is the clear, bright, com-
> plete, and thick *ch'i* and must make a good man. If the sun and the moon are dark, and
> the cold and hot weather is not normal, all this is the perverse *ch'i* of heaven and earth.
> If a man is endowed with this *ch'i*, then he becomes a bad man. How can this be
> doubted?[22]

Thus it is that men born at different times and in different regions show different
qualities.[23] Chu Hsi also maintained that "the fate" of a man is determined by the
ch'i with which he is endowed at birth: "Death and life have the fate, [which was]
fixed at the time when [one] was originally endowed with *ch'i*."[24] As for wealth and
nobleness, poverty and lowliness, long and short life, these all have "fixed *shu* (*ting-
shu*) residing inside it [namely, inside the endowed *ch'i*]," and it is "the *shu* of the
ch'i with which he is endowed at the time of birth [that] fixed it like this."[25]

   This belief gave rise to certain questions. Among the most frequently asked was
why a sage like Confucius remained poor and failed to occupy a high position. A
common answer, which was Chu Hsi's also, was that there were different sets of
characteristics accounting for different aspects of man. A typical conversation discussing the question ran as follows:

> QUESTION: If one gets clear and bright *ch'i*, one becomes a sage; [if one gets] dark and
>   turbid *ch'i*, one becomes stupid and unworthy. If one's *ch'i* is thick, one becomes rich
>   and noble; if it is thin, one becomes poor and lowly. . . . Yet, Confucius on the contrary
>   was poor and lowly. Why was this so? . . .
> ANSWER: It was because what he was endowed with had a deficiency. That clearness and
>   brightness of his [endowed *ch'i*] could only make a sage, but could not get that rich-
>   ness and nobility. If one is endowed with such high [*ch'i*], one is noble; endowed with
>   the thick [*ch'i*], one is rich; endowed with the long [*ch'i*], one lives long. Poverty, low
>   position, and early death are the opposites. Although Confucius got the clear and
>   bright one to become a sage, he was [also] endowed with the low and thin, and thus
>   was poor and lowly.[26]

Chu Hsi noted that there indeed were those who had clear *ch'i* and were intelligent
but unfortunate and those who had turbid *ch'i* and were ignorant but fortunate, and
he concluded that "the *shu* of their *ch'i* made it so."[27] That a sage like Yao had a
delinquent like Tan Chu for a son and, conversely, that a villain like Kun fathered
a sage like Yü also posed a problem, but Chu Hsi could still explain it in terms of
the *ch'i* at the time of the sons' birth: "When the two *ch'i* and the five phases meet
together and move around, there are the clear and the turbid. Men fall in with the
moment. Therefore, it was like that."[28] Chu Hsi could even explain why "great men
are always rare and small men are always abundant":

Naturally, the *ch'i* of those [men] is impure and mixed. It is sometimes in front and sometimes behind. Thus, one cannot get it to be exactly [good]. How can one get it balanced?
Talking about it in terms of a day, it is sometimes dark and sometimes clear, sometimes
windy and sometimes rainy, sometimes cold and sometimes hot, sometimes peaceful and
sometimes confused. . . . [From this] it is possible to see [why that was so].[29]

What actually fills man's body is not the formless *ch'i* of heaven and earth with
which man is originally endowed, but gaseous and fluid substances possessing various qualities and performing various functions. Traditional Chinese medical theories generally considered them as varieties of *ch'i* and usually gave them names
coined by attaching various labels to *ch'i*. Manfred Porkert has listed thirty-two
such names that appeared in medical texts.[30] Some of the labels refer to aspects of
formless *ch'i*, such as "the correct *ch'i*" (*cheng-ch'i*), "the original *ch'i*" (*yüan-ch'i*),
and "the essence *ch'i*" (*ching-ch'i*); but others refer less ambiguously to aggregated
states of *ch'i* that have acquired physical form and tangible qualities, such as "the
formed *ch'i*" (*hsing-ch'i*), "the blood *ch'i*" (*hsueh-ch'i*), and "the evil *ch'i*" (*li-ch'i*).
Sometimes the character *ch'i* was confined to a narrower meaning and was contrasted with other forms of bodily contents, such as blood (*hsueh*), essence (*ching*),
shen, and *p'o*. There were also other single-character words designating different
constituents of the body: *chin* and *yeh*, *ying* and *wei*, for example.[31] *Ch'i* and these
terms stood in various dualistic yin-yang relations with one another and could be
incorporated into a complex associative system: *ch'i* as yang and blood as yin, *ch'i*
as yang and essence as yin, *wei* as yang and *ying* as yin, and so on.[32]

Many of these words entered the common language, and we have already come
across Chu Hsi's use of them on various occasions. Chu Hsi also spoke of various yin-
yang relations between different forms of bodily contents, as is shown in table 11.1.
But the isolated cases in which he mentioned these terms do not allow us to tell
whether he subscribed to, or even understood, the detailed technical content of the
systematic medical knowledge based on them. What we know is that he did not discuss it explicitly in his writings or conversations. Characteristically, of the many dualistic pairs mentioned above, it was the *hun-p'o* dichotomy, least often used in technical medical texts, that he discussed the most extensively.[33] Furthermore, although
most modern scholars now agree that in traditional medical theories the *ch'i* varieties
in the body were not actually different substances but rather were different forms,
qualities, and functions of the same *ch'i*, it is not clear whether Chu Hsi himself consistently held that latter view, or even whether he would have followed the modern
scholars in making a distinction between the two alternatives.[34]

The *ch'i* variety most frequently mentioned by Chu Hsi was "the blood *ch'i*." It
is not clear, however, what he meant by the term; nor did he seem to mean the same
thing always. Much of his discussion on it occurred in his comments on the following remark of Confucius:

There are three things a gentleman should guard against. In youth, when "the blood
ch'i" is not settled yet, he should guard against attractions of women [literally, "color"].

TABLE 11.1
The Yin-Yang Relations of Bodily Contents
Mentioned by Chu Hsi

Yang	Yin	Reference[a]
ch'i	essence (*ching*)	YL3.7a1
ch'i	blood (*hsueh*)	YL87.29a1
ch'i	body (*t'i*)	YL74.14a4
ch'i	tangible quality (*chih*)	YL87.26b1
ch'i	*p'o*	YL74.14a4
hun	*p'o*	YL87.26b1
essence	tangible quality	YL83.21a2

Note
[a]Only one representative reference is given for each pair.

In the prime of life, when "the blood *ch'i*" has hardened, he should guard against strife. In old age, when "the blood *ch'i*" has already declined, he should guard against acquisitiveness.[35]

Here it is obvious that "the blood *ch'i*" refers to the physical aspect—strength or energy—of man's body. Chu Hsi also interpreted the term in that sense and followed Fan Chung-yen (989–1052), who made the distinction between "the blood *ch'i*" and "the will *ch'i*" (*chih-ch'i*):

What the Sage (i.e., Confucius) has in common with [other] men is the blood *ch'i*; what is different from [other] men is [his] will *ch'i*. The blood *ch'i* sometimes declines; the will *ch'i* never declines. That which is not settled in youth, hardened in the prime of life, and declining in old age, is the blood *ch'i*. That which guards against the attractions of women, strife, and against acquisitiveness is the will *ch'i*. The gentleman cultivates his will *ch'i* and therefore is not moved by the blood *ch'i*.[36]

Again, the blood *ch'i* and the will *ch'i*, for Chu Hsi, were not different substances but simply two different aspects of the same *ch'i*: "*Ch'i* is one. What is in charge of mind is the will *ch'i*; what is in charge of physical form and body is the blood *ch'i*."[37]

The blood *ch'i* was also what made man and animals different from plants.[38] In this case "the blood *ch'i*" could simply mean blood, which man and animals have but plants do not. Chu Hsi spoke, for example, of "feeling the pulse (*ch'ieh mo*) and seeing the blood *ch'i* flow around."[39] But it is possible that the term covered other fluid substances as well. Indeed, it could mean "blood and *ch'i*," referring to both the yin and yang parts of the *ch'i*-blood dichotomy. The blood *ch'i*, then, covers all the fluid and gaseous constituents of man's body. It is in this sense that Chu Hsi said, "The blood *ch'i* [is] that which fills [man's] body."[40] He even used the expression "the body of blood *ch'i*" in referring to the human body.[41]

Another *ch'i* variety that Chu Hsi often mentioned was "the essence *ch'i*," which appeared frequently in his comments on the "Hsi-tz'u chuan" phrase "The essence *ch'i* becomes things" (*ching-ch'i wei wu*) (ch. A4).[42] Yet, Chu Hsi usually took the term as two words, "essence" and "*ch'i*." His ideas about them are discussed in section 11.6, along with *hun* and *p'o*, with which they were frequently associated.[43]

11.2. The Parts of the Human Body

Nathan Sivin has aptly characterized the conception of man's body in traditional Chinese medical theories as "an organism composed of functional systems that extracted vital substances from air and food, distributed them where they were needed, expelled the residues, and resisted the factors of disease."[44] Sivin has elaborated on this in terms of "three types of substratum for distinct functions" in the contents of the body:

> First there are the eleven visceral systems, . . . [which] ferment food, extract and store the vital essence from it and from air, maintain and regulate the distribution of the essence, and expel the residues. Secondly there is the circulation tract system, which provides a network through which the nutritive essences are distributed throughout the body, . . . Finally there are the various fluid and pneumatic sources of vitality, some extracted by the visceral systems and some inborn, stored and moved both through and outside the circulation system.[45]

This conception of the body naturally led to the predominantly functional, rather than structural, orientation of traditional Chinese medical knowledge.[46]

It is possible that Chu Hsi had the same conception and shared the same orientation, but he hardly ever showed it; he was not interested in details about the contents and structure of man's body. His sayings and writings contain little that can be called anatomical knowledge, that is, description of the different parts and organs of the body. For example, he knew that it contained the "five storing viscera" (*wu-tsang*) (the heart [*hsin*], the liver [*kan*], the spleen [*p'i*], the lungs [*fei*], and the kidneys [*shen*]) and the "six processing viscera" (*liu-fu*) (the gall [*tan*], the small intestine [*hsiao-ch'ang*], the stomach [*wei*], the large intestine [*ta-ch'ang*], the bladder [*p'ang-kuang*], and the three caloria [*san-chiao*]).[47] He said that every man "has the five storing viscera and the six processing viscera inside [his body]."[48] But he did not concern himself with anatomical description of these visceral systems.[49] The only exception was the heart, which he considered to be the site of the mind; but all he said about its anatomy was that it had empty spaces inside, and this to explain that man's mind can contain many ways and *li*, as we have already seen.[50] Rarely did he even mention the individual names of the viscera.[51] On the circulation tract system, he mentioned only the words "blood vessel" (*hsueh-mo*, or *mo*) and "spine" (*ch'i*).[52] The same can be said about the external parts of man's body. In the few cases in which Chu Hsi spoke of some very simple anatomical features of them, his actual interest lay in illustrating certain classical phrases. For example, he said that man's back cannot move, whereas "the four limbs and hundred bones can move," in discussing the *I-ching* phrase "keeping the back still" (*ken ch'i pei*).[53] He said also that the skin has many pores, some "eighty-four thousand hair-pores," which "the original *ch'i*" can pass through, but this only to illustrate the *Analects* phrase "As for my Way, it is penetrated through by one" (4.15).[54]

Chu Hsi was far more interested in associating the parts and the organs of the body with various human characteristics. The most frequent examples were that the eyes see, the ears hear, the nose smells, the mouth speaks, the hands hold things, and the feet walk.[55] It is to be noted, however, that these characteristics were not what we would call anatomical or physiological; they were almost always behavioral, which is well illustrated by the fact that as the characteristic for the mouth, he chose speaking instead of eating. Typically, the perceptual organs were associated with man's perceiving activities. The visceral organs also were linked with the perceiving activities, through their association with the perceptual organs: the liver with the eyes, and thus with seeing; the kidneys with the ears, and thus with hearing.[56] Sometimes the characteristics of the organs mentioned were normative rather than descriptive: for example, "the brightness of the eyes, and the astuteness of the ears."[57]

The parts and the organs of the body were associated with human desires also. Chu Hsi mentioned common desires associated with particular parts or organs: the mouth desires taste, or to eat; the ears desire sound; the eyes desire colors; the nose desires smell; and the four limbs desire comfort.[58] He also spoke of human desires not associated with particular parts of the body: for example, the desire for life, seeking life and avoiding death; the sexual desire, man and woman seeking each other; and the economic desire, seeking profit and avoiding loss.[59] For him these desires were a natural consequence of man's having a physical body: "Man has this body and therefore has the desires of the ears, eyes, nose, mouth, and the four limbs."[60] To be more specific, these desires are "the desires of *ch'i*";[61] they are "produced from the blood *ch'i*."[62] Thus, Chu Hsi did not reject man's bodily desires. For him such desires should not be said to be "bad, but [should] simply [be said] to be dangerous."[63] He rejected a disciple's suggestion that a man with clear *ch'i* does not have desires.[64] Even the sages, Confucius for example, cannot be free from desires: the sages also eat when hungry and drink when thirsty.[65] It is simply that "the feelings of the sage are not indulged in them."[66]

11.3. *Hsin:* Heart and Mind

The most important part of the body for Chu Hsi was the heart, for he shared the common belief that the heart was the site of the mind in man's body: the same character *hsin* was used both for the visceral organ the heart and for the mind. Chu Hsi distinguished the two senses in the following manner:

> As for the *hsin* (heart) of the five storing viscera like the lungs and the liver, in fact, there actually is a thing. If it is the *hsin* (mind), of which scholars nowadays speak of "holding, throwing away, keeping, and losing," then it is naturally *shen* and bright, and is unfathomable. Therefore, if the *hsin* (heart) of the five storing viscera gets a disease, then one

can use medicine and replenish it; but if it is this *hsin* (mind) [that gets a disease], then [even] calamus (*ch'ang-p'u*) and tuckahoe (*fu-ling*) cannot replenish it.[67]

But the mind exists not only in the heart; it can exist elsewhere in the body. Chu Hsi interpreted Ch'eng Hao's saying "What fills the cavity (*ch'iang-tzu*) is the mind of commiseration" to mean that the mind of commiseration fills man's body.[68] When a disciple quoted Chu Hsi's earlier saying that "mind is not this one lump [i.e., the heart]," and suggested that the heart "is the 'pivot' (*shu-niu*) of mind," Chu Hsi disagreed and said that instead it is the "house (*she*) for ascending and descending of mind's *shen* and brightness."[69]

The heart is the organ that "thinks" (*ssu*). Chu Hsi spoke of thinking as the proper activity of the heart as he referred to seeing and hearing as the proper activities of the eyes and the ears.[70] He interpreted the *Mencius* statement "The 'organ' (*kuan*) of the heart is thinking" (6A15) to mean that the heart takes charge of thinking, and he followed Mencius in arguing that because the heart can think it can keep itself from being blocked by external things.[71] "Evil thoughts and petty anxieties" caused by external things cannot occupy the heart or obstruct its other activities because it can think and eliminate them, whereas the eyes and ears cannot think and are liable to being blocked by them.[72]

Thinking is the key function of man's mind. For Chu Hsi, "thinking is the manifestation (*fa*) of mind."[73] It is also its continuous activity. Chu Hsi accepted the Ch'eng brothers' view that even if one tries, one cannot keep one's mind from thinking.[74] The mind can think even during sleep — in a dream, for example.[75] Because the mind can think, it takes charge of such activities as reading and writing.[76] Wisdom and knowledge also come from the mind's capacity to think:

> Wisdom and knowledge all come from mind. If the mind does not have that which takes charge of it, then while it responds to events and is in contact with things, how can it use thinking to get what is appropriate for it?[77]

Perception also falls under the purview of the mind. Chu Hsi spoke of the mind's role with respect to perception in various ways. He said, for example, that "mind is that which perceives."[78] He also referred to perception as "the manifestation," "the function" (*yung*), and "the virtue" of the mind.[79] And "to perceive is the *li* of the mind."[80] As a particular example of perception, Chu Hsi took the ability to feel pain to be evidence of the existence of the mind.[81] The mind's role is illustrated also by the fact that the sun's warmth is felt only when the sun is seen.[82] Seeing and hearing are related to the mind, too: "[As for] the ears and eyes seeing and hearing, that by means of which they see and hear is the mind";[83] "Seeing, hearing, and activities are also what the mind is turned to";[84] "When [the mind] is clear, seeing is [also] bright and hearing is also astute."[85] In a letter to a friend, Ho Kao (1128–1175), he was explicit about how the mind "controls" (*yü*) these perceiving activities:

> Seeing and hearing are shallow, stagnant, and have [concrete] locations; but the *shen* and brightness of the mind are unfathomable. Therefore, at times of seeing and hearing, [one] must control them by means of the mind. Then the correctness will not be lost.[86]

The mind controls not only thinking and perceiving, but all other activities as well. When a disciple asked, "Are the movements of the physical body and the mind related to each other?" Chu Hsi responded that "the mind makes it [i.e., the physical body] move."[87] He even said, "Of [man's] seeing, hearing, words and conduct, leaving home, and speech and silence, what can be seen outside are also the functions of this mind and can never be separated [from it]."[88] Thus it is that "when a thing errs, it is just one event that is in error; when the mind errs, the myriad events are in error."[89] It is in this sense also that the mind is what "takes charge of" (*chu*), or what "presides over" (*chu-tsai*) the body, as Chu Hsi repeatedly asserted.[90] Man's mind also rules his nature, feelings, and talent (*ts'ai*).[91]

Since man's mind controls all his activities, the mind has to attend to and accompany what he does in order that it can be really done. Chu Hsi said: "If a man has this mind and goes to do this thing, only then he accomplishes this thing; if he does not have this mind, how can he accomplish this thing?"[92] He repeated the passage from the *Great Learning* (Ta-hsueh) that says "If the mind is not there, he looks but does not see, he listens but does not hear, and he eats but does not know the taste" (ch. 7), changing the last clause to "he takes the crooked to be straight and the straight to be crooked."[93] Also, "if one reads without one's mind [attending to it], . . . it is like having never read it."[94]

Man has to be sincere (*ch'eng*) in order to have his mind attend to what he does. This was how Chu Hsi interpreted the comment from the *Doctrine of the Mean* (Chung-yung) "Without sincerity, there is nothing" (ch. 25): "If one is not sincere, the mind does not exist. One looks but does not see, one listens but does not hear. It is all right even to say that one has no ears or eyes."[95] He also said:

> In general, in responding to the coming of an event or a thing, one should always exhaust one's sincere mind to respond to it. Only then there begins to be this thing and event. When one manages an affair, if one's mind does not exist in this, then this affair is not accomplished; it is [as if] this affair did not exist. In reading a book, for example, if one's mind does not exist in this [book], it is [as if] the book were not there.[96]

Furthermore, the existence of the mind is not enough; the mind also has to attain correctness. Otherwise, it is as if the mind did not exist. Thus, Chu Hsi said: "If the mind does not attain its correctness, one looks but does not see, listens but does not hear, and eats but does not know the taste."[97]

The mind controls one activity at a time. Chu Hsi said: "The mind simply has one road; it can never take account of two things."[98] He also said, "Man has only one mind. How can he divide it and do many things [at a time]?"[99] Thus, "When one goes, then the mind simply is in [the act of] going; when one sits, the mind simply is in sitting."[100] If a person does many things at one time, all the activities other than the one being controlled (or attended to) by his mind at the time are not really being done. Chu Hsi used the Ch'eng brothers' expression "to concentrate on one" (*chu-i*), to refer to the state of the mind attending to one thing at a time: "At the time when [a man] concentrates on one, if he sits, the mind sits; if he goes, the mind goes; if the body is here, the mind is also here."[101] This state of a man "concentrated on one" can be reached when he "settles (*ting*) his mind."[102] Chu Hsi followed the Ch'engs also in equating this state with the mental state of "reverence" (*ching*).[103]

Man's mind in its ideal and original state is empty (*hsü*), not occupied by any thought. Chu Hsi said repeatedly that the mind is originally "empty," "empty and numinous," or "empty and bright."[104] It is because it is "empty" or "empty and numinous" that the mind contains "the myriad *li*" or that it enables "many ways and *li* to pass [through it]."[105] This led Chu Hsi even to say, as we have seen, that the heart has empty spaces inside so that it can contain many ways and *li*. As the empty mind — or empty heart — can contain many *li*, it can know many things and events: "This mind [or heart] is originally empty and numinous, and is complete with the myriad *li*. Events and things are all what it ought to know."[106]

The mind (or the heart) can be blocked, however, by external things, perturbing thoughts, emotions, and desires. Chu Hsi said that the mind (or the heart) "is blocked by things and desires and is therefore dark and unable to know exhaustively."[107] He also said: "The mind (or the heart) originally is a broad and large thing. It is simply [because of] embarrassment and shame that it becomes depraved and narrow, and obstructed by them."[108] The mind can be blocked not only by external things and desires but also by the dark and turbid *ch'i* endowed by man: "Those endowed with the dark and turbid [*ch'i*] also have these ways and *li* inside. But they are simply blocked by the dark and turbid [*ch'i*]."[109] When the mind (or the heart) is blocked in this manner, it is no longer empty, and its "volume" is reduced: "The volume of man's mind is originally large. Because of selfishness, [it becomes] small."[110] For Chu Hsi, this is what is meant by Chang Tsai's remark "When the mind (or the heart) is large, a hundred things are all unobstructed (*t'ung*); when the mind (or the heart) is small, a hundred things are all in disease," on which Chu Hsi commented: "'To be unobstructed' is simply to be able to penetrate that way and *li*; 'to be in disease' is to be obstructed."[111]

Of course, the mind cannot be completely free from perturbing thoughts and emotions. Chu Hsi believed that it was impossible for man not to have such feelings as happiness, anger, sadness, and fear.[112] Thus, he said: "Things like fondness and pleasure are proper to have";[113] "When there is an event [at which] one ought to be angry, how can one not be angry?"[114] It is only that things, events, feelings, and desires should not linger in the mind (or the heart) after the thought of them has passed; if they do not linger, the mind becomes empty and regains correctness.[115] Chu Hsi elaborated:

> Man's mind is originally transparent, empty, and bright. When an event or a thing comes, [the mind] follows its stimulus and responds [to it]. [The mind] spontaneously sees its height and weight. When the event has passed, [the mind] must become empty like that as before. Only then it is all right.[116]

He also said: "[Only] when there is nothing in the mind, it can respond to [another] thing."[117]

This is the state of a man at night who is well rested, for then his mind becomes "empty and calm" again.[118] When the mind is peaceful and not drifting around, "the ways and *li* spontaneously become clear."[119] Thus, to keep one's mind empty and

calm, free of any blocking, is most important in man's intellectual and moral endeavors. Chu Hsi said, "Scholars [should] simply wish to eliminate the blockings of
things and desires; [then] this mind becomes bright."[120] "This mind must always be
neat, empty, and bright; afterward things cannot block it."[121] Conversely, "if one
does not investigate the *li* exhaustively, then there will be blockings and [one will]
not have any means to exhaust the volume of this mind."[122] Therefore, in reading
books, one should first empty the mind to see the righteousness and *li* in the text.[123]
Chu Hsi also spoke of the need to "settle" and "brush, scrape, and clean" the mind
before reading books.[124]

11.4. The Mind and *Ch'i*

Chu Hsi's discussion of the mind centered around ethical and metaphysical problems. He frequently considered the relation of the mind to concepts such as nature
(*hsing*), feelings, will, intention, and talent (*ts'ai*). For example, nature is "the substance (*t'i*) of the mind," and feelings are "the functions of the mind";[125] to be more
specific, nature is "the way and *li* of the mind"; feelings are those "in which the mind
is manifest," whereas the mind itself is "what rules the body."[126] "Intention is the
manifestation of the mind; feelings are movements of the mind; will is the reaching
of the mind and is much more important than feelings and intention."[127] Talent is
"the power of the mind";[128] it is "what advocates, utilizes and does things."[129] Chu
Hsi also discussed the distinction between "the mind of man" (*jen-hsin*) and "the
mind of the Way" (*tao-hsin*). For example, "the mind of the Way is what comes out
from righteousness and *li*; the mind of man is what comes out from man's body."[130]

Such metaphysical inclination of Chu Hsi's ideas about the mind is also reflected
in his characterization, as we have seen, of the mind as "numinous" (*ling*) or as
"*shen*, bright, and unfathomable" (*shen-ming pu-ts'e*).[131] The character *hsü* (empty),
which he frequently used in reference to the mind, also had the sense of being "abstract" or "unreal." Chu Hsi said, for example: "It appears as if the mind had an image, but its body [or substance, *t'i*] is 'shapeless' (*hsü*)."[132] He also said, "The
Analects does not speak of mind; it only speaks of 'real' (*shih*) things," implying that
the mind, for him, was not "real."[133] Indeed, the mind does not have "physical form
and image" (*hsing-hsiang*) or "physical form and shadow" (*hsing-ying*)[134] and thus
cannot be seen. He even said: "When the mind has no event, it cannot be seen at
all; . . . when it responds to an event, it cannot be seen either. It is so 'unfathomable
and unpredictable' (*shen-ch'u kuei-mei*, literally, '*shen* appearing and *kuei* disappearing')."[135]

Yet, Chu Hsi did not consider the mind as something sacred beyond the realm of
ch'i; the mind could still be discussed in terms of *ch'i*—its qualities and activities.
He said, for example, that mind was nothing but "the essential and refreshing"
(*ching-shuang*) part of *ch'i*.[136] The most characteristic function of the mind, perception, is due to the "numinous" part of *ch'i*.[137] "In *ch'i* there naturally is a numinous thing," which takes charge of the activities of the heart, the eyes, and the
ears.[138] Thus, "when man's physical form and *ch'i* have become complete, that

which has perception and is able to move comes into being."[139] In contrasting "the mind of man" with "the mind of the Way," Chu Hsi even said that the former "is made through *ch'i* and blood combining harmoniously."[140]

Chu Hsi routinely attributed characteristics and phenomena involving the mind to qualities and activities of *ch'i*. We have already seen numerous examples. But to look at one particular case in some detail, daring and fearlessness, according to him, arise from the *ch'i* that is "great." The *ch'i* of those who "do not dare to do anything . . . is small"; the *ch'i* of those who "dare to do everything . . . is great." For example, when a man "has nourished and made this *ch'i* great, he does not fear it [i.e., death]."[141] Chu Hsi even described how *ch'i* can become small or great:

> Now, if there is regret and shame in man's mind, then this *ch'i* [that fills the body] spontaneously diminishes. In doing things one no longer has courage and vigor. . . . When one fights a man, if one gets another man behind, helping one, one will spontaneously feel even more that [one's] *ch'i* excels.[142]

"Courage," then, "is added to man by means of *ch'i*."[143] Chu Hsi spoke of "vigorous" *ch'i* also as a source of fearlessness.[144]

Chu Hsi also used certain terms containing the character *ch'i* that manifest certain moral and mental qualities. A foremost example is a term he took from the *Mencius*, namely "the magnanimous *ch'i*" (*hao-jan chih ch'i*), the same *ch'i* as that which fills man's body, but which "has collected and accumulated righteousness to the extent that it is full and flourishing, . . . and can be[come] 'magnanimous.'"[145] He spoke of two other Mencian terms, "the *ch'i* of peaceful dawn" (*p'ing-tan chih ch'i*), and "the nightly *ch'i*" (*yeh-ch'i*): "After resting a few hours, the *ch'i* [of peaceful dawn, or the nightly *ch'i*,] becomes clear, and 'the good mind' (*liang-hsin*) grows. When it becomes morning and day, the *ch'i* becomes turbid, and the good mind cannot be manifest."[146]

It was therefore natural, for Chu Hsi, that man's *ch'i* should influence his mind. He said, for example:

> If the *ch'i* is clear, then the mind attains what is to be nourished and can spontaneously become clear; if the *ch'i* is turbid, the mind loses what is to be nourished and spontaneously becomes turbid.[147]

He also said: "The blood *ch'i* can help the righteous mind to arise. When man's blood *ch'i* declines, the righteous mind also follows and declines."[148] "The bad *ch'i* can stimulate [anger]."[149] He explained his own tendency to frequent wrath by the "quality of [his] *ch'i* [that] has a deficiency."[150]

Man's *ch'i* can move his mind. To be sure, the mind is something that moves by itself, as Chu Hsi recognized explicitly.[151] Thought, for example, is "movement of the mind."[152] He also used such expressions as "flow," "flow and move," and "alive" (*huo*) in alluding to the movement of the mind.[153] Yet, to move was not an ideal state of man's mind. For example, the mind is moved by things if it has [something] incorrect.[154] Thus, the movement of the mind, in particular movement caused by *ch'i*, was something to be avoided. This was what Chu Hsi said repeatedly in his comments on the method of "not moving the mind" by "upholding the will and not agitating the *ch'i*," appearing in the famous passage of the *Mencius* (2A2).[155] It is important for a man "to nourish *ch'i*," "to defend *ch'i*," or "not to debauch *ch'i*" in order to keep the mind correct, settled, and not moving.[156]

Ch'i-mind interaction occurs in both directions; the mind can influence *ch'i* also. Chu Hsi said, for example: "When the mind has been loosened, *ch'i* must be dark. When *ch'i* has become dark, the mind perishes even more. The two pull and move each other."[157] "[When] one wastes the power of the mind, one damages *ch'i* and becomes ill."[158] But "if one can keep this [good] mind, then *ch'i* will always be clear";[159] "if the mind is peaceful, *ch'i* will naturally be harmonious."[160] It is because the mind can affect *ch'i* in this manner that "collecting the righteousness" makes *ch'i* "magnanimous."[161] It is for the same reason that man's moral and intellectual endeavors can change the endowments of his *ch'i*:

> One must know the harms of the [one-sided] endowments of *ch'i* and should endeavor to work hard and overcome and control [oneself]. It is all right only when one has reduced the excesses and returned them to balance.[162]

He rejected the belief that "if one were to say that the endowments of *ch'i* are fixed, then [one's being] a great man or a small man would all be fixed at birth, and the scholarly ability would not be able to change [it]."[163] Of course, Chu Hsi admitted that it is "most difficult to change the quality of [one's] *ch'i*."[164] But he still believed that study and moral exertions could change it: "You simply keep making exertions! Then the *li* will become bright, the *ch'i* will naturally become strong, and the courage (literally 'the gall' [*tan*]) will naturally become great."[165] Music also "can move and swing man's blood *ch'i*, so that even if a man has some bad intentions, he will be unable to set them forth."[166]

The aspect of *ch'i*-mind interaction that Chu Hsi mentioned most frequently is the mutual interaction of man's *ch'i* and his will (*chih*). Again, the Mencian phrases—"When the will arrives, the *ch'i* follows"; "When the will is one, it moves the *ch'i*; when the *ch'i* is one, it moves the will"—provided the occasion for Chu Hsi to discuss the *ch'i*-will interaction. He said: "When the *ch'i* is here, then the will is here.... The will and the *ch'i* naturally follow each other."[167] Thus, "if one can uphold one's will, the *ch'i* will naturally be clear and bright."[168] Chu Hsi took "shifting [one's own] anger [to an innocent person]" (*ch'ien-nu*) as an example of *ch'i* and will moving each other: "To have selfish intentions inside and to go as far as 'shifting anger' is the will moving *ch'i*. To be moved by the angry *ch'i* (*nu-ch'i*) and to shift [anger] is *ch'i* moving the will."[169] Excessive joy, as well as anger, can agitate *ch'i* and in turn move the will: "If [one] gets excessively joyful and is joyful all the time, or gets excessively angry and is angry all the time, then [one's] *ch'i* becomes coarse and agitated. [This] is 'agitating the *ch'i*.' One's will will be moved in response."[170]

Chu Hsi believed, following the Ch'eng brothers, that the case of the will moving *ch'i* was much more frequent than the converse, and he considered the will to be the more important of the two.[171] That is why *ch'i* cannot move the will if one upholds the will: "Drinking wine certainly can move the will. But if one can uphold one's will, it still cannot move."[172] Thus it is that "when the will is strong, the power of the body is also strong."[173] Chu Hsi even spoke of "a certain monk who could withstand burning" by means of keeping "the mind concentrated and not moving."[174]

Man's mind can interact not only with the *ch'i* inside his body but also with the *ch'i* of the outside world. Chu Hsi said, for example: "Once man's mind has moved, it must reach the *ch'i* [of heaven and earth] and mutually stimulate and interact with this [*ch'i*] that contracts and expands, goes and comes."[175] This was so for him because, as we have seen, "man's *ch'i* and the *ch'i* of heaven and earth are constantly in contact with each other."[176] Thus, a sage like Confucius, whose mind is "vast" (*tang-tang*), is "in a harmonious contact with heaven."[177] Chu Hsi attributed many phenomena that now appear impossible—supernatural or superhuman—to the mutual response of man's mind and the outside *ch'i*. Such response takes place during sacrificial services, for example, when the sincerity of the descendants' minds can reach and recall ancestors' *ch'i*.[178] Divination and fortune-telling are also practices in which man's mind seeks to get in touch with, and to apprehend, the *ch'i* of heaven and earth and various fortunes of men that are determined by the endowments of *ch'i*.[179] Chu Hsi even agreed with a disciple who suggested that the following can happen as a result of the mind's stimulating the *ch'i* of the outside world:

If a man accumulates many errors and sins in his life, [they] can stimulate [the outside *ch'i*] and invite what is inauspicious, and cause disasters of the blockings and eclipses of the sun and the moon, collapses of mountains and drying of rivers, and floods, droughts, and famines.[180]

Finally, man's mind can interact with the minds of other men, or even of animals. This is to be expected in principle because all these minds interact with the outside *ch'i* and are themselves attributable to their *ch'i*. It can also be a consequence of the belief that man receives the *ch'i* and the mind of heaven and earth and makes them his *ch'i* and mind.[181] But Chu Hsi spoke of specific examples of direct interactions or responses of minds. For example, when a man's "dedication (literally, 'essence and sincerity' [*ching-ch'eng*]) is extremely profound," he can read the minds of others.[182] We have seen that man's filial piety could even move a fish—or the mind of the fish.[183]

11.5. Functions of the Human Body

Although Chu Hsi might have shared, as I have suggested, the emphasis of traditional Chinese medical theories on the functional, rather than structural, aspect of the human body, he rarely discussed—described or explained—activities and functions of the human body in detail.

For instance, Chu Hsi did not concern himself with the details of how man's perceptual organs perceive or of how man's mind controls the processes of perception. He had little to say about the mechanisms of perception or about the nature of the

sensible qualities perceived by man.[184] Perhaps that visible objects should be perceived (seen) by the eyes and sounds perceived (heard) by the ears appeared to him
too obvious to necessitate further discussion. Thus, he could say: "It is simply that
if *ch'i* has aggregated, the eyes can see; if it has not aggregated, [the eyes] cannot
see."[185] Concerning tastes he was more explicit: "When one eats a sour [food], one
immediately knows that it is sour; when one eats a salty [food], one immediately
knows that it is salty."[186] His reference to perception as "*shen*" revealed the same
attitude: "Perception is *shen*. Prick the hand, then the hand perceives the pain;
prick the foot, then the foot perceives the pain. This is *shen*. *Shen* responds, and
therefore it is subtle."[187] For him, perception was *shen*—mysterious, subtle, and unfathomable—because it was beyond the reach of man's intellectual understanding or
explanation; it was simply to be accepted.

What Chu Hsi did speak of were mostly common facts that can readily be gathered from everyday experience. He said, for example, "If the sky [itself] were bright,
the sun and the moon would not be bright,"[188] suggesting that bright objects can be
seen only against a dark background. He noted that one has to see from a great distance to perceive the whole shape of a large object because at close range the field
of vision is narrower.[189] He also observed that when exposed to a particular smell
for a long time, one does not sense the smell.[190] Sometimes he even seemed to say
that one tends to feel what one sees: "When one opens the window and sits, and sees
the sunlight outside the window above the ground, then one feels hot. When one
withdraws and does not see [the sun], then one does not [feel] hot."[191]

Of course, it is not impossible to gather hints about Chu Hsi's ideas of how the
processes of perception take place. We have seen that the *ch'i* of an object has to be
aggregated for it to have physical form and to be seen by the eyes. Chu Hsi also appeared to be of the view that the light in the eyes is what enables man to see external objects, for he took the eyes' light to be their *p'o* and the ability to hear to be the
p'o of the ears.[192] He did not say, however, exactly how the eyes, with light in them,
see the objects—or their physical forms—made of aggregated *ch'i*. It cannot be determined clearly whether his view was closer to the modern view, according to
which the light from external objects reaches the eyes to give rise to the sense of vision, or to the opposite one. Sometimes he seemed to believe that perception occurred in both ways, and he distinguished the passive acts of "seeing and hearing"
(*chien-wen*) from the active ones of "looking and listening" (*shih-t'ing*): "Looking
and listening are different from seeing and hearing. When sounds and colors come
in contact with the ears and eyes, it is seeing and hearing. Looking and listening are
the ears and eyes following sounds and colors."[193] He also spoke of the difference
between the perception of vision and that of hearing: "Seeing is to pull and take out
what is in here. . . . Hearing is to hear and bring in what is outside."[194] But his criticism of Buddhist beliefs contained the following flat rejection of the view that seeing is the eyes' light reaching out to external objects:

> [The Buddhists] say: "Even if things appear in front [of me], I never see [it], and [it] has
> nothing to do with me." If it were like this, then it must be that the light of the eyes pur-
> sues, flows, enters, and disturbs [the things]. Hearing [must] be the same. How, under
> heaven, can there be this *li*?[195]

Chu Hsi's remarks about the eyes and the ears as perceptual organs did not touch the actual processes of seeing and hearing, either. He said, for example: "The virtue of the ears is astuteness; the virtue of the eyes is brightness; the virtue of the mind is humaneness."[196] Or, "the five colors nourish the eyes; sounds nourish the ears; righteousness and *li* nourish the mind."[197] These remarks clearly suggest that his interest was not in the processes of perception. Indeed, he was frequently engaged in such philosophical problems as identifying the roles of the mind, *ch'i*, and *li* in man's perception[198] or in such moral issues as what one should see or hear as opposed to what one should not.[199]

Of the various human physiological functions, Chu Hsi spoke of respiration most often, referring to it as the "coming out and entering" of *ch'i* through the nose.[200] He frequently mentioned inhalation and exhalation as examples of the yin-yang alternation. For example, "when [*ch'i*] comes out, it must enter; coming out stimulates entering. When it enters, it must come out; entering stimulates coming out."[201] Of the *ch'i* that enters and comes out, "what comes out is yang and what returns is yin."[202] Using the yin-yang scheme, he could explain why the exhaled breath can be seen in winter but not in summer:

> Spring and summer are yang; autumn and winter are yin. [If one] takes yang *ch'i* [i.e., the exhaled *ch'i*] and scatters it inside yang *ch'i* [i.e., the *ch'i* of summer], then, like pouring hot soup into [another] hot soup, it will not be seen at all. In autumn and winter, this *ch'i* [i.e., the exhaled yang *ch'i*] is like mixing hot soup into water; it will be seen.[203]

For Chu Hsi, however, what came in and out through the nose was not the outside *ch'i*. It was the *ch'i* produced inside man's body. This *ch'i* comes out from the body through exhalation, but the body is not depleted of *ch'i* because it is continuously produced inside the body. Chu Hsi seemed to consider exhalation of the *ch'i* to be essential for man's life and the ceasing of it to be a sign of death, for he said that when this *ch'i* has been exhausted completely and cannot come out any longer, man dies.[204]

It is not clear, however, what Chu Hsi thought about inhalation—whether the entering *ch'i* is the fresh *ch'i* from outside or the same *ch'i* that has been exhaled. Although common sense points to the former alternative, his comparison of the movement of *ch'i* during respiration to "the snail, having come out of the shell, contracting and entering [again]," points to the latter.[205] His other remarks are not clear on this. For example,

> [Consider] man's respiration. If he exhales all the time, the *ch'i* will become extinct. [Thus,] he must inhale also. If he inhales all the time, the *ch'i* will have no place to go and will not be received.[206]

In a long conversation summing up much of what has been discussed above, he even said explicitly that what happens in inhalation is not an entering of the outside *ch'i* but a temporary halting of the process of the *ch'i* coming out:

> When man exhales *ch'i*, the belly still swells; when he inhales *ch'i*, the belly still repels. . . . At the time of exhalation, although this one mouthful of *ch'i* has come out, the second

mouthful of *ch'i* is produced again, and therefore the belly swells. When it comes to the time of inhalation, the *ch'i* that has been produced comes out from inside in haste, and therefore the belly still repels. In general, in man's life till he dies, his *ch'i* comes out all the time. When it has come out completely, he dies. When he inhales the *ch'i*, for example, it is not that he inhales the outside *ch'i* into [his body]; it simply is holding [the process of exhaling the *ch'i*] for one moment. [Afterward,] the second mouthful of *ch'i* comes out again. When it cannot come out, he dies.[207]

Chu Hsi had remarks about certain other aspects of respiration as well. For example, he praised Hu Yüan's saying that man breathes "about thirteen thousand and six hundred times" a day.[208] He also said that "*ch'i* in the mouth is warm when it is exhaled and cold when inhaled."[209]

On digestion and nutrition, Chu Hsi spoke of some simple common-sense notions. For example, food has to be chewed into little pieces so that "[it may] be dissolved and [may] produce essence and blood; if [a large piece] . . . is swallowed, it is of no help [to the body]."[210] He even likened the process to "melting" (*jung*):

> [Take] the example of a man eating a thing. If it does not disappear but stays without change inside the belly, how can it nourish and benefit the body and skin? It must be melted and transformed: the sediments go down; the exquisite [portions] fill the body and skin and therefore can nourish and enrich [them].[211]

Concerning human reproduction, Chu Hsi seemed to hold the common belief that the father plays the more important and active role. He said, for example: "[As for] the reason that man has this body, he receives the physical form from the mother, but the basic quality (*tsu*) begins with the father."[212] A pair of *I-ching* phrases about its first two hexagrams—"The myriad things use [the *ch'ien*] to begin" (*wan-wu tsu shih*); "The myriad things use [the *k'un*] to come into being" (*wan-wu tsu sheng*)—could be the source of this idea, for the *ch'ien* and *k'un* hexagrams were usually associated with father and mother.[213] In his comments on the phrases, Chu Hsi said:

> The myriad things use the *ch'ien* to begin and have *ch'i*. [They] use the *k'un* to come into being and have physical form. After the *ch'i* has arrived, [they] come into being. When they come into being, that is the origination of the *k'un*.[214]

Thus, *ch'ien* and *k'un* were often used in metaphors of human reproduction. For example, "if *ch'ien* acts on things and *k'un* does not respond, then it cannot produce things."[215] "In general, yang acts and yin receives. *Ch'ien's* production of things is like a bottle bestowing water."[216] He even said: "When the *ch'i* of *ch'ien* comes from above, *k'un* simply opens and follows out to the two sides."[217]

Other remarks touching human reproduction came up on various occasions in Chu Hsi's conversations. For example, asked about the expression from the *Tso Commentary* (Tso-chuan) "the first transformation" (*shih-hua*) of man's life, he said: "It is the time when the physical form has been accomplished slightly at the beginning inside the womb."[218] In illustrating the "Hsi-tz'u chuan" phrase "That which succeeds it is good" (*Chi-chih-che shan*) (ch. A5), he said that the fetus "receives the *ch'i* of the parents while inside the womb."[219] His discussion of the first appearance of a yang line in the *fu* hexagram made use of the fact that "when [a woman is] pregnant, a whole baby is formed after ten months have been complete."[220]

The above instances, however, did not make Chu Hsi curious about the actual processes of conception and the growth of the fetus. Instead, he was interested in a consequence of reproduction, namely the passing of *ch'i* from father to son, to grandson, and so on.[221] As a result of such transmission, the ancestors' *ch'i* can exist inside a descendant's body,[222] and Chu Hsi frequently said that the ancestors' and the descendants' *ch'i* are the same.[223] He even said that "the body of one man is divided to form two men [i.e., the father and the son]"[224] and called the descendant "a blood vessel" (*hsueh-mo*) of the ancestor.[225] This suggests that Chu Hsi held the idea of transmission quite seriously and literally. We have already seen that he used the idea to explain such things as sacrificial services and the spontaneous love between father and son.[226] Questions raised during conversations showed that his interlocutors also understood the idea quite literally. We have come across a typical example: how could sages like Yao and Shun, whose *ch'i* were clear and bright, beget villains like Tan Chu and Shang Chün?[227] The question of how sacrificial services can reach maternal ancestors also seems to imply a belief, held both by the disciple and by Chu Hsi himself, that the *ch'i* passes to a child only from the father and not from the mother.[228] To someone who pointed out the contradiction of this idea of the transmission of *ch'i* with the theory that man receives the *ch'i* of heaven and earth, Chu Hsi replied: "It is simply that this *ch'i* [of heaven and earth] must come and pass through man's body [i.e., through the father]."[229]

Chu Hsi did not have much to say about childbirth, either. He quoted the remark from *Ts'an-t'ung-ch'i* (Kinship of the three) about different positions of male and female infants at birth, that male babies are born facing down and female babies are born lying on their backs. He seems to have accepted this, since he offered an explanation for it: "The male has yang *ch'i* [i.e., the lighter portion of *ch'i*] in the back, whereas the female has yang *ch'i* in the belly."[230] But his real interest was in arguing, just as the original *Ts'an-t'ung-ch'i* passage did, that these positions, assumed by men and women during sexual intercourse, are their spontaneous positions. On that basis it was also natural that the drowned bodies of men and women should show the same difference.

Concerning death Chu Hsi had more to say, mainly because of his interest in sacrificial services for dead ancestors.[231] Basic to his discussion of the topic, for example, was the belief that man's *ch'i* is exhausted or dispersed upon death, as we saw in chapter 6. But most of his descriptions of what happens to the body upon death were in terms of *hun* and *p'o*.

11.6. *Hun* and *P'o*

A key source for the concepts of *hun* and *p'o* is the passage from the *Tso Commentary* containing the above-mentioned expression "the first transformation": "In man's life, the first transformation is called *p'o*. Once the *p'o* has been produced, yang is called *hun*."²³² The passage apparently speaks of the formation of *hun* and *p'o* in man, as K'ung Ying-ta's subcommentary interprets it:

> As for the birth of man, the first change and transformation produce physical form. The numinous part of the physical form is named "*p'o*." After the *p'o* has been produced, there spontaneously is yang *ch'i* inside the *p'o*. The *shen* part of the *ch'i* is named "*hun*."²³³

Chu Hsi took the same view. In his own passage that quoted and praised the remark of the *Tso Commentary*, he said: "At the beginning of man's life, there first is *ch'i*. When physical form has already been accomplished [it means] that there has been *p'o* beforehand."²³⁴

What seems to have been a more important source for Chu Hsi, however, was a passage in the *Record of Rites* that speaks of what happens to *hun* and *p'o* when man dies: "*Hun* and *ch'i* return to heaven; physical form and *p'o* return to earth."²³⁵ Chu Hsi frequently quoted and commented upon it.²³⁶ He also repeatedly said that upon death *hun* rises and *p'o* descends.²³⁷ He had an explanation: "When a man is about to die, hot *ch'i* comes out from the top. Thus it is said that *hun* rises. The bottom [part of the] body gradually becomes cold. Thus it is said that *p'o* descends."²³⁸

Still another ancient source, discussed frequently by Chu Hsi in connection with *hun* and *p'o*, is a remark attributed to Confucius that appears in the chapter of the *Record of Rites* dealing with sacrificial services:

> *Ch'i* is the flourishing of *shen*; *p'o* is the flourishing of *kuei*. Combining *kuei* and *shen* is the supreme of teaching. All living things must die. Having died, they must return to earth. This is called *kuei*. Bones and flesh die [and go] down. The yin becomes the earth of the fields. Its *ch'i* is emitted and displayed up high; it is "bright" (*chao-ming*), "fuming up" (*hsün-hao*), and "pathetic" (*ch'i-ch'uang*). This is the essence of the hundred things and "the manifestation" (*chu*) of *shen*.²³⁹

Chu Hsi seemed to interpret the beginning sentence as referring to man's *hun* (or *ch'i*) and *p'o* while the person is alive: according to him the word "flourishing" referred to "the living human body."²⁴⁰ But the bulk of the above remark speaks of what happens to man's body after death: its yin part (bones and flesh) returns to the ground and decays; its yang part (the *ch'i*) rises and is dispersed. In his comments on it, Chu Hsi identified the yin and yang parts of the body with *p'o* and *hun*.²⁴¹ He was particularly interested in the description, in the last part of the remark, of the rising *hun*, or *hun-ch'i*, which he discussed very frequently. For example:

> When a man dies, his *hun-ch'i* is emitted and displayed up high. "Brightness" is the scene in general [that appears] spontaneously when man dies. "Fuming up" is . . . the warm *ch'i*. "Being pathetic" is the "solemn" (*su-jan*) *ch'i* in general.²⁴²

Chu Hsi's overall view concerning *hun* and *p'o* was a combination of the ideas of these ancient sources: man's *hun* and *p'o* are united in the body when he is alive;

they are separated from each other and are dispersed when he dies. His view is summed up in the following remark:

> When a man is alive, *hun* and *p'o* meet each other. When he dies, they are separated and each is dispersed. The *hun*, being yang, is scattered upward; the *p'o*, being yin, descends downward.[243]

Later in the same conversation, he elaborated on how it is that they are united while the man lives and separated when he dies:

> In general, *hun* is hot and *p'o* is cold; *hun* moves and *p'o* is at rest. If it can be that *p'o* is protected by means of *hun*, then *hun*, for the sake of protecting, is also at rest. *P'o*, because of *hun*, has life intent. *Hun*, being hot, produces coolness; *p'o*, being cold, produces warmth. Only when the two are not separated from each other, the yang is not dry, and the yin is not impeded, and their harmony is achieved. Otherwise, the more *hun* moves, the more at rest is *p'o*; the hotter *hun* becomes, the colder becomes *p'o*. If the two are separated from each other, then their harmony is not achieved, and man dies.[244]

This passage clearly shows that Chu Hsi saw a role of *hun* and *p'o* in maintaining man's life. Indeed, he thought that *hun* and *p'o* took charge of the various parts, functions, and activities of a living man. Many examples can be found in table 11.2, which lists the *hun-p'o* associations mentioned by Chu Hsi.

Certain general characteristics can be gathered from the table. Of the human parts, functions, and activities, the more active, outward, subtle, and formless ones are associated with *hun*, and the more passive, inward, fixed, and corporeal ones with *p'o*. Such differences were mentioned in some of Chu Hsi's own words not listed in the table. For example, *hun* is "that which has no physical form or trace in the essence *ch'i*"[245] and "that which is manifest and coming out."[246] *P'o*, on the other hand, "has physical form and shape inside . . . like quartz,"[247] "is a crystal, bright, hard, and concentrated thing,"[248] "is a thing that sinks and is blocked,"[249] and "is relatively more settled."[250] He also illustrated characteristics of *hun* and *p'o* by comparing them to nonhuman things. For example, "to compare [them] with burning incense, the sap coming out through burning is *p'o*; that which is fragrant after forming the smoke is *hun*. *Hun* is the light and flame of *p'o*; *p'o* is the root and base of *hun*."[251] Of a tree, "the vapor coming out when cut is *shen*; the nature of nourishment is *p'o*."[252] And in the moon, the dark part is *p'o* and the light is *hun*.[253]

The *hun-p'o* association of human functions that Chu Hsi mentioned most frequently was taken from a comment by Cheng Hsüan (127–200) on the passage from the *Record of Rites* quoted earlier: "*Ch'i* refers to that which is exhaled and inhaled, and comes out and enters; the astuteness and brightness of ears and eyes are *p'o*."[254] Chu Hsi quoted, praised, and discussed this comment repeatedly; he associated *hun* with *ch'i* and respiration and *p'o* with essence, astuteness, and brightness.[255] Thus, *p'o*, for him, was that which makes the ears hear (the astuteness) and the eyes see (the light, or brightness). In other words, *p'o* is what enables the perceptual organs to perceive. To a questioner who identified the eyes' light as their *p'o* and asked

TABLE 11.2
The *Hun-p'o* Associations Mentioned by Chu Hsi

hun	p'o	References[a]
yang	yin	YL87.26b1
shen of yang	*shen* of yin	YL3.4a0[b]
shen	*kuei*	YL63.23b0
ch'i	essence (*ching*)	YL3.1b3
shen of *ch'i*	*shen* of essence	YL3.7b1
ch'i	blood (*hsueh*)	YL3.4b0
ch'i	body (*t'i*)	YL3.4a0
ch'i	physical form (*hsing*)	YL74.14b0
ch'i	tangible quality (*chih*)	YL94.11a4–11b0
shen of *ch'i*	*shen* of physical form	YL87.27b0
shen	essence (*ching*)	YL87.26b1–27a0
essence (*ching*)	tangible quality	YL83.21a2
movement	rest	YL3.8a3
warm *ch'i*	cold *ch'i*	YL3.7b1
the sun	the moon	YL79.26b2
Fire	Water	YL3.6b1
Wood	Metal	YL3.9a1
three (the number for Wood)	seven (the number for Metal)	YL3.9a1
two	one	YL125.8b1
fire and the sun, which have shadow outside	metal and water, which have shadow inside	YL87.28a2
light of the moon	dark portion of the moon	YL87.26b1
moving and using	storing and receiving	YL87.26b1[c]
able to move, use, and take action	unable to move, use, and take action	YL3.8a3
respiration of mouth and nose	astuteness and brightness of ears and eyes	YL3.7b1[d]
respiration of mouth and nose	essence and brightness of ears and eyes	YL87.29a1[d]
the *ch'i* exhaled and inhaled by mouth and nose	the essence of ears and eyes	YL3.8a5
respiration of mouth and nose	the likes of ears, eyes, mouth, and nose	YL63.23a3–23b0
perception and movement	physical form and body	YL3.4a0[c]
speech and action[e]	essence and blood	YL63.25a0
mental spirit (*ching-shen*) and perception and their operation[f]	the four limbs and the nine holes (*chiu ch'iao*)[g] and their essence and blood	YL87.28a2
manifesting and using (*fa-yung*)[f]	settling of *ch'i* (*ch'i-ting*)	YL63.25a0

TABLE 11.2 (*continued*)

hun	*p'o*	*References*[a]
knowledge[f]	memory	YL63.25a0
ability to think and account	ability to memorize	YL3.7b1
ability to think and plan	ability to memorize and distinguish	YL3.9a2
perceiving and manifesting outward	ability to perceive	YL87.26b1
manifesting outward	ability to memorize	YL87.26b1
(similar to) lantern	(similar to) mirror	YL87.28a2[h]

Notes

[a] Only one representative reference is given for each pair of associations.
[b] Quoting the commentary of Kao Yu (fl. 205) on *Huai-nan-tzu*, 16.1a.
[c] Associated indirectly through associations with the yin-yang.
[d] Quoting Cheng Hsüan's commentary on *Li-chi*, ch. 24 (47.14a).
[e] Associated indirectly through association with *ch'i*.
[f] Associated indirectly through association with *shen*.
[g] The nine holes of the human body: eyes (2), ears (2), nose (2), mouth (1), anus (1), genital organ (1).
[h] Originally from *Chuang-tzu*; see YL3.8a3.

what the ears' *p'o* was, he replied: "The ability to hear. That is [their *p'o*]. For example, the nose knowing smells and the tongue knowing tastes—these are all [*p'o*]."[256] Chu Hsi himself frequently identified the eyes' light with *p'o*, and he even mentioned "people [who] say that the light of the eyes falls down [upon death]," in speaking of the descending of a dead man's *p'o* down to earth.[257] There also were those who said that "when a tiger dies, the light of its eyes enters the earth."[258]

P'o is only the ability to perceive, however; perception itself is not *p'o*. Chu Hsi said: "That which is able to perceive is *p'o*; but that which perceives and manifests outward is also *hun*."[259] He added the following to the remark about "the nose knowing smells and tongue knowing tastes."

> But [one] cannot take the word "knowing" for *p'o*. When only "knowing" is spoken of, it is taken charge of by the mind. The mind can know only. As for the sweet, bitter, salty, and insipid [tastes], they must pass on to the tongue.[260]

He made a similar distinction between man's ability to memorize and memorization itself, which he explained in terms of a yin-yang association.

> Yin is mainly storing and receiving; yang is mainly moving and using. In general, the ability to memorize is always what the *p'o* stores and receives. But when it comes to what moves, uses, and manifests outward, it is *hun*.[261]

Chu Hsi mentioned other *hun-p'o* associations of human functions and activities. Speech, action, thinking, and planning are those associated with *hun*, for example. But he spoke of *p'o* far more frequently. He even argued, from the *Tso Commentary* passage identifying the first transformation of man's life with *p'o*, that "first there is *p'o* and afterward is there *hun*, and therefore *p'o* is always the primary and main part."[262] He spoke of man's growing up and aging in terms of the growth and decline of his *p'o* and attributed various deficiencies and weaknesses of children and old persons to their deficiency of *p'o*. For example,

> When a man is first born, [he has] much *ch'i* and a little *p'o*. Afterward, the *p'o* gradually flourishes. Reaching old age, the *p'o* is again in small quantity, and therefore the ears are deaf and the eyes are unclear, "the power of essence" (*ching-li*) is not strong, and the memory is not sufficient. I [myself] now feel that yang [i.e., *hun* or *ch'i*] is plentiful, but yin [*p'o*] is deficient, and [thus I] cannot remember events. Small children do not have memory. It is also [because their] *p'o* is deficient. They like to play and are not settled. It is also [because their] *p'o* is deficient.[263]

Table 11.2 shows also that *hun* and *p'o* were associated with many dualistic pairs such as yin-yang, *kuei-shen*, essence-*ch'i*, and other pairs of human bodily contents that we came across in section 11.1. As noted there, however, Chu Hsi did not make clear how different pairs are related to one another. His various assertions involving these dualities sometimes contradict one another and do not yield to attempts to reconstruct a neat scheme, which suggests that he was not interested in an exact demarcation of the purviews of the different dualities themselves or the different terms that constitute the dualities.

Chu Hsi characterized the relation among the essence-*ch'i*, the *hun-p'o*, and the *kuei-shen* pairs in the following manners:

> When the essence and *ch'i* aggregate, they produce things. When the essence and *ch'i* are dispersed, the *ch'i* becomes *hun* and the essence becomes *p'o*. The *hun* rises and becomes *shen* and the *p'o* descends and becomes *kuei*.[264]

> Inside man, the essence is *p'o*, and the *p'o* is the flourishing of *kuei*; the *ch'i* is *hun*, and the *hun* is the flourishing of *shen*. Essence and *ch'i* aggregate and become things.[265]

From these remarks it can be gathered that the essence and *ch'i* are the fundamental constituents forming man and things and that inside man the essence and *ch'i* are *p'o* and *hun*.[266] Chu Hsi said, "Man's essence and *ch'i* flow around up and down in the body, and [there is] no place [where they are] fixed."[267] He elaborated:

> Essence and *ch'i* flow around and fill the inside of the body. Respiration, astuteness, and brightness are only what they manifest and are easily seen. But once [they] flow around and fill the inside of the body, is the nose knowing smells or the mouth knowing tastes not *p'o*? The inside of the ears and eyes always has warm *ch'i*. Is this not *hun*? To extend this to the whole body, all must be the same.[268]

The above remarks also imply that when *hun* and *p'o* are dispersed, they become *shen* and *kuei*. But *kuei* and *shen* refer also to all other aspects of the world, as we saw in chapter 6. Chu Hsi said, "*Kuei* and *shen* refer to the one *ch'i* between heaven and earth; *hun* and *p'o* refer mainly to the human body."[269] This did not mean, however, that *kuei* and *shen* change into *hun* and *p'o* when they are inside man's body; it was rather that the aspects of *kuei* and *shen* in the body were referred to as *hun* and *p'o*. Thus, he could say that man's body "also is *kuei* and *shen*,"[270] and that "when a man is born, one half naturally is *shen* and one half *kuei*."[271]

Chu Hsi was not clear as to how the individual terms of these various pairs related to the living and dead states of man. Of the *kuei-shen* pair, he was of the view that *shen* is more pronounced during life and *kuei* is so in death: "Before [man] dies, *shen* is in control; after death *kuei* is in control."[272] He must have meant the same thing when he said, "In man's body it is called *shen*, and when dispersed it is called *kuei*."[273]

As for the *hun-p'o* pair, the situation is more ambiguous. To be sure, what we have seen so far suggests that *hun* and *p'o* refer both to the living and the dead states. Yet, we have also noted that from the ancient source of the *Record of Rites* on, the *ch'i-p'o* pair was frequently used in place of the *hun-p'o* in reference to the living body. Chu Hsi also showed a tendency to use the words *ch'i* and *shen* when speaking of the living human body, reserving the word *hun* for the dead. Thus, when asked to explain *hun* and *p'o*, he had the following to say, obviously concentrating on *hun* and *p'o* in man's (living) body:

> *P'o* is a speck of essence and *ch'i*. When the *ch'i* meet together, there is this *shen*. *Hun* is that which is manifest and coming out, like the coming in and out of *ch'i* [in] respiration. *P'o* is like water. [Because of it] man's seeing can be bright, hearing can be astute, and the mind can be vigorous and can memorize [well]. When a man has this *p'o*, then he has this *shen*. It is not what has entered from outside.[274]

He even said: "When dead, it is called *hun* and *p'o*; when alive, it is called the essence and *ch'i*."[275]

Chu Hsi's characterizations of the relationship of *hun* and *p'o* with such terms as "tangible quality," "physical form," "body," and *ch'i* were less ambiguous. He said, for example: "*Ch'i* and tangible quality are real (*shih*); *hun* and *p'o* are half real and half imaginary (*hsü*); *kuei* and *shen* are in a large part imaginary and in a small part real."[276] *Hun* and *p'o*, referring frequently to the parts and functions of man's body, seem to have appeared to Chu Hsi more tangible than *kuei* and *shen*; but compared with *ch'i* and tangible qualities, *hun* and *p'o* still had some of the numinous character of *kuei* and *shen*: They were "half real and half imaginary." Thus, he characterized *hun* and *p'o* as "the exquisite [aspects] of physical form and *ch'i*, which are referred to as 'numinous.'"[277] It was in this sense also that he referred to *hun* as "*shen* of *ch'i*" and *p'o* as "*shen* of physical form."[278] Distinguishing *p'o* from one of its associations, the body, was more straightforward: the eyes themselves are the body, whereas their light, or the brightness of the eyeballs, is the *p'o*; the ears themselves, or "the holes," are the body, whereas their astuteness, or the ability to hear, is the *p'o*.[279]

We have seen in section 11.1 that certain dualistic pairs were used as single words: the blood-*ch'i*, the essence-*ch'i*, the *kuei-shen*, the essence-*shen* (the mental spirit, *ching-shen*), for example. The *ch'i-p'o* pair is another such example, with the meaning of mental vigor and strength. Chu Hsi said: "If a man has '*ch'i-p'o*,' he can do and accomplish things. Faced with disasters and fortunes, gains and losses, and profits and damages, of the world, [he] can match them and is not moved in fear of them."[280]

11.7. Disease and Medicine

Chu Hsi's remarks about disease and medicine were frequently intended as analogies in discussing other problems. For him, taking medicine to cure disease seems to have been among the most familiar activities of man, one to which he could compare more difficult and complex moral, social, and philosophical problems.[281] For example, in arguing that only a continuing exertion of effort leads one to the understanding of the *li*, he noted that medicine shows its effect only after one has taken it continuously for a long time.[282] That medicine is effective only when one keeps taking the same medicine was used to support the argument that "scholars should 'concentrate on one [thing]' (*chüan-i*)."[283] To illustrate the manifestation of man's nature as concrete virtues of humaneness, righteousness, propriety, and knowledge, he spoke of the manifestation of "the nature of medicine" (*yao-hsing*): "As for the things like the nature [of medicine] being cold and being hot, there is no place to discuss these appearances inside medicine, either. Only after taking it, [it] can produce cold and hot."[284] Chu Hsi also mentioned the difficulty of curing disease by medicine, when what he had in mind was the problem of handling troubles in the affairs of the world.[285] He spoke of the method of preparing medicine by decoction (first boiling over a strong fire, then nurturing with a weak fire) in relation to the proper method of reading a book.[286] He even drew direct analogies between some philosophical terms and different aspects of curing by medicine. For example, "If reverence is compared to medicine, then self-esteem (*chin-chih*) is taking medicine."[287] "Self-control" (*k'e-chi*) is like "seeing an effect after taking [medicine] once," whereas "reverence and considerateness" is like "taking medicine gradually and grinding the disease away."[288]

Chu Hsi seldom discussed details of the knowledge of medical specialists, and there is no evidence that Chu Hsi's medical knowledge reached the level of his knowledge in calendrical astronomy or harmonics (see chapter 12). The remaining discussion of this section is based on isolated facts, mostly simple and familiar ones that he mentioned on various occasions.

Chu Hsi occasionally referred to particular symptoms and diseases: for example, stomachache, dropsy, paralysis of the arms and legs.[289] In old age he frequently complained of the symptoms of "old ailment" (*lao-ping*): poor eyesight, hearing, and memory; weakness of the legs; diarrhea; and insomnia.[290] But more often he simply spoke of the "hot" (*je*) and "cold" (*han* or *leng*) — or "cool" (*liang*) — diseases in general.[291]

On the cause of disease, Chu Hsi shared the common belief that man becomes sick when his *ch'i* is damaged or weakened.[292] When he spoke of the causes of particular symptoms and diseases, however, his actual interest often lay elsewhere. For example, when he attributed disorders of the eyes and ears to damage to the visceral organs associated with them, the liver and the kidneys, he was really interested in illustrating the association schemes involving various aspects of man's mind.[293] The remark that stomachache is caused when food is stuck in the stomach, forming a "cold accumulation" (*leng-chi*), was made to support his point that deficiency in the moral mind causes harm and thus should be eliminated.[294] He spoke of "a man [who] had eaten a cold thing, [which] had remained between the spleen and the stomach for more than ten years, causing damages," but again, this was to illustrate the effects of difficult passages in reading: if one continues without fully understanding them, the passages will "make roots of disease in the mind."[295]

A method universally used in Chinese medicine for the diagnosis of disease was taking the pulse, that is, to feel the pulse by hand. This method makes diagnosis possible because, as Chu Hsi said, it enables one "to see the blood and *ch'i* flow around."[296] He touched upon some details of the technique in his preface to a medical book.[297] He also spoke of diagnosis by just looking at patients, but he seemed to consider that an extraordinary ability of exceptional persons, the famous physician Pien Ch'üeh (fl. 501 B.C.) and a certain "medical monk" (*i-seng*), for example. The former was so skilled in "seeing symptoms (*cheng-hou*) that merely by looking at the outside [of a person] he could know the conditions of the five storing viscera and the six processing viscera."[298] The latter

> never felt the pulse. He only saw the man, and could tell what disease the man had. Afterward, he did not even see the man, and simply told [other] men to come to speak [about the man's condition]. Based on what they said, he simply knew [what the disease was].[299]

It was Chu Hsi's view that in curing disease with medicine, one should first know the disease, or about "how the disease has started," and prescribe medicine accordingly;[300] when a medicine does not fit the disease, not only does it have no effect, but it can even be harmful for the patient.[301] Thus, it was natural for him that the medicine for stomachache should be directed at eliminating "the cold accumulation" that had caused it.[302] Inducing diarrhea and vomiting can be used as cures also: "If 'the cold damage' (*shang-han*) is in the upper [part of the body], vomit. If it is in the lower [part], [induce] diarrhea. In this way, one can eliminate the disease."[303] He spoke of a poisoned person who, by drinking a large amount of water, caused vomiting and diarrhea and neutralized the poison.[304]

Chu Hsi shared the idea that the purpose of a medicine should be to restore the balance in the body by strengthening the aspect that has been weakened or by counteracting the quality causing the disorder with an opposite quality. For example, the eyeballs of the tiger, the animal whose *p'o* is the strongest, are used as "a drug that settles the *p'o*" of patients whose *p'o* is declining, whereas the bones of the dragon, whose *hun* is the most flourishing, are used as "a drug that aids *hun*."[305] At a more general level, one who has "a hot disease" (with symptoms of excessive heat) should take "a cool medicine" (which produces an effect of coolness), whereas "a cold disease" should be cured by "a hot medicine."[306]

Of course, Chu Hsi knew that things could not be so simple. He said that, though taking a cold medicine for a hot disease and a hot medicine for a cold disease is "the constant *li*," there also are times when "having a hot disease, one still uses a hot medicine and gets rid of the disease; and also, having a cold disease, one still uses a cold medicine and gets rid of the disease."[307] He also spoke of the difficulty of keeping a stable balance by medicine:

> For example, a man had a cold disease, and took hot medicines. After a while, [the symptoms] changed again to become dry and hot. When [it became] a hot disease, he took cold medicines. After a while, [the symptoms] again changed to cold [ones].[308]

Chu Hsi noted that the effect of medicine depends on the condition of the patient. Medicine can help only when the patient "himself has the life-*ch'i*. Then the *ch'i* of the power of medicine relies on it and the life intent naturally grows."[309] For a middle-aged man, whose *ch'i* and blood are no longer flourishing, medicine does not produce effects easily.[310] Other conditions of preparing and taking medicine, not only the weights of its ingredients, but also the methods of refining, roasting, mixing, dividing, boiling, and even of drinking it can all affect the medicine's curing effect.[311] Thus, Chu Hsi said that in refining herbal medicines, one has to be careful not to lose "the nature of medicine," for if it is lost, "it cannot cure the disease."[312] One has to follow "the proper sequence" of taking medicine, too.[313] He warned that exceeding the proper dose can even "produce a source of another disease."[314] He also noted that when the wolfsbane is taken raw, it can kill a man.[315]

Chu Hsi spoke of actual names of some particular medicinal plants: for example, rhubarb, which can induce diarrhea; wolfsbane, which can warm the body; and "*shang-lu*," which can cure the dropsy.[316] As for calamus and tuckahoe, he implied that they had great curing powers.[317] He also noted that the roots of the ginseng and the *chu* plant can cure diseases.[318]

There are, of course, methods of curing disease other than taking medicine. For example, Chu Hsi mentioned the widely used method of moxibustion—cauterizing the surface of the body mainly to relieve pain.[319] And although he did not explicitly speak of the even more widespread practice of acupuncture, we have a poem written by him as a gift to a certain Taoist Master Ch'eng, who administered acupuncture and temporarily cured Chu Hsi's foot ailment.[320]

Much more important, however, was taking rest. Rest alone can restore the balance in the body and cure diseases. Chu Hsi even thought that rest was the first thing to try before taking medicine: "When taking rest is not sufficient [to cure disease], take medicine afterward. If taking rest is sufficient, then naturally there is no disease. Why should one waste medicine by taking it?"[321] Sometimes rest is combined with other meditational and respiratory techniques, generally referred to as "nourishing life" (*yang-sheng*)—or "nourishing the mind" (*yang-hsin*), "nourishing the *ch'i*" (*yang-ch'i*), or "nourishing the disease" (*yang-ping*).[322]

There are diseases that cannot be cured by medicines. For example, there are terminal diseases, which Chu Hsi referred to as "diseases necessarily [leading to] death" (*pi-ssu chih ping*), and which "taking hot medicines cannot cure, nor can taking cool medicines."[323] Mental diseases also cannot be cured by medicine, not even by such medicines as calamus and tuckahoe.[324] Chu Hsi even had an explanation for how mental disorder can arise: "When the eyes receive [something] but the mind fears it, then the body is not at ease."[325] As examples of the symptoms of such mental diseases, he spoke of persons with morbid fears of sharp objects and those who had hallucinatory visions of lions. The cures he proposed for these disorders were not medicines but were mental treatments: making the patients realize that sharp objects by themselves do not hurt them and that the lions they see cannot actually be touched.[326] As for those who see ghosts, he explained that their mental spirit is not complete.[327]

Notes

1. A Taoist-inspired version of this Confucian aim was how to live long in the world; it was concerned with alchemical, meditational, and "macrobiotic" techniques. For some recent discussions of those techniques, see Kohn, *Taoist Meditation and Longevity Techniques*. See also Needham, *Science and Civilisation*, vol. 5, pts. 3–5; Sakade, *Chūgoku kodai yōsei shisō no sōgōteki kenkyū*. Chu Hsi also commented upon this tradition on various occasions, but most notably in *Ts'an-t'ung-ch'i k'ao-i*. See chap. 12, sec. 12.6.

2. For an outline account of traditional Chinese knowledge of the human body and its functions, see Sivin, *Traditional Medicine in Contemporary China*.

3. We have noted a similar lack, in Chu Hsi's thought, of the matter-life distinction; see chap. 3, sec. 3.1. It should also be kept in mind that although we use such words as "anatomical," "physiological," and "psychical," they represent distinctions that we make for our convenience and do not reflect Chu Hsi's understanding.

4. *YL*92.10b1.

5. E.g., *YL*5.12a4; 52.13b0, 25b3.

6. *YL*52.19b2.

7. *YL*52.9b1.

8. *YL*5.3b4.

9. *CS*49.5a2.

10. *YL*3.1b4–2a0. See also *YL*52.25b3.

11. *YL*4.17b2. Chu Hsi added later that it was "the public (*kung-kung*) *ch'i* of heaven and earth" and that "man cannot monopolize in possessing it."

12. E.g., *YL*8.8a5; 52.19b2.

13. *YL*23.12b5.

14. *YL*4.9a1.

15. *YL*4.16b1. Here, Chu Hsi is referring to the minds of "four beginnings" (*ssu-tuan*), which first appeared in *Mencius* (6A6) and which are the beginnings of the four virtues—humaneness, propriety, righteousness, and knowledge. For Mencius's ideas on these, see, e.g., Ames, "Mencian Conception of *Ren Xing*"; Bloom, "Mencian Arguments on Human Nature." See also *YL*59.12a2, where Chu Hsi says, "Endowed with much Wood *ch'i*, one is seldom tough; endowed with much Metal *ch'i*, one is seldom benign"; and *YL*59.13a1, where he says, "[Some] are rich in humaneness and short in righteousness; some have surpluses in propriety and are not sufficient in knowledge. [Such differences] come up from the quality of [their] *ch'i*."

16. *YL*6.5a3.

17. *YL*4.16b1, immediately following the remarks cited in note 15.

18. *YL*4.12a0.

19. *YL*4.17a0.

20. *YL*4.2ao.

21. *YL*1.6b3. See also *YL*4.17ao.

22. *YL*4.11b5–12ao. See also *YL*59.10bo.

23. E.g., *YL*4.21b1, 22a1; 114.3b2; 119.5b1; 127.2b1; 135.1a4; 138.4b4, 4b5–5ao.

24. *YL*3.9a6. See also *YL*4.18b4–19ao, 20a2.

25. *YL*4.22a2. On this aspect of the concept of *shu*, see chap. 5, sec. 5.1. In *YL*4.20a1 Chu Hsi even said that "the fate of the endowment of *ch'i* . . . cannot be altered." Cf. p. 218.

26. *YL*4.20b1. Chu Hsi even added: "Yen-tzu [i.e., Yen Hui] was not even like Confucius. [He] was endowed also with that short [*ch'i*], and thus also died young." See also *YL*59.11ao.

27. *YL*1.7ao. See also *YL*4.20a2–20bo; 59.11ao.

28. *YL*4.17ao. To the same question in *YL*4.17b2, however, Chu Hsi answered that "things like this are not possible to understand."

29. *YL*4.20b1–21ao. In *YL*59.11ao Chu Hsi even said that "bad *ch'i* is always plentiful and good *ch'i* is always rare." Cf. *YL*4.21ao, where he did not directly respond to a disciple who quoted Shao Yung's explanation that "Yang is one and yin is two, and therefore great men are rare and small men are abundant."

30. Porkert, *Theoretical Foundations of Chinese Medicine*, pp. 168–173.

31. Porkert has provided an analytical discussion of these forms of bodily contents in ibid., pp. 173–196. See also Sivin, *Traditional Medicine in Contemporary China*, pp. 147–163.

32. See, e.g., the tables in Porkert, *Theoretical Foundations of Chinese Medicine*, p. 195, and in Sivin, *Traditional Medicine in Contemporary China*, p. 148.

33. On *hun* and *p'o* in a technical medical context, see, e.g., Porkert, *Theoretical Foundations of Chinese Medicine*, pp. 184–185.

34. Thus, although the character *ch'i* in the names of *ch'i* varieties has often been translated or interpreted as "energies" or "vitalities" (e.g., the references cited in note 31 above), I have chosen to leave it untranslated and retain the ambiguity of the word *ch'i*.

35. *Analects*, 16.7.

36. *SSCC* (*Lun-yü*), 8.10b. See also *YL*46.2b2, 104.11a3.

37. *WC*62.23a. In *YL*52.10b4 Chu Hsi said the same thing about the relation of the blood *ch'i* and "the magnanimous *ch'i*" (*hao-jan chih ch'i*): "*Ch'i* simply is one *ch'i*. But that which comes out from within righteousness and *li* is the magnanimous *ch'i*. That which comes out from the body of blood and flesh is the *ch'i* of the blood *ch'i*. That is all." See also *YL*46.2b3; 52.11b1, 13bo.

38. *WC*59.35a–35b. See chap. 10, p. 174.

39. *WC*43.26b.

40. *YL*5.12a4.

41. E.g., *YL*118.3ao, 8b1.

42. E.g., *YL*3.1b3, 8b1; 68.3a2; 74.14a4; 87.29a1.

43. The words "essence" and *shen* were also frequently combined and used as one word, "*ching-shen*," meaning "mental spirit." See, e.g., *YL*3.12b2, 15a1; 73.23b4; 101.9ao.

44. *Traditional Medicine in Contemporary China*, p. 14.

45. Ibid., p. 124.

46. This widely recognized feature of Chinese medicine is emphasized by Sivin in ibid., pp. 117–121. He has noted that even in modern writings, "what we learn about the Chinese conception is not anatomical but physiological and pathological—as usual, not what the viscera are but what they do in health and sickness" (pp. 120–121).

47. I have based my translation of the characters *tsang* and *fu* on the following *Huang-ti nei-ching* remark: "The so-called 'five *tsang*' store the essence *ch'i* without draining it. Therefore they are full but cannot be replete. The 'six *fu*' transmit and transform things without storing them. Therefore they are replete but cannot be

full." For discussions of this remark, which appears in *Huang-ti nei-ching su-wen* (SPPY ed.), 3.14a, see Porkert, *Theoretical Foundations of Chinese Medicine*, p. 110, where *tsang* and *fu* are translated as yin and yang "orbs"; and Sivin, *Traditional Medicine in Contemporary China*, p. 132, where they are translated as yin and yang "visceral systems." Porkert, *Theoretical Foundations of Chinese Medicine*, chap. 3, contains a detailed analytical discussion of the five *tsang* and the six *fu* in a technical medical context.

48. *YL*14.6bo.

49. For a brief discussion of early Chinese anatomical information, mainly of the visceral systems, see Watanabe, "Genson suru Chūgoku kinsei made no gozō rokufuzu no gaisetsu."

50. E.g., 57.7b2; 98.7b1. See chap. 10, p. 197.

51. For such rare examples, see, e.g., *YL*5.5a1; 107.14a4; *WC*63.20bo, where the lungs and the liver are mentioned, and *YL*56.2a1, where the spleen and the stomach are mentioned.

52. E.g., *YL*22.1a4; *WC*67.23b.

53. E.g., Y73.10a1, 11b1. The *I-ching* phrase is the first sentence on the *ken* hexagram.

54. *YL*27.24a4.

55. E.g., *YL*5.4b2; 6.2b1; 9.2b2; 18.3a1; 32.8a1; 57.8bo; 74.20bo; 109.3a1; 117.14ao.

56. E.g., *YL*52.5a1; 53.10a1; 79.17a1; 87.29a1. Since the heart, a visceral organ, is also the site for the mind, the basis of man's perception, it is to be expected that other visceral organs should be similarly associated with perceptual organs. Also, since both the visceral and the perceptual organs are associated with the five phases, they become associated with one another. In *YL*23.15a1; 138.7a8, Chu Hsi spoke of the medical specialists' association of the visceral organs with mental functions. See chap. 12, pp. 276–277.

57. *WC*36.13a. It is to be noted that Chu Hsi went on to mention "the affection of the father and the filial piety of the son" in this passage. See also *YL*6.14a2; 31.5b1.

58. E.g., *YL*31.14b2; 61.3b3; 95.12ao; 98.20b5. See also *YL*14.13a1; 78.29b3; 101.30a2, which quote the phrases from the *Mencius*: "[As for the way] the mouth is [disposed] to tastes, the eyes to colors, the ears to sounds, the nose to smells, and the four limbs to comfort, that is the nature" (7B24).

59. E.g., *YL*4.2ao; 65.6a4.

60. *WC*77.15a.

61. *YL*98.20b5.

62. *YL*78.29a1.

63. *YL*78.29b3. See also *YL*78.33b1.

64. E.g., *YL*95.12ao.

65. E.g., *YL*8.1a3; 78.28a1; 101.30a2.

66. *YL*101.30a2.

67. *YL*5.5a1.

68. E.g., *YL*53.5b2; 6a1, 2, 3. Ch'eng Hao's remark appears in *Ho-nan Ch'eng-shih i-shu*, ch. 3 (*ECC*, p. 62) and is, in turn, a comment on a *Mencius* passage (2A6). Chu Hsi also discussed a similar saying by one of the Ch'eng brothers, "Mind ought to be inside the cavity," but I have not been able to locate it in the Ch'eng sources. E.g., *YL*5.5a2; 96.2b3, 3a1.

69. *YL*5.5a2.

70. E.g., *YL*5.4b2; 32.8a1.

71. E.g., *YL*59.33b1–34a2. The *Mencius* phrase reads as follows: "The organs of the ears and eyes do not think, and are blocked by [external] things. If a thing is in contact with another thing, it attracts it, and that is all. The organ of the heart is thinking. If it thinks, it gets it; if it does not think, it does not get it." In *YL*59.34a1; *WC*40.18b, Chu Hsi glossed the word *kuan* as *chu* ("to take charge of").

72. E.g., *YL*59.33b2.

73. *YL*62.17b2.

74. E.g., *YL*97.11a7–11bo; 118.19b5.

75. *YL*34.6a3.

76. E.g., *YL*21.18b1; 47.11a2.

77. *YL*44.24b4–25ao.

78. *YL*31.5b1. See also *YL*60.8ao; *WC*76.21b, where Chu Hsi speaks of "the perception of the mind."

79. E.g., *YL*5.3a4; 20.17a2; *WC*45.12a–12b.

80. YL5.3b1.

81. E.g., YL53.5b2, 6a1. Again, these are Chu Hsi's comments on the saying of Ch'eng Hao that "what fills the cavity is the mind of commiseration."

82. YL107.17a4.

83. YL5.4b3.

84. YL5.4a3. Chu Hsi assigned the perception of sensible material qualities like color and sound to the purview of "the mind of man" (jen-hsin), in contrast to "the mind of the Way" (tao-hsin), which perceives the ways and li. See, e.g., YL78.27a3; 27b0, 1, 3. For "the mind of man" and "the mind of the Way," see p. 216.

85. YL113.7a0.

86. WC40.18b.

87. YL5.4a3.

88. WC45.12a–12b.

89. YL51.5a1.

90. E.g., YL5.12a4; 12.1a4; 20.15b6; 96.2b3; WC67.18b.

91. E.g., YL5.6b4, 7a3, 12b3. This idea can be traced to Chang Tsai's famous saying "Mind controls the nature and feelings." *Chang-tzu ch'üan-shu*, 14.2a. For Chu Hsi's comments on this, see, e.g., YL98.6b2–8a3.

92. YL13.12a1.

93. YL24.22a3.

94. YL64.16b3. See also YL64.16b4.

95. YL64.16a0.

96. YL21.18b1.

97. YL16.32a3–32b0.

98. YL16.9b6.

99. CS44.5b1.

100. YL12.2b4.

101. YL119.9a1. For the Ch'eng brothers' ideas about the word chu-i, see Graham, *Two Chinese Philosophers*, pp. 68–72, where the term is translated as "making unity the ruler."

102. YL96.6b4.

103. E.g., YL96.6b1; 96.7a1.

104. E.g., YL5.4b3, 6a0; 16.26a2; 44.25a0; 57.7b2; 96.2b1; 126.7b3; WC76.21b; CS44.5a3. It is obvious that the state of mind characterized as "not yet manifest" (wei-fa) refers to this empty and

numinous mind. E.g., YL53.10a1; WC32.5a; 64.28b–29a. Although "open" or "unoccupied" may be a better and more idiomatic translation of the character hsü in most cases, I translate it consistently as "empty"— its most common meaning—in order to indicate clearly that the Chinese character is "hsü." In the next section, however, when the character refers unambiguously to the "abstract" and "unreal" aspect of the mind, I adopt the translation "shapeless."

105. YL5.6a0; 9.6a3; 57.7b2; 67.12b1; CS44.5a3–5b0; SSCC (Meng-tzu), p. 7.1a.

106. CS44.5a3–5b0.

107. CS44.5b0.

108. YL16.21a1. See also YL16.21a4. Here, Chu Hsi is commenting on the *Ta-hsueh* statement "The heart is broad and the body is at ease" (ch. 6). Cf. YL18.12b2, where Chu Hsi used the expression "By profits and desires this mind . . . is 'contained' (pao)."

109. YL4.19a0.

110. YL43.2a2.

111. YL98.20a1. See also YL98.20a2. Chang Tsai's remark appears in *Chang-tzu ch'üan-shu*, 5.6b.

112. E.g., YL16.23b2, 3, 4, 5; 24a1; 24b3; 25a1; 26b2; 29a1. All these passages are comments on Ta-hsueh, ch. 7.

113. YL16.23b1.

114. YL16.24a3. See also YL13.14b3, where he says, "[As for] the anger of blood ch'i, one should not have [it]; [as for] the anger of righteousness and li, one is not allowed not to have [it]."

115. E.g., YL16.23b1, 24a3, 24a4–24b0.

116. YL16.26a2–26b0. See also YL96.2b2. The mind of a sage is so "broad and large, empty and bright that not a thing remains [in it]." YL16.28a0.

117. YL16.24b2. He compared this to the weighing of things by the balance: if there is something already on the balance, it cannot measure the correct weight. See also YL16.26b1, 27a2. In the latter passage, he also compared the mind to a mirror: "If a mirror has a doll inside, then [even if] a

second man comes [before it], it would not be able to shine upon [him]."

118. *YL*59.16a1. Chu Hsi added: "Soon afterward, [when it] is in contact with things, it declines again as before." See also *YL*16.28b1; *WC*40.18a–18b.

119. *YL*120.28a2.

120. *YL*20.27b0.

121. *YL*44.25a0.

122. *SSCC* (*Meng-tzu*), 7.1a.

123. E.g., *YL*11.3b5.

124. E.g., *YL*11.2a2, 4.

125. *YL*117.14a0

126. *YL*5.7a3. For his other comments on the relation between mind, nature, and feelings, which can be traced to the Chang Tsai saying quoted in note 91, see, e.g., *YL*5.3a3, 5b2–6a0, 6a4, 6b4.

127. *YL*5.12a4. Thus it is that the will is "the deep place of mind." *YL*25.13a1.

128. *YL*5.12b3.

129. *YL*59.10b0, where Chu Hsi distinguishes between feelings and talent.

130. *YL*78.28a1. Thus, Chu Hsi equates "the mind of man" with human desire and "the mind of the Way" with the *li* of heaven. For his other comments, see, e.g., *YL*78.26b3–33b1.

131. E.g., *YL*5.3a3, 3b3, 5a1; 18.10a1, 12b2; 24.11a3; *WC*40.18b.

132. *YL*5.6a0.

133. *YL*19.2a4.

134. E.g., *YL*5.4b3; 15.19a3. See also *YL*51.5a1, quoted in chap. 1, p. 5: "Things are easy to see; mind has no physical form or measure. The weight and length of things are easy to measure; the weight and length of the mind are difficult to measure."

135. *YL*17.11a0.

136. *YL*5.3b2.

137. E.g., Y5.3b1; 60.8a0.

138. *YL*5.4b2.

139. *WC*50.30a.

140. *YL*78.33b1. This, however, is not surprising at all because there was no mind-body distinction for Chu Hsi; the same *ch'i* was responsible for processes of matter, life, and mind. To be sure, Chu Hsi did speak, as

we have seen, of the distinction between "the will *ch'i*" and "the blood *ch'i*," which sounded like two different kinds of *ch'i* for the mind and the body. But he made it clear that they were different aspects of the same *ch'i* and that they affected each other. See p. 210.

141. *YL*52.19b2.

142. *YL*52.25b3–26a0.

143. *YL*47.11b2.

144. *YL*34.24a1.

145. *YL*52.13b0.

146. *YL*59.15b2. These terms appear in the *Mencius* (6A8), Chu Hsi's commentaries on which are gathered in *YL*59.15a2–21b2. See also *YL*16.28b1.

147. *YL*59.17b3. In *YL*59.15b2, which has just been quoted, Chu Hsi spelled out that what is to be nourished in the mind is "the good mind." See also *YL*59.15b1.

148. *YL*46.2b3.

149. *YL*30.11a0. Thus, for Chu Hsi, "the anger of even the Sage [i.e., Confucius] is a bad thing."

150. *YL*104.11b1.

151. E.g., *YL*5.4a1; 34.6a3; 62.17b2.

152. *YL*34.6a3. Cf. *YL*41.20a2, where Chu Hsi says: "Thought is 'the extreme smallness' (*wei*) of movement; action is 'the manifestation' (*chu*) of movement. . . . Thought is the movement inside; action is the movement outside."

153. E.g., *YL*59.32a0; 71.10b0; 118.19b5.

154. *YL*16.22a3.

155. E.g., *YL*52.1a3–9a0. It was in the same vein that Chu Hsi followed Confucius's admonition in the *Analects* (16.7) and said: "The great man . . . [should] be on guard not to be employed by the blood *ch'i*." *YL*46.2b1.

156. E.g., *YL*18.29b1; 52.4b0, 9b1; *CS*20.24b0.

157. *YL*59.21b2.

158. *WC*48.25b.

159. *YL*59.16a0.

160. *YL*12.5b4.

161. E.g., *YL*52.13a1, 13b0, 14a0.

162. *YL*4.12a0.

163. *YL*27.29a1. Cf. *YL*113.1a1; 117.21a1.

164. *YL*113.1a1.

165. *YL*117.21a1.

166. *YL*35.20b0.

167. *YL*26.12a1. The Mencian phrases come from the same passage quoted above (2A2).

168. *YL*17.3a0.

169. *YL*30.5a3. Here, Chu Hsi is commenting upon Confucius's characterization of Yen Hui as a person who "does not shift anger." *Analects*, 6A2. See also *YL*16.23b5, 24b0. For Chu Hsi's other comments on the *Analects* phrase, see *YL*30.4b2–12b0.

170. *YL*52.7a0.

171. E.g., *YL*52.14a0; 59.21a1; *SSCC* (*Meng-tzu*), 2.5a.

172. *YL*52.26a0.

173. *YL*87.31a4.

174. *YL*107.17a4.

175. *YL*3.2a0.

176. *YL*3.1b4–2a0.

177. *YL*87.26a1. See also *YL*34.6b2, where Chu Hsi spoke of "[Confucius] and heaven and earth responding to each other."

178. See chap. 6, sec. 6.2.

179. E.g., *YL*3.2a0; 4.20a1, 2. See chap. 6, pp. 97–98.

180. *YL*62.19b0.

181. See chap. 7, pp. 112, 116; chap. 11, pp. 206–207.

182. *YL*44.23a1.

183. *YL*136.8b2. See chap. 8, p. 123.

184. See chap. 10, sec. 10.3.

185. *YL*99.2b3.

186. *YL*115.13a0. See also *YL*121.1b1.

187. *YL*94.26b2.

188. *YL*1.5a7.

189. *YL*118.1b3. What Chu Hsi actually said was:

> Wanting to get the whole shape [literally, "the wicked and correct, the bent and straight" (*hsieh-cheng ch'ü-chih*)], one must see from a far [distance]. Only then can one fix it [i.e., the shape]. If one sees from a close [distance], [the vision] becomes narrower, and one cannot see.

190. *WC*41.11a.

191. *YL*107.17a4.

192. *YL*87.27b0.

193. *WC*42.29a–29b. In most cases, however, Chu Hsi used *shih* and *t'ing* to refer to both the active and the passive processes of perception. Thus, I will stick to translating the characters as "to see" and "to hear" except where the distinction is unambiguously intended.

194. *YL*41.17b2. Here, Chu Hsi is commenting on Ch'eng I's essay "Ssu-chen" (The four admonitions), which in turn commented on the following passage of the *Analects*: "If it is not in accordance with propriety, do not look; if it is not in accordance with propriety, do not listen" (12.1).

195. *YL*41.10a0.

196. *YL*6.14a2.

197. *YL*95.35b2.

198. E.g., *YL*5.3a4, 3b1; 60.8a0; *WC*50.30a–30b.

199. E.g., *YL*41.9b1–10b1, where Chu Hsi comments on the phrases of the *Analects* passage quoted in note 194.

200. E.g., *YL*72.2b2; 74.10b1; 125.11b3.

201. *YL*72.2b2.

202. *YL*74.10b1.

203. *YL*63.21b3–22a0.

204. E.g., *YL*1.6b2; 74.10b1; 115.10b0, 11a0. This is why Chu Hsi was so interested in the breathing techniques practiced by the specialists in "nourishing life" (*yang-sheng*). See chap. 12, sec. 12.6. For more on Chu Hsi's views about such breathing techniques, see Miura, "Shushi to kokyū."

205. *YL*74.10b1.

206. *YL*115.10a2–10b0. See also *YL*12.12b1; 115.11a0.

207. *YL*1.6b2.

208. *YL*68.16b4. I have not succeeded in finding the source of this number of Hu Yüan, which amounts to nine and a half times per minute, or about half the normal rate of respiration, as we now know.

209. *YL*6.19b2. See also an identical sentence in *YL*95.17b2.

210. *YL*19.5a4.

211. *YL*24.4b1. Here, Chu Hsi is illustrating the phrase "melting of the mind" (*hsin jung*), which appears in his commentary on the *Analects* (2.9). See *SSCC* (*Lun-yü*), 1.9a.

212. *WC*12.10b.

213. E.g., *YL*47.2b1; 65.12b0; 98.12a4; *WC*37.29b.

214. *YL*69.20b3.

215. *YL*69.20b4.

216. *YL*74.6a1.

217. *YL*67.17a5.

218. *YL*68.3b0. The *Tso-chuan* phrase appears in the records for the seventh year of Chao-kung (44.13a).

219. *YL*94.19b0. The same discussion appears in *YL*116.8b0.

220. *YL*71.8a0.

221. E.g., *YL*90.18b0; *WC*52.16a.

222. *YL*63.21a1.

223. E.g., *YL*3.12b1, 13a1; 17.11b3; 63.26a0. Chu Hsi also quoted the theory of Hsieh Liang-tso (1050–1103) that descendants have the same mental spirit as their ancestors; e.g., *YL*25.13b1; 14a1, 3; 63.21b0, 26a0.

224. *YL*17.11b3. See also *YL*23.16a4.

225. *YL*22.1a4.

226. See chap. 6, sec. 6.2; chap. 8, p. 126.

227. E.g., *YL*4.4a1, 17a0. See p. 208.

228. *YL*3.17a1.

229. *YL*4.17b1. For his distinction between the production of original man through "transformation of *ch'i*" and the subsequent reproduction through "transformation of physical form," see chap. 10, sec. 10.4.

230. *YL*76.4b0. The original *Ts'an-t'ung-ch'i* passage can be seen in *Ts'an-t'ung-ch'i k'ao-i*, p. 20a, and is translated in Needham, *Science and Civilisation*, vol. 5, pt. 3, p. 71.

231. Cf. *YL*126.15b4: "The Sage (i.e., Confucius) did not speak of death. Once dead, what should one still speak of?"

232. *Tso-chuan*, Chao-kung, the seventh year, 44.13a. Cf. Chan, *Source Book in Chi-*

nese Philosophy, p. 12, where *hun* and *p'o* are translated as the "earthly" and the "heavenly" aspects of the soul. On the ancient origins and development of the ideas of *hun* and *p'o*, see Yu, "'O Soul, Come Back!,'" esp. pp. 369–378.

233. *Tso-chuan chu-shu*, 24.13b.

234. *YL*3.8a2. Chu Hsi then went on to quote from Chou Tun-i's *T'ai-chi-t'u shuo*: "Physical form having been produced, *shen* starts to know," before quoting and praising the *Tso-chuan* passage itself. We have also seen his gloss on the expression "the first transformation" as the accomplishing of physical form inside the womb. *YL*68.3b0. See p. 222. In the case of the first transformation of the production of nonhuman things also, "once *p'o* has been produced, the warm part became *hun*. First there is *p'o* and afterward there is *hun*." *YL*3.8a1.

235. *Li-chi*, ch. 16 (26.1b).

236. E.g., *YL*3.4a0, 11a0; 87.26a2. The *Li-chi* passage goes on to say, "Hence the idea that sacrificial services seek from yin and yang," on which Chu Hsi commented: "The ancients, in offering sacrificial services, burn [fire] to seek from yang [i.e., *hun*] and pour [water or liquor] to seek from yin [i.e., *p'o*]." *YL*87.26a2. See *YL*74.14b0, where Chu Hsi interprets "to seek from yang" as "to seek from *hun*."

237. E.g., *YL*63.20b0, 24a2; 74.14b0; 83.21a2.

238. *YL*3.4a0.

239. *Li-chi*, ch. 24 (47.14a–15a).

240. *YL*87.26b1.

241. *YL*3.6b0; 87.27b1, 29b1; *WC*44.30b.

242. *YL*3.6b0. See also *YL*63.20b0; 21a1; 22a0, 1; 68.3a2; 87.28a3, 28b1, 2, 3; 28b4–29a0; 30b0.

243. *YL*87.26b1. See also *YL*3.9a4, 5; 13a1, where Chu Hsi speaks of "dispersion" or "scattering" (*san*) of *hun*, *hun-ch'i*, or *hun-p'o* upon death. Sacrificial services, then, are the means to reach such dispersed *hun* and *p'o*, as well as *ch'i*. See, e.g., *YL*3.5b1–6a0, 11b3, 15b1; 63.24a2.

244. *YL*87.27a0. Chu Hsi had begun by glossing the *Lao-tzu* phrase "to carry the *p'o*" (*tsai-ying p'o*) (ch. 10) as "protecting *p'o* by means of *hun*." See also *YL*125.8b1.

245. *YL*3.8b1.

246. *YL*3.7a3.

247. *YL*87.26b1.

248. *YL*3.7b1.

249. *CS*51.28b0.

250. *YL*3.15b1.

251. *YL*68.3a2.

252. *YL*63.25a0.

253. *YL*3.8a3; 87.26b1. Chu Hsi even expressed the moon's receiving the sunlight as "*hun* added upon *p'o*" and as "*p'o* carrying *hun*." *YL*79.26b2–27a0, where he comments upon the *Lao-tzu* phrase mentioned in note 244.

254. Comment on *Li-chi*, ch. 24 (47.14a), quoted on p. 224 (see note 239).

255. E.g., *YL*3.7b1, 11a0; 87.28a1, 2; 29a1.

256. *YL*87.27b0. See also *YL*87.29a1, where Chu Hsi spoke of the same thing in terms of "essence and blood" (*ching-hsueh*), which are associated with *p'o*: "When the essence and blood are flourishing, the ears are astute; when the essence and blood are wasted, the ears are deaf."

257. *YL*3.11a0.

258. *YL*3.9a5. Chu Hsi also spoke of the *p'o* of tigers and the *hun* of dragons. These were thought to be the animals whose *p'o* and *hun*, respectively, were the strongest. See also *YL*63.20b0.

259. *YL*87.26b1. To say that perception itself is *p'o* would be in conflict with the association of perception and movement with yang (associated, in turn, with *hun*) and physical form and body with yin (associated with *p'o*); e.g., *YL*3.4a0.

260. *YL*87.27b0 (continuing the passage cited in note 256).

261. *YL*87.26b1.

262. *YL*3.8a1.

263. *YL*63.25a0. See also *YL*87.27a0, 27b0. Once at least, however, he said that there are those whose *hun* decline first, al-though he placed himself among those whose *p'o* decline first, on account of his weak hearing and forgetfulness. *YL*3.7a3–7b0. He also said: "I feel myself that when [my] *ch'i* flourishes, the *p'o* declines. When young boys and girls die, the *p'o* is trans-formed first." *YL*3.8a4. Cf. *WCH*8.2b, where he said, "In middle age, the *ch'i* and blood cannot be compared with earlier days."

264. *YL*87.29a1. The first sentence is Chu Hsi's explanation of the "Hsi-tz'u chuan" phrase "The essence-*ch'i* becomes things" (A4), which we have come across earlier. See chap. 10, note 181.

265. *YL*3.1b3.

266. See also *YL*3.8b1; 68.3a2. In *Ts'an-t'ung-ch'i k'ao-i*, pp. 10b–11a, Chu Hsi even said: "*K'an* and *li* [trigrams], Water and Fire, dragon and tiger, and lead and mer-cury. . . . [They] actually are merely essence and *ch'i*."

267. *YL*125.12b1.

268. *YL*3.8b2. Chu Hsi went on to say that this theory is congruent with the Bud-dhist theory of "the four elements" (*ssu-ta*). For more on this theory, see chap. 13, p. 296.

269. *WC*44.30b.

270. *YL*74.14b0.

271. *YL*3.7a1.

272. *YL*3.7a1 (continuing the passage cited in note 271).

273. *YL*87.27b0. Obviously he was speaking of the "living" body and the dis-persion "upon death." See also *YL*3.4a0, where he said: "When essence and *ch'i* con-geal, they become man; when they are dis-persed, they become *kuei*."

274. *YL*3.7a3.

275. *YL*63.21b3.

276. *YL*3.7a2.

277. *YL*87.27b0. In *YL*68.3b0 Chu Hsi approved of a disciple's assertion that "'the essential and refreshing' [aspects] of the mind are called *hun* and *p'o*."

278. *YL*87.27b0. *Hun* and *p'o* were called *shen* of yang and yin, and of *ch'i* and essence as well. See table 11.2.

279. E.g., *YL*3.8b2; 87.27b0.

280. *YL*52.11a1. Here, Chu Hsi is saying that if one has *ch'i-p'o*, one has "the magnanimous *ch'i*," and thus courage.

281. For the use of medical metaphors in the case of a later thinker, see Birdwhistell, "Medicine and History as Theoretical Tools."

282. E.g., *YL*10.10b1; 35.20a1–20b0.

283. *YL*19.11a1.

284. *YL*4.7b0. Cf. *YL*5.8a1; 95.20a5–20b0, where he referred to such effects of the cold and the heat of medicine as "feelings" of medicine.

285. *YL*108.10b1.

286. E.g., *YL*10.3a1; 115.8b2.

287. *WC*53.26a.

288. *CS*17.33b2.

289. E.g., *YL*16.18b0; 72.22a5; 121.1b2; *WC*43.26b.

290. E.g., *YL*63.25a0; 104.11a3, 11a4–11b0. In *YL*46.2b1 Chu Hsi also spoke of the change of a man's disposition after suffering a disease.

291. E.g., *YL*37.8b1; 108.10b1. For the ideas of "symptom, syndrome, and disease" in Chinese medicine, see, e.g., Sivin, *Traditional Medicine in Contemporary China*, pp. 106–111, which includes brief comments on the symptoms of "cold" and "hot" diseases. Chu Hsi also used the word "*shang-han*" (cold damage), in an apparent reference to diseases caused by foreign agents. *YL*72.7a0. For the meaning of this word, see, e.g., Sivin, *Traditional Medicine in Contemporary China*, pp. xxiv, 84.

292. E.g., *YL*63.8b2; *WC*48.25b. For a brief account of Chinese ideas about the causes of medical disorders, see Sivin, *Traditional Medicine in Contemporary China*, pp. 100–102.

293. E.g., *YL*52.5a1; 53.10b0.

294. *YL*16.18b0.

295. *YL*121.1b2.

296. *WC*43.26b.

297. *WC*83.21b–22b, the preface to the *Shang-han pu wang lun* by Kuo Yung (1091–1187).

298. *YL*107.14a4.

299. *YL*44.23a1. Chu Hsi went on to say that this was similar to the ability of "reading the mind of others" (*t'a-hsin t'ung*).

300. E.g., *YL*10.1b2; 107.14a4.

301. E.g., *YL*73.8a1; 107.14a4.

302. *YL*16.18b0.

303. *YL*72.7a0. For the word "*shang-han*," see note 291.

304. *WC*71.13a.

305. E.g., *YL*63.20b0; 138.7a7.

306. *YL*37.8b1.

307. *YL*37.8b1. Here Chu Hsi is glossing the word *ch'üan*, which appears in the *Analects*, 9.29, and means "temporary expedient," as opposed to "*ching*," the constant norm.

308. *YL*108.10b1.

309. *YL*63.26b2.

310. *WCH*8.2b.

311. E.g., *YL*10.1b2; 18.16a0.

312. *YL*107.12a4.

313. *WC*46.18a–18b.

314. *WC*53.26a.

315. *WC*71.12b–13a.

316. *YL*60.8a0; 72.22a5; *WC*71.12b.

317. *YL*5.5a1.

318. *WC*43.10b. See chap. 10, note 188.

319. *YL*114.7b3.

320. On the history and techniques of acupuncture and moxibustion, see Lu and Needham, *Celestial Lancets*.

321. *YL*9.3b1. In *YL*104.11a3, 11a4–11b0 it is recorded that disciples asked Chu Hsi to get up late in the morning to take rest and "nourish disease."

322. For Chu Hsi's ideas on the various techniques of "nourishing life," see chap. 12, sec. 12.6.

323. *YL*135.10b2.

324. *YL*5.5a1. Chu Hsi distinguished the disease of the mind from the disease of the heart, which can be cured by medicines; see pp. 212–213.

325. *YL*107.17a4.

326. *YL*96.10b4–11a0.

327. *YL*138.9b1. See chap. 6, p. 99.

PART THREE

Chu Hsi and the "Scientific" Traditions of Specialized Knowledge

12. Chu Hsi on Specialists and Their Specialized Knowledge
13. Comparison with the Western Scientific Tradition

In parts 1 and 2 I have referred to Chu Hsi's ideas as "natural knowledge," or at most as "natural philosophy." I avoided the words "science" and "scientific" intentionally, because those two words do not adequately characterize the thought and knowledge of Chu Hsi's that I was discussing. Not only are his ideas and remarks different from what one would find in the Western scientific tradition—which is perhaps not very significant, for no one would expect that a thinker in a non-Western traditional culture would show characteristic features of Western science—but Chu Hsi's views and attitudes as considered thus far also do not fully represent the traditions of specialized knowledge that existed in China and for which the term "science" would appear less inappropriate.

In part 3 I pursue the problem of "Chu Hsi and science" by looking at Chu Hsi and his natural knowledge from different perspectives, in relation to the "scientific" traditions that existed in China and in the West.

Chu Hsi on Specialists and Their Specialized Knowledge

In addition to the kind of knowledge about the natural world discussed in the last three chapters, Chu Hsi wrote and spoke about more specialized knowledge in such areas as calendrical astronomy, harmonics, geography, medicine, alchemy, numerology, and divination. I have already touched upon some of these subjects — calendrical astronomy and geography in chapter 9, harmonics in chapter 10, and medicine in chapter 11. In those chapters, however, I have not included much of Chu Hsi's discussion of the content of these subjects, and that is for several reasons. First, although these subjects touched on the natural world in various ways, they were not primarily knowledge and understanding of things and events in that world but instead represented the application of such knowledge to human purposes — calendars, music, healing, divination, and so on. Furthermore, Chu Hsi's knowledge on these topics was not really his own but in large part adoptions from the specialist traditions. The content of his knowledge, when it comes to the technical details, did not depart much from what can be found in the existing secondary literature on the traditions.[1]

Thus, in this chapter I do not dwell much on the technical content of Chu Hsi's knowledge in these areas; I concentrate mainly on Chu Hsi's "perceptions" of and "attitude" toward the specialists and their specialized knowledge. How much and how well did he understand the technical content? What were his views about the importance of such knowledge? What did he think about the specialists in these areas and about their authority as experts? These are the main questions addressed in this chapter.

12.1. The Traditions of Specialized Knowledge

Different branches of specialized knowledge occupied different intellectual and social statuses in traditional China. Joseph Needham has divided the Chinese scientific traditions into "the orthodox" and "the unorthodox" branches according to whether they were "considered as an appropriate pursuit for Confucian gentlemen."[2] In Needham's scheme of division, mathematics, astronomy, harmonics, agriculture, and engineering activities were orthodox; alchemy, geomancy, and divination were unorthodox; and medicine lay somewhere on the borderline. Needham has characterized the "unorthodox" areas also as "pseudoscientific," and has included in that category such topics as "genethliacal" astrology, physiognomy, and chronomancy. Chu Hsi's attitude toward and interest in specialized knowledge was also different for different branches. The differences reflected his views about the places of the various scientific and technical traditions in the hierarchy of traditional Chinese learning.

The specialized subjects that Chu Hsi discussed most frequently were calendrical astronomy (*li*), harmonics (*lü*), and geography (*ti-li*), in all of which his understanding sometimes reached a fairly high level of sophistication. These subjects, for him, were clearly part of the Confucian tradition. But toward the practices connected with these subjects, such as astrology (*t'ien-wen* or *chan-hsing*), music (*yüeh*), and geomancy (*feng-shui*, literally, "winds and waters"), his attitude varied. He discussed music frequently, but on astrology and geomancy he did not have much to say. It must have been that he did not fully accept the latter activities, whereas music, a part of the Confucian rituals, was important for him.

Another subject discussed frequently by Chu Hsi was "images and numbers" (*hsiang-shu*). Consisting mainly of numerological speculations involving simple numbers and the *I-ching* diagrams, the study of this subject was based essentially on the *I-ching* texts and commentaries; Chu Hsi referred to it as "the study of the *i*" (*i-hsueh*) also. He considered the subject to be fully worth the attention of Confucian scholars, though various post-Han influences, including much that could be called Taoist, had infiltrated it. The study of "images and numbers" was also applied to other practices, such as divination (*chan* or *pu*) and alchemy (*tan* or *lien-tan*). Chu Hsi did not refrain from discussing either of these activities, which Needham has characterized as "unorthodox"; he wrote quite extensively about various aspects of both practices. There were various other techniques linked with these practices, experts in which were called "the masters of the Way" (*tao-shih*). Chu Hsi had less to say about, and perhaps rather low opinions of, such techniques—except for the technique of "nourishing life" (*yang-sheng*), the "internal alchemy" (*nei-tan*) in which he had a considerable interest, especially late in his life.

Needham's "borderline" science, medicine (*i*), did not command Chu Hsi's interest quite as much as the four subjects calendrical astronomy, harmonics, geography, and "images and numbers." Chu Hsi mentioned medicine among his examples of "the small ways" (*hsiao-tao*) in his comments on Tzu Hsia's saying recorded in the *Analects:* "Even 'the small ways' must have what are worth 'looking at' (*kuan*). But if pursued too far, one may be bogged down. For this reason great men do not 'do' (*wei*) them" (19.4). "The small ways," for Chu Hsi, also included such topics as agriculture (*nung*), horticulture (*p'u*), and divination, and crafts (*kung*).[3] And for him, medical specialists (*i-chia*) belonged to the same category as Taoists, Buddhists, diviners, craftsmen, and "the nourishing-life specialists" (*yang-sheng-chia*).[4] It is understandable, then, that though he frequently mentioned various drugs and other remedies, Chu Hsi rarely touched on the technical content of medical knowledge. Nor did he speak much of the related subject "materia medica" (*pen-ts'ao*); he did record descriptions of many plant and animal species, but most of these were in his commentaries on the *Book of Poetry* and the *Songs of Ch'u.*

About the remaining specialized branches, mathematics (*suan*, literally, "computation"), agriculture, and crafts, all of which belong to Needham's "orthodox" sciences, Chu Hsi had even less to say. But he could not ignore them altogether, for he must have faced problems involving knowledge of these subjects, agriculture in particular, in performing his official duties as a local administrator.

The areas of knowledge mentioned so far, then, are the ones covered in this chapter. It has to be noted, however, that, along with these subjects and activities, Chu Hsi also spoke and wrote about many other specialized topics, such as the protocols for rites and ceremonies, burial methods, military strategies and transportation vehicles, methods of calligraphy and painting, laws and criminal justice, land, taxes and finance, civil service administration, and other institutions. These latter subjects, which take up large portions of his conversations and writings, were not different, to his mind, from the ones mentioned in the preceding paragraphs in that they were also specialized, practical branches of knowledge with their own experts.[5] I do not discuss these areas because they did not concern things and events of the natural world, but it has to be borne in mind that this distinction did not exist for Chu Hsi himself.[6] In addition, there were the traditional "six arts" (*liu-i*), the six basic skills that Chu Hsi considered essential for the education of children (*hsiao-hsueh*): rites, music, archery, charioteering, calligraphy, and computation.[7]

Chu Hsi's basic position on the specialized subjects in general was that they should be studied also and should not be ignored. He said, for example: "As for things like harmonics, calendars, criminal justice, laws, astronomy and geography, armies and official positions, [these] must all be understood."[8] In an essay expressing his personal views on schools and civil service examinations, he wrote:

> For example, the categories of rites, music, institutions, astronomy, geography, military strategy, and criminal justice also are all necessary for the world and are not possible to do without. All [these] must be studied.[9]

This attitude of Chu Hsi was closely linked with his doctrine of *ke-wu*, which, interpreted to mean "investigating the *li* of things," tended to emphasize studying all concrete events and things in all areas of human concern.[10] Chu Hsi said repeatedly that every thing or event in the world has its *li* and should be studied and understood.[11] He had this to say in the essay on schools and examinations, before the passage previously quoted:

> All events under heaven are what scholars should know. And as for those [events] whose *li* are recorded in the classics, each has its main [point] and cannot be interchanged. . . . [If one] discards what is difficult but takes up what is easy, and looks only at the one but does not reach the rest, [then] among events under heaven there will necessarily be those whose *li* cannot be exhaustively understood.

In a letter discussing the method of study with a disciple, he wrote:

> The way of the *Great Learning* must begin with "investigation of things and extension of knowledge" and then [move] to the *li* of all under heaven. Of the books under heaven, there is none not to be "broadly studied" (*po-hsueh*).[12]

Later in the same letter, he added: "Studies of calendars and images are themselves one school. If one wants to investigate the *li* exhaustively, one must also discuss them." [13]

Chu Hsi interpreted certain expressions from the classics, the *Analects* in particular, in this spirit of the *ke-wu* doctrine. For example, he used the emphasis in the *Analects* on "broad study" in supporting his insistence upon studying and understanding everything: "Therefore, the Sage [i.e., Confucius] taught men that it is necessary to 'study broadly.'" [14] Chu Hsi believed that was what the ancients actually did, and he criticized his contemporaries who neglected concrete things. [15] Confucius's teaching "study down below and attain up above" (*hsia-hsueh shang-ta*) was used in the same vein by Chu Hsi, who emphasized that one should start with concrete things that are clearly manifest and easy to understand. [16] While commenting on another Confucian teaching, "Depend on the humaneness and play with the arts (*i*)," he said:

> "The arts" also should be understood. If any one of the things like rites, music, archery, charioteering, calligraphy, and computation is not understood, this mind will feel obstructed. Only when every one of them is understood, every one of these ways, *li*, and circuits will begin to be circulated, without that obstruction. [17]

There were other reasons that Chu Hsi should be interested in the specialized branches of knowledge. For instance, many of them were associated with important philosophical terms and concepts. The importance of the concept of "heaven," for example, made calendrical astronomy, the subject that deals with the physical heaven, important to him. Geography and geomancy could be seen to be connected with the other half of the term "heaven and earth." Because music was a vital part of Confucian rituals, the related subject of harmonics was also important. Similarly, the significance of the *I-ching* and the ideas and diagrams in that classic could be translated into the need to study the subjects of "images and numbers," and divination and alchemy, which used them. Alchemy, especially in the form of "the internal alchemy," could be related to the concept of "the Way," because it was among the techniques practiced by those who sought the Way, the "masters of the Way." Investigating these subjects would clearly help one understand the *li* of the ideas and concepts associated with them.

Moreover, knowledge of some of the subjects was present in the texts widely studied by scholars — the standard commentaries of the classics and the official dynastic histories, in particular. The latter almost always included treatises on astronomy, calendars, harmonics, and geography, as well as on rites and music. Chu Hsi studied the relevant portions of those commentaries and treatises, and his understanding of them reached a considerable level. He could make his own judgment as to which of them were best for a particular subject or problem. Indeed, this was what he had to do, for, having asserted the importance of the specialized subjects and the necessity to study them, he had to decide which texts were the best or the correct ones to be studied, just as he did for the moral and social philosophies. [18]

There were also treatises on specialized subjects written by the scholars themselves. A foremost example is Shen Kua's *Meng-hsi pi-t'an* (Brush talks of dream brook), which dealt with all kinds of subjects and to which Chu Hsi constantly referred.[19] Another is Su Sung's *Hsin i-hsiang fa-yao* (New method and synopsis on the armillary spheres and celestial globes), with which Chu Hsi struggled, as we shall see. Then, there was Chu Hsi's friend Ts'ai Yüan-ting, who was well versed in various topics. Chu Hsi had corresponded extensively with him and wrote a preface for his treatise on harmonics, *Lü-lü hsin-shu* (New book of the pitches).[20] Chu Hsi also wrote a preface for a medical treatise of Kuo Yung (1091–1187), who was known to have written many books on medicine and calendrical astronomy.[21]

Finally, it should not be ignored that knowledge of some of these subjects was actually needed by Chu Hsi for performing his official duties. To be sure, traditional Chinese civil service did include offices devoted to specialized branches and filled by specialists. But generalist officials like Chu Hsi also could face tasks involving specialized knowledge and, in any case, had to manage and supervise the specialist officials, who were usually of lower official status.[22] This need was at least in part the reason why Chu Hsi included the subjects in his proposal for the civil service examinations, classifying them under the category of "the current tasks" (*shih-wu*).[23]

Yet, in spite of his emphasis on the need to study and understand specialized subjects, Chu Hsi did not hide his belief that there were more important subjects— moral and philosophical problems. In fact, he said repeatedly that one has to understand "the basis" (*pen* or *pen-ling*), or what is "great," before moving on to "small" matters.[24] Otherwise,

> if one does not understand this basis first and merely desires to take up [particular] events and to understand them, then even if one understands many curiosities, [they will] only add to much confusion and disorder, and only to much overbearing and parsimony.[25]

Thus, after stating, as we have seen, that "the studies of calendars and images" should be included in the *ke-wu* endeavor, Chu Hsi added:

> After all, however, what is great should be established first. If one moves on to them [i.e., the studies of calendars and images] afterward, then they also will be not very difficult to understand, and there will be nothing that is not comprehended.[26]

When he referred to some of the specialized branches as "the small ways," although the point was that they should not be ignored, what he actually said clearly implied that they were not quite the "real" ways:

> The small ways are not heterodox; they are also ways. It is simply that they are small. [Subjects] like agriculture, horticulture, medicine, divination, and "the hundred crafts" also have the ways and *li* in them. If one seeks the ways and *li* only in the upward direction, they will not be comprehended.[27]

It must have been for this reason that, though Chu Hsi studied specialized subjects and attained various levels of knowledge in them, his understanding was never up to that of the specialists. He admitted that it was not necessary to try to reach a complete understanding of all the details of these subjects. For example, to his remark, quoted earlier, on the need to understand specialized subjects, he added: "Although one may not be able to see through their essences and subtleties, one should nevertheless know the general outlines."[28] Indeed, people with adequate knowledge of these subjects were rare. On Chu Hsi's proposal that topics like astronomy, geography, music, and harmonics should be included as subjects of the examinations, a disciple even feared that "there may be no [qualified] examining officer after all."[29]

Yet, this did not lead Chu Hsi to have very high opinions of the specialists. In his view they were merely technical experts in specialized areas that he had not mastered himself. As we shall see, sometimes he appeared confident that he could have mastered them if he had tried. We shall also see that such low opinions were reflected in his tendency to criticize contemporary specialists whose understanding did not reach the high standard that he believed to have existed in the golden ages of the ancient sages.[30]

Finally, it should be noted that Chu Hsi's attitude toward specialists was not same for all areas. For subjects like calendrical astronomy, which he valued relatively more and thus studied more and knew better, he did not quite accept the expertise of specialists. For subjects that he knew less about, he tended to accept the specialists' expertise, but he did not value what they did very much. In fact, at times he did not hide his feelings of disdain and distrust toward specialists of certain techniques, called "the masters of the Way," "the masters of methods" (*fang-shih*), and "the yin-yang specialists" (*yin-yang-chia*).

12.2. Calendrical Astronomy

One reason for the importance of calendrical astronomy for traditional Chinese government and scholars was, as we have seen, the importance of the concept of heaven. But perhaps a more weighty factor, at least for the court and officials, was the political and ritualistic significance of establishing the "correct" calendar as a symbol of the ruler's legitimacy.[31] Because of that need, the court had to make and maintain accurate calendars and to create a new calendar at the beginning of a new dynasty or a new era. Thus, the bureaucracy of the successive Chinese dynasties included offices devoted to calendrical astronomy, where such activities as calendar making and astronomical observations and predictions were carried out. The official dynastic histories also routinely included treatises on calendars (*li-chih*) and astronomy (*t'ien-wen-chih*).[32]

Chu Hsi showed a considerable interest in calendrical astronomy; his conversations and writings contain a fairly large amount of discussion on the subject. He derived such knowledge from various sources, of which the more important were the calendrical treatises of such dynastic histories as the *Record of the Historian* (Shih-chi), the *History of the [Former] Han Dynasty* (Han-shu), the *History of the Later Han Dynasty* (Hou-Han-shu), and the *History of the Chin Dynasty* (Chin-shu);[33] the subcommentaries (*shu*) of the "Yao-tien" (Canon of Yao) and "Shun-tien" (Canon of Shun) chapters of the *Book of Documents* (Shu-ching)[34] and of the

"Yüeh-ling" (Monthly ordinances) chapter of the *Record of Rites* (Li-chi);[35] and the writings of the Northern Sung scholars, such as Shen Kua's *Meng-hsi pi-t'an* and "Hun-i i" (Discussion of the armillary sphere),[36] Su Sung's *Hsin i-hsiang fa-yao*,[37] and Chang Tsai's *Cheng-meng* (Correct teaching for youth).[38] Chu Hsi's calendrical discussions also referred to Tu Yu (735–812), who wrote *T'ung-tien* (Comprehensive canon),[39] and the calendars of Shao Yung.[40] Of his contemporaries, Chu Hsi spoke frequently of Ts'ai Yüan-ting and his two sons, Ts'ai Yüan and Ts'ai Ch'en (1167–1230).[41] With the Ts'ais he also had extensive correspondence dealing with various specialized subjects.[42]

These, then, were the sources from which Chu Hsi gained his knowledge on calendrical astronomy. They were sources also for much of his knowledge on the heavens, discussed in chapter 9, especially on the more technical topics, such as the eclipses and the "dark gap" theory, the twenty-eight lunar mansions, the star maps and the individual stars, the movements of the earth, and the theory of "four wanderings." Chu Hsi did not simply accept all that was given in these sources, however; he expressed his own opinions, sometimes making judgments on the discussions in the sources.

In particular, Chu Hsi felt that the various sources were strong in different topics. For example, he praised the subcommentary of the "Yüeh-ling" chapter for its statement that heaven makes one full rotation plus one degree a day.[43] He even said that "no other books on the calendar were as good as this theory."[44] The subcommentary on the "Shun-tien" chapter, which contained Wang Fan's *Hun-t'ien* theory, quoted in chapter 9, was praised by Chu Hsi for its account of the structure of the heavens in general.[45] He said that its explanation of the ever visible portion of the vault within thirty-six degrees of the north pole was "very detailed."[46] He also mentioned the subcommentary on the "Yao-tien" chapter in connection with the problem of the leap month (*jun-yüeh*).[47] Another old source that he valued highly was the astronomical treatise in the *History of the Chin*,[48] which, together with the subcommentary on the "Yüeh-ling," he recommended as works that "no one can do without reading."[49] He also praised the calendrical treatise in the *History of the Later Han*.[50] Of the works of Sung scholars, Chu Hsi praised Shen Kua's *Meng-hsi pi-t'an* for its theories of the movements of the sun and the moon[51] and Chang Tsai's *Cheng-meng* for its "leftward rotation theory" and the explanation of meteorological phenomena.[52] He also had a great respect for Ts'ai Yüan-ting;[53] he said that "since the ancient times, no one's consideration [of the calendars] reached this place [i.e., the level of Ts'ai Yüan-ting's knowledge]."[54]

Chu Hsi also spoke of weak points of some of the sources. For example,

> the places where the calendrical treatise of the Former Han [i.e., *Han-shu*] discusses [the heavens in general] in accordance with the way and *li* are rare. It does not match the treatise of the Eastern Han [i.e., the *History of the Later Han*, which is] relatively detailed.[55]

He complained, as we shall see, of the insufficient information in Su Sung's *Hsin-i-hsiang fa-yao* about the actual production of the armillary sphere.[56] In *T'ien-ching* (Classic of the heavens), written in 1160 by Wang Chi-fu, which Chu Hsi characterized as a book that "collected in categories the ancient and current sayings on the heavens, and is extremely complete,"[57] he could find problems and criticisms — on its discussion, including a diagram, of the shape of the heaven's vault, for example.[58] For Chu Hsi, even Ts'ai Yüan-ting was not good enough at times, for example when he spoke of the movement of heaven without first discussing "the supreme void."[59]

Chu Hsi's attitude toward calendrical astronomy and its specialists, the "calendar specialists" (*li-chia*), was basically in line with what we have seen in the previous section about his attitude toward specialized subjects in general. There were clear limits to his interest in the specialized knowledge of calendrical astronomy. For example, he spoke of "the great things" that were more important than the study of calendars and thus "should be established first."[60] In a letter to Ts'ai Yüan-ting, he said that "[as for] the calendrical method, it may also be all right only to discuss the general outlines."[61] He even said, about a passage in the "Yao-tien" chapter of the *Book of Documents:*

> In reading the *Book of Documents*, just select from it what can be easily understood. As for [the passage] "One year is three hundred and sixty-six days. By means of leap month, fix the four seasons and complete a year," for example, even if one does not understand this kind [of things], it is not important.[62]

In his view, the subcommentary on the "Shun-tien," which he praised repeatedly, was "also not very important."[63]

Such limits were reflected in Chu Hsi's views about calendar specialists. He frequently took them as mere technicians who could make observations of obvious facts and perform practical computations but could not penetrate profound cosmological problems. Indeed, such a view was not inappropriate for the calendar specialists of Chu Hsi's time, who devoted themselves to routine astronomical observations and calendar making, with little interest in cosmological problems or even in theoretical problems of calendrical astronomy.[64] Thus, after speaking of Shao Yung's speculation on the problem of whether there could be an "inside" and an "outside" of the world, Chu Hsi added:

> When calendar specialists compute the *ch'i*, they can only compute and reach the movements of the sun, the moon, and the stars but cannot compute beyond that. How [then] could [they] get [to know] whether this has an "inside" or an "outside"?[65]

In a letter written in response to a disciple, who went as far as saying that Shao Yung's theory of "heaven and earth depending on and attached to each other . . . are not what calendar specialists can observe," Chu Hsi said that "the theories of calendar specialists must be studied also" but added: "Then, one will see the fine and delicate points."[66] The following remark, made earlier in the same letter, also reflects his view that the job of calendar specialists was computation and not theoretical speculation, although in this case that was his reason for accepting their theories:

As for the theory of the "four wanderings," it cannot be known. But the theories of the calendar specialists are reached by computation of numbers. They are not "talking while piercing through the void" (i.e., being engaged in abstract speculations).

In rejecting the view that four stars near the north pole do not move, he said: "This is a shallow matter of the 'star specialists' (*hsing-chia*) and is not worth profound discussion."[67]

To be sure, Chu Hsi was aware of the deficiency in his and his fellow scholars' knowledge of calendrical astronomy. He said, for example, that he did not understand Ts'ai Yüan-ting's calendrical theories and thus could not tell whether they were correct or not.[68] He and a disciple even spoke of the problem of the lack of qualified examiners for specialized subjects, including calendrical astronomy. Thus, naturally, he was willing to rely on calendar specialists for technical details. For example, he admitted that he had not understood the one additional degree in heaven's daily rotation until he read the subcommentary on the "Yüeh-ling."[69] In the same passage he said that his understanding had never reached the theory of the earth's ascending in winter and descending in summer, which was treated in the same subcommentary, and added: "These will be understood, if, after having read and understood the general outlines, one makes computation using [actual] degrees."[70] On another subject that he did not fully understand, the theory of "four wanderings," he believed, as we have seen, that calendar specialists could obtain the details by using numbers and making computations.[71]

Chu Hsi emphasized the need to understand the technical content properly before discussing problems in calendrical astronomy:

> Even though it is a "matter of physical form and concrete things" (*hsing-ch'i chih shih*), if one has not understood it exhaustively, one should not begin discussions lightly. . . . Even if it is astronomy and geography, one may discuss them only after reading and completely understanding them.[72]

The very fact that he made this remark implies that there were many scholars who treated calendrical knowledge lightly and jumped into discussion without adequately understanding its technical details. Indeed, it was after criticizing Hu Hung's theory of three pole stars that do not move that he made that remark. Moreover, Chu Hsi's own discussion does not seem to have been based always upon such a thorough understanding as he demanded from others. We have already come across, in chapter 9, his casual mistakes about the relative positions of the sun and the moon and about the movements of the Water star (Mercury) and the Metal star (Venus).[73] Nor did he fully accept the authority of calendar specialists as experts on the subject; he criticized them casually when their views were in conflict with his own.

Such an attitude is clearly manifest in Chu Hsi's thought about a few particular topics of calendrical astronomy. It is reflected, for example, in his criticism that calendar specialists did not possess a "determinate method" (*ting-fa*) of calendar making. He considered that lack to be the cause of many errors in the calendrical astronomy of his time, but this was not based on an accurate perception of the actual situation.

The basic task in making the luni-solar calendar used in traditional China was to group days into lunar months and solar years while keeping them in accord with the moon's phases and the sun's movement along the ecliptic. From very early in Chinese history, the lengths of a solar year and a lunar month were fairly accurately known: by the first century B.C. at the latest, the former was known to be approximately $365\frac{1}{4}$, or $365 + 235/940$ days and the latter, $29 + 499/940$ days. Problems arose because the length of a solar year is not an integral multiple of the length of a lunar month. Multiplying the latter by 12 made it $354 + 348/940$ days, shorter than the former by $10 + 827/940$ days. It became necessary, thus, to insert a "leap month" every two or three years. That the number of days in a lunar month is not an integer was another source of problems. That necessitated the mixing of 29-day and 30-day months (called "small months" and "large months"). Of course, these problems had been solved for all practical purposes long before Chu Hsi's time,[74] but the solutions could only be approximate. The phenomenon of the precession of the equinoxes (*sui-ch'a*, literally "yearly deviation"), known in China from the fourth century A.D., also made accurate calendrical computations difficult.[75] Given all these problems, errors in calendrical computations were unavoidable.[76] It was possible to reduce the magnitude of errors with ever more accurate computations, but it was not possible to eliminate them altogether. Calendar specialists had been aware of this impossibility for a long time.[77]

Chu Hsi seems to have known all these problems. He frequently mentioned the method of "placing leap [month]" (*chih-jun*), and he praised Ts'ai Ch'en's account of the common method of "placing seven leap months for every nineteen years."[78] He also mentioned the method of selecting "large" and "small" months.[79] And as we have seen, although he did not explicitly use the expression "yearly deviation," he spoke of its consequences: the long-term variations in the positions of stars and the resulting variations in the position of the earth's center.[80] Chu Hsi also knew of various calendars based on different choices of numerical constants for calendar computations—from the "T'ai-ch'u" calendar of the *Record of the Historian* to the "Chi-yüan" calendar of his time—and of the fact that none of them were free from deviations.[81]

Chu Hsi nevertheless maintained that an exact method without error was possible and that it was the calendar specialists who were responsible for errors in calendars. He knew, as we have seen, that movements in the heavens were not always uniform, at times faster and at times slower.[82] But he was convinced that there was a regularity even in such variations. Commenting upon Ts'ai Yüan-ting's remark that "movements of the heavens are not constant. . . . The degree and the speed of the movements are sometimes more and sometimes less, and they naturally are not uniform," Chu Hsi said:

> What Chi-t'ung [i.e., Ts'ai Yüan-ting] meant was not that movements of the heavens are not determinate but that the degrees of the movements are so [i.e., not determinate]. In the deviations of the movements, there also are constant degrees. It is simply that the

[ranges of] numbers which later calendar makers handled were narrow and could not cover them.[83]

Chu Hsi went as far as saying that "although sometimes the degrees of movements [of heaven and the stars] have small deviations, after a long time they recover their constancy." It was his belief, then, that by properly accounting for such deviations one could describe the movements of the heavenly bodies exactly, without error:

Although there may be deviations, one can infer and compute them all without losing any. How? By regulating the lack of determinateness in them [i.e., the movements of the heavens] by means of [the fact] that our method has a determinateness. Naturally, there will be no error.[84]

In other words, the "determinate method" would enable one to handle the deviations in the movements of the heavens.

Chu Hsi even asserted that such an exact calendrical method, the "determinate method," did exist at the times of the ancient sage kings Yao and Shun but disappeared afterward, by Han times to be more specific.[85] He praised Ts'ai Yüan-ting's following account of the original calendrical method:

Originally, when the calendar was made, the degrees of the deviation of movements of the heavens were summed up and were all accounted for. Many years later [the calendar] deviated by several minutes; many years later it deviated by several degrees. All these deviations were counted and made into correct numbers, and this [process] was simply carried out to a completion. It must have been in this manner that the calendar could be correct and would not have errors.[86]

Given the loss of such an exact method, there was no longer a "determinate method" for the calendar makers of Chu Hsi's time. In his judgment they were busy merely adding and subtracting numbers to fit the calendar to the movements of the heavens. He said, "Calendar specialists of today do not have any 'determinate method,' but merely increase or decrease the degrees of the movements of the heavens to seek agreement [with the calendar]."[87] Naturally, Chu Hsi did not consider this a "determinate method." It could ensure agreement of the calendar with movements of the heavens for a given year, but he thought that such a calendar would show deviations the very next year and would accumulate errors as the years went by.[88] In his view, it was inevitable that even the "Ta-yen" calendar of T'ang, considered to be the most accurate up to that time, could not be free of errors as long as it used a method that fell short of the "determinate method."[89] He even spoke as though calendars were becoming more inaccurate with growing errors, although he knew perfectly well that what was growing was not the magnitudes of the errors themselves but the errors in the numbers used in the numerators as the increasing precision of calendars necessitated the use of large denominators.[90]

Chu Hsi believed that if the "determinate method" were used, the calendars would have no errors. He said, "[I]f one can investigate [the calendars] thoroughly, there are 'determinate numbers' (*ting-shu*), and there can never be deviations."[91] He even believed that once the "calendrical epoch" (*li-yüan*) was established, there would be no need of calendar reform, because a single method could be used to account for the entire period from the ancient times to his day.[92]

Chu Hsi's characteristic attitude toward calendrical knowledge and its specialists is also reflected in his discussion of astronomical models and instruments. Names of various models and instruments are found in Chu Hsi's writings and conversations: for example, the celestial globe (*hun-hsiang*), the sighting tube (*kuan*), the *Kai-t'ien* model (*kai-t'ien-i*), the clepsydra (*hsia-lou*), and the sundial (*kuei*).[93] In a letter to Ts'ai Yüan, Chu Hsi spoke of very complicated observational devices that appear in the *T'ien-ching*.[94] Chu Hsi also knew about the instruments of earlier times that no longer existed in his own day, and he seemed to have some knowledge about their historical development. He pointed out, for example, that what people made in his day were mostly small celestial globes and not the armillary spheres (*hun-i*) of the past.[95] Elsewhere he asserted that the method of making instruments had become more elaborate over the ages.[96]

It was the armillary sphere that interested Chu Hsi the most. The *History of the Sung dynasty* (Sung-shih) records that he had one in his house.[97] It might have been this one that his disciple referred to when he mentioned "an armillary sphere upstairs" while discussing movements of the heavens with Chu Hsi.[98] In a letter, Chu Hsi regretted that he could not go to see an armillary sphere in the capital because of a foot ailment.[99] He gave a very detailed description of one in his commentary on the "Shun-tien" chapter of the *Book of Documents*.[100]

Chu Hsi even tried to construct an armillary sphere himself. He did not succeed because he could not construct the water-powered device to be used to operate it. He frequently complained to people like Ts'ai Yüan-ting and Ts'ai Yüan about the lack of information on its construction.[101] In particular, the content of Su Sung's *Hsin i-hsiang fa-yao*, the key source describing the famous armillary sphere constructed under his supervision,[102] was neither clear nor sufficiently detailed for Chu Hsi. In a letter, he wrote that "in it there are a few mistakes, and in a few essential places the discussions cannot be connected together."[103] The *History of the Sung* also records, after mentioning Chu Hsi's failure in making the water-powered device: "There was the book of Su Sung. But, though in general it was detailed about the celestial globe, frequently it did not record the sizes and dimensions, and thus it was difficult to reconstruct based upon [the book]."[104] Chu Hsi deplored such lack of detailed records of necessary information and even ascribed it to the secretiveness of instrument makers: "It must have been that the makers, not wishing to tell people completely [about it], kept that one section secret."[105]

Chu Hsi's strong interest in models and instruments reflects the importance he attached to observation in calendrical astronomy. He said, for example:

If one wants the details [of calendrical astronomy], one must make "observations" (*yang-kuan fu-ch'a*, literally, "to look up and observe; to look down and examine"), and then one can "verify" (*yen*). Now there are no instruments for it, and I am afraid that it is also difficult to investigate completely.[106]

Far more clearly manifested in his sayings and writings about the models, however, was the attitude of a scholar interested in cosmological problems, such as the actual structure of the heavens and movements of celestial bodies—rather than in detailed calendrical computations. To Chu Hsi, the armillary sphere was significant as something that represented the actual structure and operation of the heavens, and it was for that reason that he was interested in the waterwheel, the device used for the actual operation of armillary spheres. At times he compared the movements of heaven and earth directly to the movements of a waterwheel.[107] His belief that the model should represent the actual world also underlay the reason he offered for accepting the *Hun-t'ien* theory but not the *Kai-t'ien*:

> Ask a *Kai-t'ien* theorist to build a model [for it]. How would he make it? [If he makes it] just like an umbrella, [he will] not know how to attach it to the earth. . . . If [it is made] in this manner, the four sides must have places where winds leak out. Therefore, it [i.e., the *Kai-t'ien* theory] is not as [good as] the *Hun-t'ien* [theory], for which a model can be made.[108]

Whereas he could accept the *Hun-t'ien* theory because a model for it, that is, the armillary sphere, could be made, he could not accept the *Kai-t'ien* theory, for which no model was possible.

The manner in which Chu Hsi rejected the "rightward movement theory" (*yu-hsing shuo*) of the calendar specialists in favor of the "leftward rotation theory" (*tso-hsüan shuo*) of Chang Tsai also shows both the simplistic attitude he had with respect to the "determinate method" and his strong commitment to the actual structures and movements of the heavens.

The rightward movement theory maintained that the sun, the moon, and the five planets turned around the earth in a direction opposite to the leftward rotation of heaven. It identified and isolated the apparent daily rotation of heaven—the consequence of the actual daily rotation of the earth—as "the leftward rotation" and used this as the standard for comparison in dealing with the "rightward movements" of the sun, the moon, and the planets. There was a computational advantage to that view, and because of it the theory had been generally accepted by calendar specialists by Chu Hsi's time.[109] Chu Hsi rejected this theory, however, and maintained that not only heaven and the fixed stars, but also the sun, the moon, and the planets, all rotated leftward. In his view, the rightward movement theory merely took the difference between the faster leftward rotation of heaven and the slower leftward rotation of the sun or the moon and regarded the latter as rotating rightward with respect to heaven by as much as the difference between the two rotations. He showed this in detail in the following manner employing actual numbers:

> Heaven, the sun, the moon and the stars all rotate leftward. Heaven moves relatively fast: during one day and one night it turns around the earth once for $365\frac{1}{4}$ degrees and proceeds still one degree farther. The sun moves a little slower: during one day and one night it turns around the earth exactly once, and lags behind heaven by one degree. After one year [the sun] meets heaven at the exact place. This is called "one rotation around heaven in one year." The moon moves even slower: during one day and one night it

cannot turn around the earth fully once but always lags behind heaven by 13^7/$_{19}$ degrees. After somewhat more than 29½ days, [the moon] meets heaven at the exact place. This is called "one rotation in one month."[110]

Chu Hsi repeatedly stated that the rightward movement theory did not represent the actual movements but was merely an "expedient" (*chieh-fa*) used for convenience in computing.[111] In his words, "Calendar specialists regard the rightward rotation as a [good] theory, only [because they] accept [the fact that] it easily shows the degrees of [the movements of] the sun and the moon."[112] If one were to use the leftward rotation theory,

> then one computes those distances by which they are separated and thus the number of degrees is large. But now [when one uses the rightward movement theory] one only speaks in terms of distances close to each other, and thus it is easy to compute.[113]

It was to show this that Chu Hsi resorted to the analogies of three persons running around a circle with different speeds[114] and of two wheels rotating around a single axis but at different speeds.[115] These arguments that Chu Hsi provided in rejecting the rightward rotation theory were those of a scholar who had a broad interest in the actual structure and movements of the heavens, expressing dissatisfaction and distrust toward specialists who, putting aside such fundamental and theoretical problems, looked only for computational convenience.

Chu Hsi thought that the leftward rotation theory, which he adopted in place of the rightward movement theory, would produce the same observational data as the latter, while correctly accounting for the actual movements of heaven, the sun, and the moon. But the real situation was more complicated: the observational consequences of the two theories were not equivalent to each other. The path of the sun or the moon in heaven does not coincide with the equator but makes an angle with it, which means that the axis of the leftward rotation of heaven and that of the rightward rotation of the sun or the moon are at an angle with respect to each other. As a result, to describe the combined motion of the two rotations as a single leftward rotation would not only necessitate the use of large and cumbersome numbers, as Chu Hsi pointed out, but would also misrepresent the actual movement of the sun or the moon, which consists of the displacement above and below the equator and of the leftward rotation, thus tracing a spring-like shape.[116]

Chu Hsi, who did not have to do the actual computations, could not see this difficulty, although he knew quite well that the solar and the lunar paths do not coincide with the equator. He was convinced that the rotation of the sun or the moon was a single leftward rotation that could simply be subtracted from that of heaven to yield the apparent rightward rotation. Thus, he even argued that when reading the assertion of calendar specialists that the moon rotates faster than the sun, "faster" should be changed into "slower" and "slower" into "faster."[117] Moreover, his failure to understand the actual situation led him simply to ignore the phenomenon of the "retrograde motion" (*ni-hsing*) of the planets, a problem that could not be avoided as long as the actually heliocentric planetary rotations were viewed in a geocentric framework. He regarded the retrograde motion as merely a consequence of the "imaginary" rightward movement theory and believed that if the movement of a planet was viewed as a single leftward rotation, the retrograde motion would become merely a variation in the speed of rotation, not a change in the direction of rotation. He thus asserted that "the five stars also move conformably (*shun-hsing*)"[118] and said that if one accepted the leftward rotation theory, "the word 'retrograde' of calendar specialists should be changed into 'conformable' (*shun*) and the word 'retreat' should be changed into 'advance.'"[119]

Of course Chu Hsi had to use the terminology and the numbers of the rightward movement theory in his own discussion of calendrical knowledge. That was unavoidable because they were convenient and because his sources were from the hands of calendar specialists who all accepted that theory. He said that he had to put the rightward movement theory in one of his books because he was "afraid that people might not understand" had he used the other theory.[120] He even mentioned the "retrograde motion" of the five irregular stars, which he had rejected.[121] His belief that the actual movements of celestial bodies are leftward rotations, however, was firm. And once the leftward rotation theory was accepted by him, it became the orthodox theory of the post-Sung Neo-Confucian scholars, while calendar specialists continued to hold the rightward movement theory.[122]

12.3. Harmonics and Music

Music occupied an important place in Chinese culture from the beginning. One of the six Confucian classics was the *Classic of Music* (Yüeh-ching), and music was considered a part of Confucian rituals, as can be seen from the frequent combination of the characters for "rituals" (*li*) and "music" (*yüeh*) into a single word "*li-yüeh*."[123] Sometimes music was even thought to influence the political state of the time.[124] Thus, it was natural that scholars and officials, and at times emperors, should show much interest in music.[125] Because of the importance of music, harmonics (*lü*), which deals with the numerical relationships of the musical notes and the instruments that produce them, was also given importance. The dynastic histories always included treatises on harmonics, as well as on music. There also existed many specialized monographs on the subjects.[126]

Chu Hsi also had a considerable interest in harmonics and music. A separate *chüan* (volume), the ninety-second, of the *Classified Conversations*, titled "*yüeh*," is devoted to the two subjects. He composed treatises on them, "Ch'in-lü shuo" (Explanation of musical instruments and pitches)[127] and "Sheng-lü pien" (Discussion of sounds and pitches),[128] and wrote a preface to Ts'ai Yüan-ting's *Lü-lü hsin-shu*.[129] His letters to other scholars also frequently included discussion of various topics in harmonics and music.[130] These conversations and writings show that Chu Hsi's understanding of the specialized knowledge in these topics reached a certain level of sophistication, though not quite that of his knowledge in calendrical astronomy.

The topic most frequently discussed by Chu Hsi was the procedure by which the twelve pitches are produced through successive multiplications of the length of pitch pipes by ⅓ or ⅔. We have already come across the basic account of this procedure in chapter 10, but Chu Hsi made additional observations. For example, he used the expressions "upward production" (*shang-sheng*) and "downward production" (*hsia-sheng*)—the former referring to the production of a new pitch through multiplication by ⅓ and the latter by ⅔—and observed that every pitch from *huang-chung* (the 1st pitch) down to *chung-lü* (the 6th) produces a new pitch by a downward production, whereas the pitches from *jui-pin* (the 7th) to *ying-chung* (the 12th) produce new ones by upward productions.[131] In the actual sequence, which can be seen in table 10.3, the upward and downward productions alternate to keep the length of the pitch pipes within a given range: when a downward production would produce a pitch with a length less than half that of the principal *huang-chung* pitch, an upward production has to be used; when an upward production would produce a pitch length larger than that of the principal *huang-chung*, a downward production has to be used. Thus, *huang-chung* produces *lin-chung* (the 8th) by a downward production, *lin-chung* uses an upward production to produce *t'ai-ts'ou* (the 3rd), which in turn produces *nan-lü* (the 10th) by a downward production, and so on. But Chu Hsi noted that the upward and downward productions do not always alternate: from *ying-chung* (the 12th) to *jui-pin* (the 7th) and from *jui-pin* to *ta-lü* (the 2nd), two successive upward productions take place.[132] Such successive upward productions could also take place from *wu-i* (the 11th) to *chung-lü* (the 6th) and from *chung-lü* to *huang-chung*, the length of which would then be $524,288/531,441$. But, as Chu Hsi said, "*huang-chung* is the image of the ruler, [which] is not what can be performed by many *kung* [notes]," and thus, one should rather employ a downward production and take, as a new *huang-chung*, half the length of what one would get from an upward production.[133]

This new *huang-chung* was called "the clear sound" (*ch'ing-sheng*), "the half sound" (*pan-sheng*), or "the son sound" (*tzu-sheng*) of *huang-chung*.[134] Chu Hsi noted that if the first two strings of the lute are *kung* at *huang-chung* and *shang* at *t'ai-ts'ou*, then the sixth and the seventh are the "clear sounds" of *huang-chung* and *t'ai-ts'ou*.[135] He said that "although [the clear sound is produced by] decreasing [the length of the basic pitch] to one-half, it is just the same pitch, and therefore they also can respond to each other."[136] Each of the twelve pitches can have its "clear sound," and he believed that all had been used in ancient times; his contemporary music used only four of them because all but the "four clear sounds"—those of *huang-chung*, *ta-lü* (the 2nd), *t'ai-t'sou* (the 3rd), and *chia-chung* (the 4th)—had been lost.[137] He seems to have been rather uncertain, however, about the details of the use of the four clear sounds in music.[138]

What was used in composing music were the five- or seven-note scales, not the twelve pitches. Chu Hsi thus noted that "although there are twelve pitches, when one uses them [in music], one only uses seven of them."[139] He interpreted the term *chün* (literally, "even" or "equal") from the *Kuo-yü* (Words on the states) as referring to such a seven-note scale.[140] Because these scales are produced through simple numerical multiplications, all the notes are in fixed numerical relations with one another; once a given note is fixed, all the other notes are also fixed. Chu Hsi said, for example: "Once 'the original sound' (*yüan-sheng*) is fixed, all below it are fixed; once the original sound deviates, all below it deviate."[141] For example, once the *kung* note is set at *huang-chung* pitch, all the other six notes from *shang* to *pien-kung* are set at fixed pitches. This is what Chu Hsi meant when he said, "One *kung* simply begets the seven notes."[142]

The *kung* note does not have to be fixed at the *huang-chung* pitch, for, as Chu Hsi noted frequently, the twelve pitches "rotate and become *kung* one by one" (*hsüan hsiang wei kung*).[143] *Ta-lü* (the 2nd), for example, can be chosen as *kung*, in which case,

> *chia-chung* (the 4th) is *shang*, *chung-lü* (the 6th) is *chiao*, *lin-chung* (the 8th) is *pien-chih*, *i-tse* (the 9th) is *chih*, *wu-i* (the 11th) is *yü*, and *huang-chung* is *pien-kung*. As for the remaining [pitches, they] "rotate and become *kung* one by one." [Having completed] one round, [the process] begins again.[144]

Chu Hsi illustrated this process frequently, choosing different pitches as *kung*.[145] He proposed a method for illustrating it using two concentric circles, as depicted in figure 12.1.[146] As the internal circle, on which the five notes are marked, is rotated, while the external circle, marked by numbers from one to twelve, denoting the twelve pitches, is fixed, the *kung* note is matched with different pitches. For each different matching of *kung*, a different set of assignments of the five notes to the twelve pitches is obtained. In figure 12.1, for example, where *kung* is matched with *chung-lü* (the 6th), *shang* is *lin-chung* (the 8th), *chiao* is *nan-lü* (the 10th), *chih* is *huang-chung*, and *yü* is *t'ai-ts'ou* (the 3rd).

The length for *huang-chung* in figure 12.1 should be half the length of the basic *huang-chung*, for otherwise *chih* would become longer than *kung*, the note associated with the ruler. It was by using this scheme of "rotating *kung*" that Chu Hsi illustrated the possibility of "ministers abusing the ruler":

> If *ying-chung* (the 12th) is *kung*, its sound [i.e., length for the pitch] is shortest and clearest. . . . The *shang* note is taller [i.e., greater in length] than the *kung* note. This is "ministers [associated with *shang*] abusing the ruler [associated with *kung*]" and cannot be used. Consequently one should . . . decrease the pitch to one-half and make a clear sound.[147]

The intervals between the twelve pitches are not exactly equal; the ratio of some adjacent pair of pitches, *huang-chung* and *ta-lü* for example, is $2^{11}/3^7 = 0.9364$, whereas that of the other pairs, *ta-lü* and *t'ai-ts'ou* for example, is $3^5/2^8 = 0.9492$. Thus, a given five-note scale beginning at a different pitch would represent a different "mode" (*tiao*), characterized by different intervals, and the rotation of *kung* produces twelve different "modes" for each five-note scale. Since there are five different five-note scales, starting from each one of the five notes (*kung, shang, chiao, chih, yü; shang, chiao, chih, yü, kung;* and so on), there can be sixty such modes. When the seven-note scales are used, the number of possible modes becomes eighty-four. Chu Hsi mentioned both the sixty and the eighty-four modes, although he seemed to prefer the former.[148] At times, however, he seemed uncertain about what the sixty "modes" were, for he used such expressions as "the sixty 'notes' (*sheng*)" and "the sixty 'pitches' (*lü*)."[149]

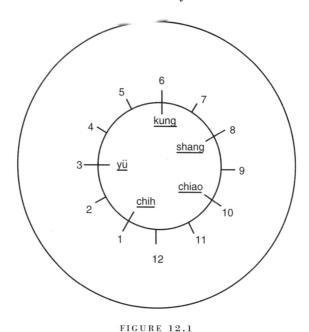

FIGURE 12.1
The Relation between the Five Notes and the Twelve Pitches
(in the figure the twelve pitches are represented by the numbers 1–12;
kung *is matched with* chung-lü*)*

Chu Hsi used the character *tiao* in the sense of *ch'iang-tiao* also, referring to "tunes" of music. He mentioned the actual names of some tunes found in various kinds of music: for example, "the *huang-chung kung* tune," "the *chung-lü* tune," "the *ta-shih* tune," and "the *Yüeh* tune."[150] What he spoke of more frequently, however, were simple tunes named by the note with which a given piece of music began and ended: A *kung*-tune music, for example, begins and ends with a *kung* note.[151] For the remaining notes, all the five, or seven, notes can be used;[152] Chu Hsi in fact said that "if [even] one of the five notes is lacking, one cannot form a music."[153] Thus, when a disciple asked about Ssu-ma Kuang's saying that there was no *chih* in the music of the Sung, Chu Hsi interpreted it as referring to the absence of the *chih*-tune and not of the *chih* note.[154] Similarly, though the *Rites of Chou* (Chou-li) does not mention *shang* in discussing the music for sacrificial services, what is excluded, in Chu Hsi's belief, was not the *shang* note but the *shang*-tune; he explained this by means of the common saying that the *shang*-tune carries "murderous" and "fierce" feelings.[155]

Chu Hsi knew also about different kinds of music.[156] He spoke frequently about the characteristics of the popular music of his time: for example, that only the three tunes—the *kung, shang,* and *yü*—were used in it[157] and that clear sounds were used more frequently than in the music of earlier times.[158] For him, a greater use of clear sounds was characteristic of the music of his time in general, which in his view was more "insipid" and "reserved."[159] The ninety-second *chüan* of his *Classified Con-*

versations contains many remarks, often quite long ones, about the actual music of various historical periods.[160]

Chu Hsi derived his knowledge of harmonics and music from various sources. The most basic ancient source was the "Lü-shu" (Pitch numbers) chapter (25th) of the *Record of the Historian*, which he praised frequently.[161] In his view its account of harmonics, although brief, covered the essential points, which were not all present in the more detailed accounts in the treatises of the *History of the Han*.[162] A few passages of the *Analects* mentioning music provided occasions for Chu Hsi to discuss the subject.[163] Some passages of various other ancient books, such as the *Record of Rites*, the *Rites of Chou*, *Kuo-yü* and the *Tso Commentary*, touch on more concrete aspects of harmonics and music and were referred to by Chu Hsi in discussing relevant points.[164] Commentaries on these passages also were sources of information for Chu Hsi. For example, he praised the long discussion on "rotating *kung*" in the subcommentary to the "Li-yün" (Revolving of the rites) chapter (22nd) of the *Record of Rites*.[165] He noted that the *pien-kung* and *pien-chih* notes first appeared in the commentary to *Kuo-yü*.[166]

Chu Hsi's sources included various post-Han works also. He frequently spoke of *T'ung-tien* of Tu Yu, praising its clear exposition. In particular, he mentioned its accurate numbers and its account of "the son sounds."[167] The strong points of Shen Kua's *Meng-hsi pi-t'an* lay in its "discussion of instruments and numbers, [which were] very thorough."[168] Chu Hsi's greatest praise, however, went to Ts'ai Yüan-ting and his book *Lü-lü hsin-shu*.[169] Chu Hsi emphasized that Ts'ai Yüan-ting not only read many books but also understood them thoroughly. In Chu Hsi's view no one else had reached the level of Ts'ai Yüan-ting in understanding the sections on harmonics and calendars in the *Record of the Historian*, for example;[170] and the excellent discussions in the *Lü-lü hsin-shu*, some of which had never been presented before, were all firmly based on established earlier methods.[171] Thus, Chu Hsi sided with Ts'ai Yüan-ting when the latter's view differed from those of such earlier authors as Tsu Hsiao-sun (early T'ang), Tu Yu, and Wang P'o (fl. 959).[172]

Chu Hsi's attitude toward "music specialists" (*yüeh-chia*) and their specialized knowledge was, on the whole, similar to his attitude toward calendar specialists:[173] he generally accepted the expertise of the specialists. He said repeatedly that when one does not understand certain points, one should consult "music specialists" or "those who know sounds and pitches,"[174] and he did so himself in his letters to scholars such as T'sai Yüan-ting who had a better knowledge of the subjects.[175] He spoke of "a certain person nearby with some knowledge of popular music," whom he wished to visit and to ask about what he did not understand himself.[176] He also spoke of persons with extraordinary abilities in recognizing notes and pitches.[177]

Chu Hsi's respect for the expertise of music specialists seems to have been somewhat greater than that for calendar specialists. This could have been because his mastery of the specialized knowledge of harmonics and music was less complete than his knowledge of calendrical astronomy, as can be seen from the casual mistakes that were more frequent in his discussions of the former subject.[178] In any case, there was no major issue in harmonics or music over which he advocated a view directly opposite to that of the specialists as he did with the leftward rotation theory. His criticisms were directed more frequently to scholars. He criticized such Northern Sung scholars as Hu Yüan, Juan I, Li Chao, Ssu-ma Kuang, and Fan Chung-yen for discussing music without sufficiently understanding it.[179] Ssu-ma Kuang and Fan Chung-yen, in particular, were engaged in a debate on harmonics; in Chu Hsi's view neither of them fully understood the subject—they had not even read *T'ung-tien*, which could hardly be said to be a rare book.[180] He spoke of deficiencies in the knowledge of other scholars: Chang Tsai, for example, who knew only of ancient music, and Hu Hung, who did not know that each of the twelve pitches could become *kung* through "the rotation of *kung*."[181] He pointed out mistakes of his disciples also: missing characters in Ts'ai Yüan's writing and mistaken remarks by Ch'en Ch'un (1159–1223) about the "drifting sounds" (*fan-sheng*) of the lute.[182] Chu Hsi was not even sure whether Tu Yu, the author of the *T'ung-tien*, which he had praised greatly, could be said to have understood music.[183] Chu Hsi also criticized contemporary scholars' neglect of the actual practice of music. For example, noting that even Ts'ai Yüan-ting could not play the lute, Chu Hsi added that it was like discussing military tactics while seated.[184] This could be contrasted with his belief that "those who tune the strings" could spontaneously identify different musical notes.[185]

Yet, Chu Hsi did not have a full intellectual respect for music specialists and their knowledge; in this respect his attitudes toward music and calendar specialists were basically the same. He seemed to believe that he and other scholars would be able to master music, had they applied themselves to it: "A music study ought to be established. Let scholar-officials study it. Then after a long time, there necessarily will appear those who have mastered it."[186] His lack of respect was reflected also in his casual rejection of some music, still performed in his time, as "personal fabrications" (*tu-chuan*) of earlier music specialists, the famous Wang P'o for example.[187]

Chu Hsi's low opinion of contemporary music specialists can also be seen in the great admiration he expressed for the ancient music. According to him, the ancients had a true understanding of music and harmonics: they knew about music and actually performed, using instruments.[188] He said repeatedly that such music of the ancients had been lost; people in his time did not possess a true knowledge of it or have the means to study it.[189] He said:

> The ancient music cannot be found [today]. In short, [the ancient] notes and pitches are now also difficult to encounter. But today's song also must have the so-called "five notes and twelve pitches," so that a piece can be composed, and [thus] it is also similar to the ancient music. Performing the lute is so, too. Only, that [i.e., today's song] is evil, [whereas] the ancient music is correct. Therefore they are not the same.[190]

He even said, "The music of today is all music of barbarians."[191]

The decline of music had begun early, but Chu Hsi specified the troubled times of the late T'ang as the period when the ancient music, which had existed until then, disappeared.[192] It was then, for example, that Wang P'o came up with his "fabrications," including "the four clear sounds."[193] Chu Hsi's brief description of the historical situation of music and harmonics in his preface to Ts'ai Yüan-ting's *Lü-lü hsin-shu* was along essentially the same line.[194]

12.4. Geography

Geography was another subject in which Chu Hsi had a considerable interest and of which he attained some knowledge. For example, he wrote a rather long essay on waterways and mountains—"the Nine Rivers" (Chiu-chiang) and P'eng-li Lake in particular—that is recorded in the chapter titled "Yü-kung" of the *Book of Documents*.[195] Detailed geographical discussions were included also in his various other essays and treatises[196] and in his letters to scholars such as Ch'eng Ta-ch'ang (1123–1195), Li Pi (1159–1222), Tung Chu (1152–1214), and Wu Pi-ta.[197] *Ch'u-tz'u chi-chu* (Collected commentaries on the *Songs of Ch'u*) also contained much information on the numerous geographical names appearing in the *Songs of Ch'u*. He was frequently engaged in discussions on geographical topics in his conversations, too.[198] In these writings and sayings, he spoke in detail of the geography of various areas of China, including many cities, mountains, and rivers. He also discussed various maps and mentioned a method of mapmaking.[199] He was said to have made relief maps in wood, which he carried while traveling.[200]

Much of Chu Hsi's geographical discussion appeared in his comments on the "Yü-kung" chapter.[201] Geographical information also came up in his discussion on the *t'u-kuei* method of determining the earth's center in the "Ti-kuan" chapter of the *Rites of Chou*.[202] Chu Hsi referred to other ancient sources of Chinese geographical knowledge, such as the geographical treatise of the *History of the Han*[203] and works like *Shan-hai-ching* (Classic of the mountains and rivers) and *Shui-ching* (Classic of the waters).[204] Buddhist canons were mentioned as sources of geographical information about the far western regions, beyond K'un-lun Mountain, for example.[205] Among scholars of later periods whose expert geographical knowledge Chu Hsi cited were Li Tao-yüan (d. 527), author of the commentary on the *Shui-ching*, and Hsueh Ch'ang-chou (fl. 1075), author of the *Nine Region Map* (Chiu-yü t'u).[206]

I restrict myself here to mentioning general characteristics of traditional Chinese geographical knowledge that Chu Hsi shared with the specialists, rather than discussing the actual content of Chu Hsi's geographical knowledge.[207] For one thing, Chinese geographical knowledge, including Chu Hsi's, was thoroughly centered around China; it was based on the belief that China was at the center of the world and was its most important part.[208] Sometimes it can even be sensed that for the Chinese, China *was* the world. Thus, descriptions of China were offered frequently as if they were descriptions of the world. For example, much of what Chu Hsi said about the earth's shape and the features of the earth's surface in general, which we have seen in sections 9.2 and 9.4, was based on the known geographical features of China.[209]

Chu Hsi shared the emphasis of Chinese geographical knowledge upon human, rather than physical, aspects. At times he provided a physical description of a place in order to explain its richness in human resources.[210] Obviously, for him human resources depended on physical geographical conditions, as did the mineral and agricultural resources, which was a natural consequence of the belief in the dependence of man's qualities upon his *ch'i.* Thus, Chu Hsi attributed social customs and personal characteristics, as well as such different human qualities as voices and proneness to disease, to the *ch'i,* and so to the physical geographical conditions, of the area in which men lived.[211] It was frequently in this context that he discussed the physical conditions for a good capital city.[212]

A belief in the dependence of human conditions on the physical geographical ones was the basis of Chinese geomancy, or *"feng-shui"* (wind and water), the task of which was to select auspicious sites for residences and graves. For the *"feng-shui"* practice is based on the belief that the state of the *ch'i* and its flow at and near a given site, determined by its physical— or "topographical"—features, influences the conditions of those who reside in the site or those whose ancestors are buried in it.[213] Chu Hsi did not actively endorse that belief. He sounded rather apologetic when he admitted that his own family had used a sitting method, which "cannot help being 'vulgar' (*su*) but is still nothing but seeking a peaceful and stable place."[214] He did not explicitly reject the belief, either. His attitude toward it was similar to his attitude toward the *kuei-shen* and other strange phenomena we have seen in chapter 6. For him, it represented possible manifestations of qualities and activities of *ch'i.* He said that some do not believe in the efficacy of *feng-shui* practices because they do not understand their *li.*[215] He mentioned some "geography specialists" (*ti-li-chia*) who "select directions of mountains and forests,"[216] those ancients who "divined omens of their houses having good or bad fortunes,"[217] and those families that "invited 'the masters of techniques' (*shu-shih*) . . . to select the best [site for their ancestors]."[218] He spoke of the names and views of such past *feng-shui* experts as Kuo P'u (late third century) and Lu Yü (fl. 760).[219] Once, at least, he offered a description of the *feng-shui* features of an ancient capital region, employing such specialist terms as "tiger" (*hu*) and "dragon" (*lung*) forms.[220]

Chu Hsi noted that geography was "very difficult to understand,"[221] a comment that he did not make about calendrical astronomy or harmonics. But the source of the difficulty he mentioned was not the difficulty of the content of geographical knowledge, but rather discrepancies between different accounts or between given accounts and the geographical facts. He pointed out many such discrepancies, those in the "Yü-kung" chapter in particular. In fact, much of his geographical discussion on the "Yü-kung" was about such problems in its descriptions of various rivers and mountains.[222] Chu Hsi himself found many errors from his own limited observations and suspected that there would be many more of them in the areas where he had not traveled.[223] In his view the main source for the errors was that King Yü, the author of the geographical description in the chapter, did not actually observe all the regions whose geography he was recording; the chapter's descriptions of mountains and rivers in the southern areas, for which King Yü had to rely upon second-hand reports, contained many discrepancies.[224] But Chu Hsi also spoke of historical changes in the names and locations of cities, mountains, and rivers as possible sources of the discrepancies.[225] He did not rule out the possibility of alterations in geographical features over a long period of time. The course of the flow of the Yellow River, for example, had changed since King Yü's time.[226] He even spoke of the following possibility:

> "Yü-kung" only records the Nine Rivers but no Tung-t'ing [lake]. Now checking the area to verify it, there is Tung-t'ing but no Nine Rivers. Thus there is no doubt that Tung-t'ing is the Nine Rivers. Tung-t'ing and P'eng-li [Lakes] are also dried up during winter months, and there only are several stripes of rivers in them.[227]

Thus, Chu Hsi's geographical discussion does not show the admiration of ancient knowledge that is so characteristic of his treatments of calendrical astronomy and harmonics. On the contrary, he said that one should not pay too much attention to the geography of "Yü-kung": "Understanding 'Yü-kung' is not like understanding today's geography."[228] He criticized those who, being afraid of pointing out errors in classical texts, continued to record them.[229] He even found those "laughable" who slavishly followed Mencius's erroneous interpretation of what was said in the "Yü-kung" chapter.[230] He criticized other authors for relying on speculation rather than actual observation: Su Shih, for example, "did not see the condition of the southeastern waters himself, [but] merely thought [about them] and insisted on his sayings."[231] But as for those who "'verified' [their sayings] with the eyes," he said that "their theories must be reliable and can still be studied today."[232] Of course, Chu Hsi's geographical criticism resorted to means other than observation as well. While discussing mistakes in the famous map *Yü-chi-t'u* (Map of the traces of Yü), carved in stone in 1137, which represented two branches of a river as one, he said: "To judge it by means of the *li* and situations, how can there be these?"[233]

12.5. "Images and Numbers" (*Hsiang-shu*), Divination, and Alchemy

In chapter 5 we noted that, to Chu Hsi and other traditional Chinese thinkers, "images and numbers" ranked among the fundamentals that underlie the workings—or the order, or the secrets, or even the mysteries—of the world. There thus arose a tradition of specialists who attempted to master the secrets of the world by means of study and manipulation of images and numbers.

The most important source for the study of "images and numbers" was the *I-ching*, the "Hsi-tz'u chuan" and "Shuo-kua chuan" commentaries in particular.[234] Charts consisting of various arrangements of simple numbers (in lines and dots) and the *I-ching* diagrams—*Ho-t'u*, *Lo-shu*, and *Hsien-t'ien-t'u*, for example—also came up frequently in Chu Hsi's discussion of the subject.[235] Although all of these charts were allegedly of ancient origin, it was only in Shao Yung's writings that one can find anything resembling a system incorporating them.[236] Those who came after Shao Yung always took his theories as the source and starting point of their numerological discussions. Chu Hsi's immediate sources also were Shao Yung's theories.[237]

Chu Hsi did not fully accept Shao Yung's theories of images and numbers, however. He did praise the latter's ability to deal with numbers: "After the *I-ching*, no one has accomplished a thing in such an orderly manner, or could cover [everything so] exhaustively."[238] In Chu Hsi's view Shao Yung's numerological theories were "based on making the *li* clear."[239] Thus, Chu Hsi thought that Shao Yung's ability to know future events was different from the foreknowledge of mere fortune-tellers, who were "far from the Way" and whose "knowledge of K'ang-chieh [i.e., Shao Yung] was scarce." Shao Yung "could play with this *li* competently. When an event or a thing reached before him, he saw [the *li*] right away, without waiting to think [about it]."[240] Yet, Chu Hsi could not understand "why one should know the numbers also" once one has already known the *li* of heaven and earth.[241] Thus, for him, what Shao Yung did with numbers was still basically "techniques" (*shu*).[242] Chu Hsi said:

> [Shao Yung's] learning is merely the learning of techniques and numbers. [If] a man of a later age has intelligence and is able to calculate, he will also be able to infer [and understand it].[243]

> [Whereas] the Sage [i.e., Confucius] knew the decree of heaven through the *li*, he [i.e., Shao Yung] [did so] simply through "techniques." Although he could attain the essential points of the techniques, [the decree of heaven] is still not what the techniques can exhaust. Nevertheless, the beginning was just techniques.[244]

Chu Hsi likened Shao Yung to the famous ancient tactician Chang Liang and rejected the Ch'eng brothers' saying that Shao Yung was "pure and unadulterated."[245] He even admitted that "K'ang-chieh's learning was similar to Buddha['s]."[246]

Chu Hsi spoke of Ch'en T'uan (ca. 906–989) as the source of Shao Yung's learning of numbers.[247] Concerning earlier sources, however, he was not quite certain. At least, he did not think that all of Shao Yung's numerological thought had originated from Ch'en T'uan. He noted that the great *Taoist Corpus* (Tao-tsang) contained similar diagrams and numbers.[248] As for the *Hsien-t'ien-t'u* (Chart of the "Prior to Heaven"), it had existed before Ch'en T'uan but had been kept secret, being transmitted, for example, among the "masters of methods" (*fang-shih*), practitioners of various techniques, including alchemy, macrobiotics, and so on.[249] In particular, Chu Hsi saw the connection of the chart with *Ts'an-t'ung-ch'i*, an alchemical text supposedly written by Wei Po-yang in the second century A.D.[250] He thus discounted the role of the supposed forerunners of Shao Yung, saying that Mu Hsiu (979–1032) and Li Chih-ts'ai (d. 1045), who were considered generally as the links between Shao Yung and Ch'en T'uan, "merely received [the chart], not necessarily understanding it." He even said that Shao Yung "came up with [the understanding through] his own thinking."[251]

In spite of such Taoist connections, Chu Hsi did not shun the study of images and numbers. He himself wrote many separate works on the subject: in particular, *Chou-i pen-i* (Original meaning of the *I-ching*), a commentary on *I-ching*; *I-hsueh ch'i-meng* (Introduction to the study of the *I-ching*), an introductory manual on *I-ching* numerology and divination; and *Ts'an-t'ung-ch'i k'ao-i*, a commentary on *Ts'an-t'ung-ch'i*.[252] His conversations and writings also contained a great amount of quite detailed discussion on speculations and manipulations of diagrams and numbers, as well as practices of divination and alchemy involving concrete examples of them.[253] In addition, he recommended that others study them. For example, he said to a disciple:

> Have you seen the numbers of *Ho-t'u* and *Lo-shu?* It is worth looking at when there is nothing to do. Although [they are] not the most important matters, when one plays with these one will be able to get one's mind to flow, change, and move.[254]

As Chu Hsi implied in those words, there were more important things for a scholar than to study images and numbers. After discussing a few hexagram associations—*chung-fu* with an egg, *ting* with a cauldron, and so on—he made the following remark:

> What is said here and elsewhere has some meaning. But if one [takes up] the one book of *I*[*-ching*] and wishes to be forced and far-fetched like this, then in a while one will become loose and broken. Scholars should understand the proper way and *li* first.[255]

He was thus critical about numerological speculations that appeared too far-fetched. For example, he refused to accept the numerological significance of "there being 360 degrees in the heavens"; for him one degree is defined simply as the difference that arises between the daily rotations of heaven and of the sun, and there are thus 365 ¼ degrees in the heavens and so many days in a year.[256] He also rejected the numerological association of the number of days in a leap year with the number of 384 single lines of the 64 hexagrams:

> [If so] it [i.e., this explanation] can be used just once in three years, and cannot be used in the other years. Moreover, the leap months are necessarily small [i.e., 29 rather than 30 days long]. If we examine as you say, the leap years will have only 383 days, and the additional one single line will have no use.[257]

Nor did Chu Hsi claim that he fully understood images and numbers. He admitted readily that "the images" of the *I-ching* diagrams were difficult to understand.[258] He used the term "*shu* specialists" (*shu-chia*) in obvious references to experts of the subject.[259] For example, he spoke of a certain country monk named Tsung-yüan, who, after spending a few months on a mountain, became enlightened in *shu* and could readily understand Shao Yung's *Huang-chi ching-shih* (Supreme rules governing the world).[260]

Yet, Chu Hsi did not seem to have much intellectual respect for these specialists. In addition to his critical remarks about Shao Yung's *shu*, there was his judgment about Chan T'i-jen (1143–1206), who "spoke only of *ch'i, shu,* and the apocryphal texts (*ch'en-wei*)"; Chu Hsi said, "These are not sufficient to rely on."[261] Chu Hsi even ranked the *shu* specialists with those occultists whom he called "the specialists of techniques" (*shu-chia*) and "the masters of methods."[262]

On contemporary scholars' knowledge of images and numbers in general, Chu Hsi was usually critical. In his view they tended to indulge in "abstruse and subtle" points and "forced, far-fetched" interpretations.[263] Yet, there were scholars whose knowledge of the subject he was willing to rely upon. In his correspondence with men like Ch'eng Chiung, Yüan Shu (1131–1205), and Ts'ai Yüan-ting, Chu Hsi frequently asked questions and expressed the desire to receive instruction on particular problems.[264] His opinion of his own knowledge of images and numbers does not seem to have been low, either. He was confident enough, for example, to make judgments on Tung Chu's discussions on specific numerological issues, using such words as "What you said is correct," "It caught the point," "That is clear," and "That is not right,"[265] or to reject Ts'ai Yüan-ting's view that "Fu Hsi must have known" Shao Yung's theory of *shu*.[266]

The main application of the study of "images and numbers" was to divination. Indeed, for Chu Hsi, the basic source for such study, the book *I-ching* itself, was originally intended for use in divination. He said repeatedly that "the *I* [-*ching*] was originally [written by the sages] for divination."[267] He criticized contemporary scholars who neglected this aspect of the book while concentrating on "the righteousness and *li*" (*i-li*) hidden in it.[268] Even Ch'eng I, "who spoke of just one [aspect of the] *li*," could not escape such criticism.[269] Chu Hsi's purpose in writing the *I-hsueh ch'i-meng* was, then, to correct this situation:

> Those who have discussed the *I*[-*ching*] in recent times have been completely "extravagant and sketchy" with respect to images and numbers. Those who have not been so have been too restricted and fragmented, [and thus it] was not possible to examine them closely. Therefore, going back to what the sages originally discussed on images and numbers in the classics and commentaries and inferring the intentions from just these several passages, I take this to be sufficient by means of which to examine upward the original intention of the sages' writing the *I*, and to help downward the practical utility of contemporary people's "observing changes and pondering about the prognostications" (*kuan-pien wan-chan*).[270]

Thus, for Chu Hsi, divination based on the *I-ching* was a perfectly legitimate activity of a Confucian scholar:

> As for divination, since the time of Fu Hsi, Yao, and Shun all have used it, and there is *li* for it. Now, if people today have doubts about an affair, they reverently use divination to decide on it. What is wrong with this?[271]

As we have seen in chapter 6, he viewed the divination procedure as parallel to that of sacrificial service, the most important Confucian ritual. In fact, he was of the view that everyone—"literati, farmers, artisans, and merchants"—will find a use for divination for every affair.[272]

Chu Hsi did not forget to put divination in a broader context of moral self-cultivation. He had the following to say in commenting on the passage from the *Doctrine of the Mean* involving the possibility of foreknowledge—"By means of the Way of extreme sincerity, one can foreknow. . . ." (ch. 24):

All this is the *li* manifesting beforehand. But only the one whose sincerity has reached the extreme and who does not have a trace of selfishness and falsehood remaining between the heart and the eyes can have [the means] by which to observe the 'incipiency' (*chi*).[273]

On divination based on the *I-ching*, he said:

In reading a hexagram and a line, [do] just as the prognostications obtained: empty the mind to seek what the words and meanings signify, and consider it as a decision of a good or a bad fortune. Afterward, examine what the image has been earlier, seek the reason for the *li*, and then extend them to the event. [This will] allow [everyone] from kings and nobles down to common people to use it for self-cultivation and governing the state.[274]

There is only one recorded case of Chu Hsi's own recourse to the *I-ching* divination—to decide whether or not to submit a controversial memorial to the emperor.[275] One may or may not agree with Joseph A. Adler's suggestion that "it is . . . likely that Chu [Hsi] felt himself capable of knowing what to do in most cases without resorting to divination."[276] Nevertheless, Chu Hsi was well versed in the actual methods of the *I-ching* divination. He spoke frequently of the procedure of divination using milfoil stalks, in particular the method of "sorting out milfoil stalks" (*she-shih*), based on the fragmentary information in chapter A9 of "Hsi-tz'u chuan."[277] He wrote a critical essay, titled "Shih-kua k'ao-wu" (Examination of milfoil stalks and hexagrams), surveying various versions of the method.[278] What he considered correct, and what has since become the standard procedure, seems to have been the version presented in chapter 3 of *I-hsueh ch'i-meng* as a detailed commentary upon the "Hsi-tz'u chuan" chapter.[279]

As a result of the milfoil-stalk divination, one comes up with hexagrams, which need to be interpreted as signs or omens representing one's situations or "fortunes." Chu Hsi frequently spoke of ways to interpret the hexagrams and their individual lines.[280] There were other sorts of signs and omens that could be used in obtaining foreknowledge.[281] He spoke, for example, of the divination method that uses tortoise shells.[282] Actual numbers—and the stems and branches—of the hours, dates, months, and years of people's birth, for example—could also be used for "fate calculation," as noted in chapter 5. We have spoken of other examples of omens in chapter 8 in connection with Chu Hsi's ideas of "the mutual stimulation of heaven and man." Man's facial features could also be used in foretelling his fortunes. Chu Hsi said of a certain monk, for example, that his physiognomy would certainly have made him a bandit leader, had he not become a monk.[283]

Yet, though not rejecting these practices of seeking foreknowledge, Chu Hsi did not fully accept their value. He had acquaintance with practitioners of fate calculation, some of them known to be very efficacious, as the prefaces he wrote for them show.[284] He even praised their abilities: "Although their techniques appear easy to understand, those who study them often cannot reach their profundity."[285] He also mentioned the names of expert practitioners of other sorts of fortune-telling—those who could foretell disastrous death and ascension to the throne or could interpret dreams, for example.[286] Chu Hsi never explicitly denied such abilities, for, as we have noted, they were entirely possible through the interaction of man's mind and the *ch'i* of the world. But as he said in one of the prefaces that he wrote, these abilities were of secondary importance: "One must cultivate oneself and wait till one is able to establish the fate."[287] To the passage quoted earlier to show his critical opinion of Shao Yung's thoughts about *shu*, Chu Hsi added: "Whether one is to die tomorrow, one cannot know; nor can one know if one is to be in the world for twenty or thirty years. [One should] simply cultivate oneself. Why must one know it beforehand?"[288] It is no wonder, then, that Chu Hsi had generally low opinions of the specialists of divination and fortune-telling.

Another major application of the study of "images and numbers" was to alchemy. The basis for this application had been laid out in *Ts'an-t'ung-ch'i*. In this abstruse text, various alchemical procedures—including the related chemical, respiratory, and meditational ones—were recorded, frequently in metaphors using associations of hexagrams with alchemical agents (mercury and lead, for example), symbols (dragons and tigers), procedures ("fire-phasing" [*huo-hou*]), and apparatus, as well as with the usual categories of yin-yang, the five phases, the ten stems and the twelve branches, the compass directions, the hours of the day, the days of the month, the twelve pitches, and so forth.[289] Chu Hsi's discussion of alchemy was also centered around this book, in which he showed a great interest in his later years, especially in the late 1190s. His correspondence and conversations during those years frequently mentioned the book and its alchemical associations and procedures.[290] *Ts'an-t'ung-ch'i k'ao-i*, which he published shortly before his death, was a kind of commentary that summed up his understanding of the book.

I am omitting the detailed contents of Chu Hsi's alchemical discussions in *Ts'an-t'ung-ch'i k'ao-i*; it is filled with terms and expressions that are hard to interpret unambiguously.[291] They were difficult for Chu Hsi himself. He said that the *Ts'an-t'ung-ch'i* was difficult to understand and that people do not dare to discuss it lightly.[292] In the *K'ao-i* also, he said repeatedly things like "I do not know the detail of the theory," "It is not clear what this refers to," and "I cannot understand in detail."[293] He believed that the difficulty of the *Ts'an-t'ung-ch'i* lay in the text itself and that the words in the book were "difficult and profound" because the author, "being afraid of revealing the secrets of heaven, did not wish to speak straightforwardly."[294] He had written the *K'ao-i* because "the arcane and obscure" style of the *Ts'an-t'ung-ch'i* was "difficult to master," and thus it contained many mistakes.[295] According to him, the difficulty increased just where the book began to deal with the actual alchemical content.[296]

Chu Hsi thus relied heavily on Ts'ai Yüan-ting, to whom he wrote repeatedly, asking questions and requesting advice on what he did not understand. In 1197 he spent many days with Ts'ai Yüan-ting, discussing difficult parts of the *Ts'an-t'ung-ch'i* when the latter visited him.[297] Later, he deplored that though he had desired to discuss the theory with Chi-t'ung, the latter died before he had written it up and sent it.[298]

Yet, Chu Hsi seemed to believe that he had reached an understanding of the essentials of the *Ts'an-t'ung-ch'i*. For him, the book "borrowed the *na-chia* method to convey the conditions of the action, transfer, advance, and retreat."[299] Concerning its alchemical content in particular, the basic point was that "[things that are] of the same category change each other" (*t'ung-lei hsiang pien*) and that "[things that are] of different categories cannot form each other" (*i-lei pu-neng hsiang ch'eng*).[300] Chu Hsi thought that the key ideas were the essence-*ch'i* dichotomy and its associations with various other dualistic pairs, including the hexagram pairs of *k'an-li*:

> The categories of "*k'an-li*, Water and Fire, dragon and tiger, lead and mercury," spoken of in the *Ts'an-t'ung-ch'i*, simply are [results of] exchanging names. Actually, [they are] nothing but the two things — essence and *ch'i*. The essence is Water, *k'an*, dragon, and mercury; the *ch'i* is Fire, *li*, tiger, and lead. The method is to move, by means of *shen*, essence and *ch'i* to congeal and to make the elixir (*tan*). The yang *ch'i* is below. It first forms Water. Smelt (*lien*) it by means of Fire, then it condenses and forms the elixir.[301]

"If one gets the outline from these points," said Chu Hsi, "then [one will get] the principle of the effort. What Mr. Wei [Po-yang] did not say can naturally be made out through [the] meanings."[302]

There is no evidence that Chu Hsi himself was engaged in alchemical practice, and he did not show a full respect for the actual techniques and practitioners of alchemy. He once referred to the alchemical procedures as "'trivial techniques' (*mo-chi*) of oven and fire."[303] In publishing *Ts'an-t'ung-ch'i k'ao-i*, he did not sign his name but used a pseudonym, Tsou Hsin, and added the title "Taoist master" (*Tao-shih*).[304]

12.6. "Nourishing Life" (*yang-sheng*) and Other "Taoist" Techniques

The *Ts'an-t'ung-ch'i* contained remarks that could be interpreted in the spirit of the "internal alchemy" (*nei-tan*), "the physiological analogue of alchemy," to use Nathan Sivin's words, "which uses alchemical language to describe the pursuit of immortality through breathing or meditative disciplines."[305] Indeed, by the time of the Sung most commentators took it mainly as a book of internal alchemy.[306] Chu Hsi himself seems to have shared that view: he said repeatedly that such frequently used alchemical terms as "lead and mercury" and "dragon and tiger" are all things "inside man's body."[307]

Chu Hsi used the expression "nourishing life" in referring to various techniques of internal alchemy.[308] What he spoke of most often were the breathing and meditating exercises. Such terms as "holding the *ch'i*" (*ping-ch'i*), "reducing the breath" (*chien-hsi*), and "regulating the *ch'i*" (*t'iao-ch'i*) referred to the former, whereas "emptying the mind" (*hsü-hsin*), "keeping the mind" (*ts'un-hsin*), and "keeping the thought" (*ts'un-hsiang*) meant the latter.[309] Chu Hsi had a considerable degree of interest in and knowledge of them, at least late in life. Compared with alchemy — or "external alchemy" (*wai-tan*) — he seemed to have more knowledge, and a higher opinion, of these techniques. He composed the brief essay "Admonition on Regulating the Breath" (T'iao-hsi chen).[310] He asked Lin Ch'eng-chi about the practice of the breathing method and its effect.[311] In a letter to a disciple, Chu Hsi even spoke of his own experience of practicing a meditation technique when he was ill:

> I simply . . . sat quietly. The eyes looked at the end of the nose. I directed the mind below the navel and the belly. After a long time, [the body] spontaneously [became] warm, and [the method] gradually showed [its] efficacy [of curing the illness].[312]

That quotation shows Chu Hsi's belief that the meditating technique had an effect in curing illness. Another letter also indicated his belief in the curing effect of the breathing and meditating techniques:

> The *ch'i* and blood at middle age cannot be compared to [those of] earlier days. Taking medicine hardly shows effect, either. There only is [the method of] "emptying the mind and regulating the *ch'i*." Quietly nourish them, then you can perhaps hope that they will be of some help.[313]

He even said that the Taoist meditating technique of "keeping the *shen* and inwardly illuminating (*ts'un-shen nei-chao*) . . . is not necessarily useless for nourishing illness."[314]

Chu Hsi also spoke of "the *li* of nourishing life" in general. It can, for example, be obtained by "studying medication recipes when there is nothing to do."[315] He seemed to think that he had obtained the essence of it. In a conversation recorded very late in his life (not earlier than 1198), he said that he had understood what Ts'ai Yüan-ting had said about the *li* of nourishing life.[316] He must have had such a *li* in mind when, in another conversation, recorded about the same time, perhaps even later, he commented on the *Lao-tzu* phrase "carrying the *p'o* and embracing the One" (ch. 10):

> Water is the One; Fire is the Two. Carry the *hun* by means of the *p'o*. Protect the One by means of the Two. Then Water and Fire are sure to become orderly and are not separated from each other. Therefore, one can [live for] everlasting years. The theories of "nourishing-life specialists" exhaust a thousand sayings and myriad words. [They] speak of dragon and tiger, lead and mercury, and of *k'an* and *li*. [But] their techniques do not go further than this.[317]

The purpose of nourishing life, as the above quotation shows, was to live long— or to live forever. Chu Hsi thought that those whom people called "immortals" (*hsien*) were the ones who had mastered these techniques. Again, his attitude toward stories about immortals was similar to that toward *kuei-shen:* he was generally skeptical but tried to explain them rather than reject them outright. For example, he explained stories about the immortals in the following way:

> It is not that [the immortals] do not die. They can refine their physical form and *ch'i*, and make the sediments all melt. [They] only have that clear and empty *ch'i*, and therefore can rise up [in the sky] and [undergo] changes.[318]

This was how he explained, as we have seen, stories about people who could fly and whose corpses melted away.[319] But as he said, he did not believe that they could live forever. He mentioned actual names like Chung Li-ch'üan and Lü Tung-pin, who were believed to be immortals and who, according to the records, were seen by people many times over a long span of time, but he emphasized that they were not seen anymore (implying that they must have died).[320]

Chu Hsi did not claim that he had a full understanding of "nourishing life." His comments on it in *Ts'an-t'ung-ch'i k'ao-i* were usually very brief, in sharp contrast with the commentary's very detailed discussion on the theories of "images and numbers" involving the *I-ching* diagrams.[321] And though he said that he had understood Ts'ai Yüan-ting's remarks about "the *li* of nourishing life," he added immediately: "Only, the frames (literally, 'the walls,' *ch'eng-kuo*) are not completed so that there is no place to apply its effect."[322]

Nor did Chu Hsi fully accept the techniques and theories of nourishing life. Perhaps he could not, for their Taoist association was too unmistakable. Chu Hsi frequently noted the ideas of immortals and "long life" (*ch'ang-sheng*) contained in the *Lao-tzu*.[323] He even said that "Lao-tzu only wanted a long life."[324] The *Lao-tzu* also contained many other expressions that could be interpreted as alluding to various techniques of nourishing life; much of Chu Hsi's own discussion of such techniques actually came up in commenting on them.[325]

Not only alchemy and "nourishing life," but various other beliefs and techniques, frequently connected in some way with images and numbers, were associated with Taoists. In Chu Hsi's view, military strategy, computation, and the technique of "performance and title" (*hsing-ming*) all originated from the *Lao-tzu*.[326] He used the word "Taoist techniques" (*tao-shu*) to refer to these techniques;[327] the expression "the Taoist masters" (i.e., "the masters of the Way," *tao-shih*) was used in referring to the practitioners of these techniques. Chu Hsi spoke of the *Yin-fu-ching* (Canon of secrets and tallies), on which he wrote a brief commentary, as a text dealing with such techniques.[328] He also mentioned other titles that belong to the great *Taoist Corpus* (Tao-tsang).[329]

Chu Hsi's opinion of the Taoist techniques and their practitioners, however, was not very high. For example, he noted disapprovingly that "those who study [*Lao-tzu*] frequently stray into 'techniques and numbers' (*shu-shu*)."[330] He even said, "To be concerned with tactfulness and to be engaged exclusively with techniques and numbers under heaven is 'the failure of Lao-tzu.'"[331] When Ts'ai Yüan-ting spoke of a Taoist master capable of an invocation technique called "the five thunder method" (*wu-lei-fa*), Chu Hsi responded harshly: "Now, the extremely vulgar are the Taoist masters. They say a great deal, [but] all is lies."[332] The problem with these theories, for Chu Hsi, was that they "were only for the self; their own body is all that matters [for them; they] do not care about other persons."[333]

Chu Hsi claimed that the situation was different in the beginning of Taoism; it was the later Taoists who had become so preoccupied with the techniques.[334] Thus, he denied that books like the *Tan-ching* (Canon of the elixir) and the *Ts'an-t'ung-ch'i* belong to the original learning of Lao-tzu.[335] He criticized contemporary Taoists who "only busy [themselves] over [techniques of] external [alchemy]," while not even understanding what is said in the *Lao-tzu* text.[336]

Of course, Chu Hsi did not totally lack intellectual respect for the Taoist masters. There were some who were sufficiently learned, with whom Chu Hsi associated. His letters to men like Ts'eng Chi and Fang I, who are known to have been Taoist masters, clearly show his respect for and reliance on them.[337] The *Collected Writings* also contains letters he wrote to persons whom he simply called "Taoist Master Kan" and "Taoist Master Ch'en," prefaces for "Taoist Master Ch'en Ching-yüan" and "Taoist Master Ch'ing-chiang, Mr. Chou," and poems for "Taoist Master Li."[338] Furthermore, he would not have chosen the pseudonym "Taoist Master K'ung-t'ung" for his own authorship of *Ts'an-t'ung-ch'i k'ao-i* if all he had had for Taoist masters was contempt or suspicion.

12.7. Medicine

We have seen that medicine, for Chu Hsi, belonged to "the small ways," whereas the subjects of calendrical astronomy, harmonics, geography, and "images and numbers" did not.[339] We have also noted that he ranked medical practitioners along with such groups as Taoists, Buddhists, "nourishing-life specialists," fortune-tellers, and craftsmen. In commenting on the saying in the *Analects* "When a man has no stability, he will not even make a shaman or a medical man" (13.22), Chu Hsi said:

> Shamans are those through whom one can interact with *kuei* and *shen;* medical men are those to whom one entrusts one's life and death. Therefore, even though they are lowly jobs, it is all the more impermissible for them to be without stability.[340]

This does not mean, however, that medicine was an unacceptable subject for a Confucian scholar to be interested in, for "the small ways" were "ways," after all, and were worth "looking at."[341] Chu Hsi showed some degree of interest in the subject. He was aware of various medical texts, which he seems to have read and studied. Indeed, as Robert P. Hymes has shown, the intention of the original *Analects* passage mentioning "the small ways" and of Chu Hsi's commentary as well must have been to distinguish the acceptable acts of "studying, reading, intellectual acquaintance" (i.e., "looking at" [*kuan*]) from the unacceptable acts of "practicing," or "pursuing a mere occupational skill" (i.e., "doing" [*wei*]).[342]

Thus, although Chu Hsi spoke of names and effects of many drugs and remedies and of diagnosis by feeling the pulse (see section 11.7), he rarely touched upon the detailed technical content of the knowledge of those whom he called "the medical specialists" (*i-chia*).[343] His account of methods of locating the pulse, in a preface to a medical book, was virtually the only exception. He did refer to "theories" of medical specialists, but they were quite elementary ideas, sometimes with philosophical implications, mentioned simply as isolated examples; they were seldom explained systematically or discussed in detail. For example, he quoted the medical specialists' theory concerning human mental functions that the five storing viscera "store": "The heart stores *shen*. The spleen stores the intention. The liver stores *hun*. The lungs store *p'o*. The kidneys store the feelings and the will."³⁴⁴ He also spoke of the "theory of nonhumaneness" (*pu-jen chih shuo*) of the medical specialists who "consider [the symptom of] not perceiving pain or itching as 'nonhumaneness.'"³⁴⁵ Chu Hsi attributed to medical specialists the idea that "small children do not need to be too warm"³⁴⁶ and stated that medical specialists prescribed pills made of a drug mixed with meat for those who had lost their appetite for meat.³⁴⁷

Chu Hsi seemed to be quite familiar with the classical and other important medical texts. He felt that he knew the two main parts of the *Yellow Emperor's Inner Canon* (Huang-ti nei-ching) well enough to say that "the words spoken in the *Su-wen* (Basic questions) are profound. [Those in] the *Ling-shu* (Numinous axis) are shallow, and comparatively easy."³⁴⁸ In a letter to Ts'ai Yüan, for example, Chu Hsi asked him to lend him a book called *Su-wen yün-ch'i chieh-lüeh* (Outline of the movement and *ch'i* in the *Basic Questions*).³⁴⁹ It is recorded that Chu Hsi, on his sickbed a few days before his death, asked Ts'ai Ch'en to consult the standard etiological text, *Chu-ping yüan-hou lun* (Treatise on origins and symptoms of various diseases) of Ch'ao Yüan-fang (fl. 610).³⁵⁰ Chu Hsi also knew and spoke about more recent and less well known medical texts. In a letter he expressed his desire to obtain and learn about the commentary of P'ang An-shih (fl. ca. 1080) on the *Nan-ching* (Classic of difficult problems).³⁵¹ He approvingly mentioned a certain Mr. Hsü's "prescriptions that must be used" (*pi-yung fang*).³⁵² He also wrote a brief introductory comment on a medical book by a certain "Mr. Hsia," which he sent to someone along with the book,³⁵³ and arranged the publication of Kuo Yung's *Shang-han pu wang lun* (Treatise on repairing cold damage), to which he wrote the above-mentioned preface.³⁵⁴

The prefatory comments show some elements of Chu Hsi's attitude toward medicine. For example, his characteristic respect for ancient knowledge in classical texts—not restricted to the branch of medicine alone—can be seen in his praise of "Mr. Hsia's" medical book.

> Mr. Hsia's [theories of] medicine, and prescriptions and uses of drugs are unusual and absolutely unparalleled. Some appear far from men's feelings [i.e., usual knowledge], but they are effective after all. If it is asked why they are so, [the answer is] that all were based on the [medical] classics and study of the ancients, and there were none that did not have sources. . . . [I am] sending the book in order to communicate his techniques to the present age and also to ridicule those of us who do not respect the ancients but are on their own.³⁵⁵

Chu Hsi's praise of Kuo Yung's book is also based on his judgment that Kuo Yung had rendered difficult parts of the medical classics into easily understandable form:

> Generally, what he says appears as though it altogether has come from the ancient [medical] classics, without any addition or omission. Yet, the ancient classics, being profound, great, and broad, are difficult to consult, whereas this book, being clearly delineated and classified, is easy to read.³⁵⁶

The preface went on to speak about the need to make such medical knowledge available to many people:

> How should we broaden its distribution and enable [those in] the world who study the preparation of prescriptions to keep it at home and [let] people recite it, so that [they] know all the details of the ancient and past sages' "ways of medicine" (*i-tao*), without blaming their difficulties?[357]

Chu Hsi himself seems to have been familiar with what was available to him. His comments on different methods of locating the pulse discussed in the book, with which he ended the preface, was fairly detailed. He preferred the method of Wang Shu-ho (210–285), the author of the *Mai-ching* (Classic of the pulses)—though in his view Kuo Yung's treatment of it in the book was quite inadequate—to the method of Ting Te-yung, the author of an eleventh-century commentary on the *Nan-ching*. And although he said that he was "not well versed in the ways [of medicine],"[358] he was not ambiguous about his judgment.

12.8. Other Areas: Mathematics, Animals and Plants, Agriculture, and Crafts

Traditions of specialized knowledge also existed in other areas: mathematics and computational skills, detailed animal and plant knowledge, agriculture, and crafts, for example. Chu Hsi did not discuss much of the technical content of these subjects, however, and for some of them, what he did speak of came up in his discussion of problems other than the subjects themselves.

Chu Hsi could perform simple mathematical computations. This was to be expected because, as we have noted, computation was one of the basic skills considered to be compulsory subjects for the education of children.[359] We have seen that Chu Hsi was quite familiar with calendrical astronomy and harmonics and engaged frequently in discussions of those subjects, which required certain computational skills. His numerological discussions also often used basic arithmetic operations and relations among simple integer numbers. He spoke of the numerical symbols used in everyday computations: "One vertical line is five. Draw one horizontal line below [it], then it is six. Draw two horizontal lines, then it is seven."[360] His discussions of rituals and music—descriptions of ceremonial vessels, costumes, and musical instruments—also contained numbers and computations. For example, in a brief essay on ceremonial vessels, he spoke of methods of computing their volumes, which included computing squares and square roots of numbers.[361]

To be sure, there were some key technical topics of mathematics that Chu Hsi knew fairly well. A good example was the "*kou-ku*" method concerning the relation among the three sides of a right triangle.[362] In his discussions of that method, frequently found in his letters to Ts'ai Yüan-ting, he spoke of its sources—the two ancient mathematical texts *Mathematical Classic on the Chou Gnomon* (Chou-pei suan-ching) and *Nine Chapters on Mathematical Techniques* (Chiu-chang suan-shu)—and differences between its various versions and even expressed his disagreement with Tsa'i Yüan-ting.[363] When someone asked why the length of the "*t'u-kuei*" gnomon should be eight feet, he readily responded: "This, one must compute using the *kou-ku* method."[364] For another example, Chu Hsi spoke of the nonary system of units of length, according to which 1 *ts'un* = 9 *fen* = 9 × 9 *li* = 9 × 9 × 9 *ssu* = . . . , and pointed out that in computations of harmonics, which involve frequent multiplications by ⅔ and ⅓, it is more convenient than the usual decimal system given in the *T'ung-tien*.[365] He also spoke of mathematical content found in the commentaries and subcommentaries to the classics, such as the *Record of Rites* and the *Rites of Chou*.[366]

But, as we have already noted, Chu Hsi did not value the computational skills of calendar or music specialists very highly. His mathematical knowledge on the whole did not reach the level of the specialists, who were called "computation specialists" (*suan-chia*). In his letter to Ts'ai Yüan, he expressed his judgment on the deficiency of his own knowledge in the following words:

> As for the writings of "mathematics" (*suan-hsueh*), I have not understood them so far. I shall just learn from a wise man [like you]. But [your teachings] should be brief and simple to be good [for me], [which] I hope you will bear in mind.[367]

Traditional Chinese knowledge about animal and plant species did not form a single tradition like that of natural history in the West. The literature covering such knowledge was found in various different genres representing distinct traditions. The genres included handbooks, dictionaries and encyclopedias, classified compendia, specialized monographs, and tractates, but above all, the uniquely Chinese genre of "materia medica" (*pen-ts'ao*).[368] Books on agriculture also contained information on agricultural plant species.[369]

Chu Hsi spoke of animals and plants in various different contexts also. Most often, however, what he said about them, sometimes fairly detailed descriptions, came up in his comments on the *Book of Poetry* and the *Songs of Ch'u*, which contained names of many animals and plants: his commentary on the latter book, *Ch'u-tz'u chi-chu*, for example, identified and described many of them. Animal and plant names appearing in other classics also provided occasions for him to speak of them.[370] In doing so, Chu Hsi of course could refer to the specialized literature—the *Shan-hai-ching*, for example.[371] Poems written by him contained names and descriptions of various plant species.[372] He also discussed plant species found in paintings.[373] It appears from these that Chu Hsi had a fair amount of detailed knowledge about animal and plant species, especially about plants. At times, he could offer criticism of inaccurate accounts in the specialized literature, for example, the *Shan-hai-ching* and T'ao Hung-ching's (456–536) *Pen-ts'ao-ching chi-chu* (Collected commentaries on the *Classic of Pen-ts'ao*), which were not based on actual observations.[374] He also noted frequently that some plant species recorded in ancient texts either were not found in his time or were different from the ones called by the same names.[375]

Yet, all this did not represent sustained interest on Chu Hsi's part in the specialized knowledge of the subject and thus did not add up to a comprehensive system of knowledge, either on his part or on the part of his followers. A good deal of his remarks about animals and plants formed part of the 138th *chüan* of his *Classified Conversations*, which collected, under the title "Miscellaneous Categories" (*tsa-lei*), various pieces of information, sometimes quite odd ones, on animals and plants, together with bits of information about books, words, characters, family names, geographical regions, and all kinds of strange things and events. Nor did Chu Hsi value the specialized knowledge on animals and plants very highly. While discussing the lichee plant, he said: "But as for the trivial things like these, it does no harm even if one does not know them."[376] He even characterized detailed plant knowledge as a "trivial branch" (*mo-liu*) of "the evidential research" (*k'ao-cheng*), which, for him, was already a "trivial branch" of learning.[377]

Agriculture was a subject to which Chu Hsi's official responsibilities at times required considerable attention. During his tenures as prefect at Nan-k'ang in 1179–1181 and at Chang-chou in 1190–1191, he wrote many public notices touching on agricultural affairs.[378] In particular, he wrote several "proclamations for encouraging agriculture" (*ch'üan-nung-wen*), which showed that he had some knowledge of agricultural practice in his time.[379] He began the first of those by saying that "having been in rural areas (literally, 'fields and gardens' [*t'ien-yüan*]) for a long time, I know about agricultural affairs well."[380] The items he specified in it covered key points on important agricultural tasks and topics—tilling, manuring, rice transplanting, weeding, alternative crops, irrigation, silks and hemps, and so forth. There is no evidence that he mastered detailed agricultural knowledge, however; apart from this sort of writing, he did not discuss agricultural topics in any detail.[381] He did say that "the basis of people's life lies in sufficient food; the basis of [providing] food lies in agriculture,"[382] but when he listed lowly subjects of "the small ways," he included agriculture among them, as we have already seen.

Chu Hsi had even less to say about the various crafts, which were also included in his list of "the small ways." He had the same characteristic attitude that he showed with regard to other specialized branches of knowledge, saying, for example: "Those who have accomplished refinement in the hundred crafts, skills, and arts also become refined [only] after [having become] familiar [with them]."[383] But he did not value specialized knowledge about them very much. The only exception would be his interest in and knowledge about astronomical models, the context of which has been discussed in section 12.2.

Notes

1. For a survey of literature on Chinese scientific and technical traditions, see Sivin, "Science and Medicine in Imperial China."

2. E.g., "Social Position of Scientific Men and Physicians in Medieval China."

3. E.g., YL49.2a3; SSCC (*Lun-yü*), 10.1b.

4. E.g., *YL*65.3a4; 67.14a1; *WC*71.8a; 81.11b.

5. For discussions on some of these spe-

cialist traditions in the Sung, see, e.g., Hartwell, "Financial Expertise, Examinations, and the Formulation of Economic Policy in Northern Sung"; McKnight, "Mandarins as Legal Experts."

6. Most of these specialized subjects are discussed together in Ch'ien Mu, *Chu-tzu hsin hsueh-an*, 5:296–409.

7. E.g., *YL*7.1a1, 1b4. Although the Chi-

nese character Chu Hsi used for the subject that I translate as "computation" was *shu*, it is unlikely that he was referring to the sort of numerological and divinatory skills mentioned earlier.

8. *YL*117.22b0.

9. *WC*69.21b. For a brief discussion of this essay, titled "Personal Proposal for Schools and Official Recruitment" (Hsueh-hsiao kung-chü ssu-i), see de Bary, "Chu Hsi's Aims as an Educator," pp. 206–209.

10. On Chu Hsi's ideas of the *ke-wu* doctrine, see chap. 2, sec. 2.2.

11. E.g., *YL*15.4b2; 18.22b0; 34.33b0; 116.13b0; 117.12b0.

12. *WC*60.16b.

13. *WC*60.17a.

14. *YL*117.22b0 (in the passage cited in note 8). See also the quotation cited in note 12. The expression "*po-hsueh*" appears, e.g., in the *Analects*, 12.5, 19.6; *Li-chi*, 53.2a.

15. E.g., *YL*15.4b2–5a0; *WC*47.13a.

16. E.g., *YL*44.19b0–21b2; *WC*47.13a. See also *YL*117.21a3, where Chu Hsi criticized those who "study down below today and wish to attain up above tomorrow." The Confucius quotation appears in the *Analects*, 14.37.

17. *YL*34.9b2. Here, Chu Hsi is interpreting "the arts" as the six basic skills mentioned above. The Confucius saying appears in the *Analects*, 7.6.

18. For this aspect of Chu Hsi's "program of learning" in general, see, e.g., de Bary, "Chu Hsi's Aims as an Educator"; Gardner, *Learning to Be a Sage*, pp. 35ff.

19. The content of the book is discussed in Needham, *Science and Civilisation*, 1: 136; Sivin, "Why the Scientific Revolution Did Not Take Place in China," p. 66; Fu, "Contextual and Taxonomic Study of the 'Divine Marvels' and 'Strange Occurrences' in the *Mengxi bitan*."

20. *WC*76.17b–19a. Chu Hsi's letters to Ts'ai Yüan-ting are compiled in *WC*44.1a–16b; *WCH*2.1a–3.6b.

21. *WC*83.21b–22a. For a brief account of this, see Hymes, "Not Quite Gentlemen," pp. 49–50.

22. For a general account of the Chinese civil service institutions, including the technical branches, see Chang, *Chung-kuo wen-kuan chih-tu shih*.

23. *WC*69.22a.

24. E.g., *YL*64.5b1; 84.3b0; 116.13b0; *CS*1.20a1. This is how Chu Hsi interpreted Mencius's remark "When one has first established oneself on what is great, then what is small cannot be taken away" (6A15); e.g., *YL*59.34a3; *WC*31.18a.

25. *YL*84.5a0. See also *YL*57.7a1, 84.3b0.

26. *WC*60.17a (in the letter cited in notes 12 and 13).

27. *YL*49.2a3.

28. *YL*117.22b0 (continuing the passage cited in note 8).

29. *YL*109.8b0. Chu Hsi's response to this was that one "should first order the examining officers to study them."

30. This reflects the common restorationist tendency of Neo-Confucian thought. See, e.g., de Bary, "Some Common Tendencies in Neo-Confucianism." Of course, Chu Hsi did not believe that everything was better in ancient times. In *YL*83.14a0, for example, he spoke of the ancient small bridges, which "were not as good as stone bridges and pontoon bridges" of his own time.

31. My article "Chu Hsi on Calendar Specialists and Their Knowledge" is an earlier version of parts of this section. For brief discussions of the significance of calendrical astronomy, see, e.g., Eberhard, "Political Function of Astronomy and Astronomers in Han China"; Nakayama, "Characteristics of Chinese Astrology." The straight astrological belief that celestial phenomena are connected with events in human society and thus that one can understand or predict the latter through study of the former does not seem to have played as great a role, especially in the post-T'ang times. Chu Hsi, for example, seldom discussed astrological practices. For a rare exception, see *YL*2.9a7, where he commented on various early astrological theories, including the

ancient *"fen-yeh"* (field allocation) theory. He concluded by saying that although there have been many efficacious astrological practitioners, he could not "understand" them. On the history of Chinese astrology in general, see Hashimoto, *Chūgoku sensei-jutsu no sekai.*

32. For a general discussion of Chinese calendrical astronomy and its historical development, see Yabuuchi, *Chūgoku no tenmonrekihō.* For a brief account of the astronomical institutions in Chinese bureaucracy, see Nakayama, *History of Japanese Astronomy,* chap. 3. Yamada, "Jujireki heno dō," contains a more detailed account for the Yüan dynasty.

33. Chu Hsi mentioned the calendrical treatises of *Shih-chi,* e.g., in *YL*2.11a2, 12b3; *Han-shu,* *YL*2.2a1, 2b0, 12b3; *Hou Han-shu,* *YL*2.2b0; *Chin-shu,* *YL*2.4b3, *WC*62.39a.

34. E.g., *YL*2.2a1, 2b0, 3a2, 6b3–7a0; 78.5a0, 5b3–6a0, 13b2.

35. E.g., *YL*2.2a0, 1; 2b0; 3b1; *WC*62.39a.

36. E.g., *YL*2.2a1, 7a3, 12a4; *WC*45.37b; *CS*50.4a0.

37. E.g., *WC*44.47b; *WCH*2.7a.

38. E.g., *YL*2.4b3, 10a2.

39. *YL*2.12b3.

40. E.g., *YL*2.12b3; 86.9a1, 10a0.

41. E.g., *YL*2.3b1–4b0; 11b1; 12a5; 12b2, 3; 86.9b0–10a0.

42. Chu Hsi's letters to the Ts'ais are collected in *WC*44.1a–16b; *WCH*2.1a–3.6b (Ts'ai Yüan-ting); *WCH*3.6b–10a (Ts'ai Yüan); *WCH*3.10a–11b (Ts'ai Ch'en).

43. E.g., *YL*2.2b0, 3b1. The subcommentary was by K'ung Ying-ta, and the relevant phrase appears in 14.3b. See chap. 9, p. 148, for Chu Hsi's explanation of why this had to be so.

44. *YL*2.3b1. Indeed, as a disciple said earlier in the passage, even Ts'ai Yüan held that heaven makes just one full rotation a day, which Chu Hsi rejected.

45. E.g., *YL*2.2b0, 3a2. The subcommentary was also by K'ung Ying-ta, and the relevant portions are in 3.6a–7a. See chap. 9, p. 150, for the translation of Wang Fan's "Hun-t'ien shuo."

46. *YL*2.7a0. In the text Chu Hsi actually said "the subcommentary on the Yao-tien," which obviously is a mistaken reference to "the subcommentary on the Shun-tien" (3.6b). See chap. 9, p. 149, for discussion of this passage. In the same passage, Chu Hsi also criticized the *Chou-pei suan-ching* for its explanation of the movements of the sun and the moon.

47. E.g., *YL*78.5b3–6a0, 13b2. The relevant portion of the subcommentary is 2.10b. In *YL*78.13b2 Chu Hsi split the difference between the solar year (365 + ¼ days) and the twelve lunar months (354+ days) into two parts—the *"shuo-k'ung"* (360 − 354+ days) and the *"yü-fen"* (365 ¼ − 360 days). Cf. note 78.

48. E.g., *YL*2.4b3; *WC*62.39a. In the former passage Chu Hsi said that much of the treatise, generally considered to have been written by Li Ch'un-feng (602–670), was written actually by Hsü Ching-tsung (fl. seventh century). Cf. Ho, *Astronomical Chapters of the Chin Shu,* p. 13.

49. *WC*62.39a.

50. *YL*2.2b0.

51. E.g., *YL*2.7a3; *CS*50.4a0.

52. E.g., *YL*2.4b3, 10a2.

53. E.g., *YL*2.12b3; 86.9b0–10a0.

54. *YL*2.12b3.

55. *YL*2.2b0.

56. E.g., *WC*44.47b; *WCH*2.7a–7b.

57. *WC*62.39a. The author's name and the date of this book are recorded in Wang Ying-lin (1223–1296), *K'un-hsueh chi-wen,* 9.12a.

58. *WCH*3.6b–7b.

59. *YL*2.12b2.

60. *WC*60.17a.

61. *WCH*2.2b. See also the same remark in *WCH*2.21a.

62. *YL*78.5b3–6a0.

63. *YL*78.5a0.

64. Many calendar specialists of the T'ang and the Sung times neglected actual observation and merely adjusted available astronomical constants and numbers. E.g., Yabuuchi, *Chūgoku no tenmonrekihō,* p. 142. For more on such lack of interest by

calendar specialists and on the development of this situation, see, e.g., Nakayama, *History of Japanese Astronomy*, pp. 40 ff.; Sivin, "Limits of Empirical Knowledge in the Traditional Chinese Sciences," esp. pp. 155–159; Henderson, *Development and Decline of Chinese Cosmology*, pp. 111 ff.

65. *YL*1.6a1. See also *YL*100.6a4.

66. *WC*62.39a.

67. *WC*72.1a.

68. *YL*2.12b3.

69. *YL*2.2bo.

70. The reference to the earth's ascending and descending movements appears in *Li-chi chu-shu*, p. 14.2b.

71. See also *YL*86.10bo: "Though I am not able to understand it, when calendar specialists made computations, the numbers all agreed. So there may be a *li* for this."

72. *YL*101.32a3. See also *YL*97.3b1: "Each of the degrees of the movements of the sun, the moon, and the stars has an accomplished theory, and cannot be concluded by talking."

73. See chap. 9, notes 138, 174.

74. For brief discussions of the actual problems of Chinese calendar making, including the ones mentioned in this paragraph, see Yabuuchi, *Chūgoku no tenmon-rekihō*, pt. 3.

75. On the ways the Chinese handled the problem, see ibid., p. 97, passim.

76. Of course, there was the additional problem, which could not have been known in traditional China, of having to employ uniform motions along geocentric circular orbits in treating what are actually non-uniform motions along the heliocentric elliptical orbits.

77. The recognition of such impossibility by calendar specialists and by some scholars ever since the Han times is documented briefly in Henderson, *Development and Decline of Chinese Cosmology*, pp. 110–117.

78. E.g., *YL*2.12a2, 3. Chu Hsi's praise of T'sai Ch'en appears in *YL*2.4bo, after the following long discussion by the latter of the basic points in the calendrical astronomy:

The sun lags behind heaven by 1 degree a day. Multiply this by $365 + {}^{235}\!/_{940}$ days; then it meets [the same position of] heaven. This is the number of the sun's movement for a year. The moon is even slower than the sun. It always lags behind heaven by $13 + {}^{7}\!/_{19}$ degrees per day. Multiply this by $29 + {}^{499}\!/_{940}$ days; then it meets the sun. Meeting [the sun] 12 times amounts to 348 full days plus 5,988 of the rest [i.e., $5,988 \times {}^{1}\!/_{940}$]. If one counts 940 [of the rest] as 1 day, then one gets 6 days and 348 of the rest. In sum, one gets $354 + {}^{348}\!/_{940}$ days. This is the number of the moon's movement for a year.

A year has 12 months; a month has 30 days. 360 days is the constant number for a year. Therefore, [the number of days between each] meeting of the sun and heaven is larger [than the 360-day year] by $5 + {}^{235}\!/_{940}$ days: It is called "*ch'i-ying.*" [The number of days between every 12] meetings of the moon and the sun is smaller [than the 360-day year] by $5 + {}^{592}\!/_{940}$ days. It is called "*shuo-hsü.*" Summing *ch'i-ying* and *shuo-hsü* produces the intercalation period (*jun*). Thus the intercalation rate (*jun-lü*) for a year is $10 + {}^{827}\!/_{940}$ days. [Place] 1 leap month for every 3 years; [then 1 leap month will have to account for 3 × the intercalation rate], $32 + {}^{601}\!/_{940}$ days; [place] another leap month for the fifth year; [then 2 leap months will have to account for 5 × the intercalation rate], $54 + {}^{375}\!/_{940}$ days. [Finally], 7 leap months for every 19 years would even up the *ch'i-shuo* [i.e., *ch'i-ying* plus *shuo-hsü*, the intercalation rate]. (*YL*2.4ao–4bo)

79. E.g., *YL*2.12a1, 4.

80. E.g., *YL*2.2ao; 86.9a1. Although *CS*50.24ao records the following "explicit" account of the "yearly deviation," it appears to have been written by T'eng Kung, Chu Hsi's disciple who compiled *Ching-chi wen-heng*, from which it was reproduced:

When the Yellow path [turns] one round, it lags behind, from where it has crossed [the Red Path] before, by $\frac{1}{60}$ degree. This is called the "yearly deviation." . . . Multiply [it] by

21,915 years; then the yearly deviation [be-comes] a full round. (A9.10a)

81. E.g., *YL*2.11a2–11b0, 12b4; 86.10a0.

82. See chap. 9, p. 151. It must have been for this reason that he said that "the calendrical numbers are 'fine and subtle' (*wei-miao*)." *YL*2.12b1.

83. *YL*57.13a0.

84. *YL*2.11b1.

85. E.g., *YL*2.11b1; 86.10a0.

86. *YL*86.9b0.

87. *YL*2.11b1. See also *YL*86.9b0–10a0.

88. *YL*86.9b0. In fact, there were extremely frequent changes of calendar in the Sung dynasty. Also, it is generally accepted that calendrical astronomy declined in the Sung, reaching its lowest point around Chu Hsi's time. See, e.g., Yabuuchi, *Chūgoku no tenmonrekihō*, pp. 106–108.

89. *YL*86.10a0.

90. *YL*86.9b0.

91. *YL*86.9a1.

92. *YL*73.3b1. See also *YL*73.3b2. In these passages Chu Hsi is discussing the *I-ching* phrase "The great man brightens the times by regulating the calendar" (*ke* hexagram).

93. E.g., *YL*2.12b1, 13a1; 23.2b0; *WC*44.47b; 60.17a. For a general account of astronomical models and instruments in traditional China, see Needham, *Science and Civilisation*, 3:284–390.

94. *WCH*3.7a–7b.

95. *WC*44.48a.

96. *WC*65.10a.

97. *Sung-shih*, ch. 48, p. 966.

98. *YL*23.2b0.

99. *WC*44.48a.

100. *WC*65.10a. The source of this long description of over four hundred characters cannot be known. If Chu Hsi did more than just copy it from other sources, it demonstrates that he knew quite a lot about the structures and workings of the armillary sphere.

101. E.g., *WC*44.47b, 48a; *WCH*2.7a–7b, 3.7b. In *WCH*3.7b he mentioned the

difficulty of finding a "wheel artisan" (*ch'e-chiang*).

102. For discussions of Su Sung's armillary sphere described in *Hsin i-hsiang fa-yao*, see Needham, Wang, and Price, *Heavenly Clockwork*; Needham, "Missing Link in Horological History," pp. 210–224; Needham, *Science and Civilisation*, 3:363–366. In Chinese, see Kuan, Yang, and Su, *Su Sung yü "Hsin i-hsiang fa-yao" yen-chiu*.

103. *WC*55.31a. See also *WC*44.48a.

104. *Sung-shih*, vol. 48, p. 966.

105. *WC*44.48a.

106. *WCH*2.2b, 21a (following the quotation cited in note 61). The phrase "yang-kuan fu-ch'a" was taken from "Hsi-tz'u chuan," ch. A4. For Chu Hsi's ideas about the concept "yen" ("verification," "test"), see chap. 14, note 60.

107. E.g., *YL*116.7b0, 8a0.

108. *YL*2.13a1. Actually, this is not the problem of the *Kai-t'ien* theory but that of the idea of "the circular heaven and the square earth." Such criticism of the latter idea is found in texts of earlier times, going as far back as the Han. E.g., *Ta Tai Li-chi*, ch. 58.

109. For brief accounts of the calendrical astronomy of the Sung times that adopted the rightward movement theory, see Yabuuchi, *Chūgoku no tenmonrekihō*, pp. 104–110; Yabuuchi, "Sō-gen jidai no tenmon-gaku."

110. *YL*2.5a2–5b0.

111. *YL*2.2a1.

112. *YL*2.3a1.

113. *YL*2.5a1.

114. *YL*2.2a0.

115. *YL*2.4b2. On these analogies, see chap. 13, p. 297.

116. It is not clear how well the calendar specialists of Chu Hsi's time understood this problem. But at least one Korean scholar-official of the early Chosŏn dynasty (early fifteenth century), who was well versed in calendrical astronomy, knew and resorted to the problem in his criticism of the leftward rotation theory of the conven-

tional Confucian scholars. Yi Sun-ji, *Chega Yŏksangjip*, 1.19b–20a.

117. *YL*2.4b3.

118. *YL*2.4b3.

119. *YL*2.4b2. See also *YL*2.5a1, where he added that he had heard from Ts'ai Yüan-ting that the "Chiu-chih" calendar used the "conformable" computation based on the leftward rotation theory.

120. *YL*2.4b2.

121. E.g., *YL*2.9a2; 57.12a1.

122. There existed a similar gap of interest between astronomers and philosophers of medieval Europe. But during the early stages of the European scientific revolution, it was the astronomers who contributed to the narrowing of that gap by becoming interested in cosmological discussions. See, e.g., Westman, "Astronomer's Role in the Sixteenth Century."

123. Chu Hsi also frequently spoke of *li* and *yüeh* together and discussed the relation between them. E.g., *YL*22.8a3–8b5, 10a3–11a1.

124. In *YL*92.1a3, for example, an interlocutor even said: "The music that Emperor T'ai-tsung (r. 626–649) of T'ang established and the music of our dynasty are all peaceful and harmonious. Therefore, the blessing of the age is long-lasting." Chu Hsi's response, which he said with a smile, was: "If argued in this way, then it [i.e., the cause of the long-lasting peace] would appear to exist in the music and not in the virtue."

125. In *YL*92.3a0; 8a1, 2, for example, Chu Hsi said that Emperors T'ai-tsu (r. 960–976), Jen-tsung (r. 1023–1064), and Hui-tsung (r. 1101–1126) had a great interest in music.

126. For discussions of traditional Chinese music and harmonics, see, e.g., Yang, *Chung-kuo yin-yüeh-shih*; Wu, *Lü-hsueh hui-t'ung*. For an English account, see Needham, *Science and Civilisation*, vol. 4, pt. 1, pp. 157–228; Chen, *Early Chinese Work in Natural Science*, chap. 2.

127. *WC*66.27b–36a.

128. *WC*72.1b–3a.

129. *WC*76.17b–19a.

130. Such discussions can be found in his letters, for example, to such scholars as Liao Te-ming (*WC*45.34b–37b), Chang I (*WC*58.2a–2b), Yü Fan (*WC*60.41b–42a), and Wu Yüan-shih (*WC*63.34a–37b).

131. E.g., *YL*92.2a2, 2a5–2b0.

132. *YL*92.2b0.

133. *YL*92.2b0. Chu Hsi referred to this whole process as "the method of mutual production" (*hsiang-sheng chih fa*) (*YL*92.2a5) or as "the way of mutual production" (*hsiang-sheng chih tao*) (*YL*92.2b0). Part of Chu Hsi's saying quoted here seems to have been derived from *Han-shu*: "[Huang-chung's role] is not performed again by other pitches" (ch. 21A, p. 962). Cf. *YL*92.10b0, where he actually refers to the *Han-shu* passage.

134. E.g., *YL*92.1b5; 2b0, 1; *WC*45.36b–37a, 58.2a.

135. *YL*35.24a0.

136. *YL*92.3a0.

137. E.g., *YL*35.23b1; 92.3a0, 10a2; *WC*45.36b–37a. In *YL*35.24a0, in response to someone who said that "the son sounds" did not exist in ancient times, Chu Hsi said, "If the son sounds had not been used, how could [they] have obtained harmony?" In *YL*92.3a0 Chu Hsi even spoke of "the sixteen," which include the twelve "correct pitches" plus "the four clear sounds."

138. In *YL*92.3a1, for example, he said that originally there were only the twelve pitches, to which the four clear sounds were added later. But in *YL*92.5a0 he said that the ancient music used "the four clear sounds mixed among the correct sounds."

139. *YL*35.23a0. See also *YL*92.3b1.

140. *YL*92.3b4–4a0. In *YL*92.8b2; *WC*44.15a, Chu Hsi spoke of the seven-note scale based on *kung* at *huang-chung* pitch, calling it "the *huang-chung* scale" (*huang-chung i-chün*). Cf. *Kuo-yü*, 3.15b.

141. *YL*92.3a0. See also *YL*92.1b4, 8b2.

142. *YL*25.24b0.

143. E.g., *YL*92.2a5, 2b1; 101.31b4.

144. *YL*92.2a5.

145. E.g., *YL*92.3bo; *WC*45.36a–37a, 63.34b–35a.

146. *WC*58.2a–2b. Chu Hsi may have been speaking of the same kind of diagram in *WC*45.37a, where he recommended that a disciple "draw a diagram and recite [what is drawn] in the mornings and evenings . . . [while] rotating it, holding it in the hand." Cf. *YL*92.6bo also, where he told disciples to draw a diagram with the five notes and the twelve pitches, saying: "One must [first] understand this. [Then] one can also discuss the others."

147. *YL*92.3ao. In the conversation Chu Hsi mistakenly assigned *shang* to *jui-pin* (7th) and not to *ta-lü* (2nd). See note 178.

148. E.g., *YL*92.4a1, 6a3; *WC*44.3b, 45.37a.

149. E.g., *YL*92.4a3; *WC*63.34b. In *YL*92.4a3–4bo Chu Hsi compared the production of "the sixty sounds"—"the five notes multiplying the twelve pitches"—to the production of the sixty stem-branch pairs, or "the sixty *chia-tzu*," discussed in chap. 5, sec. 5.4. In *YL*35.23b1 Chu Hsi even said, "Each [of the five] notes is divided further into twelve grades."

150. E.g., *YL*80.2a3, 3ao. For different kinds of tunes in traditional Chinese music, see, e.g., Yang, *Chung-kuo yin-yüeh-shih*, pp. 151–188, esp. the table on p. 183.

151. *YL*92.5bo. See also *YL*92.8a2.

152. E.g., *YL*92.5bo.

153. *YL*86.18b1. In *YL*92.5a1 a disciple even said: "The five notes are like renewals of the four seasons. One cannot do without [even a single] one [of them]." Cf. *YL*92.3b3, however, where he said that in banquets the *kung* note is not used.

154. E.g., *YL*92.5bo, 8a2. In *YL*92.8a2 he even spoke of a person who, ordered by Emperor Hui-tsung to compose a *chih*-tune, was not able to do it: the person was able to begin with a *chih* note but could not end with one.

155. E.g., *YL*86.18b1, 92.5ao. The relevant *Chou-li* passage appears on p. 22.17b.

156. E.g., *YL*80.2a3, 3ao; 92.10a1.

157. *YL*92.8a2.

158. E.g., *YL*35.24ao; 92.9b2, 11a6.

159. E.g., *YL*92.4b4–5ao, 6b1, 9b1.

160. E.g., *YL*92.5b2–6ao, 6b1–7ao, 8a3, 9b1, 9b2–10ao, 10a3–10bo. See also his preface to Ts'ai Yüan-ting's *Lü-lü hsin-shu*, reprinted in *WC*76.17b–19a,.

161. E.g., *YL*92.1b1, 11bo; *WC*66.27b.

162. *YL*92.10a2. Elsewhere, however, in *YL*92.1b1, 6b1, for example, he praised the treatises on "harmonics and calendar" (*lü-li*) and on "rituals and music" (*li-yüeh*) of *Han-shu*.

163. E.g., *YL*25.24a1–bo on the *Analects*, 3.23, and *YL*35.19b4–24a1 on the *Analects*, 8.8.

164. E.g., *YL*92.10bo on *Li-chi*, 37.5b; *YL*86.18b1; 92.3a3–3bo on *Chou-li*, 22.17b; *YL*92.4b3 on *Chou-li*, 41.9a; *YL*92.3b2, 4 on *Kuo-yü*, 3.15b; *YL*92.6a3 on *Tso-chuan*, 41.25b.

165. *YL*92.2a3. The relevant discussion of the subcommentary appears in *Li-chi chu-shu*, 22.6b–10a.

166. E.g., *YL*92.3b2; *WC*45.37a. The relevant passage of the commentary appears in *Kuo-yü*, 3.17b–18a.

167. E.g., *YL*92.1b1, 3ao, 6a4, 6b1, 7a1, 10a2, 11bo; *WC*45.36b.

168. E.g., *YL*92.6a4; *WC*45.36b. In *YL*92.6a4–6bo Chu Hsi added that although Lü Tsu-ch'ien (1137–1181) disliked the *Meng-hsi pi-t'an*, the dislike was directed actually against Shen Kua's personality and not against the quality of the book.

169. E.g., *YL*92.8a5, 6; 8b1; *WC*45.36a, 37a.

170. *YL*92.8b1.

171. E.g., *YL*92.8a5; *WC*76.18a. In *WC*76.18a Chu Hsi traced sources of key subjects discussed in the *Lü-lü hsin-shu* to various earlier works.

172. E.g., *YL*92.6a3, 4; *WC*45.37a.

173. In fact, he sometimes referred to the two groups with a single name, "harmonics–calendar specialists" (*lü-li-chia*); e.g., *YL*92.3ao.

174. E.g., *YL*92.5a1, 5bo, 8bo.

175. E.g., *WC*44.13b; 66.36a; *WCH*2.2b, 21a; 3.10a.

176. *WC*45.41b. Chu Hsi added, however, that he had too many things to do to find time for that.

177. E.g., 92.11a8, 11b1, on an official, Liu Chi; *YL*92.11b2 on a certain girl who had "an inborn ability to understand music and pitches." He even spoke of Liu Hsi-sou (1017–1060), who could predict from the court music that the reigning emperor would suffer from a mental illness. *YL*92.7b1–8ao.

178. E.g., in *YL*25.24bo; 35.23ao, where it was implied that the seventh of the twelve pitches was *ku-hsien*, whereas in fact it had to be *jui-pin*. In *YL*78.23b3; 92.3ao, mistakes were made in the assignments of the five notes to the twelve pitches: in the former, *t'ai-ts'ou* should be read as *nan-lü*, and in the latter, *jui-pin* should be read as *ta-lü*. In *YL*35.23b1 the length of the *wu-i* pitch, when the *huang-chung* is set at 9 inches, is given as 4.6 or 4.7 inches instead of 4.99 . . . inches. In *YL*92.2a5 it was said that all the *lü* (the yang pitches or the odd-numbered pitches) produced the *lü* (the yin or the even-numbered pitches) by downward production, whereas in fact it was so only for the first half of the sequence of production. In *YL*92.1b6 it was asserted that only five notes within one five-note scale can be used in music. Finally, we have already seen Chu Hsi's misleading remarks about each of the five notes "divided into twelve grades." *YL*35.23b1. See note 149.

179. E.g., *YL*92.6b1, 10a2.

180. E.g., *YL*92.1b1, 6a4, 6b1, 7a1. Chu Hsi had a low opinion of both scholars' knowledge of the subject. Of the two, Ssu-ma Kuang was considered even less well informed. E.g., *YL*92.1b1, 11a8–11bo. For the actual issue of the debate, see *YL*92.7b1.

181. E.g., *YL*92.9b1; 101.31b4, 32a1.

182. E.g., *YL*92.8b2; *WCH*3.10a.

183. *YL*92.7bo.

184. *YL*92.9ao. On Chu Hsi's own skill in lute playing, there have been conflicting accounts. Ch'ien Mu, for example, has emphasized that Chu Hsi was good at the lute. *Chu-tzu hsin hsueh-an*, 5:357–358. Ch'en Jung-chieh (Wing-tsit Chan), on the other hand, asserts that Chu Hsi was not good at it. *Chu-tzu hsin t'an-so*, p. 132.

185. *YL*92.8b2.

186. *YL*92.10b2–11ao. See also *WC*45.37a.

187. E.g., *YL*92.6b1; 8a3, 4; 10a2; *WCH*2.26a.

188. E.g., *YL*2.11b1; 92.7b1, 11a1. In *YL*2.11b1 he even said that the ancients' computation of "the bells and pitches . . . all had 'the determinate method.'"

189. E.g., *YL*25.24bo; 35.24ao; 92.5ao, 7b1, 11a1.

190. *YL*35.22bo.

191. *YL*92.9b2.

192. E.g., *YL*92.6a4, 6b1, 7a1, 7bo, 10a2.

193. E.g., *YL*92.7a1, 10a2.

194. *WC*76.17b.

195. The essay, titled "Discussion of the Nine Rivers and P'eng-li" (Chiu-chiang P'eng-li pien) and included in *WC*72.5a–11a, in time became something of a standard reference on the topic. The Ming scholar Chang Huang, for example, frequently referred to it in his own essay on the "Yü-kung" chapter. Reiter, "Change and Continuity in Historical Geography."

196. E.g., *WC*71.9b–10a, 11a–12a, 17a–18a, 18a–18b, 18b–19a; 76.26b–27a.

197. E.g., *WC*37.37b–38a; 38.40b–41a; 51.16b–17a; 52.4a.

198. E.g., *YL*2.13a3–16b6; 79.1a1–5a1; 86.7b2–9ao.

199. E.g., *YL*2.15b4, 5; 16ao; 79.5a1; *WC*38.40a, 40b, 42a–40b. In *YL*2.15b3, for example, he spoke of cutting paper in the shapes of prefectures (*chou*).

200. Lo, *Ho-lin yü-lu*, 3.5b. See Needham, *Science and Civilisation*, 3:579 ff., for a brief account of relief maps in China, including Chu Hsi's.

201. E.g., *YL*2.13a3; 79.1a1–5a1; *WC*37.37b–38a.

202. E.g., *YL*2.13a3; 86.7b2–9a0, 10h1–11a0. On the *t'u-kuei* method, see chap. 9, pp. 144–145.

203. E.g., *WC*51.16b; 71.9b, 18a, 19a.

204. E.g., *YL*79.4a2; 86.8a0; 138.1b5; *WC*71.18a–18b; *Ch'u-tz'u chi-chu*, 3.106.

205. E.g., *YL*2.13b0; 86.8b0.

206. E.g., *YL*79.5a1. Yü ching, the author of a famous treatise on the sea tides, can be added here because that subject was frequently classified as belonging to geography, as it was by the editors of Chu Hsi's *YL* and *CS*.

207. For historical surveys of Chinese geographical knowledge, see Needham, *Science and Civilisation*, 3:497–590; Wang, *Chung-kuo ti-li-hsueh-shih*.

208. When they spoke of particular locations of the earth's center, which can be obtained by the method of "*t'u-kuei*," as we have seen in chap. 9, they all fell within China.

209. It was thus that the geographical description of China, as the description of the world, came to have a degree of generality similar to that of the astronomical description of the heavens. For example, that the Yellow River makes a right-angle turn in the course of its flow (e.g., *YL*2.14b0, 2) seems to have held, to Chu Hsi, the same degree of generality as the fact that the full moon repeats itself at an interval of $29\frac{1}{2}$ days, an astronomical regularity.

210. E.g., *YL*2.15a0; 15b1, 2.

211. E.g., *YL*25.15b1, 2; 119.5b1; 138.4b3, 4; 4b5–5a0; 12b5.

212. E.g., *YL*2.14a8–14b0, 14b1.

213. For brief discussions of the "*feng-shui*" tradition, see the references in note 121 of chap. 9.

214. *WCP*3.4a.

215. *YL*138.10a3.

216. *YL*4.17b1.

217. *YL*114.13a0.

218. *WC*15.33a.

219. E.g., *YL*79.3a0; *Ch'u-tz'u chi-chu*, 7.312.

220. *YL*2.14a8–14b0.

221. *YL*79.4b1.

222. E.g., *YL*2.13a3; 79.3b2–4a0; 4a2; 4b0, 1; 83.28a2; *WC*72.10a.

223. *YL*83.28a2; *WC*72.10a.

224. E.g., *YL*79.3b2, 4a2, 4b0.

225. Chu Hsi's "Chiu-chiang P'eng-li pien" spoke of many such instances in discussing the locations of "the Nine Rivers." See also *YL*127.10b2.

226. *YL*2.16b0. On the change of the Yellow River's course, see also *YL*2.16a0.

227. *YL*79.3a1.

228. *YL*79.2b1.

229. E.g., *WC*51.17a; 71.18a; 72.8a.

230. *YL*79.4a0.

231. *YL*79.2b2. See also *WC*37.38a.

232. *WC*72.11a. This is in line with his emphasis on "verification" (*yen*) in general; cf. chap. 14, note 60.

233. *WC*38.41a. The *Yü-chi-t'u* is reproduced in Needham, *Science and Civilisation*, vol. 3, fig. 226.

234. Yang Hsiung's system based on the number three could ultimately be seen also as a variation of the binary system of the *I-ching*. Nylan and Sivin, "First Neo-Confucianism." Chu Hsi himself said:

> Yang Hsiung's *Ta-hsüan[-ching]* completely imitates the *I*[-*ching*]. What he used was the number three, while the *I* uses the number four. He basically imitated the *I*. Therefore, taking up the passages where he imitated [the *I*], one can see the *I*, and also can roughly see the *I*'s meaning. (*YL*65.13a2)

For Chu Hsi's other references to Yang Hsiung's system, see, e.g., *YL*65.7b2; 100.4a1. The *Lao-tzu* sequence of "one producing two, two producing three, and three producing the myriad things" (ch. 42) was also interpreted by Chu Hsi in terms of the yin-yang, and the even-odd, associations of the numbers two and one, respectively.

235. These charts are presented, along with other charts, in the appendix of Chu Hsi's *I-hsueh ch'i-meng* and are discussed in detail in the same book, ch. 1. The *Ho-t'u* and *Lo-shu* are discussed also in *YL*65.8a1–

9a5; *WC*37.36a; 38.1a–3a, 4b–5a; 44.7b–8a; 45.38a–38b; 84.3b–4a. See also *YL*65.9a2, where Chu Hsi asserted that "The *Ho-t'u* and the *Lo-shu* were just what heaven and earth drew up." For modern discussions of these charts, including their origins and developments, see Needham, *Science and Civilisation*, 3:56–69; Cam-man, "Magic Square of Three in Old Chinese Philosophy and Religion"; Saso, "What Is the *Ho-t'u*?"; Henderson, *Development and Decline of Chinese Cosmology*, pp. 82–86; Chang, "Analysis of Chu Hsi's System of *I*," pp. 301–305. Most of these references include the charts themselves. The *Hsien-t'ien-t'u* is discussed in the passages gathered in *YL*65.9b1–15a2. For more on these charts, see Phelan, "Neo-Confucian Cosmology." In *YL*87.10b4–11b0; *WC*68.11a–12a, Chu Hsi discussed the related diagram called "*ming-t'ang*." For the *ming-t'ang* diagram, see Henderson, *Development and Decline of Chinese Cosmology*, pp. 75–82.

236. Smith et al., *Sung Uses of I-ching*, pp. 110–122.

237. For opinions on Shao Yung held by contemporary and later thinkers, including Chu Hsi, see, e.g., Birdwhistell, *Transition to Neo-Confucianism*, chap. 9. For Chu Hsi's views in particular, see, e.g., Wyatt, "Chu Hsi's Critique of Shao Yung."

238. *YL*100.4b1–5a0.   See also *YL*100.4b0.

239. *YL*100.4b1.

240. *YL*100.4b1. See also *YL*4.19b1, where Chu Hsi criticized the shallow level of his contemporaries' discussion of Shao Yung's *shu*.

241. *YL*100.11a0. Chu Hsi went on to quote Ch'eng I's saying "Thunder comes from where it comes from," which had been given in response to Shao Yung's question "Where do you think [thunder] comes from?" *Ho-nan Ch'eng-shih i-shu*, ch. 21a (*ECC*, p. 270). Chu Hsi then added, "Why must one know where it comes from?"

242. *YL*100.4b1. See also *YL*4.19b1.

243. *YL*100.11a2. See also *YL*100.1b2, 2a1.

244. *YL*100.1b2.

245. *YL*100.2a1.

246. *YL*100.2b2. Here, Chu Hsi could have had the theory of cosmic cycles (*yün-hui*) in mind, which, as we have seen in chapter 9, sec. 9.1, he did not fully accept.

247. E.g.,   *YL*67.3b3;   100.11a2; *WC*81.11b. For brief discussions of Ch'en T'uan, see, e.g., Birdwhistell, *Transition to Neo-Confucianism*, pp. 207–209; Imai, *Sōdai Ekigaku no kenkyū*, pp. 192–201.

248. *YL*67.3b3.

249. E.g., *YL*65.13a2; 100.9a2.

250. E.g., *YL*65.13a2, 13b4; 100.9a2. In *YL*65.3a4 Chu Hsi seemed to believe that the learning of Ch'en T'uan and *Ts'an-t'ung-ch'i* went back to the same sources.

251. *YL*65.14a0.

252. *WC* contains many of Chu Hsi's separate essays on the subject; see, in particular, "I-hsiang shuo" (*WC*67.1a–2a) and "Ts'an-t'ung-ch'i shuo" (*WC*67.25a–26b).

253. Most of Chu Hsi's conversations on these subjects are gathered in *YL*65–77. His correspondence on the topics is scattered all over *WC*. *Wen-kung i-shuo*, compiled by Chu Chien, also contains Chu Hsi's sayings about the *I-ching* that are not included in *YL* or *WC*.

254. *YL*65.8a1.

255. *YL*66.20b3.

256. E.g., *YL*2.1a2, 1b1.

257. *CS*27.33b0.

258. E.g., *YL*66.19a1, 2.

259. E.g., *YL*2.13a2; 4.19b1.

260. *YL*100.11a2.

261. *YL*138.7a6.

262. E.g., *YL*65.13a2; *WC*81.11b.

263. E.g., *YL*66.19b0; *WC*67.1a–1b; *I-hsueh ch'i-meng*, preface.

264. E.g., *WC*37.32a–33b, 38.1a–19b, 44.1a–16b.

265. E.g., *WC*51.13a–13b, 20a–21b.

266. *YL*65.7a1.

267. E.g., *YL*66, passim; 67.5b3, 14a1; *WC*31.15a; 33.32a–32b; 38.21a. Thus, Chu

Hsi frequently noted the difference of the character of the *I-ching* from that of the other classics. For example:

[Whereas] the other classics first based [themselves] on the event and then had the writing [for it], . . . as for the *I-ching*, . . . while there had not yet been this event, it foretold this *li* beforehand. (*YL*66.10b2)

[When] the *I-ching* speaks of one thing, it is not truly the thing. For example, when it speaks of a dragon, it is not a true dragon. As for the other books, they are truly real facts. (*YL*67.13b1–14a0)

For a good discussion of Chu Hsi's thought about the *I-ching* and the divination based on it, see Smith et al., *Sung Uses of I-ching*, chap. 6 (written by Joseph A. Adler).

268. E.g., *YL*66.19b0; *WC*33.32a–32b; 38.21a.

269. *YL*67.5b3.

270. *WC*36.5b.

271. *YL*32.12a1.

272. *YL*66.5b0.

273. *SSCC* (*Chung-yung*), p. 17b. Here, Chu Hsi used the concept of "*chi*" to refer to the signs that enable man to have foreknowledge by allowing the *li* to be manifest beforehand. Cf. *CS*4.15a3: "When one knows the *li* before the event has arrived, it is called 'foreknowledge' (*yü*)." For more discussion on the concept of "*chi*," see chap. 13, p. 304.

274. *WC*33.32b. See also *WC*31.15a–15b. Joseph A. Adler has summed it up in the following apt words:

Divination was a valid practice for literati only when it was employed seriously in the process of self-cultivation. It could be used to acquire knowledge of the self and external events; it could be used to purify oneself spiritually by making critical self-judgments concerning one's ideas and intentions; and it could be used as a guide to moral practice. (Smith et al., *Sung Uses of I-ching*, pp. 202–203. See also pp. 188–189.)

275. Wang Mao-hung, *Chu-tzu nien-p'u*, p. 216. *YL*107.10b4–11a0 records a disciple's performing the *I-ching* divination in Chu Hsi's absence, but it is not clear whether it was approved by Chu Hsi. Cf. Ch'en, *Chu-tzu hsin t'an-so*, pp. 91–93.

276. Smith et al., *Sung Uses of I-ching*, p. 234. Adler adds, "A sage, of course, had no need for divination." Also: "While the sage does not need divination (since he already possesses the spiritual clarity of mind that makes possible knowledge of the future and perfect moral responsiveness), the ordinary person can make use of the *I*—and through it the sages—in his effort to achieve on his own the sagely capacity for moral responsiveness" (p. 194).

277. E.g., *YL*66.14b1, 16b1; *WC*37.33b; 38.2b, 6b; 44.8a, 12a, 13b, 17a; 45.1b; 60.15b–16a.

278. *WC*66.11b–27b.

279. It was outlined also in "I wu-chen" (*WC*85.6a–8b) and in an appendix to *Chou-i pen-i*. For an outline description in English, see Wilhelm, *The I Ching*, pp. 721–723.

280. E.g., *YL*65.6b2, 12a2–12b0; 68.12a2, 12a4–12b0, 12b1–13a0, 13a4–13b0; *WC*38.6b; 44.12a, 17a; 59.21b. These interpretation procedures were sometimes referred to as the theory of "seven (i.e., the young yang line), eight (young yin), nine (old yang) and six (old yin)." E.g., *WC*38.6b; 44.7b, 12a, 17a; 59.21b.

281. For various forms of divination in China, see, e.g., Needham, *Science and Civilisation*, 3:346–364; Smith, *Fortune-Tellers and Philosophers*, chaps. 5–6.

282. E.g., *YL*66.17a1, 2; 17b1, 2. In *YL*66.17a2 Chu Hsi spoke of the shapes of the cracks on the tortoise shell as corresponding to omens associated with the five phases: for example, "The Earth omen (*t'u-chao*) is greatly horizontal; the Wood omen is straight."

283. *YL*4.21b0. Chu Hsi even used the expression "the method of physiognomy" (*hsiang-fa*) in referring to his preference for "hard-looking and lean man." *YL*121.8a1.

284. E.g., *WC*75.3b–4b, 12a–12b, 16a–16b.

285. *WC*75.4a.

286. E.g., *YL*138.7a1; 10a1, 2; 11a1.

287. *WC*75.4a.

288. *YL*100.11a0.

289. For a brief account of the *Ts'an-t'ung-ch'i*, see Needham, *Science and Civilisation*, vol. 5, pt. 3, pp. 50–75, which is largely based upon the translation by Wu Lu-ch'iang, "Ancient Chinese Treatise on Alchemy Entitled 'Ts'an T'ung Ch'i.'" See also Nathan Sivin's account in Needham, *Science and Civilisation*, vol. 5, pt. 4, pp. 248–279. For a more recent English translation, see Zhou, *The Kinship of the Three*. For a Japanese translation and commentary, see Suzuki, *Shueki sandōkei*. For traditional Chinese alchemy in general, see Needham, *Science and Civilisation*, vol. 5, pts. 3, 4; Chao, *Chung-kuo lien-tan-shu*.

290. E.g., *YL*65.3a4, 13a2, 13b4; 100.9a2; 107.11a2; 125.12a2–13a1; *WC*38.19a; 44.16a; 67.25a–26b.

291. For a brief discussion of the content and context of the *Ts'an-t'ung-ch'i k'ao-i*, see Azuma, "Shu Ki 'Shueki sandōkei kōi' ni tsuite." My own work on it, in collaboration with Dong Won Shin, is in progress.

292. E.g., *YL*125.12a2, 13a1; *WC*38.19a; *Ts'an-t'ung-ch'i k'ao-i*, p. 1b.

293. E.g., *Ts'an-t'ung-ch'i k'ao-i*, pp. 4a, 10b, 14b.

294. *YL*125.13a1.

295. *WC*84.26b. See also *YL*125.12b1.

296. *Ts'an-t'ung-ch'i k'ao-i*, p. 9a.

297. *YL*107.11a2.

298. *WC*67.26a.

299. *WC*38.19a; *Ts'an-t'ung-ch'i k'ao-i*, p. 1b. The *na-chia* method refers to the scheme of associating the *I-ching* diagrams with such things as the ten stems and the twelve branches, the twelve months, the five phases, and so forth. For a brief discussion, see Lo, *Chung-kuo che-hsueh ssu-hsiang-shih, Liang-Han Nan-pei-ch'ao p'ien*, pp. 481–488.

300. *Ts'an-t'ung-ch'i k'ao-i*, pp. 12a–12b.

301. *YL*125.12b1, which is appended to *Ts'an-t'ung-ch'i k'ao-i*, pp. 10b–11a.

302. *WC*67.25b.

303. *WC*81.11b.

304. For the circumstances surrounding Chu Hsi's choice of this pseudonym, see, e.g., Azuma, "Shu Ki 'Shueki sandōkei kōi' ni tsuite," p. 178.

305. Sivin's characterization of "internal alchemy" in "Chinese Alchemy and the Manipulation of Time" continues: "This 'internal' (*nei*) form and 'external' (*wai*) alchemy were so closely complementary, and were so regularly practiced in conjunction before the eleventh century (when external alchemy began to die out), that it is often impossible to distinguish which sort of operation a text is concerned with. Their theoretical basis was largely identical" (p. 514 n. 2).

306. See, e.g., Ch'en Kuo-fu, "Shuo Chou-i Ts'an-t'ung-ch'i yü nei-tan wai-tan."

307. *YL*113.7a1. See also *YL*8.11a1, 9.6b1.

308. For some recent discussions of theories and techniques of "nourishing life," see the references cited in chap. 11, note 1.

309. E.g., *YL*113.7a1; 125.13b1; *WC*51.27a; *WCH*8.2b.

310. *WC*85.6a.

311. *WCP*4.13b.

312. *WC*51.27a. To "look at the end of the nose" was, according to Chu Hsi, a method to provide the mind with something to depend on when it has eliminated thought entirely. See, e.g., *YL*120.3b2–4a0. The position "below the navel and the belly," called "true origin" (*chen-yüan*) or "*tan-t'ien*," (literally, "the elixir field"), is supposed to be the source from which man's *ch'i* originates. See, e.g., Miura, "Shushi to kokyū."

313. *WCH*8.2b.

314. *WCH*6.1b. It is not difficult to imagine how such beliefs could have been possible for Chu Hsi, for he accepted the interaction between the mind and *ch'i*. What is difficult to understand is that he seemed to

separate the breathing and the meditating techniques, although he frequently mentioned them together. For example, he did not seem to accept the view, which he called "the theory of earlier people," that "when one holds the *ch'i* and reduces breathing, [then] thoughts naturally decrease." *YL*125.13b1. He followed Ch'eng I in rejecting the saying of Lü Ta-lin (1046–1092) that "nourishing the *ch'i* can be of help for nourishing the mind." *YL*97.5b1, 2.

315. *YL*107.16b4.

316. *YL*125.11a0.

317. *YL*87.27a0 (immediately after the quoted portion of the same passage cited in chap. 11, note 244).

318. E.g., *YL*125.13a2, 16a1.

319. E.g., *YL*63.20b0–21a0; 125.13a2–13b0, 16a1. See chap. 6, p. 98.

320. E.g., *YL*63.21a0; 125.13b0. For the stories of Lü Tung-pin, see, e.g., Baldrian-Hussein, "Lü Tung-pin in Northern Sung Literature."

321. See, e.g., Azuma, "Shu Ki 'Shueki sandōkei kōi' ni tsuite."

322. *YL*125.11a0. The expression "frames" (*ch'eng-kuo*) appears in the *Ts'an-t'ung-ch'i. Ts'an-t'ung-ch'i kao-i*, p. 17b.

323. E.g., *YL*16.3a0; 125.2b3, 14b5.

324. *YL*126.6a1.

325. E.g., *YL*87.27a0; 125.11a0, 13b2. The *Ts'an-t'ung-ch'i k'ao-i* also contains numerous quotations from the *Lao-tzu*.

326. E.g., *YL*125.9b0; 126.5b4. On the origin and the meanings of the term "*hsing-ming*," see, e.g., Creel, "The Meaning of *Hsing-ming*."

327. E.g., *WC*82.18a.

328. *YL*125.9b0. His commentary on it is titled *Yin-fu-ching k'ao-i*.

329. E.g., *YL*126.6b4.

330. *YL*125.9b0.

331. *YL*126.5b4.

332. *YL*125.5a2. On the "*wu-lei-fa*," see Skar, "Ethical Aspects of Daoist Healing."

333. *YL*126.2b0.

334. E.g., *YL*125.14b5; 126.6b4.

335. *YL*126.6b4. It is not clear which of the many *tan* texts Chu Hsi meant by "*Tan-*

ching" here, although it is likely to have been *Huang-ti chiu-ting shen tan-ching*.

336. *YL*87.27a0.

337. The *WC* contains seven letters that Chu Hsi wrote to Ts'eng Chi (*WC*61.33a–36a) and fifteen to Fang I (*WC*56.9a–22a). Cf. Azuma, "Shu Ki 'Shueki sandōkei kōi' ni tsuite," p. 188.

338. *WC*63.9b; 76.14b; 83.24a–24b; *WCP*7.2b. For more on Chu Hsi's relationship with Taoist masters, see Ch'en, *Chu-tzu hsin t'an-so*, pp. 605–607. Ch'en considers Wu Hsiung as the only person among Chu Hsi's disciples who can be identified as a Taoist master. Cf. Ch'en, *Chu-tzu men-jen*, p. 99.

339. To be sure, divination (which applied "images and numbers") was among the subjects that Chu Hsi enumerated as examples of "the small ways," and he may have felt the same about "*feng-shui*" (applied geography) and alchemy (applied "images and numbers"), although he did not say so explicitly. But the subjects of geography and "images and numbers" themselves did not belong to "the small ways."

340. *SSCC* (*Lun-yü*), 7.6a–6b. In the *Analects* passage, the remark is attributed to "the southerners" and is praised by Confucius.

341. See p. 246.

342. Hymes, "Not Quite Gentlemen," esp. pp. 48–49. For Hymes it was another piece of evidence supporting his general conclusion that, whereas in Sung times there was a disagreement "as to the social acceptability of medical practice, particularly as a career for gentlemen," there also was "a rather broad acceptance of medicine as a respectable field of knowledge [for scholars], especially as manifested in texts" (p. 47). Chu Hsi's remark that "it is not harmful to study medication recipes when there is nothing to do" (*YL*107.16b4), clearly illustrates this attitude.

343. For a good introduction to traditional Chinese medical knowledge, see Sivin, *Traditional Medicine in Contemporary China*. For a theoretical analysis from

a modern perspective, see Porkert, *Theoretical Foundations of Chinese Medicine*. For historical surveys, see, e.g., Unschuld, *Medicine in China*; and in Chinese, Ma Po-ying, *Chung-wai i-hsueh-shih chiang-i*, vol. 1. For a brief account of Chinese medicine in the Sung-Yüan times, see Miyashita, "Sō-gen no i-ryō."

344. *YL*138.7a8. See also *YL*23.15a1: "The medical specialists say that the will belongs to the kidneys."

345. *CS*47.12a2–12b0. See also *WC*58.1a. In *WC*43.26b he spoke of the medical specialists' references to "the paralysis of hands and feet."

346. *YL*105.2b2.

347. *WCH*3.9b.

348. *YL*138.1b6.

349. *WCH*3.9a.

350. Ts'ai Ch'en, "Meng-tsun-chi," quoted in Miura, *Shushi*, p. 261.

351. *WCH*8.4b.

352. *YL*138.7a7. The prescription reads, "The eyeballs of the tiger settle the *p'o*; the teeth of the dragon stabilize the *hun*." I have not succeeded in identifying the "Mr. Hsü." It is possible that Chu Hsi may be speaking of Hsü Shu-wei (fl. 1132), who wrote many medical books.

353. *WC*76.2b. I have been unable to identify the "Mr. Hsia," though he could be the Sung medical author Hsia Te, who wrote *Wei-sheng shih-ch'üan fang*.

354. *WC*83.21b–22b.

355. *WC*76.2b.

356. *WC*83.21b–22a.

357. *WC*83.22a.

358. *WC*83.22a–22b. See also *YL*138.7a8, where, after pointing out that Shao Yung's theory was different from the above-mentioned associations of medical specialists involving the storing viscera, he said that "this is not possible to understand."

359. In *YL*14.10a2 Chu Hsi said that computation, which had been considered "the most trivial" among the six arts, "is still very useful."

360. E.g., *YL*100.4b0. For the Chinese

numerical symbols, see Needham, *Science and Civilisation*, 3:5–17.

361. The essay is titled "Hu shuo" (Explanation of sacrificial wine vessel) and appears in *WC*68.4b–5b.

362. For a brief discussion of this method, which has often been compared to the Pythagorean theorem, see Needham, *Science and Civilisation*, 3:22 ff. For general surveys of traditional Chinese mathematics, see, e.g., Needham, *Science and Civilisation*, 3:1–150; Martzloff, *History of Chinese Mathematics*; Yabuuchi, *Chūgoku no sugaku*. For a more detailed study on an important mathematical text of the late Sung, see Libbrecht, *Chinese Mathematics in the Thirteenth Century*.

363. E.g., *YL*86.10b1; *WCH*2.4b, 5b, 12a.

364. *YL*86.10b1.

365. E.g., *YL*92.1b1, 6a4, 10a2. Various units of measure often appeared in Chu Hsi's use of numbers and computations. We have seen, for example, that his discussions of music and harmonics frequently included units and standards of length; he even considered the pitch pipe as part of the system of weights and measures. Units of measure came up frequently also in his writings dealing with financial and tax problems. E.g., *WC*20.19a; 24.8a; *WCP*10.1a–2b, 17a–19a.

366. E.g., *WC*68.4b, which quotes and discusses the *Li-chi* subcommentary (58.16b–17b), and *WCH*2.12a, which refers to the *Chou-li* commentary (14.7a).

367. *WCH*3.10a.

368. For these various genres, see, e.g., the botanical section (sec. 38) of Needham, *Science and Civilisation*, vol. 6, pt. 1, esp. pp. 182–471. See also Unschuld, 'Pen Ts'ao.' Needham's zoological section has not been published yet. On compilers of the encyclopedias in the Sung, including their relation with the Neo-Confucian scholars, see, e.g., Tillman, "Encyclopedias, Polymaths, and *Tao-hsueh* Confucians."

369. On traditional Chinese agriculture, see Needham, *Science and Civilisation*, vol. 6, pt. 2, written by Francesca Bray.

370. In *YL*61.16a1, for example, Men-

cius's remark "Tseng Hsi liked jujubes" (7B36) led Chu Hsi to discuss jujubes. Indeed, identifying and describing the species whose names appear in these ancient books, the *Shih-ching* in particular, had become an established branch of specialized knowledge for scholars to be engaged in. E.g., Needham, *Science and Civilisation*, vol. 6, pt. 1, pp. 463 ff. See chap. 10, p. 190.

371. E.g., *YL*138.1b5; *WC*71.18b; *Ch'u-tz'u chi-chu*, pp. 1.37; 3.110, 111.

372. See especially the series of poems devoted to plants and flowers, e.g., in *WC*1.23a–23b, 3.4b–5b, 9.10a.

373. E.g., *YL*138.8b5, 9a1,

374. E.g., *YL*138.1b5, 15a3; *WC*71.18b.

375. E.g., *YL*138.8b1, 14a5–14b0; *WC*59.24a–24b.

376. *YL*138.14a1.

377. *WC*59.24b.

378. E.g., *WC*99.6b–8a, 8a–9a, 9a, 9a–10b, 11b–12b, 12b, 12b–13a; 100.9a–11b; *WCP*9.2a–2b, 2b–3a. For Chu Hsi's career as a local administrator, see, e.g., Schirokauer, "Chu Hsi as an Administrator."

379. Four "proclamations for encouraging agriculture" are found in *WC*99.6b–8a (dated 1179), 8a–9a (dated 1181); 100.9a (dated 1192, but must have been written earlier); *WCP*9.2b–3a (dated 1181). Chu Hsi's and other Sung "proclamations for encouraging agriculture" are discussed briefly in Sudō, *Sōdai keizaishi kenkyū*, pp. 45–48.

380. *WC*99.6b. See also *WC*99.8b.

381. In a poem recorded in *WC*7.11a, which he wrote for his friend Ch'en Sheng-ssu, Chu Hsi spoke of his wish to "spend nights studying [the latter's] agricultural books." But those books could not be identified in any list of Sung agricultural treatises.

382. *WC*99.8a.

383. *YL*118.13b0.

Comparison with the
Western Scientific Tradition

So far in my discussion of Chu Hsi's understanding of the natural world, I have tried to adopt his perspective. I have focused upon what Chu Hsi himself knew, thought, believed, spoke of, and questioned. I have emphasized what Chu Hsi himself was interested in and considered to be important and basic. This chapter looks at the subject from a different, and to a large degree comparative, viewpoint. I discuss what Chu Hsi thought about those ideas that were considered important by the Western scientific tradition and by modern science: matter and material qualities, motion and change, and so on. In doing so, I allow myself to make comparisons—sometimes quite speculative ones—between Chu Hsi's ideas and those of his Western counterparts; I also comment quite frequently on what Chu Hsi did not do that westerners did. Of course, this approach has its dangers, especially that of distorting the context of Chu Hsi's views. But I believe it can enhance our understanding of how his thought differed from ours, and if that objective can be achieved with minimum distortion, it will keep us from imposing our own standards upon him and will help us better understand his thought in its own context.

Chu Hsi did speak of such concepts as matter, motion, and change, but in ways vastly different from those of the West. Not only were the contents of the concepts different, but so also were the contexts in which they came up in his discussion. Nor were they among the concepts that Chu Hsi considered basic and important. This chapter thus deals both with the contents of Chu Hsi's ideas and with the contexts in which he considered them; comparisons with the West are made with respect to both aspects.[1]

13.1. Matter and Material Qualities

The basis of Chu Hsi's ideas about matter is that all material substances are made of *ch'i*. They are produced as the formless *ch'i* aggregates to acquire physical forms and tangible qualities; various substances differ from one another only in the manner of their aggregation. Thus, my discussions on *ch'i* in chapter 3 and on actual material substances in chapter 10 have already touched upon various aspects of Chu Hsi's views about matter and material qualities. Yet, he did not say much about details, and it is not possible to construct from his remarks a coherent theory of matter, of the sort found in the Western scientific tradition.

For instance, although some of Chu Hsi's remarks implied that *ch'i* is very minute, so minute that it can "permeate even gold and stone,"[2] he did not enter into discussions of its actual size or of whether the basic ingredients of matter are particulate or continuous.[3] And though the names of the five phases are those of five of the most common material substances, they were not "elements" in the sense of being the basic ingredients constituting all material substances. Indeed, this notion does not seem to have occurred to Chu Hsi. He mentioned "the four elements" (*ssu-ta*, literally "the four greats") of the Buddhists—earth (*ti*), water (*shui*), fire (*huo*), and wind (*feng*)—but does not seem to have been interested in relating them to, or comparing them with, the five phases.[4] Nor did his realization that "although between heaven and earth . . . there is nothing that does not have these five [i.e., the *ch'i* of the five phases], there are [differences of] larger and smaller proportions among them"[5] lead him to consider the general problem of the composition of compound substances.

We have seen that Chu Hsi considered material qualities and tendencies to be innate in the actual material substances and in the *ch'i* that constitutes them. Thus, they were simply accepted by him, without any need to explain in terms of external causes or hidden mechanisms. A good set of examples were those qualities that are the objects of sense perception: light, color, sound, taste, and smell. As we have already noted in chapter 10, all these sensible qualities were viewed by Chu Hsi as innate in material substances and *ch'i* and were casually accepted rather than investigated or analyzed. For example, he attributed the qualities of light directly to the "light-*ch'i*" and did not try to explain them. Although he spoke of motions of light, or light-*ch'i*, he was not concerned with the details of such motions.[6] Thus, while explaining colors of the rainbow in terms of the splitting of the sun's light-*ch'i* by thin rain drops, he did not go into detail about the mechanism of the production of colors and the eye's perception of them.[7]

In this connection, it should be noted that, in speaking of sensible material qualities, Chu Hsi's interest frequently lay elsewhere and not in the phenomena involving the qualities themselves. For example, the characters *ming* (bright) and *an* (dark) did not simply refer to the intensity of light but often had metaphysical connotations as well and were sometimes involved in quite ambiguous discussions of uncertain meaning.[8] We have seen many other examples. In his discussion of the production of "the five intermediary colors" by mixing "the five regular colors," his interest was not in the actual processes of mixing and producing colors but in the kinds and classifications of colors to be used for gentlemen's clothes.[9] Much of Chu Hsi's discussion of sound also arose not out of interest in sound itself but from the importance of music as part of the Confucian rituals. Even in discussing music, various associative schemes of the five notes, *kung* with rulers and *shang* with ministers, for example, were used, usually in contexts unrelated to music and acoustics.[10] Other material qualities and tendencies were also employed by Chu Hsi mainly for analogies in discussing moral and philosophical problems, of which we saw many examples in chapter 10. For a fresh example, there was the following set of analogical comparisons: "[Man's] mind is like water, nature is like the stillness of water, feelings are the flow of water, and desires are waves of water."[11]

13.2. Motion

For Chu Hsi, the world is in constant motion: "Looking at the motion of heaven and earth, day and night, cold and hot weather, there is not a moment of rest."[12] We have seen that movement and rest constitute a most important pair of characteristics of *ch'i*; indeed, they were among the most typical yin-yang pairs and were sometimes substituted for yin and yang themselves.[13]

Since such an importance was accorded to the concept of motion, it is to be expected that Chu Hsi made frequent remarks about it. But movement was an innate tendency of *ch'i*, and there was no need to seek external causes for movements of *ch'i* or of things in general, all of which were made of *ch'i*. Chu Hsi almost always took phenomena of motion for granted, hardly ever getting into details.[14] Thus, although he mentioned many phenomena involving motion, which, if analyzed, may yield what can be regarded as basic principles of motion, he never went on to make such an analysis. Nor did he cast his discussions in general forms; they always turned on particular facts about particular phenomena. Ideas similar to some of the basic general principles in the Western tradition of studies of motion did come up in his discussion of particular phenomena. But his understanding and acceptance of those phenomena did not imply any general understanding of the basic principles embodied therein.[15]

Take the idea of inertia, for example. Chu Hsi frequently said that pushing a cart requires exertion of force at the beginning to start the motion, but that once the motion has started, force is no longer needed because it keeps moving of itself.[16] Of course, it cannot be denied that he was speaking of the tendency of a cart to continue in motion once it has started to move. He noted the same tendency in the movement of waterwheels and boats[17] and even said that a waterwheel once in motion is difficult to stop.[18] But he did not go on to infer a general notion of inertia applicable to all motion; instead, he seemed to regard the tendency to be particular to these vehicles and machines.

Ideas similar to that of the relativity of motion turned up in a similar way, though in somewhat more general terms. Chu Hsi noted, for example, that when two wheels rotate around an axis in the same direction, the one rotating more slowly can be viewed as rotating in the opposite direction.[19] He compared the situation to the case of three persons running around a circle on the ground; the slower ones may appear as if they were running in the opposite direction.[20] He mentioned these examples to illustrate motions of the sun, the moon, and the five stars: all rotate along with heaven in the same direction though at different speeds.[21] But again, Chu Hsi did not abstract from these examples a general understanding of the relativity of motion that he could then use in discussing the motions of the luminaries. He did discern the resemblance of the phenomena but never came up with the idea of relativity in general terms. Thus, although he mentioned the common experience of a man on a boat that "while a boat without a boatman may drift to east and west, no one on the boat knows it,"[22] the very experience that men like Galileo used in explaining why man on earth does not feel its motion, it did not lead Chu Hsi to come up with the general idea that a man on a moving body does not perceive its motion, that is, the relativity of motion.[23]

This situation is easy to understand if we remind ourselves that in many cases when Chu Hsi spoke of phenomena involving motion, he was not interested in the phenomena themselves but used them as familiar and obvious facts in analogies in which less obvious problems were compared to them.[24] Thus, in the example of the cart, his interest was not in the general tendency of motion to continue but in showing that study requires a strong exertion of effort only at the beginning, after which it is easy to continue.[25] Similarly, he spoke of a man on a drifting boat not to discuss the relativity of motion but to illustrate the mental state of a man whose mind is not firmly placed within himself.[26] Indeed, in most of Chu Hsi's discussion of "movement" and "rest," what the words actually referred to was the state of man's mind rather than the motion (or lack of motion) of a physical object.[27]

Chu Hsi's perspective is in sharp contrast with that of his European counterparts, the medieval scholastics.[28] The latter started from basic principles, for example that every motion needs a constant action by an external mover. When a common empirical fact, for example that a thrown body continues in motion after being thrown, stood in conflict with the principle, the scholastics took that particular fact as a troublesome problem difficult to understand in terms of the general principle. But the fact could not, by the contradiction alone, lead to a rejection of the principle. The general principle prevailed; it was the particular fact that became the target of continuous efforts for explanation, as is very well illustrated by the long history in the West of the problem of "mover." When the principle was finally overthrown, it was by the emergence and acceptance of a new general principle, namely the principle of inertia, and not by particular empirical facts.[29] Thus, all along in the Western tradition of studies of motion, it was general principles that took precedence; particular facts were subject to explanation in terms of general principles.

With Chu Hsi, it was almost the opposite. Particular empirical facts were accepted: there was no search for basic general principles embodied in the facts, which he accepted in their entirety without any detailed analysis. For example, that a cart — or a boat, or a waterwheel — once moved keeps moving without much additional exertion of force was accepted by Chu Hsi; but that this implies a general principle that every motion has a tendency to continue did not matter to him and perhaps did not occur to him. It was natural, then, that he should not be interested in a general and fundamental examination of the principles of motion, without which there could be no coherent system of knowledge about motion that rested on basic principles. Thus, whereas in the West the notions of inertia and of relativity of motion in combination helped to produce a revolutionary transformation in the ideas about motion, and eventually a new system of knowledge called "classical mechanics," in Chu Hsi's case accepting and understanding the facts embodying the same basic notions did not carry him beyond the particular facts themselves.[30]

The way Chu Hsi dealt with a few problems and phenomena related to the idea of weight illustrates that particularistic character very well. He noted that water tends to move downward, whereas warm air and smoke move upward.[31] This is similar to the views of the medieval scholastics: whether an object falls or rises is determined by what material substance it is made of; to fall or to rise is the "nature" of the material itself. But Chu Hsi's was not a general idea applicable to all heavy and light objects. To flow downward, for him, was an innate tendency of a particular substance, water, not of all heavy objects. It is even unclear whether he realized that the downward flow of water is a particular case of the falling of heavy objects. Similarly, although he noted that the *ch'i* above a fire stove rises,[32] this does not mean that he had the general idea that light things tend to rise or that warm things are lighter. He was merely speaking of an innate tendency of a particular substance, fire.

Furthermore, for the medieval scholastics, the falling of heavy objects and the rising of light objects were tied with their conceptions of the structure of the world: heavy things fall down as they tend to their natural place, the center of the earth, which for the scholastics was the center of the world.[33] Thus, the problem of the weight of the earth, that is, the cause of the stability of the heavy earth in the middle of the sky, never arose. The concept of weight was built into the world picture itself. The earth, made of the heaviest of the four elements, lies at its natural place, the center of the world, and thus does not move. But Chu Hsi, for whom the problem of weight was separate from that of the structure of the world, had to deal with the problem of the earth's weight. Whereas the scholastics' world picture included the particular empirical fact of weight as an integral part of it, Chu Hsi's had to take account of the notion of weight as an additional and independent fact. To his mind, the fact that certain heavy things tend downward was independent of another particular empirical fact, the structure of heaven and earth.

Chu Hsi did have certain general things to say about motion. For example, he seemed to think that variations in motion, rather than uniform motions, are natural and to be expected: "The sun, the moon, and the stars . . . are all moving things. Their degrees of movement and speed are sometimes more and sometimes less; they naturally are not uniform."[34] On the shape of moving objects, he observed that circular things tend to move easily because they can roll around whereas square ones are difficult to move.[35] He also seemed to separate the motion of the water itself from the wave motion: "The later water is not the earlier water. The later wave is not the earlier wave. Nevertheless, they can be [considered] together [as] a single water wave."[36]

In his frequent comparisons of the rotations of heaven and the luminaries with those of waterwheels and millstones,[37] Chu Hsi had occasion to observe certain general points concerning rotation. For example, he noted that the central point of a rotating waterwheel or a millstone does not change its location, to show that the center of rotation does not move during rotation.[38] But there can be only one such point: however close a point may be to the center, if it is not exactly at the center, it moves, though by an imperceptible degree.[39] Thus, he rejected Hu Hung's theory that there are three pole stars by saying that "if [there are] three points that do not move, then it is not possible [for heaven] to rotate."[40]

Chu Hsi even spoke of what we would call a "centrifugal" tendency, that is, the tendency of a rotating body to move away from the center. He noted that water in a revolving vessel does not spill even when the vessel is upside down.[41] But the way he used this tendency illustrates how, in the absence of general basic principles, he was ready to resort to casual, and often misplaced, analogies. For he mentioned this tendency in order to illustrate the power of the rapidly rotating *ch'i* of heaven that keeps the heavy earth from falling down.[42] This power, we know, is not unique to the rotating *ch'i* but is common to any kind of movement of a gaseous substance. Chu Hsi also knew that. He spoke of the strength of a strong wind—movement of *ch'i*—in high places[43] and said that *ch'i* can manifest great power when they are confined to a closed space without outlet: the pent-up state of *ch'i* that explodes as thunder, for example.[44] But he did not seem to note the different natures of the two types of power between which he was drawing the analogy.

Chu Hsi's use of the "centrifugal" tendency shows still another aspect of the particularistic character of his views about motion. For while using this tendency to illustrate the power of the rotating *ch'i* of heaven that sustains the earth's weight, he also spoke of the opposite tendency of rotating objects to move toward the center. In the beginning of the world, rapid rotation of *ch'i* caused sediments of *ch'i* to move toward the center to form the earth.[45] Yet, Chu Hsi did not seem to see the contradiction between the two tendencies. It is remarkable that he brought out these two tendencies, one right after the other, in a single conversation, in dealing with the same problem of explaining the structure of the world in which the earth is at the center. Even while discussing a single subject, he could refer to such conflicting tendencies without feeling a need to relate them to each other.[46]

13.3. Change

Chu Hsi was of the view that all corporeal things are subject to change. To a question of whether heaven and earth are subject to decay, he replied: "Once they [i.e., heaven and earth] have physical form and *ch'i*, how can they avoid decaying?"[47] Thus, for Chu Hsi, changes were natural processes for things, and he accepted all kinds of changes in a matter-of-fact manner.

Yet, Chu Hsi had little to say about the details of actual changes. He spoke of changes caused by fire and its heat, as we have seen in chapter 10, but he did not say much about how these changes proceed. He was not more forthcoming with other changes. For example, although, as we have seen, he used the transformation of water into earth to explain the formation of mountains,[48] all that he said about the actual process was that the earth thus transformed was very soft at the beginning and became hard afterward.[49] A related change that he mentioned was that of the soft mud of a sea bottom becoming hard stones on a mountain.[50] A disciple suggested a general way to interpret these types of change. Ch'en Ch'un said, after mentioning the change of sea water into high mountains:

> Generally, all things are so. Take the example of [the formation of] the shell of a chicken's egg. [It is formed through a change] from *ch'i* to water and [then] from water to tangible quality.[51]

It is difficult for us not to see a resemblance of these three—*ch'i*, water, and tangible quality—to our own notions of gas, liquid, and solid: *ch'i* could be taken to correspond to gaseous substances in general, and tangible quality to the qualities of solids.[52] But Chu Hsi's response to the above remark was simply "[It is] correct." It did not lead him to consider in general the existence of different states of material substances or contemplate in detail the changes between those states. We have also seen the casual ways in which Chu Hsi compared the relation between different meteorological phenomena—clouds turning into rain, and rain and dew freezing into snow and frost—to that between the three states of water.[53]

Such lack of interest, both in general schemes and in the detailed processes of change, is not surprising if we consider, again, that Chu Hsi mentioned most of these changes for other purposes. While speaking of the mixture of silver with gold, for example, his real interest was in showing that when impurities enter the pure mind, it loses "sincerity."[54] Some of his remarks about alchemical practices came up in similar contexts in discussions of study and book reading.[55]

When Chu Hsi spoke of the change of ice into water, his interest also lay elsewhere. For example, in commenting upon Chang Tsai's saying "The existence of heaven's nature in man is exactly like the existence of the nature of water in ice," he made the following remark to show how the two modes of existence of "nature" are different from each other:

> "The existence of the nature of water in ice" simply is that [water] is frozen and congealed to form [ice]. What creative transformation [like heaven's nature] can there be? When it melts, this ice returns again into water, and it has traces. It is naturally different from "the existence of heaven's nature in man."[56]

He spoke of the melting of snow to illustrate the meaning of his own expression "melting of the mind" (*hsin jung*).[57] He touched upon the fluid nature of the liquid state of water, that is, that it does not have fixed form; but again, his interest in the passage lay somewhere else:

> Although [the ways and *li* of different activities are] different, they are also simply the same way and *li*. It is like water. When it meets a circular place [it assumes] a circular [shape]; when it meets a square place, a square [shape]. . . . But it is also just the same water.[58]

Although Chu Hsi did make distinctions between different kinds of change, between sudden change (*pien*) and gradual transformation (*hua*), in particular, they were not what would have interested a person in the Western scientific tradition. He did not distinguish, for example, between what we would call "physical" changes (changes in the ways the constituent *ch'i* are aggregated) and "chemical" ones (changes of material substances). Concerning many changes that he mentioned, it is difficult for us to tell which of the above two kinds of changes he had in mind. To take the example of the change of seawater into mountains, he could have been referring either to the precipitation of sediments out of the water or to transformation of the entire bulk of water to *ch'i*, or to both.[59] It is equally unclear which kind of change he had in mind when he spoke of water in a well becoming clear at night.[60] In fact, using so adaptable a concept as *ch'i*, which, through aggregation, can form every material substance, he could not see such a distinction.

Changes of qualities that occur upon mixing different material substances are of the same kind. He had several examples suggesting the view that, when two material substances are mixed, the resulting substance has properties quite distinct from those of the two pure substances. But this did not lead him to consider a technical problem like that of "*mixtio*," hotly debated in the medieval West.[61] Thus, although he mentioned the loss of the quality of gold when a small amount of silver is mixed, and the great increase of hardness when pure lime is mixed with sand,[62] he did not go on to ask, as the medieval scholastics did, questions about the exact manner in which the constituent substances exist in the mixture or about why the properties of the mixture cannot be deduced from those of the original substances. He simply said that silver ore, though it contains silver, cannot be called silver because it is mixed with other substances.[63] It is not possible to determine whether the changes he had in mind were in the internal states of the substances or from one substance to another. Sometimes he did mention what to us are unequivocally changes of material substances—the change of the yin portions of bones and flesh of dead body into earth;[64] the brewing of liquor by using ferments,[65] and even some alchemical processes,[66] for example. But he did not seem to treat these changes differently.

13.4. Other Concepts Important in the Western Scientific Tradition

We have noted that, although Chu Hsi did speak of many facts and problems involving the ideas of matter, motion, and change, he did not pursue them for elaboration or further development. We have seen that he casually mentioned various facts involving these concepts, which, if pursued further, would have produced some of the key ideas and issues in the Western scientific tradition—elements, sensible qualities and man's perception of them, notions of inertia and of the relativity of motion, weight and the tendency of rotating bodies, properties of compound substances, and so on. In contrast, about such concepts as space, time, the atom, infinity, minima, and a void, which were also involved in some key problems intensively discussed in Western natural philosophy, he had much less to say. To be sure, occasions did come up for him to discuss such concepts, especially when passages in the classics contained words related to them, but his interest usually lay elsewhere. He seemed either to understand the concepts intuitively or to consider them obvious and even trivial so that they did not require discussion.

For instance, the passage from the *Doctrine of the Mean* "When a great man speaks of greatness, nothing under heaven can contain it; when he speaks of smallness, nothing under heaven can divide it" (ch. 11) provided Chu Hsi an occasion to touch upon such ideas as infinite greatness, infinite smallness, the outside of heaven and earth, and the indivisibility of extremely small things. Commenting on the passage, he said, for example: "Being great, there is no 'outside' to it; being small, there is no 'inside' to it."[67] When asked about the meaning of this comment, he said:

> When it is said that there is a thing that is extremely small but can still be divided and made into two sides, then it can take a thing inside. If it is said that there is no inside [to a thing], then it is extremely small, and furthermore it does not allow division.[68]

But this is as far as his interest went. There was no possibility of debates of the sort that continued in the medieval West about infinity, about indivisibility, and about the space outside the cosmos.[69] Thus, Chu Hsi responded simply by saying, "Yes, it is so," to the following remark of a disciple:

> Now, as for the minuteness of a piece of hair, there still is a possibility of splitting it and making it into two. So, when it is said that "nothing can divide it," it is sufficient to see its smallness. What [you mean when] you say in [your] commentary that "being small, there is no inside to it" also is to say that [it is] extremely small and has no place to go [into].[70]

The problem of "the outside of heaven and earth" did come up in Chu Hsi's comments on Shao Yung's remark "Heaven depends on the physical form (*t'ien i hsing*); the earth is attached to the [formless] *ch'i* (*ti fu ch'i*)."[71] Chu Hsi's final view on this, as we have seen in chapter 9, was that there is nothing outside heaven and earth.[72] But again, the problem was not pursued further, in the manner of the Western debate about "the infinite void space beyond the cosmos," for example.[73] At times he seemed to be more interested in opposing the contemporary tendency of speculating on affairs outside the actual world: "[Shao Yung said this] only [because he] was afraid that people may go to investigate other places outside heaven and earth."[74]

When Chu Hsi spoke of "void" (*k'ung*) and "nothingness" (*wu*), it was also to criticize and refute Buddhist and Taoist doctrines involving the terms, not to discuss the ideas themselves.[75] He said, for example: "Buddhists say that the myriad *li* are all void; we Confucians say that the myriad *li* are all real."[76] He also said:

> When Buddhists and Taoists claim to have seen [something], it is only that they could see what is void, empty, "quiet and extinct" (*chi-mieh*). [But] if it is truly empty and truly quiet and nonexisting, I do not know what it is that they say they have seen.[77]

It was in the same context that he distinguished two kinds of void:

> [Buddhists] speak of "the subtle void" (*hsüan-k'ung*) and also speak of "the true void" (*chen-k'ung*). The subtle void is the void in which there is nothing. The true void, on the other hand, has something [in it]. [This] is somewhat similar to our Confucian theory. But they [i.e., Buddhists] all disregard heaven and earth and the four sides. [They] just understand the one mind.[78]

When he mentioned "emptiness" (*hsü*), it was usually in reference to the desirable empty—thus open—state of mind, which is required for moral cultivation and intellectual activities.[79]

On the general idea of space itself, Chu Hsi had little to say. It can at least be said, however, that his idea of space was different from the sort of isotropic or geometrical space that modern science adopted. Not only were there associations of the four compass directions with various five-phase characteristics and of the two sides (right and left, or west and east) with yin and yang, but also the four directions and the two sides were not symmetric. They were considered qualitatively different and, frequently on various occasions, one side or one direction was preferred. For example, Chu Hsi noted: "[In the court in the past] the right side was respected; but afterward [people] considered the left side to be respectable."[80] There were protocols stipulating particular compass directions that different persons are supposed to face during different ceremonial acts: for example, the emperor faces south while mourning, the master of a house mourns facing north standing on the western steps.[81] Chu Hsi also wrote a rather long essay dealing with ceremonial significances of the compass directions of different parts of a palace.[82]

Nor did Chu Hsi have much to say about the concept of time in general. We can assume, however, that he shared the traditional Chinese notion of cyclical time.[83] For, as we have seen, he mentioned cyclical repetitions of various units of time—the cosmic cycles, the four seasons, the twelve lunar months, day and night, and the twelve double hours, and so forth—and their associations with such cyclical categories as the twelve terrestrial branches, the five phases, the four cosmic qualities, and yin-yang. The twelve epochs and the twelve double hours were named by the twelve branches themselves.

The "Hsi-tz'u chuan" passage "'Incipiency' is 'the extreme smallness' (*wei*) of movement; it is the first showing of good fortune" (ch. B5) provided him an occasion to discuss the concept of "*chi*" ("incipient force" or "incipiency"), which appeared in various ancient texts.[84] Taking the first half of the passage, Chu Hsi interpreted the term to mean the beginning of movement: "'Incipiency' is the extreme smallness of movement. It is between [the point at which] it is about to move and [that at which] it has not yet moved."[85] But this did not lead him to consider details of the initial stage of motion; much of his discussion of the term was concerned with the incipient states of good and bad fortunes or of virtues and evils.[86] Nor did the characterization of *pien* as a sudden change "from nothing to something" lead Chu Hsi to consider the problem of how something can result from nothing, a key element of the problem of change, which nearly all ancient Western philosophers after Parmenides had to solve before dealing with change.[87]

While commenting on the passage from the *Doctrine of the Mean* "Extend balance (*chung*) and harmony. [Then] heaven and earth will take [their proper] positions and the myriad things will be nourished" (ch. 1), Chu Hsi touched upon the idea of "harmony" (*ho*).[88] He mentioned natural disasters like "solar eclipses, meteoroids, earthquakes, and mountain collapses" as examples of what happens "when balance and harmony cannot be extended, and heaven and earth did not get their proper positions."[89] But he did not elaborate on this idea of "harmony." He simply said: "It is merely that, if the *ch'i* is harmonious and the physical form is harmonious, the harmony of heaven and earth responds to it";[90] "If the mind is peaceful, then the *ch'i* is harmonious."[91] Questions of how the harmony of *ch'i* produces such effects or is itself produced did not occur to him.[92]

Chu Hsi used certain words that are usually translated as "cause" in modern Chinese: *ku* and *yin*. He said, for example, that *ku* "has the meaning of 'that by which [a thing] is as it is' (*so-i-jan*)."[93] He also spoke of Chang Tsai's apparent distinction of *yin* from *ku*, that is, that *yin* referred to what is hidden or dark ("*yu chih yin*"), whereas *ku* referred to what is manifest or bright ("*ming chih ku*").[94] But Chu Hsi's interest in these terms did not lie in the idea of causality or of the cause-effect relation in general. Most of his discussion turned on *ku* being "traces of that which is already so" (*i-jan chih chi*) and thus easy to see.[95] On the difference between *yin* and *ku*, he simply said: "Aggregation is the *yin* of dispersion; dispersion is the *ku* of aggregation."[96] Also, though, as we have noted in chapter 8, some stimulus-response relations were of the sort that we would consider as cause and effect, most of them were not; moreover, he did not differentiate between the two sorts. It cannot be said, however, that the concept of cause and effect was absent from Chu Hsi's thought. It is merely that his notions of how cause and effect act in the world were different from the modern concept of causality: they were never understood in mechanical terms; nor were they rigorously defined.[97] His ideas about stimulus and response, then, could be seen as his version of the cause-effect relation, different from the modern version in content, emphasis, and scope.

We have seen that many of Chu Hsi's examples of stimulus-response interactions were cyclical repetitions occurring regularly in the world. These were what could be called natural—or social and historical—"regularities." Of course, he also spoke of natural regularities that are not cyclical but occur constantly: for example, "the constant *li*" that winter should be cold and summer should be hot,[98] and "the constancy" (*ch'ang*) in the frequency and magnitude of the tides.[99] The passage from the *Record of Rites* "All living things must die. Having died they must return to earth," which he quoted repeatedly, can be seen as a similar example.[100] His characterizations of the upward growth of a tree and the downward flow of water as "following the *li*" (*shun li*) and the opposite cases as "against the *li*" (*ni li*) also imply a constant *li* that the tree should grow upward and water should flow downward.[101] Such regularities mentioned by Chu Hsi also included certain social and historical instances. For example, "where the [political] power is heavily [concentrated], there are harmful effects."[102] He even mentioned what sounds like Gresham's law, that is, that "pure (good) coins are always rare; impure (bad) coins are always abundant."[103]

Chu Hsi expressed some of these regularities in a form that may be called "laws of nature," "of history," or "of the economy." But he did not use any such vocabulary in referring to them. Although at times he called them "the *li*" or "the constant *li*," we have already seen that his idea of *li* was altogether different from the concept of laws of nature. The way Chu Hsi treated these regularities was also different from the attitude of Western thinkers toward laws of nature. A regularity was considered by him as a particular fact rather than as a general law or principle covering many particular facts. He did not need to analyze them or attempt to abstract from them simple, general laws.

Moreover, Chu Hsi frequently mentioned the regularities not for their own interest, but for their usefulness as analogies to similar regularities in human conduct and norms. For example, he resorted to the fixed and unchangeable order of the four seasons to make his point that the three basic human relations (*san-kang*) and the five constant virtues (*wu-ch'ang*) cannot be changed.[104] He made the remarks about the *li* of the growth of tree and the flow of water while discussing the point that the teachings of Yang Chu and Mo Ti were "against the *li*." The Gresham-law-like remark was made to illustrate that great men are always rare, whereas small men are always abundant. At times this tendency led him even to offer a basically human-centered explanation for regularities in the natural world:

> If there is day, there must be night. If it were day for a long time and there were no night, how could [one get] rest? And if there were no day, how could there be this brightness? . . . If there were spring and summer but no autumn or winter, how could a thing settle down? [If there were] only autumn and winter but no spring and summer, then again, how could it come into being?[105]

In Chapter 7 we came across the word *tse* (rule) in Chu Hsi's comments on the passage from the *Book of Poetry* "When heaven produces masses of people, if there is a thing there is a rule."[106] This passage appears to imply not only laws of nature but also a supreme being responsible for them. But that impression does not survive a closer examination. For most of the examples Chu Hsi provided for such rules were about norms of moral conduct, to use his own words, "the rules according to which one ought to be so" (*tang-jan chih tse*): for example, the rules of how rulers and subjects ought to behave, the eyes ought to see, and the ears ought to hear.[107] Moreover, he never said explicitly that these rules were laid down by heaven. Indeed, it is far more likely that Chu Hsi had the idea of a rule to be followed by heaven in producing men and things rather than that of a law provided by heaven to be followed by men and things.

This interpretation is in accord with Joseph Needham's thesis that the concept of law of nature did not develop in Chinese scientific thought because of the absence of the idea of a Creator who also laid down "laws of nature" to be obeyed by His creatures.[108] Needham reviewed occurrences of the term *tse* in various early Chinese texts and concluded, for reasons similar to those given above, that *tse* cannot mean law of nature.[109] My conclusion is also that the term was different from the law of nature, but I cannot go along with Needham when he concludes, based on his survey of terms like *tse* and *li*, that the idea of laws of nature was absent in China. For it cannot be denied that Chu Hsi did recognize regularities in natural phenomena. We have seen that some regularities even led him to speak of the possible existence of a person in heaven presiding over them, though in the end he rejected that notion.[110] To be sure, his ideas about these regularities were different from the

Western concept of laws of nature (and he did not use such a term), but it is still possible to say that they represent Chu Hsi's notions of laws of nature.

Then there were expressions resembling some aspects of the Western idea of god. For example, the term *t'ien* (heaven), in particular its *chu-tsai* (to preside) aspect, appeared somewhat similar to the notion of a divine ruler. But we have seen in chapter 7 that what Chu Hsi emphasized with the expressions was the spontaneous character of natural phenomena; neither the sense of anthropomorphic deity nor that of divine lawgiver was evident. The expression *tsao-hua* (creative transformation), was also used in ancient texts with meanings quite similar to "the Creator."[111] In one passage Chu Hsi himself seemed to use it in that sense: "If the '*tsao-hua*' used this thing [i.e., a lizard] to make hails, then this *tsao-hua* is small indeed."[112] Yet, this did not lead him to accept, or even to debate, the idea of the creation of men and things by a divine creative agent. Even when he said that heaven "produced" men and things, what he had in mind was heaven as the *li* of their "coming into being" rather than an actual act of creation. It could hardly have been otherwise, considering that *ch'i* has innate qualities of life, which made it unnecessary to look for an external agent that created life from *ch'i*.

Finally, the idea of "transformation of *ch'i*" appears to be somewhat similar to the Western concept of "spontaneous generation," to which scholars have compared it.[113] But this idea was never considered as a serious problem by Chu Hsi and his interlocutors; no sustained debate developed involving it in the manner of the persistent controversy in the West over spontaneous generation.[114] It would have raised such a problem only if *ch'i* were inert and the transformation imparted life to it. This was not the case with Chu Hsi, in whose view *ch'i* was not merely inert matter but was inherently endowed with many other qualities, including life. The prevailing belief, which Chu Hsi also accepted, that life results from the aggregation of *ch'i* and death from its dispersion, clearly illustrates such a congruent background.[115] Thus, he could accept the idea of transformation of *ch'i* without feeling a need to provide explanations. As we have already seen, his descriptions of the process were in very general terms; nor was his use of the term "transformation of *ch'i*" restricted to the processes that produce life.

13.5. The Lack of Abstract, Theoretical Speculations and Debates

Problems involving concepts such as element, mixture, infinity, indivisibility, space, time, void, causality, and law, which received so little attention from Chu Hsi, were the subjects that were pursued in great depth in the Western scientific tradition and generated intense debates and controversies. It was such controversies and the consequent close examination of those concepts that eventually led to the resolution of the problems during the European scientific revolution.

Part of the reason for Chu Hsi's lack of interest in such problems may lie in his ideas about the concepts that he did consider basic and important—*ch'i*, yin-yang, the five phases, and so on. As the earlier chapters have shown, they were not rigorously defined; they were quite ambiguous and adaptable. Thus, not only was there little possibility for technical and complex problems involving these concepts, but such problems, had they occurred to him, would have been dealt with easily using the concepts themselves. *Ch'i*, with both the innate capacity for movement and qualities of life, was a good example. It was possible to explain all kinds of phenomena in terms of it in a quite matter-of-fact manner. It did not give rise to discussion of the problems of the sort that occupied Western scholastics.

The Confucian emphasis on the reality of the external world was also in part responsible for Chu Hsi's lack of concern with concepts like space, void, and infinity. Characteristic of Confucian thought from its ancient beginning, this emphasis was sustained in the Neo-Confucian phase despite the powerful infusions of influence from Taoist and Buddhist philosophies, both of which denied the reality of the phenomenal world. Neo-Confucians like Chu Hsi considered their acceptance of the reality of the world to be what distinguished them from Taoists and Buddhists, with their otherworldly tenets. Chu Hsi said, for example:

> The difference between Confucians' and Buddhists' sayings about [human] nature is simply that Buddhists speak of the void [whereas] Confucians speak of reality, and that Buddhists speak of nothingness [whereas] Confucians speak of existence.[116]

Concepts like "void" and "nothingness"—as well as infinity and space—were too easily associated with Taoists and Buddhists, who tended to lead men to concentrate on introspection without paying attention to the actual world. To Chu Hsi these concepts could at best be imaginary, of no help in reckoning with the reality of the actual world.

They were not useful in dealing with the moral and social problems of the world, either. And for that matter, problems involving such other notions as motion, change, element, and indivisibility could be hardly any better. It must have appeared useless, for most Neo-Confucians, to be engaged in abstract, theoretical speculations involving those problems. Chu Hsi confessed that his influential friend Chang Shih (1133–1180) did not approve of his desire to write a commentary on Shao Yung's theory about the outside of the world.[117] To be sure, he did speak of the above concepts, as we have already seen. But his discussion remained on a casual level. Chu Hsi also allowed himself to discuss imaginary, theoretical situations. For example, we have seen that he could imagine what a man, placed outside heaven and earth, would see.[118] While discussing the Buddhist doctrine of the other worlds, he speculated about a consequence of it, namely that the night would then have to be very long because the sun in its daily rotation would have to travel around the other three worlds, all below the earth's horizon.[119] But these were exceptions; on the whole, he avoided abstract, theoretical—useless—speculations. Furthermore, even these exceptional cases could hardly match his discussions of moral and social problems in the levels of elaboration, seriousness, and sophistication.

Again, the contrast with the situation in the Western scientific tradition is both striking and interesting. Much of the medieval European discussion of the concepts of motion, mixture, space, void, and infinity was undertaken in theological-philosophical contexts.[120] But although similar contexts did exist in Chinese Buddhism and Taoism, they were not picked up by the Chinese because the dominant Confucian literati opposed both.[121] And it is ironic that a basis of this rejection was the emphasis on the actual world and the shunning of "useless" theoretical speculations. For abstract, theoretical speculations about such basic concepts could have contributed to a fundamental understanding of phenomena in the actual world. In the West at least, continuing debates over the interpretation of precisely such concepts helped bring modern science into being during the Scientific Revolution, which ultimately ushered in the "useful" science that we have today.[122] But excessive emphasis on the reality of the actual world and on the necessity of the usefulness of discussions made it difficult for men like Chu Hsi to consider in detail those very concepts that could have proved helpful in understanding and living in that actual world.

Notes

1. What I have discussed in chapter 12 also has significance in this comparative respect, for Chu Hsi's attitude toward specialized traditions of scientific knowledge and their practitioners can be compared with the situation in the West, in particular with the marked increase, among scholars during the Scientific Revolution, of interest in natural phenomena and science, which went along with a changed attitude toward technical arts and their practitioners. For this aspect of the Scientific Revolution, see, e.g., Rossi, *Philosophy, Technology and the Arts in the Early Modern Era*.

2. E.g., YL8.8a3; 74.24b2.

3. Yamada Keiji, for example, begins his discussion of Chu Hsi's matter theory with the concept of "sediments" of *ch'i* but concludes that *ch'i* is "continuous." *Shushi no shizen-gaku*, pp. 134 ff.

4. E.g., YL3.7b1; 8b1, 2; 126.16b1; 21a2, 3. In YL3.8b1, however, he spoke of actual associations of the Buddhist four elements with constituents of the human body: skin and flesh with earth, tears and saliva with water, warm *ch'i* with fire, and movement with wind. In YL126.21a2 he associated earth and water with *p'o* and fire and wind with *hun*. Cf. YL126.21a3, where earth was associated with the body.

5. WC47.11a.

6. It was unthinkable for Chu Hsi to be interested in explaining the qualities and motions of light at a microscopic level, employing corpuscles with unobservable sizes and processes different from what are observed at a macroscopic level, as did Western thinkers such as Descartes. For an account of the theories of light held by seventeenth-century Western thinkers including Descartes, see Sabra, *Theories of Light from Descartes to Newton*.

7. E.g., YL2.10b3, 4.

8. E.g., YL1.8b3, 4; 4.16b3.

9. WC32.12a. See chap. 10, pp. 181–182.

10. See chap. 10, pp. 183–184.

11. YL5.10a3. See also YL95.34b3, where Chu Hsi approved of a disciple's comparison of "considerateness" to the flow of water.

12. YL34.28a3. See also YL71.7b0.

13. In YL12.16b0, for example, Chu Hsi said: "As for man's *ch'i*, inhalation is rest and exhalation is movement. Also, when one questions and answers, answering is movement and stopping is rest. Things generally are all thus."

14. In contrast, when a similar importance was accorded to the idea of motion in the mechanical philosophy that dominated

seventeenth-century Europe, it gave rise to a tremendous growth of detailed studies of motion. The difference lay in the fact that in the Western scientific tradition, matter was inert and thus required external causes to put it in motion. See, e.g., Westfall, *Construction of Modern Science*, chaps. 2, 7.

15. We have already noted, in chapter 2, a similar aspect of *li: li* is not a general principle or law underlying a particular object or phenomenon; *li* refers to an object or a phenomenon in its entirety. A similar point will be made concerning Chu Hsi's ideas about causality and regularity in the natural world; see sec. 13.4.

16. E.g., YL31.8a0, 1; 8b0, 1, 2; 9a1; 9b2; 78.35b1; CS1.19a4; 2.11a1.

17. E.g., YL31.9b2; 116.8a0; 121.12a1.

18. YL116.8a0.

19. YL2.4b2.

20. YL2.2a0.

21. See chap. 9, p. 148.

22. YL96.3a0. In fact, the Han apocryphal text *Kao-ling-yao* used the same experience in explaining the "four wanderings" of the earth: "The earth constantly moves and does not stop. [It is] like a man sitting in a boat. The boat moves, but the man does not feel [the movement]." Quoted in Chang, *Po-wu-chih*, 1.1b. For "the four wanderings," see chap. 9, p. 152.

23. Somewhat related to the idea of the relativity of motion is Chu Hsi's remark that the results of the observation of the luminaries in the sky must "have small differences according to [the positions] where [people] observe [them]." WCH3.7a. But here again, it cannot be concluded that Chu Hsi had a general understanding of the dependence of observations on the frame of reference; he merely noted a particular fact that embodied the idea.

24. For the same point in a broader, more general context, see chap. 1, sec. 1.1.

25. In YL10.6a1 Chu Hsi actually described how the efforts required for reading books decrease: "In the beginning, one book uses up ten portions of effort; the next

one book uses up eight or nine portions; afterward, it uses up six or seven portions; still afterward, it uses up four or five portions." In YL31.8b1 he compared the situation to the growth of a tree, which requires care at the beginning but proceeds of itself afterward.

26. YL96.3a0.

27. E.g., YL12.16b0, 17a5; 41.20a2. Also, when Chu Hsi spoke of the words "heavy" (*chung*) and "light" (*ch'ing*), it was mostly in reference to man's behavioral characteristics; e.g., YL21.17b2, 20b1, which comment on the *Analects* phrase "If a great man is not weighty [in his behavior], he will not be dignified" (1.8).

28. For a brief discussion of the medieval studies of motion, see Murdoch and Sylla, "The Science of Motion."

29. Nor did the new principle emerge from empirical facts: although empirical facts may have played some role in it, it was more, and mainly, owing to theoretical considerations. For example, the principle of inertia arose from the primacy of circular motion as the most natural and perfect motion in the case of Galileo, and from the perfection and immutability of God in the case of Descartes. For a brief discussion of the emergence of classical mechanics, including the principle of inertia, see Westfall, *Construction of Modern Science*, chaps. 2, 7, 8.

30. It is not impossible even to discern a germ of the idea of Newton's second law embedded in Chu Hsi's remark that light things tend to move easily in various ways, "flying, fluttering and floating." YL21.17b2. That light things are easier to move than heavy things is not very difficult to interpret in terms of "$f = ma$."

31. E.g., YL3.6b0; 57.11b2, 12b1; 72.15a2.

32. YL72.15a2.

33. For a brief account of the medieval Western world picture, see Grant, *Physical Science in the Middle Ages*, chaps. 4–5.

34. YL2.11b1.

35. YL69.26b0.

36. YL3.13a1.

37. E.g., *YL*23.1b1, 2a2; 101.32a3; *CS*50.12a1. Chu Hsi even compared the workings of the entire heaven and earth to the rotation of a waterwheel. See, e.g., *YL*116.7b0, 8a0.

38. E.g., *YL*23.1b1, 2; 2a2; 101.32a3; *CS*50.12a1.

39. E.g., *YL*23.2a2.

40. *YL*101.32a3. See also *WC*72.1a–1b, where he similarly rejected the belief that there are four stars that do not move as mistakes of the "star specialists."

41. *YL*1.6a5.

42. E.g., *YL*1.5a1, 2; 6a5; 2.13b0; 68.4a1–4b0, 16b4; 100.6a2.

43. See chap. 9, p. 139.

44. See chap. 9, p. 159.

45. E.g., *YL*1.4b3, 5a1. See chap. 9, sec. 9.1.

46. The "new scientists" of seventeenth-century Europe also struggled with the centrifugal tendency of rotating bodies. But the final understanding of rotating motion came only when they had learned to balance the centrifugal tendency against a force that pulls the rotating object toward the center. See, e.g., Westfall, *Construction of Modern Science*, chaps. 7–8.

47. *YL*45.7a1. See also *CS*49.27b2.

48. E.g., *YL*1.5b2; 45.7a2.

49. *YL*1.5b2.

50. *YL*94.3a0.

51. *YL*45.7b0.

52. In general, Chu Hsi seemed to consider only solid and liquid substances to have tangible quality or tangible body and only visible substances to have physical form. See chap. 3, sec. 3.1.

53. E.g., *YL*70.11b2; 99.4a3. See chap. 9, sec. 9.8.

54. E.g., *YL*16.19b0.

55. E.g., *YL*8.7b3; 114.12a2. He even used an idiomatic expression, "forming gold from small grains of iron," in describing the impossibility of attaining moral righteousness from concerns of practical profit (*li*). See *WC*36.26a, 27a–27b.

56. *YL*99.4a3. Chang Tsai's saying appears in the "Ch'eng-ming" (6th) chapter of *Cheng-meng. Chang-tzu ch'üan-shu*, 2.18a.

57. *YL*24.4b1. The expression "*hsin-jung*" appears in *SSCC* (*Lun-yü*), p. 1.9a, in his comments on the *Analects*, 2.9.

58. *YL*120.19a3.

59. See chap 9, p. 146.

60. *YL*59.15b1.

61. For a brief discussion of the problem of *mixtio* in the medieval West, see Dijksterhuis, *Mechanization of the World Picture*, pp. 200–204.

62. E.g., *YL*16.19b0; 89.13b0.

63. *YL*59.36a2.

64. *YL*87.30b0.

65. *YL*41.16a1.

66. For Chu Hsi on alchemical practices, see chap. 12, sec. 12.5.

67. *SSCC* (*Chung-yung*), p. 6b. See also *YL*63.11a4, where he identifies the source of his comment as the *Ch'u-tz'u* comment "Being small, it has no 'inside' to it; being great there is no 'boundary' to it." *Ch'u-tz'u chi-chu*, 5.203.

68. *YL*63.11a3. See also *YL*63.11a2.

69. For ancient and medieval Western discussions of such concepts, see, e.g., Lloyd, "Finite and Infinite in Greece and China"; Grant, "Cosmology."

70. *YL*63.11a1.

71. E.g., *YL*1.5a2; 100.6a2; 115.5a0. The Shao Yung remark appears in *Yu-ch'iao wen-tui*, 13.4a.

72. E.g., *YL*98.11a4; 100.6a2.

73. E.g., Grant, "Medieval and Seventeenth-Century Conceptions of an Infinite Void Space beyond the Cosmos."

74. *YL*100.6a2.

75. Chu Hsi's discussions of the Buddhist ideas of "void" are gathered, e.g., in *YL*126.1b0, 2a1–2b0; 7a3; 7b2, 3; 8a1; 19a0. In *YL*126.5a2, 5a3–5b0, 5b1, he contrasted them with Lao-tzu's theory of "void" and "nothingness."

76. *YL*17.9a0.

77. *YL*126.7a3. The expression "*chi-mieh*" is often used to designate the Buddhist idea of "nirvana."

78. YL126.6a2. Cf. CS60.13a2, in which the same remark is made with the word "the dull void" (*wan-k'ung*) substituted for "the subtle void." See also YL126.1b0.

79. E.g., YL5.4a4; 96.2b1; 113.7b0; CS8.30a1; 27.19b1. See chap. 2, sec. 2.2.

80. CS40.2a1. Chu Hsi then went on to associate the left side with lucky events. For more on the imbalance in traditional Chinese conceptions of left and right, see, e.g., Demiéville, "Gauche et droite en Chine." The source for these associations must of course be the yin-yang associations. See, e.g., WC76.1a, where the left and right sides are connected with east and west, respectively.

81. WC63.29a.

82. Titled "I-li shih-kung." WC68.12b–24b.

83. For a brief account of the traditional Chinese ideas about space and time, see Granet, *La Pensée chinoise*, pp. 77–99. For the cyclical conception of time in particular, see, e.g., Needham, "Time and Eastern Man"; Sivin, "Chinese Conceptions of Time."

84. E.g., YL76.7b3–8b2.

85. YL76.8a3. See also YL94.24b0.

86. E.g., YL94.23b5–25b1, containing Chu Hsi's comments on the statement from Chou Tun-i's *T'ung-shu* "Sincerity has no action, but 'the incipient force' is the power of good and evil" (ch. 3). Indeed, *chi* remained a term with predominantly moral implications, as has been aptly characterized by Wing-tsit Chan: "The word *chi* means an originating power, an inward spring of activity, an emergence not yet visible, a critical point at which one's direction toward good or evil is set." *Source Book in Chinese Philosophy*, p. 467. For more on Chu Hsi's discussion of the term, see, e.g., Smith et al., *Sung Uses of I-ching*, pp. 194–199; Ch'ien Mu, *Chu-tzu hsin hsueh-an*, 2:446–452.

87. For the ancient Greek discussion of the problem of change, see, e.g., Lloyd, *Early Greek Science*, chap. 4.

88. E.g., YL62.33a1–34a2.

89. YL62.34a2.

90. YL62.34a1.

91. YL12.5b4.

92. The same could be said about his account of the harmony of musical notes that produces music, discussed in chap. 12, sec. 12.3.

93. E.g., YL57.13a1, 13b1. See also *Ta-hsueh huo-wen*, 1.11b, where he used the expression "*ku* by which [a thing] is as it is" (*so-i-jan chih ku*).

94. YL99.2b3. Chang Tsai's distinction appears in the "T'ai-ho" (1st) chapter of *Cheng-meng*. *Chang-tzu ch'üan-shu*, 2.3a.

95. E.g., YL57.11a2, 12a1, 12b1; SSCC (*Meng-tzu*), 4.21a. In all these passages, Chu Hsi was commenting on the cryptic saying of Mencius "In discussions of human nature by people under heaven, there is *ku* and that is all. *Ku* takes 'ease' (*li*) as the basis" (4B26).

96. YL99.2b3.

97. For brief discussions of various aspects of Chinese ideas about causality, see, e.g., Needham, *Science and Civilisation*, 2:280 ff., 288 ff.; 3:415, 483 ff.; vol. 4, pt. 1, pp. 135, 233; vol. 5, pt. 4, pp. 308 ff.

98. E.g., YL79.6b2.

99. E.g., YL2.14a4.

100. *Li-chi*, ch. 24 (47.14b). See chap. 11, p. 224.

101. YL55.11b1.

102. CS6.67b2.

103. YL4.20b1.

104. E.g., YL24.26a1.

105. YL72.4b1 (the same passage cited in chap. 10, note 198).

106. See chap. 7, pp. 110–111.

107. E.g., YL18.17b1–18a0; 59.6b1–7a0.

108. E.g., Needham, *Science and Civilisation*, 2:518–583, esp. pp. 543–570 (sec. 18f, "Chinese Thought and the Laws of Nature").

109. Ibid., pp. 559–562. Derk Bodde's responses to Needham have been focused on the same points, that is, whether the *tse* were meant to be obeyed by things and

events of the natural world and whether they were ordained by a supreme being that created those things and events. "Evidence for 'Law of Nature' in Chinese Thought"; "Chinese 'Law of Nature.'"

110. *YL*4.4b5. See chap. 7, p. 109.

111. E.g., Schwartz, "On the Absence of Reductionism in Chinese Thought."

112. *YL*3.3a0. On the belief that lizards make hail, see chap. 9, p. 160.

113. E.g., Needham, *Science and Civilisation*, 2:481, 487; Hatton, "Comparison of *Ch'i* and Prime Matter," p. 166.

114. For a discussion of the spontaneous generation controversy in the West, see Farley, *Spontaneous Generation Controversy from Descartes to Oparin.*

115. E.g., *YL*3.3b3; 126.5b2; *WC*52.15b. One source of this belief is *Chuang-tzu,*

7.23a: "Birth of a man is aggregation of *ch'i*. When aggregated, it is birth; when dispersed, it is death." Cf. *YL*3.11b3, where Chu Hsi said, "When *ch'i* is aggregated, it becomes a man; when dispersed, it becomes a *kuei* (spirit)."

116. *YL*126.7b2.

117. *YL*115.5a0.

118. E.g., *YL*2.3b1; *WCH*3.7a; *Ch'u-tz'u chi-chu*, 3.101.

119. *YL*86.8b0–9a0.

120. E.g., Murdoch, "From Social into Intellectual Factors," pp. 274 ff.

121. For more discussion on this and related points, see my "Some Reflections on Science and Religion in Traditional China."

122. See, e.g., Grant, *Foundations of Modern Science in the Middle Ages.*

Concluding Remarks: General Features of Chu Hsi's Natural Knowledge

14.1. Chu Hsi's Natural World

The topics of part 2 of this book, heaven and earth, the myriad things, and man, represent the three basic constituents of Chu Hsi's natural world. The three stand in various relations to one another.

To begin with, heaven (or heaven and earth) produces men and the myriad things. Thus produced by heaven and earth, men and things live — or exist — between heaven and earth. They receive the *ch'i* and the mind of heaven and earth and have them as their *ch'i* and minds. Of all that is produced by heaven and earth, man is the most numinous, for he is endowed with the *ch'i* that is most correct, clear, complete, and so on. Man, therefore, forms a triad with heaven and earth and complements the activities of heaven and earth. Chu Hsi also spoke of many ways in which men and things, especially men, are parallel to heaven and earth. Sometimes the parallelism changes into an identity, giving rise to the notion that man is one with the whole world of heaven and earth and with everything in it.

The world made of these three constituents encompassed everything, not merely the things that can be characterized as "physical" or "material." If what I have discussed in part 2 gives a different impression, it is because I have drawn an imaginary boundary and excluded what appeared to be lying beyond it. For Chu Hsi himself, that boundary did not exist. Objects and phenomena involving life and the mind, and even morality, were included in his world of heaven and earth, the myriad things, and man; there was no clear distinction between "natural" and "nonnatural" realms in that world. This lack of distinction was evident also in such basic concepts as *ch'i*, yin-yang, and the five phases, which were endowed with characteristics of life, mind, and morality as well as matter.

One consequence of this lack of distinction was that for Chu Hsi the "natural" world existed in harmony with the "nonnatural" — human and social — world. There could be no possibility of tension between the morally neutral "natural" world and the human world, which is governed by morality. On the contrary, and in part owing to the idea of parallelism — and even identity — between man and heaven and earth, the "natural" world, referred to as "heaven and earth," was frequently invested with moral qualities. The idea of the "cosmic basis of morality," discussed in chapter 1, can be understood in this context. It also led to Chu Hsi's frequent use of natural phenomena in discussing analogous moral problems of the human world. In sum, Chu Hsi's "natural" world was an integral part of the larger world that also contained human and social realms, with no boundary between them. Nothing was excluded from this world of Chu Hsi.

14.2. Conceptual Schemes

If the subjects of part 2 were the basic constituents of Chu Hsi's natural world, the concepts discussed in part 1—yin-yang, the five phases, the four cosmic qualities, *shu* and "images," and so on—provided "conceptual schemes." His perception and understanding of the things and events of the natural world reflected certain features of those schemes.

Most of the basic concepts form sets of categories. As categories, they are associated with various sets of characteristics. The different characteristics associated with a given category are connected to one another, giving rise to a network of mutual associations. In fact, this kind of association was a key mode of explanation in Chu Hsi's discussion of natural phenomena; and indeed, such categorical and associative character was a universal feature of the traditional Chinese discourse about the natural world, which many commentators have noted and referred to variously as "correlative thinking" and "the system of correspondence."[1]

We have seen many examples showing this character of Chu Hsi's thought. For one, the four seasons and the four cosmic qualities formed a network of fourfold sets of mutually associated characteristics, through their respective five-phase associations with the weather, the compass directions, and the constant human virtues.[2] They were further associated with four of the seven sentiments, love, joy, hatred, and desire, and with various other fourfold sets of human characteristics—for example, brightness, penetration, fairness (*kung*), and extensiveness (*p'u*); humaneness, centrality, righteousness, and correctness; and regret (*hui*), good luck (*chi*), parsimony (*lin*), and bad luck (*hsiung*).[3] Chu Hsi could even include four parts of a day—day, night, dusk, and dawn—and the four legs of a stove.[4] Some sets of characteristics were associated directly with each other, without bringing in as intermediaries associations with basic categories like yin-yang and the five phases. Thus, the five musical notes were directly associated with a group of five different things: the *kung* note with rulers, *shang* with ministers, *chiao* with people, *chih* with events, and *wu* with things.[5] The twelve musical pitches were associated with the twelve months.[6] Chu Hsi also mentioned associations of man's perceptual organs with visceral organs: the eyes with the liver and the ears with the kidneys, for example.[7]

These associations, and many more examples that we have seen in previous chapters, appear quite arbitrary to us. We have come across cases in which Chu Hsi himself felt a need to explain some of the associations, humaneness with yang and righteousness with yin, or appearance with Water and propriety with Fire, for example.[8] But more often he simply stated the associations without any explanation; all he did for certain sets of terms was to associate them with a known set of categories, as though such association constituted sufficient explanation. For example, he explained the cryptic passage of the *Hsün-tzu* "Clear brightness has inner shadow and turbid brightness has outside shadow" merely by associating the former with metal and water and the latter with fire and the sun.[9]

We have seen another, related tendency when Chu Hsi merely mentioned a few distinguishing characteristics for certain sets of related terms without actually discussing them, not even associating them with known categories. After dividing the void into two kinds, "the subtle void" and "the true void," all he said was, "The subtle void is the void in which there is nothing; the true void, on the other hand, has something [in it]."[10] Chu Hsi's discussion of different kinds of changes is basically of the same type, because all he did in numerous passages dealing with them was to distinguish the sudden change, *"pien"* or *"shen,"* from the gradual one, *"hua."*[11] His distinction between *kuei-shen* and *shen* in terms of "tangible" and "subtle" effects is similar.[12] The same tendency found its way into his discussion of human characteristics. For example, "knowledge is 'the clear of the clear'; wisdom is 'the correct of the correct'; stupidity is 'the turbid of the clear'; delinquency is 'the one-sided of the correct.'"[13] He also said: "Thought is the hidden (*wei*) [aspect of mind's] movement; action is the manifest [aspect of mind's movement]. . . . Thought moves inside; action moves outside."[14] He simply mentioned two kinds of reverence—"the dead reverence" (*ssu-ching*) and "the live reverence" (*huo-ching*)—without elaborating on them.[15]

These categorical and associative basic concepts are also cyclical: they come in cycles that repeat fixed sequences. Not only concepts like yin-yang and the five phases, but also characteristics associated with them, show cyclical character. We have seen numerous examples in which various yin-yang characteristics follow each other continuously, forming cycles that have no beginning or end: movement and rest, contracting and expanding, vanishing and growing, going and coming, opening and closing, day and night, life and death, hot and cold weather, and so on. Many sets of five-phase characteristics, the four seasons, the four cosmic qualities, and the life cycle of plants, for example, also repeat their fixed sequences endlessly. Chu Hsi even said that regret, good luck, parsimony, and bad luck, which are associated with the four seasons, "circulate like spring, summer, autumn, and winter."[16] Thus, for him, such endless cyclical repetition was a universal feature of natural phenomena, which is not surprising because the cyclical nature of many natural phenomena— the movement of the luminaries in the sky, the change of the seasons, the tides, the plant life cycles, and even the bending and stretching movements of the measuring worm—must have been obvious even to a most casual observer. In fact, cyclical repetition became another key feature of traditional Chinese perceptions of natural phenomena.[17]

Yet, Chu Hsi's knowledge of the natural world was not completely conditioned by these conceptual schemes. It was never Chu Hsi's intention to use these schemes in constructing a coherent system of natural knowledge covering all the particulars; nor were the schemes the sole means for explaining all natural phenomena. Thus, the presence of the schemes should not lead one to ask, or to answer, such questions as whether the yin-yang—or the five-phase, or the *I-ching* diagram—schemes "helped" or "hindered" the understanding of natural phenomena.[18] For, when alternative means of explanations, not employing such schemes, were available, they could always be adopted. The categorical schemes could not hinder, inhibit, or stand in the way of the adoption of such explanations.[19]

Consider the example of the yin-yang scheme. We have seen numerous cases in which Chu Hsi used it in explaining natural phenomena. The idea of the yin-yang cyclical alternation dominated his discussions of many periodical phenomena, such as lunar eclipses, characteristics of the seasons, and sea tides. But Chu Hsi's adherence to the idea did not prevent his reaching what we take to be correct explanations of these phenomena, that is, in terms of the relative geometrical positions of the sun, the moon, and the earth. For he was not forced to use the idea of yin-yang alternation in explaining every phenomenon. When he could adduce a more concrete explanation, he could adopt it. His explanation of the phenomenon of the moon's phases is a good example: he chose to account for it in terms of the relative positions of the sun and the moon even though the yin-yang alternation could have easily explained it.[20] Thus, what "prevented" Chu Hsi from reaching the "correct" explanation of the other phenomena must lie elsewhere—perhaps in the difficulties that the correct explanation posed, or in the lack of the additional knowledge necessary for it.[21]

Similar things can be said about Chu Hsi's use of the five-phase scheme. Consider his discussion of the five regular and the five intermediary colors.[22] The five-phase scheme did not play the role of a coherent theoretical framework covering all phenomena involving light and color. Nor did all his discussions of color necessarily use five-phase associations; more often they did not. It was only because Chu Hsi on one particular occasion was concerned with colors for gentlemen's clothing, a problem for which certain five-phase associations were well suited, that he brought in the five-phase scheme. Moreover, the five-phase concepts and associations were ambiguous enough to accommodate any particular color phenomenon and any interpretation of it in the scheme.

14.3. "Particularistic" Character

The presence of the conceptual schemes did not encumber the particularistic character of Chu Hsi's knowledge of the natural world. He treated most natural phenomena, and problems involving them, basically as particulars. He did not generalize from them: he took each phenomenon or problem as it came along, without much concern to correlate it with his views about the rest of the natural world. If a fact had been explained in terms of one or more of these schemes, he was satisfied. When another fact came up for explanation or as an illustration, it was that fact alone that needed to be dealt with; other facts that had once been explained or used for illustration were not considered again.

The adaptability of the categorical schemes seems to have facilitated the particularistic character of Chu Hsi's discussion. The concepts and associations constituting the schemes were never rigorously or exactly defined; they were frequently based on vague and ambiguous ideas and relations. Indeed, they were so adaptable that instead of forming a framework that would impose coherence on the understanding of natural phenomena, they easily accommodated all kinds of phenomena or interpretations, involving inconsistencies and even contradictions. In this sense, Chu Hsi's natural knowledge could afford to be particularistic not because of an absence of general theoretical schemes, but in spite of, or even because of, their presence.

We have seen numerous examples in which natural phenomena were treated by Chu Hsi in such a "particularistic" manner. For instance, he discussed the problem of the earth's weight or the geographical variation of weather as a particular problem in isolation from other problems that, we know, are relevant to it.[23] We saw in chapter 13 that though his remarks about motion contained what could be generalized as basic principles of motion, he always considered them as particular tendencies of particular objects and phenomena. Consider Chu Hsi's report of someone's difficulty in boiling rice gruel on top of a mountain.[24] For Chu Hsi this was an interesting but isolated geographical fact about a particular mountain, the Omei (E-mei) Mountain, not a general fact applicable to high altitude. It goes without saying that this did not lead him to think of general problems concerning the relationship of boiling, air "pressure," altitude, and so on.

As a consequence, inconsistencies or contradictions inevitably occurred between Chu Hsi's different accounts of the same fact or problem. For example, in chapter 9 we came across his conflicting thoughts about the relative distances of the sun and the moon from the earth, different explanations of why nights are short in the extreme north, and even different notions about the size and shape of the earth. But in none of these did the contradictions seem to pose problems for him; he might not even have considered them as contradictions.

Chu Hsi did not press his discussions about natural phenomena by questioning and answering all possible details and consequences—and making sure all contradictions were checked and resolved. Once an apparently reasonable explanation was obtained for a particular problem, he was satisfied and moved to other problems. When, later, he came upon the same problem again, he did not necessarily attempt to assure consistency with his earlier views. To be sure, there were exceptions. We have seen, for example, that Chu Hsi and his interlocutors pursued certain questions concerning sacrificial service in some detail.[25] He was also able to note inconsistencies in his various discussions of *pien* and *hua*[26] and in his different five-phase associations of the four sagely qualities.[27] But what was at issue in these exceptional cases was not concrete natural phenomena; nor did he make efforts to resolve the inconsistencies.[28]

Given such a particularistic bent, it is not surprising that Chu Hsi's discussion of natural phenomena did not show an understanding of different levels of generality, that is, that when there are a number of particular facts related to one another, one of them can be more general and fundamental than the rest and thus constitute the cause of them. We have seen, for example, that, of many seasonal characteristics—deviation of the sun's path from the equator, variations of temperature, length of the day, length of the sun's shadow, and so forth—Chu Hsi did not choose any single

one as the cause for the rest; for him all of them were particular phenomena, somehow related to one another.[29]

Nor did Chu Hsi have a clear idea about the differences in the levels of importance or generality of various qualities and concepts. He did have some notion that
certain qualities and tendencies were more basic and important than others. We
have seen, for example, that two pairs of dual qualities of *ch'i*—the clear-turbid and
the light-heavy dichotomies—played important roles in his discussion of natural
phenomena. They underlay, among other things, his idea of the heaven-earth dichotomy and the distinction between man and nonhuman things. But this did not
mean that the two pairs of qualities were accorded a special status that could take
account of all other qualities.[30] Also, while commenting on a "Hsi-tz'u chuan"
phrase, "accomplishing the myriad things and leaving out nothing" (ch. A4), Chu
Hsi listed attributes of things that he considered essential for understanding their *li*:

> Take the amount, physical form, and tangible quality (*fen-liang hsing-chih*) of a thing. Fol-
> low its size (literally, "the large and the small" [*ta-hsiao*]), width ("the broad and the nar-
> row" [*k'uo-hsia*]), and shape ("the square and the circular" [*fang-yüan*]). [Then] each
> will certainly accomplish the *li* of this thing. There will not be remaining deficiencies.[31]

But this did not form a fundamental distinction in which a few essential qualities—
size, width, and shape, for example—were distinguished from other qualities that
were to be explained in terms of the former.[32] For Chu Hsi, all qualities were innate
in material substances; no set of them could be inherently more fundamental than
others.[33]

14.4. "Common-Sense" Natural Knowledge

Somewhat related to the particularistic character of Chu Hsi's natural knowledge is
his lack of methodological concern. In this way he was like most traditional Chinese
thinkers.[34] When he did discuss method, it almost always had to do with the method
of study, the "method of reading books" in particular. And there the target was the
li contained in books. The problem for him was how to get at the *li* from the information recorded in books.[35] How to know—understand—what is recorded in books
was not much of a problem.

Thus, Chu Hsi did not engage in discussions of how one can obtain knowledge
or how one can be sure that what one knows is sound, the key questions in Western
epistemology. In fact, "true knowledge" (*chen-chih*), for him, was not any special
kind of knowledge: "It is not that there is a 'true knowledge' apart from these many
pieces of simple knowledge."[36] He also said, "'To extend knowledge' is not 'to know
those ways and *li* that other people do not know,' but simply [to know what is] in
front of people."[37] No special ability was required to have knowledge: "It is not necessary . . . [to know every thing of the world]. If one knows the main points of the
way and *li* for being a man, then it is all right."[38] The way or *li* was not anything special, either: "'The way' is simply the way and *li* that are clear before the eyes";[39]

"Looking before oneself, it is simply the *li*."[40] Chu Hsi even said that "all the ways and *li* are the things that I have in myself, and not [what I] get from outside."[41] This, then, was a "common-sense" epistemology, and at its basis lay Chu Hsi's belief that man's mind in its original state can "spontaneously" grasp the ways and *li* of things and events.[42]

The method of discourse, that is, the method of presenting what one knows, was not much of a problem for Chu Hsi, either. He showed little concern with rigorous logical methods, for example. If there was logic for him, it was a "common-sense" sort. Occasionally he did touch on some basic logical points. For example, he said: "When this is right, that is wrong; when this is wrong, that is right. The two standing together [as right] is not allowed."[43] Or, "From the existence of this, one can see the nonexistence of that."[44] But his logic was not of a sort that would make him consider the conditions under which those statements hold. Also, he noted that a thing is either moving or at rest, that a man is either speaking or quiet, and that there can be no state between the two alternatives. But he went on to argue from these that man is either good or bad, as if there could be no intermediate state in this case also.[45] When a disciple suggested that the three categories of "friends," "elders," and "youngers" cover all men in the world, he simply said, "Yes."[46] And although, as we have seen, he made, and spoke about, various kinds of categorical classifications, he seemed to consider it useless to make too rigorous or elaborate a linguistic distinction. For example, he refused to discuss the distinction between "not to stop" (*pu hsi*) and "no stop" (*wu hsi*), saying: "[To say] 'not to stop' is just like saying 'no stop.'"[47]

We have also seen that Chu Hsi showed little concern for ensuring consistency between his different statements. Frequently he did not even seem to notice contradictions in them.[48] When faced with different, often apparently conflicting, accounts, he could always reconcile them by pointing out that they merely represented different ways of looking at the same problem or referred to different aspects of the same fact. Thus, he frequently noted that different results arise depending on how one views a given problem: for example, whether one looks at it from inside or from outside,[49] whether one discusses it with reference to mind or to event,[50] and whether its "*i-fa*" (already manifest) or its "*wei-fa*" (not yet manifest) aspect is under consideration.[51] In a similar, characteristic example, he said:

> It is possible to say that the supreme ultimate "contains" (*han*) movement and rest. [It is] speaking in terms of the main substance. It is possible to say that the supreme ultimate "has" (*yu*) movement and rest. [It is] speaking in terms of activity (literally, "flowing and moving" [*liu-hsing*]).[52]

He even said that the two characters "*chung*" and "*yung*" in the book *Doctrine of the Mean* (Chung-yung) refer to different aspects of the same thing.[53]

For Chu Hsi, it was simply to be taken for granted that when one sees something or reads something in a book, one knows it, and that when one knows something, one can speak or write about it. Given this attitude, it is quite natural that Chu Hsi would not worry about rigorous methodological problems of how to obtain knowledge or how to present it to others.[54] What mattered to him was rather how to set one's mind upon the knowledge or how to act upon it. This was the direction that his *ke-wu* doctrine took, as we saw in chapter 2.

Such lack of concern with methodological problems was, if anything, more pronounced in Chu Hsi's discussions of natural phenomena. For most natural phenomena were simply accepted in the way they were perceived. That was partly the reason for the basically empirical character of his natural knowledge. Yet, if his natural knowledge can be characterized as "empirical," it was a "common-sense" empiricism. Most of his "empirical" knowledge was about objects and phenomena so commonplace that they would hardly have required fresh observations. When observations did play a role, they were usually made by other persons. A source for them was books, which recorded the experiences of others. At times, books were thought even to contain the words, and hence the *li*, of the sages and thus to constitute the most important source for Chu Hsi.[55] Indeed, for information about natural phenomena, he frequently turned to books rather than to the objects and phenomena of the external world.

To be sure, Chu Hsi sometimes emphasized the importance of observation, for calendrical astronomy for example.[56] He spoke of errors and discrepancies appearing in accounts not based on actual observations. We have seen that he criticized the authors of many geographical writings that contain discrepancies because they had based their discussions on speculation and hearsay.[57] The descriptions of some animals in the *Shan-hai-ching* contained errors because they relied on drawings.[58] Chu Hsi also noted that T'ao Hung-ching's materia medica included errors because the author lived in the south, and the circumstance of his time prevented him from traveling to northern China.[59] He considered those people "laughable" who held to such erroneous accounts in books and "forced interpretations of them" without checking them.[60] At times his critical attitude was expressed in a quite general manner. For example, he criticized those who "do not doubt what ought to be doubted and doubt what should not be doubted"; the former are prone to make many mistakes in their understanding, and the latter tend to waste effort.[61] He took the *Analects* passage "Hear much, and lay aside what is doubtful (*ch'üeh-i*)" (2.18) in the same vein.[62]

Yet, on the whole, Chu Hsi was ready to accept accounts of things and events by those who actually saw them; his critical attitude did not prevent him from lapsing into a rather credulous habit of accepting what was said to have been observed or what was recorded in books.[63] The adaptability and the wide purview of concepts like *ch'i* contributed to such an attitude, for all kinds of phenomena could be explained in terms of them. We saw numerous examples in chapter 6 in which strange phenomena, often associated with *kuei-shen*, were accepted and were explained in terms of *ch'i*. Indeed, no phenomenon had to be ruled out; if it was observed, it could be accepted. In one of his reports to the emperor, he accepted a strange meteorological event that he had not seen himself; his ground for accepting it was that many people had seen it and their accounts of it all agreed.[64]

What resulted, then, was a thoroughly "common-sense" natural knowledge that covered everything in the world. Chu Hsi accepted objects and phenomena of the natural world in a quite matter-of-fact manner and did not feel the need to explain them in terms of hidden mechanisms or external causes. Thus, most of what we have seen in the previous chapters has been "common-sense" knowledge of concrete things and events. Even when Chu Hsi provided explanations, they were mainly "common-sense" explanations. There were no theoretical speculations about problems involving abstract concepts such as space, time, void, infinity, indivisibility, mixture, and so on. Detailed elaborations using mathematical or other techniques were also out of the question. For why would he have needed them?

Notes

1. E.g., Needham, *Science and Civilisation*, vol. 2; Porkert, *Theoretical Foundations of Chinese Medicine*; Henderson, *Development and Decline of Chinese Cosmology*; Graham, *Yin-Yang and Correlative Thinking*. Henderson has seen a "mnemonic function" in this type of association. *Development and Decline of Chinese Cosmology*, p. 172.

2. See chap. 5, sec. 5.4.

3. E.g., YL87.14a0, 1; 94.15b3, 34a2. For details of the five-phase associations of these characteristics, see table 4.2.

4. E.g., YL20.14b0; 119.4b0–5a0.

5. E.g., YL78.36b0; 92.10b0.

6. E.g., YL87.11b2.

7. E.g., YL53.10a1. In YL79.17a1, where Chu Hsi said that "the eyes take charge of the liver, and thus belong to Wood," he seemed to use the association of the eyes with the liver to explain the association of the eyes with Wood (taking the liver-Wood association for granted).

8. See chap. 4, sec. 4.4.

9. YL1.8b4. The original passage is from the "Chieh-pi" chapter of the *Hsün-tzu*.

10. See chap. 13, p. 303.

11. See chap. 8, sec. 8.3.

12. See chap. 6, sec. 6.4.

13. WC62.17a.

14. YL41.20a2.

15. YL12.14b2.

16. YL74.9b0.

17. It is in reference to such cyclical repetition that Needham has characterized "Chinese physics" by the concept of "wave" as opposed to "particle"; e.g., *Science and Civilisation*, vol. 4, pt. 1, pp. 3–14.

18. Needham, for example, believed that the sixty-four-hexagram system of the *I-ching* was a "hindrance" to the development of scientific ideas, whereas the yin-yang and the five-phase schemes "helped" it. E.g., ibid., 2:304. Graham, however, thought that the five-phase associations, unlike the yin-yang characteristics, lacked objectivity and thus were not given much attention, perhaps because they were felt to be "less useful in practice." *Two Chinese Philosophers*, p. 33.

19. Of course, there are other problems for questions of this type. We have noted, for example, that these schemes were used more often in discussing "nonnatural" rather than "natural" phenomena, which suggests that they could not have influenced—"helped" or "hindered"—the development of natural knowledge decisively.

20. The explanation of the moon's phases using the idea of the yin-yang cyclical alternation was given by Ch'en Ch'ang-fang (fl. 1140), Chu Hsi's contemporary. See *Pu-li k'e-t'an*, 2.5a. Cf. Needham, *Science and Civilisation*, vol. 4, pt. 1, p. 7.

21. The "correct" understanding of the tidal phenomena, for example, required knowledge of gravitation and of the earth's rotation, which Chu Hsi could never have imagined. In the absence of such knowledge, some medieval Europeans also re-

sorted to the idea of "microcosmic-macrocosmic respiration." Leonardo da Vinci, who accepted that explanation, even tried to calculate the size of "the world lung." See, e.g., Needham, *Science and Civilisation*, 3:494. For a historical discussion of the tidal theory in Europe, including reference to modern works, see Burstyn, "Galileo's Attempt to Prove that the Earth Moves."

22. See chap. 10, pp. 181–182.

23. See chap. 9, pp. 156–157, chap. 13, p. 299.

24. YL138.5a1.

25. See chap. 6, sec. 6.2.

26. See chap. 8, note 72.

27. See chap. 4, p. 60.

28. Of course, there must have been times when Chu Hsi expressed different views about a problem because of genuine "development"—conscious change—of his ideas over time. This book does not deal with that possibility fully. But far more often, his varying statements simply resulted from the lack of such a "consistency check."

29. See chap. 9, sec. 9.7. Robert M. Hartwell has noted the lack of a similar understanding in traditional Chinese economic thought of Chu Hsi's time, in which "the failure to distinguish different orders of conceptualization severely limited the possibilities for integrating the separate ideas of economic doctrine into an explanatory system and precluded the broadening of abstraction essential to the progress of a science." Hartwell attributed this to "the habitual use of the historical-analogical method," according to which, "once the analogy was discovered, the problem was often deemed solved." "Historical Analogism, Public Policy, and Social Science in Eleventh- and Twelfth-Century China," esp. pp. 726–727. Cf. Derk Bodde's remark about "the alleged Chinese tendency to see the abstract and general only in terms of concrete and particular." *Chinese Thought, Society, and Science*, p. 37 (see Bodde's note 22 for earlier references).

30. Such a special status was given, for example, to the Aristotelian four qualities. See, e.g., Dijksterhuis, *Mechanization of the World Picture*, pp. 22 ff.

31. YL74.16a4. The following remark of Ts'ai Yüan-ting, quoted by Chu Hsi, refers to the same attributes and some others as key aspects of the things and phenomena of the world:

> The myriad sounds under heaven come from the opening and closing; the myriad *li* under heaven come from the movement and rest; the myriad numbers under heaven come from the odd and even; the myriad images under heaven come from the square and circle. These all arise from the two diagrams, *ch'ien* and *k'un*. (YL65.7a4; see chap. 5, note 71, of this book.)

Chu Hsi did not discuss, however, the following remark of Ch'eng I, which also speaks of important material qualities:

> When men of antiquity investigated the *li* of a thing exhaustively, they ate [and tasted] its taste, smelled its odor, distinguished its color, and knew what characteristic is formed when a certain thing combined with another. (*Ho-nan Ch'eng-shih i-shu*, ch. 15, ECC, p. 162)

Elsewhere, Ch'eng I said: "When a thing has physical form, it must have the four [qualities of sound, color, smell, and taste]." *Ho-nan Ch'eng-shih i-shu*, ch. 15, ECC, p. 193.

32. Such was the distinction between the "primary" and the "secondary" qualities maintained by the mechanical philosophy of seventeenth-century Europe. See, e.g., Boas, "Establishment of Mechanical Philosophy," esp. p. 436.

33. Chu Hsi also made remarks that appear to speak of three different levels of reality, referred to by the concepts of *li*, *ch'i*, and things (*wu*)—or "tangible quality" (*chih*). He said, for example: "To say it in terms of man's body, the *ch'i* of respiration is yin-yang; body, blood, and flesh are the five phases; its nature is the *li*." YL94.11b2–

12a0. Here, Chu Hsi is commenting on the *T'ai-chi-t'u*. In the same passage he says:

> The *ch'i* are spring, summer, autumn, and winter. The things are Metal, Wood, Water, Fire, and Earth. The *li* are humaneness, righteousness, propriety, knowledge, and faith. . . . The *ch'i* is just *ch'i*, and the tangible quality is just tangible quality. [The two] must not be mixed in discussion.

Yet, he did not pursue these ideas systematically. The associations of yin-yang with *ch'i* and the five phases with tangible quality was also a part of this three-level distinction. But again, as we noted in chapter 4, the distinctions were neither rigorously defined nor consistently maintained in Chu Hsi's discussions of the relations between *li* and *ch'i* and between yin-yang and the five phases.

34. A growing number of studies on epistemological, logical, and methodological aspects of early Chinese discourses and arguments have appeared recently. See, e.g., Graham, *Later Mohist Logic, Ethics, and Science*; Graham, *Disputers of the Tao*; and the articles in Lenk and Paul, *Epistemological Issues in Classical Chinese Philosophy*.

35. See Tillman, *Confucian Discourse and Chu Hsi's Ascendancy*, pp. 225–228, for Chu Hsi's debate with Lu Chiu-yüan (1139–1193) on this problem. For a brief discussion of Chu Hsi's ideas about the "method of reading books," see Gardner, *Learning to Be a Sage*, pp. 42–54.

36. *WC*59.40a.

37. *YL*15.13b4.

38. *YL*26.17a0.

39. *YL*26.16b1.

40. *YL*117.11b1.

41. *YL*17.11a1.

42. See chap. 2, sec. 2.2.

43. *WC*53.9b.

44. *YL*74.13b4–14a0.

45. *YL*116.7b0.

46. *YL*29.17a4.

47. *YL*64.19a1.

48. Of course, he was fully able to note "self-contradictions" (*tzu-hsiang mao-tun*) in other persons' arguments. E.g., *WC*37.30a, 58.37a.

49. E.g., *YL*30.3b2; 34.33b0.

50. E.g., *YL*15.13a1; 42.14b2.

51. E.g., *WC*55.2b.

52. *WC*45.12a.

53. *YL*15.13a1.

54. Thus, his discussion of the method of "analogical extension" (*lei-t'ui*) did not show much concern with rigorous methodological issues. What the method involved, the extension of the knowledge of a thing or event to that of other things or events belonging to the same category, or the inference from what one knows to what one does not know, was frequently based on crude, and at times far-fetched, common-sense analogies. For more discussion of the "*lei-t'ui*" method, see my forthcoming article, "'Analogical Extension' in Chu Hsi's Methodology."

55. See chap. 7, p. 114.

56. E.g., *WCH*2.21a. See chap. 12, p. 256.

57. See chap. 12, sec. 12.4.

58. E.g., *YL*138.1b5; *WC*71.18b.

59. *YL*138.15a3.

60. *YL*79.4a0. Chu Hsi used the character *yen* in this sense of "checking a fact by actual experiences or observations": e.g., *YL*2.6a0, 138.9a3. In the latter passage he spoke of checking himself the different rate of growth of the bamboo shoot during day and night. The character had such other meanings as "to examine," "to produce an effect," "to verify," and so forth. For Chu Hsi's use of the character in those other senses, see, e.g., *YL*39.3a4; *WC*14.23b, 44.15b.

61. *YL*121.10b1.

62. E.g., *YL*24.19a1–21b1.

63. What Hu Shih noted some decades ago concerning "scientific spirit and method in Chinese philosophy" turns out to have been essentially right after all: it was books and words, not objects and phenomena of the natural world, that Chu Hsi

turned to with such a critical spirit of "lay-
ing aside what is doubtful [till it is verified
later]." His critical "spirit" did not make
him a pioneer in a critical tradition of empirical natural knowledge; instead, he was
a forerunner of the tradition of "evidential
research" (*k'ao-cheng* or *k'ao-chü*) that was
overwhelmingly textual in nature. See Hu

Shih, "Scientific Spirit and Method in Chinese Philosophy." For Chu Hsi's remarks
on various books in the spirit of evidential research, see, e.g., *YL*138.1b6–2b3;
*WC*38.4b–5a. See also Ch'ien, *Chu-tzu hsin
hsueh-an*, 5:266–341.

64. *WC*14.23b–24a.

Glossary

For the Chinese characters for titles of books and articles and the names of modern authors, see the bibliography. For the Chinese characters for the following sets and categories, see the sources indicated below.

The eight trigrams (*pa-kua*): table 5.1.
The sixty-four hexagrams: Needham, *Science and Civilisation*, 2:315–321.
The ten celestial stems (*shih-kan*): table 5.1.
The twelve terrestrial branches (*shih-erh-chih*): table 5.1.
The four cosmic qualities: table 5.1.
The five notes (*wu-sheng*): table 10.1.
The twelve pitches (*shih-erh-lü*): table 10.3.

Personal Names

Ai-kung　哀公

Chan T'i-jen　詹體仁	1143–1206
Chang Huang　章潢	1527–1608
Ch'ang Hung　萇弘	
Chang I　張毅	
Chang Liang　張良	
Chang Shih　張栻	1133–1180
Chang Tsai　張載, Heng-ch'ü 橫渠	1020–1077
Chao-kung　昭公	
Ch'ao Yüan-fang　巢元方	fl. 610
Ch'en Ch'ang-fang　陳長方	fl. 1140
Ch'en Ching-yüan　陳景元	
Ch'en Ch'un　陳淳	1159–1223
Ch'en Sheng-ssu　陳勝私	
Ch'en Tao-shih　陳道士	Taoist Master Ch'en
Ch'en T'uan　陳搏	ca. 906–989
Ch'eng Chiung　程迥	

Ch'eng Hao　程顥	1032–1085
Cheng Hsüan　鄭玄	127–200
Ch'eng I　程頤, I-ch'üan 伊川	1033–1107
Ch'eng Ta-ch'ang　程大昌	1123–1195
Ch'ing-chiang Tao-shih　清江道士	Taoist Master Ch'ing-chiang
Chou-kung　周公	d. 1094 B.C.
Chou Tao-shih　周道士	Taoist Master Chou
Chou Tun-i　周敦頤	1017–1073
Chu Hsi　朱熹	1130–1200
Chung Li-ch'üan　鐘離權	
Fan Chung-yen　范仲淹	989–1052
Fang I　方誼	
Fu Hsi　伏羲	
Han Ying　韓嬰	fl. mid–2nd century B.C.
Ho Kao　河鎬	1128–1175
Hsia Te　夏德	
Hsieh Liang-tso　謝良佐	1050–1103
Hsü Ching-tsung　許敬宗	fl. 7th century
Hsü Shu-wei　許叔微	fl. 1132
Hsueh Ch'ang-chou　薛常州	fl. 1075
Hu Hung　胡宏	1105–1155
Hu Yüan　胡瑗	993–1059
Huang-ti　黄帝	the Yellow Emperor
Hui-tsung　徽宗	r. 1101–1126
Jen-tsung　仁宗	r. 1023–1064
Juan I　阮逸	
Kan Tao-shih　甘道士	Taoist Master Kan
Kang-hsi　康熙	r. 1661–1722
Kao Yu　高誘	fl. 205
Kun　鯀	father of King Yü
K'ung-t'ung Tao-shih　空同道士	Chu Hsi's pseudonym
K'ung Ying-ta　孔穎達	574–648
Kuo P'u　郭璞	late 3rd century
Kuo Yung　郭雍	1091–1187
Li Chao　李照	
Li Chih-ts'ai　李之才	d. 1045
Li Pi　李璧	1159–1222
Li Tao-shih　李道士	Taoist Master Li
Li Tao-yüan　酈道元	d. 527
Liang Hsiao　良霄	

Liao Te-ming　廖德明		
Lin Ch'eng-chi　林成季		
Liu Chi　劉几		
Liu Hsi-sou　劉義叟	1017–1060	
Lo Ta-ching　羅大經		
Lu Chiu-yüan　陸九淵	1139–1193	
Lü Ta-lin　呂大臨	1046–1092	
Lü Tsu-ch'ien　呂祖謙	1137–1181	
Lü Tung-pin　呂洞濱		
Lu Yü　陸羽	fl. 760	
Mo Ti　墨翟	fl. 479–438 B.C.	
Mu Hsiu　穆修	979–1032	
Pan Ku　班固	first century A.D.	
P'ang An-shih　龐安時	fl. ca. 1080	
Pao Yang　包揚		
Pien Ch'ueh　扁鵲	fl. 501 B.C.	
Po Chü-i　白居易	772–846	
Po Yu　伯有		
Shang Chün　商均	son of King Shun	
Shao Yung　邵雍, K'ang-chieh 康節	1011–1077	
Shen Hsien　沈僩		
Shen Kua　沈括	1031–1095	
Shun　舜		
Ssu-ma Kuang　司馬光	1019–1086	
Su Shih　蘇軾	1036–1101	
Su Sung　蘇頌	1020–1101	
Sun Ssu-kung　孫思恭	1015–1076	
T'ai-tsu　太祖	r. 960–976	
T'ai-tsung　太宗	r. 626–649	
Tan Chu　丹朱	son of King Yao	
T'ang　湯	the founder of Shang	
T'ao Hung-ching　陶弘景	456–536	
T'eng Kung　滕珙		
Ting Te-yung　丁德用		
Ts'ai Chen　蔡沈	1167–1230	
Ts'ai Yüan　蔡淵	1148–1236	
Ts'ai Yüan-ting　蔡元定, Chi-t'ung 季通	1135–1198	
Ts'eng Chi　曾極		
Ts'eng Hsi　曾晳		
Tsou Hsin　鄒訢	Chu Hsi's pseudonym	
Tsou Yen　鄒衍	ca. 305–240 B.C.	

Tsu Hsiao-sun　祖孝孫	early T'ang
Tsung-yüan　宗元	
Tu Yu　杜佑	735–812
Tung Chu　董銖	1152–1214
Tung Chung-shu　董仲舒	ca. 179–104 B.C.
Tzu Hsia　子夏	507–420 B.C.
Wang An-shih　王安石, Ching-kung 荊公	1021–1086
Wang Chi-fu　王及甫	
Wang Fan　王蕃	fl. 3rd century A.D.
Wang Hsiang　王祥	
Wang Mao-hung　王懋竑	1668–1741
Wang P'o　王朴	fl. 959
Wang Shih-p'eng　王十朋	1112–1171
Wang Shu-ho　王叔和	210–285
Wang Ying-lin　王應麟	1223–1296
Wei Po-yang　魏伯陽	fl. 2nd century A.D.
Wu Hsiung　吳雄	
Wu Jen-chieh　吳仁傑	
Wu Pi-ta　吳必大	
Wu Yüan-shih　吳元士	
Yang Chu　楊朱	4th century B.C.
Yang Hsiung　揚雄	53 B.C.–18 A.D.
Yang-kung　襄公	
Yao　堯	
Yen Hui　顏回, Yen-tzu 顏子	
Yi Sunji (Li Shun-chih)　李舜之	
Yü　禹	
Yü Ching　余靖	fl. 1025
Yü Fan　余範	
Yüan Shu　袁樞	1131–1205

OTHER TERMS

ai　愛	love
ai　哀	sadness
an　暗	dark
an-hsü　暗虛	dark gap
an-p'ai　安排	to arrange
an-tun　安頓	to be settled in
ang-huan　盎緩	plentiful and slow
cha-tzu　渣滓	sediments
chai-chieh　齋戒	purification and abstinence

chan	占	divination
chan-hsing	占星	astrology
chan-jan	湛然	transparent
ch'ang	暢	clear (weather)
ch'ang	常	constant
chang	長	to grow, chief
chang	丈	a unit of length (ten feet)
ch'ang-che	常者	common man
Chang-chou	漳州	a geographical name
chang-chu	彰著	manifestation
ch'ang-li	常理	constant *li*
ch'ang-p'u	菖蒲	calamus
ch'ang-sheng	長生	long life
chao	召	to beckon
chao-ming	昭明	bright
Che-chiang	浙江	a geographical name
ch'e-chiang	車匠	wheel artisan
ch'en	辰	p. 150
ch'en	臣	subject, minister
chen-chih	眞知	true knowledge
chen-k'ung	眞空	true void
ch'en-wei	讖緯	apocryphal texts
chen-yüan	眞元	true origin
cheng	正	correct, right, the first lunar month
cheng	貞	pure
ch'eng	誠	sincere, sincerity
ch'eng	成	to complete, to form, to settle down
cheng-ch'i	正氣	the correct *ch'i*
ch'eng-chiu	成就	achieving
cheng-hou	證候	seeing symptoms
cheng-hsin	正心	making the mind correct
ch'eng-i	誠意	making the intention sincere
cheng-ku	貞固	pure and firm
ch'eng-kuo	城郭	frames
"Ch'eng-ming"	誠明	a chapter of Chang Tsai's *Cheng-meng*
ch'eng-shu	成熟	complete and ripened
ch'eng-shu	成數	number of completion
cheng-wei	正位	correct position
ch'eng-wu	成務	completion of tasks
ch'i	氣	
ch'i	器	concrete things
chi	極	extreme, ultimate
chi	幾	incipiency
chi	吉	lucky
chi	祭	sacrificial service

ch'i	脊	spine
chi	寄	to consign to
chi	繼	to inherit
ch'i	擊	to strike
chi	迹	trace
ch'i-chia	齊家	regulating the family
chi-chih	極至	acme
ch'i-chih	氣質	*ch'i* and tangible quality
chi-chih-che shan	繼之者善	a phrase from the "Hsi-tz'u chuan"
ch'i-ch'ing	七情	the seven sentiments
Chi-chou	冀州	a geographical name
ch'i-ch'uang	悽愴	pathetic
ch'i-hou	氣候	situation of *ch'i*
ch'i-hsiang	氣象	image of *ch'i*
chi-hsing	極星	pole star
ch'i-hua	氣化	transformation of *ch'i*
ch'i-li	氣力	power of *ch'i*
chi-mieh	寂滅	quiet and extinct
ch'i-ping	氣稟	endowment of *ch'i*
ch'i-shu	氣數	the *shu* of *ch'i*
ch'i-shuo	氣朔	chap. 12, note 78
ch'i-ting	氣定	settling of *ch'i*
ch'i-ying	氣盈	chap. 12, note 78
Chi-yüan	紀元	name of a calendar
chia	嘉	beautiful
chia-se	稼穡	planting and harvesting
chia-tzu	甲子	first stem–first branch
ch'iang	強	strong
chiang-shen	降神	visitation of spirits
ch'iang-tiao	腔調	tune
ch'iang-tzu	腔子	cavity
chiao-i	交易	intersecting *i*
chiao-sha	焦殺	anxious and fierce
chieh-ch'i	節氣	seasonal point
chieh-chü	結聚	forming and aggregating
chieh-fa	截法	expedient
ch'ieh-mo	切脈	feeling the pulse
"Chieh-pi"	解蔽	a chapter of the *Hsün-tzu*
ch'ien	前	before
chien	見	to see
chien	健	vigorous
chien-hsi	減息	reducing the breath
ch'ien-nu	遷怒	to shift anger
chien-wen	見聞	seeing and hearing
chih	至	extreme, to arrive at

chih	知	knowledge, to know
ch'ih	赤	red
chih	直	straight
chih	質	tangible quality
chih	致	to extend, to bring about
chih	志	will
chih-chi	至極	extreme
chih-ch'i	志氣	the will *ch'i*
chih-chih	致知	extension of knowledge
chih-chüeh	知覺	perception, consciousness
chih-jun	置閏	placing leap month
chih-kuo	治國	ordering the country
chih-shou	持守	to keep on guard
ch'ih-tao	赤道	the Red Path (equator)
chin	津	constituent of a man's body
chin	金	gold, Metal
chin	進	to advance
chin	盡	to exhaust
chin-chih	矜持	self-esteem
chin-hsing	金星	Metal star (Venus)
chin-i yüan-san	近一遠三	near by one and far by three
chin sheng yü chen	金聲玉振	a phrase from the *Mencius*
ch'ing	靑	blue
ching	經	classic, constant norm
ch'ing	清	clear
ching	精	essence
ch'ing	情	feelings
ch'ing	磬	jade tube
ch'ing	輕	light
ching	靜	quiet, rest, tranquil, calm, still
ching	敬	reverence
ching-ch'eng	精誠	dedication
ching-ch'i	精氣	the essence *ch'i*
ching-ch'i wei wu	精氣爲物	the essence *ch'i* becoming things
ching-chung	靜重	tranquil and grave
ching-hsing	經星	regular star (fixed star)
ching-li	精力	power of essence
ching-mi	靜密	quiet and hidden
ching-miao	精妙	essential and subtle
ching-shen	精神	mental spirit
ch'ing-sheng	清聲	clear sound
ching-shuang	精爽	essential and refreshing
ching-tso	靜坐	quiet sitting
ching-ying	精英	exquisite
Chiu-chiang	九江	the Nine Rivers

chiu-ch'iao	九竅	the nine holes
Chiu-chih	九執	name of a calendar
chiu-t'ien	九天	the nine heavens
Chiu-yü t'u	九域圖	Nine Region Map
ch'iung-li	窮理	exhaustive investigation of the *li*
ch'o	啜	to drink
cho	濁	turbid, dark
chou	呪	incantation
chou	州	prefecture
chou-t'ien	周天	circumference of heaven
chü	聚	aggregation
ch'u	初	beginning
chü	懼	fear
chu	主	host, to take charge of
chu	著	manifestation
chu	朮	name of a plant
ch'u	處	place
ch'ü	屈	to contract
ch'ü	去	to go
chü	具	to implement
ch'ü-chih	曲直	bending and straightening
chu-ching	主敬	to maintain reverence
chü-chiu	雎鳩	name of a bird
chu-hou	諸侯	princes
chu-i	主一	to concentrate on one
ch'u-ju	出入	coming out and entering
chu-tsai	主宰	to preside over, ruler
ch'üan	全	complete, perfect
ch'üan	權	temporary expedient
chüan	卷	volume (part of a book)
chüan-i	專一	to concentrate on one
ch'üan-nung-wen	勸農文	proclamation for encouraging agriculture
chuang	壯	vigorous
ch'üeh-i	闕疑	to lay aside what is doubtful
chün	君	ruler
chün	均	seven-note scale
Chün-i	濬儀	a geographical name
chün-tzu	君子	great man
chung	中	balance, centrality
chung	鐘	bell
chung	重	heavy
chung	忠	loyalty
ch'ung	衝	opposite point
chung	種	seed

E-mei　峨眉	Omei mountain
fa　發	manifestation
fa　法	model
fa-ch'ang　發暢	emitting
fa-san　發散	diverging
fa-sheng　發生	generation, coming forth
fa-tung　發動	initiating
fa-yung　發用	manifesting and using
fan　反	to turn back from
fan-sheng　泛聲	drifting sound
fang-shih　方士	master of methods
fang-yüan　方圓	shape (the square and the circular)
fei　肺	lung
fen　忿	angry
fen　分	unit of length (p. 279)
fen-fa　奮發	aroused and coming forward
fen-jao　紛擾	varied and disorderly
fen-liang hsing-chih　分量形質	amount, physical form, and tangible quality
fen-yeh　分野	field allocation
feng　鳳	phoenix
feng　風	wind
feng-shui　風水	wind and water (geomancy)
fo-teng　佛燈	Buddha candle
fu　覆	to cover
fu　腑	processing viscera
fu　復	to return, original
fu　富	wealthy
Fu-chien　福建	a geographical name
fu-cho　附著	to adhere to
Fu-chou　福州	a geographical name
fu-ling　茯苓	tuckahoe
fu-ts'ang　伏藏	hiding and storing
fu-tzu　附子	wolfsbane
han　寒	cold
han　含	to contain
hao　好	good
hao-hao　浩浩	vast
hao-jan chih ch'i　浩然之氣	the magnanimous *ch'i*
ho　合	combination
ho　和	harmony
Ho-t'u　河圖	the Yellow River chart
hou　後	after
hou　厚	thick

hou-ch'i	候氣	watching for *ch'i*
hsi	翕	closing
hsi	息	growing, breath
hsi	習	habit
hsi	喜	joy
hsi	細	minute, thin
Hsi-ch'üan	西川	a geographical name
hsi-jun	細潤	delicate and enriching
"Hsi-tz'u chuan"	繫辭傳	a commentary of the *I-ching*
hsia-hsueh shang-ta	下學上達	to study down below and attain up above
hsia-lou	下漏	clepsydra
hsia-sheng	下生	downward production
hsiang	響	echo
hsiang	象	image
hsiang-ch'ien	向前	going forward
hsiang ch'i-se	相其色	divination method using colors
hsiang-fa	相法	method of physiognomy
hsiang-k'e-hsü	相剋序	mutual conquest sequence
hsiang-sheng	相生	mutual production
hsiang-sheng-hsü	相勝序	mutual conquest sequence
hsiang-sheng-hsü	相生序	mutual production sequence
hsiang-shu	象數	images and numbers
hsiang-shu-hsueh	象數學	study of images and numbers
hsiao	小	small
hsiao	消	to vanish
hsiao-ch'ang	小腸	small intestine
hsiao-han	小寒	small cold (a seasonal point)
hsiao-hsing	宵行	name of a worm
hsiao-hsueh	小學	education of children
hsiao-jen	小人	small man
hsiao-tao	小道	the small ways
hsieh	邪	wicked
hsieh-cheng ch'ü-chih	邪正曲直	the whole shape
hsieh-o pu-cheng	邪惡不正	deviant and incorrect
hsien	仙	immortals
hsien	顯	manifest
hsien	賢	wisdom
hsien chu jen	顯諸仁	to manifest it in humaneness
hsien-shen yeh-kuei	閑神野鬼	idle *shen* and wild *kuei*
hsien-t'ien	先天	prior to heaven
Hsien-t'ien-t'u	先天圖	chart of the "Prior to Heaven"
hsien-tsu	險阻	hazardous
hsin	辛	bitter
hsin	信	faith
hsin	心	mind, heart

hsin-jung 心融	melting of the mind
hsing 性	(human) nature
hsing 形	physical form
hsing 刑	punishment
hsing 行	to go, to act, passage
hsing-ch'en 星辰	stars
hsing-ch'i 形氣	*ch'i* with physical form
hsing-chi 星紀	name of a Jupiter station
hsing-ch'i chih shih 形器之事	matter of physical form and concrete things
hsing-chia 星家	star specialists
hsing-ch'ing 性情	disposition
hsing-erh-hsia 形而下	below physical form
hsing-erh-shang 形而上	above physical form
hsing-hsiang 形象	physical form and image
hsing-hsing 惺惺	alert
hsing-hua 形化	transformation of physical form
hsing-k'o 形殼	external shape
hsing-ming 刑名	performance and title
hsing-shu 行恕	to practice considerateness
hsing-t'u 星圖	star map
hsing-ying 形影	physical form and shadow
hsiu 秀	excellent
hsiu 宿	lunar mansion
hsiu-o chih hsin 羞惡之心	the mind of shame and dislike
hsiu-shen 修身	cultivating the self
hsiung 凶	unlucky
hsü 虛	empty, shapeless, imaginary
hsü-k'ung 虛空	empty void
hsü-ling ming-chüeh 虛靈明覺	chap. 2, note 30
hsüan-feng 旋風	rotating wind
hsüan hsiang wei kung 旋相爲宮	to rotate and become *kung* one by one
hsüan-k'ung 玄空	subtle void
hsueh 血	blood
hsueh-ch'i 血氣	blood-*ch'i*
hsueh-mo 血脈	blood vessel
hsün-hao 勳蒿	fuming up
hsün-huan 循環	circulation
hu 戶	gate
hu 虎	tiger
hua 化	(slow) transformation
hua erh ts'ai chih ts'un hu pien 化而裁之存乎變	a phrase from the "Hsi-tz'u chuan"
hua erh ts'ai chih wei chih pien 化而裁之謂之變	a phrase from the "Hsi-tz'u chuan"
hua-sheng 化生	birth through transformation

hua-wu 化物	transformed thing
Huai 淮	name of a river
huang-chung i-chün 黃鐘一均	the *huang-chung* scale
huang-tao 黃道	the Yellow Path (ecliptic)
huang-wu 黃霧	yellow fog
hui 會	epoch, to gather
hui 悔	regretful
hui-san 揮散	dissipating
hun 魂	
hun 昏	dark
hun-hsiang 渾象	celestial globe
hun-i 渾儀	armillary sphere
"Hun-i i" 渾儀議	"Discussion of armillary spheres" (an essay by Shen Kua)
hun-p'o 魂魄	
Hun-t'ien 渾天	a cosmological theory
hung 紅	vermillion red
"Hung-fan" 洪範	"Great Plan" (a chapter of *Shu-ching*)
hung-huang 洪荒	immense turbulence
huo 活	alive
huo 惑	delusive
huo 火	fire
huo-ch'i 火氣	fire *ch'i*
huo-chu-lin 火珠林	a divination method
huo-hou 火候	fire phasing
huo je wai ying 火日外影	a phrase from the *Huai-nan-tzu*
i 藝	arts
i 易	change
i 意	intention, meaning
i 醫	medicine
i 義	righteousness
i 一	uniform
i-chia 醫家	medical specialists
i-fa 已發	already manifest
i-feng 蟻封	ant hill
i-hsueh 易學	*I-ching* studies
i i kuan-chih 一以貫之	to penetrate through it by one
i-jan chih chi 已然之迹	traces of that which is already so
i-ke tao-li 一箇道理	one way and *li*
i-ke yüan-t'ou 一箇原頭	one source
i ku shen 一故神	"One, therefore shen."
i-lei pu-neng hsiang ch'eng 異類不能相成	p. 273
i-li 義理	righteousness and *li*

i-lou 蟻樓	ant tower
i-pang 依傍	to rely on
i-seng 醫僧	medical monk
i-shang ts'an-sha 夷傷慘殺	disease and killing
i-shou 義獸	righteous animal
i-tao 醫道	way of medicine
i-tieh 蟻垤	ant hill
i-yao 熠耀	p. 196
i-yüan 一原	one source
i-yüan chih ch'i 一元之氣	the *ch'i* of one origin
je 熱	hot
jen 仁	humaneness
jen 人	man
jen-hsin 人心	the mind of man
jen-shih 人事	human affairs
jen-shou 仁獸	humane animal
jen-tao 人道	the way of man
jen-wei 人爲	artificial
jen-yü 人欲	human desire
jo 弱	weakness
jou 柔	soft
juan 軟	soft
jun 閏	intercalation
jun-hsia 潤下	soaking and descending
jun-lü 閏率	intercalation rate
jun-yüeh 閏月	leap month
k'ai 開	to open, to begin
k'ai-p'i 開闢	the great beginning
Kai-t'ien 蓋天	a cosmological theory
kai-t'ien-i 蓋天儀	*Kai-t'ien* model
k'ai-wu 開物	opening up things
kan 肝	liver
kan 幹	main part
kan 感	stimulus
k'an 看	to see
kan-en 感恩	to stimulate favors
k'an-jan 欿然	dissatisfied
kan-te 感德	to stimulate favors
kang 剛	hard
kang-chi 綱紀	principles
kang-feng 剛風	hard wind
k'ao-cheng 考證	evidential research

k'ao-chü	考據	evidential research
k'e	客	guest
k'e-chi	克己	self-control
k'e-chi fu-li	克己復禮	to control the self and return to the propriety
k'e-hsing	客星	guest star
ke-wu	格物	investigation of things
ken ch'i pei	艮其背	keeping the back still
kou	姤	accidental
kou-ching	構精	sexual union
kou-ku	句股	a mathematical method
kou-wen	鉤吻	name of a plant
ku	梏	fettered
ku	故	reason
ku-shen	谷神	valley spirits
kua	卦	the *I-ching* diagrams
kua-ch'i	卦氣	chap. 5, note 89
kua-ta	掛搭	to attach to
kua-tz'u	卦辭	hexagram text
kuan	官	organ
kuan	管	sighting tube
kuan	觀	to look at
kuan-pien wan-chan	觀變玩占	observing changes and pondering about the prognostications
kuan-she	管攝	to control
kuan-t'ung	貫通	thorough penetration
kuang	光	light, bright
kuang	廣	vast
kuang-ch'i	光氣	the light *ch'i*
kuang-yao	光耀	brightness and shining
kuei	鬼	
kuei	貴	honorable
k'uei	夔	an one-legged monster
kuei	晷	sundial
kuei	歸	to return
kuei-hsing	鬼星	name of a star
kuei-huo	鬼火	ghost fire
kuei-ju	跪乳	kneel to suck
kuei-shen	鬼神	
K'un-lun	崑崙	name of a mountain
kung	工	crafts
kung	公	public, fair, unselfish
kung	恭	respectful
k'ung	空	void
kung-chuan	公轉	revolution
kung-fu	工夫	laborious efforts

kung-kung	公共	public
kung-yung	功用	tangible effect
kuo	過	to pass
k'uo-hsia	闊狹	width (the broad and the narrow)
lai	來	to come
lao-jen-hsing	老人星	Old Man Star (the South Pole star)
lao-ping	老病	old ailment
le	樂	happiness
lei-fu	雷斧	thunder ax
lei-t'ui	類推	analogical extension
leng	冷	cold
leng-chi	冷積	cold accumulation
li	理	
li	曆	calendrical astronomy
li	厲	evil spirits
li	利	profit, advantage, ease
li	禮	propriety, ritual
li	立	to stand
li	釐	a unit of length (p. 279)
li	里	a unit of length (about 400 meters)
li-chia	曆家	calendar specialists
li-chia	禮家	ritual specialists
li-chih	曆志	treatise on calendars
li-ch'un	立春	beginning of spring (a seasonal point)
li hsiang i chin i	立象以盡意	a phrase from the "Hsi-tz'u chuan"
li-hsing	力行	strenuous exertion
li-hui	理會	understanding
li i fen shu	理一分殊	a phrase from Ch'eng I
li yu tung-ching	理有動靜	"*Li* has movement and rest."
li-yüan	曆元	calendrical epoch
li-yüeh	禮樂	rituals and music
"*Li-yün*"	禮運	"Revolving of the Rites" (a chapter of *Li-chi*)
liang	涼	cool
liang	量	volume
liang-hsin	良心	the good mind
liang-i	兩儀	the two modes
liang ku hua	兩故化	"Two, therefore *hua*."
liang-li	兩立	two standing together
liang-neng	良能	innate ability
lien	煉	to smelt
lien-chü	斂聚	collecting
lien-tan	煉丹	alchemy
lin	吝	stingy, parsimonious
ling	靈	numinous

liu	霤	eaves
liu	騮	horse-brown
liu	流	to flow
liu-fu	六腑	the six processing viscera
liu-hsing	流行	flowing and moving
liu-i	六藝	the six arts
liu-tzung	六宗	the six worships
Lo-shu	洛書	Lo River diagram
lü	律	(musical) pitches, harmonics
lü	呂	the yin pitches
lü-li	律曆	harmonics and calendar
lü-shu	律數	pitch number
lü-tu-liang-heng	律度量衡	standard system of measures
luan-sheng	卵生	oviparous birth
lun-hui	輪回	cyclical transmigration
lung	龍	dragon
mao	貌	appearance
men	門	doors
meng	雺	a kind of fog
"Meng-tsun-chi"	夢尊記	an essay by Ts'ai Ch'en
miao	妙	subtle
miao-yung	妙用	subtle effect
min	民	people
ming	明	bright
ming	命	decree, fate
ming chih ku	明之故	p. 305
ming-t'ang	明堂	chap. 12, note 235
mo	磨	to rub
mo-chi	末技	trivial technique
mo-liu	末流	trivial branch
mou	謀	plan
na-chia	納甲	p. 273
nan-chi-hsing		the South Pole star
Nan-k'ang	南康	a geographical name
nei-kan	內感	internal stimulus
nei-tan	內丹	internal alchemy
neng kuang	能光	ability to be bright
ni-hsing	逆行	retrograde motion
ni li	逆理	against the *li*
ning	凝	congelation
ning	寧	tranquil
ning-chieh	凝結	congelation
ning-chü	凝聚	congelation

nu 怒	anger
nuan 暖	warm
nung 農	agriculture
o 惡	bad, evil
ou-jan 偶然	accidental
pan-sheng 半聲	half sound
p'ang-kuang 膀胱	bladder
pao 雹	hail
pao 包	to surround, to contain
pao-yü chih mu 包育之母	mother of surrounding and nourishing
pei 卑	humble
pei-ch'en 北辰	the north *ch'en*
pei-chi-hsing 北極星	the North Pole star
Pei-tou 北斗	the Big Dipper (name of a star)
pen 本	basis
pen-ling 本領	basis
pen-ts'ao 本草	materia medica
P'eng-li 彭蠡	name of a lake
pi 閉	closing
pi 碧	emerald blue
pi 蔽	screened, blocked
p'i 脾	spleen
p'i 闢	to open
pi-jan chih li 必然之理	*li* that is necessarily so
pi-ssu chih ping 必死之病	terminal disease
pi-yung fang 必用方	prescriptions that must be used
p'ien 偏	one-sided
pien 變	[sudden] change
pien-chih 變徵	a musical note
pien-i 變易	changing *i*
pien-kung 變宮	a musical note
ping 病	disease
ping 稟	endowment, to be endowed with
p'ing 平	peaceful, even
ping-ch'i 屏氣	holding the *ch'i*
p'ing-t'an 平坦	smooth
p'ing-tan chih ch'i 平旦之氣	the *ch'i* of peaceful dawn
p'ing-t'ien-hsia 平天下	bringing peace to all under heaven
p'o 魄	
po-hsueh 博學	broad study
po-wen 博文	broad culture
pu 卜	divination
p'u 溥	extensive

p'u 圃	horticulture
pu-hao 不好	bad
pu hsi 不息	not to stop
pu-hsiao 不肖	delinquency
pu-jen chih shuo 不仁之說	theory of nonhumaneness
pu-jen-jen chih hsin 不忍人之心	the mind unable to bear other men's sufferings
san 散	dispersion, scattering
san-chiao 三焦	the three caloria
san-kang 三綱	the three basic relations
"San-liang" 參兩	a chapter of Chang Tsai's *Cheng-meng*
san-t'ien liang-ti 三天兩地	three for heaven and two for the earth
san-tsai 三才	the three talents
shan 善	good
shan-jen 善人	good man
shang 賞	reward
shang-han 傷寒	cold damage
shang-lu 商陸	name of a medicine
shang-sheng 上生	upward production
she 舍	house
she-shih 揲蓍	sorting out milfoil stalks
shen 神	
shen 深	deep
shen 腎	kidney
shen 伸	to expand
shen-ch'u kuei-mei 神出鬼沒	unfathomable and unpredictable
shen-hsien 神仙	immortals
"Shen-hua" 神化	a chapter of Chang Tsai's *Cheng-meng*
shen-ling 神靈	spirits
shen-ming pu-ts'e 神明不測	*shen*, bright, and unfathomable
shen-t'ou 滲透	to infiltrate
sheng 生	birth, production
sheng 盛	flourishing
sheng 聖	sageness
sheng-ch'i 生氣	life-*ch'i*
sheng-ch'i 聲氣	sound *ch'i*
sheng-hsien 聖賢	sage
sheng-hsü 生序	production sequence
sheng-i 生意	life-intent
sheng-jen 聖人	sage
sheng-li 生理	life-*li*
sheng-sheng pu-ch'iung chih i 生生不窮之意	the intent of ceaselessly coming into being
sheng-shu 生數	number of production
sheng-ta 盛大	magnificent
sheng-wu 生物	producing things

sheng-yü chang-yang	生育長養	giving birth and nourishing
shih	事	event
shih	世	generation
shih	蓍	milfoil stalk
shih	濕	moist
shih	實	real
shih	視	to see
shih	施	to take action
shih-erh-chih	十二支	the twelve terrestrial branches
shih-erh-kua	十二卦	the twelve hexagrams
shih-erh-lü	十二律	the twelve pitches
shih-hua	始化	the first transformation
shih-kan	十干	the ten celestial stems
shih-li	實理	real *li*
shih-shen	室神	house spirits
shih-sheng	濕生	wet birth
shih-t'ing	視聽	looking and listening
shih-wu	時務	current tasks
shou	受	to receive
shou-lien	收斂	converging
shou-t'ui	收退	withdrawing
shu	恕	considerateness
shu	熟	ripe
shu	數	*shu* (number)
shu	疏	subcommentary
shu	術	technique
shu	述	to follow
shu	淑	virtue
shu-chia	數家	*shu* specialists
shu-chia	術家	technique specialists
shu-chou	樞軸	pivotal axis
shu-niu	樞紐	pivot
shu-shu	術數	techniques and *shu*
shu-tu	熟讀	careful reading
shuai	衰	declining
shui	水	water
shui-hsing	水星	Water star (Mercury)
shui yüeh nei ying	水月內影	a phrase from the *Huai-nan-tzu*
shun	順	obedient, conformable
shun-huo	鶉火	a Jupiter station
shun li	順理	following the *li*
"Shun-tien"	舜典	"Canon of Shun" (a chapter of the *Shu-ching*)
shuo-hsü	朔虛	chap. 12, note 78
"Shuo-kua chuan"	說卦傳	a commentary of the *I-ching*
shuo-k'ung	朔空	chap. 12, note 47

so-i-jan chih ku	所以然之故	a reason by which a thing is as it is
so-sheng	所生	product
so-tang-jan chih tse	所當然之則	a rule according to which a thing ought to be
ssu	私	private, selfish
ssu	思	to think, thought
ssu	絲	a unit of length (p. 279)
"Ssu-chen"	四箴	"Four Admonitions" (an essay by Ch'eng I)
ssu-ching	死敬	dead reverence
ssu-fang	四方	the four directions
ssu-i	私意	selfish intention
ssu-pang	四傍	four sides
ssu-pien	四邊	four sides
Ssu-shu	四書	the Four Books
ssu-ta	四大	the [Buddhist] four elements
ssu-te	四德	the four [cosmic] qualities
ssu-tuan	四端	the four beginnings
ssu-yu	四遊	four wanderings
su	肅	solemn, clean
su	俗	vulgar
su-jan	肅然	solemn
suan	算	computation, mathematics
suan	酸	sour
suan-chia	算家	computation specialists
suan-hsueh	算學	mathematics
suan-ming	算命	calculating the fate
sui	歲	chap. 9, note 41
sui	遂	continuation
sui-ch'a	歲差	yearly deviation
sui-hsing	歲星	Year star (Jupiter)
Sung-kao	嵩高	name of a mountain
Sung-shan	崇山	name of a mountain
ta	大	great, grand, large
ta	搭	to attach to
ta-ch'ang	大腸	large intestine
ta-chuan	大轉	great turning
ta-fu	大夫	high official
ta-heng	大亨	great success
ta-hsiao	大小	size
t'a-hsin t'ung	他心通	reading the mind of others
ta-huang	大黃	rhubarb
ta-shih	大石	name of a musical tune
ta-shu	大暑	great heat (a seasonal point)
Ta-yen	大衍	name of a calendar
ta-yüan	大原	great source

t'ai-chi 太極	the supreme ultimate
T'ai-chi-t'u 太極圖	*Diagram of the Supreme Ultimate*
T'ai-ch'u 太初	name of a calendar
"T'ai-ho" 太和	a chapter of Chang Tsai's *Cheng-meng*
t'ai-hsü 太虛	the supreme void
t'ai-hsü-k'ung 太虛空	the supreme empty void
T'ai-i 太一	name of a star
t'ai-sheng 胎生	viviparous birth
"T'ai-shih" 泰誓	"Great Oath" (a chapter of *Shu-ching*)
t'ai-yang 太陽	the supreme yang (the sun)
t'ai-yin hsüan-ching-shih 太陰玄精石	name of a stone
tan 丹	alchemy, elixir
tan 膽	gall
tan-t'ien 丹田	elixir field
tang-tang 蕩蕩	vast
t'ao 討	punishment
tao 道	way
tao-hsin 道心	the mind of the Way
Tao-hsueh 道學	Learning of the Way
tao-li 道理	way and *li*
tao-shih 道士	master of the Way, Taoist master
tao-shu 道術	Taoist technique
tao-t'i 道體	substance of the Way
t'e 慝	evil
te 得	to get, to beget
te 德	virtue
t'i 體	body, substance
ti 地	the earth
ti, Ti 帝	a ruler, name of a constellation
ti-chung 地中	the earth's center
"Ti-kuan" 地官	"Official of Earth" (a chapter of the *Chou li*)
ti-li 地理	geography
ti-li-chia 地理家	geography specialists
ti-ying 地影	the earth's shadow
tiao 調	mode, tune
t'iao-ch'i 調氣	regulating the *ch'i*
tiao-ts'an shuai-lo 彫殘衰落	withering and declining
t'ien 天	heaven, the sky
t'ien-chih 天職	heaven's duty
t'ien chih ming-ming 天之明命	heaven's bright decree
t'ien-hsia 天下	the world, all under heaven
t'ien i hsing ti fu ch'i 天依形地附氣	a phrase from Shao Yung
t'ien-jen hsiang-kan 天人相感	mutual stimulation of heaven and earth
t'ien-li 天理	the heavenly *li*, the *li* of heaven
t'ien so ming 天所命	fate decreed by heaven

t'ien-tao　天道	the Way of heaven
t'ien-ti　大地	heaven and earth
t'ien-ti chih ch'i　天地之氣	the *ch'i* of heaven and earth
t'ien-ti chih chung　天地之中	the center of heaven and earth
t'ien-ti chih hsin　天地之心	the mind of heaven and earth
t'ien-wen　天文	astronomy, astrology
t'ien-wen-chih　天文志	treatise on astronomy
"T'ien-wen-hsün"　天文訓	"Teaching on the Pattern of the Heavens" (a chapter of the *Huai-nan-tzu*)
t'ien-yüan　田園	fields and gardens
t'ien-yüan ti-fang　天圓地方	circular heaven and square earth
t'ing　聽	hearing
ting　定	settled, definite, fixed, determinate
ting-fa　定法	determinate method
ting-shu　定數	determinate number, fixed *shu*
ting-wei　定位	fixed in position
t'o-jan　脫然	sudden
t'o-man hsieh-p'i　惰慢邪僻	lazy, haughty, and perverse
to-t'ai　奪胎	robbing the fetus
t'ou　透	to permeate
tsa　雜	impure
tsa-lei　雜類	miscellaneous category
ts'ai　才	talent
ts'ai　裁	to conclude
tsai　載	to sustain, to carry
tsai-i　災異	abnormal disaster
ts'ai-liao　材料	raw material
tsai-ying p'o　載營魄	to carry the *p'o*
ts'an-jan　粲然	brilliant
tsang　臟	storing viscera
ts'ang　藏	to store, to hide, latency
ts'ang chu yung　藏諸用	to store it in function
ts'ang-shou　藏受	storing and receiving
ts'ang-ts'ang-che　蒼蒼者	the blue [sky]
tsao　竈	kitchen
tsao-hua　造化	creative transformation
tse　則	rule
ts'e-chuan　側轉	slant rotation
ts'e-yin chih hsin　惻隱之心	the mind of commiseration
tso-hsüan　左旋	leftward rotation
tsu　資	to supply, basic quality
ts'un　存	alive, to remain
tsun　尊	noble
ts'un　寸	a unit of length (inch)
ts'un-hsiang　存想	keeping the thought

ts'un-hsin	存心	keeping the mind
ts'un-shen nei-chao	存神內照	keeping the *shen* and inwardly illuminating
ts'ung	聰	clear
ts'ung-ke	從革	obeying and changing
tu	度	degree
t'u-chao	土兆	Earth omen
tu-chuan	杜撰	personal fabrication
t'u-kuei	土圭	p. 144
tu-shu-fa	讀書法	method of reading books
t'ui	推	to extend
tui	對	opposite
t'ui	退	to retreat, to retrogress
t'ui-to	隤墮	degenerated
tung	動	movement
t'ung	通	penetration, unobstructed
t'ung-lei hsiang pien	同類相變	"Things of the same category change each other."
t'ung-lei hsiang tung	同類相動	"Things of the same category move each other."
"Tung-shan"	東山	a poem of the *Shih-ching*
Tung-t'ing	洞庭	name of a lake
"Tung-wu"	動物	a chapter of Chang Tsai's *Cheng-meng*
tz'u	次	Jupiter station
tzu	滋	to nurture
tzu	紫	violet
tzu-ch'eng	自成	to accomplish by oneself
tzu-chuan	自轉	rotation around its own axis
tz'u-hsiang	慈祥	kind
tzu-hsiang mao-tun	自相矛盾	self-contradiction
tzu-jan	自然	so by itself, spontaneous
tzu-jan chih shu	自然之數	the *shu* of spontaneity
tzu-k'e	自克	self-command
tzu-sheng	子聲	son sound
Tzu-wei-han	紫微垣	name of a constellation
tzu wu erh yu	自無而有	from nothing to something
tzu yu erh wu	自無而有	from something to nothing
wai-kan	外感	external stimulus
wai-tan	外丹	external alchemy
wan-k'ung	頑空	dull void
wan-wu	萬物	the myriad things
wan-wu tsu sheng	萬物資生	a phrase from the *I-ching*
wan-wu tsu shih	萬物資始	a phrase from the *I-ching*
wang	望	full moon
wang	旺	prospering

wang 往	to go
wang-liang 魍魎	a mountain monster
wei 衛	constituent of man's body
wei 微	extreme smallness, hidden
wei 胃	stomach
wei 爲	to do
wei-ch'üan 未全	not perfect
wei-fa 未發	not yet manifest
wei-hsing 緯星	irregular star (planet)
wei-mi hsün-no 委靡巽懦	dispirited and subservient
wei-miao 微妙	fine and subtle
wen-hou 溫厚	gentle
"Wen-yen" 文言	"Words on Text" (commentary of the *I-ching*)
wu 霧	fog
wu 惡	hatred
wu 無	nothingness
wu 巫	shaman
wu 物	things
wu-ch'ang 五常	the five constant virtues
wu-cheng-se 五正色	the five regular colors
wu-chi 無極	the ultimate of nothingness
wu-chien-se 五間色	the five intermediary colors
wu chih li 物之理	the *li* of things
wu hsi 無息	no stop
wu-hsing 五行	the five phases
wu-lei-fa 五雷法	the five-thunder method
wu-lün 五倫	the five human relations
wu-sheng 五聲	the five notes
wu-ssu 五祀	the five domestic spirits
wu-tao 吾道	my way
Wu-ti 五帝	name of a constellation
wu-tsang 五臟	the five storing viscera
ya 軋	to grind
yang 陽	
yang 養	to nourish
Yang-ch'eng 陽城	a geographical name
yang-kuan fu-ch'a 仰觀俯察	observations
yang-sheng 養生	nourishing life
yao 爻	single line of the *I-ching* diagrams
yao-hsing 藥性	nature of medicine
"Yao-tien" 堯典	"Canon of Yao" (a chapter of the *Shu-ching*)
yeh 液	constituent of man's body
yeh-ch'i 夜氣	the nightly *ch'i*
Yen 燕	a geographical name

yen	言	speech
yen	驗	to prove, to verify, to test
yen-ning	嚴凝	severe
yen pu chin i	言不盡意	words not exhausting the meaning
yen-shang	炎上	blazing and uprising
yin	陰	
yin	淫	licentious
yin-te	淫慝	debauching
yin-yang	陰陽	
ying	營	constituent of man's body
ying	應	response
ying	影	shadow
ying	硬	solid
Ying-ch'uan	穎川	a geographical name
yü	御	to control
yu	幽	dark, hidden
yü	欲	desire
yü	豫	foreknowledge
yü	雨	rain
yu	愚	stupid
yu	有	to have
yu	游	to wander
yu-ch'i	游氣	wandering *ch'i*
Yü-chi-t'u	禹迹圖	name of a map
yu chih yin	幽之因	p. 305
yü-chou	宇宙	universe
yü-fen	餘分	chap. 12, note 47
yu-hsing	右行	rightward movement
yu-hun wei pien	游魂爲變	the wandering *hun* making a change
"Yü-kung"	禹貢	a chapter of the *Shu-ching*
yü-lu	語錄	recorded conversations
yu tz'u li	有此理	"There is *li* for this."
yu wei	有爲	to have action
yüan	元	origin, cosmic cycle
yüan	原	source
yüan-ch'i	元氣	the original *ch'i*
yüan-hsiao	元枵	a Jupiter station
yüan-sheng	元聲	the original sound
Yüeh	越	a geographical name
yüeh	樂	music
yüeh-chia	樂家	music specialists
Yüeh-ching	樂經	*Classic of Music*
yüeh-li	約禮	restraining propriety
"Yüeh-ling"	月令	"Monthly Ordinances" (a chapter of the *Li-chi*)
Yüeh-t'ai	嶽臺	a geographical name

yün 運   fortune, revolution
yün-tung 運動   physical activity
yün-yung 運用   moving and utilizing
yung 用   function

Bibliography

The standard abbreviations are used for the following compilations.

SKCS: *Wen-yüan-k'o Ssu-k'u ch'üan-shu* 文淵閣四庫全書
SPPY: *Ssu-pu pei-yao* 四部備要
SPTK: *Ssu-pu ts'ung-k'an* 四部叢刊

The abbreviated forms of citations to Chu Hsi sources are explained below. In addition, this bibliography uses the following abbreviation of the collected works of Ch'eng Hao and Ch'eng I.

ECC: *Erh-Ch'eng-chi* 二程集 (Collected works of the two Ch'engs). Modern punctuated ed. Beijing: Chung-hua shu-chü 中華書局, 1981.

Primary Sources

Chu Hsi sources

Chu-tzu yü-lei 朱子語類 (Classified conversations of Master Chu, compiled in 1270) and *Chu-wen-kung wen-chi* 朱文公文集 (Collected writings of Chu Wen-kung, compiled in 1534) are the two basic sources for Chu Hsi's sayings and writings. But this book also contains occasional references to a later compilation, *Chu-tzu ch'üan-shu* 朱子全書 (Complete works of Master Chu, compiled in 1713), which excerpts mainly from the two earlier compilations. The following abbreviations are used for references to the Chu Hsi sources:

WC: *Hui-an-hsien-sheng Chu-wen-kung wen-chi* 晦庵先生朱文公文集. SPPY ed. *WC*60.17a refers to the 60th *chüan* 卷, p.17a.
WCH: "Continuing Collections" (*hsü-chi* 續集).
WCP: "Separate Collections" (*pieh-chi* 別集).

YL: *Chu-tzu yü-lei*. 1270. Reprint, 1473. Modern reprint, Taipei: Cheng-chung shu-chü 正中書局, 1962. *YL*49.2a3 refers to the 49th *chüan*, the 3rd passage beginning on p.2a. The following approximate formula can be used to convert the page in the 1473 edition (p) into the page in the modern punctuated edition (q) by Chung-hua shu-chü 中華書局 (Beijing, Chung-hua shu-chü, 1986): q = (q^0 – 1) + 1.2p, where "q^0" is the first page of the relevant *chüan* in the Chung-hua shu-chü edition.

CS: *Chu-tzu ch'üan-shu* 朱子全書. 1713 ed. *CS*15.9b0 refers to the 15th *chüan*, the passage that begins on the previous page (p. 9a) and is continued on p. 9b.

SSCC: *Ssu-shu chi-chu* 四書集註 (Collected Commentaries on the *Four Books*). SPPY ed.

The following editions are used for the other Chu Hsi sources.

Chin-ssu-lu 近思錄 (Reflections on things at hand). In *Chin-ssu-lu chi-chu* 近思錄集註 (Collected commentaries on *Reflections on Things at Hand*). SPPY ed.

Chou-i pen-i 周易本義 (Original meaning of the *Book of Changes*). SKCS ed.

Ch'u-tz'u chi-chu 楚辭集註 (Collected commentaries on the *Songs of Ch'u*). Reprint, Taipei: I-wen yin-shu-kuan 藝文印書館, 1973.

I-hsueh ch'i-meng 易學啓蒙 (Introduction to the study of the [*Book of*] *Changes*). Reprint, Taipei: Huang-chi ch'u-pan-she 皇極出版社, 1980.

Shih chi-chuan 詩集傳 (Collection of commentaries on the [*Book of*] *Poetry*). Taipei: Chung-hua shu-chü 中華書局, 1982.

Ta-hsueh huo-wen 大學或問 (Some questions on the *Great Learning*). SKCS ed.

Ts'an-t'ung-ch'i k'ao-i 參同契考異 (Examination of the *Kinship of the Three*). SPPY ed.

Wen-kung i-shuo 文公易說 ([Chu] Wen-kung's explanations on the [*Book of*] *Changes*). Compiled by Chu Chien 朱鑑. SKCS ed.

Yin-fu-ching k'ao-i 陰符經考異 (Examination of the *Canon of Secrets and Tallies*). SKCS ed.

The following essays and treatises of Chu Hsi are included in *Chu-wen-kung wen-chi*.

"Ch'in-lü shuo" 琴律說 (Explanation of musical instruments and pitches).

"Ching-chai chen" 敬齋箴 (Admonitions of "the Studio of Reverence").

"Chiu-chiang P'eng-li pien" 九江彭蠡辨 (Discussion of the Nine Rivers and P'eng-li).

"Hsueh-hsiao kung-chü ssu-i" 學校貢擧私議 (Personal proposal for schools and official recruitment).

"Hu shuo" 壺說 (Explanation of sacrificial wine vessel).

"I-hsiang shuo" 易象說 (Explanation of the images of the [*Book of*] *Changes*).

"I-li shih-kung" 儀禮釋宮 (Ceremonial interpretation of palace).

"I wu chen" 易五箴 (Five admonitions on the [*Book of*] *Changes*).

"Sheng-lü pien" 聲律辨 (Discussion of sounds and pitches).

"Shih-kua k'ao-wu" 著卦考誤 (Examination of milfoil stalks and hexagrams).

"T'iao-hsi chen" 調息箴 (Admonitions on regulating the breath).

"Ts'an-t'ung-ch'i shuo" 參同契說 (Explanation of the *Kinship of the Three*).

"Yüan-heng-li-chen shuo" 元亨利貞說 (Explanation of *yüan, heng, li,* and *chen*).

OTHER PRIMARY SOURCES CITED AND EDITIONS USED

Ancient sources that are cited by the standard chapter numbers and works for which the edition does not need to be specified are listed by title only. The titles of chapters or volumes of the works whose titles are listed here, except for the "Hsi-tz'u chuan" and the "Shuo-kua chuan" commentaries of the *I-ching,* are not listed separately.

Chang Heng 張衡. *Ling Hsien* 靈憲 (Numinous constitution).

Chang Hua 張華. *Po-wu-chih* 博物志 (Treatise on natural history). SPPY ed.

Chang Tsai 張載. *Chang-tzu ch'üan-shu* 張子全書 (Complete works of Master Chang). SPPY ed.

——. *Cheng-meng* 正蒙. (Correct teaching for youth). In *Chang-tzu ch'üan-shu.*

——. *Hsi-ming* 西銘. (Western inscription). In *Chang-tzu ch'üan-shu*.

Ch'ao Yüan-fang 巢元方. *Chu-ping yüan-hou lun* 諸病源候論 (Treatise on origins and symptoms of various diseases).

Ch'en Ch'ang-fang 陳長方. *Pu-li k'e-t'an* 步里客談 (Idle talks of village strolling). SKCS ed.

Ch'eng Hao 程顥 and Ch'eng I 程頤. *Ho-nan Ch'eng-shih i-shu* 河南程氏遺書 (Surviving works of the Ch'engs of Honan). *ECC.*

Ch'eng I. *Chou-i Ch'eng-shih chuan* 周易程氏傳 (Mr. Ch'eng's commentary on the *Book of Changes*). *ECC.*

——. *I-ch'üan wen-chi* 伊川文集 (Collected writings of I-ch'üan). *ECC.*

——. *Ts'ui-yen* 粹言 (Pure words). *ECC.*

Chin-kang-ching 金剛經 (Diamond sutra).

Chin-shu 晉書 (History of the Chin dynasty). Modern punctuated ed. Beijing: Chung-hua shu-chü, n.d.

Ch'in-ting Shu-ching chuan-shuo 欽定書經傳說 (Imperial edition of commentaries and explanations on the *Book of Documents*). SKCS ed.

Chiu-chang suan-shu 九章算術 (Nine chapters on mathematical techniques).

Chiu T'ang-shu 舊唐書 (Old history of the T'ang dynasty). Modern punctuated ed. Beijing: Chung-hua shu-chü, n.d.

Chou-li 周禮 (Rites of Chou). In *Chou-li chu-shu* 周禮註疏 (Commentaries and subcommentaries on the *Rites of Chou*). Reprint, Taipei: Hsin-wen-feng 新文豐, 1977.

Chou-pi suan-ching 周髀算經 (Mathematical classic on the Chou gnomon). SPPY ed.

Chou Tun-i 周敦頤. *T'ai-chi-t'u shuo* 太極圖說 (Explanation of the *Diagram of the Supreme Ultimate*).

——. *T'ung-shu* 通書 (Penetrating book [on the *Book of Changes*]). SPPY ed.

Ch'u-tz'u 楚辭 (Songs of Ch'u). In Chu Hsi, *Ch'u-tz'u chi-chu*.

Chuang-tzu 莊子. SPPY ed.

Ch'un-ch'iu 春秋 (Spring and autumn annals). In *Ch'un-ch'iu chu-shu* 春秋註疏 (Commentaries and subcommentaries on the *Spring and Autumn Annals*). Reprint, Taipei: Hsin-wen-feng, 1977.

Ch'un-ch'iu yüan-ming-pao 春秋元命苞 (Bract of origin and fate on the *Spring and Autumn Annals*). In Ou-yang Hsün, *I-wen lei-chü*.

Chung-yung 中庸 (Doctrine of the mean).

Erh-ya 爾雅 (Close and correct). In *Erh-ya chu-shu* 爾雅註疏 (Commentaries and subcommentaries on the *Close and Correct*). Reprint, Taipei: Hsin-wen-feng, 1977.

Han-shu 漢書 (History of the [former] Han dynasty). Modern punctuated ed. Beijing: Chung-hua shu-chü, n.d.

Han Ying 韓嬰. *Han-shih wai-chuan* 韓詩外傳 (Outer commentary on the poems of Han).

Hou Han-shu 後漢書 (History of the later Han dynasty). Modern punctuated ed. Beijing: Chung-hua shu-chü, n.d.

"Hsi-tz'u chuan" 繫辭傳. (Commentary on the appended words [in the *Book of Changes*]).

Hsia Te 夏德. *Wei-sheng shih-ch'üan fang* 衛生十全方 (Complete recipes of protecting life).

Hsün-tzu 荀子.

Huai-nan-tzu 淮南子. SPPY ed.

Huang-ti chiu-ting shen tan-ching 皇帝九鼎神丹經 (The Yellow Emperor's canon of the nine-caldron divine elixir).

Huang-ti nei-ching ling-shu 皇帝內經靈樞 (The Yellow Emperor's inner canon, numinous axis). SPPY ed.

Huang-ti nei-ching su-wen 皇帝內經素問 (The Yellow Emperor's inner canon, basic questions). SPPY ed.

I-ching 易經 (*Book of Changes*).

K'ao-ling-yao 考靈曜 (Examination of the sun). In Chang Hua, *Po-wu-chih*.

Kuan-tzu 管子. In *Chu-tzu chi-ch'eng* 諸子集成 ed. Beijing, 1954.

K'ung Ying-ta 孔穎達. *Chou-i cheng-i* 周易正義 (Correct meaning of the *Book of Changes*). In *Chou-i chu-shu* 周易註疏 (Commentaries and subcommentaries on the *Book of Changes*). Reprint, Taipei: Hsin-wen-feng, 1977.

Kuo-yü 國語 (Words on the states). SPPY ed.

Kuo Yung 郭雍. *Shang-han pu wang lun* 傷寒補亡論 (Treatise on repairing cold damage).

Lao-tzu 老子.

Leng-yen-ching 楞嚴經 (Surangama sutra).

Li-chi (Record of rites). In *Li-chi chu-shu* 禮記註疏 (Commentaries and subcommentaries on the *Record of Rites*). Reprint, Taipei: Hsin-wen-feng, 1977.

Lieh-tzu 列子. Reprint, Taipei: I-wen yin-shu-kuan, 1971.

Lo Ta-ching 羅大經. *Ho-lin yü-lu* 鶴林玉露 (Dewdrops of temples). SKCS ed.

Lun-yü 論語 (Analects).

Meng-tzu 孟子 (Mencius).

Nan-ching 難經 (Classic of difficult problems).

Ou-yang Hsün 歐陽詢. *I-wen lei-chü* 藝文類聚 (Classified collections of literary writings). Shanghai: Ku-chieh ch'u-pan-she 古籍出版社, 1982.

Pao-p'u-tzu 抱朴子. SPPY ed.

Shan-hai-ching 山海經 (Classic of the mountains and rivers).

Shao Yung 邵雍. *Huang-chi ching-shih* 皇極經世 (Supreme rules governing the world). SPPY ed.

——. *Yü-ch'iao wen-tui* 漁樵問對 (Questions and answers between the fisherman and the woodcutter). In *Hsing-li ta-ch'üan* 性理大全 (Great compendium on human nature and *li*). SKCS ed.

Shen Kua 沈括. *Meng-hsi pi-t'an* 夢溪筆談 (Brush talks of dream brook). Reprint, Beijing: Wen-wu ch'u-pan-she 文物出版社, 1975.

Shih-ching 詩經 (Book of poetry).

Shu-ching 書經 (Book of documents).

Shui-ching 水經 (Classic of the waters).

"Shuo-kua chuan" 說卦傳 (Commentary on the explanation of the diagrams [in the *Book of Changes*]).

Ssu-ma Ch'ien 司馬遷. *Shih-chi* 史記 (Record of the historian). Modern punctuated ed. Beijing: Chung-hua shu-chü, n.d.

Su Sung 蘇頌. *Hsin i-hsiang fa-yao* 新儀象法要 (New method and synopsis on the armillary spheres and celestial globes). SKCS ed.

Su-wen yün-ch'i chieh-lüeh 素問運氣節略 (Outline of the movement and *ch'i* in the *Basic Questions*).

Sung-shih 宋史 (History of the Sung dynasty). Modern punctuated ed. Beijing: Chung-hua shu-chü, n.d.

Ta-hsueh 大學 (Great learning).

Ta Tai Li-chi 大戴禮記 (Ta Tai's record of rites). SKCS ed.

T'ai-p'ing yü-lan 太平御覽 (T'ai-p'ing imperial reader). SKCS ed.

T'ao Hung-ching 陶弘景. *Pen-ts'ao-ching chi-chu* 本草經集註 (Collected commentaries on the *Classic of Pen-ts'ao*).

Tao-tsang 道藏 (The Taoist corpus).

T'eng Kung 滕珙. *Ching-chi wen-heng* 經濟文衡 (Consideration of the writings on governing and aiding). SKCS ed.

Ts'ai Yüan-ting 蔡元定. *Lü-lü hsin-shu* 律呂新書 (New book of the pitches). SKCS ed.

Tso-chuan 左傳 (Tso commentary [on the *Spring and Autumn Annals*]). In *Tso-chuan chu-shu* 左傳註疏 (Commentaries and subcommentaries on the *Tso Commentary*). Reprint, Taipei: Hsin-wen-feng, 1977.

Tu Yu 杜佑. *T'ung-tien* 通典 (Comprehensive canon). SKCS ed.

Tung Chung-shu. *Ch'un-ch'iu fan-lu* 春秋繁露 (Luxuriant dew of the *Spring and Autumn Annals*). SPPY ed.

Wang Chi-fu 王及甫. *T'ien-ching* 天經 (Classic of the heavens).

Wang Mao-hung 王懋竑. *Chu-tzu nien-p'u* 朱子年譜 (Chronological biography of Master Chu). Reprint, Taipei: Shang-wu 商務, 1982.

Wang Shu-ho 王叔和. *Mai-ching* 脈經 (Classic of the pulses).

Wang Ying-lin 王應麟. *K'un-hsueh chi-wen* 困學紀聞 (Record of hard study). SKCS ed.

Wei Po-yang 魏伯陽. *Ts'an-t'ung-ch'i* (Kinship of the three). In Chu Hsi, *Ts'an-t'ung-ch'i k'ao-i.*

Yang Hsiung 揚雄. *T'ai-hsüan-ching* 太玄經 (Canon of the great mystery). SPPY ed.

Yi Sun-ji (Li Shun-chih) 李舜之. *Chega yŏksangjip* (*Chu-chia li-hsiang-chi*) 諸家曆象集 (Collection of calendrical and astronomical theories of various masters).

Yin-fu-ching 陰符經 (Canon of secrets and tallies). In Chu Hsi, *Yin-fu-ching k'ao-i.*

Yü Ching 余靖. *Hai-chao t'u-lun* 海潮圖論 (Pictorial discussion of the sea tides). Appended to *CS*50.46a1.

Modern Secondary Materials

EAST ASIAN LANGUAGE MATERIALS

Azuma Jūji 吾妻重二. "Shu Ki 'Shueki sandōkei kōi' ni tsuite" 朱熹周易參同契考異について (On Chu Hsi's *Examination of the Kinship of the Three in the Book of Changes*). *Nihon Chūgoku-gakukaihō* 日本中國學會報, no. 36 (1984), 175–190.

Chang Chin-chien 張金鑑. *Chung-kuo wen-kuan chih-tu shih* 中國文官制度史 (History of Chinese civil service institutions). Taipei, 1955.

Chang Li-wen 張立文. *Chu Hsi ssu-hsiang yen-chiu* 朱熹思想研究 (Study of Chu Hsi's thought). Beijing: Chung-kuo she-hui ke-hsueh ch'u-pan-she 中國社會科學出版社, 1981.

Chao Kuang-hua 趙匡華. *Chung-kuo lien-tan-shu* 中國煉丹術 (Chinese alchemy). Hong Kong: Chung-hua shu-chü 中華書局, 1989.

Ch'en Jung-chieh 陳榮捷 (Wing-tsit Chan). *Chu-tzu men-jen* 朱子門人 (Master Chu's disciples). Taipei: Hsueh-sheng shu-chü 學生書局, 1982.

——. *Chu-tzu hsin t'an-so* 朱子新探索 (New investigation on Master Chu). Taipei: Hsueh-sheng shu-chü, 1988.

Ch'en Kuo-fu 陳國符. "Shuo Chou-i Ts'an-t'ung-ch'i yü nei-tan wai-tan" 說周易參同契與內丹外丹 (On the *Kinship of the Three in the Book of Changes* and the inner and the outer alchemies). *Tao-tsang yuan-liu k'ao* 道藏源流考 (Study of the origins and development of the *Taoist Corpus*). Shanghai, 1949.

Ch'en Lai 陳來. *Chu Hsi che-hsueh yen-chiu* 朱熹哲學研究 (Study of Chu Hsi's philosophy). Beijing: Chung-kuo she-hui ke-hsueh ch'u-pan-she, 1987.

Ch'en Tsun-kuei 陳遵嬀. *Chung-kuo t'ien-wen-hsueh-shih* 中國天文學史 (History of Chinese astronomy). 6 vols. Taipei: Ming-wen shu-chü 明文書局, 1984–1990.

Ch'eng Wen-kuang 鄭文光 and Hsi Tse-tsung 席澤宗 (Xi Zezong). *Chung-kuo li-shih shang te yü-chou li-lun* 中國歷史上的宇宙理論 (Theories of the universe in Chinese history). Beijing: Jen-min ch'u-pan-she 人民出版社, 1975.

Ch'ien Mu 錢穆. *Chu-tzu hsin hsueh-an* 朱子新學案 (New anthology and critical accounts of Master Chu). 5 vols. Taipei: San-min shu-chü 三民書局, 1971.

Ch'in Chia-i 秦家懿 (Julia Ching). "'Sheng' tsai Chung-kuo ssu-hsiang-shih nei te to-chung i-i" 聖在中國思想史內的多重意義 (Many layers of meaning of "*Sheng*" in the history of Chinese ideas). *Ch'ing-hua hsueh-pao* 清華學報 (Tsing Hua journal of Chinese studies) *16* (1985), 15–27.

Ch'ü Wan-li 屈萬里. *Hsien-Ch'in Han Wei i-li shu-p'ing* 先秦漢魏易例述評 (Explanation and criticism of the examples dealing with the *Changes* in the Pre-Ch'in, Han, and Wei). Taipei: Hsueh-sheng shu-chü, 1975.

Chung-kuo t'ien-wen-hsueh shih cheng-li yen-chiu hsiao-tsu 中國天文學史整理研究小組 (Group for arrangement and research of the history of Chinese astronomy). *Chung-kuo t'ien-wen-hsueh shih* 中國天文學史 (History of Chinese astronomy). Beijing: Ke-hsueh ch'u-pan-she 科學出版社, 1987.

Hashimoto Keizō 橋本敬造. *Chūgoku senseijutsu no sekai* 中國占星術の世界 (The world of Chinese astrology). Tokyo: Tōhō Shoten 東方書店, 1993.

Hsü Fu-kuan 徐復觀. *Chung-kuo jen-hsing-lun shih: Hsien-Ch'in-p'ien* 中國人性論史.先秦篇 (History of discussions on human nature in China: The pre-Ch'in period). Taichung: Tung-hai University, 1963.

Huang I-nung 黃一農 (Huang Yi-Long). "Chi-hsing yü ku-tu k'ao" 極星與古度考 (Study of the pole star and the ancient "degree"). *Ch'ing-hua hsueh-pao* 清華學報 *22* (1992), 93–117.

Huang I-nung and Chang Chih-ch'eng 張志誠. "Chung-kuo ch'uan-t'ung hou-ch'i-shuo te yen-chin yü shuai-t'ui" 中國傳統候氣說的演進與衰頹 (Development and decline of the traditional Chinese theory of "watching for *ch'i*"). *Ch'ing-hua hsueh-pao* 清華學報 *23* (1993), 125–147.

Hwang Ŭi-dong 황의동. *Han'guk-ŭi yuhaksasang* 한국의 유학사상 (Confucian thought in Korea). Seoul: Sŏkwangsa 서광사, 1995.

Imai Usaburō 今井宇三郎. *Sōdai Ekigaku no kenkyū* 宋代易學の研究 (Studies on the study of the *Changes* in the Sung period). Tokyo: Meiji 明治, 1958.

Kao Heng 高亨. *Chou-i ku-ching t'ung-shuo* 周易古經通說 (Comprehensive explanation of the ancient classic, *Book of Changes*). Beijing: Chung-hua shu-chü, 1958.

Kim Yŏng-sik 金永植 (Yung Sik Kim). "Yi Hwang-ŭi igigwan-kwa sinyuhak chŏnt'ongsang-esŏŭi kŭ wich'i" 李滉의 理氣觀과 新儒學 전통상에서의 그 위치 (Yi Hwang's views on *Li-Ch'i* and its place in the Neo-Confucian tradition). *T'oegye hakpo* 退溪學報, no. 81 (1994), 70–101.

Kobayashi Nobuyuki 小林信明. *Chūgoku jōdai in'yō gogyō shisō no kenkyū* 中國上代陰陽五行思想の研究 (Studies on the ideas of the yin-yang and the five phases in early China). Tokyo, 1951.

Kuan Ch'eng-hsueh 管成學, Yang Jung-kai 楊榮垓, and Su K'e-fu 蘇克福. *Su Sung yü "Hsin i-hsiang fa-yao" yen-chiu* 蘇頌與新儀象法要研究 (Study of Su Sung and the *New Method and Synopsis on the Armillary Spheres and Celestial Globes*). Ch'ang-ch'un 長春: Chi-lin Wen-shih ch'u-pan-she 吉林文史出版社, 1991.

Kuroda Genji 黑田源次. *Ki no kenkyū* 氣の研究 (Studies on *Ch'i*). Tokyo, 1977.

Lo Kuang 羅光. *Chung-kuo che-hsueh ssu-hsiang-shih: Liang-Han Nan-pei-ch'ao p'ien* 中國哲學思想史.兩漢南北朝篇 (History of Chinese philosophical thought: The Han and the Northern and Southern dynasties). Taipei: Hsueh-sheng shu-chü, 1978.

Ma Po-ying 馬伯英. *Chung-wai i-hsueh-shih chiang-i* 中外醫學史講義 (Lectures on the history of Chinese and foreign medicine). Shanghai: Shanghai Ti-i I-hsueh-yüan 上海第一醫學院, 1982.

Miura Kunio 三浦國雄. *Shushi* 朱子 (Master Chu). Tokyo: Kōdansha 講談社, 1979.

——. "Shushi to kokyū" 朱子と呼吸 (Master Chu and respiration). In *Chūgoku ni okeru nin-genjō no tankyū* 中國における人間性の探究 (Research on human nature in China), pp. 499–521. Tokyo, 1983.

Miura Yoshiaki 三浦吉明. "Keisho yori mita ten no shisō" 經書より見た天の思想 (Views of *t'ien* seen from the classics). *Tōyōgaku* 東洋學 *34* (1975), 38–65.

Miyashita Saburō 宮下三郎. "Sō-gen no i-ryō" 宋元の醫療 (Medicine in the Sung and Yüan). In Yabuuchi, *Sō-gen ji-dai no kagaku gijutsushi*, pp. 123–170.

Morohashi Tetsuji 諸橋轍次 and Yasuoka Masahiro 安岡正篤, eds. *Shushigaku taikei* 朱子學大系 (Outline of the Chu Hsi learning). 14 vols. Tokyo: Meidoku 明德, 1974–1983.

Mou Tsung-san 牟宗三. *Hsin-t'i yü hsing-t'i* 心體與性體 (Mind and human nature). 3 vols. Taipei: Cheng-chung shu-chü, 1968.

Onozawa Seiichi 小野澤精一, Fukunaga Mitsuji 福永光司, and Yamanoi Yu 山井湧, eds. *Ki no shisō: Chūgoku ni okeru shizenkan to ningenkan no tenkai* 氣の思想:中國における自然觀と人間觀の展開 (Ideas of *Ch'i*: Development of the views of nature and the views of man in China). Tokyo: Tokyo University Press, 1978.

Sakade Yoshinobu 坂出祥伸, ed. *Chūgoku kodai yōsei shisō no sōgōteki kenkyū* 中國古代養生思想の綜合的研究 (Synthetic studies of the ancient Chinese ideas of "nourishing life"). Tokyo: Harakawa 平河, 1988.

Shimada Kenji 島田虔次. *Shushigaku to Yōmeigaku* 朱子學と陽明學 (The Chu Hsi learning and the [Wang] Yang-ming learning). Tokyo: Iwanami 岩波, 1967.

Shinjō Shinzō 新城新藏. "Kanshi gogyō-setsu to Senkyokureki" 干支五行說と顓頊曆 (The theories of the [ten] stems, the [twelve] branches, and the five phases, and the Chuan-hsü calendar). *Shinagaku* 支那學 *2* (1922), 387–415, 495–516.

Shu Ching-nan 束景南. *Chu-tzu ta-chuan* 朱子大傳 (The great biography of Master Chu). Fu-chien: Fu-chien chiao-yü ch'u-pan-she 福建教育出版社, 1992.

Sudō Yoshiyuki 周藤吉之. *Sōdai keizaishi kenkyū* 宋代經濟史研究 (Studies on the economic history of the Sung period). Tokyo: Tokyo University Press, 1962.

Suzuki Yoshijirō 鈴木由次郎. *Shueki sandōkei* 周易參同契 (The kinship of the three in the *Book of Changes*). Tokyo: Meidoku, 1977.

Tanaka Kenji 田中謙二. "Shumon teishi shijinen kō" 朱門弟子師事年攷 (Study of the dates of the disciples' study under Chu Hsi). *Tōhō gakuhō* 東方學報 (Kyoto) *44* (1973), 147–218; *48* (1975), 261–357.

T'ang Chün-i 唐君毅. *Chung-kuo che-hsueh yüan-lun: Yüan-hsing-p'ien* 中國哲學原論:原性篇 (Foundations of Chinese philosophy: On human nature). Hong Kong: Hsin Ya yen-chiu-so 新亞研究所, 1968.

Terada Gō 寺田剛. *Sōdai kyōikushi gaisetsu* 宋代教育史概說 (Introduction to the history of education in the Sung period). Tokyo: Hakubunsha 博文社, 1965.

Wang Yung 王庸. *Chung-kuo ti-li-hsueh-shih* 中國地理學史 (History of Chinese geography). Ch'ang-sha: Shang-wu, 1938.

Watanabe Kōzō 渡邊幸三. "Genson suru Chūgoku kinsei made no gozō rokufuzu no gaisetsu" 現存する中國近世までの五臟六腑圖の概說 (Introduction to the extant premodern Chinese diagrams of the five storing viscera and the six processing viscera). *Nihon ishigaku zasshi* 日本醫史學雜誌 7 (1956), 88–182.

Wu Nan-hsün 吳南薰. *Lü-hsueh hui-t'ung* 律學會通 (Complete understanding of harmonics). Beijing, 1964.

Yabuuchi Kiyoshi 藪內清. "Sō-gen jidai no tenmon-gaku" 宋元時代の天文學 (Astronomy in the Sung and Yüan times). In Yabuuchi, *Sō-gen jidai no kagaku gijutsushi*, pp. 89–122.

——. *Chūgoku no tenmonrekihō* 中國の天文曆法 (Astronomy and calendrical method of China). Tokyo: Heibonsha 平凡社, 1969.

——. *Chūgoku no sugaku* 中國の數學 (Mathematics of China). Tokyo: Iwanami, 1974.

——, ed. *Sō-gen jidai no kagaku gijutsushi* 宋元時代の科學技術史 (History of science and technology in the Sung and Yüan times). Kyoto: Kyoto daigaku Jinbun kagaku kenkyūso 京都大學人文科學研究所, 1967.

Yamada Keiji 山田慶兒. *Shushi no shizen-gaku* 朱子の自然學 (Master Chu's study of nature). Tokyo: Iwanami, 1978.

——. "Jujireki heno dō" 授時曆への道 (The way toward the Shou-shih calendar). In Yamada, *Chūgoku no kagaku to kagakusha*, pp. 1–207.

——, ed. *Chūgoku no kagaku to kagakusha* 中國の科學と科學者 (Science and scientists of China). Kyoto: Kyoto daigaku Jinbun kagaku kenkyūso, 1978.

Yamada Keiji and Tanaka Tan 田中淡, eds. *Chūgoku kodai kagakushiron* 中國古代科學史論 (Papers on the history of ancient Chinese science). Kyoto: Kyoto daigaku Jinbun kagaku kenkyūso, 1991.

Yamanoi Yū. "Shushi no shisō ni okeru ki." 朱子の思想における氣 (Ch'i in the thought of Master Chu). In Onozawa, Fukunaga, and Yamanoi, *Ki no shisō*, pp. 438–452.

Yang Yin 楊隱. *Chung-kuo yin-yüeh-shih* 中國音樂史 (History of Chinese music). 2nd ed. Taipei: Hsueh-i ch'u-pan-she 學藝出版社, 1977.

Yasuda Jirō 安田二郎. "Shushi no 'ki' ni tsuite" 朱子の氣について (On Master Chu's [ideas of] Ch'i). In Yasuda, *Chūgoku kinsei shisō kenkyū*, pp. 3–61; originally published in *Tōhō gakuhō* (Kyoto) 10 (1939–1940), 468–514.

——. *Chūgoku kinsei shisō kenkyū* 中國近世思想研究 (Studies of modern Chinese thought). Tokyo, 1976.

Yü Ying-shih 余英時. "Ts'ung Sung Ming ju-hsueh ti fa-chan lun Ch'ing-tai ssu-hsiang-shih. Shang-p'ien. Sung-Ming ju-hsueh chung chih-shih-chu-i te ch'uan-t'ung" 從宋明儒學的發展論清代思想史. 上篇: 宋明儒學中知識主義的傳統 (Discussion of the history of ideas in the Ch'ing period from the development of the Sung-Ming Confucian learning. 1. Tradition of intellectualism in the Sung-Ming Confucian learning). *Chung-kuo hsueh-jen* 中國學人 2 (1970), 19–42.

WESTERN LANGUAGE MATERIALS

Aiton, A. J., and Eikoh Shimao. "Gorai Kinzo's Study of Leibniz and the *I ching* Hexagrams." *Annals of Science 38* (1981), 71–92.

Ames, Roger T. "The Mencian Conception of *Ren Xing*: Does It Mean 'Human Nature'?" In Rosement, *Chinese Texts and Philosophical Contexts*, pp. 143–175.

Baldrian-Hussein, Farzeen. "Lü Tung-pin in Northern Sung Literature." *Cahiers d'Extrême-Asie 2* (1986), 133–170.

Bennett, Stephen J. "Patterns of the Sky and Earth: A Chinese Science of Applied Cosmology." *Chinese Science*, no. 3 (1978), 1–26.

Berthrong, John. "The Thoughtlessness of Unexamined Things." *Journal of Chinese Philosophy 7* (1980), 131–151.

Birdwhistell, Anne D. *Transition to Neo-Confucianism: Shao Yung on Knowledge and Symbols of Reality*. Stanford, Calif.: Stanford University Press, 1989.

——. "Medicine and History as Theoretical Tools in a Confucian Pragmatism." *Philosophy East and West 45* (1995), 1–28.

Birge, Bettine. "Chu Hsi and Women's Education." In de Bary and Chaffee, *Neo-Confucian Education*, pp. 325–367.

Bloom, Irene. "Mencian Arguments on Human Nature (*Jen-hsing*)." *Philosophy East and West 44* (1994), 19–53.

Boas, Marie. "The Establishment of Mechanical Philosophy." *Osiris 10* (1952), 412–541.

Bodde, Derk. "Harmony and Conflict in Chinese Philosophy." In Wright, *Studies in Chinese Thought*, pp. 19–80.

——. "Evidence for 'Law of Nature' in Chinese Thought." *Harvard Journal of Asiatic Studies 20* (1957), 709–727.

——. "The Chinese Cosmic Magic Known as 'Watching for the Ethers.'" In Bodde, *Essays on Chinese Civilization*, pp. 351–372; originally published in Glahn, *Studia serica Karlgren dedicata*.

——. "Chinese 'Law of Nature': A Reconsideration." *Harvard Journal of Asiatic Studies 39* (1979), 139–155.

——. *Essays on Chinese Civilization*. Princeton, N.J.: Princeton University Press, 1981.

——. *Chinese Thought, Society, and Science: The Intellectual and Social Background of Science and Technology in Pre-modern China*. Honolulu: University of Hawaii Press, 1991.

Bol, Peter K. "Chu Hsi's Redefinition of Literati Learning." In de Bary and Chaffee, *Neo-Confucian Education*, pp. 151–185.

——. "The Sung Examination System and the *Shih*." *Asia Major*, 3rd ser., *3*, pt. 2 (1990), 149–171.

——. *"This Culture of Ours": Intellectual Transitions in T'ang and Sung China*. Stanford, Calif.: Stanford University Press, 1992.

Burstyn, H. L. "Galileo's Attempt to Prove that the Earth Moves." *Isis 53* (1962), 161–185.

Camman, Schuyler. "The Magic Square of Three in Old Chinese Philosophy and Religion." *History of Religions 1* (1961), 37–80.

Chaffee, John W. *The Thorny Gates of Learning in Sung China: A Social History of Examinations*. Cambridge: Cambridge University Press, 1985; 2nd ed., Albany: State University of New York Press, 1995.

——. "Chu Hsi and the Revival of the White Deer Grotto Academy, 1179–1181." *T'oung Pao 71* (1985), 40–62.

Chan, Wing-tsit. "The Evolution of the Confucian Concept *Jen.*" *Philosophy East and West 4* (1955), 295–319.

——. *A Source Book in Chinese Philosophy.* Princeton, N.J.: Princeton University Press, 1963.

——. "The Evolution of the Neo-Confucian Concept *Li* as Principle." *Tsing Hua Journal of Chinese Studies,* new ser., *4,* no. 2 (1964), 123–149.

——, trans. *Reflections on Things at Hand.* New York: Columbia University Press, 1967.

——. "Chu Hsi's Completion of Neo-Confucianism." In Françoise Aubin, *Etudes Song: In Memoriam Etienne Balazs,* ser. 2, no. 1, pp. 59–90. The Hague: Mouton, 1973.

——, ed. and trans. *Neo-Confucian Terms Explained (The "Pei-hsi tzu-i") by Ch'en Ch'un (1159–1223).* New York: Columbia University Press, 1986.

——, ed. *Chu Hsi and Neo-Confucianism.* Honolulu: University of Hawaii Press, 1986.

——. "Chu Hsi and the Academies." In de Bary and Chaffee, *Neo-Confucian Education,* pp. 389–413.

——. *Chu Hsi: New Studies.* Honolulu: University of Hawaii Press, 1989.

Chang, Li-wen. "An Analysis of Chu Hsi's System of Thought of *I.*" In Chan, *Chu Hsi and Neo-Confucianism,* pp. 292–311.

Chao, Wei-pang. "The Chinese Science of Fate-Calculation." *Folklore Studies* (Peiping) *5* (1946), 279–315.

Chen, Cheng-Yih. *Early Chinese Work in Natural Science: A Re-Examination of the Physics of Motion, Acoustics, Astronomy and Scientific Thoughts.* Hong Kong: Hong Kong University Press, 1996.

Cheng, Chung-ying. "Chu Hsi's Methodology and Theory of Understanding." In Chan, *Chu Hsi and Neo-Confucianism,* pp. 169–196.

Ching, Julia. "Yi Yulgok on the 'Four Beginnings and the Seven Emotions.'" In de Bary and Haboush, *Rise of Neo-Confucianism in Korea,* pp. 303–322.

Creel, Herrlee G. *The Origins of Statecraft in China.* Chicago: University of Chicago Press, 1970.

——. "The Meaning of *Hsing-ming.*" In Creel, *What Is Taoism,* pp. 79–91.

——. *What Is Taoism? and Other Studies in Chinese Cultural History.* Chicago: University of Chicago Press, 1970.

Cullen, Christopher. "A Chinese Erastosthenes of the Flat Earth." *Bulletin of the School of Oriental and African Studies* (London) *39* (1976), 106–127.

de Bary, William Theodore. "Some Common Tendencies in Neo-Confucianism." In Nivison and Wright, *Confucianism in Action,* pp. 25–49.

——. *Neo-Confucian Orthodoxy and the Learning of the Mind-and-Heart.* New York: Columbia University Press, 1981.

——. "Chu Hsi's Aims as an Educator." In de Bary and Chaffee, *Neo-Confucian Education,* pp. 186–218.

de Bary, William Theodore, and John W. Chaffee, eds. *Neo-Confucian Education: The Formative Stage.* Berkeley: University of California Press, 1989.

de Bary, William Theodore, and Ja Hyun Kim Haboush, eds. *The Rise of Neo-Confucianism in Korea.* New York: Columbia University Press, 1985.

Demiéville, Paul. "Gauche et droite en Chine." In *Choix d'études sinologique (1921–1970),* pp. 180–194. Leiden: E. J. Brill, 1973.

Dijksterhuis, E. J. *The Mechanization of the World Picture.* London: Oxford University Press, 1961.

Eberhard, Wolfram. "Beitrage zur kosmologischen Spekulation Chinas in der Han Zeit." *Baessler Archiv* (Berlin) *16* (1933), 1–100.

———. "The Political Function of Astronomy and Astronomers in Han China." In Fairbank, *Chinese Thought and Institutions*, pp. 33–70.

Elvin, Mark. *The Pattern of the Chinese Past: A Social and Economic Interpretation*. Stanford, Calif.: Stanford University Press, 1973.

Eno, Robert. *The Confucian Creation of Heaven*. Albany: State University of New York Press, 1990.

Fairbank, J. K., ed. *Chinese Thought and Institutions*. Chicago: University of Chicago Press, 1957.

Farley, John. *The Spontaneous Generation Controversy from Descartes to Oparin*. Baltimore: Johns Hopkins University Press, 1977.

Fraser, J. T., N. Lawrence, and F. C. Haber, eds. *Time, Science and Society in China and the West*. Amherst: University of Massachusetts Press, 1986.

Fu, Daiwie. "A Contextual and Taxonomic Study of the 'Divine Marvels' and 'Strange Occurrences' in the *Mengxi bitan*." *Chinese Science*, no. 11 (1993–1994), 3–35.

Fung, Yu-lan. *History of Chinese Philosophy*. Trans. Derk Bodde. 2 vols. Princeton, N.J.: Princeton University Press, 1937, 1952.

Gardner, Daniel K. *Chu Hsi: Learning to Be a Sage*. Berkeley: University of California Press, 1990.

———. "Modes of Thinking and Modes of Discourse in the Sung: Some Thoughts on the *Yü-lu* ('Recorded Conversations') Texts." *Journal of Asian Studies 50* (1991), 574–603.

Glahn, E., ed. *Studia serica Bernhard Karlgren dedicata*. Copenhagen, 1959.

Graham, A. C. *Two Chinese Philosophers: Ch'eng Ming-tao and Ch'eng Yi-ch'üan*. London: Lund Humphries, 1958.

———. "China, Europe, and the Origins of Modern Science." In Nakayama and Sivin, *Chinese Science*, pp. 45–69.

———. *Later Mohist Logic, Ethics, and Science*. Hong Kong: Chinese University Press, 1978.

———. *Yin-Yang and the Nature of Correlative Thinking*. Singapore: Institute of East Asian Philosophies, 1986.

———. *Disputers of the Tao: Philosophical Argument in Ancient China*. La Salle, Ill.: Open Court, 1989.

Granet, M. *La Pensée chinoise*. Paris, 1934.

Grant, Edward. "Medieval and Seventeenth-Century Conceptions of an Infinite Void Space beyond the Cosmos." *Isis 60* (1969), 39–60.

———. *Physical Science in the Middle Ages*. New York: Wiley, 1971.

———. "Cosmology." In Lindberg, *Science in the Middle Ages*, pp. 265–302.

———. *The Foundations of Modern Science in the Middle Ages: Their Religious, Institutional, and Intellectual Contexts*. Cambridge: Cambridge University Press, 1996.

Haeger, John W., ed. *Crisis and Prosperity in Sung China*. Tucson: University of Arizona Press, 1975.

Hansen, Valerie. *Changing Gods in Medieval China, 1127–1276*. Princeton, N.J.: Princeton University Press, 1990.

Hartwell, Robert M. "Historical Analogism, Public Policy, and Social Science in Eleventh- and Twelfth-Century China." *American Historical Review 76* (1971), 690–727.

———. "Financial Expertise, Examinations, and the Formulation of Economic Policy in Northern Sung China." *Journal of Asian Studies 30* (1971), 281–314.

———. "Demographic, Political, and Social Transformations of China, 750–1550." *Harvard Journal of Asiatic Studies 42* (1982), 365–442.

Hashimoto, Keizo, Catherine Jami, and Lowell Skar, eds. *East Asian Science: Tradition and Beyond.* Osaka: Kansai University Press, 1995.

Hatton, Russell. "A Comparison of *Ch'i* and Prime Matter." *Philosophy East and West 32* (1982), 159–175.

Henderson, John B. *The Development and Decline of Chinese Cosmology.* New York: Columbia University Press, 1984.

Ho, Peng-Yoke. *The Astronomical Chapters of the Chin Shu.* Paris: Mouton, 1966.

Hu, Shih. "The Scientific Spirit and Method in Chinese Philosophy." In Moore, *The Chinese Mind,* pp. 104–131. Originally presented at the Third East-West Philosophers' Conference, Honolulu, 1959.

Huang, Yi-Long. "Court Divination and Christianity in the K'ang-hsi Era." *Chinese Science,* no. 10 (1991), 1–20.

Huang, Yi-Long, and Chang Chih-ch'eng. "The Evolution and Decline of the Ancient Chinese Practice of Watching for the Ethers." *Chinese Science,* no. 13 (1996), 82–106.

Hymes, Robert P. *Statesmen and Gentlemen: The Elite of Fu-chou, Chiang-hsi, in Northern and Southern Sung.* Cambridge: Cambridge University Press, 1986.

——. "Not Quite Gentlemen? Doctors in Sung and Yüan." *Chinese Science,* no. 8 (1987), 9–76.

Hymes, Robert P., and Conrad Schirokauer, eds. *Ordering the World: Approaches to State and Society in Sung Dynasty China.* Berkeley: University of California Press, 1993.

Kasoff, Ira E. *The Thought of Chang Tsai (1020–1077).* Cambridge: Cambridge University Press, 1984.

Kim, Yung Sik. "Natural Knowledge in a Traditional Culture: Problems in the Study of the History of Chinese Science." *Minerva 20* (1982), 83–104.

——. "Some Aspects of the Concept of *Ch'i* in Chu Hsi." *Philosophy East and West 34* (1984), 25–36.

——. "*Kuei-shen* in Terms of *Ch'i*: Chu Hsi's Discussion of *Kuei-shen.*" *Tsing Hua Journal of Chinese Studies,* new ser., *17* (1985), 149–163.

——. "Some Reflections on Science and Religion in Traditional China." *Han'guk Kwahak-sa Hakhoe-ji* (Journal of the Korean History of Science Society) 7 (1985), 40–49.

——. "Chu Hsi (1130–1200) on Calendar Specialists and Their Knowledge: A Scholar's Attitude toward Technical Scientific Knowledge in Traditional China." *T'oung Pao 78* (1992), 94–115.

——. "'Analogical Extension' (*lei-t'ui*) in Chu Hsi's Methodology of 'Investigation of Things' (*ke-wu*) and 'Extension of Knowledge' (*chih-chih*)." Forthcoming.

Kohn, Livia, ed. *Taoist Meditation and Longevity Techniques.* Ann Arbor: Center for Chinese Studies, University of Michigan, 1989.

Kuhn, Thomas S. *The Copernican Revolution: Planetary Astronomy in the Development of Western Thought.* Cambridge, Mass.: Harvard University Press, 1957.

Lamont, H. G. "An Early Ninth Century Debate on Heaven: Liu Tsung-yüan's *T'ien Shuo* and Liu Yü-hsi's *T'ien Lun.*" *Asia Major 18* (1973), 181–208; *19* (1974), 37–85.

Lau, D. C. "A Note on *Ke Wu.*" *Bulletin of the School of Oriental and African Studies 30* (1967), 353–357.

Le Blanc, Charles, and Susan Blader, eds. *Chinese Ideas about Nature and Society: Studies in Honour of Derk Bodde.* Hong Kong: Hong Kong University Press, 1987.

Lee, Thomas H. C. *Government Education and Examinations in Sung China.* Hong Kong: Chinese University Press, 1985.

Lenk, Hans, and Gregor Paul, eds. *Epistemological Issues in Classical Chinese Philosophy.* Albany: State University of New York Press, 1993.

Levey, Matthew. "The Clan and the Tree: Inconsistent Images of Human Nature in Chu Hsi's Settled Discourse." *Journal of Sung-Yüan Studies* 24 (1994), 101–143.

Libbrecht, Ulrich. *Chinese Mathematics in the Thirteenth Century: The Shu-shu chiu-chang of Ch'in Chiu-shao.* Cambridge, Mass.: MIT Press, 1973.

Lindberg, David C., ed. *Science in the Middle Ages.* Chicago: University of Chicago Press, 1978.

Liu, James T. C. *Ou-yang Hsiu: An Eleventh-Century Neo-Confucianist.* Stanford, Calif.: Stanford University Press, 1967.

——. "How Did a Neo-Confucian School Become the State Orthodoxy?" *Philosophy East and West* 23 (1973), 484–505.

——. *China Turning Inward: Intellectual-Political Changes in the Early Twelfth Century.* Cambridge, Mass.: Harvard University Press, 1988.

Liu, James T. C., and P. Golas, eds. *Change in Sung China: Innovation or Renovation?* Boston: Heath, 1969.

Lloyd, G. E. R. *Early Greek Science: Thales to Aristotle.* New York: Norton, 1970.

——. "Finite and Infinite in Greece and China." *Chinese Science,* no. 13 (1996), 11–34.

Loewe, Michael. *Ways to Paradise: The Chinese Quest for Immortality.* London: Allen and Unwin, 1979.

Lovejoy, Arthur O. *The Great Chain of Being: A Study of the History of an Idea.* Cambridge, Mass.: Harvard University Press, 1936.

Lu, Gwei-djen, and Joseph Needham. *Celestial Lancets: A History and Rationale of Acupuncture and Moxa.* Cambridge: Cambridge University Press, 1980.

Machle, Edward J. *Nature and Heaven in the* Xunzi: *A Study of the Tian Lun.* Albany: State University of New York Press, 1993.

Major, John S. *Heaven and Earth in Early Han Thought: Chapters Three, Four, and Five of the Huainanzi.* Albany: State University of New York Press, 1993.

March, Andrew L. "An Appreciation of Chinese Geomancy" *Journal of Asian Studies* 27 (1968), 253–267.

Martzloff, Jean-Claude. *A History of Chinese Mathematics.* Berlin: Springer-Verlag, 1997.

McKenna, Stephen E., and Victor H. Mair. "A Reordering of the Hexagrams of the *I Ching.*" *Philosophy East and West* 29 (1979), 421–441.

McKnight, Brian. "Mandarins as Legal Experts: Professional Learning in Sung China." In de Bary and Chaffee, *Neo-Confucian Education,* pp. 493–516.

Metzger, Thomas A. *Escape from Predicament: Neo-Confucianism and China's Evolving Political Culture.* New York: Columbia University Press, 1977.

Moore, Charles A., ed. *The Chinese Mind.* Honolulu: University of Hawaii Press, 1967.

Munro, Donald J. *Images of Human Nature: A Sung Portrait.* Princeton, N.J.: Princeton University Press, 1988.

Murdoch, John E. "From Social into Intellectual Factors: An Aspect of the Unitary Character of Late Medieval Learning." In Murdoch and Sylla, *Cultural Context of Medieval Learning,* pp. 271–339.

Murdoch, John E., and Edith D. Sylla. "The Science of Motion." In Lindberg, *Science in the Middle Ages,* pp. 206–264.

——, eds. *The Cultural Context of Medieval Learning.* Boston: Riedel, 1975.

Nakayama, Shigeru. "Characteristics of Chinese Astrology." *Isis 57* (1966), 442–454.

——. *A History of Japanese Astronomy: Chinese Background and Western Impact.* Cambridge, Mass.: Harvard University Press, 1969.

Nakayama, Shigeru, and Nathan Sivin, eds. *Chinese Science: Explorations of an Ancient Tradition.* Cambridge, Mass.: MIT Press, 1973.

Needham, Joseph. "Time and Eastern Man." In Needham, *Grand Titration*, pp. 218–298.

——. *Grand Titration: Science and Society in East and West.* London: George Allen and Unwin, 1969.

——. "The Missing Link in Horological History: A Chinese Contribution." In Needham, *Clerks and Craftsmen*, pp. 203–238.

——. *Clerks and Craftsmen in China and the West.* Cambridge: Cambridge University Press, 1970.

——. "Social Position of Scientific Men and Physicians in Medieval China." In *Proceedings, XIVth International Congress of the History of Science*, 4:19–34. Tokyo: Science Council of Japan, 1974.

Needham, Joseph, Wang Ling, and Derek J. de Solla Price. *Heavenly Clockwork: The Great Astronomical Clocks of Medieval China.* 2nd ed. Cambridge: Cambridge University Press, 1986.

Needham, Joseph, et al. *Science and Civilisation in China.* Multivolume series. Cambridge: Cambridge University Press, 1954–.

Nivison, David S., and Arthur F. Wright, eds. *Confucianism in Action.* Stanford, Calif.: Stanford University Press, 1959.

Nylan, Michael, and Nathan Sivin. "The First Neo-Confucianism: An Introduction to Yang Hsuing's 'Canon of Supreme Mystery' (*T'ai hsüan ching*, ca. 4 B.C.)." In Le Blanc and Blader, *Chinese Ideas about Nature and Society*, pp. 41–99.

Peterson, Willard J. "Making Connections: 'Commentary on the Attached Verbalizations' of the *Book of Change.*" *Harvard Journal of Asiatic Studies 42* (1982), 67–116.

——. "Another Look at *Li.*" *Bulletin of Sung-Yüan Studies*, no. 18 (1986), 13–32.

Phelan, Timothy. "The Neo-Confucian Cosmology in Chu Hsi's *I-hsueh ch'i-meng.*" Ph.D. diss., University of Washington, 1982.

Pollard, David. "*Ch'i* in Chinese Literary Theory." In Rickett, *Chinese Approaches to Literature*, pp. 43–66.

Porkert, Manfred. *The Theoretical Foundations of Chinese Medicine: Systems of Correspondence.* Cambridge, Mass.: MIT Press, 1974.

Reischauer, E. O., and J. K. Fairbank. *East Asia: The Great Tradition.* Boston: Houghton Mifflin, 1958.

Reiter, Florian C. "Change and Continuity in Historical Geography: Chang Huang's (1527–1608) Reflections on the 'Yü-kung.'" *Asia Major*, 3rd ser., *3*, pt. 1 (1990), 129–141.

Rickett, A. A., ed. *Chinese Approaches to Literature from Confucius to Liang Ch'i-ch'ao.* Princeton, N.J.: Princeton University Press, 1977.

Rosemont, Henry, Jr., ed. *Chinese Texts and Philosophical Contexts: Essays Dedicated to Angus C. Graham.* La Salle, Ill.: Open Court, 1991.

Rossi, Paolo. *Philosophy, Technology and the Arts in the Early Modern Era.* New York: Harper, 1970.

Rubin, Vitaly A. "The Concepts of Wu-Hsing and Yin-Yang." *Journal of Chinese Philosophy 9* (1982), 131–157.

Ryan, James A. "Leibniz' Binary System and Shao Yong's *Yijing.*" *Philosophy East and West 46* (1996), 59–90.

Sabra, A. I. *Theories of Light from Descartes to Newton.* London: Oldbourne, 1967.

Saso, Michael. "What Is the *Ho-t'u?*" *History of Religions 17* (1978), 399–416.

Schirokauer, Conrad. "Chu Hsi's Political Career: A Study in Ambivalence." In Wright and Twitchett, *Confucian Personalities,* pp. 162–188.

——. "Neo-Confucianism under Attack: The Condemnation of *Wei-hsueh.*" In Haeger, *Crisis and Prosperity,* pp. 163–198.

——. "Chu Hsi as an Administrator." *Etudes Song–Sung Studies,* ser. 1, no. 3 (1976), pp. 207–236.

Schwartz, Benjamin I. "On the Absence of Reductionism in Chinese Thought." *Journal of Chinese Philosophy 1* (1973), 27–44.

Shchutskii, Iulian K. *Researches on the I Ching.* Trans. William L. MacDonald, Tsuyoshi Hasegawa, and Hellmut Wilhelm. Princeton, N.J.: Princeton University Press, 1979.

Shih, Vincent Y. C. "Metaphysical Tendencies in Mencius." *Philosophy East and West 12* (1963), 319–341.

Sivin, Nathan. "Chinese Conceptions of Time." *Earlham Review 1* (1966), 82–92.

——. "Chinese Alchemy and the Manipulation of Time." *Isis 67* (1976), 513–526.

——. "Why the Scientific Revolution Did Not Take Place in China–Or Didn't It?" *Chinese Science,* no. 5 (1982), 45–66.

——. "The Limits of Empirical Knowledge in the Traditional Chinese Sciences." In Fraser, Lawrence, and Haber, *Time, Science and Society,* pp. 151–169.

——. *Traditional Medicine in Contemporary China.* Ann Arbor: Center for Chinese Studies, University of Michigan, 1987.

——. "Science and Medicine in Imperial China–The State of the Field." *Journal of Asian Studies 47* (1988), 41–90.

——. "Change and Continuity in Early Cosmology: *The Great Commentary to The Book of Changes.*" In Yamada and Tanaka, *Chūgoku kodai kagakushiron,* pp. 3–43.

Skar, Lowell. "Ethical Aspects of Daoist Healing: The Case of Song and Yuan Thunder Rites." In Hashimoto, Jami, and Skar, *East Asian Science,* pp. 221–229.

Smith, Kidder, Jr., Peter K. Bol, Joseph A. Adler, and Don J. Wyatt. *Sung Dynasty Uses of the I Ching.* Princeton, N.J.: Princeton University Press, 1990.

Smith, Richard J. *Fortune-Tellers and Philosophers: Divination in Traditional Chinese Society.* Boulder, Colo.: Westview Press, 1991.

Taylor, Rodney L. *The Religious Dimensions of Confucianism.* Albany: State University of New York Press, 1990.

Tillman, Hoyt C. "The Idea and the Reality of the 'Thing' during the Sung." *Bulletin of Sung and Yüan Studies,* no. 14 (1978), 68–82.

——. *Utilitarian Confucianism: Ch'en Liang's Challenge to Chu Hsi.* Cambridge, Mass.: Harvard University Press, 1982.

——. "Consciousness of *T'ien* in Chu Hsi's Thought." *Harvard Journal of Asiatic Studies, 47* (1987), 31–50.

——. "Encyclopedias, Polymaths, and *Tao-hsueh* Confucians: Preliminary Reflections with Special Reference to Chang Ju-yü." *Journal of Sung-Yüan Studies,* no. 22 (1990–1992), 89–108.

——. *Confucian Discourse and Chu Hsi's Ascendancy.* Honolulu: University of Hawaii Press, 1992.

Tjan, Tjoe Som, trans. *Po Hu T'ung: The Comprehensive Discussions in the White Tiger Hall.* 2 vols. Leyden, 1949, 1952.

Unschuld, Paul U. *'Pen Ts'ao'; Zwei tausend Jahre traditionelle pharmazeutische Literatur chinas.* Munich: Moos, 1973.

———. *Medicine in China: A History of Ideas.* Berkeley: University of California Press, 1985.

Waley, Arthur, trans. *The Analects of Confucius.* New York: Knopf, 1938.

Westfall, Richard S. *The Construction of Modern Science: Mechanisms and Mechanics.* New York: Wiley, 1971.

Westman, Robert S. "The Astronomer's Role in the Sixteenth Century: A Preliminary Study." *History of Science 18* (1980), 105–147.

Wilhelm, Hellmut. *Eight Lectures on the I Ching.* Princeton, N.J.: Princeton University Press, 1960.

———. *Heaven, Earth, and Man in the Book of Changes.* Seattle: University of Washington Press, 1977.

Wilhelm, Richard, trans. *The I Ching or Book of Changes.* Trans. into English by Cary F. Baynes. Princeton, N.J.: Princeton University Press, 1950.

Wittenborn, Allen. "*Li* Revisited and Other Explorations." *Bulletin of Sung-Yüan Studies,* no. 17 (1981), 32–48.

Wright, Arthur F., ed. *Studies in Chinese Thought.* Chicago: University of Chicago Press, 1953.

Wright, Arthur F., and Denis Twitchett, eds. *Confucian Personalities.* Stanford, Calif.: Stanford University Press, 1962.

Wu, Lu-ch'iang. "An Ancient Chinese Treatise on Alchemy Entitled 'Ts'an T'ung Ch'i,' Written by Wei Po-Yang about 142 A.D. with an Introduction and Notes by Tenney L. Davis." *Isis 18* (1932), 210–289.

Wyatt, Don J. "Chu Hsi's Critique of Shao Yung: One Instance of the Stand against Fatalism." *Harvard Journal of Asiatic Studies 45* (1985), 649–666.

Yamanoi, Yu. "The Great Ultimate and Heaven in Chu Hsi's Philosophy." In Chan, *Chu Hsi and Neo-Confucianism,* pp. 79–92.

Yu, Ying-shih. "'O Soul, Come Back!' A Study in the Changing Conceptions of the Soul and Afterlife in Pre-Buddhist China." *Harvard Journal of Asiatic Studies 47* (1987), 365–395.

Zhou Shiyi, trans. *The Kinship of the Three, according to the Book of Changes.* Changsha: Hunan Education Publishing House, 1988.

Index